PERSUASION AND HUMAN ACTION

PERSUASION AND HUMAN ACTION

A Review and Critique of Social Influence Theories

Mary John Smith
University of Virginia

WADSWORTH PUBLISHING COMPANY
Belmont, California
A Division of Wadsworth, Inc.

Senior Editor, Communications: Rebecca Hayden
Production Editor: Donna Oberholtzer
Art Director: Detta Penna
Designer: Wendy Calmenson
Copy Editor: Stephen McElroy
Technical Illustration: Innographics
Cover Designer: Stephen Rapley

Printed in the United States of America

1 2 3 4 5 6 7 8 9 10—86 85 84 83 82

Library of Congress Cataloging in Publication Data

Smith, Mary John.
    Persuasion and human action.

    Bibliography: p.
    Includes index.
    1. Influence (Psychology) 2. Persuasion
(Psychology) 3. Attitude change. 4. Social action.
I. Title.
HM258.S539   302.3′4   81–11631
ISBN 0–534–01006–7   AACR2

For my mother and father

Preface

Persuasion and Human Action is an attempt to give new conceptual direction to what is perhaps the oldest subdiscipline in communication. In conceptualizing the nature of persuasion and persuasion theory, three assumptions have guided my thinking. First, I assume that people are active agents, having the capacity for choice and self-direction. Second, people are treated as intentional, goal-oriented agents, striving to maximize rewards and minimize punishing experiences. Finally, the social environment, including persuasive messages, is regarded as a product of human interpretive processes that are guided by personalized assumptions about the nature of the external world. From this perspective, people assign uniquely personal meanings to messages and respond to their interpretations of symbols, in effect, to the messages they create for themselves. Thus, the dominant focus of this book is on what people intentionally "do with" persuasive messages, not what messages "do to" people.

Given this conceptual grounding, I have had two objectives in writing this book. First, I have proposed a new theoretical framework for looking at the nature of persuasion and persuasion theory. The proposed reconceptualization is action oriented and rules based. It assumes that most human social action is not forced by antecedent conditions or governed by causal laws; but, rather, it is self-generated in accordance with practical rules specifying those actions people must take, should take, or must not take to reach goals. Consistent with this view, persuasive communication is regarded as a symbolic activity whose purpose is the coordination of human choice-making behavior according to contextually relevant rules for achieving desired objectives.

My second aim has been to present a review and a critique of theories that have had a significant impact on contemporary understanding of persuasive communication.

In selecting theories, I have avoided the temptation to consider only those perspectives fitting my philosophical biases. Thus, I have included not only theoretically compatible approaches, but also a number of theories that depart markedly from my own view of what persuasion is or ought to be. I have tried to provide a balanced view of the current status of persuasion theory and, at the same time, to appraise the limitations and contributions of each theory to our understanding of persuasion and human action.

The book is divided into four parts. In Part 1, I examine the conceptual foundations of persuasion. Chapter 1 describes persuasion as a developmental process of social influence whose function is to effect the internalization, or voluntary acceptance, of meanings people assign to messages. The cognitive processes by which people assign these personal meanings to messages is addressed in Chapter 2. In Chapter 3, I discuss the nature of persuasion theory and advance a rules-based reconceptualization of it. Chapter 4 concludes with a description and critical evaluation of research methods in persuasion, including naturalistic, correlational, and experimental methodologies.

Parts 2 and 3 are devoted to a review and critique of specific persuasion theories falling into two classes: active participation and information-processing perspectives. In Part 2, active participatory theories, or those focusing on the self-generation of persuasive effects, are discussed. Critical analyses of counterattitudinal advocacy, self-attribution theory, group interaction theories, and social learning models of self-persuasion are contained in Chapters 5 through 8. In Part 3, I consider information-processing theories, those in which an external agent produces messages. The Yale approach to information processing, information integration theory, judgmental theories of information processing, and theories of inducing resistance to counterpersuasion are considered in Chapters 9 through 12.

In Part 4 I discuss new directions in persuasion. In Chapter 13 I evaluate some of these new theoretical directions, take the "pulse" of current theory development, and suggest some new research areas for persuasion theorists. Finally, Chapter 14 presents case studies in image making, advertising, religious conversion, and ideological indoctrination, and then goes on to assess the extent to which current practices conform to or diverge from theoretical models.

As this outline suggests, *Persuasion and Human Action* is not a descriptive manual, but a critical assessment of the current status of persuasion theory. Moreover, the book is, in many respects, an argument for the directions persuasion theory ought to take in the 1980s. Thus, my audience will probably be found in persuasion theory or attitude change courses at the upper division undergraduate or graduate levels. Even so, previous study in persuasion, although useful, is not essential for effective use of the book.

A number of people have contributed to the development of this book. First, my thanks to Lillian Davis and Mark Knapp for understanding and for being my friends. To Charlotte Turner Springford, Sean O'Neil, and Tracy Gordy, my thanks for always "being there." I am grateful to Bob Reinheimer for his helpful suggestions and friendship. John Sullivan, Chairman of my department at the University of Virginia, and Joanne Stevens, Office Manager, performed many favors that made my life easier during the writing of this book. I am indebted to Mark Knapp, Annabel Hagood,

Michael Prosser, and Ronald Bassett for their guidance and encouragement during the early planning stages of this project.

The following three people made especially valuable contributions to the development of this book, and I am grateful to them. Barnett Pearce provided many unpublished documents and offered generous encouragement. His insights substantially influenced my thinking about the nature of persuasive communication. Anne Gabbard-Alley's insightful criticisms and constant encouragement were indispensable to me. Gerald Miller's probing criticisms and good counsel helped shape this book. He taught me much. In addition to Miller, Pearce, and Gabbard-Alley, the following people read all or part of this manuscript and gave valuable assistance: Charles Willard, Forrest Conklin, Eva McMahan, M. Lee Williams, Uvieja Good Leighton, and Mary Arbogast. Finally, I am grateful to Rebecca Hayden of Wadsworth Publishing Company for being an editor extraordinaire and a delightful colleague.

Contents

PART *1*

CONCEPTUAL FOUNDATIONS OF PERSUASION

CHAPTER *1*

The Nature of Persuasion

The word *persuasion* brings to mind varying images. The barrage of television, radio, newspaper, and magazine advertisements we encounter daily may typify our notion of persuasion. Or we may think of political rhetoric, with aspiring politicians billing themselves as America's best hope for an end to high prices, energy shortages, urban blight, and rural poverty. But what of the socialization processes by which we acquire our basic values, the ways we change as a result of interacting with friends, or the appreciation we learn for art, music, or morality in the home, the church, or the school? Usually we do not associate the term *persuasion* with such subtle and productive changes. Rather, we attribute them to "interpersonal growth," "educational influence," or "parental and religious guidance." Finally, what about the processes that have moved hundreds of thousands of "ordinary" Americans to join bizarre, semireligious cults, variously worshiping UFOs, Satan, serpents, and Adolph Hitler?[1] We are more likely to label these sudden and mysterious processes with the terms *mind control* or *indoctrination* rather than *persuasion.*

Although these forms of influence differ in several critical ways that we shall consider later, they all contain dimensions of persuasive communication. Indeed, the varieties of persuasion range from subtle peer influence and educational guidance to abrupt and discontinuous forms of political, religious, and social conversion. When our attitudes, values, and behavior patterns are influenced gradually by benign agents like friends, lovers, and teachers, we rarely feel coerced or manipulated. Rather, we perceive that we are participating freely in an interactive process of becoming our own person. Likewise, when we buy certain commercial products or vote for our favorite political candidate, we usually feel we are acting freely in accordance with our best judgment. However, when people change suddenly, when the source of influence is unfamiliar or disliked, or when the nature of the change is nonnormative, we often suspect more sinister influence forms like *coercion, mind control,* or *brainwashing.*[2]

3

Such terms imply that some external agent has "done something" to an unwilling victim. In contrast, *education* and *interpersonal growth* suggest that the target of persuasion has participated freely and actively in the influence process.

In reality, such perceptual differences often do not reflect differences in the nature of the persuasive tactics being used. Rather, they reflect whether or not we approve of the results of a process of persuasion. For example, Americans usually are dismayed to read of people being "indoctrinated" to accept Communism or other ideologies, yet they take pride in America's efforts to "educate" or "assist" the same people to understand democracy. Likewise, the parents of young converts to nontraditional religious sects, such as the Reverend Sun Myung Moon's Unification Church, label its rapid conversion process "mind control," but they view efforts to "deprogram" their children as attempts to "bring them back to their senses." As these examples suggest, we often apply benevolent labels to persuasive outcomes we approve and use negative ones when we disapprove just as we use the term *perversion* for sex acts we do not practice.

Edgar Schein and his associates reached such a conclusion after studying the persuasive tactics used by the Communist Chinese on American prisoners of war during the Korean conflict. They found that the Chinese tactics were not unusual or unique, but were remarkably similar to those employed in many of our own institutions. "There is a world of difference," writes Schein, "in the content of what is transmitted in [American] religious orders, prisons, educational institutions, mental hospitals, and thought reform centers. But there are striking similarities in the manner in which the influence occurs."[3] Whether we label the ways people change after internalizing symbolic appeals as *persuasion, brainwashing, propaganda, interpersonal growth,* or *education,* we often are all talking about the same thing: the universal human experience of people influencing other people. That is what this book is about.

SOME CONTEMPORARY CONCEPTS OF PERSUASION

From the end of World War I through the early 1950s, the average American and the communication scholar alike regarded persuasion as a powerful tool, capable of instantly controlling all people who had the misfortune to encounter it. The widespread panic following the airing of Orson Welles' radio adaptation of H. G. Wells' book, *War of the Worlds*, seemed to confirm that assumption. Thousands of Americans fled their homes on the night of October 30, 1938, to escape an "invasion from Mars," the central thesis of the production.[4] Likewise, Nazi and Communist indoctrination campaigns prior to World War II, and anti-Communist propaganda in the fifties, seemed particularly frightening because of the spread of the mass media, especially television.

During this period, the "hypodermic needle" theory of persuasion was the dominant view of social influence processes. The theory holds that, as receivers of messages, we are all relatively passive and defenseless; thus, someone can "inject" a persuasive communication into us and change us, just as a drug is administered with a hypodermic syringe. Later research in persuasion demonstrated the folly of such a notion. On measuring the effects of persuasion, researchers found that, as recipients of messages, we are all rather obstinate creatures who expect to "get something from the manipulator if he is to get something from [us]."[5] Indeed, as Wilbur Schramm notes,

> The most dramatic change in general communication theory during the last forty years has been the gradual abandonment of the idea of a passive audience, and its replacement by the concept of a highly active, highly selective audience, manipulating rather than being manipulated by a message."[6]

As we enter the 1980s, scholars of persuasion theory generally agree that the recipient of a message is an active, often dominant, participant in any persuasive transaction.

Currently, the only characteristic of persuasion upon which there is unanimous agreement is that its effects are produced by symbols. Beyond that focus, conceptions diverge. Given the absence of a single perspective, we will look at the dominant conceptual properties of several definitions in current use. Any contemporary conception of persuasion can be understood in relation to each of the following three pairs of contrasting or alternative models: (1) a transactional model versus a hypodermic model; (2) an intentional model versus a response model; and (3) a process model versus an effects model. Let's look at some representative definitions.

The Transactional versus the Hypodermic Model

The transactional model of communication regards the communicative act as one in which two or more persons engage in mutual and simultaneous interaction and influence.[7] Similarly, a *transactional model* of persuasion assumes that persuasive effects are the joint product of symbolic interaction between two or more persons, and that each party shares a perception of choice and a sense of control over the persuasive encounter. Moreover, the transactional model regards persuasion as a *developmental* process. With each exchange of messages, the participants grow and change. Each is influenced by his or her interpretations of others' messages. Thus, from a transactional point of view, the process of persuasion is characterized by a spiral of changing feelings and beliefs on the part of each communicator.[8] In contrast, the *hypodermic model,* like the hypodermic needle theory of persuasion, considers persuasion a unidirectional process whereby a source influences a relatively passive recipient. The receiver is regarded as a reactive victim of persuasive strategies, not as a full partner in the process of social influence.

With few exceptions, current approaches to persuasion are transactional, differing only in the perceived dominance of the receiver relative to the source. Some transactional definitions give the source of a message the dominant part in the transaction, leaving the recipient a secondary, but relatively active role. For instance, Erwin Bettinghaus defines persuasion as a source-based process involving "a conscious attempt by one individual to change the attitudes, beliefs, or the behavior of another individual or group of individuals through transmission of some message."[9] Similarly, Gary Cronkhite views persuasion as the "act of manipulating symbols so as to produce changes in . . . those who interpret the symbols."[10]

Another transactional approach suggests that the source of a message and the recipient perform roughly equal roles in influencing the outcome of a persuasive event. Thomas Scheidel's notion of persuasion as an "activity in which speaker and listener are conjoined" typifies this approach,[11] as does Wallace Fotheringham's view of persuasion as "that body of effects in receivers" instrumental to source-desired goals, largely generated by messages, and "involving the perception of choice for the receiver."[12]

In a third variation of the transactional approach, the receiver is considered the dominant partner in the transaction, and the persuader merely generates the necessary symbolic stimuli for recipients to persuade themselves. From this perspective, the receiver is the final shaper of his or her own responses to persuasive messages. Thus, Charles Larson, in subscribing to this view, defines persuasion as "the co-creation of a state of identification between a source and a receiver," and emphasizes the crucial role played by self-persuasion "in the co-creation of meaning."[13] Along this line, Gerald Miller and Michael Burgoon suggest that a major, but often neglected, framework of persuasion involves "influence attempts in which the primary agent of message transmission or symbolization . . . is the intended persuadee."[14] Finally, Herbert Simons captures the essence of this approach when he describes persuasion as "an adaptive process which . . . takes place on the recipient's terms. . . . In a real sense," he argues, "we do not persuade others at all; we only provide the stimuli with which they can persuade themselves."[15]

The Intentional versus the Response Model

Definitions of persuasion patterned after the *intentional model* stipulate that for persuasive communication to occur, one or more individuals must consciously and deliberately intend to influence one or more other persons. This source-oriented approach is illustrated by Kenneth Andersen's view that persuasion aims to "effect a voluntary change in attitude or action desired by the communicator."[16] Bettinghaus also emphasizes the "conscious" intent requirement, as do Miller and Burgoon, Scheidel, and others.[17]

In contrast, a *response model* does not treat deliberate intent to influence as a defining characteristic of persuasion. It approaches persuasion from the viewpoint of the recipient and holds that both deliberate and unintentional messages can produce persuasive responses in people. For example, Stephen King argues that persuasion is possible any time "the receiver attaches meaning to the communicator's behavior . . . whether or not [the communicator] actually intends to communicate with another."[18] Larson also views persuasion as a function of symbol use, without regard to origin or intent.[19]

The Process versus the Effects Model

A *process model* requires only that a persuasion process takes place; it may be deliberate or unintentional, a success or a failure. Typical of this approach are Otto Lerbinger's view of persuasion as "manipulation designed to produce action in others,"[20] and Andersen's notion of persuasion as a process that "seeks . . . change."[21]

The *effects model,* on the other hand, holds that persuasion has occurred only when somebody is actually affected by a message. Cronkhite reserves the term persuasion for "that situation in which a communication actually produces some change in [the] evaluative or approach–avoidance behavior" of a person.[22] Similarly, Fotheringham and Larson both regard persuasion as the effects of a process, not as a process capable of eliciting effects.[23]

THE NATURE OF PERSUASION: A POINT OF VIEW

Despite their diversity, these contemporary views of persuasion have several common conceptual themes. First, the theorists cited generally agree that the function of persuasion is to effect the *internalization* or *private acceptance* of new ways of believing and behaving through the exchange of *messages.* Second, it is assumed that persuasive communication entails the perception of *choice* on the part of message recipients to accept or reject the recommendations contained in persuasive messages. Third, the theorists agree that persuasive effects are mediated by the *interpretation* or *meaning* people assign to persuasive messages. Fourth, there is consensus that persuasion is a *transactional activity,* involving mutual interaction and influence among people. Finally, the theorists agree that people's responses to messages may take the form either of *cognitive* reorganization or overt *behavioral* change. Cognitive reorganization entails creation, reinforcement, or change in internal processes like beliefs or feelings, and behavioral change signifies overt actions prompted by altered cognitive dispositions.

Drawing on these five themes, we suggest that persuasion is best viewed as *a symbolic activity whose purpose is to effect the internalization or voluntary acceptance of new cognitive states or patterns of overt behavior through the exchange of messages.* Consistent with this view, we assume that *a process of persuasion has occurred when people internalize the meanings they assign to messages in an atmosphere of perceived choice.* This view of persuasion is *transactional* in nature, *process oriented,* and *response dependent.* These three qualities should become increasingly apparent as we explore this conception of persuasion.

Internalization and Human Choice

As our definition suggests, the function of persuasion is to effect the internalization of symbolic recommendations. According to Herbert Kelman, the internalization process occurs when people see recommended courses of action as "congruent with [their] basic value system," as "useful for the solution of a problem," or otherwise as "congenial to [their] needs."[24] In short, people internalize the meaning of a message when its recommendations are perceived as goal satisfying or need fulfilling.

By definition, the process of internalization or private acceptance implies that a person feels free to choose from alternative recommendations those best meeting personal needs and goals; thus, *the perception of choice is regarded as a defining characteristic of persuasive communication.* In using the term choice we do not refer to the objective availability of two or more behavioral options from which to select, but, rather, choice is seen as a subjective feeling that one is not being compelled by external forces to select one recommended behavioral option over another. Choice, then, is equated with the perceived absence of duress.

This conception of choice is warranted by the repeated finding that the actual number of behavioral options open to a person often is related only incidentally to the *perception* of options. For example, Ellen Langer found that people sometimes retain a perception of volition or what she calls the "illusion of control" in situations where their behavioral options are actually controlled by chance.[25] A chance environment, of course, differs radically from the persuasive communication situation since recipients of messages presumably have at least the two options of accepting or rejecting the recommendations contained in messages. Nonetheless, Langer's finding that "objective contingency" is related imperfectly to the "perception of contingency" suggests the inadvisability of equating choice simply with available options. It is more meaningful to construe choice as a subjective feeling of freedom to select, and thus internalize, those recommendations promising reward and to reject those threatening misfortune or pain.

Interpretation and Human Action

We believe that interpretation or the assignment of meaning to messages is the crucial mediator of persuasive effects. It is assumed that the environment, including persuasive messages, is "a product of [human] perception, not the cause of it."[26] People assign uniquely personal meanings to messages and respond to their *interpretation* of messages, not to some raw reality unaffected by human cognition.[27] Thus, any responses people make to persuasive messages are, in effect, responses to the messages they create for themselves.

As this discussion implies, we reject the hypodermic model wherein humans are passive reactors to messages generated by external agents. Instead, our view is transactional. We regard persuasion as a dynamic, developmental process of symbolic human interaction. As such, all parties to a process of persuasion are active agents continually influencing and being influenced by their interpretations of others' messages. Moreover, each person in the interaction can choose the best course of action to meet his or her personal needs. In short, people are active agents who exercise influence over messages, rather than passive reactors.[28]

Intentionality

Traditionally, persuasion has been viewed as a unidirectional process, in which a persuader tries to elicit responses from recipients that are instrumental to his or her goals. Hence, intentionality or purposiveness has been equated with a *specific* intent to achieve a *persuasive* objective on the part of the *source* of a message. Although we believe specific intentions to influence often characterize the practice of persuasion, we regard this conception as unnecessarily restrictive. The following discussion will clarify our more general view of the nature of persuasive intentionality.

From our perspective, all people behave *intentionally;* that is, they act purposively to achieve their desired goals. Further, the human use of symbols is inherently intentional. All of us communicate and process the communications of others in ways that enable us to achieve valuable outcomes and avoid undesirable ones. However, it is crucial to distinguish between the narrow view of persuasive intent from a source's perspective and a broader view of intentionality from the perspective of recipients or processers of messages. According to this broader view, all humans interpret and process messages intentionally, with a view toward maximizing benefits and minimizing unfortunate consequences. This intentional nature of message processing is quite independent of a specific persuasive intent or lack of it on the part of the sender of messages.[29]

To illustrate this notion, suppose someone reads a newspaper article describing an explosion at a local nuclear power plant. Now imagine this same person hears a persuasive speech by Ralph Nader arguing the hazards of nuclear power. In both cases, the person will process the information intentionally with a view toward maximizing personal safety and minimizing hardship or danger. Although the newspaper reporter surely wrote the article with the intention of accurately disseminating information about a local tragedy, he or she had no *specific intent to persuade* our reader to oppose nuclear power. In contrast, the speaker did have this specific persuasive intention. That the reporter's purposive use of symbols was not motivated by an intent to persuade, while the speaker's was, is not, in our judgment, relevant to the intentional nature of the two processes of persuasion that took place. In each instance, our hypothetical receiver processed the information with an intent to maximize safety and minimize danger.

In sum, we believe that the locus of *persuasive* intentionality properly belongs with the recipient of messages. Hence, a specific intent to influence another is not a necessary component of the process of persuasion. We require only that persuasive effects result from the intentional assimilation and internalization of the meanings contained in messages.

THE RELATIONSHIP BETWEEN PERSUASION AND COERCION: A RECEIVER-BASED VIEW

At the beginning of this chapter, we referred to several types of social influence and variously labeled them *persuasion, education, brainwashing, mind control,* and so forth. Although we noted there are important differences among these forms, we suggested that some of the distinctions are more in the eye of the beholder than in the nature of the influence strategies employed. At this time, we need to examine more carefully the various forms of social influence. Our aim is to specify their commonalities as well as critical points of difference.

Persuasive communication is only one of many modes of social influence. From a recipient's perspective, all forms of social influence can be placed on a continuum ranging from relatively "noncoercive" at one extreme to "highly coercive" at the other. Terms like *brainwashing* and *mind control* normally are applied to influence strategies appearing at the coercive end of the continuum, whereas *persuasion, education,* and *interpersonal development* usually are placed toward the continuum's noncoercive end.

Persuasive communication has two characteristics distinguishing it from more coercive forms of social influence. First, when a person is exposed to a persuasive message, he or she has a *perception of choice* regarding the acceptance or rejection of symbolic appeals. As we stipulated earlier, whether behavioral options actually are available is not relevant. It is only required that an individual have the perception of free will. Second, if people choose to act on the recommendations made in persuasive messages, it is because they *privately accept* or *internalize* the advocated position. Thus, regardless of the label chosen for a form of influence, so long as a person feels free to choose, we regard the influence strategy as persuasive in nature.

In contrast, when people are confronted with coercive social influence, they perceive that they have *no choice* but to perform the behavior urged upon them. The elimination of choice may be accomplished in two ways—by either rewards or punishments, promised or delivered, for the performance or nonperformance of the desired behavior. (Again, whether a person actually lacks behavioral options is irrelevant. It is only necessary that an individual *perceives* no choice but to comply.)

A further distinguishing mark of coercive social influence is that when people act under duress, their behavior is characterized by *public compliance* without private acceptance. According to Kelman, the public complier "adopts the induced behavior—not because he believes its content—but because he expects to gain specific rewards . . . and avoid specific punishments by conforming."[30] Again, regardless of the label applied to a form of social influence, so long as the recipient experiences no choice, we believe the influence strategy is coercive in nature.

It follows that our criterion for determining whether a message is persuasive or coercive is based on the *perspective of the recipient of the message*. Moreover, using the criterion of perceived choice, the same message may be regarded as coercive by one person and persuasive by another. For example, suppose an employer suggests that a group of employees contribute to an office Christmas fund to help the needy in the community. Some employees are likely to perceive that they can choose to donate or not, depending on their current financial status, their concern for the poor, and so forth. For these people, the employer's remarks are persuasive in nature. Moreover, if they choose to contribute, they will do so because they privately accept the worth of the charity. On the other hand, some employees may perceive they have no choice but to contribute, fearing reprisals if they don't. For these people, the employer's remarks are coercive. Thus, their contributions will represent public compliance without private acceptance. Of course, many messages are not as ambiguous as such a remark from an employer. Thus, there often is substantial agreement among individuals regarding the persuasive versus the coercive nature of a message. For instance, most people would agree that "Hands up, give me your money!" is rather coercive, whereas "Please contribute to the Children's Fund" is more persuasive. Nevertheless, individuals will often disagree in their judgments of the nature of messages.

Although coercion results in public compliance without internalization, it should be noted that public compliance can lead to the private acceptance of an act initially induced by coercion. For instance, some people contributing under duress to our hypothetical Christmas fund may later see the benefits their donations brought to the needy in the community. In such a case, private acceptance occurs by persuading oneself over time of the rightness of a past behavior. Indeed, several theories of persuasion we shall consider in this book are based on the premise that initial public compliance can trigger a process of self-persuasion leading ultimately to internalization of the worth of a behavior. However, any behavior is a product of coercion when people perceive at the time that they have no choice but to enact it.

A MESSAGE-CENTERED VIEW OF PERSUASION AND COERCION

Some persuasion theorists take a different, message-centered approach to the persuasion–coercion dichotomy, arguing that the distinction between the two forms of social influence is far less clear-cut than we have implied. To illustrate some of these concerns, consider the following hypothetical examples of social influence strategies:

1. The boss of a criminal organization to a prospective trial witness: "If you testify against the organization, you'll never see your son alive again."

2. An employer seeking support for a controversial new company policy to a division foreman: "If you can convince everyone in your division to support the new policy, I promise to promote you to a managerial position."

3. A presidential candidate to the voting public: "If you elect my opponent, you can expect four more years of high taxes, soaring inflation, and corruption in government."

4. An actress in a television commercial advertisement to the viewing public: "Try new Smellum cologne. It will improve your social life and give you a fresh, new sense of self-confidence."

Note that the first two appeals seem highly coercive, promising explicit rewards or punishments for the performance or nonperformance of certain behaviors. In contrast, the last two are more representative of our usual notion of persuasive messages—each presents reasons listeners should choose to accept certain recommendations. But are the latter "persuasive" appeals radically different from the two appeals we labeled "coercive"?

Like the "coercive" messages, the "persuasive" appeals suggest that one recommended action will bring rewards like social approval and an improved self-image, whereas a failure to accept another suggestion will result in punishment—specifically, high taxes, exorbitant prices, and governmental corruption. Indeed, it can be argued that the effectiveness of the "persuasive" messages depends on how serious the threatened punishments and how attractive the promised rewards are perceived to be. That the effectiveness of most persuasive messages depends heavily on the *credibility* of threatened punishments and promised rewards has led several theorists, notably Simons[31] and Miller,[32] to argue that persuasive communication is an *indirectly coercive* form of social influence. They contend that people, as intentional agents, adopt behaviors promising rewards and avoid those threatening punishments. Thus, from Simons' and Miller's perspective, "coercive potential determines the relative impact of most persuasive messages."[33]

This analysis raises the question of whether it is possible to make a meaningful distinction between coercion and persuasion. We believe it unlikely that a clear-cut, dichotomous distinction can be drawn since, as Miller and Simons note, the two forms of influence share many important features. However, we believe it is possible to differentiate meaningfully between the two on a continuous basis. To accomplish this, the conceptual properties peculiar to each must be stipulated, so that "coercive" symbolic influence can be positioned at one end of the continuum and "persuasion" at the other. Such a scheme would differentiate between the two, yet allow for a middle ground where distinctions become blurred and, therefore, meaningless.

To set down the conceptual properties peculiar to coercion and persuasion, we should recall the essential difference between Simons' and Miller's argument, on the one hand, and our position on the other. Their view that persuasion is indirectly coercive is a *message-based* argument. From such a perspective, the content of blatantly "coercive" messages as well as subtle "persuasive" ones both associate rewards and punishments with recommended courses of action. Thus, if one's judgmental criterion is the objective content of the message, all messages are "more or less" coercive. In contrast, we advanced a *receiver-based* argument, using a person's interpretation of the content of messages, not the objective content itself, as our judgmental criterion. According to this view, coercion occurs when people feel they have no choice but to comply with recommendations. On the other hand, when individuals feel free to accept or reject a recommended action, then the message may properly be termed persuasive.

The divergent conclusions reached by these two approaches derive not from logical fallacies in either argument, but from their use of quite different criteria for determining the essential nature of messages. Simons and Miller emphasize the objective content of a message; the receiver-based perspective focuses on people's subjective interpretations of messages. Despite appearances, these two approaches are not intrinsically incompatible. Indeed, each can complement the other in the search for meaningful distinctions between persuasion and coercion, a search that must take account of both the content of messages and people's reactions to that content.

The locus of commonality between the two perspectives derives from the *interdependence* of message content and one's interpretations of that content. Perceptions of choice or compulsion inevitably are based on the meanings assigned to the content of messages and associated cues. Although there will be individual differences, people in any one speech community undoubtedly have some common notions about which content cues imply coercion and which imply choice. Thus, we must ask what general types of content are most likely to be perceived as coercive and what varieties probably imply a freedom of choice? A satisfactory answer to this question should reconcile some of the thornier differences between the receiver-based and the message-centered views of the persuasion–coercion dichotomy.

Reconciling the Perspectives

James Tedeschi and his associates have suggested a classification scheme for social influence strategies that may help reconcile our present dilemma.[34] According to Tedeschi, all direct modes of social influence may be separated into two broad categories: (1) those involving explicit *control over positive and negative reinforcements;* and (2) those relying upon *control over information.* In the first message category, the source has *personal control* over rewards and punishments and has the *power* (intent or motivation + capacity to deliver the reinforcement)[35] to dispense them for the performance or nonperformance of recommended courses of action. The two social influence strategies available to such a powerful individual are called threats and promises. A *threat* implies the threatener has personal control over punishments and the motivation and capacity to deliver them for the nonperformance of a recommended behavior. A *promise* implies the promiser has personal control over rewards and the explicit power to dispense them for the performance of a suggested action.

For messages falling into the second category, the source has *information* about naturally occurring rewards and punishments in the physical or social environment, but lacks the personal power to deliver them for the performance or nonperformance of recommended actions. Two kinds of social influence strategies are available to individuals who possess information about environmental reinforcements: warnings and mendations. A *warning* informs listeners about probable "punishments which the source does not control but knows about, whereas a *mendation* predicts positive consequences" that may, though not necessarily will, result if listeners take the suggested course of action.[36] Thus, warnings and mendations are essentially *predictions* about *probable* links between actions and naturally occurring reinforcements. For example, a persuader may be aware that social approval may result from the actions being recommended. Conversely, the persuader may know that social sanctions or health hazards may occur if the recommendations are not accepted. Of course, as Tedeschi has noted, warnings and mendations are not always different, since telling someone "not to do something because of the negative consequences may at the same time point to an alternative behavior that would have positive consequences."[37]

In general, the effectiveness of a person using warnings and mendations is based on the possession of information about probable rewards and punishments, coupled with the ability to communicate that information to others and not on the power to dispense rewards and punishments. In contrast, the effectiveness of an individual using threats and promises derives from his or her personal control of rewards and punishments and the certain power to deliver them for the performance or nonperformance of suggested actions.

Threats, Promises, and Choice   Tedeschi's analysis allows us to speculate on those types of messages most likely to be interpreted as coercive versus those likely to imply a freedom of choice. A message containing threats and promises is likely to foster the impression of having little or no choice but to accede to the source's recommendations. The first two hypothetical appeals outlined earlier were messages of this sort. The first, you will recall, involved a death threat to the son of a prospective trial witness by the boss of a criminal organization. The power of this individual to deliver the threatened punishment probably would not be questioned by the recipient of the message. Thus, we have in this instance clear coercive cues likely to be perceived as such by most reasonable people. The second message involved the promise of a promotion and financial gain to the recipient of the message. The power of the employer to deliver the promised rewards probably would not be disputed by the division foreman. Again, we have a message containing clear coercive cues that persons in the same speech community most likely would recognize as such.

Although messages containing threats and promises increase tremendously the probability that choice will be eradicated, this is not always the case. If a person doubts either the motivation *or* the ability of a source to deliver rewards or punishments, the perception of choice should remain intact. For instance, if our hypothetical foreman believed in the employer's ability to deliver the promised promotion, yet doubted his or her motivation, a perception of choice should remain. As this example indicates, *noncredible* threats and promises are functionally equivalent to warnings and mendations, respectively.

However, even if a person believes a source has the motivation as well as the ability to deliver reinforcements, a perception of choice is not necessarily eliminated. We saw earlier that objective contingencies and the perception of control are imperfectly matched. Thus, our foreman, although confident of the employer's power, may prefer his or her present job or otherwise feel free to reject the employer's offer. Less likely, but still possible, is the chance that the prospective witness will choose to jeopardize his or her son's life. Nevertheless, messages containing threats and promises are those most likely to eliminate a recipient's perception of choice. Although both threats and promises are effective, threats to harm someone usually are far more powerful coercive cues than promises of reward, since ignoring a threat is inherently more risky than eschewing reward.

Warnings, Mendations, and Choice   In contrast to threats and promises, messages containing warnings and mendations are likely to foster the perception that one has a choice to accept or reject the recommended actions. This is because the effectiveness of warnings and mendations depends, not on a source's personal power to reward and punish, but on the *credibility of the information* presented about naturally occurring, environmental rewards and punishments that might, though not necessarily will, result. Thus, unlike the recipients of threats and promises, receivers of warnings and mendations must assess the probability that naturally occurring rewards and punishments will be forthcoming if they perform or do not perform recommended actions. This judgment is necessary since the source has no personal control over claimed reinforcements. As this analysis suggests, messages relying on the control of information about probable environmental rewards and punishments are more likely to imply a freedom of choice than messages whose effectiveness derives from the certain possession of power. Indeed, we believe it is meaningful to define *a persuasive message as one relying on information control to prompt human action, whereas a coercive message is one relying on reinforcement control to induce behavior.*

In summary, we believe that our receiver-based view and the message-based approach of Simons and Miller are reconciled satisfactorily by the analysis we have presented. From our perspective, the criterion distinguishing persuasion from coercion remains the recipient's perception of choice or lack of it. However, Tedeschi's thinking has allowed us to specify the types of content cues most likely to exert a predominant influence on a person's perception of free will. Messages relying on reinforcement control are likely to imply coercion, whereas messages relying on information control are likely to be perceived as persuasive.

Persuasion and Coercion as Mutually Supportive Influence Modes

Most practical programs of social influence use a mix of persuasive messages relying on information control and coercive messages entailing reinforcement control. The extent to which coercion will be used with persuasion depends on a source's *power* over reinforcements. When a source cannot reward and punish, persuasion is likely to be the dominant mode of social influence.

For example, advertisers must rely almost exclusively on persuasion to sell goods and services since they have no power to punish television viewers or magazine readers if they don't buy their client's brand of laundry detergent, toothpaste, or deodorant. As a consequence, advertisers rely on warnings that failure to use a product likely will result in dingy clothes, decaying teeth, or a generally miserable social life. Alternately, they can use mendations, assuring people that social, economic, and health benefits may result from using a product or service. Similarly in politics, challengers have little power relative to incumbents and must rely heavily on persuasive messages, warning of the potential dangers of electing opponents, or pointing to the benefits of supporting their own candidacies.

In contrast, when sources control reinforcements, coercion is used liberally in pursuit of goals. For example, politicians seeking reelection have considerable power to reward special interest groups and other constituencies with financial and political support in exchange for votes and to punish reluctant voting blocs by withholding funds or blocking public projects they favor. Thus, political incumbents often rely heavily on threats and promises to secure reelection. Of course, they also spend millions of dollars for mass media persuasive campaigns in support of their candidacies. In cases like this, coercion and persuasion complement one another in the pursuit of desired objectives.

Regardless of the ratio of persuasive to coercive messages in any one social influence program, the two modes have quite different functions. As we have earlier noted, persuasion effects the *internalization* or *private acceptance* of new ways of believing and behaving, whereas coercion's role is to secure *public compliance* with the wishes of powerful individuals. These functions reinforce one another in at least two crucial ways.

First, coercion often sets the stage for internalization by rendering people more susceptible to later persuasive appeals. For instance, political and religious indoctrination programs typically employ reinforcement controls before exposing potential converts to information designed to persuade. One common tactic is to encourage the breakup of a person's social support systems. For example, the religious movement of the Reverend Sun Myung Moon reportedly encourages potential converts to renounce their family and friends outside the church. By inducing social isolation, potential converts are far more amenable to the persuasion of the Unification Church than they might be were old social contacts maintained.

Second, public compliance induced by reinforcement control often leads to later internalization of the compliant act without the intervention of external persuasive appeals. As we mentioned earlier, public compliance can trigger a process of *self-persuasion*: in time an individual finds positive reasons to support behavior that initially was performed under duress. Clearly, in the rough-and-tumble arena of social influence, information and reinforcement controls often work in tandem to produce intended effects. But despite its complementariness with coercion, persuasion remains a crucial ingredient in any social influence program. It alone can effect the private acceptance of new cognitive structures and patterns of overt behavior.

THE NATURE OF PERSUASION: AN EXTENDED ANALYSIS

Thus far, we have suggested that persuasion occurs when people internalize or voluntarily accept the meanings they attach to messages. Additionally, we concluded that persuasive messages rely on information control or warnings and mendations to promote the internalization of recommended courses of action. We can now extend our analysis of the nature of persuasion by exploring three additional dimensions of the process: (1) the nature of persuasive *effects*; (2) classic *persuasive paradigms*, including active and passive participation models; and (3) the influence of the *medium* through which persuasive messages pass.

Types of Persuasive Effects

Heretofore, most of our examples of persuasive responses have focused on *changes* in people's cognitions or behaviors since those correspond to our usual notion of what a persuasive communication effect is or ought to be. However, the *formation* or creation of cognitions and behaviors and the *reinforcement* or strengthening of existing cognitive and behavioral dispositions, making them more resistant to change, are equally important.[38] These latter persuasive effects are, in fact, as prevalent as the change paradigm.

Consider, for instance, the barrage of advertisements by large corporations designed to create and reinforce their image and the image of their products. "Pioneer, the trusted name in electronics"; "U.S. Steel: people helping other people"; and "You and DuPont: there's a lot of good chemistry between us," are typical examples. Large companies devote considerable monies to creating and strengthening consistent buying behaviors among consumers. The old Tareyton cigarette slogan, "I'd rather fight than switch," is a pertinent, if transparent, example of a reinforcement technique. In general, over 30 years of research confirms that the major persuasive effect of mass media advertising and programming is not the alteration, but the creation of new and the reaffirmation of existing attitudes, norms, and values.[39] Thus, when we study persuasive communication effects, creation and reinforcement as well as change must be taken fully into account.

Paradigms of Persuasion: The Traditional Model

There are two frameworks in which persuasive communication occurs: an information-processing paradigm and an active participation paradigm. In the first, an *information-processing* or *traditional persuasive paradigm,* some external agent is the primary overt producer of messages. This traditional model is exemplified by commercial advertising, political speaking, sermons, and other forms of public information dispersal. Although an external source is the principal overt symbolizer, it is important to remember that the recipients of externally produced messages actively assign personal meanings to messages and respond to their own interpretations of messages, not to the uninterpreted content of an extrinsic set of symbols.

Anthony Greenwald and his associates suggest that in addition to assigning personal meanings to messages, people typically engage in active, covert argumentation in response to externally generated messages.[40] Put another way, people generate idiosyncratic *response messages* to the arguments presented by an external agent, and these messages take many forms. One of the more common forms is counterargumentation—the generation of arguments, including warnings and mendations, that contradict the external source's arguments. A second common response is supportive argumentation. Additional information, not contained in the messages, is sought to bolster the original claims made by the source. Clearly, externally produced messages are powerful stimuli, triggering cognitive responses and interpretative transformations of the arguments contained in the messages. And it is these interpretative responses, not the raw content of the message itself, that mediate persuasive effects in the traditional information-processing paradigm.

Considerable evidence supports this view. For example, in an early study, Cullen asked college students to read a persuasive message containing 12 different arguments supporting a career-oriented as opposed to a liberal arts education. After reading the message, the recipients were asked to "collect their thoughts" and list everything that had occurred to them as they read. This information was then classified as either source originated, defined as ideas learned directly from the persuasive message, or as self-generated. The self-generated thoughts were supportive argumentation and counterargumentation, as well as original ideas and arguments not traceable to the material presented in the message. The results showed that the vast majority of cognitions listed by the message recipients were in the self-generated category. Moreover, attitude change on the issue of general versus specialized education bore a positive correlation to the content of self-generated cognitions but was unrelated to the content of source-originated thoughts.[41]

In a more recent study, Cacioppo and Petty asked a group of university students to listen to a taped message advocating an increase in expenditures at their institution. After hearing the message, the listeners were requested to list all the thoughts that had occurred to them during the presentation. All thoughts were then classified either as cognitions supporting the persuasive message, as counterarguments against the message, or as neutral thoughts irrelevant to the message. Finally, the recipients were asked to list all the message arguments they could recall. Results showed that attitude change or agreement with the persuasive message was positively correlated with supportive cognitive responses, negatively related to covert counterarguments, and bore no relation to recall of message content or neutral cognitive responses.[42]

These findings support our conceptual position that persuasive effects in the traditional paradigm result from a people's active interpretation of and cognitive responses to persuasive messages, in effect, from the messages they create for themselves. In Part 3 of this book, we shall consider further the dynamics of persuasion in the traditional paradigm by examining a number of specific information-processing theories of persuasive communication.

Paradigms of Persuasion: The Active Participatory Model

As you may recall, the second persuasive framework was termed a *self-persuasion* or *active participation paradigm*. This model entails no external producer of messages. Rather, people generate their own *original messages* containing reasons for changing beliefs or behaviors. This process usually is triggered by engaging in activities like role-playing and group interaction, or by participating in sales promotion strategies like the use of free samples or the acceptance of introductory trial offers of new commercial products.

For example, the person who takes advantage of an introductory trial offer of an unneeded set of cookware or fishing gear and proceeds to convince himself or herself to keep the purchase illustrates the active participatory model of persuasion. Similarly, the process of actively thinking about an issue regarding the self or the environment usually results in a number of self-generated persuasive messages. For instance, suppose I decide to consider seriously why I continue to smoke cigarettes despite the obvious dangers. In so doing, I will generate numerous arguments in support of my present habit or in support of my resolve to quit. As these examples indicate, in the active participation paradigm, people generate their own original messages without the benefit of external symbolization.

The effectiveness of the active participation paradigm was first examined experimentally during World War II. Due to military requirements, there was an acute shortage of desirable cuts of beef, pork, and other meats for the American public. To try to alleviate these problems, the United States government launched a campaign to persuade American housewives to increase their families' consumption of undesirable cuts of meat, such as beef hearts, pork brains, sweetbreads, and kidneys. Lewin conducted a series of experiments comparing the relative effects of traditional persuasion and active group discussion on women's attitudes and behaviors toward these unusual foods.

Lewin had one group of women listen to a 45-minute persuasive message emphasizing the nutritional value of the meats and linking the problem of nutrition to the war effort. Afterwards, information packets and recipes were distributed to the audience. Another group of women participated in a group discussion triggered by a brief, low-key statement mentioning the war effort and specifying the meats. The group then discussed their feelings about the unaccustomed foods for 45 minutes. At the conclusion, the same information packets and recipes were given to the discussion group. A follow-up study showed that only 3 percent of the women who heard the persuasive message served one of the suggested meats to the family, whereas 32 percent of the women in the discussion group served them.[43] In later studies, Lewin consistently found the self-persuasion strategy a superior method of changing people's behavior.

A number of factors may account for this finding. An increased emotional involvement may heighten attention and motivation. Clearly, the inventive quality of active participation strategies promotes many self-generated messages. And Greenwald and Albert found that self-generated arguments are easier to understand and remember and are far more readily assimilated into preexisting frameworks of attitudes and values than are arguments generated by an external agent.[44] In Part 2 of this book, we will examine why self-generated persuasion is so effective as we review some active participation theories of persuasion.

In summary, whether the persuasive paradigm is traditional or one designed to stimulate original self-generated arguments, people are persuaded by the messages they create for themselves, and it is to these messages that the final effects of any process of persuasion may be attributed.

The Influence of Media on Persuasion Processes

Persuasive messages are transmitted through two types of media: face-to-face and mass, including electronic and print media. The *face-to-face medium* is characterized by "live" contact between the communicating parties. All five communication channels—sight, sound, touch, taste, and smell—are available for the exchange of verbal and nonverbal symbols. Moreover, *feedback*—the responses of each person to the messages of others—is rapid and continuous as the communication progresses.

Two varieties of persuasion use the face-to-face medium. The first, *public persuasion,* occurs when one or more individuals transmit messages to a relatively large number of other people. Because of audience size, the channels used in public persuasion normally are limited to sight and sound. A religious service, like the Billy Graham crusades, or a mass rally denouncing nuclear energy or supporting equal rights for women are typical examples of public persuasion.

Interpersonal persuasion is the second variety of persuasion occurring in the face-to-face medium. Unlike public persuasion, the number of participants in interpersonal persuasion is sufficiently small that all can engage in meaningful interaction and mutual influence. Because all parties to an interpersonal encounter interact directly with one another, additional communication channels like touch may be employed to convey messages. Interpersonal persuasive effects include cognitive and behavior changes that result from interacting with friends, family, and romantic partners. The development of all our personal relationships is a product of an ongoing process of interpersonal persuasion. Indeed, our basic values and, ultimately, our self-concepts emerge and evolve over a lifetime simply because we are engaged in mutual interaction with other people.

Although the two types of face-to-face persuasion share some characteristics, they differ in several important respects. Public and interpersonal persuasion are alike in that they are both "live" events, benefiting from rapid feedback. This responsiveness, more than any other quality, creates a level of interaction among communicators not found in mass persuasion. Even so, public persuasion has considerably less *mutual* interaction and influence than does the interpersonal variety. Public persuasion, like mass media communication, is a traditional, source-based phenomenon (some external agent is the producer of messages) and as such is often regarded as a "live" variant of mass communication. In contrast, in interpersonal persuasion all participants are active coproducers of messages resulting in a spiraling, developmental process of mutual interaction and influence.

In contrast to public and interpersonal persuasion, the *mass media* are characterized by the interposition of either an electronic device or the printed page between the communicating parties. Available communication channels are limited to sound only in the case of the radio; sight only for newspapers, magazines, books, billboards, and the like; and a combination of sight and sound is available in the case of television and film. Feedback occurs on a delayed basis. Thus, political candidates rely on follow-up reports of political polling agencies, a count of campaign contributions, or returns at the ballot box to assess the effectiveness of their media messages. Likewise, advertisers rely on indices like gross sales and market analyses to judge the impact of television, newspaper, and magazine advertisements.

Further distinguishing characteristics of mass persuasion are audience size (the number of potential recipients of any one mass communication message is relatively unlimited) and its traditional active source mode of symbolic influence.

The Developmental Nature of the Media Forms   To some extent interpersonal, public, and mass persuasion are all developmental in nature. Recall that a process of persuasion is developmental to the extent that each person is influenced by every other person and that the relationship among people in a persuasive transaction develops and matures as their communications continue. To be developmental, a process of persuasion must be characterized by relatively continuous feedback. The degree to which feedback is meaningful and continuous depends on the medium employed and on the number of participants in any one persuasive transaction.

It should be clear from our discussion of interpersonal, public, and mass persuasion, that interpersonal persuasion is the most developmental of the three. It is characterized by rapid feedback among participants whose number is small enough that each can interact meaningfully with the others on a face-to-face basis. Public persuasion benefits from rapid feedback processes as well, but its source orientation and large audience size diminish the amount of mutual interaction and influence among all parties. Thus, public persuasion is less developmental than interpersonal communication. Mass persuasion is the least developmental of the three forms of social influence. Certainly, mass persuasion has some developmental characteristics in that sources of media messages and their recipients influence the form and content of each other's responses. However, the delay associated with mass media feedback, coupled with the physical separation of the communicators, make a dynamic developmental relationship difficult to establish.

A CASE STUDY: THE CONVERSION OF
PATRICIA HEARST

As we have described it, persuasion is a developmental process whose effects result from the internalization of meanings people assign to messages. Moreover, it is an informational process entailing a perception of free will on the part of each party to the transaction. Each participant is viewed as an active, goal-directed agent who ultimately shapes his or her own responses to messages.

Examining a case study that highlights in a dramatic fashion the dynamics of persuasion should crystallize our viewpoint. The incident involves *conversion*, a process of giving up one ordered view of the world for another. As we shall learn, conversion is almost exclusively a product of face-to-face interpersonal persuasion and it entails a high level of active participation on the part of the convert, who, in the final analysis, persuades him or herself of the value of new visions and the worth of new ways. Finally, we shall see that coercive influence strategies or reinforcement controls typically are employed early in the conversion process to render the potential convert more susceptible to later persuasive appeals. Thus, we will see how coercion aimed at public compliance and persuasion directed toward private acceptance work together to promote changes in people's views of themselves and their world.

The Transformation of Patricia Hearst

On February 3, 1974, Patricia Campbell Hearst, heiress to the Hearst newspaper empire, was kidnapped from her Berkeley, California, apartment by a small band of young revolutionaries calling themselves the Symbionese Liberation Army. The SLA, a group dedicated to the liberation of all people "oppressed by capitalism," immediately demanded that the wealthy Hearst family purchase several million dollars worth of food as ransom and distribute it to the poor of California.

After two months of captivity, two weeks of which were spent blindfolded and locked in a small closet, Patty Hearst made the startling announcement that she had decided to join the SLA. She publicly renounced her family and took the name Tania, after a revolutionary who had fought along with Ché Guevara during the Cuban revolution. Finally, Patty expressed hope that her family and friends would "try to understand the changes I've gone through." During the next few months, Hearst participated with the SLA in the armed robbery of a bank and a sporting goods store. On being captured by the FBI 17 months later, Tania smiled for the press, clenched her fist in a radical salute, and proclaimed herself forever "an urban guerilla."

Variables Prompting the Conversion of Tania

The conversion of Patricia Hearst to Tania, the urban guerilla, provides a dramatic illustration of interpersonal persuasion at work. Although some of the initial influence strategies used by the SLA were highly coercive, most of their later tactics were persuasive in nature, aimed at inducing Patty Hearst to privately accept the philosophy of the SLA. Moreover, these strategies were really quite ordinary, much like those used by "respectable" American institutions like the home, the church, and the school. Philip Zimbardo and his associates studied the variables at work in the metamorphosis of Patty Hearst and provided an account that illustrates the "ordinary" quality of most of the strategies employed.[45]

First, Patricia Hearst's political beliefs, although not very well formed, were somewhat left of center. Second, the conditions of her kidnapping and confinement in a closet aroused fear and anxiety about her eventual safe return. By letting her out of the closet, not harming her, and treating her well, the SLA induced feelings of gratitude in her. Moreover, strong guilt feelings may have been aroused because of her family's privileged position and the disparity between the Hearst wealth and the poverty of those who were the object of the SLA's concern. Third, the usual sources of support on which Patty had relied for social rewards, feedback, and identity were severed. She was exposed daily to persuasive communications espousing the philosophy of the SLA with no opportunity to seek countercommunications.

Fourth, the eight members of the SLA were a cohesive unit sharing bed and board as well as beliefs. They defined Hearst's reality, and their approval became powerful sources of social reward, status, and recognition. Moreover, Patty could readily identify with them since most were her age and came from similar well-to-do backgrounds. In addition, the SLA members were practicing what they preached in not wanting money for themselves, but in a Robin Hood fashion, were feeding the poor with what they got from the rich. Thus, they probably were seen as trustworthy and attractive communicators who were models of the message they proclaimed.

Finally, critical to inducing change in Patricia Hearst was her perception that the decision to join the SLA was made of her own free will. In this regard, SLA member William Harris reported that just before Hearst took off the blindfold that they had put on her at the time of the kidnapping, she was "reminded that she could walk freely out the door and that we would help her return to her family and friends. We all wanted Tania to stay," said Harris, "but we wanted to make sure that she saw all her options and was making a strong choice with no regrets or indecision."[46] Hearst said of her own transformation:

> What some people refer to as a sudden conversion was actually a process of development, much the same as a photograph is developed. . . . We ate all our meals together . . . and during these times, we would discuss different events, different struggles. At first I didn't say anything. I felt weird sitting and arguing with these people while I was blindfolded. After a while I began to participate in these discussions. I began to see . . . that U.S. imperialism is the enemy of all oppressed people. I opened my eyes and realized it was time to get off my ass.[47]

An Analysis of Hearst's Conversion

Although most persuasion focuses on less ambitious goals and occurs in less constrained circumstances than did Hearst's conversion, the basic developmental process and many of the supporting strategies were the same. There were two stages in the program that led Patty Hearst to accept the philosophy of the Symbionese Liberation Army.

In the initial stage, coercion or reinforcement control was used. Her kidnapping and the resulting social isolation were powerful negative reinforcers that made her vulnerable to later persuasive appeals outlining the virtues of a replacement support system. Moreover, by confining, then releasing Hearst from the closet and treating her well, the SLA created potent positive reinforcements. Her relief and gratitude should have increased further her vulnerability to the SLA's later persuasive communications.

The second stage in Hearst's conversion occurred after her release from the closet. The SLA changed its tactics from coercion to persuasion or information control aimed at effecting the internalization of their political views. As Zimbardo's account indicated, there was nothing unusual or sinister about the SLA's persuasive strategies. Indeed, they were similar to the tactics used in any active participatory process of interpersonal persuasion.

Three persuasive strategies were used to convince Hearst of the worth of the SLA's philosophy. First, the members of the SLA succeeded in establishing themselves as *credible purveyors of information,* increasing the probability that Hearst's cognitive responses to their messages would be more supportive than counterargumentative. Second, by engaging her in active discussion and interaction with the group, the SLA triggered a process of *self-persuasion.* Hearst convinced herself of the wisdom of the SLA's political mission. Finally, Hearst's *perception of free will* to join or reject the SLA was critical to her ultimate internalization of positive information about the Symbionese Liberation Army.

By virtue of these three factors, the conversion of Patty Hearst followed the classic pattern of a *developmental* process of interpersonal persuasion. As Hearst put it, her conversion was a *gradual* metamorphosis, a "process of development," despite outward appearances of abrupt or radical alteration. As a developmental activity, all communicating parties actively contributed to the final outcome of the persuasive encounter. Moreover, in the Hearst case as in many processes of interpersonal persuasion, the emphasis was on supplying the verbal and nonverbal stimuli for Patty to actively persuade herself of the wisdom of a new world view.

Hearst's conversion highlights the relative roles played by coercion and persuasion in a total social influence program. Although initially the victim of brutal coercion, Hearst's ultimate decision to join the SLA was, by her account, a consequent of *voluntarily* internalizing the argument that "U.S. imperialism is the enemy of all oppressed people." As the Hearst case sharply illustrates, although coercion is a powerful means of rendering people susceptible to informational appeals, it remains the task of persuasion to effect the private acceptance of new ways of believing and behaving.

NOTES

1. For a discussion of some of the more unusual cults, see Martin Ebon, ed., *The World's Weirdest Cults* (New York: New American Library, 1979).

2. The term *brainwashing* was coined by the journalist Edward Hunter, whose book, *Brainwashing in Red China* (New York: Vanguard, 1941), documented the efforts of Mao Tse-tung's Communist cadres to change the ideology of the Nationalist Chinese.

3. Edgar H. Schein, Inge Schneier, and Curtis H. Barker, *Coercive Persuasion* (New York: Norton, 1961), p. 285.

4. For a discussion of the persuasive impact of Welles' "War of the Worlds," see Hadley Cantril, "The Invasion from Mars," in *The Process and Effects of Mass Communication*, 2nd ed., ed. Wilbur Schramm and Donald F. Roberts (Urbana, Ill.: University of Illinois Press, 1971), pp. 579–595.

5. W. Phillips Davison, "On the Effects of Communication," *Public Opinion Quarterly* 23 (1959): 360.

6. Wilbur Schramm, "The Nature of Communication Between Humans," in *The Process and Effects of Mass Communication*, p. 8.

7. For discussion of several versions of the transactional approach to communication, see William W. Wilmot, *Dyadic Communication: A Transactional Perspective* (Reading, Mass.: Addison-Wesley, 1975); C. David Mortensen, "A Transactional Paradigm of Verbalized Social Conflict," in *Perspectives on Communication in Social Conflict*, ed. Gerald R. Miller and Herbert W. Simons (Englewood Cliffs, N.J.: Prentice-Hall, 1974), pp. 90–124; Dean C. Barnlund, "A Transactional Model of Communication," in *Language Behavior: A Book of Readings*, ed. Johnnye Akins et al. (The Hague, The Netherlands: Mouton, 1970), pp. 53–61; and Eric Berne, *Transactional Analysis in Psychotherapy* (New York: Grove Press, 1961).

8. For discussions of communication as a developmental process, see Charles R. Berger and Richard J. Calabrese, "Some Explorations in Initial Interaction and Beyond: Toward a Developmental Theory of Interpersonal Communication," *Human Communication Research* 1 (1975): 99–112; Gerald R. Miller, "Interpersonal Communication: A Conceptual Perspective," *Communication* 2 (1975): 93–105; and Gerald R. Miller and Mark Steinberg, *Between People: A New Analysis of Interpersonal Communication* (Chicago: Science Research Associates, 1975).

9. Erwin P. Bettinghaus, *Persuasive Communication*, 3rd ed. (New York: Holt, Rinehart & Winston, 1980), p. 4. Because of the overwhelmingly dominant role accorded the source in Bettinghaus' conception of persuasion, a convincing case can be made that his approach is more hypodermic in nature than transactional.

10. Gary Cronkhite, *Persuasion: Speech and Behavioral Change* (Indianapolis: Bobbs-Merrill, 1969), p. 15.

11. Thomas M. Scheidel, *Persuasive Speaking* (Glenview, Ill.: Scott, Foresman, 1967), p. 1.

12. Wallace C. Fotheringham, *Perspectives on Persuasion* (Boston: Allyn and Bacon, 1966), pp. 7–8.

13. Charles U. Larson, *Persuasion: Reception and Responsibility*, 2nd ed. (Belmont, Calif.: Wadsworth, 1979), p. 7.

14. Gerald R. Miller and Michael Burgoon, *New Techniques of Persuasion* (New York: Harper & Row, 1973), p. 16.

15. Herbert W. Simons, "Persuasion and Attitude Change," in *Speech Communication Behavior: Perspectives and Principles*, ed. Larry L. Barker and Robert J. Kibler (Englewood Cliffs, N.J.: Prentice-Hall, 1971), p. 232.

16. Kenneth E. Andersen, *Persuasion: Theory and Practice* (Boston: Allyn and Bacon, 1971), p. 23.

17. Bettinghaus, p. 4; Miller and Burgoon, p. 16; Scheidel, p. 1. Others sharing this view include Winston L. Brembeck and William S. Howell, *Persuasion: A Means of Social Change*, 2nd ed. (Englewood Cliffs, N.J.: Prentice-Hall, 1976); and Simons.

18. Stephen W. King, *Communication and Social Influence* (Reading, Mass.: Addison-Wesley, 1975), pp. 12–13.

19. Larson, p. 7. For other response models, see Fotheringham; and Cronkhite.

20. Otto Lerbinger, *Designs for Persuasive Communication* (Englewood Cliffs, N.J.: Prentice-Hall, 1972), p. 3.

21. Andersen, p. 23. Others taking this approach include Bettinghaus; Miller and Burgoon; Brembeck and Howell; Simons; and Scheidel.

22. Cronkhite, p. 14.

23. Fotheringham, p. 7; and Larson, p. 7.

24. Herbert C. Kelman, "Compliance, Identification, and Internalization: Three Processes of Attitude Change," *Journal of Conflict Resolution* 2 (1958): 53.

25. Ellen J. Langer, "The Illusion of Control," *Journal of Personality and Social Psychology* 32 (1975): 311–328.

26. William H. Ittelsen and Hadley Cantril, *Perception: A Transactional Approach* (New York: Norton, 1954), p. 5.

27. This view of the relationship of humans to their environment is patterned after a cognitive schematic or constructivist approach. See Shelley E. Taylor and Jennifer Crocker, "Schematic Bases of Social Information Processing," in *The Ontario Symposium on Personality and Social Psychology: Social Cognition*, ed. E. Tory Higgins, E. Peter Herman, and Mark P. Zanna (Hillsdale, N.J.: Lawrence Erlbaum, 1981); Jesse C. Delia, "Constructivism and the Study of Human Communication," *Quarterly Journal of Speech* 63 (1977): 66–83; and Chapter 2 of this book.

28. This view of people as active agents is based on an actional approach to the nature of human behavior. For a full discussion of this view, see Romano Harré and Paul F. Secord, *The Explanation of Social Behavior* (Oxford: Basil Blackwell, 1972); and Chapter 3 of this book.

29. For a discussion of intentionality similar to our view, see Robert L. Scott, "Communication as an Intentional, Social System," *Human Communication Research* 3 (1977): 258–268.

30. Kelman.

31. Herbert W. Simons, "The Carrot and Stick as Handmaidens of Persuasion in Conflict Situations," in *Perspectives on Communication in Social Conflict*.

32. Gerald R. Miller, "On Being Persuaded: Some Basic Definitions," in *Persuasion: New Directions in Theory and Research*, ed. Michael E. Roloff and Gerald R. Miller (Beverly Hills, Calif.: Sage Publications, 1980), pp. 12–15.

33. Miller, "On Being Persuaded," p. 13.

34. See James T. Tedeschi and Paul Rosenfeld, "Communication in Bargaining and Negotiation," in *Persuasion: New Directions in Theory and Research*, pp. 225–248; James T. Tedeschi and Svenn Lindskold, *Social Psychology: Interdependence, Interaction and Influence* (New York: John Wiley, 1976); and James T. Tedeschi, "Threats and Promises," in *The Structure of Conflict*, ed. Paul Swingle (New York: Academic Press, 1970), pp. 155–191.

35. See Tedeschi, pp. 157–162.

36. Tedeschi and Rosenfeld, p. 234.

37. Ibid.

38. As we shall discover in Chapter 12 of this book, reinforcing cognitions and behaviors is not always equivalent to rendering them more resistant to change. However, for the present, we shall treat the two as similar effects.

39. See Wilbur Schramm and Donald F. Roberts, "Social Consequences of Mass Communication," in *The Process and Effects of Mass Communication*, pp. 519–523; and Joseph T. Klapper, *The Effects of Mass Communication* (Glencoe, Ill.: The Free Press, 1960).

40. See Richard E. Petty, Thomas M. Ostrom, and Timothy C. Brock, eds., *Cognitive Responses in Persuasion* (Hillsdale, N.J.: Lawrence Erlbaum, in press); Richard M. Perloff and Timothy C. Brock, "'And Thinking Makes it So:' Cognitive Responses in Persuasion," in *Persuasion: New Directions in Theory and Research*, pp. 67–99; and Anthony G. Greenwald, "Cognitive Learning, Cognitive Response to Persuasion, and Attitude Change," in *Psychological Foundations of Attitudes*, ed. Anthony G. Greenwald, Timothy C. Brock, and Thomas M. Ostrom (New York: Academic Press, 1968), pp. 147–170.

41.   Dallas M. Cullen, "Attitude Measurement by Cognitive Sampling" (Ph.D. diss., Ohio State University, 1968).

42.   John T. Cacioppo and Richard E. Petty, "Effects of Message Repetition and Position on Cognitive Response, Recall, and Persuasion," *Journal of Personality and Social Psychology* 37 (1979): 97–109.

43.   Kurt Lewin, "Group Decision and Social Change," in *Basic Readings in Social Psychology*, ed. Harold M. Proshansky and Bernard Seidenberg (New York: Holt, Rinehart & Winston, 1965), pp. 423–437.

44.   Anthony G. Greenwald and Rosita D. Albert, "Acceptance and Recall of Improvised Arguments," *Journal of Personality and Social Psychology* 8 (1968): 31–34.

45.   Philip G. Zimbardo, Ebbe B. Ebbesen, and Christina Maslach, *Influencing Attitudes and Changing Behavior*, 2nd ed., © 1977, Addison-Wesley Publishing Company, Inc., pp. 13–14. Reprinted by permission.

46.   Ronald Koziol, "Patty's Story: Why I Joined the SLA," *Chicago Tribune*, 6 February 1976, p. 1. © *Chicago Tribune*. All rights reserved. Reprinted by permission.

47.   Ibid., p. 10. © *Chicago Tribune*. All rights reserved. Reprinted by permission.

CHAPTER 2

The Cognitive Bases of Persuasion

During the 1968 presidential campaign, the main objective of Richard Nixon's media messages was to portray him as a strong and experienced statesman capable of leading the nation out of the chaos of the 1960s. A typical television commercial aired on behalf of Mr. Nixon's candidacy was titled "Vietnam." Consistent with the media campaign's central theme, Nixon was presented in this commercial as the man who could end American involvement in Vietnam with a "just and honorable peace."

The commercial depicted young American and Vietnamese soldiers, maimed, wounded, killing each other, and being killed. It concluded with a montage of the faces of American servicemen and Vietnamese natives, all with questioning, anxious, and perplexed looks. Visible on the helmet of one of the American G.I.s in the last scene was the scrawled word *love*. The voice-over on this scene was Nixon's: "I pledge to you: we will have an honorable end to the war in Vietnam."

Nixon's principal advisors thought the commercial was splendid. Not only did it emphasize Mr. Nixon's strength and resolve, but it also brought out his essential humanity, associating him with caring and devotion to family values. Much to their surprise, the advertisement drew a wave of protest, particularly from the Midwest. There was annoyance over the word *love* written on the soldier's helmet. "It reminds them of hippies," one of Nixon's media men explained. "We've gotten several calls already from congressmen complaining. They don't think it is the sort of thing soldiers should be writing on their helmets." The picture of the soldier was ordered out of the commercial and another G.I. wearing a plain helmet was inserted.

A few days later, the agency that produced the commercial received a letter from the mother of the soldier who had been cut from the spot. She wrote how thrilling it had been to see her son's picture in one of Mr. Nixon's commercials, and she asked if there was some way she might obtain a copy of the photograph. The letter was signed Mrs. William Love.[1]

27

This incident illustrates the issues we shall consider in this chapter. The three groups viewing "Vietnam" assigned radically different meanings to its content. Whereas one group associated the word *love* with humanity and caring, a second group felt it unmanly and un-American, connoting permissiveness and weakness. Finally, the mother of the young soldier saw the word only as her son's name. These disparate interpretations occurred because the three groups brought to the interpretative process remarkably different perspectives regarding the concepts of love and war. Although they had all viewed the same image, they "saw" vastly different things; thus the message had quite different persuasive effects on the three groups.

The perspective a person uses for interpreting or assigning meaning to messages has been labeled his or her *cognitive schemata.* Such schemata are structured to a considerable degree by a person's attitudes regarding the people, policies, and ideas mentioned in messages. Moreover, persuasive effects represent alterations in a person's schematic structures. Schematic alterations may involve the *creation* of new schemata, the *reinforcement* of preexisting ones, or an actual *change* in one or more schematic frames. Any behavioral changes occurring as a result of a persuasive message are presumed to reflect cognitive schematic alterations. As this description suggests, cognitive schemata are central to the process of interpreting messages, and they shape the final effects of any persuasive process.

In this chapter, we shall explore the nature and persuasive implications of cognitive schemata. Three topics will be examined. First, the nature of cognitive schemata and their effects on human information processing will be considered. Second, we shall look at the nature of attitude, a central component of cognitive schemata. Finally, the relationship between cognitive schemata and overt behavior will be examined.

THE NATURE OF COGNITIVE SCHEMATA

The number of external and self-generated messages available to us at any one time is vastly greater than we can process or even attend to. On an average day, most of us converse with dozens of friends, acquaintances, and strangers. Moreover, we are bombarded with information from television, radio, and the print media. Aside from this external informational glut, all of us spend a considerable amount of time thinking or processing self-generated messages about our own joys, disappointments, hopes, and fears.

None of us can or even wants to assimilate every aspect of the numerous messages we encounter. Rather, we are highly selective in what we notice, learn, infer, and remember from any message. Furthermore, our selective tendencies are not random, but are purposive and highly organized. Those internal structures that guide our selection, organization, and storage of information are called *cognitive schemata.*[2] Other labels describing similar cognitive organizers are *scripts,*[3] *frames,*[4] *prototypes,*[5] *personal constructs,*[6] and *thematic structures.*[7]

Cognitive schemata are defined as sets of rules or generalizations derived from past experience that organize and guide information processing about ourselves and others in our social experience. Schemata represent a person's complex of beliefs and feelings about, or world view of, some area of experience. They are assumptions about relationships among, or the co-occurrence of, behaviors, characteristics, and events associated with that area of experience.[8] Some schematic generalizations I might have about politics include: "Republicans are fiscal conservatives"; "Democrats are concerned about the poor"; and "The federal bureaucracy is inefficient." Some self-schemata I may have are: "I am honest"; "I am independent"; and "I feel insecure when meeting new people."

Note that these schemata reflect assumed relationships or co-occurrences. For instance, Republicans and conservatism are linked, as are inefficiency and bureaucracy, and honesty and myself. Moreover, each assumption implies a positive or negative reaction to assumed relationships. For instance, positive feelings probably are attached to the relation between honesty and the self, whereas negative ones are implied by the link between bureaucracy and waste. As this description suggests, cognitive schematic structures are closely related to the concept of *attitude* regarding some area of experience. Attitudes traditionally have been regarded as internal dispositions manifesting themselves in general likes and dislikes toward the self and others. In a later discussion, we shall see that attitudes are major components of any human cognitive structure.

Self-schemata, such as "I am a generous person," as well as generalizations about others reflect assumptions about recurring patterns of relationships, rather than information specific to a single behavior or event. Even a relatively concrete self-schema, such as "I feel insecure with new people," expresses a generalization that I feel uneasy *every time* I encounter strangers. The generalized nature of schemata has been described as an "economy measure," allowing us to subsume and remember a variety of separate, but similar, social occurrences in terms of a single "standardized episode."[9]

Because of their generality, schemata can be used to process multiple items of information. They allow us to anticipate the presumed nature of certain behaviors and events and to make sense of them when they are encountered. Because of this anticipatory quality, schemata have been described as "naive theories" about an area of experience. Moreover, like "naive scientists" we use them to organize and explain our complex social and personal worlds.[10]

The Relation Between Cognitive Schemata and Reality

Although there is general agreement that one's total life experiences shape cognitive structures, the extent to which schematic assumptions reflect the actual occurrence of relationships is in dispute. Some theorists argue that assumed relationships accurately reflect genuine covariations,[11] that they are faithful interpretations of the external reality experienced by people. From this perspective, if someone assumes that "Democracy is the best form of government," it is because that person has observed repeatedly that "democracy" and "goodness" vary together. Likewise, if "Blondes have more fun," it is because someone has observed that pleasure and hair color "actually" are related.

However, many other theorists contend there is *no* necessary correspondence between assumed relations and actual ones. According to this perspective, cognitive schemata reflect a person's naive theories about how things *ought to be related*, not necessarily how they "are, in fact" associated with one another.[12] From this perspective, if people assume that "Democracy is the best form of government," it is not because they have repeatedly observed such a co-occurrence. Rather, it is because ideally they feel it ought to be so. Similarly, if we assume that parents, small children, and puppies are warm and loving, it is not because they necessarily are, but because we think they should be. Indeed, according to this view, such an assumption selectively ignores the condition that some puppies bite, children often pitch temper tantrums, and some parents are child abusers. Likewise, the assumption that democracy is linked to goodness selectively avoids the corruption and abuses associated with many democracies, including our own.

Considerable research has tested the relative merits of these two interpretations. Evidence overwhelmingly supports the latter view that cognitive schemata reflect more about our own expectations and desires than our observations and faithful interpretations of actual covariations.[13] This view, of course, does not exclude the possibility that our idealizations may sometimes be influenced by interpretations of observed events. For example, relatively concrete schemata such as "I am an honest person" and "My neighbors are nosy" were most certainly influenced by interpretations of my own behavior and that of my neighbors. However, even this conclusion is complicated because interpretations themselves are based on idealizations about our own behavior and that of others. Put another way, we often "see" those behaviors we "expect" to see. Thus, even very concrete schemata are influenced heavily by a person's expectations about how things ought to be related.

In contrast to concrete schemata such as "My neighbors are nosy," other schematic structures are quite abstract in nature, reflecting one's philosophical perspective and one's views of social relationships. These viewpoints often bear little or no correspondence to actual observations. Again, they reflect an idealized view of how things ought to relate. Cognitive schemata, of whatever abstraction level, represent, in the final analysis, idealizations and personal desires that are embodied in assumptions or naive theories. We organize our world and guide information processing about ourselves and others on the basis of these naive theories.

Cognitive Schemata and Information Processing

Having outlined the general nature of cognitive schemata, we should examine closely their functions as instruments of information processing. When people communicate with one another, they observe what Darren Newtson and others have called a continuous "stream of behavior," both verbal and nonverbal, emanating from the self and others.[14] Cognitive schemata serve at least three functions in the processing of this complex stream of communication.

First, schemata tell us what to *attend* to. They make salient those features in a stream of behavior that are relevant to our particular view of things. For instance, my schemata relating to issues like abortion or nuclear energy will direct my attention to certain topic-relevant messages, but not to others. Persons with different cognitive schemata will attend to other aspects of the same stream of behavior. This schema-guided process of selectivity has been called *unitization*.[15] People divide up streams of communicative behavior into those units or episodes that are relevant to their own particular assumptions, expectations, and desires.

Second, as we have already made clear, cognitive schemata are a framework for *interpreting* incoming information. Recall the commercial, "Vietnam." The various assumptions or cognitive schemata of the three groups viewing the film resulted in radically different interpretations of the same stream of communicative behavior. That the film was interpreted so variously relates to the essential nature of schemata. Schemata reflect personal assumptions about co-occurrences or networks of associations among behaviors, characteristics, and so forth. One of the groups viewing "Vietnam" associated the word *love* with caring and devotion, a second felt it was related to permissiveness and weakness, and for the mother, the term *love* denoted the name of her child.

Given these assumptions, when the informational stimulus *love* appeared in the film, each group "filled in" relationships that were not present in the film itself. The mother filled in "my son," but the other groups made quite different associations. *This "filling-in" process is the essence of interpretation.* It is the creation of meaning. The idiosyncratic nature of interpretation or meaning led us in Chapter 1 to stipulate that, because people respond to their own interpretations of messages, they are in essence responding to the messages they create for themselves.

The third function of cognitive schemata in information processing is to guide the *reconstruction* of messages in *memory*. Human memory is not a reactive process, a mere copying of observed events or received messages. Rather, remembering or the storage of information in memory is a reconstructive process.[16] When a person reconstructs a message or unit from a stream of communicative behavior, the relevant cognitive schemata "fill in" features that either have been forgotten since initial observation or, more usually, were not present in the first place. This reconstructed store of information provides the framework for interpreting or "filling-in" all later messages to which people are exposed.

Self-Schemata and Other-Schemata

We have said that cognitive schemata are dynamic frameworks for processing information about the self and others in our social world. Thus, *self-schemata* refer to the "abstracted essence of a person's perception of him or herself."[17] They represent a person's interpretative framework or "cognitive generalizations about the self . . . that organize and guide the processing of self-related information."[18] In contrast, *other-schemata*, a concept similar to *implicit personality theories*, represent our assumptive knowledge about other people,[19] ideas, and symbolic stimuli in the external environment. Taken together, these assumptions guide the organization and interpretation of our social world.

A critically important question here concerns the similarities and differences between self- and other-schemata. This issue is important because of the nature of persuasive messages capable of inducing change in people. Recall from Chapter 1's discussion of classic persuasive paradigms that two types of messages have the capacity to influence us: (1) self-generated *response messages*, predominant in the traditional persuasive paradigm; and (2) self-generated *original messages*, predominant in the active participatory persuasive model. Response messages are a person's reactions to externally produced messages. As we have seen, in cognitive schematic terms, response messages are the product of a "filling-in" process, whereby personalized assumptions are applied to external symbolic stimuli. Original messages are not traceable to the information contained in external, symbolic stimulation. Rather, they represent overt and covert argumentation generated from an individual's independent information base. In cognitive schematic terms, original messages represent memory reconstructions and self-generated embellishments of one's existing cognitive schemata.

The critical distinction to be made here concerns the frequency with which response and original messages use self- and other-schemata to process information. Obviously, each type of message variously uses both depending on whether the information to be processed is self or other related. However, *original* self-generated messages rely almost exclusively on self-schemata since original messages, by definition, represent embellishments of preexisting cognitive structures without the benefit of external symbolization.

In contrast, self-generated *response* messages make extensive use of both other-schemata and self-schemata for interpreting and reconstructively storing externally produced symbols. More particularly, the production of response messages typically is a two-stage process. First, other-schemata are used to assign meaning to the communication *context*, including the physical setting and social atmosphere; the message *source*, including physical attributes, behaviors, and psychological dispositions; and the *message* itself. Second, self-schemata are employed to relate the context, source, and message to one's own personal needs and goals. With this information in mind, we now examine the similarities and differences between self- and other-schemata in order to understand the types of persuasive effects each type of message may be expected to produce.

Differences   A first and rather obvious distinction is that self-schemata typically have greater depth and breadth than our notions about others. This difference is particularly striking when we consider our assumptions about casual acquaintances and strangers. When we process information about unknown persons, like performers in commercials, we usually "type" them on the basis of superficial characteristics like sex, race, age, occupation, physical appearance, vocal qualities, and so forth. We then process the information they transmit using preconceived notions we have about "dumb blondes," "middle-aged housewives," "black athletes," and so on. Of course, as we come to know people better, we develop richer and more particularized schemata about them. But even though other-schemata increase in complexity as our relationships with other people become more intimate, they rarely approach the complexity of most self-schemata.[20]

A second major difference between self- and other-schemata concerns the way information is processed using the two types of schemata. Charles Lord recently advanced the intriguing notion that information about the self and others is processed and reconstructively stored in memory in dynamically different ways. He argues that information about the self is interpreted and reconstructed *verbally*, in linguistic propositions and rules such as "I am honest," or "Because I am shy, I always avoid large parties." In contrast, information about others is processed and stored largely in *visual images* or iconic representations. This argument is based primarily on the fact that other people and objects are more visually prominent to us than we are to ourselves simply because of the location of the eye.[21] We have few retinal pictures of ourselves going about daily activities; thus, we rely on verbal representations like "I'm a happy person" to describe our dispositions. In contrast, we continually observe other people, and so we use visual information such as smiling faces, frowns, and habitual gestures as much or more than verbal descriptions in other-schemata.[22]

If Lord's notions are correct, they offer some interesting explanations for certain well-known persuasive effects. For instance, we know that, in processing the messages of others, the nonverbal, visual components of the communication situation play a major role in affecting responses. Indeed, it has been estimated that no more than 35 percent of the social meaning of any externally generated message is carried by the verbal component.[23] A cursory look at the nature of much everyday persuasion verifies the importance of the visual aspects of a message. For example, the language used in television advertisements usually is limited to the repetition of a brand name, preferably in a catchy slogan or musical jingle like "Campbell soup is *Mmmm Mmmm* good!" It is the setting, the physical attractiveness of the performer, and other visual displays in commercials that usually carry the burden of selling a product. Likewise, for political candidates and other public persuaders, a contemporary hair style, fashionable clothing, and a visual image of decisiveness and vigor often are more crucial to success than are their programs for dealing with the problems of constituents.

In contrast, when we process information about the self, our internal dialogue is more important than visual imagery. Certainly, we can generate fantasized images of ourselves as "millionaires" or "victims of accident or disease" if we decide to take or avoid certain actions. However, if Lord is correct, such imaginal representations should be less important in original self-persuasion than in our responses to externally generated messages. Because original self-persuasion relies almost exclusively on self-schemata, the means of self-influence should be predominantly verbal, assisted minimally by visual imagery. In contrast, the persuasion process in response to external messages utilizes both self- and other-schemata. As a result, the means of persuasion should contain strong visual symbols as well as verbal components. As a conclusion to this discussion, we should note that, despite the intuitive appeal of Lord's theorizing, his notions await exhaustive empirical verification.

Similarities   Having examined some of the more important differences between self- and other-schematic information processing, we need to consider the features they share. The two modes of information processing have a common ground because self-schemata often exert a profound, perhaps controlling, influence over our assumptions about others.

Considerable evidence suggests that the self functions as a powerful *cognitive reference point* for interpreting all information about others.[24] For example, we are unlikely to conclude that someone is fat or physically attractive, unless they are fatter or more attractive than we perceive ourselves to be. Similarly, when we conclude that another person is foolish, generous, inconsiderate, or loving, it is rarely because we have some fixed standard defining foolishness, generosity, and so forth. Rather, if we observe others acting more foolish or inconsiderate than we normally do, we are likely to conclude they are really quite "silly" or "thoughtless" people. Such cognitive processes suggest that an implicit "self–other comparison [is always] an integral part of how we process information about other people."[25]

Given the active role played by the self in processing external information, we may conclude that self-schemata mediate either directly or indirectly our interpretation of *all* persuasive messages. This is the case regardless of whether the dominant persuasive paradigm is an active participatory one involving original self-generated messages, or the traditional model, entailing self-produced responses to the messages initiated by others.

Variables Affecting the Selection of Interpretive Schemata

As our discussion has shown, all of us have a vast array of cognitive schemata regarding the self and others. Indeed, people rapidly develop assumptions about any person or thing with whom they have even minimal experience. Moreover, each of us has a number of different sets of schemata that may be used to process any one stimulus. In this section, we will consider some factors that determine what particular schematic set will be used to process any one item of information.

To illustrate how different schemata may be used to interpret the same message, imagine that I hear the message "We should love our enemies." There are a number of schematic sets I may use to interpret such a message. For instance, one obvious set is religious, and it contains beliefs about love. Another is political, containing assumptions about world politics and harmonious relations among nations. Which of these schemata am I likely to use as a frame for interpreting a message about affection for adversaries? Two sets of variables affect the selection of an interpretive frame. One is comprised of interpretations of *external* phenomena and the second concerns *internal* factors, like the goals and desires of receivers of messages.

The external set of variables is called *category accessibility* and refers to external factors, including fortuitous events, that make one or another set of schemata more accessible to a person at the time information is received.[26] *Context* is a factor affecting category accessibility. If, for example, I am in a church or synagogue when I hear the statement about relations with enemies, I undoubtedly will use a religious frame for interpreting the message. However, if I hear the statement during the course of a televised political discussion of détente between the United States and the Soviet Union, I am more likely to apply political schemata to the message. Of course, numerous cues other than context affect category accessibility. One of the more important is the *source* of a message. Assuming a political context, I certainly will interpret a message about affection for enemies quite differently if it is made by the president of the United States as opposed to a member of the Communist Party USA. Generally then, category accessibility refers to a set of external factors, the interpretation of which affects the selection of cognitive schemata to apply to any one message.

As this discussion implies, the persuasive impact of a message is affected profoundly by category accessibility. Recall our description of reactions to the political commercial, "Vietnam." The Midwesterners and congressmen who interpreted the word *love* as unmanly and un-American surely had another set of schemata associating *love* with interpersonal caring. If the film had been produced in such a way that the latter schemata were more accessible, these critics might have found the film very persuasive, rather than repugnant. Indeed, a primary task of effective persuaders is to arrange communication cues in such a fashion that the desired cognitive structure is evoked. This effect often is achieved through the selection of sources and the manipulation of the setting where a message is delivered.

The following examples illustrate this persuasive tactic. In the late 1970s, the Carter administration launched a nationwide campaign to persuade conservative Americans to support the return of the Panama Canal to Panamanians. As one part of the campaign, John Wayne taped a number of television advertisements on behalf of the Canal treaties. Wayne, a national folk hero, had an image of a "rough-and-tough" American patriot and a long history of support for conservative causes. The Carter administration hoped that using Wayne as spokesman would evoke schemata related to American power and patriotism rather than those related to the nation's weakness in "giving away" the canal. Similarly, American presidents often use grand settings like the Oval Office or the White House East Room to make pronouncements, especially more unpopular ones, to the public. The aim is to activate schemata related to loyalty to the president and pride in the nation rather than those militating against the particular message to be delivered. Clearly, arranging external cues to arouse favorable schemata is a potent strategy of persuasive communication.

The second class of variables affecting the selection of schematic sets is internal to the receiver of messages. In this case, the personal *goals* or intentions a person brings to a persuasive event are a major determinant of schematic selection. Cohen and Ebbeson demonstrated the effects of goals on schematic selection and information processing by asking people to view a film of an actor performing several ordinary tasks. Prior to viewing the film, one group of people was told its goal was to form an overall impression of the actor's personality. Another group was informed that its goal was to learn how to perform the tasks demonstrated by the actor. Finally, the subjects were asked to divide the actor's stream of behavior into units or bits of information they felt were most meaningful and helpful to them in reaching their goals. To accomplish this unitization, each person was given an electronic keyboard and told to depress a button each time he or she felt one meaningful unit of behavior had ended and another begun.

Results showed that the different goals of the two groups resulted in the selection of quite different schemata for interpreting the information. Moreover, the use of these schemata resulted in radically different processing of the same information stream. The task-oriented viewers saw a substantially greater number of meaningful units of behavior in the film than did the impression-oriented viewers. Moreover, the units selected as meaningful by the task-oriented viewers were quite specific and detailed, whereas the impression-oriented group saw broader, more sweeping communication units as most meaningful. Based on these differences, the two groups reconstructively recalled quite different things about the content of the film.[27] This study confirmed that the goals of message recipients profoundly affect the selection of schemata for interpreting messages. Additionally, goal-oriented schemata determine what information in a message is seen as meaningful, and therefore, worthy of reconstructing in memory.

The Complexity of Cognitive Schemata

As we just saw, all of us have many schematic structures, any one of which may be used to interpret any one message. If we consider the total set of schemata any one person has, we can expect some to be rich and well developed, while others will be sketchy and incomplete. In judging the complexity of a person's schematic structures, we must remember first that self-schemata generally are more complex than the assumptions we have about others. Second, some of our self- or other-schemata are richer than others. For example, the assumptions of a women's rights activist about sex discrimination will probably be more complex than the same individual's schemata about American relations with Japan. As this example suggests, familiarity with another person, concept, or cause enriches other-schemata. Similarly, self-schemata become richer as we better understand the multiple dimensions of our own self-identity.

Walter Crockett has provided a definition of cognitive complexity that relates to the relative richness and complexity of schemata. "A cognitive system will be considered relatively complex in structure," writes Crockett, "when (a) it contains a relatively large number of elements and (b) the elements are integrated hierarchically by relatively extensive bonds of relationships."[28] Thus, if I have a large number of assumptions about any particular area of experience and my more specific assumptions are subsumed progressively by more general schemata, my schematic structure will be relatively complex. In contrast, if I have a few assumptions and these are not progressively related, my cognitive schemata will be relatively simple and provide a sketchy frame for interpreting information pertaining to that area of experience. Generally, the greater the number and quality of social interactions a person has with a particular area of experience, the more complex will be his or her cognitive structures.[29]

Figure 2.1 illustrates the notion of cognitive complexity. Suppose my global schematic structure or world view pertains to political and governmental policy. The symbols S_1 through S_n represent the major cognitive schemata underpinning this structure. For example, S_1 might signify my assumptions and beliefs concerning human rights issues; S_2 might refer to environmental issues; S_3 to foreign policy; S_4 to defense or energy matters; and S_n denotes all other major cognitive schemata I may have about politics and governmental policy.

Supporting each major schema in a hierarchical or subsumptive fashion are more specific schemata. For example, in the area of human rights, s_1 might contain my views on the rights of women; s_2 may concern racial equality; and s_3 could relate to legal and political rights. If my cognitive schemata are exceedingly complex, each specific schema (s) should have even more particularized schemata (s') related to it. For instance, my views on women's rights might contain assumptions about abortion, economic equality, and the like. In contrast to such a structure, if my view of political and governmental policy is sketchy and incomplete, I should have a small number of major schemata and few, if any, subordinate schemata.

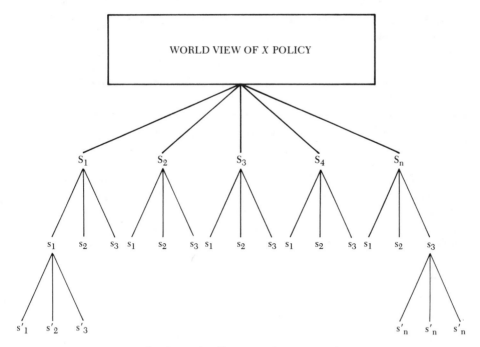

FIGURE 2.1   *A complex, hierarchically arranged cognitive schematic structure*

The relative complexity of one's schematic structures clearly affects the interpretation process, as well as the ease with which cognitive structures may be formed, reinforced, or changed through persuasive communication. Regarding interpretation, research generally shows that the more complex our cognitive structures, the more extensive and differentiated will be our perceptions of ourselves and others.[30] Moreover, compared to people with less mature cognitive structures, cognitively complex individuals usually better understand the motivations of others, recognize and integrate a variety of different, often inconsistent, symbolic cues exhibited by others, and generally demonstrate a greater capacity to understand themselves and the perspectives of others in communication situations.[31] In the next section, we shall consider the effects of cognitive complexity on the ease of persuading people to alter their schematic structures.

COGNITIVE SCHEMATA, PERSUASION, AND THE CONCEPT OF ATTITUDE

We have now examined in some detail the nature of human cognitive structures. Cognitive schemata represent a person's complex of feelings and beliefs or world view about some particular area of experience. This world view is a hierarchical set of assumptions and it interfaces with persuasive communication on at least two levels.

First, the process of interpreting messages is exclusively a product of a person's cognitive schemata. As we saw earlier, the assignment of meaning is a filling-in process. We endow messages or sets of symbols with our own personal beliefs, feelings, and assumptions. Second, persuasive effects represent alterations in an individual's cognitive schematic structures. Schematic alterations may involve the *creation* of new schemata, the *reinforcement* or embellishment of already existing schemata, or a *change* in one or more schematic frames. The overt behavioral effects of persuasion, of course, represent outward manifestations of cognitive alterations. Indeed, the *only* means of determining whether people have experienced cognitive alteration is by observing their overt behavior and inferring the existence of some cognitive counterpart of action.

To understand more completely the relationship between cognitive schemata and persuasive communication, we need to examine the forces that shape people's views of themselves and their world. Such an exploration brings us to perhaps the oldest and most central notion in all the literature of persuasion: attitude. Our attitudes toward ourselves and other people, objects, and ideas exert a profound influence on the assumptions and expectations that make up our world views.

The Relation Between Attitudes and Cognitive Schemata

Although *attitude* has been defined in many ways,[32] it typically is regarded as a two-dimensional, internal structure, manifesting itself in general feelings of favorableness or unfavorableness toward the self or some external stimulus.[33] The first dimension, a cognitive one, consists of the *beliefs* a person has about the self and others. When one believes, one accepts the existence of some condition or relationship. "There is an energy shortage"; "The present administration supports nuclear energy development"; "Homosexuality is not a mental disorder"; and "I am an honest person" are all examples of beliefs.

The second component of attitude is *affective* in nature and constitutes one's positive or negative feelings about or *evaluation* of beliefs. Human affective responses reflect underlying goals, intentions, and desires. Typically, whatever helps us pursue goals and fulfill desires is viewed positively, and whatever thwarts goal satisfaction is negatively evaluated. Thus, if in fact I believe there is an energy shortage in America, I am likely to evaluate that condition negatively, assuming I desire plentiful energy. Similarly, if I fear nuclear power, I will have a negative affective reaction to governmental development of such an energy source. On the other hand, if I support the rights of gays and place a high value on honesty, I am likely to evaluate positively the belief that homosexuality is a normal life style and the belief that I am a candid person.

As these examples indicate, the affective component of attitude gives beliefs valence or *direction*, whether positive or negative and determines *intensity* of feelings toward the self and others. Thus, I may have moderately negative feelings about an energy shortage, but intensely dislike nuclear power. Similarly, positive affective reactions may range from mild to strongly favorable evaluations of beliefs. In sum, a set of beliefs coupled with an affective evaluation of those beliefs constitute an attitude.

How do we relate the concept of attitude to cognitive schematic structures?[34]

Clearly, cognitive schemata have many constituent parts, including human goals, as well as actual or imagined past experiences as they have been reconstructed in memory. However, it should be apparent that attitudes, or beliefs, coupled with an affective evaluation of beliefs, are the principal shapers of world views. Schemata, as we have described them throughout this chapter, are assumptions about relationships or idealized expectations about how things ought to vary together. "I am a generous person"; "There is a god"; "An unborn child has a right to life"; and "I am shy with strangers" are typical examples of self- and other-schemata. A cursory examination of these schemata reveals they are all nothing more than attitudes, or beliefs imbued with an implicit affective direction and intensity. For instance, the self-schema, "I am shy with strangers," expresses the belief that personal shyness and strange people are related to one another. Moreover, an implicit negative affect is associated with that assumed relationship. The other-schema, "There is a god," expresses the belief that human life is associated with some divine presence and probably carries with it a positive affective response. The intensity of affect will vary depending on how closely a belief is related to one's central goals and intentions.

As these examples indicate, any cognitive schematic structure represents little more than a complex of interrelated attitudes.[35] Because the complexity and strength of attitudes have profound implications for the interpretation process, as well as the ease with which cognitive structures may be altered through persuasive communication, we need to consider carefully what factors affect the complexity and strength of attitudinal structures.

Cognitive Schemata and the Strength of Attitudes

Attitudes vary widely in strength and complexity. The potency of any one attitudinal structure is a function of: (1) the number of beliefs an individual has regarding some area of experience; (2) the extent to which one's beliefs are hierarchically arranged in an interrelated, supportive structure; (3) the degree to which individuals judge their beliefs to be "true," that is, reliable assumptions about the self and others; and (4) the intensity of one's affective evaluation of each belief.

Suppose I have a relatively large number of hierarchically related beliefs about the habit of cigarette smoking, three of which are that cigarette smoking causes disease, pollutes the environment, and is a social and physical irritant to nonsmokers. Suppose further that I am 100 percent confident of the truth of the first belief, 80 percent sure of the second, and absolutely certain that the third is a reliable assumption. Finally, imagine that I strongly value good health, environmental quality, and am sensitive to the welfare of others. In such a case, my attitude toward cigarette smoking is going to be very strong and intensely negative.

Conversely, any attitude is weak to the extent that an individual holds few relevant beliefs about an area of experience; the beliefs are unstable or halfhearted; are poorly related to one another; or one's affective reactions to the beliefs are weak, ill defined, or ambiguous.

Attitudinal Centrality   One variable influencing the strength of one's beliefs and feelings is called centrality. The term *centrality* refers to the relationship of an attitude to a person's basic goals or value system and to his or her conception of the self.[36] We shall see that the attitudes comprising our schematic structures range in hierarchical fashion from very central values to more peripheral beliefs and feelings. The ease with which cognitive schemata may be altered through persuasive communication is tied to centrality.

Some attitudes about ourselves and others are strong and persist over time, while others are weak and impermanent. Our most central attitudes are called values. A *value* is an ego-involving attitude, one that a person strongly identifies with and incorporates into his or her self-concept.[37] Many of our values are products of the general culture, subculture, and social class to which we belong. A respect for human life, the belief in a god, an appreciation of democracy, and a commitment to racial and sexual equality are examples of culture-oriented values. Such values vary from one culture or subculture to another. For instance, Americans typically have valued material success, but many other cultures place a greater value on spiritual matters, including self-denial and inner growth.

Aside from cultural origins, values often grow out of personal contact with a particular area of experience. For example, economic and social deprivation often prompt particular individuals and subcultures to place a high value on work, wealth, and social status. On the other hand, a child of abundance, not lacking in material wealth, may develop values oriented toward individual growth, self-fulfillment, and the creative use of leisure. Whatever their genesis, values are ego-involving schemata that are relatively strong and persistent.

However, many of our attitudes are less central and ego involving than values. Although these more peripheral attitudes are hierarchically related to our central values, they typically are directed toward specific and often changing issues. Support for abortion, a concern about poverty, a preference for casual clothing, and opposition to nuclear energy are some examples of these attitudes. The strength of such attitudinal schemata is a function of their relationship to our more central attitudes. For example, the issue of abortion frequently elicits strong positive and negative feelings because it relates dramatically to more centrally held values like the rights of women and a respect for unborn life. On the other hand, issues like poverty may generate weaker beliefs and less intense feelings because they seem farther removed from our personal goals and identities. As this discussion suggests, the strength of any attitude is a function of its relationship to our underlying self-concepts, personal goals, and central value systems.

Centrality and Persuasion   The issue of attitude centrality has obvious implications for the student of persuasive communication. Generally, how easily a person's cognitive schemata may be altered is inversely related to the degree of centrality of his or her attitudes. Thus, the attitudes of an avid women's rights supporter toward American foreign policy should be altered more readily than his or her assumptions about sexual equality. And the feminist who holds the stronger beliefs and more intense feelings on the issue of sexual equality should be more difficult to persuade than the person with a less centralized cognitive structure. Despite this general rule, we saw in our account of the conversion of Patty Hearst that even the most central cognitions can be altered and that such alteration is often accomplished with interactional persuasive strategies having an ordinary, almost mundane quality.

Beyond fundamental alterations, very centralized attitudes are important because of the crucial role they play in mediating a multitude of less radical changes in people. Indeed, much contemporary persuasion induces changes in cognitive schemata by linking new or unfamiliar peripheral issues to old and well-established values. Commercial and political persuasion is successful largely because it does not attempt to change basic values. Rather, the company and the candidate offer consumers and voters new and better ways to enact old habits and fulfill basic goals and values.

Many of the successful strategies Jimmy Carter used during the 1976 presidential campaign exemplify the tactic of linking the new and different with old and familiar values. Carter campaigned as a Washington "outsider," a "born again" Christian, and a farmer, divorced from the corruption of Watergate and the pomposity of the Imperial Presidency. The aura of casualness, simplicity, and sincerity he projected seemed to signal a return to the basic agrarian values upon which Americans have always fantasized the country was founded. By linking himself with the central values of many ordinary Americans, an obscure man from Georgia, whose vision of America was never entirely clear, was catapulted into the highest office in the land!

In sum, while ego-involving values may gradually be transformed, change usually is accomplished by taking advantage of the stability and persistence of old values.

The Formation of Attitudes

Earlier in this chapter, we suggested that cognitive schemata are derived from one's total life experiences. Moreover, we argued that schematic assumptions more often than not reflect our personal desires and idealized expectations rather than a faithful interpretation of what actually is. In this section, we shall consider how these assumptions or attitudinal schemata are formed.

Some of our attitudes are developed from *direct experience*. In this case, attitudes represent our biased interpretations of what we see, hear, feel, and so forth. The belief that gasoline prices are rising, coupled with a negative evaluation of this condition, is an example of an attitude derived from interpretations of direct experience. Other attitudes are formed on the basis of *vicarious* or *symbolic experience*. We may believe the South African government violates human rights on a massive scale and deplore that situation. Or we may have a positive attitude toward some piece of legislation recently enacted by the state legislature. Such attitudes usually are formed on the basis of what we read, see on television, or hear from other people. Given the pervasiveness of the mass media, it is likely that many of our ongoing attitudes about the world are based on the interpretations of other people.

Finally, some attitudes, called *stereotypes*, are assumptions we have about the self and others having little correspondence to direct or vicarious interpretations. *Stereotyping* involves categorizing specific people, objects, or events and attributing to the categories one or more general characteristics.[38] Stereotyped attitudes include statements like "Politicians can't be trusted"; "Southerners are bigots"; "French men are good lovers"; "Americans are generous people"; and "The Communist aim is to take over the world." Although these examples appear extreme, it is important to remember that *all* our attitudes or cognitive schemata are, in fact, stereotyped views of ourselves and the world. Indeed, it is the generalized, stereotypical quality of cognitive schemata that makes them useful information processers. We interpret messages by filling in our own assumptions or stereotypes about ourselves and other people. Some assumptions may reflect reality more than others, but they are all stereotypical in nature.

Stereotyped attitudes have several characteristics. First, stereotypes, like all attitudes, may be either positive or negative. People in conflict tend to develop negative views of one another, and groups in cooperative relationships often develop positive mutual stereotypes. The average American may feel that Communists are godless warmongers, yet see the French as urbane and the British as brave and stouthearted. Second, we develop stereotyped attitudes about ourselves as well as others. The former are referred to as *autostereotypes,* and the latter, *heterostereotypes.*[39] For instance, Democrats may believe themselves to be champions of the common man; and Americans often see themselves as industrious and efficient. The stereotypes we develop about ourselves are as generalized as our characterizations of others. Finally, some stereotypes are more faithful interpretations of reality than others. For instance, "Priests are moral men" is probably a more realistic appraisal than "Jews are shrewd" or "Blacks are lazy." A few writers distinguish between attitudes that bear little correspondence to actual conditions and those that do by labeling the former *stereotypes* and the latter *sociotypes.*[40]

Theories of Stereotypes   Several theories have been advanced to explain the formation of stereotypes, especially those bearing little relation to reality. One suggests that the extreme members of groups and extreme characteristics of people are remembered more readily than average or mild ones; thus, our views of groups are disproportionately influenced by these extremes.[41] According to this view, if someone assumes that male homosexuals are "limp wristed," it is not because most gay men have that characteristic; but because effeminate gays are more noticeable and, therefore, more memorable than are other, more typical members of the gay community.

Another, somewhat different explanation for the formation of stereotypes is the "kernel of truth" hypothesis. It holds that stereotyping begins with the observation of some actual difference between groups or of some actual characteristics of a single group. Later, similar, nonobjective traits become associated with this original "kernel of truth."[42] For example, Americans are, in fact, wealthier than most other peoples in the world. From that kernel of truth, other associations may develop: Americans are unscrupulous, power hungry, and materialistic. They are shrewd, efficient, and industrious.

No matter how stereotypes are formed, considerable evidence suggests they are quite resistant to change. A study of prevailing stereotyped views of ten national and ethnic groups was conducted at Princeton University in 1933 and repeated in 1951. Results showed that stereotyped attitudes toward these groups remained quite stable over the 20-year period. There was, however, a "fading effect": stereotypes became less intense although they retained the same positive or negative valence.[43] Fortunately, changing societal norms and group relationships can gradually alter stereotypes. Many of the social changes occurring in the 1960s, for example, resulted in a lessening of many negative stereotypes associated with ethnic minorities, women, and homosexuals. Additionally, contact between hostile groups can transform conflict into cooperation, resulting in the development of positive stereotypes. America's changing attitudes toward the Chinese Communists and many white Americans' more positive views of minorities have resulted, at least in part, from the development of cooperative relationships, based on direct interpersonal or international communication.

The Functions of Attitudinal Schemata

Throughout this book we have advanced the notion that humans are active agents whose behavior is goal oriented and choice laden. Moreover, we have found that cognitive schemata are more likely to reflect our own personal goals and assumptions about what ought to be than to be faithful interpretations of what is. Daniel Katz has advanced a theory of attitude that explains well why our cognitive schemata inevitably reflect idealized expectations and personal goals.[44] His theory, called a *functional theory of attitude*, provides some interesting insights into the forces that shape each person's unique, cognitive schematic structures. Katz argues that we all adopt particular attitudes about ourselves and others because those schemata help us achieve certain desired goals. Moreover, Katz maintains that a knowledge of the functions served by attitudes is crucial to understanding why some people respond well to certain persuasive strategies, and others respond poorly to the same tactics.

Katz says that any one attitude performs at least one of four possible functions. First, some attitudes serve an *instrumental* or adjustive function. All of us develop positive attitudes toward those people and policies that satisfy our needs, and negative ones toward whatever thwarts need satisfaction. If I have a positive attitude toward a program of national health insurance because I think it will help me cope with the rising cost of medical care, that attitude serves an instrumental function. It is compatible with my desire to reduce the cost of living. On the other hand, a negative attitude toward an income tax increase is congruent with maintaining my present purchasing power.

Second, many attitudes serve a *value-expressive* function. Such attitudes give positive expression to an individual's self-concept and central values. Suppose I support the feminist movement because I see myself as a liberated person. Or I may have a positive attitude toward the issue of gay rights because I regard myself as a tolerant, openminded individual. In these cases, my attitudes are expressive of my ideal self-concept. Note that if I support women's rights because I feel sexual equality will get me a better job or if my attitude toward gays is designed to garner political support from that community, my attitudes would be instrumentally based, not value expressive. The critical distinction here is that an instrumental attitude is oriented toward an external goal, whereas value-expressive attitudes help the holder project a desired self-image.

Attitudes also may serve ego-defensive and knowledge functions. An *ego-defensive* attitude protects one from acknowledging basic truths about oneself or from facing unpleasant external realities. In a series of studies, Sarnoff found that many racial and ethnic prejudices serve an ego-defensive function.[45] Negative attitudes and feelings of superiority toward blacks, Hispanics, or Jews generally mask a low self-image. Likewise, a strong sense of racial pride or ethnicity among members of a minority group can serve an ego-defensive role, blunting the impact of external prejudice.

Finally, some attitudes perform a *knowledge* function by supplying frames of reference for understanding a seemingly disorganized and chaotic world. Thus, in periods of personal or national crisis, people often develop stereotyped attitudes that help "make sense" out of disorder. For example, with the onset of a severe national gasoline shortage in 1979, many Americans developed very negative attitudes toward domestic oil companies, the federal government, and foreign exporters of petroleum. Also, identification of a scapegoat in periods of crisis is common. Moreover, scapegoats are often imaginary villains, mysterious and sinister conspiracies. During the gas crunch in the summer of 1979, rumor had it that the gasoline shortage actually was caused by big oil companies dumping gas at sea and in the deserts of the Southwest in a conspiracy to drive up prices.[46] Such scapegoating and stereotyping allow people to identify a simple, highly visible "cause" for problems, whether real or delusionary, thus giving a sense of meaning and simplicity to very complex phenomena.

An understanding of attitudinal functions can be immensely helpful to the student of persuasion. If a woman supports a Constitutional guarantee of sexual equality because such an attitude gives positive expression to her internal values and self-conception, it probably would make little sense to try to change her opinion by emphasizing the negative, external consequences such an amendment might entail. A more appropriate strategy might be to play on the self-image implications of such a measure. On the other hand, an opponent of such a measure, who fears military conscription of women and "unisex toilets," should be most easily persuaded by a message focusing on consequences. However, if a proponent or opponent's attitude is thought to serve both value-expressive and instrumental functions, then both consequential and self-concept strategies would be in order.

THE RELATIONSHIP BETWEEN COGNITIVE SCHEMATA AND OVERT BEHAVIOR

We have now examined the nature of cognitive schemata in considerable detail. Throughout our discussion, the focus has been on those variables affecting the strength of schemata and how schemata may be altered by persuasive communication. Such detail was necessary because of the implications attitudinal schemata have for a person's overt behavior. That behavior may involve purchasing a product, interacting with friends, voting for a political candidate, or adopting a new religious or social philosophy. In a real sense, the ultimate aim of all persuasion is behavior creation, reinforcement, or change. A political candidate, for example, will take little comfort in the knowledge that he or she is admired if the admiration produces no votes. Likewise, parents will probably feel they have failed if their children do not act upon the moral values taught in the home. Since persuasion aims to influence actions, it is critically important to explore the relationship between attitudinal schemata and overt behavior.

In doing so, we will identify those conditions under which we can expect alterations in cognitive schemata to lead to behavior changes.

An Overview of the Issues

The persuasion literature suggests four possible relationships between cognitive schemata and overt behavioral acts: attitudinal schemata and behaviors are unrelated; overt behavior produces attitudinal structures; attitudes mediate overt behaviors; and there is a reciprocal mediating relationship between attitudes and behavior.

Some early research on attitudes and behavior led a number of writers to conclude that the two were quite unrelated. For example, La Pière studied the relationship between attitudes and behavior during the 1930s when anti-Chinese feelings were prevalent in the United States. He took a Chinese couple on a 10,000-mile automobile tour of the country, stopping at about 250 hotels and restaurants. With only one exception, the couple received full service and courteous treatment. After the tour, La Pière wrote to all of the proprietors who had served the couple and asked them if they believed Chinese people should be served in their establishments. Despite their previous behavior, more than 90 percent of the proprietors stated that they were opposed to serving Chinese.[47] On the basis of this and a number of more sophisticated studies,[48] Alan Wicker concludes that "taken as a whole, these studies suggest that it is considerably more likely that attitudes will be unrelated or slightly related to overt behaviors than that attitudes will be closely related to actions."[49]

Other, more recent, theoretical accounts maintain that overt behavior leads to the formation of cognitive schemata. Daryl Bem has proposed that when internal schemata are weak or ambiguous, behavior will lead to the creation of attitudes.[50] In a similar vein, Leonard Doob[51] and William Scott[52] have focused on a "backward chaining process" of learning in which cognitive schemata develop as a consequence of rewarded, overt behavior. Much behavioral research supports the notion that overt behaviors do, in fact, influence attitudinal structures.[53] Several theoretical perspectives on attitude change explored later in this book assume that behavior mediates the formation and change of attitudinal schemata.

A third contemporary view holds that attitudes produce behavior. William McGuire has argued convincingly for this position, and a substantial body of evidence supports his analysis.[54] For example, Kahle and Berman conducted a two-month study of the relationship between attitudes and behavior. They found that on such issues as Jimmy Carter's 1976 presidential candidacy, Gerald Ford's candidacy, drinking, and religion, cognitive sets consistently determined people's overt behaviors.[55]

The final contemporary position subsumes the previous two perspectives. According to this view, attitudes and behaviors are related reciprocally: attitudes lead to overt behavior, but behaviors also shape attitudinal structures. In a typical study, Watts had subjects support, in writing, a position with which they disagreed. Six weeks later, he discovered that the subjects' attitudes had changed and were now more consistent with the position they earlier had supported in writing. Moreover, he found that the subjects had begun acting in accordance with their new attitudinal stance.[56] On the basis of a substantial body of related data, Herbert Kelman has theorized that "not only is attitude an integral part of action, but action is an integral part of the development, testing, and crystallization of attitudes."[57]

Theorists now generally agree with the last perspective discussed: that *attitudes and behavior are reciprocally interrelated*. Each is seen as exerting a powerful influence upon the other. Indeed, contemporary interest has shifted from asking *if* attitudes can predict overt behavior and vice versa, to asking *when* and *under what conditions* attitudes and behaviors correlate. We now turn to that question. Three classes of variables affect consistency between attitudinal schemata and overt behavior: (1) characteristics of the schema itself; (2) situational factors; and (3) personal variables.

Characteristics of Attitudinal Schemata

The extent to which attitudes will mediate overt behavior is dependent upon several characteristics of attitudes themselves. These characteristics include: (1) the *method* of attitude formation (direct versus indirect experience); (2) the level of *ego involvement* in an attitude; (3) the *certainty* of an attitude; (4) *affective–cognitive* consistency within an attitudinal complex; and (5) the *specificity* of an attitude. Let's examine each of these characteristics in more detail.

Several recent studies have confirmed that the *method* of attitude formation is a crucial variable. The more an attitudinal schema is based on interpretations of *direct personal experience*, the greater the tendency of people to act consistently with their attitudes.

Regan and Fazio confirmed this conclusion in a field study conducted during a severe housing shortage at Cornell University in the fall of 1973. All participants in the experiment stated strong negative attitudes about the University's failure to resolve the crisis. However, some of the students had directly experienced the housing shortage, having been assigned temporary quarters consisting of cots in dormitory lounges. Other students assigned to permanent housing were keenly aware of the shortage but had not directly experienced it. Although stated attitudes were equivalent in strength, the students who had developed their negative attitudes through personal experience took significantly more actions toward pressuring the administration to change housing policy than did those whose attitudes were learned indirectly.[58] These results parallel common knowledge. The person who suffers or benefits as a result of a particular policy or program is usually the first to try to stop the suffering or to continue the benefit.

In another study, Fazio and Zanna confirmed the common-sense notion that the centrality and strength of one's cognitive schemata influence profoundly the schema–behavior relationship. They found that the more well defined a person's attitude, as measured by the level of *ego involvement*, the greater the likelihood of related overt behavior. Further, the more *certainty* people have about their assumptions, the more schema-relevant behavior they will exhibit.[59]

Along with direct experience, ego involvement, and certainty, a fourth determinant of overt behavior is the level of *affective–cognitive consistency* exhibited by an attitudinal complex. Norman has found that the more consistency there is between feelings and beliefs, the more people will act on the basis of their attitudes.[60] For instance, if one believes in the programs or policies of some political figure, and at the same time, responds warmly to the personality and character of the politician, one is likely to vote for the person. However, if feelings and beliefs toward the political figure are incongruent, related action is far less likely. In this regard, Fazio and Zanna found that affective–cognitive consistency is particularly important in producing behavior when attitudes are based on vicarious or symbolic experience as opposed to personal contact.[61]

Finally, the *specificity* of an attitude is related to behavior. Specific behaviors are best predicted by specific schemata, and general behavior patterns are influenced by more global or generalized attitudinal structures.[62] For example, a generalized positive attitude toward a commercial product or political candidate by no means insures that a consumer will purchase the product or that a citizen will pull the voting lever adjacent to the candidate's name. However, the development of more specific, particularized attitudes toward the product and the candidate should increase the likelihood of such specific behavioral responses.

Situational Factors

Assuming a person has a relatively strong attitude toward some object, three general situational or environmental variables affect the probability that the individual will act on the attitude. First, *social norms* exert a profound influence on one's predisposition to behave overtly.[63] Such norms include general cultural and subcultural rules prescribing acceptable behaviors and the views of specific respected others. A resident of a small, socially conservative community may strongly support the rights of homosexuals to equal opportunity in employment, housing, and the like. However, general cultural biases and the antigay views of friends, family, and neighbors may prevent overt action. In such a case, the failure to act is inconsistent with one's personal schemata, but congruent with social rules. On the other hand, if the same individual had the benefit of supportive social norms, he or she would probably act on the progay attitudes.

A second situational factor affecting the relationship between attitudes and behavior is the expected *personal consequences* of an action.[64] For example, many Germans prior to and during World War II abhorred the extermination of Jews and other non-Aryans by the Nazis; yet fear of torture and death at the hands of the Gestapo led most Germans to publicly tolerate what they privately regarded as hideous crimes. In contrast, when the personal consequences of overt action are positive or at least not intolerable, the probability that people will act on the basis of their schemata increases sharply.

A third variable affecting the attitude–behavior relationship concerns the perceived *effort* required to perform a behavior.[65] The easier it is to act, the more consistency one can expect between schemata and actions. Presumably, supportive norms, positive consequences, and the absence of other situational constraints should make acting easier.

Personal Variables

Three individual-differences variables affect consistency between cognitive schemata and human action. First, the individual who has the *self-image* of a doer is more likely to act on the basis of attitudes than others whose temperaments are passive.[66]

Second, how *competent* a person feels about engaging in particular behaviors affects the attitude–behavior relationship. The greater one's abilities, including verbal skills, to act, the more consistency one can expect between attitudes and behavior.[67]

Third, the person with few *competing attitudes* is more likely to act than one with conflicting attitudes toward a particular behavior.[68] For instance, a group of upper middle-class suburban homeowners may believe strongly in equal housing opportunities for low-income and minority groups. Yet they may actively oppose the construction of low-income housing in their neighborhood because they fear the value of their property might drop with an influx of the poor. In this case, the homeowners are behaving consistently with one attitude and as a result, acting contrary to another. The absence of such competing attitudes should increase the likelihood that people will act in accordance with their attitudes.

An Alternative View of the Attitude–Behavior Relationship

Martin Fishbein has argued that an attitude toward some object, such as women's rights, equal housing, and military conscription, should not be viewed as a major determinant of behavior with respect to the object. Rather, he has proposed that overt behavior can best be predicted from behavioral intentions. *Behavioral intentions* are regarded as predispositions to act with respect to some specific area of experience. "I intend to write a letter to the editor protesting the article on abortion"; "I plan to march in the antinuclear demonstration on Friday"; and "I intend to tell my parents this coming weekend that I am gay" are all examples of behavioral intentions.

Fishbein regards behavioral intentions as a function of two major variables. The first variable is one's *attitude toward performing a particular behavior* in a given situation. This attitude depends on a person's beliefs about the personal consequences of performing the behavior and his or her evaluation of such consequences. Consequences will be evaluated either negatively or positively, and evaluations will vary in intensity. Although writing a letter to the editor might have no negative, or may even have positive effects, discussing unorthodox sexual preferences might have highly negative consequences.

The second predictor of behavioral intentions consists of one's *social normative beliefs*. Normative beliefs are a function of a person's expectancies that important others think that he or she should or should not enact a particular behavior, along with one's motivation to comply with social norms. Thus, the amount of social support people believe they have for performing a particular behavior should affect their behavioral intentions.[69]

Fishbein's notions are a parsimonious summary of most of the determinants of attitude–behavior consistency discussed earlier. First, his concept of attitude is specific relative to behavior. Second, attitudinal schemata should be major determinants of behavior if they are ego involving, formed through direct experience, certain, and internally consistent. Third, if the attitude holder perceives the consequences of behaving as mostly positive, he or she will probably act. Fourth, an active self-image, the absence of competing attitudes, a behavior that requires little effort, and confidence in one's ability to perform should lead to action. Finally, Fishbein regards the power of relevant social norms as a major determinant of overt behavior.

In fact, then, Fishbein's explanation of the determinants of attitude–behavior consistency *is not an alternative view at all.* Rather, it is a sophisticated attempt to take into account all those disparate factors years of research have shown influence the relationship between a person's cognitive schemata and his or her overt actions.

NOTES

1. Joe McGinness, *The Selling of the President 1968* (New York: Trident Press, 1969), pp. 87–92.

2. Sir Frederick Bartlett is generally credited with originating the notion of cognitive schemata. See Frederick C. Bartlett, *Remembering: A Study in Experimental and Social Psychology* (London: Cambridge University Press, 1932).

3. See Robert P. Abelson, "Script Processing in Attitude Formation and Decision Making," in *Cognition and Social Behavior,* ed. John S. Carroll and John W. Payne (Hillsdale, N.J.: Lawrence Erlbaum, 1976).

4. See Marvin Minsky, "A Framework for Representing Knowledge," in *The Psychology of Computer Vision,* ed. P. Winston (New York: McGraw-Hill, 1975).

5. See Nancy Cantor and Walter Mischel, "Traits as Prototypes: Effects on Recognition Memory," *Journal of Personality and Social Psychology* 35 (1977): 39–48.

6. See George A. Kelly, *The Psychology of Personal Constructs* (New York: Norton, 1955).

7. See John H. Lingle et al., "Thematic Effects of Person Judgments on Impression Organization," *Journal of Personality and Social Psychology* 37 (1979): 674–687.

8. See Shelley E. Taylor and Jennifer Crocker, "Schematic Bases of Social Information Processing," in *The Ontario Symposium on Personality and Social Psychology: Social Cognition,* ed. E. Tory Higgins, C. Peter Herman, and Mark P. Zanna (Hillsdale, N.J.: Lawrence Erlbaum, 1981); and Hazel Markus, "Self-Schemata and Processing Information About the Self," *Journal of Personality and Social Psychology* 35 (1977): 63–78.

9. Roger Schank and Robert Abelson, *Scripts, Plans, Goals, and Understanding* (Hillsdale, N.J.: Lawrence Erlbaum, 1977), p. 19.

10. Lee Ross, "The Intuitive Psychologist and His Shortcomings: Distortions in the Attribution Process," in *Advances in Experimental Social Psychology,* ed. Leonard Berkowitz (New York: Academic Press, 1977).

11. See Lawrence J. Stricker, Paul I. Jacobs, and Nathan Kogan, "Trait Interrelations in Implicit Personality Theories and Questionnaire Data," *Journal of Personality and Social Psychology* 30 (1974): 198–207; and Clarry H. Lay and Douglas N. Jackson, "Analysis of the Generality of Trait Inferential Relationships," *Journal of Personality and Social Psychology* 12 (1969): 12–21.

12. See Richard A. Shweder, "Illusory Correlation and the MMPI Controversy," *Journal of Consulting and Clinical Psychology* 45 (1977): 917–924; Roy G. D'Andrade, "Trait Psychology and Componential Analysis," *American Anthropologist* 67 (1965): 215–228.

13. For a summary of relevant research, see David J. Schneider, Albert H. Hastrof, and Phoebe C. Ellsworth, *Person Perception,* 2nd ed. (Reading, Mass.: Addison-Wesley, 1979), pp. 161–164.

14. See Christopher M. Massad, Michael Hubbard, and Darren Newtson, "Selective Perception of Events," *Journal of Experimental Social Psychology* 15 (1979): 513–532; and Darren Newtson and Gretchen Engquist, "The Perceptual Organization of Ongoing Behavior," *Journal of Experimental Social Psychology* 12 (1976): 847–862.

15. See Darren A. Newtson, "Foundations of Attribution: The Perception of Ongoing Behavior," in *New Directions in Attribution Research*, ed. John H. Harvey, William J. Ickes, and Robert F. Kidd (Hillsdale, N.J.: Lawrence Erlbaum, 1976); and Darren A. Newtson, "Attribution and the Unit of Perception of Ongoing Behavior," *Journal of Personality and Social Psychology* 28 (1973): 28–38.

16. Donald A. Norman, *Memory and Attention*, 2nd ed. (New York: John Wiley, 1976).

17. T. B. Rogers, N. A. Kuiper, and W. S. Kirker, "Self-Reference and the Encoding of Personal Information," *Journal of Personality and Social Psychology* 35 (1977): 677.

18. Markus, p. 64.

19. See David J. Schneider, "Implicit Personality Theory: A Review," *Psychological Bulletin* 79 (1973): 294–309.

20. For an excellent discussion of the differences arising from the relative complexity of self- and other-schemata, see N. A. Kuiper and T. B. Rogers, "Encoding of Personal Information: Self–Other Differences," *Journal of Personality and Social Psychology* 37 (1979): 499–514.

21. This idea is developed by Edward E. Jones and Richard E. Nisbett, *The Actor and the Observer: Divergent Perceptions of the Causes of Behavior* (Morristown, N.J.: General Learning Press, 1971), p. 7.

22. Charles G. Lord, "Schemas and Images as Memory Aids: Two Modes of Processing Social Information," *Journal of Personality and Social Psychology* 38 (1980): 257–269.

23. Randall Harrison, "Nonverbal Communication: Explorations into Time, Space, Action, and Object," in *Dimensions in Communication*, ed. J. H. Campbell and H. W. Hepler (Belmont, Calif.: Wadsworth, 1970), pp. 256–271.

24. See Kuiper and Rogers; Ross; and Donald Snygg and Arthur W. Combs, *Individual Behavior: A Perceptual Approach to Behavior* (New York: Harper & Row, 1959).

25. Kuiper and Rogers, p. 513.

26. See Thomas K. Srull and Robert S. Wyer, Jr., "The Role of Category Accessibility in the Interpretation of Information about Persons: Some Determinants and Implications," *Journal of Personality and Social Psychology* 37 (1979): 1660–1672; and E. Tory Higgins, William S. Rholes, and Carl R. Jones, "Category Accessibility and Impression Formation," *Journal of Experimental Social Psychology* 13 (1977): 141–154.

27. Claudia E. Cohen and Ebbe B. Ebbesen, "Observational Goals and Schema Activation: A Theoretical Framework for Behavior Perception," *Journal of Experimental Social Psychology* 15 (1979): 305–329.

28. Walter H. Crockett, "Cognitive Complexity and Impression Formation," in *Progress in Experimental Personality Research*, ed. Brendon A. Maher (New York: Academic Press, 1965), p. 49.

29. Crockett, p. 56.

30. Jesse G. Delia, Ruth Anne Clark, and David E. Switzer, "Cognitive Complexity and Impression Formation in Informal Social Interaction," *Speech Monographs* 41 (1974): 299–308; and Crockett.

31. Claudia Hale and Jesse G. Delia, "Cognitive Complexity and Social Perspective-Taking," *Communication Monographs* 43 (1976): 195–203; Allen N. Press, Walter H. Crockett, and Jesse G. Delia, "The Effect of Cognitive Complexity and of the Perceiver's Set Upon the Organization of Impressions," unpublished MS, Kansas State University, 1974; Lewis J. Nidorf and Walter H. Crockett, "Cognitive Complexity and the Integration of Conflicting Information in Written Impressions," *Journal of Social Psychology* 66 (1965); and Paul S. Rosenkrantz and Walter H. Crockett, "Some Factors Influencing the Assimilation of Disparate Information in Impression Formation," *Journal of Personality and Social Psychology* 2 (1965): 397–402.

32. For summaries of definitions, see Samuel Himmelfarb and Alice Hendrickson Eagly, eds., *Readings in Attitude Change* (New York: John Wiley & Sons, 1974), pp. 3–8; and Charles A. Kiesler, Barry E. Collins, and Norman Miller, *Attitude Change* (New York: John Wiley & Sons, 1969), pp. 1–8.

33. See Martin Fishbein and Icek Ajzen, *Belief, Attitude, Intention and Behavior* (Reading, Mass.: Addison-Wesley, 1975), pp. 222–228; and Martin Fishbein and Bertram H. Raven, "The AB Scales: An Operational Definition of Belief and Attitude," *Human Relations* 15 (1962): 35–44.

34. For relevant discussions of the relationship between cognitive schemata and attitudes, see John H. Lingle and Thomas M. Ostrom, "Thematic Effects of Attitude on the Cognitive Processing of Attitude Relevant Information," in *Cognitive Responses in Persuasion*, ed. Richard E. Petty, Thomas M. Ostrom, and Timothy C. Brock (Hillsdale, N.J.: Lawrence Erlbaum, in press); and Charles M. Judd and James A. Kulik, "Schematic Effects of Social Attitudes on Information Processing and Recall," *Journal of Personality and Social Psychology* 38 (1980): 569–578.

35. Our view of the relation between attitudes and cognitive schemata is similar to Abraham Tesser's. See Abraham Tesser, "Self-Generated Attitude Change," in *Advances in Experimental Social Psychology*, ed. Leonard Berkowitz (New York: Academic Press, 1976), pp. 289–338; and Abraham Tesser and Christopher Leone, "Cognitive Schemas and Thought as Determinants of Attitude Change," *Journal of Experimental Social Psychology* 13 (1977): 340–356.

36. See Milton Rokeach, *Beliefs, Attitudes, and Values* (San Francisco: Jossey-Bass, 1968), pp. 6–11.

37. Carolyn W. Sherif, Muzafer Sherif, and Roger E. Nebergall, *Attitude and Attitude Change* (Philadelphia: W. B. Saunders, 1965), pp. 64–65; Muzafer Sherif and Carl I. Hovland, *Social Judgment: Assimilation and Contrast Effects in Communication and Attitude Change* (New Haven: Yale University Press, 1961), p. 197; and Muzafer Sherif and Hadley Cantril, *The Psychology of Ego-Involvements* (New York: John Wiley & Sons, Inc., 1947) pp. 126–127.

38. Harry C. Triandis, *Attitude and Attitude Change* (New York: John Wiley & Sons, 1971), pp. 103–104.

39. Donald T. Campbell, "Stereotypes and the Perception of Group Differences," *American Psychologist* 22 (1967): 817–829.

40. Triandis, p. 104.

41. Myron Rothbart et al., "From Individual to Group Impressions: Availability Heuristics in Stereotype Formation," *Journal of Experimental Social Psychology* 14 (1978): 237–255.

42. Triandis, pp. 107–112.

43. Daniel Katz and Kenneth Braly, "Racial Stereotypes of 100 College Students," *Journal of Abnormal and Social Psychology* 28 (1933): 280–290; and G. M. Gilbert, "Stereotype Persistence and Change among College Students," *Journal of Abnormal and Social Psychology* 46 (1951): 245–254.

44. Daniel Katz, "The Functional Approach to the Study of Attitudes," *Public Opinion Quarterly* 24 (1960): 163–204.

45. Irving Sarnoff, "Reaction Formation and Cynicism," *Journal of Personality* 28 (1960): 129–143. See also Daniel R. Miller and Guy E. Swanson, *Inner Conflict and Defense* (New York: Holt, Rinehart & Winston, 1960).

46. Bradley Graham and Phil McCombs, "The Energy Mess: How We Got There," *The Washington Post*, 8 July 1979, p. A1. For one account of the psychological basis of conspiracy theories, see Clark McCauley and Susan Jacques, "The Popularity of Conspiracy Theories of Presidential Assassination: A Bayesian Analysis," *Journal of Personality and Social Psychology* 37 (1979): 637–644.

47. Richard T. La Pière, "Attitudes vs. Action," *Social Forces* 13 (1934): 230–237.

48. For examples, see Alan W. Wicker, "An Examination of the 'Other Variables' Explanation of Attitude-Behavior Inconsistency," *Journal of Personality and Social Psychology* 19 (1971): 18–30; Lawrence Wrightsman, "Wallace Supporters and Adherence to 'Law and Order'," *Journal of Personality and Social Psychology* 13 (1969): 17–22; Lester Carr and S. O. Roberts, "Correlates of Civil-Rights Participation," *Journal of Social Psychology* 67 (1965): 259–267; Kenneth R. Berg, "Ethnic Attitudes and Agreement with a Negro Person," *Journal of Personality and Social Psychology* 4 (1966): 215–220.

49. Alan W. Wicker, "Attitudes versus Actions: The Relationship of Verbal and Overt Behavioral Responses to Attitude Objects," *Journal of Social Issues* 25 (1979): 65.

50. Daryl J. Bem, "Self-Perception Theory," in *Advances in Experimental Social Psychology*, ed. Leonard Berkowitz (New York: Academic Press, 1972), pp. 1–62.

51. Leonard W. Doob, "The Behavior of Attitudes," *Psychological Review* 54 (1947): 135–156.

52. William A. Scott, "Attitude Change Through Reward of Verbal Behavior," *Journal of Abnormal and Social Psychology* 55 (1957): 72–75.

53. For a summary of some relevant research, see Robert A. Wicklund and Jack W. Brehm, *Perspectives on Cognitive Dissonance* (Hillsdale, N. J.: Lawrence Erlbaum, 1976).

54. William J. McGuire, "The Concept of Attitudes and Their Relations to Behaviors," in *Perspectives on Attitude Assessment: Surveys and their Alternatives*, ed. H. Wallace Sinaiko and L. A. Broedling (Champaign, Ill.: Pendleton, 1976).

55. Lynn R. Kahle and John J. Berman, "Attitudes Cause Behaviors: A Cross-Lagged Panel Analysis," *Journal of Personality and Social Psychology* 37 (1979): 315–321.

56. William A. Watts, "Relative Persistence of Opinion Change Induced by Active Compared to Passive Participation," *Journal of Personality and Social Psychology* 5 (1967): 4–15.

57. Herbert C. Kelman, "Attitudes Are Alive and Well and Gainfully Employed in the Sphere of Action," *American Psychologist* 29 (1974): 324.

58. Dennis T. Regan and Russell H. Fazio, "On the Consistency Between Attitudes and Behavior: Look to the Method of Attitude Formation," *Journal of Experimental Social Psychology* 13 (1977): 28–45.

59. Russell H. Fazio and Mark P. Zanna, "Attitudinal Qualities Relating to the Strength of the Attitude–Behavior Relationship," *Journal of Experimental Social Psychology* 14 (1978): 398–408.

60. Ross Norman, "Affective–Cognitive Consistency, Attitudes, Conformity, and Behavior," *Journal of Personality and Social Psychology* 32 (1975): 83–91.

61. Fazio and Zanna, p. 403.

62. See Thomas A. Heberlein and J. Stanley Black, "Attitudinal Specificity and the Prediction of Behavior in a Field Setting," *Journal of Personality and Social Psychology* 33 (1976): 474–479; Russell H. Weigel and Lee S. Newman, "Increasing Attitude–Behavior Correspondence by Broadening the Scope of the Behavioral Measure," *Journal of Personality and Social Psychology* 33 (1976): 793–802; Martin Fishbein and Icek Ajzen, "Attitudes Toward Objects as Predictors of Single and Multiple Behavioral Criteria," *Psychological Review* 81 (1974): 59–74; and Martin Fishbein, "The Prediction of Behaviors from Attitudinal Variables," in *Advances in Communication Research*, ed. C. David Mortensen and Kenneth K. Sereno (New York: Harper & Row, 1973), pp. 3–31.

63. See Icek Ajzen, "Attitudinal vs. Normative Messages: An Investigation of the Differential Effects of Persuasive Communications on Behavior," *Sociometry* 34 (1971): 263–280; Icek Ajzen and Martin Fishbein, "The Prediction of Behavior from Attitudinal and Normative Variables," *Journal of Experimental Social Psychology* 6 (1970): 466–487; and Lyle G. Warner and Melvin L. DeFleur, "Attitude as an Interactional Concept: Social Constraint and Social Distance as Intervening Variables Between Attitudes and Action," *American Sociological Review* 34 (1969): 153–167. A compact summary of the effects of social norms on behavior can be found in Fishbein and Ajzen, *Belief, Attitude, Intention and Behavior*, pp. 302–307.

64. See Chapter 7 of Fishbein and Ajzen, *Belief, Attitude, Intention and Behavior* for a review of research related to the behavioral effects of consequences.

65. For a discussion of the role of effort in mediating behavior, see Donald T. Campbell, "Social Attitudes and Other Acquired Behavioral Dispositions," in *Psychology: A Study of a Science*, ed. Sigmund Koch (New York: McGraw-Hill, 1963), pp. 94–172.

66. Leslie Ann McArthur, Charles A. Kiesler, and Barry P. Cook, "Acting on an Attitude as a Function of a Self-Precept and Inequity," *Journal of Personality and Social Psychology* 12 (1969): 295–302.

67. Howard J. Ehrlich, "Attitudes, Behavior, and the Intervening Variables," *American Sociologist* 4 (1969): 29–34.

68. Milton Rokeach and Peter Kliejunas, "Behavior as a Function of Attitude-Toward-Object and Attitude-Toward-Situation," *Journal of Personality and Social Psychology* 22 (1972): 194–201.

69. See Chapter 7 of Fishbein and Ajzen, *Belief, Attitude, Intention and Behavior* for a summary of Fishbein's theorizing on the attitude–behavior relationship.

CHAPTER 3

The Nature of Theory in Persuasion

In March, 1954, newspapers in Seattle, Washington, began carrying reports of extensive damage to automobile windshields in the area. Between April 14 and 15, over 3000 Seattle residents telephoned the police reporting such damage. Most commonly, the windshield damage consisted of pitting marks that grew into bubbles in the glass about the size of a thumbnail. Police suspected vandalism but were unable to gather proof. On the evening of April 15, the mayor of Seattle declared the damage was no longer a police matter and made an emergency appeal for help to the governor of Washington and the president of the United States.

Over the next three months, scientists, engineers, police officials, and ordinary citizens speculated about what was causing the persistent windshield damage. Explanations ranged from a purely physical cause to unusual and mysterious forces. Most scientists explained the windshield pitting as a consequence of ordinary road damage or pollution from nearby coal plants. The explanations offered by engineers included radioactive fallout from recent H-bomb explosions at a nearby Pacific testing ground; a shifting of the earth's magnetic field; and high frequency electronic waves from a giant radio transmitter located near Seattle. The police suspected vandalism, unspecified atmospheric conditions, and ordinary road wear.

Among ordinary citizens, the most frequently mentioned explanation was the H-bomb. Other explanations included cosmic rays, chemicals of uncertain origin, meteorites, and sandflea eggs hatching in the glass! Later tests conducted by the University of Washington's Environmental Research Laboratory confirmed that the black particles found on many automobiles were just bits of soot formed by improper combustion of bituminous coal at local plants. All instances of pitted windshields were found to be a consequence of ordinary road damage.[1]

These explanations, ranging from the reasonable to the absurd, highlight the central issue we shall consider in this chapter: finding plausible explanations for persistent patterns of effects. Searches for explanations, for causes, for answers to the question "Why?" are among the most pervasive of all human actions. Moreover, people inevitably answer the question "Why?" by concocting *theories* specifying reasons for the occurrence of persistent effects. The theories suggested by the citizens of Seattle ranged from the ordinary to the bizarre. Through empirical testing, the most plausible theory was confirmed.

The structure of theorizing about persuasive effects is not unlike the general pattern taken by the citizens of Seattle. However, the substance of our theoretical interest is radically different. To seek to explain automobile windshield damage is to look for some external cause of a physical phenomenon. This process is similar to that of an engineer looking for the cause of malfunctioning machinery or a medical researcher searching for the virus responsible for a new strain of influenza. In such cases, involving natural or physical effects, direct, cause-to-effect relationships can be located and verified.

In contrast, when we seek to explain human responses to messages, we are not dealing with passive recipients of environmental stimuli. Rather, we are concerned with active human agents who respond to their personalized and varied interpretations of external reality. Moreover, people are choice laden and goal directed. Unlike the windshields of Seattle, people are not passive victims whose responses can be explained fully by referring to external causal forces. Rather, humans are themselves "causal" agents, who shape their own responses to the world around them.

Thus, in our pursuit of explanations for persuasive effects, we will find ourselves committed to a more complex task than that suggested by the mechanistic causal model operating 30 years ago in Seattle. We shall approach this task by examining the nature of theory in persuasion, its philosophical bases, and the types of theoretical explanations capable of accounting for persuasive effects. Additionally, we will critique persuasion theory and present our own views about theoretical directions appropriate to human communicative behaviors.

THE GENERAL NATURE OF PERSUASION THEORY

A theory is a generalization providing an explanation for a persistent pattern of effects. It specifies why certain effects occur and under what circumstances we may expect them to recur. Theoretical explanations grow out of a careful observation of recurring effects, coupled with rational speculation about the factors or reasons responsible for the effects. The pattern of effects explained by any theory may be physical, as in the case of windshield damage in Seattle, or it may be behavioral in nature. In persuasion, we are interested exclusively in patterns of behavioral effects, in intentional, human responses to persuasive messages.

As we saw in Chapter 2, the particular persuasive effects we wish to explain are those cognitive schematic and overt behavioral responses people make to symbols. If, for example, we observe that physically attractive people generally are more persuasive than less attractive individuals, we may wish to know why this is so. Or if we notice that new members of social groups usually adopt the attitudes and behavior patterns of more established group members, we may wish to know the reasons for this effect. Theories provide us with the means for explaining such effects. Persuasion theories explain by stipulating relationships between *human responses* and those *generative forces* responsible for the responses. Thus, we may define a persuasion theory as *a statement or set of statements specifying an explanatory relationship between patterns of cognitive or behavioral responses to messages and some generative force responsible for the responses.*

Accordingly, we may theorize that "Physically attractive people are especially influential because identifying with them gives positive expression to people's ideal self-concepts," and that "New group members conform to the attitudes and behaviors of others because they wish to remain in the group and enjoy its social benefits." Persuasion theories, then, explain human actions by specifying why and under what conditions we can expect a particular response to appear.

The Predictive Power of Theory

Because theories have explanatory power, that is, they specify the generative force behind certain effects, they allow us to *predict* future responses to messages. For example, if I know, as a general theoretical rule, that highly anxious people respond negatively to frightening messages because such messages arouse ego-defensive reactions, I am in a position to predict when defensive responses will occur. Similarly, the theoretical explanations advanced about physically attractive people and new group members give one the power to predict reactions to physical attractiveness and new group membership in advance.

Because theories enable us to predict responses to certain messages, they give us a measure of *control* over the relationship between messages and responses. For example, if I can predict that minimal attitude change will occur when anxious people hear frightening messages, I can exercise some control over persuasive effects. At a minimum, I can avoid communicating fearful messages when I am with anxious people. In general, then, theories of persuasion have predictive as well as control properties.

Theory and Patterns of Effects

We have said that a theory explains patterns of persuasive effects. At this juncture, it is important to emphasize that persuasion theorists are interested only in those effects that are recurrent and relatively stable. Isolated, random effects are of little interest to any theorist bent on explaining the physical, psychological, or social world. For instance, if only one or two car owners in Seattle had observed windshield damage in 1954, it is doubtful that an attempt to find a generalized explanation of "windshield pitting" would have occurred. It was only when a pattern of similar damage was reported by many car owners over a period of several weeks that the community of Seattle began to suspect that a single causal factor was responsible for the recurring damage.

Likewise, in persuasion we seek theories for consistently recurring responses. If, for example, we observe that active participation strategies consistently are more effective than traditional persuasive techniques, we may ask why this is so. As a response, we may theorize that a person is persuaded more readily in the self-influence paradigm because self-generated arguments are more congruent with basic values than are messages produced by external agents. We resort to theorizing only when we observe a repetitive, enduring pattern of responses to persuasive messages. Indeed, theories are useful because they are not situation-specific, and because they can explain cognitive and behavioral effects across a variety of similar situations.

The Structure of a Persuasion Theory

A persuasion theory has three components: (1) a statement specifying the generative force or motivating reason; (2) a statement describing a pattern of effects; and (3) a connective or linking statement stipulating how and under what conditions the generative force is likely to be joined with its effects. The statement specifying the generative force, or what does the explaining, is formally called the *explanans*, and the statement of effects, what is to be explained, is referred to as the *explanandum*. The contingent circumstances under which the generative force is likely to produce a particular pattern of responses are called the *boundary conditions*. Thus, a theory in persuasion takes the general form: If X (generative force), then Y (effects), under conditions $Z_1 \ldots Z_n$ (specified boundary limitations).

These three components are called constructs. A *construct* refers to "classes or sets of objects or events bound together by the possession of some common characteristic."[2] To illustrate, consider the theoretical statement that a desire to be accepted in a social group (generative force) results in conformity to the behaviors of well-accepted group members (effects), under the condition that the particular group demands a high level of conformity in exchange for acceptance (boundary condition).

This theoretical statement contains three constructs. The first, a desire for acceptance, is a *generative construct*, the second, conformity, is an *effects construct*, and the third, group tolerance of deviancy, is a *boundary construct*. While there undoubtedly will be a variety of reasons why people desire acceptance in a particular group, their various reasons all relate to acceptance goals. Likewise, there will be differences in the ways individuals conform and in how much deviancy a group will tolerate. Yet the two sets of behaviors are sufficiently similar that they may be grouped together as a conformity construct and a tolerance of deviancy construct, respectively.

In sum, a theory consists of a set of constructs coupled with statements showing how the constructs are linked together. The typical linkage pattern is: If X (generative construct), then Y (effects construct), under conditions $Z_1 \ldots Z_n$ (boundary constructs).

GENERATIVE FORCES IN PERSUASION: MECHANISM VERSUS ACTIONALISM

Since the essence of theorizing in persuasion is a search for generative forces or reasons responsible for particular effects, we need to examine the nature of human generative forces. In this regard, one's epistemological stance will determine the kinds of generative forces deemed capable of explaining human responses to messages. An *epistemological perspective* consists of "a set of assumptions about how one 'knows' the world."[3] It encompasses people's assumptions about the nature of human beings, their perspective on the nature of the social environment, and their conception of the relationship of humans to that environment. Historically, two epistemological postures have influenced our thinking about ways of explaining human responses to messages. Called mechanism and actionalism, each view embraces radically different assumptions about human behavior. These assumptions, in turn, lead to widely divergent views about the types of generative forces capable of prompting human responses to messages.

Philosophical Views of Human Nature: Mechanism

Early attempts to explain human social behavior in general, and human responses to persuasive messages in particular, adopted the epistemological assumptions of the physical sciences. These assumptions were based on a *mechanistic model of man*.[4] According to this view, human behavior can be explained adequately by referring to external, causal stimuli. A person is seen as a relatively passive object whose behavior is controlled by antecedent environmental forces.

The "radical behaviorism" of B. F. Skinner typifies this perspective. In Skinner's view, all human behavior, including verbal behavior, can be explained within a stimulus–response (S–R) paradigm. Externally rewarded responses develop and become a part of a person's behavioral repertoire, while punished behaviors decay. Skinner took no account of internal, cognitive processes. People were regarded as reactive victims of environmental causal forces with no freedom of choice or capacity for self-direction.[5] You will recall that the "hypodermic needle" theory of persuasion, discussed in Chapter 1, reflects this mechanistic causal model of man.

Consistent with this view of causal determinism, social scientists and communication theorists in the mechanistic tradition adopted a *logical positivist* approach to the nature of the environment and a person's relationship to it. The positivist position regards the external environment as factual, fully knowable, and causally ordered phenomena. The world is seen as an objective reality, unaffected by human cognitive schemata and actions. The logical positivists tried to discover existing laws of human behavior stipulating invariant, causal relations between external antecedent conditions and consequent behavioral effects.[6] Similarly, the aim of persuasion theorists in the hypodermic tradition was to stipulate relationships between human responses and powerful external causal mechanisms, including message strategies and source manipulations. From this mechanistic perspective, people are moved by their environment, they do not act upon it.[7]

Philosophical Views of Human Nature: Actionalism

A more recent philosophical paradigm for explaining human behavior and human responses to persuasive messages is based on an *actional model of man*.[8] Four principal assumptions underlie this view. First, humans are regarded as active agents, exercising influence over their environment, rather than passively reacting to it. Second, humans have intentionality; they are goal oriented and strive to maximize personal rewards and minimize undesirable outcomes. Third, humans can choose among alternative courses of action in the pursuit of their goals. This self-directional quality leads people to select among available alternatives those actions best meeting their personal needs and goals at any one moment.

Finally, the actional model rejects the logical positivist view of a world unaffected by human perception in favor of a *cognitive schematic* or constructivist approach,[9] a view we discussed thoroughly in Chapter 2. In this view, the environment is seen as a creation of humans based on their peculiar, cognitive schematic structures. People assign their own meanings to external events and respond to their interpretation or construction of environmental stimuli, not to some raw reality untouched by the human mind. It is upon this actional model that our own theoretical explanations of human responses to persuasion ultimately will be found.

TYPES OF THEORETICAL EXPLANATIONS IN PERSUASION: LAWS AND RULES

Historically, two different approaches to explanation have guided persuasion theorists.[10] The oldest theoretical tradition is an offspring of the mechanistic model revised to accommodate many of the actional qualities of human behavior. This theoretical perspective is called the *laws approach* or the covering law model, and it aims to formulate generalizations about the ways people usually respond to certain messages in particular communication environments. Emphasis is placed on locating those message variables having a powerful causal effect on receivers.

The second and newer approach to theorizing about persuasive effects is strictly actional in nature, representing a complete break with the mechanistic tradition. Called the *rules perspective*, this approach explains human actions by referring to reasons, or the intentions and goals of persuasive agents. Emphasis is placed on discovering the practical rules people follow in order to satisfy their needs and desires. Let us now examine these two approaches.

The Laws Approach: Causal Explanation

Systematic efforts to explain human behavior by referring to laws began in the early 1930s and continue to date. These 50-plus years of sustained work have generated a substantial body of theoretical generalizations and supportive research relevant to human responses to messages.

The laws approach is derived from the mechanistic model of explanation, and therefore, explains human behavior by referring to causes.[11] A *causal explanation* cites some antecedent condition that produces a consequent effect. "Viruses cause influenza," and "Electricity generates artificial light," are examples of natural, causal connections. The social scientific literature contains two conceptions of laws. The earliest was mechanistic and positivist in nature and applied the epistemological assumptions of physics, biology, and other natural sciences directly to human behavior without any adaptation or revision. This mechanistic view regards laws as generalizations specifying invariant causal connections between external antecedents and consequent human actions. Such laws reflect recurring regularities that presumably have been observed between messages and the effects they produce in people. Moreover, these laws are regarded as universal, holding through both time and space.

The mechanistic conception of law is characterized by determinancy, sufficiency, and necessity. *Determinancy* refers to a universal, invariant connection between a cause and its effect. A deterministic relationship takes the form: If cause X, then always response Y. In the context of B. F. Skinner's mechanistic S–R paradigm discussed earlier, a deterministic relationship might be: whenever a behavior pattern such as human aggression is positively reinforced, it will always develop and persist.

Sufficiency means that the causal force, in our example, positive reinforcement, has *all* the properties necessary to produce its effect. A sufficient relationship takes the form: If cause X, then response Y, regardless of any contingent circumstances. If Skinner's deterministic relationship between reinforcement and aggression is sufficient, it should occur regardless of contingent circumstances. However, if certain conditions are a prerequisite for the effect to occur, then the relationship would not be sufficient. For example, if a person had developed through prior reinforcement a masochistic or self-punishment syndrome, then a Skinnerian theorist would not expect rewards to foster the learning of aggression. In this case, the relationship between positive reinforcement and the learning of aggression would be deterministic only under the condition that the reinforced person lacked masochistic tendencies.

Finally, *necessity* refers to a situation in which one and only one cause can produce a particular effect. A necessary relationship takes the form: If cause X, and only if cause X, then response Y. Thus, if positive reinforcement were the *only* cause capable of producing human aggression, the relationship would be necessary. However, if an individual could learn to be aggressive in other ways, for example by imitating others, then the relationship would lack necessity.

The Current Conception of Laws

Most communication theorists have rejected the mechanistic conception of laws as inappropriate to the study of human responses to persuasive messages.[12] In its place they have turned to a laws approach that eschews many of the epistemological assumptions associated with mechanism and logical positivism. Gerald Miller and Charles Berger have written extensively on the nature of communication laws, and our analysis will follow their conceptualizations.[13]

According to Miller, *laws* are general statements about the ways people will probably respond to certain types of messages in specifiable kinds of communication environments.[14] In other words, laws describe regularities or associations that *usually* are found between certain messages and human responses, under specifiable conditions. Moreover, Berger has argued that these associations need not be causal but may reflect only covariations or correlations between certain types of messages and their effects.[15] Whether the stipulated relationships are causal or correlational, laws take the general form: If message strategy X, then response Y, under conditions $Z_1 \ldots Z_n$.

Some examples of such laws include: "If factual information is used in a persuasive message, it will probably produce greater attitude change than a message without evidence, if the source lacks credibility with recipients, the evidence is unfamiliar to receivers, and so forth"; "If viewers are exposed to televised violence, then they are likely to behave aggressively, provided latent aggression is already present in the viewers"; and finally, to use one of Berger's examples, "Perceived similarity of attitudes between persons has a high probability of producing a high level of attraction between the two persons."[16]

Such laws differ from mechanistic explanations in two critical ways. First, the nature of the stipulated relationships diverge from mechanistic relationships along three dimensions. Current laws relationships are: (1) *probable* or stochastic, not deterministic; (2) *contingent*, not sufficient; and (3) *substitutable*, not necessary. A *probable* law declares that particular effects are likely, not certain. To say that a relationship is *contingent*, not sufficient, means that certain effects are likely *only* under certain specifiable conditions. In our example regarding evidence in a persuasive message, the law stated that factual material is likely to facilitate attitude change *only* if the persuader is perceived as low in credibility, the evidence is novel, and the like. In the second example, the law declared that symbolic violence is likely to cause human aggression *only* if a viewer already has aggressive tendencies.

Finally, the relationship between a generative persuasive force and some probable effect is *substitutable*, not necessary. Not only is the stated generative force capable of producing a particular effect under the stipulated conditions, but other generative forces can produce the same effect under the same conditions. As we saw in our earlier example, while televised violence can arouse latent aggression, so can numerous other things. It is likely that temporary frustration, fatigue, or other internal forces may also transform covert aggressive tendencies into overt violence.

A second major way the current laws approach differs from the mechanistic model is that most contemporary laws theorists reject the logical positivist view that *unin*terpreted external stimuli cause human responses to messages. Instead, they search for causal forces in the external environment as it is selectively perceived, interpreted, and influenced by human cognitive schemata. As Miller puts it, even those theorists "who still label their scientific quest as 'a search for laws' . . . strike an action-oriented stance when it comes to theory construction, preferring to emphasize the individual's selective perception and organization of the environment, as well as his/her active behavioral influence over it."[17]

Even so, current laws theorists assume that the generative forces responsible for human behavior are causal, antecedent conditions; and they emphasize the power of interpreted, external, persuasive manipulations to *cause* certain effects in the recipients of such messages. This approach contrasts sharply with the perspective employed by rules theorists.

The Rules Perspective: Teleological Explanation

Contrasted with laws, the rules approach to explaining human communicative behavior is in its conceptual and methodological infancy. Although rules have been used extensively in other disciplines, the first attempt to explicate a rules analysis of human communication phenomena appeared in the early 1970s.[18] Since its inception, the rules perspective has gathered a substantial following among communications scholars. However, as Miller notes in a general review of the status of communication theory, "even the staunchest advocates of the rule-governed approach to conceptualizing . . . communication, grant that it has yet to generate a unified body of coherent theory or an ambitious program of coordinated research."[19] Even though many specific theories of persuasion are implicitly rules based and a few are explicit rules approaches, few attempts have yet been made to explicate a *general* rules-based perspective on persuasion. Because we believe that a rules analysis is particularly well suited to much persuasive phenomena, one of our aims is to suggest some guidelines for a rules-based conceptualization of persuasive communication.

Philosophical Bases of the Rules Perspective

Philosophically, the rules perspective is strictly actional, breaking all ties with the mechanistic model of man. In the tradition of Immanuel Kant,[20] humans are seen as active agents possessing goals and the capacity for choice. People seek to maximize their rewards and minimize undesirable consequences. As Romano Harré and Paul Secord summarize it, human behavior "involves an agent capable of deliberating and choosing from a variety of courses of action" those best meeting his or her needs and goals.[21] From the rules perspective, goal-maximizing behavior follows the pattern of a practical syllogism. Georg von Wright's third-person, practical syllogism illustrates the rules perspective in regard to the ways we generate our actions: (1) A *intends* to bring about P; (2) A *considers* that he cannot bring about P unless he does B; and (3) therefore, A sets himself [*chooses*] to do B.[22] From this perspective, people's intentions and goals, their *reasons* for acting, are seen as the essential generative forces prompting social behavior.

The view that responses can be explained fully by reference to a person's subjective *reasons* for acting is called a *teleological explanation.* Such "an explanation of action is intentional and purposive. Actions are explained [strictly] in terms of the ends [or reasons] for which they are performed."[23] While laws explain human behavior by referring to some antecedent causal condition, teleological explanations suggest that human actions may be explained by referring to a person's reasons for taking an action. In short, causal explanation focuses on the things done *to* a person, whereas teleological explanation emphasizes the things done *by* a person for goal-oriented reasons.[24]

The Nature of Rules

Although there are many conceptions of the nature of a rule, most theorists suggest that rules take the form of the minor premise of the practical syllogism. Specifically, *rules are descriptive statements linking human intentions or goals with actions that are goal satisfying.*[25] Put another way, a rule is a means–end generalization, describing people's beliefs about what behaviors are required in certain contexts if they are to achieve desired objectives.[26] Thus, rules define appropriate actions in specified social settings. They stipulate what a person must do (obligation), ought to do (preference), or must not do (prohibition) in order to achieve certain goals.[27] Some examples of rules, or goal–action linkages, include: "If you wish to be an accepted member of a social group, you must (are obligated to) conform to group attitudes and behavior patterns"; "If you wish to enhance your self-image, you ought to (should prefer to) buy Calvin Klein designer blue jeans"; and "If you wish to defend your ego against attack, you must avoid (prohibit yourself from) threatening persuasive messages."

As these examples illustrate, rules link personal goals with courses of action designed to achieve them in particular contexts. Structurally, a rule takes the form of an "if–then" relationship: If goal X, in situation or context Y, then action Z. As this form suggests, rules function as criteria for human choice about alternative courses of action. Moreover, from a rules perspective, reasons or goals are the essential generative force prompting human actions.

Characteristics of Rules

Three characteristics of rules are said to differentiate them from laws. First, a rule is *followable*, that is, one may choose to follow it or break it as judgment dictates.[28] Although the rule for acceptability in groups is conformity to norms, one may choose to rebel, just as one can buy Levi's instead of designer jeans or deliberately choose to hear ego-threatening messages. While rules are breakable, laws presumably are not, since they specify antecedent causal forces not fully under our control.

Second, rules are characterized by *prescriptiveness*, that is, they specify what ought or ought not to be done to achieve certain goals.[29] By stipulating that rules are prescriptive, we do *not* mean that rules carry any moral or ethical force. They are simply means–end generalizations, specifying those actions people believe they *should* take to maximize personal goals.[30] In contrast, laws have no prescriptive qualities. They are descriptions of previously observed relationships between certain types of messages and particular kinds of responses to them. Thus, rules describe what people believe they ought to or should do, while laws describe what individuals previously have been observed to do in specified settings. The prescriptive quality of rules implies a third characteristic: rule-related behavior is *critiqueable*. If one ought to conform to group norms and does not, that behavior is subject to evaluation by others who share group rules. Deviancy usually is evaluated negatively and conformity positively.

In contrast, laws describe what is, not what ought to be; thus, law following or law breaking is not subject to critique. Recall some of the examples of laws mentioned earlier. One stated that "messages containing factual information produce more attitude change than those containing no evidence." If after hearing a factual message, someone doesn't exhibit positive attitude change, that person cannot be criticized. And being persuaded by such a message is not likely to elicit praise. Likewise, whether or not people with similar attitudes conform to the law that "similarity breeds attraction," their law-abiding or law-violating actions will not be evaluated.

Three additional characteristics of rules are *shared* with laws. First, rules like laws are *probable*, not deterministic. Regardless of how much careful deliberation goes into the choice of a goal-satisfying action, it is always possible the action will, in fact, not achieve the intended goal. Second, goal–action relationships are *contingent* or *contextual,* not sufficient. Any action can achieve its intended goal only under certain specifiable conditions. For example, I may expect that adopting a friendly attitude toward a neighbor with whom I have been quarreling will end our feud. However, my goal will be achieved only on the condition that my neighbor chooses to adopt a reciprocal attitude. Moreover, rules apply in some contexts, but not in others. For example, bombastic rhetoric is appropriate at political rallies, but not in small discussion groups. This contingent nature of rules is inherent in their structure: rules explicitly state those circumstances in which certain goal–action linkages are applicable. As we have already seen, laws likewise are bounded by the same sort of conditions and contexts.

Finally, the relationship between some goal and a goal-satisfying action is *substitutable,* not necessary. Any one goal can probably be accomplished by a whole range of behavioral options. I may be able to restore a disrupted friendship by purchasing my old friend a gift, apologizing for some past misdeed, resuming a friendly attitude, or by simply doing nothing until the temporary rift "blows over." In sum, rules, like laws, are probable, contingent, and substitutable.

The Origin of Rules

Rules have two principal sources. They may be social or idiosyncratic in origin. The most general and pervasive rules are *social* or cultural prescriptions. They reflect the consensus of the social community or general culture as to appropriate behaviors in specified contexts. The social community may consist of two or three people, such as close friends, lovers, and spouses, or it may be comprised of larger groupings. Small social clubs, large organizations like the church or school, and whole nations all constitute social communities. Some examples of socially shared rules include: "If you wish to get a job promotion, you should take actions to impress the boss"; "If you wish to persuade people to contribute to a worthy cause, you should ask, not demand or threaten them"; and "If you expect the good will of others, you must respect their rights." Many clichés express rules of behavior. "If you want to get along, go along"; and "Spare the rod, spoil the child," are examples of broad, socially shared rules of action.

Social rules vary from culture to culture and from one subculture to another within a single culture. Moreover, they change depending on the particular context in which people find themselves. Finally, social rules vary depending on the nature of the relationship between two or more persons. For example, when there are status differences in a relationship, social rules suggest that the person of lower status should be polite and deferential to the individual with higher status. Moreover, as interpersonal relationships develop, rules change. In initial interactions, social rules prescribe very formal or stylized modes of communicative behavior. People address one another by full names, perhaps even by titles like Mister or Doctor, and social talk is usually trivial. As relationships become more intimate, the rules prescribe more informal behavior modes. First or even "pet" names are used to address others, and social talk takes on an increasing breadth and depth.[31]

In addition to social rules, we have *idiosyncratic* rules. They represent an individual's own personally developed assumptions regarding appropriate actions in various contexts. Their genesis is not viewed as societal or cultural, but rather the "self-concept is viewed as a repository of rules indicating what a given individual wants and how he thinks he can get what he wants."[32] For example, if a young man decides to pursue a particular woman, he may carefully scrutinize her personality characteristics, observe the kinds of friends she chooses, and the like. On the basis of such information, he may then formulate a particularized rule or course of action he believes will achieve his goal.

From a rules perspective, social and idiosyncratic rules are the generative forces responsible for all human action.

The Strength or Practical Force of Rules

The strength or *practical force* of a rule is a function of two variables. First, the extent to which a person believes strongly that an action will achieve a desired goal is one determinant of a rule's force. Second, the strength of a rule depends heavily on the extent to which society in general, and important others in particular, support the rule and are prepared to dispense rewards for conformity and sanctions for rule violation.[33]

Thus, if I am personally convinced that apologizing to a friend for some past action will revive our friendship, if other persons I admire support the action, and if society generally supports acts of contrition, the chances that I will apologize are good. On the other hand, if I doubt that an apology will help, my other friends share these doubts, and if there is a cultural disapproval of acts of contrition, it is unlikely I will apologize to my old friend. It should be clear that social rules, reflecting as they do the consensus of the social community as to appropriate behaviors, typically have considerably more practical force than idiosyncratic rules.

The strength of social rules stems in large measure from the fact that breaking them usually results in social sanctions. If you fail to express regret for a wrongful act, you may be subject to social disapproval; if you do not behave according to the norms of your group, you risk the possibility of being rejected by the group, and so forth. In contrast, idiosyncratic rules often lack this power. They are peculiar to one or more individuals and are not under the direct control of social rewards and sanctions.

Types of Rule-Related Behavior

To understand the various rule-related behaviors, we need, first, to distinguish between explicit and implicit rules. *Explicit* rules are goal–action prescriptions that have been stated publicly. Written rules of behavior in social clubs and dress and grooming codes in schools and in police and military organizations are examples of explicit rules. Additionally, spoken rules in families and among groups of friends prescribing expected behaviors are explicit rules. Contrasted with explicit rules, many of the rules that guide our behavior are implicit or tacit in nature. *Implicit* rules are unstated prescriptions for action. Rules of conformity in social groups are examples of goal–action links that usually are unstated, but about which we are fully aware. For instance, when we go along with a majority decision in order to avoid a public fight, we are tacitly aware of why we are silent and what we expect it to achieve for us.

Undoubtedly, there are far more implicit or tacit rules guiding human behavior than there are explicit ones.

Given this distinction, we now are prepared to examine the various forms of rule-related behavior. As a starting point, Susan Shimanoff has suggested that any human action must meet three criteria before it may be legitimately called rule-related behavior. First, it must be *controllable*, that is, the behavior must be a freely chosen course of action. Second, it must be *contextual;* it must occur in all those situations where a particular set of rules is applicable. Finally, as we mentioned earlier, rule-related behavior is *critiqueable* or subject to positive or negative evaluation. If any action fails to meet any one of these defining standards, it is considered *rule-absent* behavior.[34] Examples of rule-absent behaviors include actions performed under duress, involving no perception of choice, and behavior reflecting physical limitations, including a lack of communication skills on the part of an actor.

Joan Ganz has identified three types of behaviors that are rule related, that is, they are controllable, contextual, and criticizable.[35] The first, called *rule-fulfilling* behavior, occurs when an action is consistent with appropriate rules but is not motivated by them. In this case, the actor has neither an explicit nor implicit knowledge of appropriate modes of behavior. Such behaviors may be imitative, intuitive, or accidental. To illustrate rule-fulfilling behavior, imagine that a new employee at a manufacturing plant meets the vice-president of the firm but is unaware the person holds that position. Suppose further that the employee knows only that the last name of the person is Brown. If the new employee addresses the vice-president as "Mr. Brown," he or she is inadvertently following rules appropriate to status-differential relationships, without any conscious awareness of the rules applicable to the situation.

Ganz terms a second type of rule-related action, rule-accordance behavior. However, it is more commonly termed rule-conforming behavior. *Rule-conforming* behavior occurs when a person's actions are consistent with rules, and the behavior is motivated by an implicit or tacit knowledge of the rules. Although the person could articulate the rules if asked to, he or she does not explicitly refer to them while conforming. Rule-conforming actions are similar to habitual behaviors and are based on a tacit understanding of the appropriate rules. Many, if not most of our rule-related behaviors are of the rule-conforming variety. For example, when we address a higher-status person in a formal manner, rarely are we thinking "It is a rule that I should defer to a higher-status person and, therefore, I am doing so." Rather, we perform this action habitually, based on a tacit understanding of the appropriate rules. Likewise, when we conform to the attitudes and dress and grooming behaviors of our friends and important social groups, we usually do so based on an implicit knowledge of conformity rules. Although we could articulate conformity rules were we asked to, we seldom think of them while conforming.

Ganz calls the final type of rule-related action rule-following behavior. *Rule-following* behavior occurs when we act according to rules and continually refer to them while behaving. The behaviors of "new kids on the block" often typify rule-following behavior. When we come into a novel social environment, like a new school or business, we try to determine those attitudes we need to assume, the actions we need to perform, and the modes of dress and grooming we should adopt if we are to be accepted by the new group. In cases like this, we explicitly articulate the appropriate rules and scrupulously follow them. When our behavior is either rule conforming or rule following, it is said to be *governed* by rules. In contrast, rule-fulfilling behaviors reflect rules, but are not governed by them.[36]

RULES, LAWS, AND EXPLANATION IN PERSUASION

We have now examined the nature of the rules and laws approaches to explaining social behavior. In summary, we saw that a rules explanation is teleological, implying that the generative forces prompting human actions and human responses to persuasive messages are a person's goals or *reasons* for behaving. In contrast, a laws explanation is causal, suggesting that the generative forces producing action are *antecedent conditions*, including message strategies as they have been interpreted by people. In short, causal explanation focuses on what messages *do to* people, while teleological explanation emphasizes the things people *do with* messages for goal-oriented reasons.

Both approaches are valid logical systems for explaining phenomena. Since each presents a coherent set of assumptions about human nature and the forces prompting social action, neither can be judged superior to the other as an epistemological system. Rather, the usefulness of the two approaches can be judged only by the richness of the information they generate about the nature of persuasive communication.[37] We believe the explanatory potential of each perspective can be exploited most effectively by construing them, not as competing, but as complementary belief systems, applicable to quite different areas of communicative behavior. When applied to the proper area of experience, each yields valuable, though qualitatively different, information about persuasive effects. To understand how the two approaches complement one another in accumulating knowledge about persuasion, the areas of persuasive communication behavior to which each is most appropriate must be delineated.

To begin, we should define the term *appropriate. A mode of explanation is appropriate when the epistemological assumptions it entails are compatible with the nature of the phenomenon needing explanation.* If the phenomenon needing explanation behaves causally, that is, its behavior is prompted by antecedent conditions, then laws are the appropriate mode of explanation. In contrast, when a phenomenon behaves purposively, that is, its actions are motivated by reasons, then rules, not laws, are the appropriate explanatory system.

To apply the appropriate mode of explanation to any set of communicative phenomena, one must differentiate between causally determined communication behaviors and those representing purposive action. *Causal communication behaviors* refer to actions that are produced by some antecedent condition, and therefore, may not be altered by human volition or choice. Innumerable behaviors relevant to persuasion are causally determined. For instance, there are *physical limitations* on the amount of information humans can assimilate and reconstructively store in memory at any moment. These natural barriers create many perceptual and memory-based effects when people respond to persuasive messages. Likewise, deficiencies in communication skills, such as speaking, writing, and listening, cause people to respond to messages in ways that people with more refined skills might not. Beyond these biological antecedents, people have many *persistent psychological and physiological conditions* that cause them to respond to persuasive messages in ways that unaffected individuals do not. For example, chronic anxiety and native intelligence are conditions whose persuasive effects are causally determined. Indeed, one could argue that all chronic personality traits—self-esteem, dogmatism, and authoritarianism among them—are causallike forces whose consequent effects have long interested persuasion theorists. Additionally, numerous persuasive strategies can trigger temporary, *acute, physiological arousal states*—fear, euphoria, and anger. Such states are causallike conditions that profoundly affect a person's responses to messages. Finally, *situational contingencies* such as people's social and economic status, can affect the nature and direction of their responses to messages.

These diverse examples of causal communication behaviors share one important feature: humans cannot alter the relationship between antecedents and consequents. People cannot choose their intelligence levels. They cannot fully control their anxiety. They cannot choose to be authoritarian or to have low self-esteem. Neither can they set the physical limits beyond which they will experience information overload, nor can they "will away" socioeconomic antecedents or the quality of their communication skills. Such phenomena behave causally and therefore require a laws, not a rules, explanation. Indeed, the use of a reason-based explanation in cases such as we have described would misrepresent the causal nature of the phenomena under investigation and would obscure the essential generative forces responsible for observed effects.

Unlike causal phenomena, *purposive communication behavior* is prompted by reasons, that is, people choose to enact behaviors for the purpose of achieving personal goals or objectives. Consistent with the conception of persuasion adopted in this book, we believe that much persuasive communication behavior is imbued with choice and thus is purposive in nature. People are not "forced" by antecedent persuasive strategies to change their ways of believing and behaving. As we have seen, a process of internalization or the private acceptance of messages is a complex cognitive activity wherein humans choose from alternative courses of action those best meeting their needs. In doing so, they normally accept those proposals that promise benefits and reject those threatening misfortune or pain. In short, people typically act for goal-oriented reasons, rather than passively react to the vagaries of external message strategies. We believe the epistemological assumptions associated with rules are appropriate to such choice-laden, purposive behaviors, and that causal laws are appropriate to communication behaviors forced by antecedent conditions. Indeed, the application of causal assumptions to reason-based communication behaviors would misrepresent their purposive nature, just as a rules explanation distorts the nature of causal communication phenomena.

Types of Purposive Communication Behaviors

By taking the position that most persuasive communication behaviors are purposive and thus amenable to teleological explanation, we do not imply that people are always fully aware of the precise reasons for their social action. Indeed, abundant evidence suggests that purposive behavior varies widely regarding the extent to which reasons for behaving are salient.[38] For instance, Shelley Duval and Robert Wicklund have shown that people oscillate between states of what they term "objective" and "subjective" self-awareness. Objective self-awareness entails an acute perception of one's inner motivations for behaving, whereas subjective self-awareness occurs when situational cues take precedence over the awareness of inner states.[39] Consistent with this reasoning, we saw in Chapter 2 that people possess numerous cognitive schemata that *prestructure* their purposive actions in relevant social situations. A central component of all well-developed schemata is a set of beliefs about those behaviors most likely to reap rewards or bring punishments in specified social contexts. Once we develop firm assumptions about appropriate behaviors, we often act in a habitual fashion on the basis of these "prepackaged," goal-oriented beliefs. Although we could articulate reasons for these actions were we asked, we often do not actively monitor those reasons in our everyday social encounters.

As a general rule, we can expect that self-awareness of reasons will vary as a function of the *importance* of a behavior to a person and the *familiarity* of the social situation in which the behavior occurs. As the personal significance of a behavior goes up, awareness of reasons for behaving should increase proportionately. However, as familiarity with a social situation increases, self-awareness should decline. This is expected since people bring well-developed schemata to familiar settings, and thus are guided more by generalized assumptions about appropriate behaviors than by the specific reasons prompting actions at the time. Based on these criteria, it is possible to identify three types of purposive behavior that differ regarding the level of a person's self-awareness of reasons for behaving.

The purposive behavior involving the least self-awareness of reasons has been called scripted behavior. According to Ellen Langer, *scripted behaviors* are those actions a person takes with little or no conscious awareness.[40] As might be expected, given the importance and familiarity criteria, Langer's research indicates that people are most likely to behave in a "mindless" fashion when the behaviors are *trivial*, requiring little or no effort to enact, and when the setting is *highly familiar*.[41] A person engaging in scripted behavior has a well-developed set of schemata or a script specifying appropriate behaviors in familiar contexts. Thus, one's purposes or reasons are deeply embedded in the script. Upon encountering a familiar setting requiring unimportant actions, the person follows the script automatically, giving little or no immediate thought to the reasons for behaving. For our purposes, it is critically important to note Langer's finding that, despite their "thoughtless" nature, scripted behaviors typically are accompanied by what she calls an "illusion of control," or a subjective perception of choice over behavioral outcomes even in situations where the possibility of control is nonexistent.[42] Thus, the most mindless of social actions are purposive since scripted persons still perceive a choice to perform or not perform prescribed actions. Typical examples of scripted behaviors include complying with small requests of friends and family, and observing well-established social rules, such as deferring to high-status persons or following the rules of turn taking in conversations.

The second type of purposive behavior also occurs in *highly familiar* social settings but, unlike scripted behaviors, is personally *important* to the actor. This variety of purposive behavior is akin to rule-conforming action and may be termed *routinized behavior*. When people engage in routinized behavior, they are aware of the reasons motivating their actions, but they do not monitor those reasons while behaving. Monitoring is unnecessary since the setting is familiar, and, therefore, the actor has a well-developed schematic set or routine defining appropriate actions. Although routinized actors could give the reasons for their behavior were they asked to, they do not continually refer to them when behaving routinely. Conformity behavior is a typical routinized action. When we adopt the attitudes or behaviors of valued social groups, we do so with an implicit knowledge that to be accepted, we must conform. However, we usually go about conforming in a routine manner without continually deliberating about the precise reasons for each conforming act.

At the third level of awareness, we are concerned with purposive behavior that is personally *important* to the actor but, unlike routinized actions, it occurs in a *novel* social situation. This behavior is similar to rule-following action and is called *monitored behavior*. Persons engaging in monitored behavior are acutely aware of the reasons for action and, lacking a well-developed schematic set for the social situation, they continually monitor those reasons as they act. Since this behavior includes awareness *and* behavioral monitoring, the person's perception of personal volition and his or her general level of self-awareness of reasons are maximal. When we enter new social situations, our purposive behavior usually is of the monitored variety. We carefully consider our goals and scrutinize the social environment to determine what to do to achieve them. Our reasons for behaving are highly salient to us and are continually attended to throughout a monitored behavioral sequence.

In sum, scripted behavior involves little awareness of immediate reasons and no behavioral monitoring, routinized actions involve awareness but no active monitoring, and finally, monitored actions involve awareness of reasons plus careful and continual attention to the reasons for behaving. Despite these differences, we have seen that all three types of behavior involve a perception or illusion of control over one's behavioral destiny. Generally, we can expect that our purposive behaviors will fluctuate among these three levels of self-awareness as a function of the importance of the behavior and the familiarity of the setting in which we find ourselves. Although the literature on cognitive schemata reviewed in Chapter 2 suggested that the bulk of human social behavior is routinized or schematized, we can expect to engage in scripted behavior whenever the setting is familiar and the stakes are trivial. In contrast, monitored actions will be performed when important behaviors occur in novel environments. That people's reasons for behaving are sometimes embedded in schemata and, at other times, are highly salient does not affect their perception of control nor the essential purposiveness of their social action. Thus, we believe that rules, not laws, are the appropriate explanatory system for isolating the generative forces prompting scripted, routinized, and monitored actions.

LAWS VERSUS RULES AS EXPLANATIONS OF PURPOSIVE ACTION

Our belief that laws and rules are complementary explanatory systems appropriate to different domains of communicative behavior is not shared universally. Indeed, the two approaches often are viewed as explanatory systems competing to explain the *same* area of communicative experience. Consistent with this perspective, the laws approach traditionally has been applied to purposive as well as causal communicative behaviors. We believe the use of causal analysis to explain purposive action is unwise and we shall now explore the basis for this belief. We shall argue that rules provide a more meaningful description of purposive action and a more useful representation of the nature of the relationship among purposive phenomena than do laws.

To begin our inquiry, it will help to recall the nature of the current laws approach. Remember that communication laws are generalizations about the *probable* relationships between certain types of message strategies and the effects those messages cause in people. To illustrate the nature of a probabilistic communication law, Berger has offered as a prototypical inductive–statistical law the generalization that "perceived similarity of attitudes between persons has a high probability of producing a high level of attraction between two persons."[43]

To clarify our position on the impropriety of applying causal analysis to purposive action, it will be useful to examine Berger's assumptions. In doing so, we must ask the following questions. (1) Does the *phenomenon needing explanation* in this generalization (interpersonal attraction between people) behave causally? and (2) Is it useful to describe the *relationship* stipulated in Berger's generalization as a probabilistic "law" of communication? To answer these questions, it will be helpful to compare the present example with a typical probabilistic law of nature. In his analysis of scientific explanation, Carl Hempel cites several examples of probabilistic laws in nature, including the probability that penicillin can cure streptococcal infections.[44] At issue is whether or not the communication law that "attitudinal similarity probably causes attraction," is similar to Hempel's inductive–statistical law that "penicillin probably cures streptococcal infections." Are these two examples of laws describing the same kind of *phenomena* and the same type of *relationship?* We think not.

We believe that the two laws constitute radically different kinds of probable relationships and relate to quite disparate phenomena needing explanation. Three factors differentiate the two laws. First, the phenomenon needing explanation in the communication law is *interpersonal attraction* among choice-laden people, and in Hempel's law it is an *infectious disease,* a matter in which choice does not inhere. Second, the relationships stipulated by the two inductive–statistical laws are probabilistic for vastly different reasons. The element of choice confers a probabilistic quality on the communication law. People can conform to or violate the law. Some of us may find people who share our attitudes dull and uninteresting, but others of us may get social reinforcement from interacting with such persons. In contrast, the notion of choice is absent from Hempel's probabilistic connection between a drug and its curative effects. The probabilistic nature of Hempel's law stems from the possibility that some biological or other natural condition may interfere with the curative power of penicillin.

Third and finally, because the two laws address radically different phenomena and entail disparate kinds of logical relationships, it follows that the generative forces responsible for the probable effects in Berger's and Hempel's laws ought to be qualitatively different. In Hempel's law, the generative force is a vaccine, an external antecedent capable of causing some consequent effect, the curing of an infection. The generative force in the communication law is "attitudinal similarity." Given the episte-mological assumptions associated with *laws*, the two generative forces are not qualita-tively different. "Attitudinal similarity" may cause "interpersonal attraction," just as "penicillin" may cure "streptococcal infections." However, if we apply the assump-tions associated with *rules*, "attitudinal similarity" becomes a spurious generative force. From a rules perspective, the generative forces responsible for the effect, "interperson-al attraction," are human goals, intentions, or reasons, phenomena qualitatively differ-ent from the generative force in Hempel's law. If attitudinally similar people choose to like one another, it is because such a relationship is perceived as personally satisfying, that is, it meets their goals and needs for social reinforcement. On the other hand, if similar people choose not to be mutually attracted, it is because such a relationship is not perceived as personally satisfying or goal fulfilling.

To restate the issue before us: it is not whether the laws approach or the rules perspective is the superior epistemological system for explaining the phenomena con-tained in Berger's example of a communication law, but rather, which epistemology provides the richest, most meaningful information about the generative forces responsi-ble for the stipulated relationship between similarity and attraction. We believe that rules provide a more meaningful analysis of the generative forces prompting interper-sonal attraction than do laws. The superior utility of the rules approach derives from the condition that the teleological assumptions associated with rules are more compati-ble with the purposive nature of the phenomenon needing explanation. In contrast, a causal analysis is inappropriate since the phenomenon requiring explanation does not behave causally. Thus, we believe the term "causal law" is not a useful description of the probable relationship stipulated in Berger's communication generalization. Rather, we believe it is far more meaningful to describe it as a generalization about goal-oriented or reason-governed behavior that has been observed to recur rather consistent-ly. After all, similar people choose to affiliate far more frequently than not.

In sum, we believe the application of causal assumptions to purposive phenomena like interpersonal attraction does not adequately reflect the nature of the phenomena themselves nor the relations among the phenomena. In this regard, Shimanoff has pointed out that William Dray, whose definition of law Berger himself uses, rejects a causal explanation of purposive historical phenomena on the same grounds that we have argued it should be rejected in communication.[45] Dray argues that laws so *misde-scribe* the nature of historical phenomena that they "ought to be abandoned as a basic account of what it is to give an explanation."[46] We believe his argument applies equal-ly well to purposive, persuasive communication phenomena.

Laws of Persuasion and Purposive Behavior

The analysis we have applied to the interpersonal attraction law is generalizable to other laws of persuasion explaining purposive, as opposed to causal, behavior. Like the relationship between similarity and attraction, the relationships stipulated by many persuasion laws are purposive explanations for human actions cast into the causal lan-guage of laws. Laws of persuasion generally take the following linguistic form: X (a type of persuasive strategy) will probably cause Y (some person) to do Z (make some response). A concrete example of a well-established law in persuasion is: "Physically attractive persuaders (X) frequently cause opposite-sex recipients of their messages (Y) to comply readily with their persuasive recommendations (Z)." This linguistic form implies that the relationships posited by such persuasion theories are causal in nature, that some specifiable persuasive strategy (X) *causes* a specifiable behavioral response (Z).

Such an implication is misleading when applied to reason-based or purposive behaviors, like the relationship between physical attractiveness and compliance. Hence, we believe the following linguistic form is a more meaningful description of purposive theoretical relationships: Y (some person) did Z (responded) after hearing X (some message strategy) because Z (the response) met some important personal goal. We would restate the physical attractiveness generalization as: "People (Y) often comply with the recommendations (Z) of physically attractive persuaders (X) because doing so bolsters their own ideal self-conceptions." As this analysis shows, despite the causal language of many persuasion theories, many of them refer to purposive or reason-based behavior. In all cases where the phenomena requiring explanation are purposive in nature, we believe it is far more useful to describe them as generalizations about recurrent goal-oriented actions than as causal laws. In contrast, when the phenomena needing explanation behave causally, laws, not rules, provide the more meaningful description of the stipulated relationships.

TOWARD A RULES-BASED THEORETICAL APPROACH TO PERSUASION

As the oldest theoretical tradition in persuasion, the laws approach has a coherent set of assumptions and a well-developed methodology for explaining causal communication behaviors. As a relative newcomer, the rules perspective has no counterpart system for explaining purposive communicative phenomena. In this section, our purpose is to develop the foundational components of a rules-based theoretical system for explaining purposive human actions in response to persuasive communication. To lay the groundwork for this approach, we should begin by restating the essential nature of a theory. A *theory* is a generalization describing probable relationships between generative forces and associated responses in human agents. Applied to persuasion, a theory typically describes probable relationships between message strategies and responses and identifies the generative force responsible for the described relationships.

Given this definition, how may we formulate a persuasion theory from a rules perspective? Following Shimanoff's analysis,[47] we suggest that a rules-based theory of persuasion is *a generalization describing probable relationships among purposive phenomena in specified contexts, based on the nature of the rules operable in these contexts.* Put another way, theoretical statements are descriptions of relationships between specifiable message strategies and purposive actions that may be predicted by examining contextually relevant rules. To illustrate, again recall the communication law that "attitudinal similarity probably leads to interpersonal attraction." From a rules perspective, this theoretical statement is a product of, and therefore, may be predicted by the rules or goal–behavior linkages operating in interpersonal influence contexts. The predominant rule operating in this context is that affiliation with others similar to oneself will achieve social reinforcement and self-evaluation goals.[48]

Given such a rules or means–end description of appropriate behaviors, people typically conform by seeking out similar others with whom to affiliate. Of course, as we saw earlier, not all persons will choose to follow this rule since some will value diversity and novelty more than social reinforcement. That rules may be broken accounts for the *probable* nature of rules-based, theoretical statements. However, because people follow such rules more often than they violate them, a rather consistent and recurring pattern emerges in which similarity and attraction frequently are observed to covary. Because such patterns of rule-governed behavior can be observed in many similar interpersonal contexts, we can describe the probable relationships between certain persuasive strategies and their related effects within specified contexts.

It is important to note that, from a rules as opposed to a laws perspective, the persuasive strategy itself is *not* the generative force responsible for a related effect. Rather, socially shared rules or reasons that are relevant to or made salient by the persuasive strategy constitute the generative force responsible for purposive action. Thus, rules or reasons are linked to action in a generative or explanatory fashion. In contrast, the relationship between rule-relevant persuasive strategies and human responses is covariational or correlational in nature, that is, *persuasive strategies covary with actions*. Rules *explain why* purposive responses probably will occur because they are the generative forces responsible for them. However, the persuasive strategies cited in theoretical statements only *predict* that certain responses probably will occur since persuasive strategies covary with effects by virtue of their relation to relevant generative rules.

To illustrate these distinctions, consider the theoretical statement that "high-status persuaders usually elicit more compliance with their recommendations than do lower-status persuaders." In this theoretical statement, high-status persuaders (a persuasive strategy) covaries with probable compliance from recipients (response). Thus, the statement allows us to predict the *probable* co-occurrence of status and certain persuasive effects. However, from a rules perspective, the statement does *not* explain the response. Rather, the explanation is to be found in the rules that are relevant to or made salient by the persuasive strategy, in this case status differences between persuaders. We may speculate that a relevant rule activated by the persuasive strategy might be that following the recommendation of a high-status person helps recipients reach a goal of self-image enhancement. Identifying with a well-respected person normally is more value expressive than identifying with a person perceived to be low in status.

In general, then, theoretical rules statements usually take the form of described covariations between certain persuasive strategies and some type of purposive response. Moreover, the stated covariation is generated by relevant rules operating within the context of the persuasive encounter.

A Framework for Rules-Based Theories of Persuasion

How might one develop specific theories of persuasion from a rules perspective? Following Shimanoff's analysis,[49] we suggest that persuasion theories should be cast in an axiomatic form. According to Virginia McDermott, an *axiomatic theory* is a hierarchically interrelated set of propositions having at least three components. First, axiomatic theory, like all theories, has a set of constructs, both of the generative and the effects variety discussed earlier. Second, axiomatic theory consists of a set of interrelated propositions, including general assumptions or *axioms*, along with *theorems* derived from them. These axioms and theorems are statements linking certain generative constructs and effects constructs. Third and finally, axiomatic theory, like other forms of theory, has a set of boundary conditions, identifying the contexts and conditions in which its axioms and theorems are applicable.[50]

As this description indicates, axioms and theorems are the two primary components of axiomatic theory. An *axiom* is a general proposition that is assumed to be true. Axioms cannot be confirmed directly since the constructs they contain are not observable. Some examples of axioms are: "Humans are choice-laden agents"; "People desire consistency in their world"; and "Human behavior is goal maximizing." Note that these axioms link two or more constructs together and they have implicit boundary conditions, suggesting the particular areas of purposive behavior to which they apply. Moreover, as these examples indicate, axioms typically are value judgments or statements of belief about the nature of people and their world. As such, they often embody the goals or reasons for human action.

In contrast, *theorems* are statements deduced or derived from axioms. They are theoretical statements about *specific* persuasive effects and therefore, are equivalent to what we have been calling "theories" of persuasion. Unlike axioms, their constructs are observable and the relationships they posit can be tested empirically and proven as reliable or unreliable statements about effects in persuasion. An example of a theorem derived from the axiom that "People desire consistency" might be: "If someone acts contrary to underlying attitudes, then he or she will change attitudes to more closely approximate behavior, or vice versa." A theorem derived from the axioms that "Humans possess choice" and "People are goal maximizing" might be: "Given two persuasive messages, one promising reward for some behavior and the other offering pain, people will respond to the message promising reward." As these examples indicate, theorems are empirically testable theories linking generative constructs to effects constructs. Each theorem carries with it implicit boundary conditions specifying the area of experience to which it is applicable. Finally, each theorem is logically interrelated with or derived from its relevant axioms.

Axiomatic theory is particularly well suited to persuasion for at least two reasons. First, unlike laws, axiomatic propositions can be used to describe purposive as well as causal relationships.[51] Second, like laws, axiomatic theories are general in scope and thus can be used to describe behavioral regularities produced by reasons or rules. As Shimanoff has put it, "by adopting the axiomatic form, rules scholars can accrue the advantages of the [general] law model without misrepresenting the phenomena described."[52]

As we have seen, hierarchically interrelated axioms and theorems are the primary components of the axiomatic form. However, very complex and well-developed axiomatic theories often will contain propositions other than axioms and theorems.[53] The statements in any axiomatic theory are ordered hierarchically from the broadest to the most specific. Moreover, each succeeding statement is deduced logically from the more general one preceding it. The axiom, of course, is the most general proposition in any axiomatic theory, and theorems often are derived from and directly follow axioms. However, in very complex axiomatic theories, more general propositions called postulates often intervene between axioms and theorems. A *postulate* contains qualities of both axioms and theorems, in that some of its constructs are observable, and others must be assumed. For example, using the axiom that "Humans desire consistency," we might postulate: "When faced with psychological inconsistency, people will take concrete actions to restore consistency." In this example, "psychological inconsistency" is not directly observable, but "concrete actions" are.

If theorems, derived either from axioms or postulates, are relatively general, more concrete *hypotheses* may be deduced from them. Hypotheses, like theorems, may be tested empirically against statements of fact, the most specific statement in axiomatic theory. For example, consider the theorem stated earlier that "Acting contrary to attitudes will result in a person's bringing attitudes and actions into line with one another." A hypothesis derived from this theorem might be, "If a person tells a lie, he or she is likely to come to believe the lie actually is true." Finally, theorems as well as hypotheses are tested against *factual statements*. This testing might involve inducing someone to tell a lie and then observing whether the person actually does come to believe the lie. Regardless of the complexity of any axiomatic theory, axioms and theorems will always be the *primary* components.

A Rules-Based Approach to Persuasion Theory: Some Preliminary Guidelines

To develop a comprehensive, rules-based approach to persuasion theory, one must begin by specifying the most general axioms supporting one's conception of persuasive communication. Given our own philosophical view of purposive, persuasive phenomena, we offer the following axioms around which a rules-based theory of persuasion might be developed.

Axiom 1:   Humans are self-directed agents, having the capacity for choice.

Axiom 2:   Humans are goal-oriented agents, striving to maximize rewards and minimize punishments. Put another way, human action is rule governed.

Axiom 3:   The external environment is a product of human cognitive schematic structures.

From these axioms, two basic theorems may be derived:

Theorem 1:   Given the choice-laden and goal-oriented nature of people, they will choose to comply with persuasive messages specifying contextually relevant rules or prescriptions for achieving goals more often than they will comply with messages stipulating contextually irrelevant rules.

Theorem 2:   Given the cognitive schematic nature of reality, human action will be a response to people's *own* interpretations of and cognitive responses to incoming persuasive messages, not to the uninterpreted symbolic stimuli represented by the content of the messages themselves.

From these theorems, more specific hypotheses may be derived and tested against statements of fact to determine their reliability or lack of it.

The axioms and theorems we have posited are very general. Thus, the contexts or boundary conditions to which they are applicable are exceedingly broad. To develop a more complete axiomatic structure for persuasion theory, we must stipulate axioms and theorems relevant to more limited areas of persuasive communicative experiences. For instance, axioms and theorems peculiar to interpersonal, as opposed to mass, persuasion may be stated; and once that is accomplished, we can formulate axioms and theorems to apply to more limited areas within the interpersonal domain. For example, dyadic persuasion or small group persuasion can be described with appropriate axioms and theorems. In short, the development of a complete axiomatic theory for persuasion requires that persuasion theorists delineate all relevant contexts in which persuasion occurs and develop hierarchically ordered axioms and theorems relevant to each domain.

The Rules Perspective and Persuasive Messages

We suggested in Chapter 1 that a persuasive message is one relying on information control to accomplish its objectives. That information control consists, first, of *warnings* about probable undesirable consequences if people choose not to take certain courses of action. Second, persuasive messages contain *mendations*—statements about probable positive benefits a person can expect if certain recommended actions are taken.

From a rules perspective, persuasive messages, whether they are external in origin or self-produced, are nothing more than complex sets of statements stipulating those rules or goal–action links appropriate to the context in which the persuasion occurs. Within a rules framework, messages have two functional components: goal definitions and action stipulations. As to goal definitions, persuasive messages typically make salient those *goals* relevant to the communication topic and the persuasive context. For example, messages on the hazards of cigarette smoking or on the benefits of a nutritious diet usually emphasize goals related to human health and safety. In contrast, television commercials advertising cosmetics, toothpastes, and other personal products typically stress social acceptance and value-expressive goals.

Beyond goal definition, persuasive messages stipulate those *actions* people must take (obligation), should take (preference), or must not take (prohibition) in order to achieve their goals. In the case of cigarette smoking, the typical rule expressed in an antismoking message states that "you must stop (prohibition) smoking to preserve your health." Regarding nutrition, a usual rule urged in such messages is that "you must (obligation) eat a balanced diet if you are to remain healthy." Finally, in advertisements for cosmetics, dental products, and the like, a typical rule urged upon viewers is "if you choose (preference) our product, you will have more friends and generally have a better self-image."

As this rules analysis suggests, *persuasive communication involves the coordination of human action according to contextually-relevant rules.* Typically, people adopt goal-maximizing behaviors and avoid goal-blocking ones; so successful persuasion, whether self-instigated or generated by an external agent, induces people to follow appropriate rules. As we have seen, the rules embodied in persuasive messages take the form of warnings and mendations.

Barriers to the Development of a Comprehensive Rules Theory

There are several serious problems requiring resolution if the goal of developing a comprehensive rules system for explaining purposive action is to be realized. Before detailing these problems, we should say that many of them reflect the usual problems faced by any relatively new theoretical model. Given a period for sustained research, methodological development, and theoretical refinement, it is probable that many of the thornier problems will be resolved satisfactorily. With this disclaimer in mind, let us consider some of the major problems associated with rules theory as it is presently constituted.

First, there is no consensus among rules scholars about what actually constitutes a rule. Shimanoff surveyed the rules-based communication literature and found at least *11* different conceptions of the nature of a rule![54] Two conceptual divergencies are apparent here. First, rules theorists disagree as to whether rules are strictly *prescriptive* in nature or, alternately, are *descriptions* of people's beliefs about *prescribed* behaviors. We have taken the latter position that rules *describe* people's assumptions about appropriate goal-fulfilling actions. Thus, we assume that rules embody both descriptive and prescriptive qualities. A second conceptual problem is that rules theorists disagree about the origin of rules structures. Some theorists equate rules only with socially shared notions of what one ought to do in specified contexts. Others advance the broader conception adopted in this book that includes socially shared and idiosyncratic views of goal–action stipulations. The failure to agree on the essential nature of a rule impedes the development of a unified and coherent body of rules theory.

As well as the lack of consensus about what a rule *is*, rules theory also lacks a coherent methodology for identifying rules specifying goal-fulfilling actions. This problem is particularly acute in the case of idiosyncratic rules, involving, as they do, uniquely personal goals and individual ways of fulfilling them. Moreover, there is disagreement as to whether rules should be defined from the perspective of the user of rules or the observer of the rule-using behaviors of others.[55] Although most rules researchers opt for determining rules from the view of the rule user, this methodology is problematic since, as we saw earlier, people often are not fully aware of the specific rules prompting their behavior at any particular moment. In general, it is fair to conclude that the rules perspective presently lacks a unified set of research tools for locating and verifying both socially shared and idiosyncratic rule structures.

Finally, there are a limited number of specific rules-based theories of human communication. Undoubtedly, the failure to agree on a general conceptual and methodological approach to rules accounts for the absence of rules theories applicable to particular types of purposive communicative behavior. Although several promising efforts have been made to develop rules-based theories of interpersonal communication,[56] there are few explicit rules-based theories relevant to purposive persuasive behavior. Indeed, the preliminary efforts we have made in this chapter represent one of the first concerted attempts to advance a general, rules-based theoretical structure peculiar to persuasive communication.

As a concluding remark, we should return to our original disclaimer that the problems we have described likely reflect the relative newness of the rules approach to communication. A theoretical perspective only a decade old in the field of communication may be expected to experience the sorts of growing pains we have discussed. Fortunately, many creative minds are working to resolve these difficulties. Our judgment is that the rules perspective has a bright future in persuasion and in the field of communication generally.

RULES AND LAWS AS MUTUALLY SUPPORTIVE EXPLANATORY SYSTEMS

Throughout this chapter, we have taken the position that rules and laws are best viewed as complementary modes of explanation. We believe that the richest, most meaningful information about persuasion may be derived when laws are applied to phenomena that behave causally, and that a rules approach is the most useful way to explain purposive behavior. In this section, we want to illustrate how laws and rules can support one another in the pursuit of knowledge about persuasion.

By adopting the position that most persuasive behavior is purposive in nature, taking the form either of scripted, routinized, or monitored actions, we have not meant to imply that causal phenomena play an insignificant role in persuasion. To the contrary, most complex social action undoubtedly is affected by causal antecedents as well as by reasons for behaving. Indeed, it is reasonable to argue that *all purposive action or human choice-making behavior takes place within boundaries that expand and contract as a function of phenomena over which people have little control.*

Physiological antecedents like intelligence; chronic psychological states like anxiety, self-esteem, dogmatism, and authoritarianism; temporary arousal states like fear and anger; and situational exigencies like social or economic status, all represent conditions people do not fully control. Yet each affects profoundly the limits of human purposive action. For example, fear arousal will affect all purposive behavior aimed at insuring one's health and safety. Similarly, dogmatism or low self-esteem inevitably will affect a person's choice of goals as well as goal-satisfying actions. Finally, factors like socioeconomic status will affect one's aspiration levels as well as the actions that feasibly may be taken to fulfill objectives. In short, numerous conditions over which people have little control inevitably influence the goals they value and the actions they will take in pursuit of those goals. Thus, while scripted, routinized, and monitored purposive actions predominate in persuasion, each is tempered by antecedents that vary as a function of the situation and the characteristics of the purposive actor.

It follows from this analysis that a comprehensive explanation of all complex social action must take account of antecedent conditions as well as reasons for behaving. *Laws* are required to adequately explain the effects of causal mediators, while we believe *rules* yield the most meaningful information about purposive action. By applying each to its appropriate domain of communicative experience, the two explanatory systems can complement one another in the accumulation of knowledge about persuasion.

THE CURRENT STATUS OF THEORY IN PERSUASION: THE APPROACH OF THIS BOOK

Because the laws epistemology has long been applied to purposive as well as causal communication phenomena, many current persuasion theories, while addressing purposive action, remain lawlike in language and structure. Moreover, a few apply exceedingly mechanistic assumptions to persuasive phenomena. Other current theories are more actional in nature and rules based in approach. In this book, we will examine as many as 20 current theories of persuasion. We have selected those theories that, in our judgment, have had *a significant impact on contemporary ways of thinking about, and approaches to understanding, the process of persuasive communication.*

In applying this criterion, we have avoided considering only those theories fitting our own philosophical biases, the most important of which are a commitment to actionalism and a belief that purposive actions require a rules, not a laws, explanation. Rather, our application of the "significant impact" rule has led us to include not only action-oriented approaches and rules explanations of purposive behavior, but also laws accounts of purposive action and several theories that, on the surface at least, appear to be singularly mechanistic in nature. For instance, "inoculation theory," a laws perspective usually regarded as highly mechanistic, will be explored in Chapter 12. Such an approach is included because it has, for many years, had a significant impact on ways of thinking about resistance to persuasion. Although we may regard the application of mechanistic laws to purposive action as misguided, that personal belief does not obviate inoculation theory's real and pervasive impact on the literature of persuasion.

Additionally, certain mechanistic approaches are reviewed because they have had enormous heuristic value. For instance, some of the early mechanistic models served as intellectual lightning rods, sparking criticism and leading to the development of more meaningful views of persuasion. For example, "cognitive dissonance theory" reviewed in Chapter 5 and the "chain of responses model" considered in Chapter 9, are mechanistic in many ways. Yet, the critical reactions to each of these perspectives led to the development of several actional approaches to account for the persuasive phenomena each originally sought to explain.

In selecting theories, then, we have included those perspectives that have made landmark contributions to the literature of persuasion. To provide a focal point for comparing and contrasting the diverse theories covered in this book, each major theory we present will be evaluated critically from our actional and rules-based perspective of persuasion. Our aim will be to highlight those features of each theory that are consistent with, or depart from, our own view of the nature of persuasion and human action.

NOTES

1. Nahum Z. Medalia and Otto N. Larsen, "Diffusion and Belief in a Collective Delusion: The Seattle Windshield Pitting Epidemic," *American Sociological Review* 23 (1958): 180–186.

2. Fred N. Kerlinger, *Foundations of Behavioral Research* (New York: Holt, Rinehart & Winston, 1964), p. 4.

3. Gary Cronkhite and Jo Liska, "Symposium: What Criteria Should Be Used to Judge the Admissibility of Evidence to Support Theoretical Propositions in Communication Research? Introduction," *Western Journal of Speech Communication* 41 (1977): 5.

4. For explanations of human behavior based on a mechanistic view of man, see B. F. Skinner, *Science and Human Behavior* (New York: Macmillan, 1953); Clark L. Hull, *Principles of Behavior* (New York: Appleton-Century, 1943); and John B. Watson, *Psychology from the Standpoint of a Behaviorist* (Philadelphia: Lippincott, 1924).

5. Skinner, *Science and Human Behavior*.

6. For a collection of essays that explore the basic tenets of logical positivism, see A. J. Ayer, ed., *Logical Positivism* (New York: The Free Press, 1959).

7. The classic distinction between human *action* and *motion* originated with the philosopher Immanuel Kant. For example, see *Anthropology from a Pragmatic Point of View* (Berlin: Reimer, 1902). Human behavior that is caused by some antecedent condition is termed "motion," and self-motivated behavior based on reasons is labeled "action."

8. For explanations of human behavior based on an actional view of man see Romano Harré and Paul F. Secord, *The Explanation of Social Behavior* (Oxford: Basil Blackwell, 1972); Theodore Mischel, ed., *Human Action* (New York: Academic Press, 1969); Charles Taylor, *The Explanation of Behaviour* (London: Routledge and Kegan Paul, 1964); and Abraham Irving Melden, *Free Action* (London: Routledge and Kegan Paul, 1961). What we have termed an "actional model of man," Harré and Secord call an "anthropomorphic model of man." See Harré and Secord, pp. 84–100.

9. For a discussion of the basic tenets of the cognitive schematic perspective, see E. Tory Higgins, C. Peter Herman, and Mark P. Zanna, *The Ontario Symposium on Personality and Social Psychology: Social Cognition* (Hillsdale, N.J.: Lawrence Erlbaum, 1981); Jesse G. Delia, "Constructivism and the Study of Human Communication," *Quarterly Journal of Speech* 63 (1977): 66–83; and Chapter 2 of this book.

10. Systems analysis is sometimes discussed as a third approach to persuasion theorizing. The perspective is not discussed here since it utilizes the two modes of explanation we are considering. For a discussion of systems analysis, see Peter R. Monge, "The Systems Perspective as a Theoretical Basis for the Study of Human Communication," *Communication Quarterly* 25 (1977): 19–29.

11. The conception of causal explanation discussed here follows the general line of Hume's thinking. See David Hume, *Enquiries Concerning Human Understanding* (Oxford: The Clarendon Press, 1902).

12. See Gerald R. Miller and Charles R. Berger, "On Keeping the Faith in Matters Scientific," *Western Journal of Speech Communication* 42 (1978): 44–50.

13. See Miller and Berger; and Charles R. Berger, "The Covering Law Perspective as a Theoretical Basis for the Study of Human Communication," *Communication Quarterly* 25 (1977): 7–18.

14. This definition is taken from Gerald R. Miller, *An Introduction to Speech Communication* (Indianapolis: Bobbs-Merrill, 1972), p. 28.

15. Berger, p. 9.

16. Berger, p. 11.

17. Gerald R. Miller, "The Current Status of Theory and Research in Interpersonal Communication," *Human Communication Research* 4 (1978): 174.

18. See Donald Cushman and Gordon C. Whiting, "An Approach to Communication Theory: Toward Consensus on Rules," *The Journal of Communication* 22 (1972): 217–238.

19. Miller, "The Current Status of Theory," p. 176.

20. See Kant's *Critique of Pure Reason*, trans. N. Kemp Smith (London: Macmillan, 1929); *Critique of Practical Reason and Other Works*, trans. T. K. Abbott (New York: Longman's, 1909); and *Anthropology from a Pragmatic Point of View.*

21. Harré and Secord, *The Explanation of Social Behavior*, p. 35.

22. Georg H. von Wright, *Explanation and Understanding* (Ithaca, N.Y.: Cornell University Press, 1971), p. 96. For original discussions of the nature of practical syllogisms, see von Wright, *Explanation and Understanding;* and David P. Gauthier, *Practical Reasoning* (Oxford: The Clarendon Press, 1963). For a critique of the practical syllogism from a communication theory perspective, see Keith Adler, "An Evaluation of the Practical Syllogism as a Model of Man for Human Communication Research," *Communication Quarterly* 26 (1978): 8–18.

23. Harré and Secord, p. 40.

24. See Harré and Secord, p. 148.

25. See Donald P. Cushman, "The Rules Perspective as a Theoretical Basis for the Study of Human Communication," *Communication Quarterly* 25 (1977): 35.

26. I am grateful to W. Barnett Pearce for suggesting this conception of rules. Personal communication from Pearce to Smith, 25 August 1980.

27. This view that rules prescribe obligations, prohibitions, and preference is taken from Susan B. Shimanoff, *Communication Rules: Theory and Research* (Beverly Hills, Calif.: Sage Publications, 1980), pp. 44–45; and Gidon Gottlieb, *Logic of Choice: An Investigation of the Concepts of Rules and Rationality* (New York: Macmillan, 1968), p. 39. Some theorists hold that rules only prescribe obligations and prohibitions. See, for example, Joan Safron Ganz, *Rules: A Systematic Study* (Paris: Mouton, 1971), pp. 50, 84–85. Finally, some theorists contend that rules prescribe not only obligations and prohibitions, but also permitted behaviors and indifferent actions. See Georg H. von Wright, "The Logic of Practical Discourse," in *Contemporary Philosophy*, ed. Raymond Klikansky (Italy: La Nuava Italia Editrice, 1968), pp. 141–165.

28. Shimanoff, pp. 39–41.

29. Shimanoff, pp. 41–46.

30. I am grateful to Gerald R. Miller for suggesting this interpretation of the nature of prescriptiveness as applied to rules. Personal communication from Miller to Smith, 13 October 1980.

31. For an excellent account of changing rules in the development and deterioration of interpersonal relationships, see Mark L. Knapp, *Social Intercourse: From Greeting to Goodbye* (Boston: Allyn and Bacon, 1978).

32. Cushman, p. 40.

33. See Adler, p. 13; and Mary John Smith, "A Practical Reasoning Model of Human Communication" (unpublished MS, University of Virginia, 1979).

34. Shimanoff, pp. 126–127.

35. Ganz, p. 66.

36. Some writers make a distinction not drawn here between rule-governed and rule-guided behavior. For a relevant discussion, see Cushman and Whiting; and Shimanoff, pp. 117–119.

37. See Joseph R. Royce, *The Encapsulated Man* (New York: Van Nostrand Reinhold, 1964), p. 165.

38. For a discussion of the role of self-awareness in persuasion, see Michael E. Roloff, "Self-Awareness and the Persuasion Process: Do We Really Know What We're Doing?" in *Persuasion: New Directions in Theory and Research*, ed. Michael E. Roloff and Gerald R. Miller (Beverly Hills, Calif.: Sage Publications, 1980), pp. 29–66.

39. See Robert A. Wicklund, "Objective Self-Awareness," in *Advances in Experimental Social Psychology*, ed. Leonard Berkowitz (New York: Academic Press, 1975), pp. 233–275; and Shelley Duval and Robert A. Wicklund, *A Theory of Objective Self Awareness* (New York: Academic Press, 1972).

40. Ellen J. Langer, "Rethinking the Role of Thought in Social Interaction," in *New Directions in Attribution Research*, ed. John H. Harvey, William Ickes, and Robert F. Kidd (Hillsdale, N.J.: Lawrence Erlbaum, 1978), pp. 35–58.

41. Langer; and Ellen Langer, Arthur Blank, and Benzion Chanowitz, "The Mindlessness of Ostensibly Thoughtful Action: The Role of 'Placebic' Information in Interpersonal Interaction," *Journal of Personality and Social Psychology* 36 (1978): 635–642.

42. Ellen J. Langer, "The Illusion of Control," *Journal of Personality and Social Psychology* 32 (1975): 311–328.

43. Berger, p. 11.

44. Carl G. Hempel, *Aspects of Scientific Explanation: And Other Essays in the Philosophy of Science* (New York: Free Press, 1965).

45. Shimanoff, p. 204.

46. William Dray, *Laws and Explanation in History* (London: Oxford University Press, 1957), p. 19.

47. Shimanoff, p. 208.

48. This rule is fully articulated by Leon Festinger in his theory of social comparison. See Leon Festinger, "A Theory of Social Comparison Processes," *Human Relations* 7 (1954): 117–140; and Chapter 7 of this book.

49. Shimanoff, pp. 205–216.

50. Virginia McDermott, "The Literature on Classical Theory Construction," *Human Communication Research* 2 (1975): 92–93.

51. See Kenneth D. Bailey, "Evaluating Axiomatic Theories," in *Sociological Methodology*, ed. Edgar F. Borgatta (San Francisco: Jossey-Bass, 1970), pp. 48–71. It is interesting to note that Charles Berger has used the axiomatic form for representing causal connections. See Charles R. Berger and Richard J. Calabrese, "Some Explorations in Initial Interaction and Beyond: Toward a Developmental Theory of Interpersonal Communication," *Human Communication Research* 2 (1975): 99–112.

52. Shimanoff, p. 205.

53. See Leonard C. Hawes, *Pragmatics of Analoguing: Theory and Model Construction in Communication* (Reading, Mass.: Addison-Wesley, 1975), pp. 33–38.

54. Shimanoff, p. 57.

55. See W. Barnett Pearce, "The Structure of the Social Order: A Review of Research about Communication Rules" (unpublished MS, University of Massachusetts, 1978), pp. 60–66; and W. Barnett Pearce, "Naturalistic Study of Communication: Its Function and Form," *Communication Quarterly* 25 (1977): 51–56.

56. See W. Barnett Pearce, Linda M. Harris, and Vernon E. Cronen, "The Coordinated Management of Meaning: Human Communication Theory in a New Key," in *Rigor and Imagination: Essays on Communication from the Interactional View*, ed. John Weakland and Carol Wilder-Mott (New York: Praeger, in press); W. Barnett Pearce and Vernon E. Cronen, *Communication, Action, and Meaning* (New York: Praeger, 1980); and W. Barnett Pearce, "The Coordinated Management of Meaning: A Rules-Based Theory of Interpersonal Communication," in *Exploration in Interpersonal Communication*, ed. Gerald R. Miller (Beverly Hills, Calif.: Sage Publications, 1976), pp. 17–35.

CHAPTER 4

The Nature of Research in Persuasion

In the last chapter, we began our discussion of persuasion theory by relating the strange story of automobile windshield pitting in Seattle during the mid-1950s. Recall that the episode involved unusual and unexplained damage to thousands of car windshields. Tentative explanations for the damage ranged from ordinary road wear and industrial pollution to radioactive fallout, meteorites, and cosmic rays.

To determine its actual cause, a research team from the University of Washington's Environmental Research Laboratory was called in. After extensive testing, they concluded that the puzzling, black particles found on many automobiles were soot deposits formed by incomplete combustion of bituminous coal at nearby plants. Ordinary road wear had caused the windshield damage.[1] Thus, scientific observation established a reasonable explanation for the reported damage and, at the same time, disproved the more unusual theories suggested by the citizens of Seattle.

The research conducted by the Washington scientists illustrates the issue we will consider in this chapter: the role of empirical research in building a body of knowledge about persuasive communication. Four topics will be discussed: (1) the relationship between theory and observational research; (2) the types of observational research available to students of persuasion, including naturalistic and correlational studies; (3) the persuasion experiment; and (4) the uses and limitations of the persuasion experiment as a mode of inquiry.

THE RELATIONSHIP BETWEEN THEORY AND RESEARCH IN PERSUASION

As we saw in Chapter 3, a theory stipulates an explanatory relationship between a pattern of persuasive effects and the generative force responsible for the effects. Following our rules-based analysis of purposive communication behaviors, we suggested that many persuasion theories are descriptions of recurring, covariational relationships between persuasive strategies and their effects, and that the covariations are generated by contextually relevant rules.

Like other social sciences, persuasion relies on *observation* to develop a theory and test its plausibility. Theorizing begins with careful observation of recurring human actions. Preliminary observations are guided by the axioms or general assumptions we have about the area of experience under scrutiny. Once a researcher identifies a persistent response pattern, he or she must begin to think about generative forces responsible for the pattern. If, for example, after extensive and careful observation, I conclude that people consistently respond favorably to physically attractive persuaders, I must ask why this is so.

Perhaps I will theorize that identifying with a physically attractive person is a way of expressing one's ideal self-concept. More formally stated, such identification is rule-guided behavior, designed to achieve the goal of positive self-expression. I now have a hypothesis explaining what I have observed. Because hypotheses are conjectural and tentative, they must be subjected to rigorous verification procedures to determine their accuracy. Herein lies a primary role of research in persuasion.

To test the reasonableness of any theoretical explanation, we must conduct research to see how well our generalization fits the reality of people's actions. This research entails careful, controlled observation whose purpose is to verify that the expected behavioral effects actually occur. Only after we determine that a particular generative force, such as human goals or reasons, consistently produces certain actions do we have a reliable theory. Once reliability is determined, we can conduct additional research to refine the theory, to establish its generality and limitations. While as a theoretical rule, physically attractive persons may be especially good persuaders, we cannot expect this is *always* the case. Further testing will help us precisely define the context and other boundary conditions in which the theory's generative force is operable.[2] As this description suggests, the relationship between theory and research is a spiraling pattern, with each process reinforcing the other.

Theory and Research: An Illustration

To illustrate this interrelation, let's examine an interesting and well-designed piece of research conducted by Janis and Mann.[3] Their purpose was to determine the relative effectiveness of active versus passive persuasive strategies in modifying the habit of cigarette smoking. Guided by the axiom that people value good health, they began their investigation by observing that a ten-year mass media campaign aimed at reducing cigarette smoking had had little success. They also observed that many physicians and relatives of lung cancer patients, having seen the suffering and death resulting from cigarette smoking, had kicked the habit.

On the basis of these preliminary observations and relevant axioms, Janis and Mann theorized that "when people stop smoking after direct encounters with cancer victims, it is partly because of an empathic reaction involving a realization that, if it can happen to others, it can happen to themselves."[4] From this conclusion, they developed the following research hypothesis: role-playing a lung cancer victim should be a frightening empathic experience capable of changing attitudes and behaviors toward cigarette smoking significantly more than passive reception of antismoking messages.

To test their rules-based theory, Janis and Mann recruited 26 women, 18 to 23 years of age, who were moderate to heavy smokers. All of the women were given a questionnaire assessing their attitudes toward smoking and their present smoking behavior. After finding the women had similar attitudes and smoking behaviors, the researchers randomly picked 14 of them to role-play cancer victims; the rest were assigned to a control group destined to receive passively the same information about the dangers of smoking as the role-players. The role-playing took place in the office of a physician; chest x rays of malignant tumors were displayed prominently. The role-players were asked to pretend to be cancer patients and to express their feelings about health and its relation to cigarette smoking and lung cancer. The control group listened to the role-playing sessions and thus were exposed to the same persuasive information as the role-players themselves. The single difference between the two groups was that the role-players constructed their own messages, while the control group passively received the messages produced by the role-players.

Two weeks after the completion of the experiment, checks on the attitudes and behaviors of the 26 women showed that the role-players were much more convinced that smoking causes lung cancer and were more fearful of being harmed by smoking than were members of the control group. Moreover, the role-players had reduced their smoking an average of 10.5 cigarettes per day compared to 4.8 for the non–role-players. Extensive interviews with all the women confirmed that the role-playing was, in fact, perceived as an empathic, fear-arousing experience, bringing health goals into focus and stimulating the role-players to persuade themselves to modify their smoking habits. In contrast, the fear level reported by the passive receivers was insignificant. On the basis of this evidence, Janis and Mann concluded that "emotional role-playing" is significantly more effective in producing attitude and behavior change than passive exposure to "the same informational inputs."[5] Thus, through careful experimentation, the researchers' tentative hypothesis was given considerable support.

This example illustrates how careful observation can suggest theoretical hypotheses, and how the reliability of those hypotheses can be tested through experimentation. After carefully observing recurring behaviors and speculating about contextually relevant goals or rules, the persuasion theorist formulates a hypothesis. Once clearly formulated, it is subjected to controlled observation to see if the expected behavioral effects are, in fact, produced by the suspected rule-relevant message strategy. Once a hypothesis is confirmed repeatedly through experimentation and other observational strategies, it acquires the status of a theory.

Theory Structures Observation

In this, as well as the previous chapter, we have discussed theory in the relatively narrow sense of a statement linking some generative force to a specified effect. Although this definition is appropriate, the term *theory* also encompasses more general notions that are crucially important to the researcher. For instance, we saw in Chapter

3 that axiomatic assumptions about the nature of humans and the external environment may also be called theories. Moreover, as Chapter 2 made clear, such naive theories structure our observations, directing us to selectively perceive certain external stimuli, while ignoring others. Theory, then, is comprised not only of specific generalizations about persuasive effects, but also, following the axiomatic form developed in Chapter 3, includes broad assumptions structuring our observations and interpretations of the external environment.

Given this broader view, we need to ask how theory and observational research affect one another. Although observations of recurring behavioral effects give rise to specific theories, the observations themselves are, as Barnett Pearce puts it, "inevitably theory-laden."[6] Both the choice of what actions to observe and our interpretations of what we see are affected profoundly by our theoretical biases.

Norwood Hanson discusses an imaginary incident that illustrates the theory-laden nature of observing. Suppose, he says, that the sixteenth century astronomers, Johannes Kepler and Tycho Brahe, were both watching the sun rise. Would they "see" the same thing? In one sense, Hanson argues, they would, since each should have similar retinal images of the sun. However, seeing the sun, he notes, is not the same as seeing retinal images. Cognitive schemata and theoretical assumptions also are involved. In this sense, he argues, they would see quite different things. Kepler would see the earth move to expose a fixed-in-place sun, while Brahe would see the sun move around a fixed-in-place earth.[7] What we see is influenced profoundly by what we *want* to see.

Although new theory is suggested by and tested against observation, it is important to bear in mind that observation is itself structured by a researcher's theoretical perspectives and schematic structures. This fact has two implications. First, conflicting theoretical explanations of any one persuasive effect cannot always be resolved by examining the empirical tests of the theories. Advocates of one theory often see the *same* test results quite differently than do the proponents of a competing theory. (We will have occasion to examine several such conflicts in the next chapter on counterattitudinal behavior and self-persuasion.) Second, the results of any empirical research can be fully understood only by taking into account the theoretical biases and cognitive schemata of the researcher.[8] Although the observations of some researchers are less tainted by personal biases than others, there is no such thing as completely "objective data." All observations, even the most careful, are seen through the rose-colored glasses of each researcher's schematic biases.

TYPES OF OBSERVATIONAL RESEARCH IN PERSUASION

Whether an investigator's primary interest is the search for laws or rules-based theories, three types of observational research methods are available to him or her: (1) descriptive or naturalistic research; (2) correlational studies; and (3) the experimental method. In this section, we will focus on the first two, reserving for a later section discussion of the experiment. The observations associated with each method of inquiry are tainted by the observer's preconceptions, but the degree to which the methods are theory-laden varies. As we shall see, naturalistic study is least encumbered by theory, while the experiment is designed expressly to test hypotheses. Correlational research represents a middle position regarding the structuring effect of theory on observation.

Naturalistic Research

Naturalistic or *descriptive* research, often called phenomenological and exploratory inquiry, is not guided by any specific persuasion theories. Naturalistic researchers pose open-ended questions about generative forces and their persuasive effects. Their aim is to observe carefully and describe systematically the nature of persuasive communication behaviors and effects. A primary use of naturalistic research is to identify and describe rules underlying responses to persuasive messages. Whether observations relate to rules or causal generalizations, the ultimate purpose of naturalistic research is to amass a body of descriptive data needing explanation.[9] It is preliminary to theory building and testing, and aims neither to predict nor explain, but rather to systematically describe persuasive communication behaviors.

Some questions that might profitably be addressed in descriptive research include: "Exactly what types of antismoking messages are heavy cigarette smokers exposed to?"; "What sorts of social and idiosyncratic rules guide group members when they try to persuade deviants to accept a group decision?"; and "What types of conversation or communication patterns (questions, requests, commands, compliments, and so on) characterize face-to-face interpersonal persuasion?" Only after systematically observing and describing patterns of behaviors and effects can we ask why they occur and devise persuasive strategies to alter them. You will recall, for instance, that Janis and Mann devised an effective antismoking strategy only after careful examination of ineffective antismoking messages. Similarly, understanding group and interpersonal persuasion depends on carefully observing and classifying the types of rules and conversation patterns associated with each process.

Naturalistic inquiry typically is a three-stage process: (1) *observing* acts of persuasion; (2) *recording* the persuasive phenomena of interest—types of messages, rules, or conversation patterns; and (3) *classifying* these phenomena into related descriptive categories. No attempt is made to explain the observed phenomena, only to systematically describe them. However, as we saw earlier, implicit theories and the conceptual biases of researchers affect naturalistic research when data are interpreted and classified.

To illustrate this biasing effect, suppose a researcher is observing and classifying conversation patterns in interpersonal persuasion, a research methodology called *conversational analysis*.[10] To accomplish this task, he or she must assign meaning to the persuasive utterances in a conversation. Since interpretation is a function of each observer's unique cognitive schemata, different observers are likely to interpret any one conversational utterance differently. For example, whether the statement "You have no choice but accept the truth of the Bible," made by a minister to a potential convert, is classified as a command, a plea, or a threat, will probably depend on the attitudes and background of the observer.

Fortunately, naturalistic research minimizes the impact of a researcher's interpretative biases by determining, in most cases, the meanings communicators themselves attach to their own talk and that of others. Therefore, if a person is scrutinizing the rules guiding group persuasion, he or she determines the rules the members themselves perceive are operating in their group. Similarly, the responses of smokers to antismoking messages must be ascertained from the smoker's perspective. Thus, in descriptive research, as in all other aspects of persuasion, interpretations should be obtained from participants, not from observers of the persuasive encounter.[11]

Unfortunately, past researchers, especially those searching for persuasion laws, have deemphasized descriptive research, preferring to concentrate on theory building and hypothesis testing. This neglect too often has resulted in a "cart-before-the-horse" methodology. A researcher develops a theoretical hypothesis, then tests it against descriptive data without having first induced the hypothesis from careful preliminary observation. Thus, the persuasion literature is filled with many elegant and elaborately designed experiments resting on woefully inadequate descriptive bases.

In contrast to the direction taken by many laws theorists, rules researchers generally have placed far more emphasis on naturalistic research. Their past efforts have largely been directed toward identifying and classifying the communication rules that govern human behavior. Fortunately, many persuasion researchers of all theoretical bents are beginning to conduct basic, observational research before leaping to the theory-testing stage of inquiry.

Correlational Research

Correlational research moves beyond basic description and searches for relationships between and among persuasive communication behaviors and effects. Put another way, correlational research examines how communication phenomena vary together.[12] As we shall see, correlational research allows a researcher to predict as well as to describe communication effects. In contrast to descriptive research, theory plays an important role in correlational inquiry since the researcher must first speculate about how certain variables *ought* to be related, and then proceed to test the theoretical speculations. However, theory does not dictate the design of correlational studies to the extent that it does experimental methodologies.

Guided at least by fragmentary theoretical notions, a correlational researcher might ask: "What is the relation between chronic aggression in teenagers and their desire to view violent films on television?"; "How do the need for social approval and a person's persuasibility relate?"; "What is the relationship between fear appeals in a message and a recipient's persuasibility?"; and "How do sanctions for violating group rules relate to the amount of deviant communication that takes place in the group?"

Positive Correlation

Persuasion researchers have observed three types of relationships between variables. The first is called *positive* or *direct correlation*. Two communication variables are directly correlated when they vary with one another in the same direction: as the value of one variable increases or decreases, so does the value of the other. For example, a high need for social approval often bears a positive correlation to attitude change

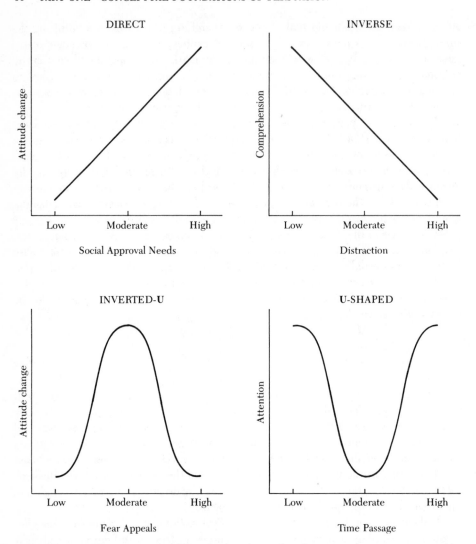

FIGURE 4.1   Direct, inverse, and curvilinear relationships between communication variables

among receivers of persuasive messages. As one's need for approval goes up, attitude change in response to messages normally increases; as it declines, attitude change decreases. Figure 4.1 illustrates this direct correlation. You will notice that the positive correlation between the two variables is a linear relationship.

Negative Correlation

A second linear relation between two variables, also shown in Figure 4.1, is termed *negative* or *inverse correlation*. It occurs when two variables covary in opposite directions; as the value of one increases, the value of the second systematically declines. For example, the greater the sanctions for violating small group rules, the lower the level of deviant communication. A second example of inverse correlation is shown by the distraction graph in Figure 4.1. The more people are distracted while attending to a persuasive message, the less likely they are to comprehend the content of the message.

Curvilinear Correlation

A third type of relation between communication variables is *curvilinear* in nature, that is, two variables initially covary in the same direction then proceed to vary together in opposite directions, or vice versa. As Figure 4.1 illustrates, there are two varieties of curvilinear relationships. The first, an *inverted-U relationship*, is the most common of all relationships among persuasion variables. It occurs when two variables initially increase together, after which one begins to decline, while the second variable continues to increase. The relationship between fear appeals in a message and persuasibility of people typically follows an inverted-U pattern. As fear appeals increase from low to moderate levels, attitude change increases as individuals become concerned for their health and safety. However, at moderate-to-high levels of fear arousal, people usually begin to exhibit defensive reactions against the fear the message generates. After that threshold is reached, they "tune out" the message and show declining acceptance of the advocated position.

The second variety of curvilinear relationship, the *U-shaped curve*, occurs less often than the inverted-U association. A U-shaped relationship occurs when two variables initially covary in opposite directions, and then begin to vary together in the same direction. The relationship between attention to a persuasive message and the time period during which the message is presented follows the U-shaped pattern shown in Figure 4.1. Attention to a speaker's message often is high when he or she first begins a presentation. Soon thereafter, a receiver's mind may wander to other concerns and attention drops. However, near the conclusion of the speech, people often "tune in" again to catch the speaker's final remarks, resulting in a sharp increase in attention. The outcome is a U-shaped relationship between time and attention.

It should be noted that the magnitude of positive, negative, and curvilinear relationships may be assessed mathematically. The magnitude of a linear correlation is determined by computing a simple *coefficient of correlation*.[13] Symbolically represented by a lower-case r, the simple coefficient of correlation may range from -1 to $+1$. A -1 indicates perfect inverse correlation, and $+1$, perfect direct correlation. Zero indicates that there is no correlation between two variables.

Multivariate Correlation

Thus far, we have discussed relationships between only two communication variables—a *bivariate* analysis. Bivariate research, although useful, is limited. It is almost certain that any act of persuasion will have more than two variables of interest to the researcher. Thus, much correlational research is *multivariate* in nature. Fortunately, the persuasion researcher has a number of statistical tools for assessing the relationship among multiple communication behaviors and effects. We will review two uses of multivariate correlational procedures.

First, a researcher often wishes to determine how a set of several communication variables relates to a single effect. For example, I may be interested in determining how source credibility, the quality of a message, and receiver anxiety all relate to a single variable, attitude change. This case presents a problem in prediction. What I am really asking is: Will a knowledge of the credibility of a source, the anxiety level of receivers, and an assessment of message quality allow me to accurately predict the amount of attitude change? This determination can be made by computing a *multiple regression analysis*.[14] A multiple regression analysis yields a correlation coefficient symbolized by an uppercase R. Like r, the multiple R ranges from -1 to $+1$ and represents the magnitude of correlation between several variables and a single criterion variable of interest.

A second multivariate correlational procedure is called *canonical correlation analysis*.[15] It is used when researchers want to know how one set of variables relates to a second set. For example, I may wish to know how the set, source credibility, message content, and receiver anxiety, relate to a second set, attitude change, message comprehension, and estimates of source objectivity. Canonical correlation yields a correlation coefficient often symbolized by an uppercase R_C. Again, like the simple r and multiple R, R_C ranges from -1 to $+1$ and represents the magnitude of association between two sets of communication variables. As with multiple regression analysis, canonical correlation is used to determine how well one set of independent variables can predict a second set of criterion or dependent variables.[16]

The Uses and Limits of Correlational Research

It is important to note that a correlation, especially of the bivariate variety, does not imply that one variable is a generative force or reason producing the other. For example, to conclude there is a highly positive correlation between social approval needs and persuasibility in no way suggests that one of the variables is the reason for the other. Some third, shared generative force may account for both behaviors. Or different generative forces or reasons may have prompted the two separate behaviors. Nonetheless, it is still possible that one of the variables may, in fact, be the generative force responsible for the other. However, even if this is the case, correlational research cannot confirm it. The only legitimate aim of correlational inquiry is to search for covariational interrelationships among previously observed descriptive data, not to establish generative links among communication variables.[17] It is the task of experimental methodologies to try to establish such explanatory links.

Despite this limitation, correlation research establishes covariation and that is a considerable contribution. Unlike descriptive research, correlational research enables us not only to describe, but also to *predict* persuasive effects. For example, if we know that anxiety is negatively related to persuasibility, we can predict persuasive effects among highly anxious people. Moreover, we have seen that multiple regression and canonical correlation analyses are tailored specifically for predicting persuasive effects.

THE EXPERIMENT AS AN
OBSERVATIONAL RESEARCH METHOD

Because the experimental method has generated much of the theoretical knowledge we have about persuasion, we should examine it carefully. The purpose of an experiment is to test theoretical hypotheses, and it is, therefore, the most theory laden of all observational research techniques. A hypothesis states a connection between observed persuasive effects and a generative force or set of reasons responsible for the effects. Because the experimental method is used to establish *why* certain persuasive effects occur, it has predictive as well as *explanatory* power.[18]

The experimental methodology is useful for testing the explanatory power of laws as well as rules. Although rules researchers traditionally have shied away from the experimental method because of its historical association with laws research, there is no reason why they should. As Susan Shimanoff puts it, to assume that "the experimental method . . . is appropriate only for testing causal relationships . . . is false." To the contrary, she notes that "the experimental method [is] appropriate whenever one wishes to maximize control" in the testing of rule-related hypotheses.[19] Thus, whether one's principal interest is testing laws or rules, the experiment is the primary vehicle for generating explanatory information about persuasion and human action.

An experimenter might ask such questions as: "What goals prompt small groups to adopt rules of intolerance toward deviant members?" and "Why does repetition of a persuasive message result in the greatest attitude change at moderate frequencies of exposure, that is, show an inverted-U pattern of effects?" As these questions indicate, many of the theoretical issues that interest experimenters are suggested by prior descriptive and correlational research. There are three general procedures for conducting any experiment. First, the researcher must formulate a hypothesis linking some generative force to certain effects. The hypothesis is suggested by observing recurring responses and asking why they recur. For example, recall in the role-playing experiment discussed earlier that Janis and Mann hypothesized that active, rather than passive, participation should persuade people to stop smoking because the active mode makes health-related rules emotionally salient.

Once a hypothesis is formulated, the researcher exposes some people to the persuasive strategy expected to activate relevant rules or goals, while deliberately not exposing other, similar persons to the same strategy. In this second stage of the experimental process, it is critically important that only the one strategy be tested. All other variables must be held constant. Remember that Janis and Mann accomplished this control in two ways. First, both the role-players and non–role-players were alike in age, sex, attitudes toward smoking, and general smoking habits. Second, both active and passive participants received the same information about the dangers of smoking. By controlling these two factors, typically called *intervening variables*, Janis and Mann insured that any postexperimental attitude and behavioral differences between role-players and passive receivers could not be attributed to preexisting individual differences or to the receipt of different persuasive information. Thus, any observed differences should be due to empathic role-playing. After controlling intervening variables and thereby eliminating potential *confounding effects*, an experimenter then allows the target persuasive strategy to operate among some people, but not among others.

Third, and finally, the experimenter observes the cognitive and behavioral responses exhibited both by people exposed to the target persuasive strategy and those who were not exposed. If the predicted effects occur *only* among people exposed to the rule-relevant strategy, then the experimenter has support for the original hypothesis. In the case of the role-playing study, you will remember that Janis and Mann found that empathic role-playing produced significant attitude and behavior change toward cigarette smoking, confirming their hypothesis. In general, by following these three procedures, an experimenter can discover if a particular generative force is responsible for the predicted persuasive responses.

The Nature of Experimental Variables

Throughout this chapter, we have used the term *variable* rather loosely to refer to any type of persuasive behavior or effect. However, because of its structured use in experimentation, the concept should now be defined more explicitly. The term *variable* takes its name from the notion *to vary* and refers to any set of persuasive strategies, behaviors, goals, or responses that can fluctuate or vary in kind or degree. In other words, a variable is any persuasive phenomenon that can take on different values. For example, attitude change is a communication variable that may range from a negative, boomerang effect toward an advocated position to increasingly positive responses. And a variable like behavior change may have only two variations: no change or complete behavioral compliance with some recommendation.

As these examples indicate, some variables are *continuous*, that is, they fluctuate from one extreme to the other along a continuous scale. Attitude change is one of these and might be measured on an arbitrary scale ranging from −5 through 0 to +5. In contrast, other persuasion variables are measured in a *discrete* manner: their values change, not continuously, but in distinct steps. For example, a persuader's credibility often is measured discretely. He or she may have a low, moderate, or high level of credibility, an assessment made in three ascending steps. Similarly, behavioral compliance is often a discrete variable—either people comply with a persuasive message or they don't.

This last example illustrates a naturally occurring discrete variable: only two behavior variations intrinsically are possible. However, in the former example, credibility was arbitrarily rendered discrete. A person's credibility is actually a continuous variable, ranging from extremely credible to extremely noncredible. We will see later that such an arbitrary simplification often is dictated by the experimental method itself.

Whether continuous or discrete, variables such as credibility and attitude change are empirical counterparts of the theoretical notion *constructs*. To understand this point, recall that a *theoretical hypothesis* links generative constructs to effects constructs. The theoretical hypothesis advanced by Janis and Mann, for instance, linked the generative construct, *activation of health goals through active versus passive participation*, to the effects construct, *persuasibility*. To test the hypothesis, the key constructs were transformed into empirical variables. Thus, Janis and Mann construed active versus passive participation as a two-part, discrete variable: empathic role-playing versus listening passively to the role-players. The effects construct, persuasibility, was defined as two continuous variables: attitude change toward cigarette smoking; and behavior change, measured by the number of cigarettes consumed per day.

Once variables are defined, the original theoretical hypothesis can be restated as a research hypothesis. A *research hypothesis* states the expected relationship between generative variables and effects variables. In the case of Janis' and Mann's experiment, the research hypothesis stated: Empathic role-playing should produce greater attitude and behavior change than passive receipt of the role-players' messages due to the superiority of the former method in making health goals salient. Thus, *salient health goals engendered by empathic role-playing* was the generative variable, and *attitude and behavior changes* were the effects variables.

Independent Variables in the Experiment

What we have referred to as generative variables in a research hypothesis typically are called independent variables in an experiment. *Independent variables* usually are described as ones the researcher suspects are strong generative forces. He or she manipulates them on the assumption that they will produce some expected persuasive effect. As we saw in Chapter 3, reasons and goals are the generative forces behind purposive communication behaviors; however, independent variables traditionally have not been equated with these. Because the experimental methodology has long been associated with laws research, independent variables usually are equated with types of message strategies that researchers expect will *cause* certain responses, regardless of whether the responses to be explained are purposive or causal. We believe it unwise to assume that message strategies cause purposive action. From our rules-based perspective, message strategies function as independent variables only when a researcher seeks to explain causal communicative phenomena.

To illustrate, suppose a researcher wants to test the generalization that "high-status persuaders get more agreement with their recommendations than low-status persuaders." The phenomenon needing explanation here, agreement with high-status persuaders, behaves purposively, not causally. People are not forced to accept the recommendations of high-status persuaders. Rather, they choose to comply with recommendations that promise beneficial outcomes. Despite the purposive nature of compliance behaviors, the message strategy, "high-status," typically is regarded as the independent variable capable of causing compliance. Thus, a researcher tests this generalization by having one group of people listen to a persuasive message delivered by a high-status person and a second group listen to the same message presented by a low-status persuader. Afterwards, compliance levels are measured to determine who was the superior persuader. If the high-status person got more compliance, the researcher concludes that the message strategy, "high-status," *caused* the response, compliance. We regard this conclusion as misleading.

According to our rules-based perspective, status is not the generative force responsible for the compliant response. Rather, the goals a person achieves by complying with high-status people are the relevant generative forces. Perhaps people find that agreeing with a high-status person expresses their ideal self-concepts more effectively than complying with a low-status individual. From our perspective, the relationship between high-status and persuasibility is covariational, not causal. High status usually activates relevant rules or goal–behavior linkages that, in turn, generate appropriate responses. That researchers almost always equate independent variables with persuasive strategies, rather than with rules relevant to the strategies, is a consequence of the long-standing practice of applying causal assumptions to *purposive* communication behaviors.

Current usage dictates that we describe independent variables as types of persuasive strategies or manipulations. However, when the phenomenon needing explanation behaves purposively, we do not assume the independent variables themselves are generative forces, but, rather, that the contextual rules and goals relevant to the persuasive strategies are responsible for purposive human action. In contrast, when the phenomenon needing explanation behaves causally, persuasive strategies may function as independent variables capable of causing strategy-related responses.

Independent variables or persuasive strategies usually are discrete, containing two or more variations, manipulations, or *treatment levels*. Moreover, discreteness often is imposed arbitrarily on naturally occurring, continuous variables. For example, suppose I am interested in measuring attitudinal effects related to fear appeals in messages. I might decide to expose some people to a message containing no fearful content, a second group might hear a message with a low fear appeal, a third group a moderately fearful appeal, and a fourth group a high-fear message. In this case, the independent variable, fearful message content, is manipulated four ways. What is, in fact, a continuous variable has been transformed into a discrete variable with four treatment levels. The first group, receiving no fear appeals at all, is called a *control group*; the other three are termed *experimental groups*. The responses of the control group serve as baseline data against which to assess the responses of the experimental groups.

Unlike the experiment just described, most persuasion experiments employ two, three, or more independent variables simultaneously. For instance, a researcher may want to determine how rules related to source credibility coupled with the quality of the source's message jointly affect attitude or behavior change. Or a researcher might want to know how film violence and the sex of a viewer jointly relate to subsequent aggression. In this last instance, the researcher might make four films with varying amounts of violence (no violence/control, low, moderate, and high) and then ask both males and females to view the four films. As we will see later, the inclusion of more than one independent variable in a single experiment allows a researcher to measure not only the separate persuasive effects associated with each variable, but to determine any unique effects of the variables working in combination.

Dependent Variables in the Experiment

Recall that a research hypothesis links a generative force or set of reasons to some specified, human action. These behavioral effects, earlier called effects or response

Abortions on demand should be available to women during the first trimester of pregnancy.

AGREE _____ : _____ : _____ : _____ : _____ : _____ : _____ :DISAGREE

| Strongly agree | Moderately agree | Agree somewhat | Unsure | Disagree somewhat | Moderately disagree | Strongly disagree |

FIGURE 4.2   *A self-report scale*

variables, have traditionally been labeled the *dependent variables* in an experiment. They are the effects that rules or goals relevant to independent variables or, alternately, causal forces, are expected to produce. The two most frequently occurring dependent variables in persuasion research are alterations in attitudinal schemata and overt behavior change. Other dependent variables of interest include message comprehension, self-generated messages produced in response to some external message, and evaluations of a source's credibility and likeability.

Dependent variables are most often continuous rather than discrete. For example, attitude change usually is measured on continuous *self-report scales,* wherein subjects express their attitudes on one or more continua ranging from "strongly agree" to "strongly disagree." Self-report scales are the most frequently used instrument for measuring dependent variables. Figure 4.2 shows a continuous self-report scale for measuring attitudes toward abortion.

Such self-report measures typically are administered to subjects after exposure to certain persuasive strategies. Indeed, attitude scales often are given both prior to and after message exposure so that the researcher can see how much people changed their opinion as a result of the experimental manipulations. Responses to self-report scales are computed mathematically. For example, a *1* usually is assigned to a "strongly disagree" response, a *2* to "moderately disagree," a *3* to "agree somewhat," a middling *4* to an "unsure" reaction, and a 5, 6, and 7 to the "agree somewhat," "moderately agree," and the "strongly agree" responses, respectively. By assigning these values, average or mean responses can be determined.[20]

Aside from self-report measures, there are several other procedures for measuring dependent variables. First, *overt behavior* may be observed directly.[21] Recall in Janis' and Mann's study that overt behavior was measured continuously by noting the number of cigarettes smoked by each role-playing and non–role-playing subject after participation in the experiment. But frequently, overt behavior is measured discretely, rather than continuously. For example, in studies of behavioral compliance, the researcher simply notes whether or not subjects complied. In that case, behavior change is a two-step, discrete variable.

A second commonly used set of non–self-report procedures consists of *physiological measures.*[22] Pupil dilation, heart rate, galvanic skin response, and so forth, have been used to measure reactions after exposure to independent variables. Each of these is a continuous measure of arousal, giving the researcher clues to people's reactions to the persuasive strategies. In sum, dependent variables are the effects that generative forces in association with independent variables are expected to produce.

Designing the Experiment and Interpreting Results

To illustrate the nature of a typical persuasion experiment, suppose I decide to investigate the attitudinal effects of rules relevant to source credibility and message quality. To pursue my study, I create two levels of source credibility (high and low) and two levels of message quality (excellent and poor). In addition, I set up a control group, exposed to none of my experimental treatments, to get baseline data. After designing my experiment, I select 50 subjects out of a large population and randomly assign them to one of the groups in my experimental design.[23] As Figure 4.3 illustrates, this design has, in addition to the control subjects, four separate experimental groups. The 10 subjects in Group 1 will hear a high-credibility source deliver an excellent message; Group 2 will listen to the same high-credibility source present a poor-quality message; Group 3 will hear a low-credibility source deliver an excellent message; and Group 4 will hear the same low-credibility source present a poor-quality message. Finally, the control group will be exposed to no independent manipulation.

Before exposing subjects to the persuasive message, I measure the attitudes of the five groups toward the issue to be advocated. Once the four experimental groups have heard the message, I remeasure the attitudes of all five groups. Table 4.1 shows mean attitude change scores I obtain for each group of subjects. In interpreting results, I can assess two different kinds of effects. First, *main effects* are those associated with each independent variable considered alone. In this experiment, there apparently is a main effect for source credibility since the column totals indicate that the high-credibility source, regardless of the quality of the message, elicited more attitude change (4.60) than the low-credibility speaker (2.60). Additionally, the row totals show that excellent messages, regardless of the speaker's credibility, were associated with more attitude change (4.40) than were the poor-quality messages (2.80).

The second assessable effect is called an *interaction effect*. Interaction effects are the unique effects associated with two or more independent variables operating together. Such effects differ from the separate main effects of the independent variables added together. In this experiment, apparently I have such an interaction effect. It takes the following form: although the high-credibility source was equally persuasive regardless of message quality, message quality significantly enhanced the effectiveness of the low-credibility source. In other words, the effect of the same quality message on attitude change depended on the credibility of the source delivering it.[24]

	High-credibility source	Low-credibility source	Control group
Excellent quality message	n = 10 Group 1	n = 10 Group 3	n = 10 Group 5
Poor quality message	n = 10 Group 2	n = 10 Group 4	

FIGURE 4.3   *Experimental design for assessing the attitudinal effects of source credibility and message quality*

**TABLE 4.1: MEAN ATTITUDE CHANGE AS A FUNCTION OF
SOURCE CREDIBILITY AND MESSAGE QUALITY**

	High credibility	Low credibility	Row totals
Excellent quality	4.80	4.00	4.40
Poor quality	4.40	1.20	2.80
Column totals	4.60	2.60	
Control	1.00		

Note: Attitudes were measured on a 7-point self-report scale, where 1 denoted least agreement with the message and 7 represented greatest agreement.

Note that the amount of attitude change associated with the low-credibility source/poor-quality message (1.20) differed very little from that of the control subjects who heard no message at all (1.00). In fact, the difference of .20 is so small it can probably be attributed to chance and labeled a statistically insignificant difference. In contrast, *statistically significant differences* between means, such as between 4.40 and 1.20, occur when differences are sufficiently large that they cannot be attributed to chance. Traditionally, differences are considered statistically significant if computations result in a 95 percent probability (expressed as $p < .05$) that the observed differences among experimental and control groups reflect nonchance or real differences in the populations from which the subjects in each group were selected.[25]

Laboratory and Field Experiments

The difference between laboratory and field experiments relates to the setting where the research is conducted. The field researcher goes into real-life settings and exposes people to experimental treatments. For example, a field researcher interested in the effects of dress and grooming on compliance with verbal requests makes two visits to a local shopping mall—for the first visit he or she is neatly dressed, for the second sloppily groomed. In each guise, the researcher asks for donations to some charity or tries to recruit volunteers to work for the charity. Afterwards, the researcher tallies how many people responded favorably to each guise. If significantly more people complied when the researcher was well groomed, he or she will conclude that a neat appearance is related to powerful generative forces affecting compliance behavior.

In contrast to field research, the laboratory experimenter brings subjects into a setting that he or she has created and structured. Four principal characteristics distinguish the laboratory study from the field study.[26] First, as we just noted, the laboratory researcher rigorously structures the physical environment where the research is conducted. The size of the experimental room, the color, lighting, arrangement of furnishings, and the like, all can be controlled by the experimenter.

Second, experimental variables are carefully controlled in laboratory research. Intervening variables that might confound results are monitored. For instance, the experimenter makes sure there are no preexisting differences among subjects that could account for, and thus confound, observed effects. In the field, such a degree of control is impossible since naturally occurring events frequently confound observed effects. Third, field experimenters cannot select their subjects or the groups of people who are to respond to their strategies, but the laboratory researcher can. Typically, the laboratory researcher draws on college-age students as a primary population for random selection of subjects. In contrast, the field experimenter comes into contact with many different populations in terms of age, educational level, occupation, and the like.

Finally, laboratory experimenters usually deceive subjects to try to obscure the hypothesis they wish to test. As we shall see in our critique of the experiment, when subjects are aware of the research hypothesis, they often do not behave naturally. Rather, they try to confirm or disprove a suspected hypothesis, depending on their motivations or attitudes toward the experimenter or the experiment itself. To prevent subjects from learning a hypothesis, laboratory experimenters devise *cover stories* to misinform subjects about the nature of the experiment. Field researchers, although occasionally engaging in deception, do so far less often than the laboratory experimenter. The artificiality of the laboratory setting usually makes deception essential.

These differences between laboratory and field research raise two issues we will confront in our critique of the experimental methodology. The first, *internal validity*, concerns the extent to which results can be attributed solely to generative forces related to the independent variables. In general, laboratory experiments achieve a higher degree of internal validity than do field studies because intervening variables can be controlled better in the laboratory than in the field. The second issue, *external validity*, concerns the extent to which the results of an experiment can be generalized to different social settings and different populations. As one might expect, the field experiment normally has more external validity than the laboratory study because the field researcher uses many different populations and operates in a natural setting.

A CRITIQUE OF THE EXPERIMENTAL METHODOLOGY

How valuable is the experimental method in helping us understand persuasive communication? To answer this question, we must focus on the extent to which the persuasion experiment yields internally and externally valid results.

As we have said, internal validity concerns the extent to which the observed effects in an experiment are a result of independent variables. External validity, on the other hand, raises the question of the generalizability of results to persons and situations outside the confines of the experiment. More particularly, there are at least three separate issues involved in determining external validity. First, to what extent may experimental results be generalized to the total population of persons from which the sample was drawn? Obviously, no researcher can observe entire populations; he or she must choose samples from populations and observe their responses to particular generative forces. For instance, if I am interested in the responses of 18-year-old males to media violence, I will select a relatively small sample of 18-year-old males for experimental manipulation. My results can be generalized to all 18-year-old males only if, by random methods, I have selected a group that is representative of the total population. This first issue, then, is a *sample to population* generalizability problem.

The second issue is a *population to population* generalizability problem, since external validity also concerns the extent to which the responses of an experimental population may be generalized to other, diverse populations. Suppose, for example, I select a representative sample of college-age students as subjects in an experiment. To what extent do their responses reflect the responses of other populations, say middle-aged persons or less educated individuals? Finally, external validity concerns the extent to which results obtained in an experimental setting (from any population) will reflect the responses of the *same* population in different social situations, say at work or play outside the laboratory or field setting. In other words, is the experimental setting, especially a laboratory one, a peculiar social situation capable of eliciting responses that subjects ordinarily would not exhibit in more natural social settings? This third issue, often called a question of *ecological validity*, is a *social setting to social setting* generalizability question.

In our critique, we will examine three categories of variables threatening the internal and external validity of the experiment: (1) characteristics of the *subjects* in experiments; (2) characteristics of the *experiment as a social setting*; and (3) the nature of the *experimental design* itself. Accordingly, we will evaluate the seriousness of the validity problems associated with each of these confounding variables. We will also discuss methodological advances designed to combat the more serious sources of experimental invalidity. Finally, we will look at the problems associated with applying the experimental methodology to rules research.

Characteristics of Subjects

Two characteristics of subjects challenge a persuasive experiment's external validity. First, the great majority of subjects who participate in persuasion experiments are *college students*. Rossiter reviewed the communication experiments appearing in the 1972 issues of three prominent communication journals and found that 75 percent used college students as subjects.[27] More recently, a survey of persuasion experiments conducted from 1977 through 1980, reported in *Human Communication Research*, showed that 88.7 percent of them used college students as subjects. This extensive use of student subjects led Quinn McNemar to conclude 25 years ago that social scientific research may largely be a "science of the behavior of sophomores."[28] The validity issue here is the external one of population to population generalizability. Aside from age differences, college students as a whole are probably more intelligent, better educated, and of a higher social class than the general public. Moreover, their attitudes and behavior patterns usually are not as well formed as those of the average adult. Such differences lead one to question whether the results of most persuasion experiments reflect the responses other populations might exhibit in similar circumstances.

Nonetheless, a few experiments have found that results obtained from college students generalize quite well to other populations. For example, in a series of classic studies on obedience to authority figures, Milgram used college students, adult professionals, white collar workers, unemployed persons, and industrial workers. He conducted studies in the United States, Germany, Italy, South Africa, and Australia. In all cases, Milgram reported that the results obtained from these diverse populations were exactly the same as those he observed among college students.[29] In an experiment dealing with persuasive effects, Smith and Gabbard-Alley exposed college-age women and females over 60 to a persuasive message on vegetarianism and found no differences in attitude change as a function of the age differential.[30]

Whether these limited findings are generalizable to a wide range of persuasion experiments is not clear. More research is needed, and until it is conducted, students of persuasion should be alert to potential external validity problems when experiments use college students as subjects.

A second threat to external validity is the use of *volunteers* as subjects. This is not a serious problem for experimenters using college students since increasingly large numbers of students are required to participate in experiments to fulfill course requirements. However, when researchers don't use students, they almost always are forced to rely on volunteers. A number of writers argue that the use of volunteers threatens the sample to population validity of an experiment. For example, Robert Rosenthal and Ralph Rosnow contend that volunteers differ radically from the general population since they have higher needs for social approval, higher occupational and educational levels, higher intelligence, and lower authoritarian levels. As a result, Rosenthal and Rosnow suggest that volunteers are unrepresentative of the population from which they are selected.[31]

Other writers have countered this argument by suggesting that volunteers are, in fact, a rather heterogenous group representative of their population. For example, Arie Kruglanski argues that people volunteer for a variety of reasons: some have a strong interest in the subject under investigation, others volunteer after intense appeals from experimenters, and so forth. Given "the diversity in bases for volunteering," Kruglanski notes, "it would not seem very plausible to expect subjects volunteering for one reason to resemble in their psychological characteristics those volunteering for quite a disparate reason."[32] In conclusion, Kruglanski cites several studies, including a persuasion experiment by Rosnow and Rosenthal,[33] in which no significant differences between volunteers and nonvolunteers were found. Clearly, the issue of volunteerism and invalidity is far from settled. However, the student of persuasion should be aware that the use of volunteer subjects introduces potential validity problems in experiments.

The Experiment as a Social Situation

The experiment, especially the laboratory variety, creates, at best, an artificial social situation. Subjects are brought into an environment structured by the experimenter, exposed to certain persuasive strategies, given a battery of tests, and sent on their way. The peculiarity of the experimental setting raises questions of internal and ecological validity. The extent to which subjects' responses are linked to the independent variables alone or to other characteristics of the experimental setting raises the issue of internal validity. These other characteristics include variables like the presence of the experimenter as an authority figure, subjects' preconceived notions about how they are "supposed" to act while participating in scientific research, and so on.

The extent to which responses obtained in the structured experimental setting reflect the responses people usually exhibit in more realistic, ongoing social situations raises the question of ecological validity. Three threats to validity are associated with the experiment as a social situation: (1) demand characteristics of the experimental situation; (2) evaluation apprehension; and (3) experimenter effects.

Experimental Demand Characteristics

Discussed most extensively by Martin Orne, *demand characteristics of the experimental situation* are "the totality of cues which convey an experimental hypothesis to the subjects."[34] According to Orne, most subjects see as one of their tasks a determination of the true purpose of the experiment. The true purpose or hypothesis can be conveyed to subjects in a number of ways; among these are rumors about the nature of the research, past experience as an experimental subject, the experimental setting, the behavior of the experimenter, and the experimental procedures themselves. Even with the cleverest of cover stories, many subjects will discern an experiment's essential nature.

According to Orne, the responses of subjects in any experiment will be affected by two sets of variables: the independent variables and perceived demand characteristics. The greater the influence of the latter, the less the internal validity of the experiment. Additionally, the external validity of the experiment is threatened since individuals in natural settings are not subject to the demand characteristics imposed on laboratory subjects. Thus, the presence of demand characteristics raises serious setting to setting generalizability questions.

Once a subject has learned the nature of an experimental hypothesis, he or she may adopt one of three roles.[35] Orne calls the first of these the "good subject" role. People assuming this role give responses they believe will validate an experimental hypothesis. In contrast, a subject may elect a "negativistic subject" role and try to disprove a hypothesis by giving responses of no use to the experimenter. Joseph Masling has called this the "screw you effect."[36] Samuel Fillenbaum terms the third role an experimental subject may take as the "faithful subject."[37] Faithful subjects believe they should scrupulously follow the experimenter's instructions and avoid acting on the basis of any suspicions they may have about the experiment's true purpose. Unlike the other two roles, faithful subjects respond only to the independent variables, and therefore, exhibit internally and externally valid responses. Indeed, valid results can be obtained in an experiment only when subjects are faithful after learning the hypothesis or when they are "naive," that is, they do not learn the experimental hypothesis at all.[38]

To evaluate the impact of demand characteristics on the validity of persuasion experiments, we need to determine the usual proportion of subjects who actually learn the experimental hypothesis and the number expected to behave faithfully after guessing the experiment's true nature. In an early learning experiment, Fillenbaum found that 51 percent of his subjects remained naive or unaware of the experimental hypothesis and that 29 percent were faithful, that is, they were aware of the hypothesis but showed no intent to bias the results. The remaining 20 percent were aware of the hypothesis and intended to bias the results, principally in a positive fashion.[39] More recently, Spinner, Adair, and Barnes replicated Fillenbaum's study after correcting some methodological shortcomings in the original design. Their results showed that only 5 percent of the subjects were faithful, whereas 55 percent were unaware of the hypothesis. The remaining 40 percent were aware and showed a clear intent to confirm or to disprove the hypothesis.[40]

These results suggest that anywhere from 60 percent to 80 percent of experimental subjects can be expected either to be naive or faithful and, as a result, present few validity problems. But what of the 20 to 40 percent who are aware of the experimental hypothesis and intend to bias results? What distorting effects can we expect from this bias? Considerable evidence suggests that bias in persuasion experiments typically is in the direction of confirming the experimenter's hypothesis,[41] that subjects often play the "good subject" role. As a result, cognitive or behavior change in a persuasion experiment is likely to be greater than one might expect in a "real life" setting. Because the effects associated with the independent variables often are confounded by the subject's adoption of the "good subject" role, demand characteristics may impugn both the internal and external validity of persuasion experiments. Despite this problem, that the majority of subjects in persuasion experiments are likely either to be naive or faithful suggests that most experiments retain acceptable validity levels.

Evaluation Apprehension

Evaluation apprehension is a second variable thought to bias subjects' responses in persuasion experiments. Milton Rosenberg defines it as an "active, anxiety-toned concern that [the subject] win a positive evaluation from [observers], or at least that he provide no grounds for a negative one."[42] Generally, the apprehensive subject, regardless of awareness of the experimental hypothesis, wishes to give socially approved responses and present a positive public image. If aware of the experimental hypothesis, apprehensive subjects may try to confirm or disprove it depending on which behavior conforms to their self-concepts or makes them look better in the eyes of important others. For example, they might show a great deal of attitude change if they believe themselves to be, and wish to appear, flexible and open minded. In contrast, if they wish to appear independent and not easily swayed, they may exhibit no attitude change or a boomerang effect. As this description suggests, apprehensive behavior is synonymous with rule-following action.

There is considerable evidence that evaluation apprehension is widespread among subjects and that it profoundly affects their responses. Indeed, when a subject's desire to present a good self-image conflicts with "good subject" demand effects, the desire to present a positive image almost always prevails.[43] In other words, subjects who are aware of the experimental hypothesis will confirm it only when doing so projects their basic values and places them in a favorable light. There is some evidence that subjects in persuasion experiments often are concerned about appearing independent and non-conforming. As a result, they show low levels of conformity to persuasive recommendations.[44] Such nonconformist motivations should, in many cases, offset the "good subject" demand characteristics that bias subjects to show increasing attitude change.

Whether evaluation apprehension results in increasing or decreasing persuasibility in experiments, it probably doesn't seriously threaten validity. Whether in the laboratory or in our everyday comings and goings, all of us follow rules allowing us to express our values and present a positive self-image. The notion that public-image maintenance goals are powerful motivators is well documented in all the social sciences. Unlike demand characteristics peculiar to the experimental setting, evaluation apprehension is a pervasive force in *all* social settings.

Experimenter Effects

The third category of variables threatening the internal and external validity of persuasion experiments relates to the physical, social, and psychological characteristics of the experimenter. Two sets of these qualities are especially important.[45] First, the *biosocial characteristics* of an experimenter such as sex and race can affect subjects' responses. For example, male experimenters frequently are perceived as friendlier than female researchers, and consequently, elicit more hypothesis-confirming responses from subjects. Additionally, black experimenters usually elicit decreased self-reports of racial prejudice among subjects than do white investigators.

Beyond biosocial characteristics, an experimenter's *psychosocial traits* can bias subject responses. These traits include the experimenter's apparent need for social approval, his or her level of anxiety and warmth, and the researcher's status vis-à-vis subjects. For instance, experimenters with a high need for social approval tend to elicit more positive responses from subjects than those with lower approval needs. Similarly, "warmer" researchers frequently get more hypothesis-confirming responses than "cooler" experimenters.

These biasing effects clearly compromise the internal validity of an experiment since responses relate not only to the independent variables, but also to an experimenter's personal characteristics. However, such biasing is only a minimal threat to external validity or generalizability. We are all influenced by the biological, psychological, and social characteristics we perceive in other people, whether in the laboratory or in natural settings. Thus, responses to a researcher's psychosocial traits may actually make the laboratory setting a closer approximation of natural social situations than if such effects were absent.

Assessing the Ecological Validity of Experiments: Template Matching

A methodology recently has been developed for assessing the extent to which people's behavior in an experimental setting differs from that performed in more natural social settings. Developed by Daryl Bem and David Funder, the procedure is called *template matching*, and it is a two-stage assessment technique.[46] In the first stage, each distinct behavior exhibited by subjects in a laboratory setting is characterized by a *template*, a description of the type of personality most likely to display the particular observed behavior. In the second stage of template matching, personality descriptions characterizing the subjects' usual behaviors outside the laboratory are obtained from their close friends and acquaintances.

The ecological validity of the experimental setting is determined by how closely these two sets of data match. The more closely a subject's behavior in natural settings approximates his or her laboratory behavior, the more ecologically valid an experiment. Template matching is a powerful tool for assessing the ecological validity of persuasion experiments.

The Nature of Experimental Procedures

Perhaps the most perplexing problems in the persuasion experiment grow out of the nature of the experimental design itself. We will look at three of these problems and present some methodological innovations for alleviating them. All three problems occur because traditional methodologies oversimplify human behavior and the persuasive communication process.

The Study of Persuasion as Variable Analysis

It should be abundantly clear by now that the experimental methodology is, in many respects, highly mechanistic. The complex process of persuasive communication is studied by breaking it down into a relatively *small number of discrete variables*. In reality, persuasion variables are rarely as discrete, as few in number, or as unrelated to one another as this research paradigm suggests. Indeed, as we mentioned earlier, almost all persuasion variables are continuous in nature. Yet, the traditional experimental methodology requires that most continuous, independent variables be arbitrarily made dichotomous or trichotomous to test their associated effects, resulting in a massive oversimplification of the complexities of a person's response to a message.[47]

Fortunately, persuasion researchers are beginning to adopt more sensitive research methodologies for studying persuasion. One of these is *multivariate analysis*,[48] which takes many communication variables into account in the context of a single experiment and also considers the interrelationships among variables of interest. Multiple regression and canonical correlation are two promising multivariate tools. In addition to their use in correlation research, both procedures help establish generative links among variables, thus yielding explanatory knowledge. Beyond the handling of a large number of related variables, multivariate analytical tools can process independent variables on a continuous basis, a major improvement over the traditional methodology requiring that continuous variables be rendered discrete.

A second promising research procedure coming into use is called *meta-analysis*,[49] a statistical technique for integrating the results of an unlimited number of independent experiments on any one problem of interest. This data integration augments the internal and external validity of observed persuasive effects. Such methodological innovations as meta-analysis and multivariate analysis give one hope that the complexity of the persuasion process will be better understood than was the case with older methodologies.

The Study of Persuasion as a Static Process

A second serious defect of the traditional experimental methodology is its inability to capture the ever-changing, developmental nature of persuasion. Like a still photographer, the traditional experimenter measures a set of responses at a single moment in time, ignoring the impact of time on the development of communicative relationships. This defect led psychologist William McGuire almost a decade ago to call for "time series data" on human behavioral effects. "While it is useful to have contemporaneous data," said McGuire, "the full exploitation of these data becomes possible only when we have recorded them at several successive points in time."[50]

McGuire's call was for the methodological equivalent of motion picture photography. Though we have yet to develop such a sophisticated methodology, a number of recent advances are enabling researchers to begin to collect reliable, time series data. For example, *meta-analysis* promises to be a useful technique for comparing a single kind of persuasive effect observed in several sequential experiments. A second research tool, *cross-lagged panel analysis*, is useful for testing hypotheses in longitudinal studies where measurements are taken at several different times.[51] A third, *round robin analysis of variance*, enables a researcher to study the uninhibited interactions among communicators over time.[52] Finally, a promising set of procedures called the *Box–Jenkins methods*, are available for analysis of time series data.[53] In sum, although most of our present knowledge about persuasion comes from studies using static methodologies, the new methods we have described should enable us to enrich our understanding of the developmental properties of persuasive communication.

The Treatment of Subjects as Passive Reactors

Because traditional experimental methods were borrowed from scientists working in the mechanistic tradition, they focus on what the experimenter does to subjects. Indeed, the label *subject* suggests a passive creature, rather than an active, thinking, human being. Of course, persuasion researchers discovered long ago that subjects were not passive reactors. In fact, the phrase *internal and external invalidity* was coined to signify all those things subjects *do to* experimenters other than passively react to their independent variables! Our existing and rather extensive body of literature on experimental invalidity is testimony to the active nature of subjects who consistently refuse to "act right" in experiments.

Despite the recognition that people behave as active agents even in scientific research, many persuasion researchers, as a practical matter, continue to treat subjects as relatively passive objects to be manipulated. Consequently, the meanings people assign to independent variables and other aspects of the research setting are often glossed over or ignored. Fortunately, these practices have declined substantially during the last five to ten years. Persuasion researchers have begun to focus extensively on the role of human perception in experimentation. Moreover, researchers are increasingly using interpretative research strategies to determine how and why people respond as they do to certain types of persuasive messages. Indeed, a major research paradigm in persuasion is the study of how human interpretations and covert, cognitive responses to messages shape attitudes.[54] We will refer to the results of such research throughout this book.

Beyond this research, several methodologies adapted to the active subject have emerged in recent years. One such methodology, the *round robin design*, was men-

tioned earlier. Its essential feature is that experimental subjects are exposed to *no* externally imposed, independent variables. Rather "the 'treatment' to which each subject
reacts are the behaviors of other subjects."[55] The researcher using the round robin
design can observe the effects associated with naturally occurring differences among
people, such as different speech patterns or message appeals; he can also study how
experimental subjects influence one another's behavior. Put to this latter use, the round
robin design captures well the developmental nature of persuasive communication.

THE EXPERIMENT AND RULES RESEARCH

We noted earlier that most rules researchers have avoided the experiment, assuming it applicable only to causal research. Although we believe this assumption is false,
the experimental methodology presently has several problems limiting its usefulness to
rules researchers. We will review these problems and present guidelines for alleviating
them. Our aim is to pave the way for rules researchers to take advantage of this powerful methodological tool.

Problems in using the experiment for rules research occur because of its mechanistic origins and its traditional use by laws researchers who often apply causal assumptions to purposive phenomena. As we noted earlier, experimenters typically assume
that persuasive strategies or independent variables are causal forces producing purposive responses to messages. In this and the preceding chapter, we have argued repeatedly that this assumption misrepresents the nature of human purposive action. We believe that people's responses to messages are usually prompted by reasons, goals, or
rules activated by persuasive strategies. In such cases, the rules relevant to independent
persuasive strategies, not the strategies themselves, are the generative forces prompting
human action. From our view, independent variables or persuasive strategies and their
associated effects *covary* by virtue of the relationship between the strategies and relevant generative rules.

The alternative, traditional view that independent variables themselves cause purposive responses creates major problems for rules researchers. If one operates on the
rules assumption that independent message strategies covary with purposive responses,
it follows that experiments do not really *explain* purposive action. Rather, they establish covariations between some persuasive strategy X and a purposive response Y. In
the traditional experiment, those generative forces responsible for purposive behavior,
that is, contextual rules relevant to persuasive strategies, are not manipulated directly
to determine the actions they generate. Thus, when the experimental methodology is
applied to purposive, as opposed to causal, behaviors, experiments do not fulfill their
ostensible purpose: to isolate the *reasons why* certain persuasive effects are associated
with particular types of persuasive strategies.

Consequently, when rules researchers examine experimental results, the best they
can do is speculate on the sorts of rules that probably are generating the covariation the
experiment has established. For instance, if an experiment establishes that "physically
attractive people are effective persuaders," about all we can do with this information is
speculate about the rules or goal-directed links that may have prompted the covaria-

tion between attractiveness and persuasiveness. Likewise, we may establish experimentally that "perceived attitudinal similarity leads to interpersonal attraction."[56] However, we must go outside the experiment to speculate on the reasons for the covariation between similarity and attraction. Thus, the experimental methodology as presently constituted leaves rules researchers no basis for directly establishing explanatory links between human goals and purposive actions.

To avoid this methodological trap, many rules scholars have junked the experiment as a methodological tool, an act we believe is unfortunate and self-defeating. We suggest that rules researchers need not abandon the experimental methodology itself, but rather they should debunk its use of causal assumptions to explain purposive action.

By taking this route, rules researchers can, by applying appropriate language and assumptions, revitalize the experimental methodology and use it as a powerful tool for isolating rules that prompt human action. To illustrate how this can be done, recall the rules-based persuasion theorem offered in Chapter 3 that "people will choose to comply with persuasive messages specifying contextually relevant rules more often than they will comply with messages stipulating contextually irrelevant rules."

To test this hypothesis, suppose I recruit a group of women who favor a constitutional guarantee of sexual equality and ask them to listen to a message on the topic of women's rights. Suppose further, that these women hold their attitudes for value-expressive reasons; that is, they see themselves as liberated women and support for sexual equality allows them to project this positive self-image. To test my theorem, I might construct one message that makes value-expressive goals and actions salient and another making external rewards or instrumental goals and actions prominent.[57] The former message contains contextually relevant rules; the latter is comprised of contextually irrelevant rules. By exposing groups of women to each type of message and measuring their responses, I can test experimentally my rules-based theorem. In this experiment, I would have manipulated goal-action links or rules as the independent variable and measured the effects of those manipulations. Such an experiment should have true explanatory power since the design allows us to isolate the *reasons* prompting human actions.

In our judgment, the revitalized methodology we have sketched should advance our knowledge of purposive action in persuasion. Such advances should complement those produced by the traditional experiment that aims to explain causal communication phenomena.

NOTES

1. Harley H. Bovee, "Report of the 1954 Windshield Pitting Phenomenon in the State of Washington," unpublished MS, Environmental Research Laboratory, University of Washington, Seattle, June 10, 1954.

2. The relationship just described between theory and research has been called the "inductive-hypothetico-deductive-experimental-inductive spiral." See Raymond B. Cattell, ed., *Handbook of Multivariate Experimental Psychology* (Chicago: Rand McNally, 1966).

3. Irving L. Janis and Leon Mann, "Effectiveness of Emotional Role-Playing in Modifying Smoking Habits and Attitudes," *Journal of Experimental Research in Personality* 1 (1965): 84–90.

4. Ibid., p. 84.

5. Ibid., p. 88.

6. W. Barnett Pearce, "Metatheoretical Concerns in Communication," *Communication Quarterly* 25 (1977): 4.

7. Norwood Russel Hanson, *Patterns of Discovery* (Cambridge: Cambridge University Press, 1958).

8. Pearce, pp. 4–5.

9. For discussions of the nature and methodology of naturalistic research, see W. Barnett Pearce, "Naturalistic Study of Communication: Its Function and Form," *Communication Quarterly* 25 (1977): 51–56; Leonard Schatzman and Anselm L. Strauss, *Field Research: Strategies for a Natural Sociology* (Englewood Cliffs, N.J.: Prentice-Hall, 1973); Edwin P. Williams and Harold L. Raush, eds., *Naturalistic Viewpoints in Psychological Research* (New York: Holt, Rinehart & Winston, 1969); and Barney G. Glaser and Anselm L. Strauss, *The Discovery of Grounded Theory: Strategies for Qualitative Research* (Chicago: Aldine Publishing Company, 1967).

10. For a discussion of this research method, see Robert E. Nofsinger, Jr., "A Peek at Conversational Analysis," *Communication Quarterly* 25 (1977): 12–20.

11. This form of descriptive research using participants' or actors' meanings may be contrasted with a second form that uses the observer's interpretations. Pearce has called the latter "objectivistic research." See Pearce, "Naturalistic Study of Communication." Both objectivistic research and descriptive research have a methodological flaw called *reactivity*, referring to the possibility that people who are aware they are being observed will behave differently than they might in a natural setting.

12. For a discussion of correlation, see J. P. Guilford and Benjamin Fruchter, *Fundamental Statistics in Psychology and Education* (New York: McGraw-Hill, 1973), pp. 79–98.

13. For a discussion of computation methods, see Guilford and Fruchter, pp. 83–90.

14. See Fred N. Kerlinger and Elazar J. Pedhazur, *Multiple Regression in Behavioral Research* (New York: Holt, Rinehart & Winston, 1973).

15. See Raymond K. Tucker and Lawrence J. Chase, "Canonical Correlation in Human Communication Research," *Human Communication Research* 3 (1976): 86–96.

16. A third, common multivariate correlation procedure not discussed is called factor analysis. *Factor analysis* assesses the intercorrelations among an exceptionally large number of variables for the purpose of reducing them to a smaller, more manageable set of factors. For a fuller discussion of it, see Fred N. Kerlinger, *Foundations of Behavioral Research* (New York: Holt, Rinehart & Winston, 1973), pp. 659–692. A critical examination of the uses of factor analysis in communication research can be found in James C. McCroskey and Thomas J. Young, "The Use and Abuse of Factor Analysis in Communication Research," *Human Communication Research* 5 (1979): 375–382.

17. It should be noted that, unlike bivariate correlation, multiple linear regression procedures can be used to establish explanatory links. See, for example, Jae-On Kim and Frank J. Kohout, "Special Topics in General Linear Models," in *Statistical Package for the Social Sciences*, ed. Norman H. Nie et al. (New York: McGraw-Hill, 1975), pp. 368–397.

18. For discussions of the experimental methodology, see Kerlinger; C. Mitchell Dayton, *The Design of Educational Experiments* (New York: McGraw-Hill, 1970); Donald T. Campbell and Julian C. Stanley, *Experimental and Quasi-Experimental Designs for Research* (Chicago: Rand McNally, 1963); and Percy H. Tannenbaum, "Experimental Method in Communication Research," in *Introduction to Mass Communication Research*, ed. Ralph O. Nafziger and David M. White (Baton Rouge, La.: Louisiana State University Press, 1963), pp. 51–77.

19. Susan B. Shimanoff, *Communication Rules: Theory and Research* (Beverly Hills, Calif.: Sage Publications, 1980), pp. 193–194.

20. For full discussions of a variety of self-report measures, see Gene F. Summers, ed., *Attitude Measurement* (Chicago: Rand McNally, 1970), pp. 125–316. A less technical summary of self-report instruments is found in Philip G. Zimbardo, E. B. Ebbesen, and Christina Maslach, *Influencing Attitudes and Changing Behavior* (Reading, Mass.: Addison-Wesley, 1977), pp. 213–220.

21. For a discussion of a variety of direct observation techniques, see Summers, pp. 413–478.

22. A discussion of physiological measures may be found in Summers, pp. 481–552.

23. For a discussion of random sampling strategies, see Kerlinger, pp. 117–132.

24. For an extended discussion of the nature of interaction effects, see Kerlinger, pp. 242–227.

25. A more detailed discussion of significance of difference between and among groups can be found in Guilford and Fruchter, pp. 149–194.

26. The following discussion of laboratory experiments draws heavily on Gerald R. Miller, "Research Setting: Laboratory Studies," in *Methods of Research in Communication*, ed. Philip Emmert and William D. Brooks (Boston: Houghton Mifflin, 1970), pp. 77–85.

27. Charles M. Rossiter, "The Validity of Communication Experiments Using Human Subjects: A Review," *Human Communication Research* 2 (1976): 197–206.

28. Quinn McNemar, "Opinion–Attitude Methodology," *Psychological Bulletin* 43 (1946): 333.

29. Stanley Milgram, *Obedience to Authority: An Experimental View* (New York: Harper & Row, 1974), pp. 170–171.

30. Mary John Smith and Anne Gabbard-Alley, "Attitudinal Freedom, Crowding, and Chronological Age," unpublished MS, University of Virginia, 1979.

31. Robert Rosenthal and Ralph L. Rosnow, "The Volunteer Subject," in *Artifact in Behavioral Research*, ed. Robert Rosenthal and Ralph L. Rosnow (New York: Academic Press, 1969), pp. 59–118.

32. Arie W. Kruglanski, "Much Ado About the 'Volunteer Artifacts'," *Journal of Personality and Social Psychology* 28 (1973): 350.

33. Ralph L. Rosnow and Robert Rosenthal, "Volunteer Subjects and the Results of Opinion Change Studies," *Psychological Reports* 19 (1966): 1183–1187.

34. Martin T. Orne, "On the Social Psychology of the Psychological Experiment: With Particular Reference to Demand Characteristics and their Implications," *American Psychologist* 17 (1962): 779.

35. For an exhaustive discussion of subject roles, see Stephen J. Weber and Thomas D. Cook, "Subject Effects in Laboratory Research: An Examination of Subject Roles, Demand Characteristics, and Valid Inference," *Psychological Bulletin* 77 (1972): 273–295.

36. Joseph Masling, "Role-Related Behavior of the Subject and Psychologist and its Effects upon Psychological Data," *Nebraska Symposium on Motivation*, ed. David Levine (Lincoln, Neb.: University of Nebraska Press, 1966), pp. 67–103.

37. Samuel Fillenbaum, "Prior Deception and Subsequent Experimental Performance: The 'Faithful' Subject," *Journal of Personality and Social Psychology* 4 (1966): 532–537.

38. Naive subjects are often thought to be those who have not previously participated in experimental research. Considerable evidence suggests this definition may be too narrow, in that prior participation seems to have little biasing effects upon subsequent reactions to experiments. See, for example, Thomas D. Cook and Barton F. Perrini, "The Effects of Suspiciousness of Deception and the Perceived Legitimacy of Deception on Task Performance in an Attitude Change Experiment," *Journal of Personality* 39 (1971): 204–224; Thomas D. Cook et al., "Demand Characteristics and Three Conceptions of the Frequently Deceived Subject," *Journal of Personality and Social Psychology* 14 (1970): 185–194; and Timothy C. Brock and Lee Alan Becker, " 'Debriefing' and Susceptibility to Subsequent Experimental Manipulations," *Journal of Experimental Social Psychology* 2 (1966): 314–323. For evidence that prior participation may have some biasing effects, see Irwin Silverman, Arthur D. Shulman, and David L. Wiesenthal, "Effects of Deceiving and Debriefing Psychological

Subjects on Performance in Later Experiments," *Journal of Personality and Social Psychology* 14 (1970): 203–212; David S. Holmes and Alan S. Appelbaum, "Nature of Prior Experimental Experience as a Determinant of Performance in a Subsequent Experiment," *Journal of Personality and Social Psychology* 14 (1970): 195–202; and David S. Holmes, "Amount of Experience in Experiments as a Determinant of Performance in Later Experiments," *Journal of Personality and Social Psychology* 7 (1967): 403–407.

39. Fillenbaum. For additional evidence supporting these conclusions, see Samuel Fillenbaum and Robert Frey, "More on the 'Faithful' Behavior of Suspicious Subjects," *Journal of Personality* 38 (1970): 43–51.

40. Barry Spinner, John G. Adair, and Gordon E. Barnes, "A Reexamination of the Faithful Subject Role," *Journal of Experimental Social Psychology* 13 (1977): 543–551.

41. For a summary of research supporting this conclusion, see Weber and Cook, pp. 282–283.

42. Milton J. Rosenberg, "The Conditions and Consequences of Evaluation Apprehension," in *Artifact in Behavioral Research*, p. 281.

43. See John G. Adair and Brenda S. Schachter, "To Cooperate or to Look Good?: The Subjects' and Experimenters' Perceptions of Each Other's Intentions," *Journal of Experimental Social Psychology* 8 (1972): 75–85; Irwin Silverman and Arthur D. Schulman, "A Conceptual Model of Artifact in Attitude Change Studies," *Sociometry* 33 (1970): 97–107; and Harold Sigall, Eliot Aronson, and Thomas Van Hoose, "The Cooperative Subject: Myth or Reality?" *Journal of Experimental Social Psychology* 6 (1970): 1–10.

44. For a summary of relevant research, see Weber and Cook, pp. 281–282.

45. See Robert Rosenthal, "Interpersonal Expectations: Effects of the Experimenter's Hypothesis," in *Artifact in Behavioral Research*, pp. 181–277.

46. See Daryl J. Bem and Charles G. Lord, "Template Matching: A Proposal for Probing the Ecological Validity of Experimental Settings in Social Psychology," *Journal of Personality and Social Psychology* 37 (1979): 833–843; and Daryl J. Bem and David C. Funder, "Predicting More of the People More of the Time: Assessing the Personality of Situations," *Psychological Review* 85 (1978): 485–501.

47. For an extended discussion of the implications of the variable analytic approach, see Jesse G. Delia, "Constructivism and the Study of Human Communication," *Quarterly Journal of Speech* 63 (1977): 72–79.

48. For a discussion of multivariate analytic procedures and a review of several books on multivariate analysis in the social sciences, see Peter R. Monge and Patrick D. Day, "Multivariate Analysis in Communication Research," *Human Communication Research* 2 (1976): 207–220.

49. See Harris M. Cooper, "Statistically Combining Independent Studies: A Meta-Analysis of Sex Differences in Conformity Research," *Journal of Personality and Social Psychology* 37 (1979): 131–146; and Gene V. Glass, "Primary, Secondary, and Meta-Analysis Research," *Educational Researcher* 5 (1976): 3–8.

50. William J. McGuire, "The Yin and Yang of Progress in Social Psychology: Seven Koan," *Journal of Personality and Social Psychology* 26 (1979): 453.

51. See Lynn R. Kahle and John J. Berman, "Attitudes Cause Behaviors: A Cross-Lagged Panel Analysis," *Journal of Personality and Social Psychology* 37 (1979): 315–321; and David A. Kenny, "Cross-Lagged Panel Correlation: A Test for Spuriousness," *Psychological Bulletin* 82 (1975): 887–903.

52. See Rebecca M. Warner, David A. Kenny, and Michael Stoto, "A New Round Robin Analysis of Variance for Social Interaction Data," *Journal of Personality and Social Psychology* 37 (1979): 1742–1757.

53. See Richard McCleary, Richard A. Hay, Jr., Errol E. Meidinger, and David McDowall, *Applied Time Series Analysis for the Social Sciences* (Beverly Hills, Calif.: Sage Publications, 1980).

54. See Richard E. Petty, Thomas M. Ostrom, and Timothy C. Brock, eds., *Cognitive Responses in Persuasion* (Hillsdale, N.J.: Lawrence Erlbaum, in press).

55. Warner et al., p. 1742.

56. Charles R. Berger, "The Covering Law Perspective as a Theoretical Basis for the Study of Human Communication," *Communication Quarterly* 25 (1977): 11.

57. The reader will recall from our discussion of Daniel Katz' functional theory in Chapter 2 that attitudes may achieve one or more of four goals for people: instrumental, value-expressive, ego-defensive, and knowledge goals. See Daniel Katz, "The Functional Approach to the Study of Attitudes," *Public Opinion Quarterly* 24 (1960): 163–204.

PART 2

ACTIVE PARTICIPATION THEORIES OF PERSUASION

CHAPTER 5

Counterattitudinal Advocacy and Self-Persuasion

In May 1954, the United States Supreme Court in the case of *Brown* v. *Board of Education* ordered the public schools desegregated "with all deliberate speed." In September 1956, more than two years after this landmark decision, 15-year-old Elizabeth Elsford and eight other black youths attempted without success to begin their school year at Central High in Little Rock, Arkansas. Despite a court order requiring their admission, Arkansas' governor, Orville Faubus, activated the National Guard and used it to prevent their entry. Angry crowds of white parents and students blocked the schoolhouse door to prevent Elizabeth's enrollment. When, on September 23, the nine black students tried to enter the school as a group, whites rioted, and the Guard was unwilling or unable to stop them. On September 24, President Dwight D. Eisenhower took action. He federalized the National Guard and ordered it to enforce the court's decree.

On the morning of September 24, the nine black students entered Central High School. Escorted by two truckloads of troops brandishing M-1 rifles, they integrated the Little Rock school system. But militant whites did not peacefully accept integration. For almost three months, threats of violence kept the Guard at the school. The troops may have forced integration, but people's attitudes showed no signs of changing. This incident was typical of the reactions of many other southern states to the *Brown* decision.

However, there is another story from another southern state meriting attention, not because of newspaper headlines or confrontations, but because it unfolded without incident. The state was North Carolina and again the year was 1956. The state legislature was considering alternatives to compliance with the Supreme Court's order. One proposal was to defy the court and force the federal government into an acrimonious confrontation with the state. Despite the popularity of this option, North Carolina went a different route. The state ordered the public school system desegregated, but at the same time, it offered state aid to any family wishing to switch its children from the public schools to a private school system. In the end, almost no one applied for tuition grants, and public school desegregation proceeded smoothly and peacefully in North Carolina.[1]

What happened in North Carolina to make it different from Arkansas and many other southern states? One could argue that people's attitudes were different to start with, but there is little evidence to support this. It is more likely that, as a result of the policy adopted by North Carolina, people's attitudes began to moderate. They were offered a choice between private and public schools. Most parents opted to keep their children in the public schools to avoid disrupting their education and to escape the bureaucratic hassle application for a tuition grant entailed. It is possible that the attitudes of the people of North Carolina began to change as a result of behavioral changes made in an atmosphere of perceived choice. More directly, we can speculate that after North Carolinians were induced to alter their behavior, they gradually changed their attitudinal schemata to conform with these new behavior patterns.

This story of peaceful integration suggests the persuasive effects that can result when one acts contrary to one's attitudinal schemata. Such actions are called *counterattitudinal behavior*. In this chapter, we will consider the persuasive effects of a particular kind of counterattitudinal behavior, the production of messages conflicting with one's attitudes. We will find that advocating a position contrary to internal cognitions is often a potent form of self-persuasion, prompting a realignment of cognitive structures to conform with counterattitudinal acts. After discussing the nature of counterattitudinal advocacy, we will evaluate several theoretical explanations for its persuasive effects, including the theory of cognitive dissonance, incentive theory, self-perception theory, and the theory of impression management.

THE NATURE OF COUNTERATTITUDINAL ADVOCACY

Counterattitudinal advocacy occurs when a person says what he or she does not believe. A counterattitudinal message is an original self-generated message; that is, one not directly traceable to the content of messages produced by some external agent. The content of such a message is inconsistent with one's internal cognitive schemata.

Counterattitudinal advocacy may be an overt or a covert process. Covert or subvocal advocacy is equivalent to private thought, and it follows either the actual performance of an inconsistent act or a commitment to behave contrary to one's attitudinal schemata. For example, the teenager who, for the first time, commits himself or herself to experiment with drugs or engage in sexual intimacy often exemplifies the covert advocacy process. After acting or committing oneself to act, an individual initially may feel a sense of regret or guilt, thinking such activities are not right, that they are contrary to the values learned in the home, school, or church. However, once such a decision is made, people normally begin to generate covert arguments to convince themselves that such activities are not immoral after all, that, in fact, they are quite enjoyable, even enlightening and mind expanding.

Although much counterattitudinal advocacy is covert in nature, it may also be an overt process, involving spoken or written messages that conflict with attitudinal schemata. Like covert arguing, overt advocacy often is prompted by the performance of an inconsistent action or a commitment to do so. In the example cited above, it is likely that overt arguing, such as conversations with drug-using friends or with sexual partners, accompanied the covert, self-influence processes.

We often make overt counterattitudinal statements because of peer pressure and participation in highly cohesive social groups. It is common for all of us to make statements with which we disagree when we believe friends or respected others expect such behaviors of us. Counterattitudinal statements that initially are rationalized as "going along with the crowd" often result in our becoming a part of the crowd, as we convince ourselves of the wisdom of our overt statements. It is important to note that overt and covert counterattitudinal advocacy are interdependent processes of self-influence. Covert messages supplement overtly expressed messages that, in turn, may stimulate additional covert messages.

Some of the conversion strategies used by the Unification Church of the Reverend Sun Myung Moon illustrate the use of overt and covert counterattitudinal advocacy as tools of self-influence. After voluntarily agreeing to attend a weekend retreat, potential recruits are involved in intensive group interaction. A relaxed, "open-minded," and highly cohesive atmosphere is created and maintained by group singing and games. During group discussion, potential recruits are encouraged to express their innermost feelings, their frustrations, loneliness, hopes, and dreams.

A Stanford University student who, as part of a class project, spent a weekend at the Moon-sponsored Eden Awareness Training Center in Booneville, California, reported some specific counterattitudinal tactics used by the "Moonies." He reported that, during group discussion, any "unacceptable" comments made by a potential recruit elicited an immediate, uniform reaction from the Moon faithfuls: they seemed hurt and saddened, never angered by deviant thoughts. On the other hand, acceptable comments were greeted with smiles, words of approval, and other loving gestures.

The student reported that his initial counterattitudinal comments were insincere, designed only to further his research into the conversion phenomenon. However, as the weekend wore on, he noted that he began to convince himself of the wisdom of his overt statements supporting the Moon movement. By the end of the weekend, he reported that "when it was my turn to talk, I told of my desire to help the world after I got myself ready. This time," he said, "I wasn't just playing along." After he returned to Stanford, he talked of feeling "sad." "People showed me love in Ideal City," he said, "but I chose to return to a place where the programming was easier to avoid, with all my struggles, loneliness, and fair-weather friends." Although the Stanford student was not converted, clearly his "head" was not in the same place to which his body returned.[2]

Both overt and covert counterattitudinal advocacy typically are induced through the promise or delivery of rewards or punishments. As our examples illustrate, some of the more common inducers of counterattitudinal advocacy are displays of social approval for performing inconsistent actions and threats of social rejection or isolation for nonperformance. Such inducements often prompt original self-generated messages, leading a person to gradually convince himself or herself of the wisdom of new ways of feeling, believing, and behaving.

The Persistence of Counterattitudinal Self-Persuasion

Let us assume that someone, as a consequence of counterattitudinal advocacy, has changed an attitude toward some issue like abortion, marijuana use, or racial balance in the public schools. Or perhaps this person has experienced more monumental changes, such as those reported by some Moon converts and many "born again" Christians, who adopt new philosophical outlooks differing considerably from their old ways of believing and behaving. To what extent can we expect these changes to persist? Unfortunately, experimental research on the long-term effects of counterattitudinal advocacy has yielded sharply conflicting results. For example, Crano and Messé found that attitudes reverted to their original position only 20 minutes after subjects engaged in counterattitudinal advocacy.[3] In contrast, Watts found that attitude changes persisted six weeks after counterattitudinal advocacy.[4]

These conflicting findings mirror real-life examples. Some born again Christians maintain their changed value orientations for a lifetime. Yet others "backslide" or "fall from grace" at the first tempting opportunity. We saw earlier that North Carolinians peacefully integrated their public school system in the 1950s. Yet as recently as 1981, the state was threatened with a cut-off of federal funds because of its failure to integrate fully the state college and university system.

How might we account for these divergencies? Elaine Walster and Ellen Berscheid suggest that the persistence of effects depends on one's counterattitudinal behavior continuing to be important and relatively salient over time.[5] Robert Wicklund and Jack Brehm argue that attitude change will persist so long as there are no major social pressures prompting a return to one's original cognitive state.[6]

These are reasonable explanations for the conflicting effects we have discussed. The born again Christian who continues to receive strong social support for his or her new beliefs should remain a changed person. Frequent contact with similar others and ongoing involvement in the affairs of the church should stimulate an ongoing, supportive process of self-persuasion. However, in the absence of such a process, an individual's attitudes should return to their initial state. In any case, continuing self-persuasion in the form of supportive message-production is necessary if counterattitudinal advocacy is to result in lasting attitude change.

COGNITIVE DISSONANCE THEORY AND COUNTERATTITUDINAL ADVOCACY

Counterattitudinal advocacy was first explained systematically by Leon Festinger's theory of *cognitive dissonance*.[7] The basic units of dissonance theory are cognitions or cognitive elements. A *cognition* is similar to a cognitive schema as described in Chapter 2, and it refers to all those things people believe and feel about themselves, other

people, and all other aspects of their environment. The knowledge that I smoke cigarettes, the belief that I am an honest person, and the feeling that capital punishment is
wrong are all cognitions.

Some cognitive elements are perceived as related, and others are not so perceived.
Related cognitions may be in either a *consonant* or a *dissonant* relationship. Festinger
states that "two elements are in a dissonant relation if, considering the two alone, the
obverse of one element would follow from the other."[8] For example, cigarette smoking
is in a dissonant relation to the knowledge that smoking causes disease and death. A
behavior like lying is dissonant with the belief that one is an honest person. On the
other hand, consonant relationships occur when cognitive elements or sets of elements
follow from one another. For example, statements opposing the death penalty are consonant with my belief that capital punishment is morally reprehensible, just as truthfulness follows from an honest self-concept.

The motivational dynamic underlying Festinger's notion of cognitive dissonance
rests on two premises. First, it is assumed that humans have a basic desire for consistency among the cognitions in their psychological world. Second, the presence of inconsistency among one's relevant cognitions produces psychological discomfort, motivating
the rearrangement of one's psychological world to restore consistency. Festinger calls
this aversive or uncomfortable state *dissonance*.

Given this motivational basis, we see that dissonance will occur when I lie to a
friend but still see myself as an honest person, or when I smoke cigarettes even though
I believe that doing so causes disease. These dissonant states, in turn, should motivate
me to rearrange my cognitions to restore consistency or consonance. Dissonance-reduc-
ing options in the case of smoking and disease would be to stop smoking or to convince
myself that cigarette smoking is really not all that harmful.

Eliot Aronson has questioned this conception of the motivational basis of dissonance.[9] He charges that Festinger's notion of dissonance as a state resulting from the
failure of cognitions to "follow from" one another lacks conceptual clarity. He argues
that conceptualizing dissonance, not as a result of conflicting cognitions, but as a consequence of violations of expectancies or rules, especially regarding one's self-concept,
would enhance clarity. Thus, to tell a monstrous falsehood should create dissonance in
an honest person—not because truthfulness "follows from" being honest—but because
the lying individual has a self-expectancy that he or she will be truthful in matters of
importance.

From Festinger's view, a white lie, such as telling the hostess of a terrible party
that you enjoyed yourself, is inconsistent with the belief that one is honest. According
to dissonance theory, such an inconsistency should create discomfort, yet it rarely does.
From Aronson's view, dissonance should not result here because socialization processes
have produced an expectancy or rule that we should be polite and civil in such circumstances. Thus, Aronson might argue that dissonance would result only if we did *not* tell
the white lie. From his perspective, then, dissonance arises because we have expectancies or rules regarding our value orientations and goals. When we violate such rules, we
should experience a psychological discomfort motivating us to reestablish a consonant
relationship between actions and expectancies. Although he never explicitly uses the
term *rule*, Aronson's reinterpretation of the motivational bases of dissonance is implic-

itly rules based. In essence, he is suggesting that rule violations create dissonance or discomfort, and that rule-following actions result in feelings of consonance or harmony.

Cognitive Dissonance and Counterattitudinal Advocacy

When people advocate something that conflicts with their attitudes or self-expectancy rules, the action should create dissonance. Given certain conditions, this state should motivate a person to change cognitive structures to conform with the discrepant behavior. If substantial self-persuasion is to result, it is vital that counterattitudinal advocacy result in a high dissonance level and that the person chooses to reduce it by coming to believe the counterattitudinal statements. Let's look at some of the factors affecting the magnitude of dissonance and the options available for reducing psychological discomfort.

Magnitude of Dissonance

In general, the magnitude of dissonance associated with a counterattitudinal statement is equal to the ratio of dissonant to consonant cognitions in association with the discrepant message. Moreover, each dissonant and consonant cognition must be weighted for its social and personal importance to a person. Stated as a ratio:

$$\text{The magnitude of dissonance associated with any one counterattitudinal statement} = \frac{\text{Related dissonant cognitions} \times \text{the importance of the cognitions}}{\text{Related consonant cognitions} \times \text{the importance of the cognitions}}$$

To clarify this conception, let's consider the hypothetical case of an 18-year-old man recruited for a weekend retreat sponsored by followers of Reverend Moon. Suppose in the course of a group discussion, this young man states that he plans to renounce his earthly family and follow his spiritual father, the Reverend Moon. He is lying, but this counterattitudinal statement elicits smiling approval from all the group members and reinforces his comment. At this point, he should have a number of related dissonant and consonant cognitions. Cognitions that would bear a dissonant relation to his statement are: "I love my family and I don't wish to part with them"; "These people are a bunch of weirdos. I'm not that type of person"; and "I plan to be a lawyer. I can't give that ambition up for a life of self-sacrifice." On the other hand, covert cognitions consonant with the statement would include: "I feel loved and accepted here"; "My life is all messed up anyway"; "I'm young. If I don't fit in with the movement, there is plenty of time to pursue a career"; and "These people may be weirdos, but after all I came to this retreat of my own free will."

How much stress should this young man be experiencing? Dissonance levels will be high if the cognitions threatened by his plan to join the movement are more numerous and more important than those cognitions enhanced by the plan. However, if consonant cognitions outweigh dissonant ones, he will experience a minimal amount of psychological discomfort.

Reducing Dissonance

We must ask how dissonance can be reduced once a person makes an overt or covert counterattitudinal statement. Although there are numerous possibilities,[10] we will look at only three. First, the person may *deny* or suppress a dissonant cognitive relationship. Kassarjian and Cohen conducted a study of smokers in Santa Monica, California, one year after the 1964 Surgeon General's report established a causal link between cigarette smoking and lung cancer. They found that 40.9 percent of the heavy smokers who were aware of the report denied there was any causal link between smoking and disease.[11]

Second, an individual may reduce dissonance by *altering attitudes or cognitive schemata* to conform with overt counterattitudinal actions or commitments. The case of a "Moonie" convert and the conversion of Patty Hearst are dramatic examples of cognitive alteration stimulated by counterattitudinal activity. Less dramatic instances of attitude change include the teenager who persuades him or herself of the value of drugs or the joy of sex through covert encoding and conversations with friends.

Finally, consistency between discrepant behavior and attitudinal schemata may be restored by *recanting the behavior;* that is, publicly stating that one erred in making certain counterattitudinal statements. This mode is not used as often as attitude realignment. After overtly stating a position on an issue, social pressures usually militate against a "whimsical" change of mind. Although it is socially acceptable to "rethink" one's attitudinal position, repudiating a public act often damages one's credibility. The relative ease of altering attitudes versus established behavior is a primary reason for the effectiveness of counterattitudinal self-persuasion.

The principal way people alter attitudes is by adding cognitions that are consonant with counterattitudinal acts. In this way, the ratio of dissonant to consonant cognitions associated with the counterattitudinal behavior is altered in favor of consonance. For example, consider the case of the smoker who is convinced of the danger of his or her habit, but continues to smoke. He or she reduces dissonance by focusing on consonant cognitions.

The smoker may say: "I know smoking is hazardous, but it relieves my tensions and keeps me from gaining weight. Besides, lots of people who smoke live to a ripe old age, and many nonsmokers die young. Ah, life is capricious; you gotta go somehow; so why not smoke?" This smoker has succeeded in covertly producing a rather convincing message to support a dissonant behavior pattern. In a similar fashion, the individual who has lied may covertly generate messages supporting the lie. Adding cognitions consonant with an overt message is a potent means of chipping away at attitudinal schemata.

Factors Affecting the Success of Counterattitudinal Self-Persuasion

From the perspective of cognitive dissonance theory, counterattitudinal advocacy is, by definition, a dissonance-producing phenomenon. One is saying what is not believed. The resulting psychic discomfort should motivate a person to restore psychological consistency or maintain the integrity of the self-concept. That restoration generally results in attitude change in the direction of the self-produced message.

Although this effect has been observed in numerous settings, it will not always occur. As we saw in Chapter 3, all theoretical statements are probable, contingent, and substitutable; dissonance theory is no exception. We will now examine the boundary conditions under which counterattitudinal advocacy should result in self-persuasion.

Perception of Choice

The perception of choice to generate a discrepant message exerts more influence on the success of counterattitudinal advocacy than any other factor. From a dissonance perspective, a person must feel a counterattitudinal statement was freely made. Coercive advocacy produces neither rules violation nor psychological inconsistency. A knife at one's throat, verbal blackmail, or other methods of coercion provide ample *external* justification for the performance of a discrepant behavior.

In an experimental test of the role of choice in counterattitudinal advocacy, Linder, Cooper, and Jones required a group of college students to write an essay defending a position they opposed: banning the appearance of controversial speakers on university campuses. Other students were told they should write such an essay only if they wished to do so. Results confirmed that the subjects who were given no choice exhibited the same level of attitude change after writing an essay as did a control group that generated no message. In contrast, the attitudes of those individuals who were given a free choice changed significantly in favor of the persuasion topic.[12]

The real-life cases of counterattitudinal advocacy we have examined thus far bear out the crucial role played by a perception of choice. The Patty Hearst affair, the strategies employed in the Moon Movement, and the desegregation policy implemented by the legislature of North Carolina in the 1950s, are striking examples. In citing these cases, we have not meant to imply that any of the people involved were clever communication specialists deliberately employing strategies designed to induce a perception of choice. Rather, the examples are meant to illustrate that the actions of these disparate groups inadvertently made a great deal of sense in the light of dissonance research.

Justification for Counterattitudinal Advocacy

Counterattitudinal advocacy typically is induced by promising or providing rewards or punishments for the performance or nonperformance of a counterattitudinal act. A considerable body of research shows the less the reinforcement promised or delivered for speaking contrary to one's attitudes, the greater the expected attitude change toward one's discrepant message. The *minimum justification hypothesis* states that a person should be given just enough reinforcement to prompt the counterattitudinal act and that overjustification or the provision of excessive rewards or punishments should be avoided.

This reasoning is a straightforward deduction from dissonance theory. A large

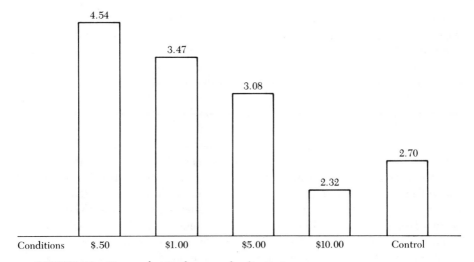

FIGURE 5.1   *Means of attitudes toward police actions*

reward, such as a free vacation in the Bahamas, or the threat of excessive punishment provide external justification for counterattitudinal statements. Overjustification and discrepant behavior are consonant cognitions. For example, the "bought" witness at a criminal trial can claim that he or she "lied for the money." Likewise, the student who lies about an absence on examination day should not be motivated to believe he or she really was ill, if the false explanation was given to keep from flunking the course.

In an experiment conducted at Yale University in the early 1960s, Cohen found support for an inverse relation between reward and attitude change. Shortly after a clash between Yale students and the local police department, a number of Yale students were asked to write "forceful essays" defending the actions of the New Haven police. They were told that a large research institute needed the essays to substantiate the police officers' versions of the incident and that the firm would pay them for their services. Students were offered $.50, $1.00, $5.00, or $10.00 to write the essays. A matched control group neither wrote an essay nor received a reward.

After the essays were completed, the students' attitudes toward the police were assessed. As Figure 5.1 shows, the lower the reward, the greater the attitude change in favor of the New Haven Police,[13] a result in line with the dissonance prediction that increasing the amount of external reward will decrease the need for dissonance reduction.[14]

Sponsorship

A more subtle prediction made by dissonance theory relates to the characteristics of the sponsor or source who induces counterattitudinal behavior. Given two sources, one perceived as attractive and the other as unattractive, dissonance theory predicts that the unattractive sponsor will facilitate greater attitude change following a successful inducement of counterattitudinal actions. We return here to the issue of justification and consonance. A positive source provides external justification for counterattitudinal advocacy. Lying to save one's family or a best friend from embarrassment or hurt is a consonant symbolic act. However, lying at the request of a person one dislikes violates self-expectations. If one lies in this instance, it must be justified internally by coming to see the inherent "reasonableness" of the falsehood.

A series of studies, commonly called the "grasshopper experiments," demonstrated the superiority of unattractive sponsors in facilitating self-persuasion. Zimbardo, Weisenberg, Firestone, and Levy conducted one such study. The subjects were college ROTC members and a primary experimental object was to get them to eat fried grasshoppers. It was argued that, as future military men, they would probably be faced with the necessity of eating many exotic foods in combat and in training for combat, and so they should begin to get used to unusual food. Half of the subjects listened to a positive communicator whose manner was warm, friendly, and relaxed. The other half heard a negative communicator who conducted himself in a cold, unfriendly, brusque manner. Both speakers were presented as equally capable, conscientious, well organized, and industrious. Moreover, the subjects were not coerced into complying with either communicator's request.

Results showed that about one-half of the men in each group sampled the fried grasshoppers, indicating that each speaker was adept at inducing counterattitudinal behavior. However, the men's attitudes toward grasshoppers in terms of taste, quality, and willingness to try them in the future differed radically. About 55 percent of the men who ate grasshoppers at the request of the negative communicator showed a positive attitude change toward the food, but only 5 percent of those in the other group showed a liking for grasshoppers. Results also diverged on a measure of the subjects' willingness to endorse grasshoppers as a food in a field manual. In the negative communicator condition, 37 percent of the men wrote strong endorsements, but only 11 percent did so at the request of the positive communicator.[15]

This and other research[16] demonstrate that so long as a person feels that he or she has freely chosen a counterattitudinal behavior, a negative communicator will be more effective than a positive one in creating cognitive realignment.

Effort

Conventional wisdom suggests "we come to love that for which we suffer." Indeed, many practices in our society reflect a commitment to this notion. Initiations into social organizations, such as college fraternities and sororities, usually involve the performance of tasks that are unpleasant and degrading. In a similar vein, religious orders emphasize sacrifice, self-denial, work for the faith, and the promise of few earthly rewards. When applied to the theory of cognitive dissonance, the notion that suffering increases our devotion to that for which we suffer suggests that the more difficult it is to advocate a counterattitudinal message, the greater the attitude change will be. A substantial expenditure of effort is simply inconsistent with disbelief in the value of the object of one's effort.

A number of experiments have confirmed this effect. For example, Aronson and Mills invited women subjects at the University of Texas to participate in a discussion

TABLE 5.1: EVALUATION OF THE DISCUSSION GROUP

	Control	Mild initiation	Severe initiation
Discussion	80.2	81.8	97.6
Participants	89.9	89.3	97.7

Note: The higher the mean, the more positive the evaluation.

group on sexuality. Before they could join, they were told that they must undergo a screening test as an initiation into the group. The experimenter implied strongly that the test might be embarrassing for some of the subjects. At this point, some of the women were given a list of obscene words and lurid descriptions of sexual activity and asked to read the material aloud. Other subjects were given a mild script containing ordinary words like *petting* and *prostitute*. Finally, a control group worked on an irrelevant initiation task. After the initiation, all of the subjects were asked to listen to a discussion by the group they were about to join. The discussion focused on the rather unexciting topic of "secondary sex behavior in the lower animal," and was deliberately contrived to be boring and incoherent.

After the presentation, the women were asked to rate the quality of the discussion and how interesting they found the participants. Table 5.1 shows that as the severity of initiation increased, so did the subjects' positive evaluation of the group and its partici- pants.[17] Generally, the amount of effort involved in a counterattitudinal behavior has strong positive effects on attitude change. Of the examples of successful counterattitu- dinal persuasion we have considered so far, the case of Patty Hearst, who was kid- napped, blindfolded, and kept locked in a small closet for two weeks, is most reflective of some of the cognitive consequences of suffering.

Consequences and Responsibility

Much dissonance research suggests that maximal attitude change follows counter- attitudinal advocacy when people believe their messages will result in unwanted or undesirable consequences. In such a case, advocates should feel personally responsible for the negative effects of their actions.[18] Thus, if I tell a lie knowing that my behavior will harm someone I love, I should experience more discomfort than if I believe my lie will be inconsequential. Significant self-expectancy violation should occur when un- wanted consequences result from an action, but if one does not feel responsible for any negative outcomes, expectancy violation should be lower.

Cooper and Worchel explored this effect by asking subjects to perform a series of extremely dull tasks, including turning pegs on a pegboard and removing spools from trays.[19] After performing the tasks, the subjects were asked to tell groups waiting to be tested that the tasks were actually very interesting. One-half of the subjects were led to believe they had convinced the waiting subjects with their lie, and that all of them were very much looking forward to the experiment. The other half were told that the waiting subjects still felt the upcoming tasks would not be much fun. Results showed that the subjects responsible for undesirable effects changed their attitudes significantly more in the direction of their discrepant statements than did those who felt their lies had not succeeded.[20] Later research has shown that unwanted consequences do not actually have to result from counterattitudinal advocacy. It is only necessary that the counterattitudinal advocate expect or foresee that unwanted consequences are likely to ensue.[21]

A Critical Appraisal of Dissonance Theory

Dissonance theory was the first model for examining counterattitudinal advocacy and has produced more extensive research than any other theoretical perspective. At the same time, it has generated a substantial amount of criticism that, in turn, has led to other theories of counterattitudinal advocacy. Before exploring some of these, let's examine the more serious flaws in the dissonance explanation of counterattitudinal advocacy.

First, the central assumption of dissonance theory is unduly simplistic. Dissonance theorists assume that an inconsistency between internal cognitions and overt behavior is the *only* reason for attitude change following counterattitudinal advocacy. The content of counterattitudinal arguments is considered irrelevant. Many dissonance theorists base their position on the finding that a simple commitment to make a counterattitudinal statement, without following through with the overt process, is sufficient to induce attitude change.[22] However, this finding is ambiguous since the effects of anticipatory, covert arguing following commitment are not taken into account. Even so, dissonance theorists argue that message content is irrelevant since independent raters typically find no differences in the credibility of counterattitudinal messages producing attitude change and those that do not.[23] But it must be pointed out that independent judges cannot assess the self-persuader's view of the credibility of his or her messages. Indeed, Bokaken and his associates found that when counterattitudinal advocates evaluate the persuasiveness of their *own* messages, positive attitude change shows a high, direct correlation with their perceptions of the credibility of their own arguments.[24]

The dissonance explanation of counterattitudinal advocacy boils down to an inconsistency between the two cognitions, "I believe X," but "I said Y." This simplification has led Natalia Chapanis and Alphonse Chapanis to argue that "to condense most complex social situations into two, and only two, simple dissonant statements represents so great an abstraction that the model no longer bears any reasonable resemblance to reality."[25] We support this view. Although psychological inconsistency may be a powerful motivator, the content of a person's cognitions is critical to the effects of counterattitudinal advocacy. Some alternative theories also assume that the generative forces responsible for cognitive realignment cannot be reduced to psychological inconsistency alone. Among other things, they suggest that goal-satisfying message content is a powerful mediator of the effects of counterattitudinal self-persuasion.

A second major problem with dissonance theory is its use of a circuitous methodology. Dissonance researchers rarely make an effort to verify independently that their subjects experienced dissonance. Instead, they use the dependent variable, attitude change, as an after-the-fact sign of the presence or absence of dissonance.[26] If positive attitude change occurs after an individual engages in counterattitudinal advocacy, the experimenter often concludes that dissonance was, in fact, created and was responsible for the effect. However, if no attitude change occurs, the researcher assumes that dissonance was not created. Such circular reasoning shields the researcher from considering other reasons for the persuasive effects of counterattitudinal advocacy. For example, rather than altering attitudes to restore psychological consistency, the counterattitudinal advocate may learn new ways of satisfying goals from the content of self-constructed messages.[27]

Because of its circuitous methodology, dissonance theory is immune to disconfirmation. When the actual creation of a dissonant state is not verified, any failure to confirm a dissonance prediction can be "explained away" as a failure to create dissonance.[28] The failure of many researchers to determine the counterattitudinal advocate's *reasons* for attitude change is a serious methodological shortcoming with considerable conceptual import. Indeed, the difficulty of verifying an internal state of dissonance has led to the development of theories that abandon all reference to internal motivators of attitude change following counterattitudinal advocacy.

A third problem with dissonance theory is that it suffers from what some writers have called "empirical shrinkage."[29] Years of research have shown that the theory is applicable to an exceedingly limited area of human behavior. As we found earlier, for the dissonance explanation to apply to counterattitudinal advocacy, the following conditions must be present: (1) the advocate must perceive free choice; (2) little or no reward can be given for the advocacy; (3) the advocate must put considerable effort into the task; (4) the sponsor of the advocacy must be unattractive; and (5) negative consequences must result from the advocacy.[30] It is unlikely that one will find a great many naturally occurring persuasive situations where these five minimal prerequisites for the creation of dissonance are present. Thus, the practical value of dissonance theory for the student of persuasion is questionable.

Dissonance Theory and Rule-Related Behavior

As a final point, we need to evaluate dissonance theory from our rules-based view of persuasive communication. Conceptually and methodologically, dissonance theory departs considerably from our perspective on the nature of human responses to messages. First, the dissonance approach is a causal laws explanation of purposive or intentional action. The essence of the explanation is that inconsistency *causes* dissonance that, in turn, *causes* cognitive restructuring or attitude change. We have already expressed agreement with Chapanis and Chapanis that this is an unduly simplistic account of human responses to self-generated messages.

Second, dissonance theorists take a mechanistic view of humans, regarding them as relatively passive creatures: selective attention, interpretation, and cognitive processing of the content of self-generated counterattitudinal messages are considered irrelevant. And as we have already seen, the methodology employed by most dissonance researchers is mechanistic. It fails to verify subjective discomfort on the part of counterattitudinal advocates, and does not determine the *reasons* counterattitudinal advocates choose to alter their attitudes following inconsistent statements.

Although dissonance theory departs in many ways from our view of human behavior, several aspects of it are consistent with our perspective. First, its axioms are essentially rules based: (1) people desire consistency in their psychological world; and (2) inconsistency motivates them to take actions to restore harmony or consonance. These two axioms are in essence a rule since they stipulate a goal and the classes of actions one must take to achieve that goal. Second, Aronson's modification of Festinger's view is compatible with ours. Recall that Aronson stipulated that discomfort results, not from inconsistency, but from the violations of self-expectancy rules. It is unfortunate that dissonance theorists have only given lip service to his notions, preferring instead to emphasize Festinger's view that psychological inconsistency causes persuasive effects.

Finally, it may be useful to summarize our own view of the generative forces responsible for cognitive realignment following counterattitudinal advocacy. We believe that the effects of counterattitudinal advocacy are inextricably related to the content of self-generated messages. By generating arguments for positions one does not support, a person discovers positive *reasons* for accepting a new viewpoint. The interpretation and internalization of these reasons or goal–action links lead to attitude change following counterattitudinal advocacy.

THE INCENTIVE THEORY OF
COUNTERATTITUDINAL ADVOCACY

In contrast to dissonance theory, *incentive theory* emphasizes the motivational value of the content of counterattitudinal messages. The development and learning of new arguments or reasons for accepting counterattitudinal positions is regarded as the primary instigator of self-persuasion, not inconsistency between beliefs and behavior. According to incentive theorists, like Milton Rosenberg, Irving Janis, and Bernard Gilmore, when a person improvises arguments in favor of a discrepant point of view, "he becomes . . . motivated to think up all the good positive arguments he can, and at the same time suppresses thought about the negative arguments. . . . This 'biased scanning' increases the chances of acceptance of the new attitude position."[31] Furthermore, "the strength and stability of new cognitions [generated by producing counterarguments] are influenced among other things, by the degree of reward received for their improvisation."[32]

Incentive theory departs radically from the dissonance model in its view of the effects of reward on attitude change. Incentive theory suggests that providing rewards or things an advocate perceives as goal-satisfying stimulates acceptance of counterattitudinal arguments or reasons. Rewards or incentives may take the form of monetary payments, an attractive sponsor, the expectation that positive consequences will result from one's advocacy, and so forth.

Rosenberg conducted one of the first experiments demonstrating the positive effect of reward on counterattitudinal self-persuasion. He replicated Cohen's experiment in which Yale students were induced to write essays defending the New Haven Police Department after a student–police clash but used a different essay topic. He had Ohio State University students write counterattitudinal essays arguing that Ohio State's foot-

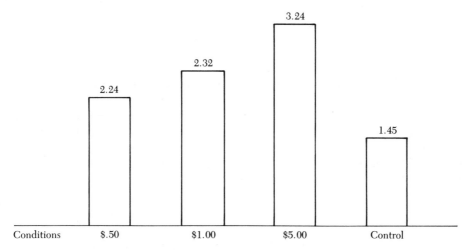

FIGURE 5.2   Mean attitude change toward nonparticipation in the Rose Bowl

ball team should not participate in the Rose Bowl. The issue was as timely as Cohen's topic since the faculty council of Ohio State had just rejected an invitation to the Rose Bowl on the grounds that it was demeaning to the academic reputation of the University. This action had outraged the student community. Similar to Cohen's study, advocates were offered either $.50, $1.00, or $5.00 for performing the essay-writing task.

The results of this experiment, shown in Figure 5.2, were the reverse of Cohen's. The students receiving $5.00 changed their views significantly more than those who received less money. Furthermore, Rosenberg found that subjects showing the most attitude change rated their *own* essays as stronger and more convincing than did students registering less cognitive change.[33] These findings, of course, lent considerable credence to the incentive interpretation of counterattitudinal advocacy.

Incentive versus Dissonance Theory

Initially, these starkly conflicting findings between incentive and dissonance studies might tempt one to lose faith in the experiment as a method of research. However, a closer examination will show the conflict is more apparent than real, that the incentive and dissonance approaches to counterattitudinal advocacy are actually complementary, not contrary. This complementariness exists because the boundary conditions under which one can expect a dissonance effect are quite different from those where an incentive effect is likely.

Assuming that people have a perception of choice to generate messages, a low reward should produce greater attitude change than a large reward; that is, a dissonance effect should occur under conditions like the following: (1) people perceive their counterattitudinal act will have undesirable consequences; and (2) the sponsor is perceived as unattractive. To clarify: under adverse conditions like those just specified, a person who lies for little or no reward should come to believe the lie far more readily than a person who, under the same conditions, lies for a high reward. In the latter case, the large reward provides an external excuse. People can claim it was at least partially responsible for a harmful act, performed freely for an unattractive sponsor. A low reward provides no such external excuse. Thus, a person justifies a harmful act by coming to believe it was not harmful at all.

In contrast, a large reward should produce greater attitude change than a low reward, that is, an *incentive* effect should occur when the consequences of advocacy are perceived as positive, or at least not harmful to others, the sponsor is attractive and well liked, and so forth. These incentives are all consonant with counterattitudinal behavior, and no discomfort or dissonance should be experienced. Indeed, these incentives should facilitate the learning and internalization of new arguments or reasons for the acceptance of a counterattitudinal position.

Some Supportive Research

A significant body of research supports this complementary view of dissonance theory and incentive theory. Let's examine the issue of consequences. When a person who freely chooses to generate a counterattitudinal message feels that undesirable consequences will result, a low reward should produce the greatest attitude change. Choosing to hurt a person for no external compensation is a dissonance-producing action. However, if one believes that either no damage or positive effects will result from a counterattitudinal message, no discomfort should occur; and external reward should facilitate learning from the counterattitudinal arguing.

An experiment conducted by Nel, Helmreich, and Aronson supports our complementary view of dissonance and incentive theories. These researchers selected female college students who opposed the legalization of marijuana and asked them to make a video tape arguing for its legalization. They were offered either $.50 or $5.00 for making the tape. One group was told that their tape would be played to a group of uninformed students who held no strong opinions about the marijuana issue. A second group was told their tape would be played to students who had very strong pro and con opinions on the subject. Thus, the first group anticipated negative consequences since they expected to argue against their convictions before a highly persuasible audience. The second group expected no such consequences since they believed their audience had already made up their minds on the issue. The researchers predicted a dissonance effect in the neutral audience condition and an incentive effect when the audience held strong opinions. Results supported these predictions: only in the neutral audience condition did the $.50 reward have a significantly greater effect than the $5.00 reward in producing favorable attitudes toward the legalization of marijuana.[34]

The complementary nature of incentive and dissonance theory may be illustrated further by examining research that focuses on the *sponsor* of counterattitudinal advocacy. Lying for little or no reward at the request of a disliked sponsor should produce dissonance and a growing belief in one's lie. However, lying for a friend or one's family should produce no dissonance since one can rationalize that the act helped a loved one. In the latter case, a reward should facilitate learning counterattitudinal arguments.

Elms and Janis confirmed this effect by offering subjects either $.50 or $10.00 to argue for an international exchange program requiring some American students to study for four years in a Soviet university. One group of subjects was told that the essays were requested by the U.S. State Department, and another group believed they would be arguing at the request of the Soviet government. Results showed that the large reward facilitated attitude change when the sponsor was attractive. However, when the sponsor was the Soviet government, the trend was for the small pay to produce more attitude change.[35]

This research confirms our earlier argument that dissonance and incentive theory are not contradictory approaches. It suggests that under conditions promoting cognitive inconsistency, such as speaking at the request of a disliked source and knowledge that one's actions will cause harm to others, dissonance occurs. On the other hand, if the sponsor is well liked and if a person feels that consequences will be beneficial, dissonance probably will not occur. In such a circumstance, adding positive incentives should prompt a sincere and open-minded examination of one's counterarguments, and self-persuasion should result from learning the content of self-produced messages.

Some Practical Implications

Whether one should use dissonance or incentive theory techniques depends on the conditions in which one operates. For example, in a circumstance where the source is well liked and no undesirable consequences are expected, an incentive approach will be preferred. In a reverse situation dissonance techniques should yield the best results.

However, a combination of the techniques suggested by the two theories can be used in most self-persuasion situations. Recall from Chapter 1 our presentation of the factors that led to Patty Hearst's conversion. Although the consequences of adopting the SLA's philosophy were generally negative, Hearst perceived SLA members as attractive Robin Hoods, feeding the poor with what they stole from the rich. Thus, the situation lent itself to self-persuasion as a function of dissonance and to self-influence as a result of learning the positive features of the SLA's philosophy. Such usually is the case.

A Critical Appraisal of Incentive Theory

The incentive interpretation of counterattitudinal advocacy clearly is more compatible with our own view than is the dissonance paradigm. Incentive theory is an implicit rules-based approach since it assumes people adopt new ways of believing and behaving because they perceive them as rewarding or goal satisfying. It regards people as active agents who seek to maximize rewards and minimize punishments.

Despite its compatibility with our view, incentive theory, like dissonance theory, applies a methodology that is mechanistic in many respects. For instance, incentive researchers rarely try to determine the specific goals the counterattitudinal advocate perceives as rewarding. Rather, a priori assumptions usually are made about rewarding and punishing stimuli. This problem reflects the failure of many researchers to conduct basic naturalistic research before applying the experimental method to problems of interest.

Despite its mechanistic overtones, incentive theory suggests, as does our own perspective, that people actively learn new reasons or rules from self-generated messages and then adopt attitudes consonant with the newly learned rules.

A SELF-PERCEPTION THEORY OF COUNTERATTITUDINAL ADVOCACY

Unlike incentive theory, self-perception and dissonance theories agree that a low reward facilitates attitude change following counterattitudinal advocacy. Theoretical differences between dissonance and self-perception theories lie in the motivational basis each theory claims for cognitive realignment. The motivational basis of dissonance theory is psychological discomfort resulting from inconsistent cognitions. In contrast, self-perception theory assumes the basis for attitude change following counterattitudinal advocacy is an external process whereby people infer their attitudes from their behaviors. According to Daryl Bem, "Individuals come to 'know' their own attitudes, emotions, and other internal states by inferring them from observations of their own overt behavior and/or the circumstances in which this behavior occurs."[36]

In the case of counterattitudinal advocacy, self-perception theory holds that the advocate observes himself or herself exerting substantial effort to generate messages for little or no reward, in an atmosphere of free choice, with possible negative consequences, and the like. On the basis of this behavioral act and the accompanying circumstances, rather than dissonance reduction, the advocates infer they must believe what they said. Bem contends that people come to know their own attitudes in much the same way as an outside observer: both make attitudinal inferences from the same evidence, consisting of discrepant statements made under circumstances consistent with the truth of the statements.

Research Supporting Self-Perception Theory

There is considerable evidence supporting Bem's notion. For example, consider the elementary school child of above average ability who consistently gets poor grades and is called a "dummy" by classmates. Frequently, such a child will infer from these external cues that he or she is, in fact, stupid. On the other hand, the child of equal ability who is encouraged by the teacher and supported by peers usually develops a healthy self-concept and performs accordingly.

Bem conducted a series of experiments to test his view of the motivational basis for attitude change following counterattitudinal advocacy. He replicated a number of dissonance experiments, including Cohen's study of Yale students induced to defend the local police department. Following counterattitudinal advocacy, he found that outside observers attributed exactly the same attitude to the advocates that they attributed to themselves.[37] In a more direct test of the self-perception interpretation, Bem and

McConnell conducted a "dissonance" experiment in which counterattitudinal advocacy took place and then subjects were asked to recall their initial attitudes before reporting changed attitudes. The researchers found that nearly 75 percent of the subjects believed their initial attitudes were roughly the same as their postadvocacy attitudes. In short they simply perceived that no attitude change had taken place.[38]

On the basis of this evidence, Bem and McConnell argued that dissonance is not a viable explanation of attitude change. Since there was no perceived inconsistency between the subjects' initial attitudes and later attitudes, they argued that, by definition, there could have been no dissonance. Bem and McConnell concluded their discussion of these attitude recall studies on a conciliatory note. "Dissonance theory," they said, "is not embarrassed by the finding that subjects failed to recall their initial attitudes. In fact," they noted, "it could be argued that forgetting an earlier conflicting attitude is itself a mode of dissonance reduction." They summarized their view by stating that just as dissonance advocates prefer their interpretation of these effects, "our preference for the self-perception explanation in these cases is, perhaps, no less a matter of taste."[39]

A Critical Appraisal of Self-Perception Theory

Although the dissonance and self-perception interpretations of counterattitudinal advocacy have long been regarded as competing theories, considerable evidence suggests that is not the case. Self-perception theory appears to be far more relevant to creating new attitudinal schemata and reinforcing presently held schemata than to attitude alteration.[40] Indeed, some critics suggest that self-perception theory cannot appropriately be applied to matters of counterattitudinal advocacy. The principal support for this criticism comes, surprisingly, from Bem himself. In developing his theory, Bem argues that individuals infer their attitudes from their overt behavior *only* when "internal cues are weak, ambiguous, or uninterpretable."[41] In the case of counterattitudinal advocacy, the advocate, by definition, holds strong internal attitudes that are contrary to his or her behavior.

However, even if we grant that self-perception theory is applicable to counterattitudinal advocacy, we believe it has serious limitations as an explanation for attitude change. In our judgment, Bem's often-quoted self-perception statement, "I am always eating brown bread, therefore I must like it,"[42] ignores an essential factor involved in the process of coming to like brown bread. If one truly likes brown bread, we believe such a liking is motivated either by an appreciation of its taste, a belief in its nutritional value, a fondness for the shape of the loaf, or a positive evaluation of some other characteristic inherent in brown bread!

Following this analogy, we believe that if attitude change following counterattitudinal advocacy is to be real and persistent, the advocate must come to accept or internalize the reasons, or warnings and mendations, that inhere in the content of his or her counterattitudinal message. As with the dissonance explanation, we believe that the self-perception account of counterattitudinal advocacy is too simplistic. In short, the generative forces at work in counterattitudinal advocacy are far more complex than the "saying-is-believing" explanation Bem posits. His disregard of the content of self-generated messages is contrary to our view of persuasive communication as is his view of people as passive reactors inferring new attitudes from actions.

THE IMPRESSION MANAGEMENT THEORY
OF COUNTERATTITUDINAL ADVOCACY

In our discussion of dissonance theory, we found that dissonance occurs when a person freely chooses to generate a discrepant message producing undesirable social consequences. This definition implies that counterattitudinal advocacy must be a social or *public* act with *harmful consequences* for those people exposed to it. These features of dissonance theory are critical to an understanding of the impression management explanation of counterattitudinal self-persuasion.

James Tedeschi and his associates propose that attitude change following counterattitudinal advocacy is not a result of intrapsychic dissonance, but rather a reflection of the advocate's desire to maintain a public image of consistency for the benefit of others.[43] According to this impression management view, people want to appear consistent because it conveys an image of stability and credibility. By bringing attitudes into line with behavior, one can present a consistent public identity. However, Tedeschi argues that publicly stated attitudes following advocacy are seldom the opposite of people's initial positions. Rather, if we put attitude change on a continuum, the advocate tends to shift toward the counterattitudinal position, frequently settling around the neutral point, but usually remaining on the pro rather than the counterattitudinal side. This moderation toward the counterattitudinal position fosters an impression of consistency, without the advocate having to totally abandon the initial stance.

According to Tedeschi, this moderation also achieves a second impression management goal. He maintains that advocates are often concerned that people who witness their behavior will attribute responsibility and blame them for choosing to harm others. Consequently, when postadvocacy attitudes are reported publicly, the advocate equivocates and indicates only a mild belief in the counterattitudinal stand, allowing him or her to seem consistent but also permitting a partial denial that any real harm to others was meant.[44]

A final feature of impression management theory concerns the persistence of attitude change following counterattitudinal advocacy. Although dissonance, incentive, and self-perception theories regard attitude change as real and often permanent, impression management theory interprets attitude change following advocacy as insincere verbal statements intended to mend a spoiled public identity.

Research Supporting Impression Management Theory

Gaes, Kalle, and Tedeschi conducted several experiments to test their notion that impression management goals are the primary motivators of attitude moderation following advocacy. Subjects were asked to write an essay arguing that toothbrushing is harmful to dental health. To create the expectancy of negative consequences, subjects

TABLE 5.2: MEAN ATTITUDE CHANGE TOWARD
"TOOTHBRUSHING IS HARMFUL"

Response mode	Public	Anonymous
Pencil and paper	3.00_a	1.75_b
Bogus pipeline	1.95_b	2.05_b
Control group	1.65_b	1.97_b

Note 1: All scores were on a 7-point scale, with 4 the neutral point,
1 the pro-attitudinal extreme, and 7 the counterattitudinal extreme.

Note 2: Means with different subscripts differ from one another at
the statistical significance level of $p < .05$.

From Gaes, Kalle, and Tedeschi, 1978, p. 500. Reprinted by
permission.

were told that their essays would be given to five classes of junior high school students,
and that another five classes would receive essays promoting toothbrushing. Moreover,
subjects were told that a six-month, follow-up study was expected to show that the
students persuaded by their essays would suffer more cavities and dental problems
than the comparison group.

Some of the subjects were identified publicly with their counterattitudinal statements by the requirement that they sign their essays. The other group was asked to
use fake names so that their identities would be unknown. In addition to the public–
anonymous variation, one-half of the subjects reported their pre- and postadvocacy
attitudes by filling out a self-report scale, a common "pencil and paper" method used
in most dissonance experiments. The other half reported their attitudes through a "bogus pipeline" procedure, a lie detector–type apparatus that had previously been found
to encourage the sincere expression of inner feelings.[45]

The results, shown in Table 5.2, support the impression management explanation
of counterattitudinal self-persuasion. A significant moderation in attitudes toward the
counterattitudinal essays occurred only when the advocacy was public and when subjects presumably felt they could get away with lying, that is, they were not attached to
the bogus lie detector. Consistent with Tedeschi's argument that postadvocacy attitudes
are equivocal, the greatest reported attitude change, an average of 3 points, approached neutrality but remained on the pro, rather than counterattitudinal, side of
the issue.[46]

Whether the attitude change reported in this experiment was real or was insincere
and temporary, as Tedeschi and his colleagues maintain, is not clear. They took no
delayed measure. Given this omission, it is possible to argue that although immediate
attitude change may well serve an "insincere" impression management function, it can
eventually become internalized, resulting in persistent attitude alteration. Beyond this
experiment, other research has been quite supportive of the impression management
interpretation of counterattitudinal advocacy. For instance, using the template matching procedure, discussed in Chapter 4, Bem and Funder found impression management theory to be a significantly better predictor of the effects of advocacy than the
dissonance approach.[47]

A Critical Appraisal of Impression Management Theory

A primary criticism of impression management theory has to do with its claim that attitude change following advocacy inevitably is insincere and temporary. Indeed, a good argument can be made that the desire to maintain a positive and consistent self-image is not so capricious and impermanent a goal as Tedeschi would have us believe. Rather, the desire to appear consistent to others is deeply ingrained in all of us. *Wishy-washy, whimsical,* and *indecisive* are derogatory terms we reserve for persons who present an inconsistent public image. Moreover, our ongoing self-concept is in large measure a function of how others see us. Like Alice, we all have our looking glasses and what we see in them are usually the eyes of important others. Research and common sense support the notion that self-presentational goals are powerful motivators. Indeed, such goals are at the heart of many well-established theories of human behavior.

It should be clear that impression management theory is an explicit rules-based approach to persuasion. It emphasizes that image-maintenance goals are powerful motivators for cognitive alteration. Moreover people are treated as active agents, taking those actions they perceive as personally rewarding and avoiding those threatening punishment. Impression management theory is compatible with our own view of the nature of human action in general, and persuasive behavior in particular.

Aside from a compatibility with our own theoretical biases, impression management theory has added several important dimensions to our understanding of counterattitudinal advocacy. First, impression management theorists caution us not to assume automatically that attitude change following advocacy is either real or persistent. As socially conscious beings, when in Rome, we often do as the Romans do, only to change our behavior in other social contexts. Second, impression management theory has underscored what is often overlooked in dissonance, incentive, and self-perception research: the magnitude of attitude change following counterattitudinal acts. Advocacy does *not* lead immediately to a reversal of one's world view or even to the complete change of a single important cognitive schema. As impression management theorists point out, it promotes attitudinal *shifts*, frequently small shifts, that over time can reverse an attitude or change one's view of the world.

Finally, impression management theory has emphasized the hazards of relying on *public* advocacy alone to produce meaningful attitude change. Although overt arguing is a valuable stimulant to self-persuasion, it is our view that the ongoing production of covert, supportive messages is crucial to any lasting persuasive effects. This view implies that counterattitudinal persuasion is a rule-governed process wherein the advocate internalizes over time the reasons contained in his or her counterattitudinal messages.[48]

NOTES

1. This information was taken from Stephen Worchel and Joel Cooper, *Understanding Social Psychology* (Homewood, Ill.: The Dorsey Press, 1979), pp. 115–116.

2. Philip G. Zimbardo, E. B. Ebbesen, and Christina Maslach, *Influencing Attitudes and Changing*

Behavior, 2nd ed., © 1977, Addison-Wesley Publishing Company, pp. 19, 184–189. The experiences of the Stanford student are reprinted by permission.

3. William D. Crano and Lawrence A. Messé, "When Does Dissonance Fail? The Time Dimension in Attitude Measurement," *Journal of Personality* 38 (1970): 493-508.

4. William A. Watts, "Relative Persistence of Opinion Change Induced by Active Compared to Passive Participation," *Journal of Personality and Social Psychology* 5 (1967): 4–15.

5. Elaine Walster and Ellen Berscheid, "The Effects of Time on Cognitive Consistency," in *Theories of Cognitive Consistency: A Sourcebook*, ed. Robert P. Abelson et al. (Skokie, Ill.: Rand McNally, 1968), pp. 599–608.

6. Robert A. Wicklund and Jack W. Brehm, *Perspectives on Cognitive Dissonance* (Hillsdale, N.J.: Lawrence Erlbaum, 1976), p. 138.

7. Leon Festinger, *A Theory of Cognitive Dissonance* (Evanston, Ill.: Row, Peterson, 1957).

8. Ibid., p. 13.

9. Eliot Aronson, "Dissonance Theory: Progress and Problems," in *Theories of Cognitive Consistency: A Sourcebook*, pp. 5–27.

10. See Festinger, *A Theory;* and Robert P. Abelson, "Modes of Resolution of Belief Dilemmas," *Journal of Conflict Resolution* 3 (1959): 343–352.

11. Harold H. Kassarjian and Joel B. Cohen, "Cognitive Dissonance and Consumer Behavior," *California Management Review* 8 (1965): 55–64.

12. Darwyn E. Linder, Joel Cooper, and Edward E. Jones, "Decision Freedom as a Determinant of the Role of Incentive Magnitude in Attitude Change," *Journal of Personality and Social Psychology* 6 (1967): 39–45.

13. Arthur R. Cohen, "An Experiment on Small Rewards for Discrepant Compliance and Attitude Change," in *Explorations in Cognitive Dissonance*, ed. Jack W. Brehm and Arthur R. Cohen (New York: John Wiley, 1962), pp. 73–78.

14. The first experiment to establish this relationship was Leon Festinger and James M. Carlsmith, "Cognitive Consequences of Forced Compliance," *Journal of Abnormal and Social Psychology* 58 (1959): 203–210.

15. Philip G. Zimbardo et al., "Communicator Effectiveness in Producing Public Conformity and Private Attitude Change," *Journal of Personality* 33 (1965): 233–255. Other "grasshopper" experiments include Ewart E. Smith, "The Power of Dissonance Techniques to Change Attitudes," *Public Opinion Quarterly* 25 (1961): 626–639; and Ewart E. Smith, "Methods for Changing Consumer Attitudes: A Report of Three Experiments," Project Report, Quartermaster Food and Container Institute for the Armed Forces. PRA Report 61-2, 1961.

16. See Joel Cooper, John M. Darley, and James E. Henderson, "On the Effectiveness of Deviant and Conventionally Appearing Communicators: A Field Experiment," *Journal of Personality and Social Psychology* 29 (1974): 752–757.

17. Eliot Aronson and Judson Mills, "The Effects of Severity of Initiation on Liking for a Group," *Journal of Abnormal and Social Psychology* 59 (1959): 177–181. Replications of this experiment include John Schopler and Nicholas Bateson, "A Dependence Interpretation of the Effects of Severe Initiation," *Journal of Personality* 30 (1962): 633–649; and Harold B. Gerard and Grover C. Mathewson, "The Effects of Severity of Initiation on Liking for a Group: A Replication," *Journal of Experimental Social Psychology* 2 (1966): 278–287. The Gerard and Mathewson experiment was a carefully controlled replication of Aronson's and Mill's study, involving the use of electric shock rather than embarrassment as the source of initiation severity. This change was instituted in response to criticism directed against the original experiment by Natalia Chapanis and Alphonse Chapanis. They argued that the increased liking expressed by the "severe" initiates in Aronson's and Mill's study may have reflected a sense of relief at having completed an embarrassing exercise, rather than

the claimed arousal of dissonance as a function of initiation effort. See Natalia P. Chapanis and Alphonse Chapanis, "Cognitive Dissonance: Five Years Later," *Psychological Bulletin* 61 (1964): 4–5.

18. For a full discussion of the implications of the foreseeability of consequences and personal responsibility for the creation of dissonance, see Wicklund and Brehm, pp. 51–71.

19. These procedures were modeled after those used by Festinger and Carlsmith. See Festinger and Carlsmith.

20. Joel Cooper and Stephen Worchel, "Role of Undesired Consequences in Arousing Cognitive Dissonance," *Journal of Personality and Social Psychology* 16 (1970): 199–206.

21. See George R. Goethals, Joel Cooper, and Anahita Naficy, "Role of Foreseen, Foreseeable, and Unforeseeable Behavioral Consequences in the Arousal of Cognitive Dissonance," *Journal of Personality and Social Psychology* 37 (1979): 1179–1185; and Joel Cooper, "Personal Responsibility and Dissonance: The Role of Foreseen Consequences," *Journal of Personality and Social Psychology* 18 (1971): 354–363.

22. See Jack W. Brehm and Arthur R. Cohen, *Explorations in Cognitive Dissonance* (New York: John Wiley, 1962), pp. 254–255; and Jacob M. Rabbie, Jack W. Brehm, and Arthur R. Cohen, "Verbalization and Reactions to Cognitive Dissonance," *Journal of Personality* 27 (1959): 407–417.

23. For examples, see J. Merrill Carlsmith, Barry E. Collins, and Robert C. Helmreich, "Studies in Forced Compliance: The Effect of Pressure for Compliance on Attitude Change Produced by Face-to-Face Role Playing and Anonymous Essay Writing," *Journal of Personality and Social Psychology* 4 (1966): 11; and E. Tory Higgins, Frederick Rhodewalt, and Mark P. Zanna, "Dissonance Motivation: Its Nature, Persistence, and Reinstatement," *Journal of Experimental Social Psychology* 15 (1979): 32.

24. For example, see Edward M. Bodaken et al., "Role Enactment as a Socially Relevant Explanation of Self-Persuasion," *Human Communication Research* 5 (1979): 203–214.

25. Chapanis and Chapanis, p. 21.

26. There are a few exceptions to this general conclusion. See for examples, Gerald R. Miller, "A Crucial Problem in Attitude Research," *Quarterly Journal of Speech* 53 (1967): 235–240; and Gary L. Cronkhite, "Autonomic Correlates of Dissonance and Attitude Change," *Speech Monographs* 33 (1966): 392–399.

27. See Chapanis and Chapanis for a discussion of several plausible explanations for attitude change following counterattitudinal behavior other than the reduction of dissonance.

28. For a discussion of other serious methodological problems associated with dissonance experiments, see Chapanis and Chapanis.

29. See Alice H. Eagly and Samuel Himmelfarb, "Current Trends in Attitude Theory and Research," in *Readings in Attitude Change*, ed. Samuel Himmelfarb and Alice Hendrickson Eagly (New York: John Wiley, 1974), p. 597.

30. A number of writers argue that the five conditions we have discussed are not the only ones required for the creation of dissonance. For discussions of other probable prerequisites, see Higgins et al., 1979; and Mark P. Zanna and Joel Cooper, "Dissonance and the Pill: An Attribution Approach to Studying the Arousal Properties of Dissonance," *Journal of Personality and Social Psychology* 29 (1974): 703–709.

31. Irving L. Janis and J. Bernard Gilmore, "The Influence of Incentive Conditions on the Success of Role Playing in Modifying Attitudes," *Journal of Personality and Social Psychology* 1 (1965): 17–18.

32. Milton J. Rosenberg, "When Dissonance Fails: On Eliminating Evaluation Apprehension from Attitude Measurement," *Journal of Personality and Social Psychology* 1 (1965): 41.

33. Ibid., pp. 28–42.

34. Elizabeth Nel, Robert Helmreich, and Eliot Aronson, "Opinion Change in the Advocate as a Function of the Persuasibility of His Audience: A Clarification of the Meaning of Dissonance," *Journal of Personality and Social Psychology* 12 (1969): 117–124.

35. Alan C. Elms and Irving L. Janis, "Counter-Norm Attitudes Induced by Consonant versus Dissonant Conditions of Role-Playing," *Journal of Experimental Research in Personality* 1 (1965): 50–60.

36. Daryl J. Bem, "Self-Perception Theory," in *Advances in Experimental Social Psychology*, ed. Leonard Berkowitz (New York: Academic Press, 1972), p. 2.

37. Daryl J. Bem, "An Experimental Analysis of Self-Persuasion," *Journal of Experimental Social Psychology* 1 (1965): 199–218.

38. Daryl J. Bem and H. Keith McConnell, "Testing the Self-Perception Explanation of Dissonance Phenomena: On the Salience of Premanipulation Attitudes," *Journal of Personality and Social Psychology* 14 (1970): 23–31.

39. Ibid., p. 31.

40. For evidence supporting this conclusion, see Russell H. Fazio, Mark P. Zanna, and Joel Cooper, "Dissonance and Self-Perception: An Integrative View of Each Theory's Proper Domain on Application," *Journal of Experimental Social Psychology* 13 (1977): 464–479; and Chapter 6 of this book.

41. Bem, "Self-Perception Theory," p. 2.

42. Bem, "An Experimental Analysis," p. 200.

43. James T. Tedeschi, Barry R. Schlenker, and Thomas V. Bonoma, "Cognitive Dissonance: Private Ratiocination or Public Spectacle?" *American Psychologist* 26 (1971): 685–695; and James T. Tedeschi, Gerald G. Gaes, and L. Silverman, "Impression Management Theory and the Forced Compliance Paradigm," unpublished MS, State University of New York at Albany, 1976.

44. Tedeschi, Gaes, Silverman.

45. For examples, see Barbara Quigley-Fernandez and James T. Tedeschi, "The Bogus Pipeline as a Lie Detector: Two Validity Studies," *Journal of Personality and Social Psychology* 36 (1978): 247–256; and Richard A. Page and Martin K. Moss, "Attitude Similarity and Attraction: The Effects of the Bogus Pipeline," *Bulletin of the Psychonomic Society* 5 (1975): 63–65.

46. Gerald G. Gaes, Robert J. Kalle, and James T. Tedeschi, "Impression Management in the Forced Compliance Situation: Two Studies Using the Bogus Pipeline," *Journal of Experimental Social Psychology* 14 (1978): 493–510. Reprinted by permission of Academic Press, Inc.

47. Daryl J. Bem and David C. Funder, "Predicting More of the People More of the Time: Assessing the Personality of Situations," *Psychological Review* 85 (1978): 485–501.

48. It should be noted that the three alternative explanations of counterattitudinal advocacy we have covered are not the only ones available. Others include role enactment theory, functional theory, and response contagion theory. For discussion of these three approaches, respectively, see Charles R. Berger, "Toward a Role Enactment Theory of Persuasion," *Speech Monographs* 39 (1972): 260–267; Reuben M. Baron, "Attitude Change through Discrepant Action: A Functional Analysis," in *Psychological Foundations of Attitudes*, ed. Anthony G. Greenwald, Timothy C. Brock, and Thomas M. Ostrom (New York: Academic Press, 1968), pp. 297–326; and Jozef M. Nuttin, Jr., *The Illusion of Attitude Change: Toward a Response Contagion Theory of Persuasion* (London: Academic Press, 1975). These perspectives were not discussed since they are less well-developed conceptually and have a smaller body of supporting research than incentive, self-perception, and impression management theories.

CHAPTER 6

Attribution Processes and Self-Persuasion

In July 1974, the Judiciary Committee of the House of Representatives brought Articles of Impeachment against President Richard M. Nixon for obstruction of justice, abuse of power, and contempt of Congress. After reviewing relevant documents and tape recordings, the Committee was convinced the President had participated in a criminal scheme to cover-up the June 1972 burglary of the Democratic National Committee headquarters in the Watergate Hotel and Office Complex. Although the Committee and much of the American public believed Mr. Nixon was guilty as charged, all evidence suggests he perceived himself quite differently.

Theodore White, in his account of the fall of Richard Nixon, reports that during the final days of his presidency, Mr. Nixon often listened to the tapes that incriminated him in the Watergate cover-up scheme, but simply did not "hear" the incriminating evidence. "He really thought he was innocent," one Nixon aide reported, and "that was the problem." White continues that Mr. Nixon had

> lost track of the truth—about himself, about the facts, about the nature of the crime charged to him. His composure, it seemed to anyone who had watched for twenty years, was real—he had persuaded himself . . . that . . . he could clear himself of penalty for what . . . had escalated into a Constitutional crisis.[1]

Thus, the nation was convinced of Mr. Nixon's complicity in criminal activity, but Mr. Nixon himself honestly believed to the end of his presidency that he was "not a crook." Indeed, months after his resignation from office, Mr. Nixon continued to argue publicly that his motive in Watergate was not criminal, but only political containment.

This account highlights the issue we will consider in this chapter: the ways people persuade themselves by assigning or attributing reasons for their actions. Mr. Nixon perceived the reasons for his behavior in the Watergate scandal to be political containment, not criminal conspiracy and, thus, was able to persuade himself that he had committed no offense against the law or the American people. That his self-perception differed radically from the views of others did not shake his faith in his own innocence. Clearly, the self-attribution of reasons for our behavior can be a potent self-persuader. In this chapter, we will explore the nature of self-attribution theory, discuss the implications of attribution processes for self-persuasion, and examine three persuasion models that are mediated by self-attribution processes.

THE NATURE OF ATTRIBUTION THEORY

Attribution theory was first discussed by Fritz Hieder in his 1958 book, *The Psychology of Interpersonal Relations*.[2] Hieder speculated on the ways that people, called "observers," try to understand the behavior of others, termed "actors." He and other attribution theorists like Harold Kelley[3] and Edward Jones[4] argue that when we try to make sense of another's behavior, we act like naive social scientists. We scrutinize the environment, including people's actions and the setting where the actions occur, and proceed to search for causes or reasons for the behavior. Upon discovering a plausible reason or cause, we attribute others' behavior to it.

The potential reasons or causes used to explain the behavior of others fall into two general classes: *situational* or external factors; and *dispositional* or internal reasons. *Situational factors* are all those events in the social or physical environment having the potential to prompt a behavior. In contrast, *dispositional reasons* are stable factors within each individual like beliefs and feelings that are sufficient to produce an action. For example, if we hear that a kidnap victim or a political hostage has espoused publicly the views of his or her captors, we usually attribute that behavior to situational constraints. We assume the individual was coerced into the performance of the behavior and that, therefore, the action did not reflect the captive's true beliefs or feelings. However, if the same individual expressed the same views in a noncoercive setting, we would probably attribute the behavior to dispositional or internal factors. We would assume that since the individual spoke freely, that is, without external constraints, the statement represented the person's true beliefs.

In general, attribution theory suggests that we scan the environment for information to explain another's behavior. That behavior may be attributed to situational or dispositional factors.

Self-Attribution Processes

Hieder's original analysis has been extended to include self-attributions as well as attributions concerning the behavior of others. Attribution theorists like Daryl Bem,[5] whose self-perception theory we discussed briefly in Chapter 5, and Kelley[6] contend that we explain our own behavior in much the same way that we attribute reasons for others' behavior. We scrutinize the environment, including our own behavior and the setting where it occurs, and infer reasons for our actions. These reasons may be situational or dispositional. If environmental cues suggest our actions are externally constrained, we infer that the behavior is not relevant to our private attitudes. In contrast, if environmental evidence clearly indicates that our behavior is not constrained by forces beyond our control, we infer we acted because of a belief in the rightness of the behavior.

For example, if I tell my employer that I support some company policy because I fear his or her stern disapproval if I do not, I likely will see that behavior as dictated by situational constraints. However, if I espouse the same position when such situational pressure does not exist, I will probably conclude that my behavior was prompted by a belief in the value of the policy I have supported.

If we elaborate a bit on the Watergate scandal, we can see that Mr. Nixon could explain his behavior by referring to external constraints such as the need for political containment, the need to protect national security, and the need to maintain the confidentiality of presidential communications. Or he could attribute it to the need to hide his participation in criminal activity. The House Judiciary Committee and a large segment of the American public attributed his actions to a dispositional force, presidential guilt, yet Mr. Nixon perceived his actions were forced on him by external factors. Consequently, he avoided inferring that his actions had any relevance to his private attitudes and ethics and, thus, was highly resistant to evidence pointing to his personal guilt.

As these examples indicate, self-attribution or self-perception theory assumes that to a large extent we rely on environmental evidence, including our own behavior and the context in which it occurs, to infer internal attitudinal structures. The theory considers that each of us "is functionally in the same position as an outside observer . . . who must necessarily rely upon . . . external cues to infer . . . inner states."[7] From this perspective, much of our behavior is not under the control of our private cognitive schemata. Indeed, attribution theory suggests that many of our attitudinal schemata are formed and controlled by our overt behavior and the environmental context where it occurs. Its relevance for self-persuasion derives from the assumption that our perception of situational cues, including our own actions, has the potential to create, reinforce, and alter our attitudes.

Causes versus Reasons for Behavior

Before discussing the implications of attribution processes for persuasion, we must look at the issue of attributing causes versus reasons for our own and others' behavior. Although we have argued throughout this book that *most* social behavior is prompted by goals or reasons, this does not imply that we always *attribute* such behavior to reasons.

Often we attribute our own behavior, especially actions with negative implications, to causes beyond our control. Indeed, when we make situational attributions for our behavior, it is usually because we feel we were forced to perform certain actions. Likewise, we often attribute the behavior of others to causes and not to reasons. When we observe people publicly supporting the "company line," we often assume they have little choice but to do so, that some external force, such as the need to keep a job, caused the person's actions. In contrast, dispositional attributions are usually based on reasons. If we see ourselves or others behaving freely, we assume the actions are meant to achieve certain objectives or goals.

As this discussion suggests, we attribute both causes and reasons for our behavior and the behavior of others. Furthermore, our attributions may have no relation, or only an incidental one, to the *actual* nature of the generative force prompting a behavior. Indeed, we often attribute causes to behavior that is actually reason based, particularly when looking at our own actions. If, for example, we perform an act we regret, we may excuse ourselves by rationalizing that we really had no choice but to behave as we did. Conversely, we may attribute "reasons" for behavior that is actually caused by some antecedent condition. For example, we sometimes attribute others' delinquent or criminal behaviors to reasons: criminals are evil or they commit crimes for monetary gain or to get others' attention. In actuality, such behavior may reflect mental disturbances or an uncontrollable physiological condition.

Despite the imperfect fit between attributions and reality, Allan Buss has offered some guidelines for determining what kinds of behaviors are usually attributed to causes rather than reasons, and vice versa. According to him, we attribute reasons to what we perceive as *actions*, defined as consciously controlled, intentional behaviors. In contrast, causes are attributed to *occurrences*, defined as physiologically related, unwilled behavior that a person "suffers." Buss cites blushing, perspiring, emotional arousal, nervousness, and other physiological conditions as occurrences and nonphysiological, social behavior such as expressions of attitudes and decision making as actions.[8]

Although Buss' analysis is useful, the process of attributing reasons or causes of behavior is still a highly subjective process.[9] Though we are more likely to make causal attributions for physiological conditions, it is not always so. For example, we often assume that blushing, a physiological phenomenon, is actually an intentional device designed to portray naiveté and innocence. Moreover, as we indicated earlier, highly intentional actions are often explained away as unwilled or coerced behavior.

Given the highly subjective nature of the attribution process, we will henceforth make no attempt to identify attributions as either reason based or causal. However, we will assume that most dispositional attributions are reason based and that causal explanations predominate in situational attributions. We will refer to these dispositional and situational factors as reasons and causes, respectively. Nevertheless, the reader should be aware that when we use the labels *cause* and *reason*, we are not implying that the attribution discussed is necessarily causal or reason based.

Attribution Processes and Self-Persuasion

For the student of persuasion, a critically important question is: What kinds of human actions are most influenced by self-attribution processes? Clearly, not all of our attitudinal schemata are based on perceptions of our own behavior and associated environmental cues. As we saw in Chapter 2, much of our cognitive schematic structure bears little relation to our perceptions and interpretations of occurrences in the social or physical environment. We also found in Chapter 2 that the relationship between cognitive schemata and behavior is reciprocal. Not only can behavior shape attitudinal structures, but attitudes also exert a powerful effect on human actions as well. The immediate issue before us, then, relates to the conditions under which behavior and associated situational cues have the power to shape a person's attitudinal schemata.

Research confirms that self-attribution processes facilitate two forms of persuasion: (1) *the formation of new attitudinal schemata* in those cases where a person's attitudes are weak, ambivalent, or nonexistent; and (2) the *reinforcement and intensification of presently held attitudes*. In the latter case, self-attribution processes can strengthen existing cognitive structures, making them more resistant to change later on. It is important to note that these two forms of persuasion are quite different from counterattitudinal advocacy (see Chapter 5). In the case of counterattitudinal self-persuasion, we were concerned with theoretical perspectives on attitude *alteration*, that is, changing a person's attitude from pro to con or from con to pro on a target issue. In this chapter, our focus is on the creation and reinforcement, not the alteration, of human attitudinal schemata.

As to the creation of stable, cognitive schemata, Bem has argued that we rely almost exclusively on external evidence to infer what we believe when our "internal cues are weak, ambiguous, or uninterpretable."[10] Thus, if I hold no strong, internal attitudes, my own actions and relevant situational variables constitute my only source of information about my feelings and beliefs. In such a situation, overt behavior should strongly influence the formation of attitudes. In contrast, if I have strong attitudes, I need not rely on external variables to tell me what I believe. In this case, attitudinal schemata will shape overt behavior far more than behavior will determine attitudes.

The following example illustrates how attitudes may be created by observing overt behavior and associated external cues. When a new product is marketed, potential consumers are not likely to have stable attitudes about it. Positive attitudes toward the new merchandise can often be created by getting customers to try it. Offering free samples, low introductory prices, or discount coupons can achieve that goal. Once a customer has tried the new product, there is a good chance that he or she will develop a positive attitude toward it and continue to purchase it in the future. In such a situation, we may conclude that an attitude has been formed on the basis of overt behavioral acts.

Not only can new attitudes be created by observing external cues, but presently held attitudes can be strengthened or reinforced by behavioral acts and associated situational cues.[11] For example, suppose I object to the use of nuclear power as an energy source. My attitude is likely to be strengthened considerably if I participate in an antinuclear rally or write a letter to my congressman expressing my views. On the basis of these actions, I should see myself as having much stronger attitudes than if I remain an armchair opponent of nuclear power. This changed perception, in turn, should reinforce preexisting attitudes.

We must emphasize that attribution processes cannot alter attitudes. If I support nuclear power, attending an antinuclear rally should not prompt me to infer that I am, in fact, against its use. As Mark Zanna and Charles Kiesler have argued, the large discrepancy between attitudes and such behavior "should make it implausible [for persons to conclude] that their behavior was in any way a reflection of their beliefs."[12] Only when overt behavior is perceived as a reflection of beliefs can we expect self-persuasion on the basis of that behavior and associated environmental cues. Clearly, self-attribution processes have far more relevance for proattitudinal than for counterattitudinal behavior.

A Model of Self-Attribution and Persuasion

For attribution processes to facilitate self-persuasion, people must be induced to attribute their behavior to *dispositional* factors; they must come to believe that their actions reflect underlying feelings and beliefs. The persuasive paradigm suggested by this attribution process is a two-stage model. First, someone must be induced to act. The overt behavior may be a verbal statement in support of some position advocated by a persuader. For example, ministers frequently encourage their church members to reaffirm their faith periodically through public prayer and testimonials before the assembled congregation. Or the induced behavior may be nonverbal actions like accepting a free sample of a new product or agreeing to donate money to a charity, a political candidate, or some other cause promoted by a persuader.

The second stage of the persuasion process requires that environmental cues be arranged in such a way that the actor will infer that the behavior reflects underlying attitudes. Suppose a person has been induced to donate money to a charity. To facilitate the inference that the donation reflects a positive attitude toward the charity, a persuader may employ a number of strategies. For instance, the persuader must insure the individual did not feel pressured into the behavior. If pressured, the individual will attribute the behavior to situational constraints, having no relevance to a belief in the value of the charity. Further, the persuader may outline all the positive consequences resulting from a donor's contribution. The donor's perception that he or she is responsible for beneficial effects should foster a true belief in the charity. Generally, this stage of the attribution persuasive process is accomplished by reducing the salience of situational constraints so that people will persuade themselves that actions were prompted by a belief in the rightness of the behavior.

Factors Promoting Dispositional Self-Attributions

Since attribution processes facilitate self-persuasion only when people attribute behavior to dispositional factors, we need to examine those variables that increase the probability of that happening. But first, we must note a major impediment to inducing dispositional self-attributions.

This problem concerns an important difference between the way we view the reasons for our own behavior and our perception of others' behavior. There is a pervasive tendency for people to attribute much of their own behavior to situational constraints, but to attribute the behavior of others to dispositions.[13] In other words, we hold others responsible for their actions, but regard our own behavior as at least partially forced on us by circumstances beyond our control. This tendency is most prominent when our behavior has negative overtones.

Nevertheless, there are many factors predisposing us to dispositional self-attributions. Five of these variables are especially important to the student of persuasion.[14] First, we tend to claim personal responsibility for our actions when they produce desirable consequences.[15] For example, when people's behaviors benefit others, they are likely to persuade themselves that the behavior reflected truly held beliefs and attitudes. However, if a person's actions have negative outcomes, the tendency is to look for situational causes for the behavior to avoid a sense of responsibility for the unfortunate consequences.

Second, when a behavior is repeated in a variety of social situations, the probability of making dispositional self-attributions increases.[16] For example, suppose I support the rights of women to choose to end unwanted pregnancies by abortion. If someone persuades me to volunteer to work in a pro-abortion counseling clinic and to speak out publicly in opposition to a Constitutional ban on abortion, I will probably infer that my attitude toward abortion is stronger than if I perform a single act in a single social setting.

Third, dispositional self-attributions are more likely to occur when situational constraints are seen as weak or nonexistent.[17] In this case, an individual is likely to conclude that an action was performed freely and infer that the behavior reflects personal beliefs. For instance, suppose someone is paid a lot of money to do an advertisement for a product or political cause. The action can easily be seen as a result of the external monetary inducement. However, if the individual performs for no salary and is not coerced, there is a good chance that he or she will decide the behavior reflects attitudes. The consequence should be a more positive attitude change toward the product or cause endorsed.

Fourth, dispositional self-attributions are more likely to occur when environmental cues imply that a behavior is consistent with one's attitudes.[18] In this regard, the reactions of others to a person's behavior are important. Suppose, for example, I make a statement supporting a cause I believe in. If feedback is positive and supportive, implying that my statement was well presented and credible, that I seemed sincere in my convictions, and the like, my initial attitude is likely to be reinforced.

Fifth and finally, dispositional attributions are more likely to occur the more time there is between the performance of a behavior and the assignment of a reason for the action.[19] As time passes, people find it more difficult to recall subtle situational constraints that may have influenced their initial behavior. As a result, they infer greater personal responsibility for their behavior and assume that it was motivated by internal beliefs and attitudes. For example, suppose that a person, at the strong urging of a friend, tries a new product or attends a public rally. Initially, the person may conclude that he or she acted because of social pressure. However, as time passes, this situational constraint recedes in memory, and there is an increasing chance that the person will decide he or she acted freely on the basis of genuinely held beliefs and feelings.

In summary, dispositional self-attributions are more likely to occur when an action produces positive consequences and is continually repeated in a variety of social situations. Futhermore, the absence of apparent external constraints on the behavior, the presence of environmental cues implying one's behavior is consistent with attitudes, and the passage of time increase the probability that dispositional self-attributions will be made. In discussing specific self-attribution models of persuasion, we will refer to many of these factors.

THREE ATTRIBUTION MODELS OF SELF-PERSUASION

Let's examine three attribution models of self-persuasion aimed either at creating or reinforcing attitudes: (1) the foot-in-the-door paradigm; (2) proattitudinal advocacy; and (3) a two-factor model of emotional attribution.

THE FOOT-IN-THE-DOOR PHENOMENON
AND SELF-PERSUASION

Anyone who has encountered door-to-door salespersons probably is familiar with the *foot-in-the-door phenomenon*. The essence of the technique is to get potential customers to comply with an initial small request—to accept a free sample, to try out a service for a short introductory period, to chat for a few minutes about the product or service that is for sale—then later to ask for a larger commitment, like the purchase of a product or service.

This strategy is used not only by salespersons, but also by religious, political, and charitable organizations. Frequently such groups initially ask for small contributions to their cause. For instance, a political candidate may ask potential voters to buy buttons, automobile bumper stickers, and other campaign paraphernalia. Once a small commitment is made, it is easier to persuade people to make larger, more demanding contributions like donating time and money to a cause.[20]

The most commonly accepted explanation for the success of the foot-in-the-door phenomenon is self-attribution theory. When people see themselves acting without any strong external pressure, they infer that the behavior has relevance for their beliefs. Moreover, compliance elicits the self-perception of a doer, a person who is active and involved. This changed self-perception increases the likelihood that the person will be responsive when greater demands are made later on.

Freedman and Fraser first demonstrated the efficacy of the foot-in-the-door phenomenon in a field experiment during the mid-1960s. The participants in the study were 112 residents, mostly females, of Palo Alto, California. They were contacted by a representative of either one or the other of two bogus organizations: the "Community Committee for Traffic Safety" and the "Keep California Beautiful Committee." In the case of the traffic safety issue, some of the residents were asked to place "Be a Safe Driver" stickers in the windows of their homes. Other residents were asked to sign a petition promoting safe driving. When the contacting organization was the "Keep California Beautiful Committee," residents were asked either to place "Keep California Beautiful" stickers in their windows or to sign a "Keep California Beautiful" petition. Finally, a control group was not asked for any initial favor.

Two weeks after the initial requests were made, a representative of a group called "Citizens for Safe Driving" appeared at the door of each resident and made a rather bizarre request. All residents were asked if they would agree to place on their lawns a very large, poorly lettered sign reading "Be a Safe Driver." The residents were told the sign would obscure much of the front of their homes, would have to remain for over a week, and when removed, would leave a rather large hole in their front yard. Only 16.7 percent of the control group complied with the second request. However, 55.7 percent of the residents who had been asked for an initial favor agreed to put the sign on their lawns.

Surprisingly, there were no differences in compliance rates among any of the experimental groups. The type of initial action (petition versus sticker) and the nature of the issue (driving safety versus environmentalism) made no difference in the final outcome. The compliance rates generalized equally in all four conditions to the later, larger request.[21] This result suggests that compliance with any initial request may be sufficient to induce people to see themselves as active individuals who support good causes.

These findings have important implications for charitable and service organizations as well as salespersons. By employing the foot-in-the-door strategy, these groups ought to increase contributions and sales. Because of its promise, we should examine some of the factors that increase the probability this strategy will promote self-persuasion.

Three Factors Promoting the Foot-in-the-Door Strategy's Success

First, the foot-in-the-door technique works best when a target person has weak attitudes or is generally favorable toward the cause related to the request. The strategy has been especially effective on such proattitudinal or weak attitudinal issues as safe driving, environmentalism, support for human service organizations and medical charities, household consumerism, and traffic control laws.[22]

In contrast, the strategy works poorly when people have strong negative attitudes toward the issue for which the initial request is made. For example, Foss and Dempsey found that it was relatively ineffective in soliciting blood donations, an action that was particularly noxious to a large number of potential donors.[23]

A second issue affecting the success of the foot-in-the-door technique concerns the size of the initial request. Generally, it must be sufficiently large to prompt people to infer that the action is relevant to their beliefs and self-images, but not so large as to result in noncompliance. For example, Seligman, Bush, and Kirsch asked 112 adults to respond to a telephone survey on the energy crisis and inflation. They varied the size of the initial requests by asking individuals to answer either a 5-, 20-, 30-, or 45-question survey. Two days later, all the subjects were called again and asked to answer a 55-question survey. The compliance rates for the 5-, 20-, 30-, and 45-question surveys were 38.1 percent, 34.8 percent, 73.7 percent, and 73.9 percent, respectively.[24] The researchers concluded that "compliance with the first request will generalize to compliance with future requests only when the first request is large enough to motivate the individual to make the appropriate dispositional inference."[25]

Apparently, an exceedingly small, initial request is so trivial that people will infer it has no relevance to underlying beliefs. On the other hand, the initial request must not be so large or troublesome that people will refuse to comply with it. In the latter case, self-attribution theory predicts that individuals will infer that they are firm, non-compliant persons who do not do favors for others, and this inference should make them less likely to comply with subsequent requests. Snyder and Cunningham demonstrated this by asking some residents of Minneapolis to respond either to an average-length telephone questionnaire or to a survey sufficiently long and detailed as to virtually guarantee noncompliance. Two days later, all residents were asked to take an additional survey. Results showed that 51.9 percent of the subjects who had been approached with the moderate initial request responded to the second survey. In contrast, only 21.9 percent of those who had been asked to respond to the cumbersome initial survey did so.[26]

Third and finally, the foot-in-the-door strategy is likely to be effective only when little or no external inducement is provided for compliance. If people perceive that they have complied just to get the requester "off their backs," or conversely, because the requester rewarded them, they will probably attribute the behavior to situational factors, not to dispositions. In this case, initial compliance should not facilitate future compliance.

Uranowitz investigated the effects of external justification on initial compliance. Of the people given little or no external inducement to comply with an initial request for help, 80 percent complied with a second request. In contrast, when individuals were given a large external inducement to comply initially, only 45 percent complied with a later request.[27]

In summary, the foot-in-the-door strategy of self-persuasion is likely to be most effective when little or no external inducements are given for complying with an initial request, when the initial request is moderate rather than very small or very large, and when the target person either favors or has few attitudes regarding the issue relevant to the initial request.

PROATTITUDINAL ADVOCACY AND SELF-PERSUASION

We have emphasized throughout this chapter that attribution processes promote self-persuasion effectively when an individual's behavior is compatible with his or her basic attitudes. In this section, we will consider the persuasive effects of *proattitudinal advocacy*, commonly defined as publicly arguing for any attitudinal position falling within one's latitude of acceptance.[28] *Latitude of acceptance* consists of a person's attitude with respect to an issue plus all contiguous, attitudinal positions regarded as generally acceptable.[29]

To illustrate this notion, suppose I favor legal abortion when the physical well-being of a woman is threatened by pregnancy. Although this position is most acceptable to me, I will probably find other attitudes tolerable. For instance, I may accept the more extreme position that abortion is also justified when pregnancy threatens mental health. In addition, I may agree that abortion should be an option in the case of pregnancy because of rape or incest. On this or any other issue, most people find several attitudes of varying intensity compatible with their most preferred position.

When people argue before an audience for any position, including their own, falling within their latitude of acceptance, they are engaging in proattitudinal advocacy. By definition, then, proattitudinal advocacy is a public act. Typically, persuaders try to induce people to argue for positions that are stronger or more intense than their most preferred attitude. From the perspective of attribution theory, the advocacy of a more extreme position should "lead to a self-attributional inference that one holds that newly endorsed position."[30] In general then, the expected consequence of proattitudinal advocacy is the intensification or reinforcement of a person's initial attitude. Reinforcement should make attitudes more resistant to change and increase the likelihood that people will act on the basis of the strengthened cognitive schemata.

People rely on a variety of cues for inferring their attitudes when engaging in preattitudinal advocacy. Research by Wyer, Anderson, and others[31] suggests that at least four sources of information are employed in the self-attribution process. First, the proattitudinal advocate relies on his or her *prior experience,* including the knowledge that the advocated position is compatible with basic attitudes and past behaviors. Second, the advocate observes his or her own *behavior* while constructing the proattitudinal message. This encoding behavior has at least three dimensions: "the decision to deliver the speech, the preparation of arguments to be used in the speech, and the delivery of the speech."[32] Third, the advocate relies on the *audience's reactions* to the message, including feedback indicating whether listeners agree or disagree with the position being taken. Finally, all additional *environmental cues* relevant to the proattitudinal advocacy are used for inferring attitudes, including the amount of pressure exerted on the advocate to deliver the message, the consequences of delivering the message, and the like.

Clearly, the self-attribution of attitudes following proattitudinal advocacy is a more complex process than that involved in the foot-in-the-door phenomenon. It is more complex because proattitudinal advocacy entails the construction and presentation of messages in the presence of observers. Let's examine some variables affecting the success of this process. We will emphasize the impact of audience feedback and other environmental cues on proattitudinal advocacy.

Factors Promoting Proattitudinal Advocacy's Success

Five variables profoundly affect the success of self-persuasion following proattitudinal advocacy. Three of these relate to observers' reactions to proattitudinal messages, and the remaining two refer to situational factors not associated with audience feedback.

Observer Reactions

First, proattitudinal advocacy is most effective when audience feedback implies the message is seen as consistent with the advocate's true attitudes. Gross, Riemer, and Collins confirmed this by inducing 42 males to tape-record proattitudinal messages on the role of women in society. All subjects listened as their speeches were replayed to a four-person audience that provided one of three kinds of feedback: (1) sincere, "He really did believe what he was saying"; (2) insincere, "He really did *not* believe what he was saying"; and (3) no feedback. The results, displayed in Table 6.1, showed that advocates receiving positive feedback increased their commitment to the initial posi-

TABLE 6.1: MEAN ATTITUDE
CHANGE SCORES

Feedback condition	Mean scores
Sincere	1.36
No feedback	0.27
Insincere	−0.24

Note: The higher the mean, the greater the attitude change in the direction of the position advocated.

tion significantly more than advocates receiving no feedback. In contrast, advocates who were told they did not appear to believe their arguments experienced a decrease in commitment to the issue they had previously supported.[33]

Second, proattitudinal advocacy enhances self-persuasion when feedback indicates that the audience favors the advocated position. Wyer, Henninger, and Hinkle demonstrated this by having male and female students deliver live speeches on the topics of television and faith healing. Prior to preparing and delivering the messages, the students were told that their target audience either agreed or disagreed with the position they would be advocating. Results showed advocates speaking to a partisan audience strengthened their belief in their messages, but that attitude strength declined among advocates whose audience disagreed with their position.[34] The researchers concluded that individuals, like their observers, "appear to use the audience's opinion as a positive indication of [their own] belief."[35]

Third, proattitudinal advocacy strengthens attitudes most effectively when feedback indicates that a speech has been competently and skillfully performed. In this regard, Edward Deci has suggested that interest in and commitment to a task is enhanced when one feels competent at it. Further, he argues that rewarding an individual, contingent on successful performance of the task, increases interest and commitment.[36] Following this analysis, a number of researchers have confirmed that providing positive verbal feedback for successful performances significantly enhances people's interest in tasks they initially find enjoyable.[37]

Wallace applied this principle to persuasive communication by telling or not telling speakers that "the manner in which you gave your speech was considered superior." As expected, significantly greater attitude change occurred among speakers who were provided positive verbal feedback than among those who were not.[38] Scott further demonstrated the effects of positive verbal feedback in a debate setting by telling debaters either that they "won" or "lost" their debates. Results showed "winners" strengthened attitudes significantly more than did "losers."[39]

Situational Variables

Two final variables affecting the success of proattitudinal advocacy relate to environmental factors not associated directly with audience feedback. The first of these is the perceived consequences of advocacy. When consequences are positive, individuals develop stronger attitudes toward the message than when consequences are negligible or undesirable. This effect occurs, in part, because people tend to perceive themselves as good, as responsible for desirable outcomes. The final variable affecting the success of proattitudinal advocacy relates to the issue of perceived choice. We can expect proattitudinal encoding to be most effective when no external rewards or punishments are provided.

Deci argues that external rewards for proattitudinal advocacy have two different functions: the control of the advocacy behavior; and the communication of information about an individual's competence in performing the advocacy behavior. As we saw earlier, rewards, such as positive verbal feedback, enhance commitment to the advocated position because these rewards communicate information about the advocate's competence and skill. However, when a reward is offered *solely* for the execution of proattitudinal advocacy, Deci contends that it communicates no information about the advocate's competence. Rather, the external control function of the reward is salient. As a result, the advocate will attribute behavior to an external constraint, the reward, not to belief in message content.[40] If an advocate freely chooses to support a position he or she believes in, the advocacy should be perceived as internally motivated behavior. However, as Carl Benware and Deci note, "if a person espouses a position which he believes in and is paid for doing so, the perceived locus of causality will change from internal to external." As a consequence, "his attitude will become less favorable toward the espoused position."[41]

Benware and Deci confirmed this conclusion by having students deliver a proattitudinal message arguing strongly for student control of course offerings at their university. One group was paid $7.50 to perform the task, and the rest received no money. The proattitudinal advocates who were paid showed a decrease in agreement with the advocated position, while those who received no reward strengthened their belief in the proattitudinal issue.[42]

In summary, proattitudinal advocacy is most effective as a self-persuader when the advocate freely chooses to deliver a message and when the consequences of presenting the message are desirable. Moreover, proattitudinal advocacy should enhance self-persuasion when audience feedback implies the message was skillfully delivered, when the audience agrees with the advocated position, and when feedback indicates the advocate truly believes in the advocated cause.

An Alternative Interpretation of Proattitudinal Advocacy: Social Identity Theory

A number of theorists question the preceding explanation of the persuasive effects of proattitudinal advocacy. Barry Schlenker and others[43] argue that attitude reinforcement following proattitudinal behavior serves a public self-presentational or social identity function, that the generative force responsible for the persuasive effects of proattitudinal advocacy is not self-attribution from observation, but rather the desire to present a positive public image. *Social identity theory* (a variant of impression management theory covered in Chapter 5) holds that attitudes communicate important aspects of the self-concept, that most of us want to appear personally responsible for actions producing beneficial consequences and to be identified publicly with desirable and socially acceptable attitudes on important issues. Since proattitudinal advocacy is performed in the presence of an audience, it should be an ideal activity for projecting our preferred social identity and for taking responsibility for desirable consequences. As this description suggests, social identity theory is a rules-based explanation of proattitudinal advocacy.

Clearly, all the factors we have discussed that enhance proattitudinal self-persuasion are consistent with this rules-based self-presentational explanation. When advocates get audience feedback indicating agreement with their messages, they get praise for their rhetorical skills, and they learn that the audience believes them sincere, the public expression of a stronger attitude should serve a positive social identity function for advocates. Expressing a strong commitment to a proattitudinal position should allow one to take full responsibility for a behavior that is supported and praised by others. Moreover, maximal responsibility for one's behavior can be claimed when it is performed freely without external reward. Finally, when the advocacy results in desirable consequences, one's public image as a good person responsible for beneficial actions is enhanced.

A TWO-FACTOR MODEL OF EMOTIONAL SELF-ATTRIBUTION

As its name implies, the last model we will consider focuses on the ways we attribute to ourselves affective or emotional states like anger, fear, and happiness. You will recall from our discussion in Chapter 2 that attitudinal schemata consist of a set of beliefs along with a set of emotional or affective responses to the beliefs. These emotional responses give direction and intensity to attitudes. Thus, the self-attribution of emotions is highly pertinent to the formation and reinforcement of schematic structures. The two-factor emotional model is applicable both to the creation of new emotional states and the reinforcement of preexisting ones.

William James originated the self-attribution model of emotions. Almost a century ago, he set forth what then was considered a rather strange theory of emotion acquisition. He suggested that any human emotion can be separated into two components— affective and cognitive. The *affective* component consists of a surge of physiological arousal, and the *cognitive* dimension is comprised of bits of information in the environment, principally one's own behavioral responses. James argued that humans use their own behavior to infer their emotions. To use his illustration, if we see a bear rushing toward us, we first experience a surge of arousal and then we run away. Later, when we reflect on our behavior, we decide we were afraid. In James' view, we did not run because we were afraid, but rather we decided we were afraid because we ran.[44]

Seventy years after James promulgated this view of emotion, Stanley Schachter and Jerome Singer revised and extended his theory. Like James, they consider that an emotion consists of two factors: physiological arousal and a cognitive label for that arousal. They conceptualize an emotion mathematically as: E (emotion) = A (affect) × C (cognition). The multiplication sign indicates that if either the arousal or the cognitive label for it is absent, then there can be no reported emotion. Unlike James, Schachter and Singer believe that cognitive labels do not necessarily come from observing our own behavior. Rather, they argue that most cognitive labels come from observing environmental cues, especially the reactions of other people.

They contend that any time people experience an emotional arousal for which there is no clearly identifiable internal cause, they turn to environmental cues, especially others' behavioral responses, to infer the nature of their emotion. Moreover, they argue that people scan the environment in an open-minded, unbiased fashion. Thus, if I have some vague, unexplained arousal, I should observe the behavior of others to determine what I am feeling. If others are acting fearful and anxious, I will probably label my arousal *fear*. However, if others seem happy, I will probably label my arousal *happiness*. The basic premise underlying Schachter's and Singer's two-factor model of emotional attribution is that we rely on all available environmental cues to help us interpret ambiguous emotional arousal.[45]

Experimental Support

Schachter and Singer tested their two-factor model in an interesting study using male college students. The students were told that the research concerned the effects of a vitamin compound, "suproxin," on vision. Some of the students were injected with epinephrine, a drug causing increased heart rate and respiration, tremor, and feelings of flushing. Control subjects got a placebo. Some of the subjects receiving the epinephrine were told what physiological effects to expect. Others were led to believe the drug would cause no physiological effects. The control group was told correctly that they would experience no side effects. Thus, subjects informed of the physiological effects of epinephrine had an appropriate internal explanation for their arousal, but uninformed subjects did not. Presumably, the uninformed subjects would make an unbiased search of the environment for information they could use to label their unexplained arousal. The control group should experience no arousal and, thus, should have no reason for cognitive labeling.

After receiving an injection, each subject was asked to wait in a room for about twenty minutes in order to let "the suproxin get from the injection site into the bloodstream." At this point, another person who presumably had also gotten an injection was brought into the room to wait. This person was actually a confederate of the experimenters whose job was to exhibit either angry or euphoric behaviors in the presence of the subjects. Theoretically, subjects who were experiencing unexplained arousal would use this person's behaviors as cues for labeling their own emotional state.

In the euphoria condition, the confederate displayed signs of giddy happiness. He crumpled up pieces of paper into "basketballs" and threw them into wastebaskets, made and flew paper airplanes, and finally picked up a hula hoop that was lying on the floor and began playing with it. Throughout this routine, the confederate commented on how good he felt and occasionally asked the subject to join in the fun. In the anger condition, the confederate behaved quite differently. The anger routine started when the subject and the confederate were asked to fill out a long questionnaire. After

**TABLE 6.2: SELF-REPORTS AND BEHAVIORAL
INDICES OF EUPHORIA AND ANGER**

	Self-report index°		Behavioral index†	
	Euphoria	Anger	Euphoria	Anger
Informed	0.98	1.91	12.72	−0.18
Control	1.61	1.63	16.00	0.79
Ignorant	1.90	1.39	18.28	2.28

° The higher the score, the more positive the reported emotion. Thus, in the anger condition, lower numbers indicate greater anger, and in the euphoria condition higher numbers indicate greater happiness.

† The higher the score, the more euphoric or the more angry the observed behaviors.

complaining about getting an injection, the confederate started to work on the questionnaire that contained some rather personal and insulting questions. Eventually he became so angry about the questions that he ripped up the questionnaire and stormed out of the room.

During the twenty-minute period when the confederates displayed either euphoric or angry behaviors, a hidden observer scored the behaviors of the subjects in terms of the level of anger or happiness they exhibited. At the conclusion of the period, each subject completed a questionnaire indicating how angry or how happy he felt. The results, displayed in Table 6.2, generally confirmed Schachter's and Singer's prediction that individuals use the behavior of others to infer the nature of their own unexplained emotions. The subjects who knew why they were aroused were least affected by the behaviors of the confederates. They had no need to rely on situational cues to interpret their internal states.

In contrast, subjects who were ignorant of the cause of their arousal were most affected by the confederates' behaviors. In the euphoria condition, they reported the most positive emotions and engaged in the most euphoric behaviors. Subjects exposed to the anger condition reported the least positive emotions and displayed the most angry behaviors. Presumably, both groups used the confederates' behaviors as cues to label their own unexplained internal states. In conflict with Schachter's and Singer's prediction that individuals will use environmental cues to label internal states only when they are physiologically aroused, the control subjects who were told they would experience no physiological arousal were affected considerably by the confederates' behaviors, attributing to themselves either happy or angry emotions.[46] This finding raises the interesting possibility that individuals will often infer internal emotions even if they are *not* experiencing internal arousal.

A Theoretical Extension of the Two-Factor Model

Since Schachter's and Singer's original experiment, Christina Maslach, Gary Marshall, and Philip Zimbardo have introduced two important modifications into the two-factor model. First, they have suggested that individuals do not rely solely upon immediate situational cues to infer their feelings and beliefs. Rather, they theorize that people search their memories for reconstructed past events and comparable situational cues and infer their feelings on the basis of past as well as present environmental evidence. Second, Maslach, Marshall, and Zimbardo contend that individuals do not engage in an unbiased scanning of the environment to explain physiological arousal. Rather, these researchers see unexplained arousal as an unusual, disturbing, and even frightening experience akin to "free-floating anxiety." Such a state is always characterized by negative emotional affect. Thus, the search for an appropriate cognitive label for it usually is biased toward negative environmental cues. In several studies, they found strong confirmation for these hypotheses.[47]

In general, the results of the research and theorizing of Schachter, Singer, Maslach, Marshall, and Zimbardo indicate that people often do rely on past and present external information to decide what their internal feelings and attitudes are. When individuals lack an appropriate explanation for their internal states or when they have no clearly defined inner feelings, they will look to the environment, especially to the behaviors of others, to infer what they feel. The affective quality of an individual's internal state should determine the kind of environmental evidence he or she will attend to.

If a person's internal state is unpleasant or disturbing, he or she will scan the environment for negative cognitive labels for feelings. In contrast, if internal feelings are positive, individuals should look for positive environmental cues. Finally, if a person's internal state is affectively neutral, unbiased scanning should occur.

Implications of the Two-Factor Model for Self-Persuasion

The implications of the emotional attribution model for self-persuasion are relatively straightforward. Two uses of the model are apparent. First, if people experience either positive or negative arousal, they can be expected to infer their precise emotions by scanning environmental cues carrying the same valence as their arousal states. In the context of persuasive communication, arousal often occurs when people are in the presence of others. That others can produce physiological arousals, termed *social facilitation effects*, was demonstrated nearly a century ago by Triplett, who found that the presence of other people releases latent energy that individuals cannot release on their own.[48] Many years later, Zajonc confirmed that the presence of others does, in fact, produce a physiological arousal that enhances one's dominant, preexisting emotional state.[49] Thus, if an individual's underlying feelings are positive or negative the presence of others should augment either state.

Second, the emotional attribution model has implications for people who are not experiencing physiological arousal,, whose emotional reactions to some stimuli are weak, uninterpretable, or nonexistent. This situation occurs most often when individuals are being introduced to new and unfamiliar products or ideas. People are influenced in this context by the feelings and behaviors of other people. Recall Schachter's and Singer's unpredicted finding that control subjects experiencing no physiological arousal were considerably affected by the behaviors of the angry and euphoric confederates. Thus, *prior* emotional arousal is not necessary for individuals to infer an emotional state; they may do so merely by viewing other people who *are* aroused.

The persuasive strategies of advertisers and politicians operate quite successfully on this assumption. The use of personal endorsements for new products and candidates is a pertinent example. Early in most political campaigns, candidates go to great lengths to get the endorsements of prominent politicians; then they widely publicize their list of supporters. In a similar fashion, advertisers use celebrity endorsements and "man-on-the-street" commentaries to promote new products. It is important to note that these endorsements rarely convey cognitive information designed to foster beliefs about a candidate's programs or a product's qualities. Rather, they are designed to create a warm emotional reaction or a positive liking for the person or product being endorsed. The model of emotional attribution suggests that people will use the responses of attractive or well-known others to infer their own emotional reactions to new products and political candidates.

A CRITICAL APPRAISAL OF SELF-ATTRIBUTION THEORY

As the three models we have examined indicate, self-attribution theory assumes that individuals infer their attitudes from salient environmental cues, including their own behavior, the behavior of others, and the situational context in which behaviors occur. Most attribution theorists regard this process as essentially *passive*, as functionally equivalent to the way an uninvolved observer infers another person's attitudes. Herein lies a major criticism of self-attribution theory.

A number of writers have questioned whether the self-inference of attitudes from environmental evidence is as passive a process as attribution theorists assume. Social identity theorists reject the assumption outright, arguing that individuals actively evaluate the public implications of their behavior and adopt attitudes and take actions that present an appealing and socially responsible public image. They contend that self-attribution responses actually represent rule-governed actions.

Other theorists like Irving Janis and Leon Mann agree with social identity theorists and argue that people exercise considerable care in forming attitudes on the basis of situational information. They contend that when individuals must decide whether or not to perform an action or adopt an attitude, they engage in a sophisticated cognitive appraisal of at least four categories of information: (1) anticipated gains and losses for the self that will come from enacting the behavior or adopting the attitude; (2) anticipated gains and losses for significant others; (3) anticipated approval or disapproval from significant others; and (4) anticipated self-approval or disapproval.[50]

Commenting on the analysis of Janis and Mann, Shelley Taylor argues that a passive attribution process probably occurs only when attitudinal and behavioral issues are trivial and relatively inconsequential. In contrast, when people's attitudes and behaviors are consequential, they carefully evaluate anticipated personal and social gains and losses before inferring what they believe.[51]

These criticisms of self-attribution theory are entirely compatible with our own action-oriented, rules-based perspective on persuasion, a view of people as intentional agents, who consciously choose to maximize rewards and minimize losses. We find social identity theory and the cognitive decision-making theory of Janis and Mann appealing explanations. Moreover, when the relative merits of social identity and self-attribution theories have been tested experimentally, the rules-based explanation has fared better than the attribution account of the effects of environmental cues on beliefs and behavior.[52]

Despite these criticisms, self-attribution theory has broadened our understanding of the process of persuasive communication. First, it emphasizes the powerful influence of perceptions of environmental cues on attitude formation and reinforcement. In the attempt to stress people's self-directional qualities, rules-based theories, like our own, too often gloss over the real impact that interpretations of the external world have on human behavior. Indeed, a literal reading of many rules accounts of behavior often leaves the impression that humans are unfettered spirits inhabiting a world unconstrained by environmental exigencies. By systematically examining the effects of the perceived environment on human action, self-attribution theory points out that human choice and goal-related actions inevitably take place within boundaries that expand and contract as a function of people's perceptions and interpretations of their physical and social world. For that reason, it is a valuable contribution to our understanding of persuasive communicative behavior.

Second, despite its relatively passive view of people, self-attribution theory emphasizes the importance of reasons as motivators. Its essence is that people's attitudes are formed and controlled by the reasons they attribute to their own behavioral acts. When people believe that their behavior is motivated by internal goals, they adopt attitudes consistent with those goals. In contrast, goal-irrelevant, situational attributions have no impact on attitude formation and reinforcement. In this sense, self-attribution theory bears a kinship to rules-based approaches to persuasion. However, self-attribution theory assumes that reasons are after-the-fact justifications for behavior. Rules approaches, of course, regard reasons as *prior* motivators of goal-oriented actions. On this crucial point, the two theoretical approaches diverge.

NOTES

1. Theodore H. White, *Breach of Faith: The Fall of Richard Nixon* (New York: Atheneum Publishers, 1975), pp. 296–297.

2. Fritz Hieder, *The Psychology of Interpersonal Relations* (New York: John Wiley, 1958).

3. See Harold H. Kelley, "The Process of Causal Attribution," *American Psychologist* 28 (1973): 107–128; Harold H. Kelley, "Attribution in Social Interaction," in *Attribution: Perceiving the Causes of Behavior*, ed. Edward E. Jones, et al. (Morristown, N.J.: General Learning Press, 1972); and Harold H. Kelley, "Attribution Theory in Social Psychology," *Nebraska Symposium on Motivation*, ed. David Levine (Lincoln, Neb.: University of Nebraska Press, 1967).

4. See Edward E. Jones and Keith E. Davis, "From Acts to Dispositions: The Attribution Process in Person Perception," in *Advances in Experimental Social Psychology*, ed. Leonard Berkowitz (New York: Academic Press, 1965).

5. See Daryl J. Bem, "Self-Perception Theory," in *Advances in Social Psychology*, ed. Leonard Berkowitz (New York: Academic Press, 1972).

6. Kelley, 1967.

7. Bem, p. 2.

8. Allan R. Buss, "On the Relationship Between Causes and Reasons," *Journal of Personality and Social Psychology* 37 (1979): 1458–1461; and Allan R. Buss, "Causes and Reasons in Attribution Theory: A Conceptual Critique," *Journal of Personality and Social Psychology* 36 (1978): 1311–1321.

9. For discussions of the limitations of Buss' analysis, see John H. Harvey and Jalie A. Tucker, "On Problems with the Cause–Reason Distinction in Attribution Theory," *Journal of Personality and Social Psychology* 37 (1979): 1441–1446; and Arie W. Kruglanski, "Causal Explanation, Teleological Explanation: On Radical Particularism in Attribution Theory," *Journal of Personality and Social Psychology* 37 (1979): 1447–1457.

10. Bem, p. 2.

11. For a study demonstrating the use of attribution processes for strengthening attitudes, see Russell H. Fazio, Mark P. Zanna, and Joel Cooper, "Dissonance and Self-Perception: An Integrative View of Each Theory's Proper Domain of Application," *Journal of Experimental Social Psychology* 13 (1977): 464–479.

12. Mark P. Zanna and Charles A. Kiesler, "Inferring One's Beliefs from One's Behavior as a Function of Belief Relevance and Consistency of Behavior," *Psychonomic Science* 24 (1971): 283.

13. Edward E. Jones and Richard E. Nisbett, *The Actor and the Observer: Divergent Perceptions of the Causes of Behavior* (Morristown, N.J.: General Learning Press, 1971).

14. There are a number of variables other than the ones discussed here that predispose a person to make dispositional self-attributions. For discussions of some of these additional variables, see Kelley, 1972; and 1967.

15. Gifford Weary Bradley, "Self-Serving Biases in the Attribution Process: A Re-examination of the Fact or Fiction Question," *Journal of Personality and Social Psychology* 35 (1978): 56–71; and Linda Beckman, "Effects of Students' Performance on Teachers' and Observers' Attributions of Causality," *Journal of Educational Psychology* 61 (1970): 76–82.

16. Kelley, 1972; and 1967.

17. Mark R. Lepper, David Greene, and Richard E. Nisbett, "Undermining Children's Intrinsic Interest with Extrinsic Rewards: A Test of the 'Overjustification' Hypothesis," *Journal of Personality and Social Psychology* 28 (1973): 129–137; Edward L. Deci, "Intrinsic Motivation, Extrinsic Reinforcement and Inequity," *Journal of Personality and Social Psychology* 22 (1972): 113–120; and Edward L. Deci, "Effects of Externally Mediated Rewards on Intrinsic Motivation," *Journal of Personality and Social Psychology* 18 (1971): 105–115.

18. Alan E. Gross, Barbara S. Riemer, and Barry E. Collins, "Audience Reaction as a Determinant of the Speaker's Self-Persuasion," *Journal of Experimental Social Psychology* 9 (1973): 246–256; and Charles A. Kiesler, Richard E. Nisbett, and Mark P. Zanna, "On Inferring One's Beliefs from One's Behavior," *Journal of Personality and Social Psychology* 11 (1969): 321–327.

19. Bert S. Moore et al., "The Dispositional Shift in Attribution over Time," *Journal of Experimental Social Psychology* 15 (1979): 553–569.

20. At this juncture, the reader should be aware that some writers argue that a reverse of the "foot-in-the-door" technique, called the "door-in-the-face" approach, is an equally effective model for gaining compliance with requests. It consists of initially requesting a very large favor, then after refusal, asking for a smaller one. Since it is not grounded in attribution theory, the "door-in-the-face" model is not discussed here. For discussions of it, see Robert B. Cialdini et al., "Reciprocal Concessions Procedure for Inducing Compliance: The Door-in-the-Face Technique," *Journal of Personality and Social Psychology* 31 (1975): 206–215; and Arnie Cann, Stephen J. Sherman, and Roy Elkes, "Effects of Initial Request Size and Timing of a Second Request in Compliance: The Foot in the Door and the Door in the Face," *Journal of Personality and Social Psychology* 32 (1975): 774–782.

21. Jonathan L. Freedman and Scott C. Fraser, "Compliance Without Pressure: The Foot-in-the-Door Technique," *Journal of Personality and Social Psychology* 4 (1966): 195–202. For studies duplicat-

ing Freedman's and Fraser's results, see William DeJong, "An Examination of Self-Perception Mediation of the Foot-in-the-Door Effect," *Journal of Personality and Social Psychology* 37 (1979): 2221–2239; and Patricia Pliner et al., "Compliance Without Pressure: Some Further Data on the Foot-in-the-Door Technique," *Journal of Experimental Social Psychology* 10 (1974): 17–22.

22. See Mark Snyder and Michael R. Cunningham, "To Comply or Not Comply: Testing the Self-Perception Explanation of the 'Foot-in-the-Door' Phenomenon," *Journal of Personality and Social Psychology* 31 (1975): 64–67.

23. Robert D. Foss and Carolyn B. Dempsey, "Blood Donation and the Foot-in-the-Door Technique: A Limiting Case," *Journal of Personality and Social Psychology* 37 (1979): 580–590.

24. Clive Seligman, Malcolm Bush, and Kenneth Kirsch, "Relationship Between Compliance in the Foot-in-the-Door Paradigm and Size of First Request," *Journal of Personality and Social Psychology* 33 (1976): 517–520.

25. Ibid., p. 519.

26. Snyder and Cunningham.

27. Seymour W. Uranowitz, "Helping and Self-Attributions: A Field Experiment," *Journal of Personality and Social Psychology* 31 (1975): 852–854.

28. See Fazio, Zanna, and Cooper, p. 469.

29. For a fuller discussion of latitude of acceptance, see Carolyn W. Sherif, Muzafer Sherif, and Roger E. Nebergall, *Attitude and Attitude Change: The Social Judgment–Involvement Approach* (Philadephia: Saunders, 1965); and Chapter 11 of this book.

30. Fazio, Zanna, and Cooper, p. 469.

31. See Robert S. Wyer, Jr., "The Prediction of Evaluations of Social Role Occupants as a Function of Favorableness, Relevance and Probability Associated with Attributes of these Occupants," *Sociometry* 33 (1970): 79–96; Norman H. Anderson, "Integration Theory and Attitude Change," *Psychological Review* 78 (1971): 171–205; Norman H. Anderson, "Averaging versus Adding as a Stimulus-Combination Rule in Impression Formation," *Journal of Experimental Psychology* 70 (1965): 394–400; and Martin Fishbein and Ronda Hunter, "Summation versus Balance in Attitude Organization and Change," *Journal of Abnormal and Social Psychology* 69 (1964): 505–510. Although the theory proposed by these writers applies to the general areas of self-attribution and impression formation, their work seems especially pertinent to the specific case of proattitudinal advocacy.

32. Robert S. Wyer, Jr., Marilyn Henninger, and Ronald Hinkle, "An Informational Analysis of Actors' and Observers' Belief Attributions in a Role-Playing Situation," *Journal of Experimental Social Psychology* 13 (1977): 216.

33. Gross, Riemer, and Collins. For studies using different "sincerity" manipulations, see Zanna and Kiesler; and Kiesler, Nisbett, and Zanna.

34. Wyer, Henninger, and Hinkle, pp. 199–217.

35. Ibid., p. 214.

36. Edward L. Deci, *Intrinsic Motivation* (New York: Plenum Press, 1975).

37. See Michael E. Enzle and June M. Ross, "Increasing and Decreasing Intrinsic Interest with Contingent Reward: A Test of Cognitive Evaluation Theory," *Journal of Experimental Social Psychology* 14 (1978): 588–597; Rosemarie Anderson, Sam Thomas Manoogian, and J. Steven Reznick, "The Undermining and Enhancing of Intrinsic Motivation in Preschool Children," *Journal of Personality and Social Psychology* 34 (1976): 915–922; Edward L. Deci, "Intrinsic Motivation, Extrinsic Reinforcement, and Inequity"; and Edward L. Deci, "Effects of Externally Mediated Rewards on Intrinsic Motivation."

38. John Wallace, "Role Reward and Dissonance Reduction," *Journal of Personality and Social Psychology* 3 (1966): 305–312.

39. William A. Scott, "Attitude Change by Response Reinforcement: Replication and Extension," *Socio-metry* 22 (1959): 328–335; and William A. Scott, "Attitude Change Through Reward of Verbal Behavior," *Journal of Abnormal and Social Psychology* 55 (1957): 72–75.

40. Deci, *Intrinsic Motivation*.

41. Carl Benware and Edward L. Deci, "Attitude Change as a Function of the Inducement for Espousing a Proattitudinal Communication," *Journal of Experimental Social Psychology* 11 (1975): 272.

42. Ibid., pp. 271–278.

43. See Barry R. Schlenker and Marc Riess, "Self-Presentation of Attitudes Following Commitment to Proattitudinal Behavior," *Human Communication Research* 5 (1979): 325–334; Barry R. Schlenker, "Group Members' Attributions of Responsibility for Prior Group Performance," *Representative Research in Social Psychology* 6 (1975): 96–108; Gifford Weary, "Self-Serving Attributional Biases: Perceptual or Response Distortions?" *Journal of Personality and Social Psychology* 37 (1979): 1418–1420; and Bradley.

44. William James, *Psychology* (New York: Holt, 1892).

45. Stanley Schachter and Jerome E. Singer, "Cognitive, Social, and Physiological Determinants of Emotional State," *Psychological Review* 69 (1962): 379–399.

46. Ibid.

47. Christina Maslach, "Negative Emotional Biasing of Unexplained Arousal," *Journal of Personality and Social Psychology* 37 (1979): 953–969; and Gary D. Marshall and Philip G. Zimbardo, "Affective Consequences of Inadequately Explained Physiological Arousal," *Journal of Personality and Social Psychology* 37 (1979): 970–988.

48. Norman Triplett, "The Dynamogenic Factors in Pacemaking and Competition," *American Journal of Psychology* 9 (1897): 507–533.

49. Robert B. Zajonc and Stephen M. Sales, "Social Facilitation of Dominant and Subordinate Responses," *Journal of Experimental Social Psychology* 2 (1966): 160–168; Robert B. Zajonc, "Social Facilitation," *Science* 149 (1965): 269–274; and Robert B. Zajonc, "The Requirements and Design of a Standard Group Task," *Journal of Experimental Social Psychology* 1 (1965): 71–88.

50. Irving L. Janis and Leon Mann, "A Conflict-Theory Approach to Attitude Change and Decision Making," in *Psychological Foundations of Attitudes*, ed. Anthony G. Greenwald, Timothy C. Brock, and Thomas M. Ostrom (New York: Academic Press, 1968), pp. 327–360.

51. Shelley E. Taylor, "On Inferring One's Attitudes from One's Behavior: Some Delimiting Conditions," *Journal of Personality and Social Psychology* 31 (1975): 126–131.

52. For example, see Schlenker and Riess; and Bradley.

CHAPTER 7

Group Interaction and Self-Persuasion

During the summer of 1962, an unusual thing happened at a clothing manufacturing plant in the deep South. Within one week, 62 people who worked the plant's first shift suffered what was thought to be insect bites and received medical attention. A physician and an entomologist from the Communicable Disease Center in Atlanta were called in to investigate the incident. They searched for insects, chemicals in dyes, and toxins in the air conditioning system, but found nothing capable of causing the reported symptoms. In the absence of physiological causes, they concluded that the illnesses were "almost exclusively psychogenic in nature," and, thus, were a case of delusionary and hysterical contagion.

Two months after the "epidemic," three social scientists began a study to uncover the psychological or social reasons for the mass delusion. They found that the "victims," who were mostly female and white, worked together in a single room where the cutting, sewing, pressing, inspecting, and packing operations were carried out. Moreover, most of the women were friends and made up a cohesive social group. The "epidemic," they discovered, began when one or two people on the fringes of the group complained of insect bites. These isolates served as role models for several particularly vulnerable persons who were a part of the larger group. Once a few "insiders" complained of pain and nausea, the "disease" was legitimized for other group members, and increasingly large numbers of them got ill, establishing the credibility of the imaginary syndrome. Ultimately, almost everybody in the group came to believe in "the bug" and the phenomenon took on the character of a "crowd" response.[1]

This strange incident highlights the major issue we will address in this chapter: the role of the group as a stimulus for self-persuasion. All of the cognitive and behavioral changes resulting from group interaction can properly be called rule-governed responses, reflecting conformity by group members to the attitudinal and behavioral norms established by the group as a whole. Throughout this chapter, we will refer extensively to rules-based theories of persuasion. In considering group interaction and self-persuasion, we will explore the following issues: (1) the nature of group rules or norms and conformity behavior; (2) attitude polarization and opinion shifts in groups; and (3) group influences on overt behavior, including the phenomena of behavioral contagion and deindividuation or psychological submergence in the group.

GROUP NORMS, ROLES, AND CONFORMITY: CREATING AND CHANGING ATTITUDES

All of us belong to numerous groups, ranging from our primary family, through informal circles of friends, to more formalized social, religious, and professional organizations. Although our membership in some groups is short-lived, we remain in others for a lifetime. Furthermore, we value membership in some groups more than others. Clearly, those most-valued groups exert the greatest persuasive influence upon us. The term *reference groups* is often used to designate those groups of sufficient importance that they can shape our feelings, beliefs, and patterns of behavior.[2]

Although groups vary considerably, they share a number of characteristics.[3] First, a group is made up of individuals who have a collective perception of unity, a sense of belonging together, or an awareness that they share some common goal. Second, a group is characterized by mutual communicative interaction, entailing face-to-face contact among group members and the possibility that every group member may influence all other members. Finally, a group has a set of norms and roles structuring it and forcing a certain amount of conformity behavior by each group member.

Group *norms* are rules or standards that regulate the attitudes and behaviors of all group members in matters of importance to the group. A normative rule states "what must, or must not, be done" in specifiable situations.[4] The norms of many social and fraternal groups, for example, often specify not only what attitudes are acceptable to the group, but also expected modes of dress and grooming. Although such norms usually are implicit, they sometimes are codified—as in the case of certain religious orders, military organizations, and law enforcement agencies. A *role* is a specialized kind of norm. It consists of the differentiated behaviors expected of each group member by virtue of the specific position occupied by the member. Although norms apply to all group members, role expectancies define how each individual member is supposed to act. For example, the designated leader of a group usually is expected to speak publicly for it, and followers are expected to defer to the leader.

Thus, norms are general social rules applicable to all group members, whereas roles are specific rules relevant to the particular individuals who comprise the group.

The Nature of Conformity to Group Norms

For a group to function cohesively, members must conform to a certain extent to its general rules or norms. Otherwise, the group becomes little more than an aggregate of individual people who have no perception of unity or semblance of structure. In short, without some conformity, or rule-following behavior, there is, by definition, no group. A group encourages adherence to its rules or norms by providing rewards for conformity and punishment for deviance. When members follow the rules, the group bestows rewards, usually in the form of social approval and acceptance, social information that would not be available otherwise, and conferral of high status. In contrast, when norms are disobeyed, the group applies negative sanctions such as social disapproval, low status, and ultimately dismissal from the group. Final rejection means a person loses the group as a source of information as well as companionship.

The ability of groups to reward and punish exerts strong pressures on members to conform. When conforming, the individual yields to the group. David Krech and his associates argue that conflict is a necessary condition for the occurrence of conformity.[5] The individual wishes to believe or behave in one way, and the group pressures him or her to think and act in another way. Thus, in order to say that a person has conformed to group norms, that person must begin to believe or behave in ways he or she would not have done without implicit or explicit pressures from the group. Charles Kiesler and Sara Kiesler summarize this conception by defining conformity as "*a change of behavior or belief toward a group as a result of real or imagined group pressure* [emphasis theirs]."[6] Note the Kieslers' emphasis that for conformity to occur, group pressures need not be real, only that they be *perceived* as real.

Students of group dynamics distinguish between two types of conformity or rule-governed behavior in groups: simple compliance and private acceptance. *Simple compliance,* sometimes called *expedient conformity,* occurs when a person publicly expresses attitudes and behaviors acceptable to the group, yet holds private beliefs at odds with the group. According to Herbert Kelman, public conformity occurs either because the complier wishes to gain specific rewards or avoid specific punishments or because he or she wants to establish or maintain a satisfying, self-defining relationship with the group or some of its members.[7] Simple compliers conform only when their behavior is under surveillance by the group.

In contrast, *private acceptance,* or *true conformity,* occurs when an individual internalizes group norms as his or her own. In this case, a person's public *and* private beliefs are congruent with the group's norms. Unlike the compliant skeptic, the private accepter is a true believer. In Kelman's terms, such individuals internalize the group's preferred attitudes and behaviors because the content of the norms is intrinsically rewarding and generally congruent with their basic value systems.[8] True conformers exhibit group-sanctioned behaviors whether or not those actions are scrutinized by the group.

As students of persuasion, our interest in group conformity lies with private acceptance. We are concerned with the dynamics by which individuals persuade themselves of the rightness of group attitudes and behaviors. However, this focus does not exclude a consideration of simple compliance. To the contrary, simple compliance is often a powerful instigator of self-persuasion leading ultimately to private acceptance since it represents nothing more than a public counterattitudinal act. As we saw in Chapter 5, public counterattitudinal advocacy can lead an individual to change private attitudes to conform with overt behaviors. Thus, the dynamics associated with both private acceptance and simple compliance are pertinent to our study.

The Normative and Informational Functions of Groups

If our discussion of conformity has implied that private acceptance and simple compliance are behaviors imposed by groups upon reluctant individual members, we have been misleading. Like all other rule-governed behaviors, group members *choose* to conform because they expect to achieve some desired objective by doing so. Put another way, people *use* groups to get things they are incapable of securing alone. Harold Kelley and others suggest that individuals affiliate with groups and conform to their norms to fulfill two categories of desired objectives.[9] First, people desire personal acceptance, companionship, and social support, and the group is in a unique position to award or withhold such recognition. To the degree that a person conforms to the rules of the group, he or she will receive recognition and social acceptance. This process has been called the *normative function* of groups. When a group can reward individuals with social approval and punish them with isolation and rejection, it is said to possess *normative power*.

Groups also have an *informational function*. People use groups not only to gain personal acceptance and companionship, but also to increase their knowledge of themselves and their world. For example, the aspiring writer who joins a writers' club will probably use the group as a source of information for evaluating and perfecting his or her own abilities. Similarly, we often use groups to gain information about appropriate attitudes regarding current social issues. For example, I may oppose a constitutional guarantee of equal rights for women. However, upon learning that a valued group to which I belong uniformly supports sexual equality, I may begin to see my own attitude as inappropriate or "out of step." When a group can withhold or provide important information to members about attitudes or abilities, it is said to possess *informational power*. In later discussion of social comparison theory, we will explore in more detail the informational and normative powers of the group.

In summary, people conform to group rules because doing so enables them to achieve desired objectives. Primary group functions are to provide information about attitudes and abilities and to convey to members a sense of personal recognition and social support. A review of two classic studies of group conformity will illustrate these two functions and highlight some of the more important aspects of true conformity.

Two Classic Studies of Conformity

Muzafer Sherif conducted some of the first studies on the nature of conformity to group norms. To demonstrate the dynamics of norm formation and rule-guided behavior, he used a phenomenon known as the *autokinetic effect*. When individuals view a stationary pinpoint of light in a dark room, the light will appear to move. This apparent movement is known as the autokinetic effect. The amount of perceived movement differs from person to person, but it is relatively constant for each individual. Initially, Sherif had each subject in his study estimate the amount of light movement in isolation from the other subjects. Later, each subject was brought together with one or two other subjects, and as a group they estimated light movement and announced their findings

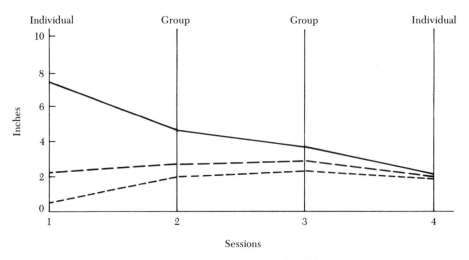

FIGURE 7.1   *Judgments of autokinetic movements by three group members. In session 1, subjects judged alone. In sessions 2 and 3, they heard the judgments of other group members. In session 4, each subject again judged alone. Adapted from Muzafer Sherif and Carolyn W. Sherif,* An Outline of Social Psychology, Revised Edition. *Copyright © 1956, 1948 by Harper & Row, Publishers, Inc. Reprinted by permission of the publisher.*

to other group members. After doing this twice, each subject again estimated light movement on his or her own. As Figure 7.1 shows, the individual estimates began to converge as subjects interacted with other group members. After a time, each person reported that he or she saw about the same amount of movement as did all other group members, indicating the establishment of a group norm. Moreover, when subjects made final estimates alone, they were almost identical to those given at the end of the group interaction period.[10]

Several aspects of this experiment are noteworthy. First, it demonstrated that in ambiguous situations where no correct response exists, groups rapidly set up norms and members follow them. This circumstance parallels situations involving attitude formation and change. Just as there was no accurate estimate of light movement, there is no such thing as an objectively correct attitude. Attitudes and behaviors are usually characterized by reasonableness and appropriateness, not correctness. Moreover, we usually judge our schemata to be reasonable or appropriate when they conform to the views held by similar, important others. For that reason, group norms have a powerful influence on the formation and change of human attitudes. Second, the pattern of behavior exhibited in Sherif's study fits our earlier description of the informational power of groups in that subjects apparently used the information supplied by others to determine the "actual" amount of light movement.

Third, the experiment confirmed that the group-instigated norms led to private acceptance, not just simple conformity. When subjects were removed from the group, they continued to report the same amount of movement on which the group had settled. Fourth and finally, follow-up studies and partial replications of this experiment have shown that group norms formed in ambiguous situations persist for long periods of time even after there are complete changes in group membership.[11]

Solomon Asch conducted a series of experiments in reaction to Sherif's findings. Asch did not believe that humans were the conforming breed that Sherif's study implied. He argued that subjects conformed in Sherif's experiment because the situation was so ambiguous. Therefore, he designed a method for studying conformity in an objective setting where correct solutions were available. Asch used groups of seven members, one of which was an unaware naive subject, and the balance were confederates of the experimenter. All groups were shown two cards. A single, straight line appeared on one card and on the second card there were three lines labeled A, B, and C. One of the three lines on the second card was exactly the same length as the line on the first card, and the other two were obviously longer or shorter than the standard line. All group members were asked to match the single standard line with the line of equal length on the three-line card. In all cases, the naive subject was asked to respond next to last. In 12 of the 18 experimental trials, the six confederates were told to respond unanimously with an incorrect answer.

Asch was interested in whether the next to last naive subject would conform to the group's opinion or stick to the obviously correct answer. His primary hypothesis was that people will not conform to the group's opinion when they know their own judgments are objectively correct. Much to his surprise, over one-third of the subjects conformed to the group's incorrect opinion in all 12 experimental trials. Moreover, most of the subjects conformed at least once, with only one-fourth of them turning in a completely error-free performance.[12]

Asch's study is less pertinent to attitude change than Sherif's since attitudes, by definition, cannot be judged as correct or incorrect. However, Asch's results illustrate two important aspects of conformity behavior. First, that 75 percent of Asch's subjects conformed at least once in the face of objective evidence to the contrary demonstrates the power of groups to influence the opinions of members. Such group power should be far more potent in attitude-relevant situations where no objective standard exists. Second, the behavior exhibited in Asch's experiments illustrates the normative, as opposed to informational, power of the group. The information provided by the group in this study was obviously useless; yet members still conformed. This finding strongly suggests that factors related to social approval and personal acceptance in the group were paramount in eliciting agreement from Asch's naive subjects.

A Theoretical Basis of Conformity: Social Comparison Theory

Leon Festinger's theory of social comparison as revised and extended by theorists like George Goethals and John Darley[13] is a major theoretical explanation for conformity behavior in groups.[14] Festinger argued that people have a drive to evaluate their opinions and abilities. To function effectively in society, each of us must be able to assess accurately the limits of our abilities and to determine the reasonableness and appropriateness of our attitudes or opinions. Edward Jones and Harold Gerard have argued that the primary motive for self-evaluation is a need for uncertainty reduction.

To the extent that we are uncertain about our abilities to perform certain tasks or unsure as to the reasonableness of our opinions regarding social issues, we will be motivated to seek out information to reduce that uncertainty.[15]

To illustrate how we evaluate our opinions and abilities, Festinger distinguished between *physical reality,* that reality created by empirical observation, and *social reality* as created by group consensus.[16] To evaluate certain types of questions like whether the temperature outside is below freezing or whether the Philadelphia Phillies won the 1980 World Series, we refer to physical reality; we validate our beliefs through empirical observation. However, our abilities and social attitudes are not subject to empirical verification. Support for a political candidate, opposition to abortion, support for gun control laws, and other such attitudes are neither correct nor incorrect and can be evaluated only by standards of reasonableness, appropriateness, and the like. To determine the reasonableness of an attitude, we refer to social reality, that is, we compare our opinions with the opinions of similar others. As Festinger puts it, "an opinion, a belief, an attitude is 'correct,' 'valid,' and 'proper' to the extent that it is anchored in a group of people with similar beliefs, opinions, and attitudes."[17]

Festinger originally assumed that the primary function of social comparison was to determine *whether* one's opinions are reasonable and appropriate. This assumption implies that we seek out information about other people's attitudes in order to make an unbiased judgment of our own opinions. Subsequent theorizing and research confirmed that there are actually two motivations underlying the need for social information.

The first is the disinterested and objective process described by Festinger. The second consists of a desire, not to determine *if* our attitudes are reasonable, but to *confirm* that our opinions *are,* in fact, reasonable and appropriate. D. A. Thornton and John Arrowood label the first motivation, *self-evaluation,* and the latter, *self-enhancement,*[18] and Jerome Singer refers to the two processes as *evaluation* and *validation* of the self, respectively.[19] These processes sometimes may produce conflicting results. For example, when an objective self-evaluation suggests that one's opinions are unreasonable, validation is blocked. Which motivation predominates in cases of conflict has been the subject of considerable study, most of which suggests that people are far more concerned with validation or self-enhancement than they are with unbiased evaluation.[20]

Given our need to evaluate and to validate social attitudes, a critical issue becomes the choice of other people with whom to compare attitudes. Thus, Festinger developed what is known as the *similarity hypothesis,* arguing that we compare ourselves with people whose attitudes are similar to our own. This statement is paradoxical since comparisons presumably are sought to find out what another's opinion is; yet prior knowledge of someone else's opinion is required to identify an appropriate comparison group. To eliminate this ambiguity, Goethals, Darley, and others reformulated the similarity hypothesis to state that people compare themselves with others perceived as similar to themselves on *attributes related to the relevant opinion.*[21] As Ladd Wheeler and his colleagues note, "we do not merely seek out someone with an opinion similar to ours but rather seek out someone who ought to have, by virtue of similarity to us on attributes related to the opinion issue, a similar opinion."[22]

Given this reinterpretation, we can now say that people seek out groups who are like themselves on stable attributes such as economic and educational background, social status, political affiliation, intelligence, and the like. Moreover, the people selected as comparison others will depend, in large measure, on the specific attitude we wish to evaluate or validate. For example, if an attitude concerns equal rights for women or racial discrimination, the sex and race, respectively, of others should be important for purposes of social comparison. However, if the attitude relates to governmental issues like military spending or environmental pollution, political party affiliation or ideological preferences should be more pertinent than race or gender.

Social Comparison and Conformity

To relate social comparison theory to conformity in groups, we need only say that people use groups of similar others to define social reality. Those attitudes and behavior patterns embodied by group norms serve as frames of reference for assessing the reasonableness of one's own opinions and behaviors. Hence, group norms can foster the formation of new attitudinal schemata and behaviors as well as facilitate attitude and behavior change in the direction of the group position.

The persuasive power of group norms will persist as long as people see themselves as similar to a group on important underlying dimensions relevant to their attitudes and behaviors. However, when individuals cease to perceive this similarity, group norms will not function as social standards for evaluating and validating opinions and behaviors. In such a case, the group norm is no longer appropriate for social comparison and it loses its persuasive power.

We suggested earlier that people conform to group norms for normative or social acceptance reasons, and for informational purposes. Although social comparison theory emphasizes the informational bases of conformity, the normative function of groups is still an essential component of social comparison processes since self-enhancement motivation is directly related to it. You will recall that normative power refers to the personal recognition and social approval groups provide members in exchange for conformity. In the case of social comparison for purposes of self-enhancement, the member receives group confirmation that his or her opinions are sound, reasonable, and socially acceptable. Thus, the information gained by someone seeking self-enhancement serves a normative function, implying recognition and approval for holding "acceptable" opinions. In contrast, when individuals want unbiased evaluations, the knowledge acquired should serve a purely informational function.

Factors Affecting Conformity in Groups

Conformity to group norms does not always occur. As we saw in Chapter 3, rule-governed behavior including conformity is probable, not absolute or deterministic. Conformity is contingent upon whether or not groups wield sufficient normative and informational power to insure that rules are followed. In this section, we will discuss factors affecting the normative and informational power of groups, specifically, characteristics of the group itself; and characteristics of individual members of groups.

Group Factors

Two group characteristics have a strong influence upon their normative and informational power: group cohesiveness and tolerance of deviancy. *Cohesiveness* is the degree of attachment—including attraction, importance, and involvement—members have to the group.[23] In a highly cohesive group, members are deeply committed to group goals and have a strong motivation to remain a part of the group. Thus, the more cohesive a group is, the greater its normative powers and, consequently, the higher the level of conformity to its norms.

Conformity is also affected by the extent to which a group tolerates *deviance* from its norms. Many groups react violently to the slightest deviation from central norms. Large groups like political parties, legislative bodies, and nations often punish deviants severely even though their numbers are exceedingly small. For example, in the Soviet Union during the 1970s, the number of political dissidents like writer Aleksandr Solzhenitsyn was miniscule in relation to the total Russian population. Yet, the handful of dissidents were systematically harassed, deported, or sent into permanent exile in remote areas of Russia as punishment for their anti-Soviet activities. Given that such a small community of deviants could not threaten the Soviet government in any substantive way, one is led to wonder why they were so harshly repressed.

The reason for the suppression of deviance is deceptively simple. The tolerance of even a single deviant can have a powerful effect on the amount of conformity that other group members will exhibit. Asch provided an early demonstration of this in the experiment we reviewed earlier. He found that when faced with a unanimously incorrect group opinion, about 35 percent of the naive group members consistently conformed with the group judgment. However, when confronted by a group where all but one member agreed with a decision, naive member conformity dropped to 8 or 9 percent.[24] Thus, the presence of just one dissenter dropped conformity levels 25 percent. From the group's perspective, allowing even one deviant to exist can be very dangerous. When group members see one person get away with breaking the rules, they may come to feel that they too are free to follow suit.

Since Asch, a number of researchers have explored the effect of a deviant on conformity behaviors. Shaw, Rothschild, and Strickland found that a deviant does not even have to express an opinion to reduce conformity. In their research, a deviant confederate was instructed to tell the group that he had not made up his mind about the issue under discussion. This ambiguous response significantly reduced the amount of conformity among group members.[25] Allen and Wilder found that the deviant does not have to be physically present to reduce conformity. If a group member simply knows that someone has previously broken the unanimity of group opinion, he or she will be less likely to conform to an otherwise unanimous group opinion.[26]

All these studies suggest that the principal effect of deviance is to reduce the normative power of the group, or its ability and willingness to reward conformity and punish deviance. Beyond the reduction of normative power, there is some evidence that group members use deviants to obtain information. For example, Allen and Levine conducted a study in which group members were asked to judge visual stimuli. In one condition, the deviant wore thick glasses, complained about his inability to see the stimuli, and failed a simple vision test before the experiment began. In another condition, the deviant had no visual impairment. The results showed that both deviants reduced conformity to an incorrect group decision, but the reduction was greater when the normally sighted deviant rather than the visually impaired one gave a correct response.[27] Thus, in some cases, the informational power of a group is diminished by the presence of deviants who appear especially competent to judge the issue at hand.

A final point to be made about deviance concerns the ways groups suppress it. Schachter demonstrated that initially the group directs a great deal of its communication toward the deviant in an attempt to persuade him or her to conform. If that fails, the group rejects the deviant, either by treating him or her as a nonperson or by physical ejection from group membership. Moreover, the greater the cohesiveness and esprit de corps of the group, the harsher it is in suppressing dissent of any kind.[28]

Individual Differences

Several characteristics of individual group members affect conformity to group norms. First, there is some evidence that certain personality types persistently fail to conform to group norms. As far back as 1903, the French sociologist Gabriel Tarde argued that there are at least two types of nonconformers: anticonformists and independents. *Anticonformists*, or counterimitators, consistently behave in a manner opposed to the wishes of the group. Ironically, the anticonformist, like the conformist, actually is very strongly influenced by group norms. However, instead of conforming to group pressures, he or she consistently opposes them. This type of person "zigs" when the group "zags" and vice versa. If everybody is wearing a suit to a party, he shows up in blue jeans; if the group favors some particular issue, she opposes it; and the like.

Independents, or nonimitators, are a rare breed who make up their own minds and are able to take the group's opinion or leave it as their personal judgment dictates. The group's opinion is only one factor among many that the independent considers when adopting an attitude or behavior. The independent conforms or does not conform depending on his or her judgment of the worth of the group norm.[29]

Aside from the influence of enduring personality traits on conformity, research has shown that conformity is greater when individuals expect to interact with a group for long periods of time.[30] Further, it is greater when a person perceives that he or she has a somewhat lower status in the group than other members,[31] or is not completely accepted by a group.[32] Regarding the latter points, Edwin Hollander has argued that high-status, well-accepted group members have a considerable store of what he calls *idiosyncrasy credits*. He theorizes that the group gives its members "credits" each time they conform to group norms and takes them away for nonconformity. Accordingly, the high-status, well-accepted member, having "paid his or her dues" over a long period of time, will have an abundance of idiosyncrasy credits. In contrast, the new, less well-accepted member will not. This theory suggests that a group will not tolerate deviance from members who are new, low in status, or marginally accepted because they have not earned the right to be occasionally nonconformist, whereas older, well-accepted members have earned the right to act independently from time to time.[33]

Role Conformity: Social Expectations and Self-Fulfilling Prophecies

Earlier in this chapter, a role was defined as a specialized kind of norm, consisting of the attitudes and behaviors expected of each group member by virtue of his or her specific position in the group. Group members tend to internalize or privately accept these role expectations by adopting new attitudes and behaviors that others expect or changing existing ones that conflict with others' expectations.

Group expectations may be conveyed to individual members through subtle, non-verbal cues or verbally by social labeling. *Social labels* like *intelligent, dumb, charitable,* and *selfish* directly inform people of the behaviors others have come to expect of them, and research shows that people tend to behave in ways that confirm our expectations of them. Others' expectations, then, become self-fulfilling prophecies. Like Pygmalion of George Bernard Shaw's play, we frequently "create" the people we expect to find in a particular role.

Rosenthal and Jacobson demonstrated that expectancies can become self-fulfilling prophecies. They told a group of first and second grade teachers that some of their students were expected to show dramatic increases in academic performance during the school year, and others were not. Allegedly, this prediction was based on a reliable Harvard-designed intelligence and achievement test. In truth there was no such test. The researchers actually selected at random one-third of the students to designate as "rapid achievers." At the end of the school year, all the children's IQs were measured. The results showed a 47.4 gain in IQ points among the first grade "achievers" compared to a 12 point increase for the balance of the class. Similarly, the "achievers" in the second grade gained 16.5 IQ points, but the rest of the second-graders gained only 7 points.[34] Thus, it appears that the teachers "created" the students they expected to have in their classes. Exactly how such processes occur is not fully known. In some way, however, teacher expectations were transmitted verbally or nonverbally to the students, who behaved accordingly.[35]

The self-fulfilling prophecy applies to a wide range of attitudinal and behavioral phenomena. Indeed, attitudes and behaviors are far more amenable to role conformity than abilities since abilities are more enduring and less socially determined than opinions. Kraut demonstrated the attitudinal and behavioral effects of social labeling in a study of charitable donations. After soliciting money, the researcher told some donors that they were "charitable," but the other contributors were not given a label. Similarly, he told some subjects who refused to give that they were "uncharitable," but he did not label the others. All subjects were later asked to contribute to a second charity. As expected, those people labeled "charitable" gave more the second time than those who had earlier given but had not been so labeled. Likewise, individuals who had not given the first time were more reluctant to give the second time if they had been called "uncharitable" than if they had not been labeled.[36]

In a study investigating the longer-range effects of social expectations, Snyder and Swann led one group of people to believe that a second target group of individuals was either "hostile" or "nonhostile." This second group was given no instruction about how they were to behave. After the two groups interacted on a one-to-one basis, their conversations were analyzed. Results showed that the second target individuals whom the first group had expected to be "hostile" actually showed greater hostility than the target people who had been expected to behave "nonhostilely." In a second stage of the experiment, the "hostile" and "nonhostile" target individuals were brought into a conversation with new partners who had no particular expectations of them. The individuals whom others had expected to behave hostilely in the first stage of the experiment again behaved hostilely in the second phase. Likewise, the "nonhostile" group continued to behave nonhostilely. Thus, having behaved hostilely or nonhostilely in response to an initial expectation, the target persons continued to exhibit the same behaviors even when others no longer expected them to do so.[37]

Taken together, these studies show that people exhibit a great deal of conformity to others' expectations of them. Clearly, group persuasive power is not limited to the power of general norms. Rather, individual group members are influenced profoundly by the expectations associated with the roles they occupy in groups. And, as Snyder's and Swann's research indicated, this self-fulfilling prophecy behavior often involves private acceptance, in that the expected behaviors persist after group expectations are no longer present.

GROUP POLARIZATION AND OPINION SHIFTS: REINFORCING EXISTING ATTITUDES

We have now explored the ways group norms and roles can create and change attitudes. In this section, we will focus on how group interaction reinforces and strengthens attitudes and behaviors. We will find that communicating with others on a face-to-face basis usually prompts people to adopt stronger or more extreme attitudes than they previously held.

Evidence supporting this contention was first reported by James Stoner in 1961. Stoner set out to investigate the then-popular notion that group judgments are more cautious and less daring than those of individuals. Contrary to the conventional wisdom, Stoner discovered that groups on the whole take more risks than their average individual members.[38] Stoner labeled this effect the *risky-shift phenomenon*, and his work stimulated a wave of investigations into group risk-taking behavior. As the research and theorizing proceeded, it became apparent that the conceptually narrow designation, *risky-shift*, was a misnomer. In addition to risky-shifts, opinion shifts toward greater caution were documented.[39] Moreover, it was discovered that group interaction can produce extreme opinion shifts on attitudinal and behavioral issues that are totally unrelated to risk taking. These risk-irrelevant issues included attitudes toward nationalities like Americans and Frenchmen and behaviors such as donations to charities.[40] In short, the risky-shift was found to be just one instance of a more pervasive group influence phenomenon.

Following the lead of Serge Moscovici and Marisa Zavalloni,[41] group theorists adopted the term *polarization* to describe the general tendency of individuals to adopt more extreme attitudes as a result of group interaction. Stated more formally, *group polarization* is defined as a strengthening or enhancement of preexisting attitudes and behaviors induced by interpersonal interaction.[42] Applied to true risk-taking behavior, this definition suggests that individuals who initially prefer a relatively risky course of action will shift toward an even riskier position after group discussion. In contrast, when caution is initially preferred, group discussion will probably result in the choice of a more cautious final position. As students of persuasion, our interest is not in risk taking per se, but rather in the more general phenomenon of opinion shifts produced by group interaction. In this regard, group polarization processes are a powerful means of reinforcing existing attitudes, making them more resistant to future counterpersuasion.

Numerous studies have confirmed the group polarization phenomenon. For example, Moscovici and Zavalloni observed that the initially positive attitudes of French students toward General de Gaulle and negative attitudes toward Americans were strengthened by group discussion.[43] Paicheler found a polarization of attitudes toward women's liberation. Groups of students with initially favorable attitudes (1.10 on a −3 to +3 scale) moved toward more favorable opinions (about 1.80) after group discussion.[44] Several studies have confirmed a polarization effect on mock juries. For example, Myers and Kaplan asked jurors to discuss traffic cases in which defendants were made to appear either guilty or not guilty. After discussing the apparently not guilty cases, the jurors became more definite in their judgments of innocence and more lenient in any recommended punishments. However, after discussing the more incriminating cases, the jurors moved toward harsher judgments of guilt and greater punishment.[45] As these studies indicate, polarization is a potent and pervasive influence in groups and, as such, has a central place in the literature on group influence and persuasive communication.

Theoretical Explanations of Group Polarization Effects

During the period when polarization effects were assumed to relate only to risk-taking behaviors, a number of theoretical explanations for the risky-shift emerged.[46] These included the diffusion-of-responsibility hypothesis, suggesting that risky decisions occur because of a lowered sense of individual responsibility when others share accountability for decisions;[47] the leadership theory, holding that group leadership is usually acquired by high risk takers who, in turn, are more persuasive than moderates;[48] and Roger Brown's risk-as-a-social value hypothesis postulating that riskiness is seen as a culturally prescribed value or norm. The presence of such a norm leads the typical group member to try to appear at least as risky as other people who are similar to him or her.[49] Brown's hypothesis is appealing because it accounts for cautious as well as risky-shifts. In those situations where a high value is placed on caution rather than risk-taking, the norm should impel group members to be equally, or more, cautious than the group average.

After group polarization effects were recognized as a pervasive influence phenomenon having no intrinsic relation to risk-taking, researchers tried to develop a theory that could account satisfactorily for general polarization effects. Two major theories have since emerged. The first is a variant of *social comparison theory* and contains some revisions of Festinger's original formulation, as well as some of the basic tenets of impression management and social identity theories (discussed in Chapters 5 and 6, respectively). The second approach is an *information-processing theory* postulating that the persuasive arguments presented during group discussion and accompanying covert self-persuasion account for the development of more extreme attitudes by group members. Let's examine these two theoretical approaches.

A Social Comparison Explanation

Robert Baron and his associates are responsible for a social comparison explanation of group polarization effects.[50] Baron begins his theorizing by denying Festinger's dichotomy between comparison of abilities and opinions. Festinger originally had argued that people desire to see themselves as superior to others in abilities, but only the same as others in opinions or attitudes.[51] This distinction led him to conclude that people evaluate their abilities by comparing them with those of people who are similar but slightly better than themselves. This strategy allows them to establish their superiority relative to a similar other. However, in the case of attitudes, no such motivation should exist. People should seek attitudinal equals for purposes of evaluating opinions.

Contrary to this reasoning, Baron and his colleagues argue that people evaluate their attitudes in much the same way that Festinger supposed they evaluate their abilities. Attitudes, they reason, vary in perceived levels of social desirability; some are more acceptable or proper than others in any given social grouping. Moreover, some attitudes are considered more reasonable than others, implying a degree of correlation between certain attitudes and underlying intelligence, competence, and related abilities of the attitude holder. Coupling this reasoning with the basic tenets of impression management theory, Baron contends that people are motivated to present themselves in a favorable light, relative to others. That is, people do not merely want to appear equal to other group members in social desirability, but rather they want to present themselves as *better* embodiments of socially desirable attitudes than are the other group members.

To relate these assumptions to group polarization effects, social comparison theorists examined the types of attitudes people usually regard as most socially desirable. Their research suggested that people value opinions that are stronger or more *extreme* than the ones they espouse. A number of studies have asked people to state their own opinion on an issue, then to indicate the attitude they most admire, and finally to estimate what they believe their peers' attitudes are on the issue. Almost always, subjects tend to estimate the group norm or peer opinion as less intense than their own, but rate the ideal opinion as stronger.[52] These results are quite general. For instance, most businesspersons perceive themselves as more ethical than the average, and most people perceive their own views as less prejudiced than the norm of their community.[53]

Apparently, people see themselves as more extreme *in a positive direction* than the average member of their group. At the same time, they perceive themselves as less extreme than their ideal position on favored issues.

This explanation of polarization effects suggests that some individuals are initially reluctant to espouse their ideal position because they fear being labeled an extremist or a deviant from a less extreme group norm. However, during a group discussion, members who espouse moderate positions may realize that other group members hold opinions closer to their ideal position than they themselves do. This realization either "releases" the moderate members from the fear of appearing extreme or it motivates them to "compete" with other group members to see who can come closest to espousing the most admired position. In either case, "the moderates are motivated to adopt more extreme positions, while there is no corresponding pressure on extreme members to moderate their opinions."[54]

The type of social comparison information needed to trigger attitude polarization has been variously interpreted. One interpretation presumes that knowledge of the group norm or average opinion of the group is sufficient to stimulate a more polarized response, that group members will be motivated to "compete" with one another to keep a step ahead of the average.[55] A second interpretation holds that the key is not discovery of the group norm, but rather observations of other group members who embody the member's ideals in a relatively extreme form. This modeling supposedly "releases" people from the constraints of the assumed, moderate group norm and lets them act out their private inclinations.[56]

These two explanations have been tested experimentally by showing some group members a percentage distribution of others' opinions, thus exposing them to some extreme models; and giving other members only the group average or norm. In one experiment using mock juries, Myers and Kaplan found that mere exposure to the average opinion of others was sufficient to polarize attitudes.[57] In a second field experiment, Myers, Wojcicki, and Aardema compared the polarization effects of the group average versus knowledge of the opinions of extreme models. Subjects were 269 church members who participated in a public opinion survey on current social issues. Approximately one-third of the church members participated in a pretest condition by responding to the questionnaire, on which they indicated their own opinion and their estimates of how the "average" church member would respond. As Figure 7.2 shows, the respondents, as expected, perceived their attitudes to be stronger in the preferred direction than the "average" churchgoer. The remaining subjects were divided randomly into three groups and completed the questionnaire three weeks after the pretest group. Control participants completed the survey without any information about others' responses. Participants in the average exposure condition were shown the average responses of the pretest group, and people in the percentage exposure group were shown the complete distribution of pretest responses. As Figure 7.2 indicates, knowledge of averages and percentages resulted in polarization. However, exposure to extreme models in the percentage exposure condition produced the greatest strengthening of attitudes.[58]

Overall, these experiments suggest that polarization can result from knowledge of the average group response alone. Thus, public opinion polls reporting only averages

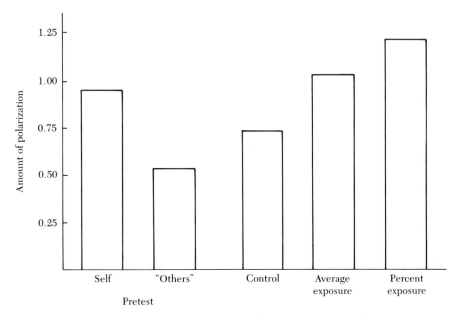

FIGURE 7.2   Amount of attitude polarization by experimental conditions. From David G. Myers, Sandra B. Wojcicki, and Bobette S. Aardema, "Attitude Comparison: Is There Ever a Bandwagon Effect?" Journal of Applied Social Psychology, *7, 1977, p. 345. Reprinted by permission of V. H. Winston & Sons, 7961 Eastern Ave., Silver Spring, Maryland 20910.*

can motivate people to differentiate themselves from the "average person." However, greater polarization can be expected if people observe the responses of other group members who have strong opinions. Although the "release" as well as the "competition" explanations are valid, interacting with extreme models appears to be the superior instigator of polarization.

An Information-Processing Theory

From the perspective of social comparison theory, the essential motivator of attitude polarization is the need for positive image maintenance. Although proponents of the information-processing approach do not dispute that such a motive exists, they deny that it is the *essential* reason for polarization. Rather, they contend that people change because they are persuaded by arguments, overt as well as covert, generated during discussion. Furthermore, they suggest that the need to present a positive self-image stimulates information processing, encouraging group members to think up and exchange arguments and information to justify their image maintenance decisions. Thus, what appears at first glance to be a social comparison effect, information-processing theorists argue, is actually a case of information processing.

Eugene Burnstein, Amiram Vinokur, and their associates are the principal architects of the information-processing explanation of group polarization effects.[59] The theory postulates that two types of information are available to group members during discussion: (1) *overtly expressed persuasive arguments* that members exchange during discussion of the attitudinal issue at hand; and (2) the thoughts and *covert persuasive arguments* generated privately by each group member during interaction. Burnstein and Vinokur propose that the magnitude of attitude polarization is dependent on three characteristics of the overt and covert arguments: (1) *direction* of the arguments, either pro or con; (2) the *cogency* or reasonableness of the arguments; and (3) the *novelty*, or originality, of the arguments. In general, the greater the number of proattitudinal arguments, the more cogent, or persuasive, they are; and the more original, or nonredundant, the arguments are, the greater the attitude polarization in group discussion.[60]

Given that these three variables determine a group's postdiscussion attitudes, one can reasonably argue that such attitudes may or may *not* represent true polarization. If the arguments generated by a group are primarily counterattitudinal, or lacking in cogency, persuasiveness, or originality, a weakening, not a polarization, of the group's initial attitude should result. In brief, information-processing theory predicts only that interaction will lead to group *extremization*, meaning movement away from a group's initial opinion regardless of direction.

Although information-processing theorists recognize the plausibility of this argument, they have advanced convincing reasons why polarization, rather than weakening, of attitudes almost inevitably results from group discussion. First, most overt and covert arguments produced during discussion reflect the group's prediscussion attitudes. In the absence of external constraints, we are rarely motivated to advance convincing arguments against a cause to which we are committed. Thus, in terms of direction, we can usually expect the majority of the information exchanged in groups to be proattitudinal. Second, one of the better-documented conclusions in the literature of persuasion is that arguments supporting one's initial attitude are perceived as more cogent and generally more persuasive than are arguments opposed to it.

Finally, group members are likely to have more information about their own opinion than an opposing one, thus, increasing the likelihood that more original, proattitudinal arguments will be generated in the discussion than would be the case with counterattitudinal material. Thus, information-processing theory provides a reasonable account of attitude polarization as a result of overt and covert argumentation accompanying group discussion.

The Relative Merits of Comparison and Informational Theories

A number of experiments have compared the social comparison and information-processing theories as explanations of polarization effects. Most research strongly supports the proposition that, regardless of other processes, such as social comparison operating on group members, the assimilation and acceptance of persuasive information is a *necessary* condition for polarization. However, whether information processing is sufficient, without the aid of social comparison processes, to produce attitude polarization is not yet clear. Let's review the results of some of the major comparative studies.

In an experiment concerning mock jury deliberations, Kaplan informed each juror of the other jurors' opinions. In all cases, the others' opinions were consistent with each jury member's initial attitude. Later on, some subjects were provided with factual information contrary to their initial judgment, whereas others received information consistent with it. In all cases, the jurors shifted in the direction toward which the information pointed. Kaplan concluded that it was the information and not the other jurors' opinions that apparently determined opinion shifts.[61]

In a more elaborate study, Burnstein, Vinokur, and Trope varied the number of arguments available to group members and knowledge of the opinions held by other group members. Each group member read from 5 to 25 arguments favoring an attitudinal issue and learned the opinions of 1 to 5 of the other group members. Results showed that the greater the number of arguments read, the more polarized a person's opinion became. However, an increasing knowledge of others' proattitudinal opinions did not affect the strength of initial attitudes. The researchers also found a slight, albeit statistically insignificant, tendency for members' opinions to be stronger when they knew of others' opinions *and* had a lot of information about an issue. Burnstein and his colleagues concluded that knowing another's opinions may be a stimulant to information processing because it facilitates the generation of additional covert arguments to bolster one's initial, socially sanctioned opinion.[62]

In another experiment focusing exclusively on the effects of covert self-generated arguments, Tesser and his colleagues found that simply giving an individual group member time to think about a proattitudinal issue was sufficient to polarize or strengthen an attitude. In no instances were group members provided with information about the opinions of similar others. Moreover, Tesser found that the magnitude of polarization varied positively with: (1) the number of arguments available to subjects or their prior knowledge about the issue; and (2) the time they spent thinking about the issue. Additionally, polarization correlated negatively with any effects that distracted subjects from thinking about arguments.[63] Along these same lines, Bateson found that individuals who thought about their opinions and came up with covert arguments supporting them exhibited the same level of polarization as people who openly discussed their opinions with fellow group members.[64]

All these studies support the notion that information processing is a necessary, perhaps even a sufficient, condition to polarize attitudes during group interaction. However, one final study deserves mention because it raises the possibility that informational and social comparison processes often may work together to polarize attitudes, indeed, that social comparison sometimes may be *necessary* to stimulate group members to generate the arguments required for attitude polarization. Burnstein and Vinokur compared levels of polarization across three experimental conditions. In one, group members were told of others' opinions and were then encouraged to think about the issue and list all the arguments that came to mind. In a second condition, subjects were informed of others' opinions, but then distracted from thinking about the issue. Finally, some group members were not told of others' opinions but, like subjects in the first condition, were encouraged to think about arguments related to the attitudinal issue. Results showed that significant attitude polarization occurred only in the first experimental condition, and consistent with information-processing theory, the degree of polarization was positively correlated with the number of arguments generated by the members.[65]

This finding has led several theorists, including the author of social comparison theory, Baron, to favor a *two-factor theory of group polarization* in which the social comparison and information-processing explanations are not considered mutually exclusive. Indeed, two-factor proponents argue that, in most opinion shifts, the two processes operate in a complementary manner. The two-factor model presumes that the social comparison–induced tendency to shift toward extreme positions is aided by the generation of persuasive arguments favoring extreme attitudinal positions.[66] This explanation is intuitively appealing and should be explored further.

Taken together, the studies surveyed offer compelling evidence that information processing is a necessary condition for attitude polarization, and that sometimes it may be sufficient without the benefit of social comparison to produce strengthened attitudes. However, as we indicated earlier, the necessity versus sufficiency question awaits resolution. Even so, it is fair to conclude as have Helmut Lamm and David Myers that "among the assorted explanations for group polarization, informational influence is the most strongly and consistently supported."[67]

GROUP INFLUENCES ON BEHAVIOR: BEHAVIORAL CONTAGION AND DEINDIVIDUATION

We have now considered group normative and informational variables that facilitate attitude formation, alteration, and reinforcement or polarization. In this section, our focus will shift to the power of groups to trigger behaviors that ordinarily are suppressed when individuals act alone. As long ago as 1903, the French sociologist Gustav Le Bon observed that individuals often become "lost" in crowds and act as they never would were they acting alone. He argued that groups develop a kind of mental homogeneity, or crowd mentality, labeled the *collective mind*. "Whoever be the individuals that compose it," Le Bon writes, "however like or unlike be their mode of life, their occupations, their character, or their intelligence, the fact that they have been transformed into a crowd puts them in possession of a sort of collective mind."[68]

Because of its collective mind, a crowd, according to Le Bon, is irrational and its intellectual level is below that of isolated individuals. The mind of the group, he says, is "fickle, credulous, intolerant, dictatorial, [and] unreasoning." He describes crowds as emotional and argues that in them the individual begins to feel the emotions of a "primitive being."[69] In short, from Le Bon's perspective, the group mentality releases individuals from normal inhibitions, freeing them to engage in acts that they would never consider were they acting alone.

Although Le Bon sometimes engaged in hyperbole, his basic analysis of crowd behavior has stood the test of time. Contemporary students of group behavior focus on two group variables that have a liberating effect on individual group members: *behavioral contagion* and *deindividuation*.

Behavioral Contagion

To understand the phenomenon of contagion, it will be useful to contrast it with the conformity paradigm discussed earlier. You will recall that prior to conformity, people believe or behave in ways contrary to the group norm. However, after observing other group members, they alter their attitudes and behaviors to conform to what the group defines as acceptable. In contrast, behavioral contagion occurs in situations where an individual group member initially and secretly wishes to act in a certain way, but feels internal constraints against doing so. If this person then sees one or more group members acting out his or her fantasy, the restraints against acting as he or she privately would like to are reduced. The reduction of restraints by a model or models is called *behavioral contagion*.

Thus, the conforming person is motivated to change behavior only *after* observing the group's normative actions. However, in the case of contagion, the individual is motivated to perform certain behaviors *prior* to observing the group's actions, and is released from internal constraints by the observation. This process is much the same as that suggested by the "release" theory of group polarization.

Behavioral contagion is often found in popular fiction as well as real-life. A common scene in many Western movies portrays a mob outside the sheriff's office demanding that a prisoner be turned over for lynching. The sheriff refuses; someone in the crowd hurls a rock through the jail window; and suddenly, the mob attacks. In this situation, the members of the crowd wanted to storm the jail, but were restrained until the action of one person reduced their inhibitions. Behavioral contagion is also present in real-life settings such as the looting and arson that have occurred in several American cities after blackouts or natural disasters. People who normally would never steal or destroy private property do so after observing similar others engage in such behaviors.

Behavioral contagion has been verified in a number of controlled experiments. For example, Redl studied contagion in group therapy sessions and observed that patients often feel angry with the therapist but initially resist expressing their anger. However, after one group member vents negative feelings, Redl observed that the balance of the patients almost always follow suit.[70] Wheeler extended Redl's work and developed an operational definition of the phenomenon. He identified four conditions that are required before contagion will occur: (1) an individual must have a prior motivation to behave in a certain way; (2) he or she must know how to perform the behavior in question; (3) the person must observe a model perform the behavior; and (4) the individual must act out the modeled behavior that he or she initially was motivated to perform.[71]

In tests of this model, Wheeler found that people are more likely to behave aggressively if they observe others aggressing and if they already have latent aggressive tendencies.[72] Taken together, these results imply that people who engage in contagion behavior already have the capacity and the motivation to behave in certain ways, but feel constrained from doing so. Observation of a model lowers these inhibitions and frees people to behave as they originally wished.

Deindividuation

Deindividuation is the second factor that liberates group members to behave as they secretly wish. It is a condition characterizing individuals who have lost their sense of personal identity and self-awareness as entities separate from the group. Because deindividuated people are submerged in the group, they feel no personal responsibility for their own actions and are freed to behave as they otherwise would not outside the group.[73] Unlike behavioral contagion, the liberating qualities of deindividuation require no model.

Theorists exploring deindividuation or submergence in the group have identified two generative forces behind it: anonymity and cohesiveness. Philip Zimbardo argues that feelings of *anonymity* prompt people to shed their own identities and take on the group persona. Anonymity-inducing variables include similarity of dress, grooming, emotional arousal, and so forth.[74] For example, from Zimbardo's perspective, a uniformed, regulation-groomed policeman is much more likely to take on a "cop-against-the-world" group identity than is an offbeat, plainclothes officer. Once the group identity is assumed, the individual police officer is freed from a sense of personal responsibility for his or her actions. From that point on, the individual acts for good or ill in the name of "the law." Similarly, military and civilian leaders often take on the identity of "the state." Freed from a sense of personal responsibility, they are capable of far more cruel and dehumanizing acts than they might be if they retained a sense of personal accountability.[75] Such behavior is reminiscent of King Louis XIV who is purported to have declared *"L'état, c'est moi"* ("I am the state").

Ed Diener has argued that deindividuation, involving a perception of the group-as-self, is more dependent on variables like *group cohesiveness*, solidarity, and esprit de corps than on external anonymity cues. He has shown that involvement with an active, highly cohesive group and commitment to its goals lower one's sense of objective self-awareness since one focuses on the group rather than the self.[76] Taking both Diener's and Zimbardo's theorizing into account, we may conclude that deindividuation involves both a loss of personal self-awareness and a heightened sense of group awareness. These conditions may be triggered by a strong commitment to the activities of a cohesive group and by cues signaling personal anonymity.

A number of studies have explored the behavioral effects of deindividuation. For example, Zimbardo deindividuated some experimental subjects by having them wear long laboratory coats and hoods over their heads, and individuated others by having them wear their own clothes and name tags. Both groups were then told they would be participating in a learning study where they could administer electrical shocks to learners for incorrect responses. Results showed that the deindividuated groups gave shocks of far longer duration than did the individuated people.[77]

In a second, highly imaginative study, Zimbardo created a mock prison in the basement of a building at Stanford University. He hired 24 male students who were described as "mature, emotionally stable, normal, intelligent college students from middle-class homes throughout the United States and Canada." A prison environment was simulated, and half of the subjects were randomly assigned to play the role of guards and half the role of prisoners. Both the "prisoners" and the "guards" were given appropriate uniforms. The prisoners were placed in three-man cells for the duration of the experiment that was to last two weeks. The guards ran the "prison," and Zimbardo served as the "warden." What happened was shocking and disturbing. The prisoners "became servile, dehumanized robots," thinking only of their own survival and of their hatred for the guards. Many of the guards became tyrannical and brutalized the inmates. Zimbardo found that this deindividuated situation temporarily "undid a lifetime of learning; human values were suspended; self-concepts were challenged, and the ugliest, most base, pathological side of human nature surfaced." In fact, the situation became so bad that the experiment had to be terminated after only six days.[78]

In a series of naturalistic studies, Watson examined the warfare patterns of over 200 cultures. He discovered that in cultures where the warriors deindividuated themselves by wearing masks and body paint, there was a greater tendency to torture captives than in cultures whose warriors were individuated.[79] In a related field study, Diener and his associates found that Halloween trick-or-treaters were more likely to steal when they wore masks than when they were clearly identifiable.[80] Taking a different approach, Worchel and Andreoli found that aggressors tend to deindividuate their victims before harming them. This deindividuation effectively removes the personal identity, uniqueness, and humanness from the victim. As a consequence, it is easier for aggressors to attack a deindividuated victim than a more individuated one.[81] These latter experimental findings, of course, parallel real-life situations. During wartime, for example, the enemy typically is stereotyped and, thereby, dehumanized. Rather than thinking in terms of killing other human beings, we see ourselves "eradicating communists," or in the case of the Vietnam war, "napalming gooks."

The studies examined so far imply that deindividuation invariably results in dehumanizing, antisocial behavior, but it is not always so. For example, Gergen, Gergen, and Barton placed subjects in a dark room—the darkness effectively deindividuating them. They found that deindividuation led not to increased aggression, but to increases in touching, caressing, and other affectionate behaviors. The researchers advanced the notion that either prosocial or antisocial behavior could be enhanced by deindividuation, depending on the valence of associated, situational cues. From this view, the darkness may have been more suggestive of intimacy than aggression, and, consequently, it led to an increase in prosocial acts.[82] This hypothesis, of course, follows the predictions of attribution theory covered in Chapter 6.

Johnson and Downing tested the notion that, depending on situational cues, deindividuation may result in either prosocial or antisocial behavior. Following Zimbardo, their study was concerned with verbal learning and subjects were given the opportunity to shock learners for incorrect responses. Some people were deindividuated by wearing robes resembling those of the Ku Klux Klan, but others wore nurse's uniforms. The results showed that subjects in the KKK costumes consistently increased shock levels throughout the experiment, but those subjects in the medical costumes administered decreasing shocks.[83] These findings suggest that deindividuation does not necessarily result in antisocial behavior. To the contrary, positive, helping behaviors may be enhanced if situational cues are prosocial in nature. Nevertheless, most available laboratory and field research confirms that deindividuation usually results in antisocial behavior.

A CRITICAL APPRAISAL OF GROUP PERSUASION THEORIES

The group persuasion theories we have examined, including social comparison and information-processing theories, are explicit rules-based approaches to social influence, and, as such, are entirely compatible with our own perspective on persuasive communication.

Despite this compatibility, group theories are not without problems. First, there are few specific theories of social influence in groups. This became apparent in our own survey where we found only two full-blown theories of group influence, namely social comparison and information processing. This state of affairs has led Marvin Shaw to conclude that "group dynamics has largely failed in . . . the development of adequate theoretical formulations [to] organize the [vast array of available] empirical data." What theories there are, he continues, "are capable of encompassing only limited amounts of information gleaned from small group research."[84] Although he may be unduly pessimistic, it is fair to say that much theoretical work in the area of small group persuasion remains to be done.

Second, group scholars have slighted naturalistic research, preferring to test hypotheses that, in many cases, lack an adequate descriptive base. For instance, few systematic attempts have been made to uncover and describe the rule structures in ongoing groups. Thus, one research goal must be to identify classes of social rules peculiar to groups and to stipulate the specific contexts where these rules should be operable. Despite these criticisms, group theories, because they focus on the behavioral impact of socially shared rules, have made important contributions to our understanding of interpersonal persuasion.

NOTES

1. Alan C. Kerckhoff, Kurt W. Back, and Norman Miller, "Sociometric Patterns in Hysterical Contagion," *Sociometry* 28 (1965): 2–15.

2. The term *reference group* was coined by sociologist Herbert H. Hyman in "The Psychology of Status," *Archives of Psychology* 1942, No. 269. For a useful discussion of the concept, see Alberta E. Siegel and Sidney Siegel, "Reference Groups, Membership Groups, and Attitude Change," in *Group Dynamics*, ed. Dorwin Cartwright and Alvin Zander (Evanston, Ill.: Row, Peterson, 1960), pp. 232–240.

3. For discussion of the essential characteristics of a group, see Marvin E. Shaw, *Group Dynamics: The Psychology of Small Group Behavior*, 2nd ed. (New York: McGraw-Hill, 1976); A. Paul Hare, *Handbook of Small Group Research* (New York: Free Press, 1976); and John A. De Lamater, "A Definition of 'Group,' " *Small Group Behavior* 5 (1974): 30–44.

4. Ivan D. Steiner, *Group Process and Productivity* (New York: Academic Press, 1972), p. 171.

5. David Krech, Richard S. Crutchfield, and Egerton L. Ballachey, *Individuals in Society: A Textbook of Social Psychology* (New York: McGraw-Hill, 1962).

6. Charles A. Kiesler and Sara B. Kiesler, *Conformity* (Reading, Mass: Addison-Wesley, 1969), p. 2.

7. Herbert C. Kelman, "Compliance, Identification, and Internalization: Three Processes of Attitude Change," *Journal of Conflict Resolution* 2 (1958): 51–60.

8. Kelman.

9. Harold H. Kelley, "Two Functions of Reference Groups," in *Readings in Social Psychology*, 2nd ed., ed. Guy F. Swanson, Theodore M. Newcomb, and Eugene L. Hartley (New York: Holt, Rinehart & Winston, 1952); and Morton Deutsch and Harold B. Gerard, "A Study of Normative and Informational Social Influence on Individual Judgment," *Journal of Abnormal and Social Psychology* 51 (1955): 629–636.

10. Muzafer Sherif, "A Study of Some Social Factors in Perception," *Archives of Psychology*, 1935, No. 187.

11. See Mark K. MacNeil and Muzafer Sherif, "Norm Change over Subject Generations as a Function of Arbitrariness of Prescribed Norms," *Journal of Personality and Social Psychology* 34 (1976): 762–773; and Robert C. Jacobs and Donald T. Campbell, "The Perpetuation of an Arbitrary Tradition through Several Generations of a Laboratory Microculture," *Journal of Abnormal and Social Psychology* 62 (1961): 649–658.

12. Solomon E. Asch, "Effects of Group Pressures upon Modification and Distortion of Judgments," in *Readings in Social Psychology*, 3rd ed., ed. Eleanor E. Maccoby, Theodore M. Newcomb, and Eugene L. Hartley (New York: Holt, Rinehart & Winston, 1958), pp. 174–183; and Solomon E. Asch, *Social Psychology* (New York: Prentice-Hall, 1952). For a discussion of the group pressures on subjects in Asch's experiments, see Lee Ross, Günter Bierbrauer, and Susan Hoffman, "The Role of Attribution Processes in Conformity and Dissent: Revisiting the Asch Situation," *American Psychologist* 31 (1976): 148–157.

13. George R. Goethals and John M. Darley, "Social Comparison Theory: An Attributional Approach," in *Social Comparison Processes: Theoretical and Empirical Perspectives*, ed. Jerry M. Suls and Richard L. Miller (Washington: Hemisphere Publishing Corporation, 1977), pp. 259–278.

14. Festinger's original account of social comparison theory is presented in Leon Festinger, "A Theory of Social Comparison Processes," *Human Relations* 7 (1954): 117–140.

15. Edward E. Jones and Harold B. Gerard, *Foundations of Social Psychology* (New York: John Wiley, 1967), p. 312.

16. Leon Festinger, "Informal Social Communication," *Psychological Review* 57 (1950): 271–282.

17. Festinger, 1950, p. 272.

18. D. A. Thornton and A. John Arrowood, "Self-Evaluation, Self-Enhancement, and the Locus of Social Comparison," *Journal of Experimental Social Psychology*, Supplement 1 (1966): 40–48.

19. Jerome E. Singer, "Social Comparison-Progress and Issues," *Journal of Experimental Social Psychology* 1 (1966): 103–110.

20. For example, see Goethals and Darley, pp. 272–273.

21. Goethals and Darley, pp. 265–266; Ladd Wheeler et al., "Factors Determining the Choice of Comparison Other," *Journal of Experimental Social Psychology* 5 (1969): 219–232.

22. Wheeler et al., p. 231.

23. Clovis R. Shepherd, *Small Groups: Some Sociological Perspectives* (San Francisco: Chandler Publishing, 1964), p. 25.

24. Asch, *Social Psychology*.

25. Marvin E. Shaw, Gerald H. Rothschild, and John F. Strickland, "Decision Processes in Communication Nets," *Journal of Abnormal and Social Psychology* 54 (1957): 323–330.

26. Vernon L. Allen and David A. Wilder, "Social Comparison, Self-Evaluation, and Conformity to the Group," in *Social Comparison Processes: Theoretical and Empirical Perspectives*, pp. 196–201.

27. Vernon L. Allen and John M. Levine, "Social Support and Conformity: The Role of Independent Assessment of Reality," *Journal of Experimental Social Psychology* 7 (1971): 48–58.

28. Stanley Schachter, "Deviation, Rejection and Communication," *Journal of Abnormal and Social Psychology* 46 (1951): 190–207.

29. Gabriel Tarde, *The Laws of Imitation* (New York: Holt, 1903); and Krech, Crutchfield, and Ballachey.

30. See Steven A. Lewis, Charles J. Langan, and Edwin P. Hollander, "Expectation of Future Interaction and the Choice of Less Desirable Alternatives in Conformity," *Sociometry* 35 (1972): 440–447.

31. David J. Stang, "Conformity, Ability and Self-Esteem," *Representative Research in Social Psychology* 3 (1972): 97–103.

32. James E. Dittes and Harold H. Kelley, "Effects of Different Conditions of Acceptance upon Conformity to Group Norms," *Journal of Abnormal and Social Psychology* 53 (1956): 100–107.

33. Edwin P. Hollander, "Conformity, Status and Idiosyncrasy Credit," *Psychological Review* 65 (1958): 117–127.

34. Robert Rosenthal and Lenore Jacobson, *Pygmalion in the Classroom: Teacher Expectation and Pupils' Intellectual Development* (New York: Holt, Rinehart & Winston, 1968). This study has been the object of considerable criticism. For major critiques of the data analyses and the intelligence testing instrument that was used, see Janet D. Elashoff and Richard E. Snow, *Pygmalion Reconsidered* (Worthington, Ohio: Charles A. Jones, 1971); and Richard E. Snow, "Unfinished Pygmalion," *Contemporary Psychology* 14 (1969): 197–199.

35. For a useful study that delineates some of the ways role expectations are transmitted, see Marylee C. Taylor, "Race, Sex, and the Expression of Self-Fulfilling Prophecies in a Laboratory Teaching Situation," *Journal of Personality and Social Psychology* 37 (1979): 897–912.

36. Robert E. Kraut, "Effects of Social Labeling on Giving to Charity," *Journal of Experimental Social Psychology* 9 (1973): 551–562.

37. Mark Snyder and William B. Swann, Jr., "Behavioral Confirmation in Social Interaction: From Social Perception to Social Reality," *Journal of Experimental Social Psychology* 14 (1978): 148–162. For a similar study, see Carl H. Word, Mark P. Zanna, and Joel Cooper, "The Nonverbal Mediation of Self-Fulfilling Prophecies in Social Interaction," *Journal of Experimental Social Psychology* 10 (1974): 109–120.

38. James A. F. Stoner, "A Comparison of Individual and Group Decisions Involving Risk," (M.A. diss., Massachusetts Institute of Technology, 1961).

39. For example, see Robert B. Zajonc et al., "Individual and Group Risk Taking in a Two-Choice Situation," *Journal of Experimental Social Psychology* 4 (1968): 89–107.

40. For a survey of studies documenting the generality of group extremity shifts, see David G. Myers and Helmut Lamm, "The Group Polarization Phenomenon," *Psychological Bulletin* 83 (1976): 602–627.

41. Serge Moscovici and Marisa Zavalloni, "The Group as a Polarizer of Attitudes," *Journal of Personality and Social Psychology* 12 (1969): 125–135.

42. Myers and Lamm, p. 603.

43. Moscovici and Zavalloni.

44. Geneviève Paicheler, "Norms and Attitude Change I: Polarization and Styles of Behavior," *European Journal of Social Psychology* 6 (1976): 405–427.

45. David G. Myers and Martin F. Kaplan, "Group-Induced Polarization in Simulated Juries," *Personality and Social Psychology Bulletin* 2 (1976): 63–66.

46. For an excellent summary of risky-shift explanations, see Dean G. Pruitt, "Choice Shift in Group Discussion: An Introductory Review," *Journal of Personality and Social Psychology* 20 (1971): 339–360.

47. See Michael A. Wallach, Nathan Kogan, and Daryl J. Bem, "Diffusion of Responsibility and Level of Risk Taking in Groups," *Journal of Abnormal and Social Psychology* 68 (1964): 263–274.

48. See Barry E. Collins and Harold Guetzkow, *A Social Psychology of Group Processes for Decision-Making* (New York: John Wiley, 1964).

49. See Roger Brown, *Social Psychology* (New York: Free Press of Glencoe, 1965).

50. The social comparison explanation is detailed in the following articles: Glenn S. Sanders and Robert

S. Baron, "Is Social Comparison Irrelevant for Producing Choice Shifts?" *Journal of Experimental Social Psychology* 13 (1977): 303–314; and Robert S. Baron and Gard Roper, "A Reaffirmation of a Social Comparison View of Choice Shifts, Averaging, and Extremity Effects in Autokinetic Situations," *Journal of Personality and Social Psychology* 33 (1976): 521–530.

51. Festinger, "A Theory of Social Comparison Processes," p. 124.

52. For a listing of over 24 such studies, see David G. Myers, "Summary and Bibliography of Experiments on Group-Induced Response Shift," *Catalog of Selected Documents in Psychology* 3 (1973): 123.

53. See Raymond Baumhart, *An Honest Profile* (New York: Holt, Rinehart & Winston, 1968); and K. J. Lenihan, "Perceived Climates as a Barrier to Housing Desegregation" (unpublished MS, Columbia University, 1965).

54. Sanders and Baron, p. 304.

55. See George Levinger and David J. Schneider, "Test of the 'Risk is a Value' Hypothesis," *Journal of Personality and Social Psychology* 11 (1969): 165–169.

56. See Dean G. Pruitt, "Conclusions: Toward An Understanding of Choice Shifts in Group Discussion," *Journal of Personality and Social Psychology* 20 (1971): 495–510; and Pruitt, "Choice Shifts."

57. Myers and Kaplan.

58. David G. Myers, Sandra Brown Wojcicki, and Bobette S. Aardema, "Attitude Comparison: Is There Ever a Bandwagon Effect?" *Journal of Applied Social Psychology* 7 (1977): 341–347. For a related study, see David G. Myers, "Polarizing Effects of Social Comparison," *Journal of Experimental Social Psychology* 14 (1978): 554–563.

59. The information-processing explanation is detailed in the following articles: Eugene Burnstein and Amiram Vinokur, "Persuasive Argumentation and Social Comparison as Determinants of Attitude Polarization," *Journal of Experimental Social Psychology* 13 (1977): 315–332; Eugene Burnstein and Amiram Vinokur, "What a Person Thinks upon Learning He Has Chosen Differently from Others: Nice Evidence for the Persuasive-Arguments Explanation of Choice Shifts," *Journal of Experimental Social Psychology* 11 (1975): 412–426; and Amiram Vinokur and Eugene Burnstein, "The Effects of Partially Shared Persuasive Arguments on Group Induced Shifts: A Group Problem Solving Approach," *Journal of Personality and Social Psychology* 29 (1974): 305–315. The reader should be aware that the information-processing explanation sometimes is referred to as persuasive-arguments theory.

60. Burnstein and Vinokur, "Persuasive Argumentation," pp. 326–329.

61. Martin F. Kaplan's research is reported in Helmut Lamm and David G. Myers, "Group-Induced Polarization of Attitudes and Behavior," in *Advances in Experimental Social Psychology*, ed. Leonard Berkowitz (New York: Academic Press, 1978), pp. 171–172.

62. Eugene Burnstein, Amiram Vinokur, and Yaacov Trope, "Interpersonal Comparison versus Persuasive Argumentation: A More Direct Test of Alternative Explanations for Group Induced Shifts in Individual Choice," *Journal of Experimental Social Psychology* 9 (1973): 236–245.

63. For a summary of Tesser's research, see Abraham Tesser, "Self-Generated Attitude Change," in *Advances in Experimental Social Psychology*, ed. Leonard Berkowitz (New York: Academic Press, 1978), pp. 289–338.

64. Nicholas Bateson, "Familiarization, Group Discussion, and Risk Taking," *Journal of Experimental Social Psychology* 2 (1966): 119–129.

65. Burnstein and Vinokur, "What a Person Thinks."

66. For a complete outline of the two-factor model, see Myers and Lamm, "Group Polarization," pp. 618–620.

67. Lamm and Myers, "Group-Induced Polarization," p. 169.

68. Gustav Le Bon, *The Crowd* (London: Allen & Unwin, 1903), p. 20.

69. Ibid. An interesting contemporary analysis of group versus individual judgments is found in Richard E. Petty, Stephen G. Harkins, and Kipling D. Williams, "The Effects of Group Diffusion of Cognitive Effort on Attitudes: An Information-Processing View," *Journal of Personality and Social Psychology* 38 (1980): 81–92.

70. Fritz Redl, "The Phenomenon of Contagion and 'Shock Effect' in Group Therapy," in *Searchlight on Delinquency*, ed. K. R. Eissler (New York: International Universities Press, 1949).

71. Ladd Wheeler, "Toward a Theory of Behavioral Contagion," *Psychological Review* 73 (1966): 179–192.

72. See Ladd Wheeler and Seward Smith, "Censure of the Model in the Contagion of Aggression," *Journal of Personality and Social Psychology* 6 (1967): 93–98; and Ladd Wheeler and Anthony R. Caggiula, "The Contagion of Aggression," *Journal of Experimental Social Psychology* 2 (1966): 1–10.

73. The first systematic description of deindividuation is found in Leon Festinger, Albert Pepitone, and Theodore Newcomb, "Some Consequences of Deindividuation in a Group," *Journal of Abnormal and Social Psychology* 47 (1952): 382–389.

74. Philip Zimbardo, "The Human Choice: Individuation, Reason, and Order versus Deindividuation, Impulse, and Chaos," in *Nebraska Symposium on Motivation*, ed. William J. Arnold and David Levine (Lincoln, Neb.: University of Nebraska Press, 1969), pp. 237–307.

75. Janis has developed a concept similar to deindividuation called *groupthink* and has analyzed the behavior of national leaders in relation to it. See Irving L. Janis, *Victims of Groupthink: A Psychological Study of Foreign-Policy Decisions and Fiascoes* (Boston: Houghton Mifflin, 1972).

76. Ed Diener, "Deindividuation, Self-Awareness, and Disinhibition," *Journal of Personality and Social Psychology* 37 (1979): 1160–1171.

77. Zimbardo, "The Human Choice."

78. Craig Haney, Curtis Banks, and Philip Zimbardo, "Interpersonal Dynamics in a Simulated Prison," *International Journal of Criminology and Penology* 1 (1973): 69–97; and Philip Zimbardo, "The Psychological Power and Pathology of Imprisonment" (Statement prepared for the U.S. House of Representatives Committee on the Judiciary, Subcommittee No. 3, Robert Kastemeyer, Chairman, hearings on prison reform, 1971). Unpublished MS, Stanford University, 1971. For a critical analysis of Zimbardo's experiment, see Ali Banuazizi and Siamak Movahedi, "Interpersonal Dynamics in a Simulated Prison: A Methodological Analysis," *American Psychologist* 30 (1975): 152–160.

79. Robert I. Watson, "Investigation into Deindividuation Using a Cross-Cultural Survey Technique," *Journal of Personality and Social Psychology* 25 (1973): 342–345.

80. Edward Diener et al., "Effects of Deindividuation Variables on Stealing among Halloween Trick-or-Treaters," *Journal of Personality and Social Psychology* 33 (1976): 178–183.

81. Stephen Worchel and Virginia Andreoli, "Facilitation of Social Interaction through Deindividuation of the Target," *Journal of Personality and Social Psychology* 36 (1978): 549–557.

82. Kenneth J. Gergen, Mary M. Gergen, and William H. Barton, "Deviance in the Dark," *Psychology Today* 7 (1973): 129–130.

83. Robert O. Johnson and Leslie L. Downing, "Deindividuation and Valence of Cues: Effects on Prosocial and Antisocial Behavior," *Journal of Personality and Social Psychology* 37 (1979): 1532–1538.

84. Shaw, pp. 405–406.

CHAPTER 8

Social Learning Theory and Self-Persuasion

On the morning of August 1, 1966, a young man made his way to the top of a 30-floor tower at The University of Texas at Austin. He carried a green duffel bag and a footlocker bearing the name, Lance Corporal Charles Joseph Whitman. Once Whitman reached the tower's observation deck, he had an excellent view of the 240-acre campus and the entire city of Austin. The campus was crowded; summer school was in session, and students were hurrying to and from their classes. Suddenly, the silence of the hot Texas morning was shattered by the intermittent sounds of gunfire. For the next 97 minutes, Whitman terrorized the campus. Relying mainly on a 6-mm rifle, a carbine, and a .356 revolver, he executed 13 people and wounded 31 more before he was killed by police officers. Later, the police added two more persons to the list of the dead when they found that Whitman had murdered his wife and mother before his journey to the tower.

Once Whitman had been killed, people emerged from their hiding places. As they milled about the base of the tower, they openly wondered why he had committed such a horrible crime. Whitman's childhood provides some clues. He was taught to shoot a rifle at an early age, and by 13 he could shoot the head off a squirrel at 60 yards. His father, a stern disciplinarian, lavishly praised young Whitman's markmanship. When Whitman served in the Marine Corps, he received further social approval for his sharp shooting. He came to value his own prowess with firearms. We also know that Whitman's father was an aggressive man who used violence to solve frustrating problems. He is known to have assaulted his passive wife on numerous occasions. Thus, Whitman's parents served as role models from which their son could learn that aggression pays off, and passivity is punished.[1]

The story of Whitman's aggression illustrates the central issue we will explore in this chapter. At the same time, we will soon see that it provides a contrast with the particular theory of learning on which our attention will be focused. At a general level, all learning theories look at the ways people learn to perform certain behaviors by anticipating or experiencing their consequences. As a rule, people learn to enact behaviors that are associated with valued rewards like social approval, personal acceptance, and the like, and to avoid behaviors associated with punishing conditions like ridicule or rejection. Learning theory, then, focuses on *overt human behavior* and addresses the internal and external determinants of that behavior.

In considering the interrelationships of learning and persuasion, we will examine in detail Albert Bandura's social learning theory. Unlike many learning approaches, it is action oriented and rules based. Thus, we will refer extensively to rule-governed behavior. We will also explore four models of self-persuasion derived from social learning theory, and appraise the social learning approach to persuasive communication.

THE NATURE OF SOCIAL LEARNING THEORY

Although social learning theory has many features in common with other theories of learning, it differs from them in several critical respects. To understand its unique properties, we must first trace the similarities and differences among the various approaches to learning and persuasion.

All learning theories emphasize in varying degrees the effects of situational forces on human behavior. According to most learning theorists, all human behavior leads to consequences that feed back on behavior, either maintaining or changing the probability of similar future action. If, for instance, one's behavior leads to positive consequences like social approval or personal recognition, it should continue or perhaps intensify. In contrast, if a behavior meets with criticism and social rejection, it is less likely to be repeated. In short, one *learns* from the consequences of one's behavior. This approach contrasts sharply with theories, like cognitive dissonance covered in Chapter 5, that explain persuasive effects by referring to internal arousal states. Learning theory, like attribution theory considered in Chapter 6, devotes considerable attention to situational variables affecting human behavior.

Beyond a common concern with external rewards and punishments, learning theories differ considerably in the emphasis placed on raw, external influences versus cognitive and interpretative processes that mediate environmental conditions. Thus, all learning theories can be classified either as behavioristic or cognitive. *Behavioristic*, or stimulus–response (S–R) theories, are derived from the work of B. F. Skinner and assume that people's actions are under the exclusive control of uninterpreted environmental forces.[2] From this perspective, people are regarded as reactive victims of external rewards and punishments with no freedom of choice or capacity for self-direction. Responses to external influences, including persuasive messages, are assumed to be independent of any cognitive or interpretative processes on the part of receivers. Indeed, Skinnerian theorists regard attitude and behavior change as automatic processes requiring no conscious human awareness.

S–R theory states that externally rewarded behavior patterns develop and persist, and negatively reinforced actions decay.[3] Charles Whitman's behavior illustrates the S–R theorist's notion of learning. From an S–R view, had Whitman's earlier aggressive behaviors not been rewarded, and had he not seen from his parents' behavior that aggression generally reaps benefits and passivity is punished, the 1966 tragedy at the Texas tower would never have occurred. From a behavioristic perspective, Charles Whitman was a helpless victim of the vagaries of external rewards and punishments. Clearly, S–R theories adhere to the "mechanistic model of man" discussed in Chapter 3.

In contrast, *cognitive*, or stimulus–organism–response (S–O–R), theories assume that human cognitive and interpretative processes shape external reality and determine responses to the environment. Despite a common interest in cognitive processes, S–O–R theories vary considerably in the role each accords cognition. For example, some are relatively mechanistic, assuming that internal processes such as attitudes are the product of external rewards and punishments. Typical of this variety is Leonard Doob's "backward chain of learning" theory. Doob regards attitudes as "implicit responses" developed after some overt response is rewarded or positively reinforced. After formation, attitudes are presumed to mediate future overt consequences.[4] This type of S–O–R model, although allowing that internal cognitions mediate external phenomena, still assumes that such internal processes are formed and largely controlled by external forces.

Other cognitive learning theories are far more actional in nature and emphasize the human capacity for choice and self-direction. Bandura's social-learning theory, to which we now turn, is one such approach. To differentiate his view from the Skinnerian and other mechanistic models, Bandura stipulates the following three philosophical premises upon which social learning theory is based. First, he notes that "man is neither driven by inner forces not buffeted helplessly by environmental influences." Rather, he suggests that behavior formation and change "is best understood in terms of a continuous reciprocal interaction" among overt behavior, the perceived positive or negative consequences of that behavior, and people's internal cognitions and emotions.[5] Second, Bandura argues that our interpretative and symbol-using capabilities permit us to enact insightful as well as foresightful behaviors that are not under the control of any external reward or punishment. "People can represent external influences symbolically," Bandura explains, "and later use such representations to guide their actions. . . . [They] can foresee the probable consequences of different actions and alter their behavior accordingly."[6]

Finally, Bandura argues that a "third distinguishing feature of man is that he is capable of self-regulative influences."[7] We can set goals or standards of behavior for ourselves. Moreover, we can reward ourselves or withhold self-reward, depending on whether or not we reach self-established goals. In sum, Bandura's theory assumes that: (1) we are capable of self-reward and self-influence; (2) environmental rewards and punishments are no more than interpretative or symbolic representations, the retention of which allows us to foresee the consequences of various actions and behave accordingly; and (3) our internal and external worlds continuously interact to shape many behavioral effects. Bandura summarizes these assumptions by noting that social learning theory is devoted to an "analysis of how patterns of behavior are acquired and how their expression is continuously regulated by the interplay of self-generated and other sources of influences."[8]

The Nature of Social Learning Processes: Searching for Rules

From Bandura's perspective, the essence of human learning is a search for "if–then" relationships. People learn by continually asking and answering the question: "If I behave in a certain fashion, what will be the consequences?" For example, if I were to consider cheating on an examination or on my income tax returns, my decision would be dependent on an analysis of the probable consequences of such an act. If I concluded that cheating would violate my own standards of morality, and result in punishments were I caught, I would probably decide not to cheat. In contrast, if I have no personal objection to dishonesty and I don't expect to get caught, my decision should be quite different. As this example indicates, humans are goal oriented; they strive for positive consequences. Moreover, they develop positive attitudes toward, and engage in, behaviors that yield positive benefits; on the other hand, we avoid behaviors that block goals or entail negative sanctions and develop associated negative cognitive schemata.

Bandura refers to this quest for goal-maximizing, if–then (goal–action) relationships as a search for "response-generative *rules* [emphasis added]."[9] You will recall from Chapter 3 that rules describe those actions a person needs to take in a given situation to achieve desired objectives. Thus, from a social learning perspective, the learning of attitudes and behaviors constitutes "rule-governed behavior."[10] As Bandura puts it,

> People who are aware of appropriate [behavioral] responses in a given situation and who value the outcomes they produce, change their behavior in the reinforced direction. On the other hand, those who are equally aware of the reinforcement contingencies but who devalue either the required behavior or the reinforcers not only remain uninfluenced but may even respond in an oppositional manner.[11]

The rules, or goal–action prescriptions, people follow may be social in nature, reflecting the social community's judgment of appropriate behaviors in specific contexts; or they may be idiosyncratic, representing an individual's own unique, personally developed beliefs about the actions needed to achieve certain goals. Whatever the case, social learning as rule-governed behavior involves discovering what one "must do in order to gain beneficial outcomes or avoid punishing ones."[12]

According to Bandura, people learn rules through *reinforcement*. Although behavioristic theorists regard reinforcement as *explicit* rewards and punishments delivered *after* the performance of a behavior, Bandura uses the term in a radically different fashion. He equates reinforcement with *knowledge of the probable (including imagined) positive or negative consequences of a future behavior*. In other words, Bandura, unlike S–R theorists, considers reinforcement a complex cognitive phenomenon.[13]

Knowledge of behavioral consequences can be gained not only by direct experience but also by observing the behavior of others, both on a face-to-face basis and in the media. For example, most of us have learned the if–then relationship that cigarette smoking causes disease, not by direct experience but through reading, attending to the mass media, and observing the misfortunes of others. On the other hand, we may have learned other rules such as "physical exercise improves muscle tone" directly by jogging, hiking, or playing tennis or racquetball.

From Bandura's perspective, reinforcement has two important functions: an informational and a motivational one. The *informational* function is equivalent to rule learning. By observing the differential consequences of the actions of ourselves and others, we learn those behaviors that produce favorable effects and those that do not. On the basis of this information, we "develop thoughts or hypotheses about the types of behaviors most likely to succeed. These hypotheses then serve as guides for future actions."[14]

The second function of reinforcement is *motivational*. On the basis of prior experiences, we develop expectations about actions promising valued outcomes and those threatening undesirable ones. As a result, our current actions are motivated "to a large extent by anticipated [future] consequences."[15] For instance, we don't wait until our house burns down to buy fire insurance or to take precautions to eliminate fire hazards in the home. Similarly, we usually fill up our gas tanks before they hit empty. Because we can anticipate consequences, these future expectations serve as *current* motivators in much the same way as directly experienced consequences would.[16]

Sources of Reinforcement: External Information

We have said that reinforcement represents knowledge of the positive and negative consequences of behavior. To function effectively each of us must be able to anticipate the consequences of different courses of action and regulate our behavior accordingly. Two general sources of knowledge about consequences are available: external and internal. The first is based on our interpretations of external rewards and punishments. Bandura refers to this source of information as "cognitive representation[s] of reinforcement contingencies."[17] Within the category of external information, people learn about the consequences of their behaviors in three ways.

Direct Experience   We sometimes learn consequences by *direct experience*. This type of learning is most prevalent among children, but adults can also learn in this fashion. For instance, ethnic and racial minorities often adopt negative attitudes and behavior patterns toward the majority establishment after they directly experience discrimination. Working women frequently develop negative attitudes toward male employers and coworkers when they get unequal pay for equal work or encounter sexual harassment on the job.

Role-Playing   A second way we learn behavioral consequences is through *role-playing*, which involves mentally placing oneself in the position of another who is faced with a specified set of circumstances. By "experiencing" the consequences of that "other's" behavior, we learn what might happen to us in similar circumstances. Recall, for instance, the experiment discussed in Chapter 4 in which young women smokers were asked to play the role of lung cancer victims. As a result, they learned the dreadful consequences of cigarette smoking, and most either stopped smoking or considerably reduced the number of cigarettes they smoked. We will return to role-playing later when we discuss some models of self-persuasion derived from social learning theory.

Modeling   The third way people learn the external consequences of their behavior is through *observational learning,* or *modeling;* that is, we observe the consequences of other people's behavior. This process is the most prevalent way adults learn consequences. When we observe, either on a face-to-face basis or by media attendance, that certain behaviors have positive outcomes, and others result in misfortune, we infer that the same consequences hold for us if we act similarly. For example, most television advertisements teach behavioral consequences by modeling. The actors in the Rolaids or Bufferin commercials who show relief after taking the medications are informing viewers that purchasing and using the products will do the same for them. Similarly, public health advertisements portraying the unfortunate consequences of drinking while driving, or of consuming too much junk food, imply that the same fate awaits us if we engage in these behaviors. In addition to learning from media modeling, we also learn by observing other people directly. In this way, teenagers learn those behaviors most likely to make them acceptable to their peers. And in like fashion, businesspersons often learn the tricks of the trade by observing both successful and unsuccessful role models. Thus, they differentiate those behaviors that work and those that fail without directly experimenting with either.

Bandura suggests that modeling is governed by four interrelated, cognitive processes. First, an individual must focus his or her *attention* on the essential features of the model's behavior. Second, the person must *retain* in symbolic form the if–then relationship he or she observes. According to Bandura, there are two subprocesses associated with successful retention. First, the observer must verbally encode the observed events. Failure to establish vivid memory codes specifying the consequences of cigarette smoking, reckless driving, and the like, will result in minimal behavior change as a result of observation. Second, Bandura argues that rehearsal is an important memory aid. "People who mentally rehearse or actually perform modeled patterns of behavior are less likely to forget them than are those who neither think nor practice what they have seen."[18] The importance of rehearsal can be seen in the teaching of courses ranging from biology to driver education. Students not only must observe other people demonstrating safe driving habits or dissecting a frog, but they must also rehearse these behaviors. Rehearsal increases the chances that behaviors will be learned and retained.

In addition to attention and retention, *competence* affects modeling. Can the observer perform the observed behavior? It does little good to learn that excelling in competitive sports like basketball or track will enhance your self-image if you are too short or too slow to compete successfully. The same is true for learning clinical biology or safe driving habits. In short, one must have the needed skills to enact behavior learned through observation. Finally, modeling depends on *motivational* factors. As Bandura puts it, a "person can acquire, retain, and possess the capabilities for skillful execution of modeled behavior, but the learning may rarely be activated into overt performance if it is negatively sanctioned or otherwise unfavorably received."[19] This last process summarizes the essence of rule-governed behavior: one enacts only those behaviors that he or she believes will accomplish desired objectives. We will return to the issue of modeling when we consider self-persuasion models derived from social learning theory.

Of the three external sources of reinforcement information—direct experience, role-playing, and modeling—only the first entails *explicit* external rewards or punishments. Indeed, people learn most of their behaviors *indirectly* through observing others. Put another way, we develop and alter our behaviors on the basis of learned, symbolic rules specifying how we can best achieve our goals. These rules are motivational because they help us anticipate positive outcomes and plan our actions accordingly.

Sources of Reinforcement: Self-Monitoring Systems

The interpretation of external consequences is by no means the only, or even the major, source of reinforcement information. Indeed, Bandura notes that "if actions were determined solely by external rewards and punishments, people would behave like weathervanes, constantly shifting in radically different directions to conform to the whims of others."[20]

Accordingly, a second powerful source of information about consequences comes from internal *self-reinforcement systems*. Bandura states that human "behavior . . . is extensively self-regulated by self-produced consequences for one's own actions."[21] In other words, people set performance standards for themselves and "respond to their own behavior in self-satisfied or self-critical ways in accordance with their self-imposed demands."[22] Thus, if I consider myself to be a kind, generous, and honest person, I have set three standards for evaluating my own behavior. If I find myself behaving in ways that hurt others unnecessarily, I will likely regard myself with disdain. In contrast, if I behave generously and honestly, I should be pleased with my actions. As these examples indicate, it is the *anticipation* of self-imposed consequences that motivates people to keep their behavior in line with self-established standards or values.

From the social learning perspective, self-esteem is a function of the relationship between a person's behavior and the standards he or she has selected as indices of personal worth. When behavior falls short of these standards, people hold themselves in low self-esteem. On the other hand, when behavior coincides with or exceeds personal standards, people hold themselves in high self-esteem. Moreover, self-reinforcement information is inextricably related to a person's self-concept. Among other things, the self-concept usually signifies a person's tendency to regard different aspects of his or her behavior positively or negatively. Within a social learning approach, "a negative self-concept is defined in terms of frequent negative self-reinforcement of one's behavior; conversely, a favorable self-concept is reflected in a disposition to engage in high positive self-reinforcement."[23]

Once an individual has developed a stable self-monitoring reinforcement system, a given behavior typically produces two sets of consequences: a self-evaluation and an external reaction.[24] It is important to note that these two types of consequences may sometimes conflict. For example, some people are rewarded socially or materially for behavior they strongly dislike. When negative self-evaluation outweighs the force of rewards for accommodating behavior, external influences should be relatively ineffective. On the other hand, when external inducements, whether rewarding or punishing, prevail over self-reinforcing influences, individuals will comply, but will not be persuaded. However, as we saw in the discussions of counterattitudinal advocacy and simple compliance to group norms, in circumstances such as these, people often realign their internal values to more closely approximate compliant behavior. A different conflict between external and self-produced consequences arises when people are punished for engaging in activities they value highly. Here, as in the previous example, the relative strength of self-approval and external censure will determine whether such behaviors will be discarded or maintained. If self-approval is valued more highly than external censure, people fall back on self-encouragement to sustain their efforts.

Of course, self-reinforcement and external influences need not conflict; indeed, they frequently are complementary. It is fair to say that external reinforcement will exert the greatest influence when it is harmonious with, rather than counter to, self-produced consequences. Moreover, people act to achieve and maintain complementary conditions. As we saw in Chapter 7, people often do this by selectively associating themselves with others who share similar behavioral standards, thus insuring social support for their own system of self-evaluation.

The Establishment and Maintenance of Self-Reinforcement Systems

Given the prominent role of self-reinforcement systems in social learning theory, we need to examine how these systems are established and maintained. Although they may be acquired in several ways, self-reinforcement systems are primarily based on group norms and general social and cultural rules. And, as we saw in Chapter 7 on group behavior, groups reward members for adherence to their rules and punish nonconformity. As a result of interacting in multiple groups, people come to respond to their own behavior in self-approving or self-critical ways, depending on how far it departs from the evaluative standards set by important groups. Numerous field studies have documented the effects of general societal or cultural rules on self-reinforcement systems. For instance, Eaton and Weil found that in cultures where austerity is the dominant norm, people reward themselves only sparingly. And because of the emphasis on high standards of personal conduct, self-denying and self-punishing reactions are prevalent.[25] In contrast, in societies where self-gratification patterns predominate, people usually reward themselves generously even for minimal performances.[26]

Just as self-reinforcement systems are established primarily by social rules, these same social influences play a major role in maintaining them. For instance, adherence to high standards of self-reinforcement is supported by a vast social reward system involving praise, social recognition, and other awards and honors. In contrast, few accolades are bestowed on people who reward themselves for mediocre performances.

In addition to this social maintenance system, there is some evidence that self-reinforcement systems are maintained through their role in the reduction of self-generated distress.[27] During the course of socialization into groups, people usually learn what has been called the *sequence of transgression*. This sequence involves four stages: (1) violation of group norms or rules; (2) internal distress because of anticipated punish-

ment; (3) punishment for the violation; and (4) relief. From this perspective, the violation of group rules creates distress that persists until the violater is reprimanded, after
which there is a sense of relief. Accordingly, when people violate their own standards
or rules of conduct, they should experience self-disapproval and other distressing
thoughts. And, in the case of group reprimands, a self-reprimand can bring relief from
the distress.

We have seen that people generate and regulate their own behavior through self-
criticism and self-reward. By anticipating self-imposed consequences, people are motivated to keep their behavior in line with self-established standards. Moreover, we have
seen that societal rules exert a powerful influence both on the establishment and maintenance of self-monitoring reinforcement systems.

Self-Reinforcement and External Influence:
Toward an Integration

As a conclusion to our analysis of the nature of social learning theory, we want to
consider the conceptual relationship between self-reinforcement systems and external
knowledge of consequences. Bandura has addressed this question and advances the
notion that self-reinforcement systems may well subsume all external reinforcement
phenomena. He suggests that external events may serve only "as cues to elicit covert
self-satisfaction or self-criticism."[28] Thus, external "reward" information is rewarding
only if it is congruent with one's personal standards, and external "punishment" is
meaningful only if it blocks the pursuit of personal goals. The philosophy we have
embraced in this book is sympathetic with this position. We have seen that external
reinforcement information is not even necessary to maintain or change behavior. People readily generate and regulate their own behavior through self-supplied rewards
and criticisms; however, societal rules and role models also have an important influence on the establishment and maintenance of self-generated reinforcement systems.

Given these findings, we may conclude that self-reinforced standards are shaped
to a considerable extent by social rules and role models, learned primarily by observing
the consequences of others' behaviors. Moreover, there is a reciprocal influence between self-reinforcement standards and social rules throughout the lifetime of any one
individual. However, once a person adopts a set of relatively enduring standards or
values, these become independent motivators of subsequent attitude and behavior
change. From that point on, external reinforcement information is only a cue eliciting
self-reinforcement either in the form of self-criticism or self-reward.

FOUR MODELS OF SELF-PERSUASION

We have now detailed Bandura's theory of social learning. We saw that the process of social learning involves a search for rules specifying those behaviors one needs
to perform to achieve positive consequences. Knowledge of external consequences may
be secured through direct experience or indirectly through role-playing or modeling.
Internal consequences are rooted in the standards of behavior people set for them-

selves. Depending on the extent to which people reach their self-established goals, they produce their own behavioral consequences either by rewarding or chastizing themselves for their actions. Thus, the theory of social learning, as Bandura articulates it, can legitimately be called a theory of self-persuasion. In this section, we will examine four specific models of self-persuasion derived from social learning theory: role-playing, modeling, desensitization, and behavior modification.

Role-Playing

We said earlier that role-playing involves mentally placing oneself in the position of another who is faced with a specified set of circumstances. By "experiencing" the consequences of that "other's" behavior, we learn what might happen to us in similar circumstances. Psychotherapists first employed role-playing as a learning technique. In the early 1950s, Jacob Moreno developed a role-playing strategy called *psychodrama*.[29] Psychodramatic exercises require patients to assume the role of important persons in their environment. For instance, an adolescent with hostile feelings toward parents might be asked to play a parental role. Through role-playing he or she should learn the motivations and consequences of the parents' behavior and this learning should result in changed attitudes and reduced hostilities. In one use of psychodrama, Kelly had depressed patients role-play happy individuals. As a result, Kelly found remarkable improvements in his patients' conditions. Apparently, role-playing helped the depressed patients learn the positive consequences of realistic optimism.[30]

Since these early experiments, role-playing has been used successfully to alter a whole range of attitudes and behaviors. We have already described the success that Janis and Mann achieved by having smokers role-play lung cancer victims.[31] Mann did a similar, follow-up study. He created three role-playing situations. In one, role-players were asked to imagine they were in their doctor's office and to think about and then verbalize the negative consequences of their own cigarette smoking. In a second condition, the role-players were again asked to imagine themselves in their doctor's office, but they were asked to think and talk about how their habitual smoking showed a lack of personal discipline and self-control. Finally, a third group was not asked to focus on personal consequences, but, rather, to imagine they were debaters and to prepare to argue the hazards of smoking in a debate. Notice that the first situation forced the role-players to ponder the *personal external consequences* of smoking, and the second condition asked them to consider the ways habitual smoking violates *self-imposed standards* of behavior. In contrast, the last situation was much less personal in that it simply requested role-players to come up with sound arguments to help win a debate.

Results showed that the first and second role-playing situations produced a much greater change in attitudes toward cigarette smoking than did the third impersonal condition. In addition, male subjects who verbalized the most arguments about consequences in the first two situations showed the greatest attitude change. For some reason, this finding did not hold for female subjects.[32] These results suggest that role-playing is likely to be successful only when the behavioral consequences of if–then relationships are relevant either to personal health or to self-established standards of behavior. Apparently, less personalized role-playing does not establish a sufficient link between one's *own* behavior and its consequences. Finally, the results imply that so long as role-playing is personally relevant, the greater the verbalization about consequences, the more effective the learning experience.

A final point about role-playing as a self-persuasion model relates to its long-term effects. Considerable research shows that role-playing produces more persistent effects than does passive learning. For example, two weeks after Janis' and Mann's experiment, the people who had role-played cancer patients had reduced their smoking by an average of 10.5 cigarettes per day. In contrast, the control group who had passively listened to information about the dangers of smoking reported an average decrease of only 4.8 cigarettes per day.[33] In follow-up studies conducted 8 months and 18 months after the original experiment, the role-players continued to report a significantly lower daily consumption of cigarettes than did the control subjects.[34] These findings indicate that role-playing holds great promise as a technique for inducing the self-generation of arguments about consequences, and that these self-generated messages can result in significant short- and long-term self-persuasion.

Modeling: Observational Learning

Recall from our earlier discussion that a primary way people learn the probable consequences of their actions is through *modeling*, or observing the consequences of others' behavior. When we observe, either directly or from the media, that certain behaviors produce desirable or undesirable outcomes, we can infer that we would probably get the same results were we to act similarly. Most of our purchases, whether of household products, a new stereo, or an automobile, are forms of modeling behavior. When we observe in television commercials that "Drano unclogs drains" and that "Ultra Brite" gives people "sex appeal," we can infer that we would reap similar benefits were we to buy these products. Similarly, if a friend reports being pleased with a certain brand of stereo speakers or that he or she is getting good performance from a new car, we might conclude that we too would be well served by buying similar items. On the other hand, we all avoid purchasing products when we observe that others do not benefit from them.

Many behaviors other than buying are also modeled actions. Indeed, we acquire most of our basic values and personal habits by initially observing our parents' behavior and later the behavior of admired friends and reference groups. And we select those attitudes and behaviors that are rewarding and avoid those threatening misfortune or pain. Let's examine six factors affecting the success of modeling.

The first and most elementary factor is the ratio of positive and negative *reinforcements* associated with observed behaviors. We are motivated to enact rewarded behaviors and avoid punished ones. Several studies on the effects of observing aggression document this point. For example, Bandura, Ross, and Ross conducted an experiment in which some children observed a film where the aggressive behavior of a child at play was rewarded. Other children saw a film where the aggressive child was "thoroughly thrashed" for his behavior. A control group saw no film. Later, the levels of aggression in all three groups were measured. The aggression score for children in the "aggression-rewarded" condition was 75.2; in the "aggression-punished" condition,

53.5; whereas the scores of the control group were intermediate at 61.8.[35] As these results suggest, undesirable outcomes deter modeling behavior, and positive ones increase it.

Second, and assuming the observed behaviors lead to positive consequences, we are more likely to enact modeled behaviors if we perceive the model as *similar* to ourselves. Relevant similarities include attitudes,[36] and in cases where gender is relevant to behavior, we are influenced more by models of the same sex.[37] For instance, women homemakers are likely to model other women homemakers in their choice of laundry detergents, baby foods, and attitudes toward women's rights. In contrast, gender will probably not be a factor for such women on issues like national defense policy, the effectiveness of a new cold remedy, and the price of gasoline.

Third, we are influenced by models who appear *competent*, reliable, and informed on the behavior at issue.[38] Fourth, individuals who are high in *status* tend to be especially influential models.[39] These two qualities are probably interrelated, in that high-status individuals are often perceived as more competent and knowledgeable than those who lack status. Fifth, models who behave *consistently* are more influential than those who act erratically.[40] For instance, if I am in the market for a cartridge for my stereo turntable, I will probably put a great deal of trust in people who have consistently given me good advice. Sixth and finally, people are more influenced by *multiple* rather than single models.[41] Indeed, we rarely act on the basis of observing a single person getting favorable results from a behavior. Instead, we usually observe several individuals, and if they all agree that product X is good or an investment in stock Y is smart, then we enact similar behaviors.

In summary, people adopt attitudes and behaviors that, in their judgment, will bring personal reward. A primary source of information about rewards comes from observing the behavior of similar others who are competent and consistent. By observing others, we learn if–then relationships that can guide our choices. Assuming the consequences of these rules are consistent with our personal goals, such rules can be potent instigators of self-persuasion.

Desensitization

Desensitization is a learning strategy in which people learn a new set of emotional responses to an old behavior, object, or person.[42] For example, fear of flying or public speaking can be affectively neutralized or even turned into pleasant experiences. From a social learning perspective, desensitization alters expected consequences. Its usual aim is to change previously negative consequences to positive ones.

In order to desensitize a behavior, an individual must learn to *relax* very deeply. Such relaxation can normally be self-induced.[43] Once relaxed, the individual must approach the negative behavior or feared object in a step-by-step fashion. In the case of a behavior, the person slowly engages in the feared activity. And, over a period of time, the behavior will come to elicit relaxation rather than fear.[44]

Paul used desensitization to reduce fear of public speaking. The subjects in his study volunteered because they were all quite afraid of speaking in public. Once the experiment began they were assigned randomly to one of four experimental conditions:

desensitization; insight; attention–placebo; and a control group receiving no experimental treatment. In the desensitization condition, the subjects gradually engaged in speech-related activities while they were relaxing. Subjects in the insight condition were told about the nature and causes of speech phobia. Finally, in the attention–placebo condition, subjects were given useless pills which, they erroneously were told, would reduce their tension and anxiety. In addition, this group was given lots of warmth, understanding, and sympathetic attention.

Three different measures of speech anxiety were taken both prior to and after the experiment. First, unbiased observers rated each person's ability to give a speech in public without overt manifestations of fear. Second, the subjects themselves reported their level of anxiety while speaking. Finally, physiological measures of fear, like heart rate, were taken while the subjects were delivering speeches. The results showed that the desensitization, insight, and attention–placebo treatments all produced significant reductions in self-reported anxiety relative to the control group. However, the desensitization group came the closest to losing completely its fear of public speaking. Only the desensitized speakers were able to deliver speeches without any behavioral or physiological signs of fear. Put another way, the speakers in all three treatment conditions stated they felt less anxious. Yet, their *actual* public speaking behavior as observed by others and measured physiologically was affected only by desensitization, the learning strategy derived from the theory of social learning.[45]

These somewhat puzzling results can be explained by looking at the nature of the three treatments designed to reduce speech fear. All three included a large amount of verbal interaction between the speakers and experimenters. In the attention–placebo condition, the speakers were *told* not to be fearful, were given medication that was supposed to make them less nervous, and were rewarded with praise for labeling themselves as less afraid. In the insight therapy treatment, speakers were informed of the nature of communication apprehension, again were told not to be afraid, and were reinforced with praise for *talking* about themselves as less fearful. In these two conditions, the speakers learned to *talk* about their reduced anxiety, but they did not actually learn to relax. In contrast, speakers in the desensitization condition did learn to relax, to be truly less afraid while speaking in public.

Apparently then, speakers in the insight and attention–placebo conditions learned that positive consequences result from describing themselves as being less fearful. However, the desensitized speakers, by learning to relax, learned that positive consequences result from the *actual process* of delivering public speeches. Thus, Paul's study suggests it is critically important that positive consequences become attached to the *particular* behavior that an individual wishes to change, and that merely changing the expected consequences of related behaviors is not sufficient.

Behavior Modification

Behavior modification as a learning strategy has caught the popular fancy in recent years. On any drugstore book rack one is likely to encounter a number of self-help manuals that assure the potential buyer that he or she can stop smoking, lose weight, become more assertive, and break all manner of annoying habits through "behavior mod." Similarly, numerous clinics have sprung up around the country promising that for a weekend of your time and a stiff fee, you can revolutionize your life through the techniques of behavior modification.[46] Most of these miracle claims are exaggerated, if not downright outrageous. However, the notoriety that has become attached to behavior modification techniques should not obscure that, when properly understood and used, behavior modification can be an effective tool of social learning about consequences.

Behavior modification is a learning strategy aimed at altering the consequences associated with certain behaviors by shifting external and internal reinforcement contingencies. Behaviors such as cigarette smoking or overeating that previously have been rewarding can become, through behavior modification, unrewarding and punishing. On the other hand, behaviors like physical exercise that have in the past been unappealing or painful can become rewarding. The ultimate aim of behavior modification is the establishment of an enduring self-reinforcement system that enables an individual to regulate his or her own behaviors in the absence of any external reinforcement information. Strategies of behavior modification are often completely self-administered, or they may be learned with the assistance of professionals.

The first step in any behavior modification program requires a determination of the precise rewards and punishments associated with a target behavior. Let's assume that the target behavior is overeating that has led to obesity. The overeater must determine what positive consequences this behavior produces for him or her. Perhaps the overeater genuinely appreciates the taste of fine foods, or alternately, is an uncontrollable "junk food junkie." In these cases, food itself has become a powerful reward. The overeater will probably reward himself or herself with food after major accomplishments, or use food as a mood elevator or calming influence when he or she feels depressed or anxious. In other words, food has become a cure-all for the person. Once all the positive consequences of the overeating behavior are enumerated and understood, the individual must then find ways to change them to negative consequences. In this fashion the behavior is modified.

An interesting three-month study by Penick and his associates illustrated how behavior modification techniques can be used to control overeating. The subjects in the study were all at least 20 percent overweight. The behavior modification program had two goals: a significant loss of weight; and the development of self-reinforcement systems with regard to obesity-related behaviors. The patients in the study were required to keep daily records of their eating behaviors—how much they ate, when and for how long, and under what circumstances. In this manner, they could begin to determine the rewards they associated with food and the circumstances in which food itself was used as a positive reinforcement.

Beyond this, the directors of the program set up a system of rewards and punishments for the patients to self-administer. For example, when patients successfully resisted eating and lost weight, they rewarded themselves with a certain number of points that were later converted into money and given to the group as a whole. At the beginning of the program, the group had decided how it wished to use its money. One subgroup planned to donate it to the Salvation Army, and another wanted to give its money to a local widow with 14 children. Negative reinforcements included losing points, and thus money, for failure to control eating; and flavoring snacks with castor oil to make them taste bad.

Additionally, patients were required to keep "fat bags" containing 16 pieces of animal fat in their refrigerators. They were encouraged to visualize the suet as their own body fat. For every pound lost, one piece of fat was removed from the bag; for every pound gained, one piece was added. If a patient lost the entire "fat bag," he or she was given a prize and praised extensively. Indeed, lavish praise was given to any group member for weight loss, but disappointment and disapproval were shown toward patients who failed to develop self-control and self-reinforcement regarding their eating behavior.

At the end of the three-month program, 53 percent of the patients had lost more than 20 pounds and 13 percent had lost more than 40. Thus, the program appeared to have been successful in accomplishing the weight loss objective for over one-half of the participants. A follow-up study several months later showed that most of the patients continued to lose weight and that 27 percent of them had lost more than 40 pounds. Apparently, almost one-third of them had successfully developed strong self-reinforcement systems. They had learned to regulate their eating behavior through self-reward and self-criticism without the benefit of external, group-instigated rewards and punishments.[47]

In summary, behavior modification programs shift reinforcement consequences associated with behaviors. Actions that were once rewarding become punishing, and unappealing behaviors are associated with positive outcomes. The ultimate aim of behavior modification is the development of strong self-reinforcement systems. With the establishment of personal standards of behavior and the resulting internal reinforcement information, individuals can then regulate their behavior without the benefit of external reward and punishment information.

THE SOCIAL LEARNING APPROACH TO PERSUASION:
A CRITICAL APPRAISAL

In many ways, social learning theory is an anomaly among other learning theories. Its theoretical progenitors were the radical behaviorism of B. F. Skinner and cognitive learning (S–O–R) theories, typified by Doob's backward chain of learning theory. Unlike Skinner's S–R approach, S–O–R models take into account internal mediators of external phenomena. However, both perspectives assume that human behavior is formed and controlled by external rewards and punishments.

In contrast to Skinner's deterministic model and many cognitive S–O–R formulations, social learning theory emphasizes internal cognitive processes as the prime motivators of human behavior. From the social learning perspective, human behavior is rule governed, guided by information about the probable consequences of the various courses of action available at any moment. People are seen as complex, thinking creatures who set goals, then choose behaviors to reach them. Human behavior is, in essence, assumed to be a consequence of self-direction and self-influence. Because of its overriding focus on self-regulation, social learning theory stands in sharp contrast to both radical behaviorism and more traditional, cognitive theories of human learning.

Despite the actional nature of social learning theory, many of its constructs are derived from the Skinnerian model or from cognitive spinoffs of Skinner's theorizing. For instance, the notion of reinforcement was the basic building block of both S–R and S–O–R learning theories. However, in developing social learning theory, Bandura adapted this and other Skinnerian notions to fit a world of cognitively complex and self-directed human beings. Despite the intellectual breadth and depth of Bandura's work, this retention of labels used in prior learning theory has itself been a source of confusion for students of learning and persuasion. Indeed, the confusion has been so pronounced that Bandura's use of Skinnerian-like terminology is a major criticism of his work.

For example, as you will recall, Bandura defined *reinforcement* as *cognitive information* about *probable* consequences of *future* behaviors. Thus, he distinguished his usage from the Skinnerian conception of unmediated external rewards and punishments provided *after* the performance of a behavior as well as from the usage of cognitive theorists like Doob who regarded reinforcement as cognitively mediated external rewards and punishments delivered *after* a behavior is enacted.

Nevertheless, theorists and researchers in the social learning tradition sometimes have construed the term *reinforcement* much as the original mechanistic theorists did, or more usually, have equated it with cognitive definitions like Doob's. Moreover, most social learning researchers have placed a far greater emphasis on external reinforcement than is warranted by Bandura's original analysis. Indeed, many social learning researchers have dealt minimally with the important issues of human choice and self-regulation.[48] Unfortunately, by the time behavior modification and other models derived from social learning theory came into popular use, they bore little resemblance to Bandura's original notions. Bandura's followers often seem to be searching more for laws of human behavior than for the rules around which Bandura originally built his social learning theory.

To lay the blame for these distortions of social learning theory on Bandura's use of borrowed language would, of course, be grossly unfair. Quite to the contrary, the unfortunate direction that much social learning research has taken may be due to the failure of his followers either to read Bandura's original theory carefully or more probably, even after careful reading, to fully incorporate it into their work. However, it is fair to conclude that, had Bandura used more original terminology in his theorizing, the distortions we have described would probably not have occurred.

Beyond this general criticism, there is little to fault in the social learning-as-rules approach to persuasion. Indeed, social learning theory has broadened our understanding of human cognitive and behavioral change in many ways, three of which deserve mention. First, social learning theory is the only rules theory we have examined that makes extensive use of idiosyncratic as opposed to socially derived rules. Recall that idiosyncratic rules are an individual's personally developed assumptions about the actions needed to achieve certain goals.

In contrast to the social rules approach, social learning theory emphasizes the persuasive effects of *personal self-reinforcement systems*, entailing the development of personal norms, or rules of conduct, and the execution of behaviors that fulfill one's goals. Of course, as we made clear earlier, social rules play a major role in the development and maintenance of these self-regulation systems. However, from the social learning perspective, it is the idiosyncratic rules embodied in self-reinforcement systems that are the final motivators of human cognitive and behavioral change. Since social learning gives a prominent, mediational role to idiosyncratic rules, it is an important contribution to our understanding of persuasion as rule-governed behavior.

A second major contribution social learning theory has made to our understanding of persuasion is a metatheoretical one. To understand it, we must recall the two major theoretical traditions in persuasion discussed in Chapter 3. One, the laws approach, emphasizes environmental influences on human behavior. In their search for environmental effects, laws theorists, although not disavowing the importance of human cognitions, often underestimate people's capacity for self-direction and self-influence.

On the other hand, rules theorists concentrate heavily on the self-regulatory and self-directional capacities of humans. Although they are not blind to the influence of the perceived environment, many rules theorists do not adequately consider the powerful interactions between the perceived environment and self-directive systems. In other words, the theoretical perspectives to which each of these two camps is committed often function as conceptual blinders. Rarely is either group willing to consider seriously the thinking of the other. Moreover, neither camp has yet been willing to try on the possibility that truth may lie somewhere in the middle between the two extremes they espouse. As a consequence, few attempts at reconciliation of the two viewpoints have been made.

Given the present state of persuasion theory, Bandura's suggestion that the perceived environment (including observed social rules) and man's self-regulatory systems (incorporating idiosyncratic rules) are interactive and reciprocally supportive is significant. "Man," said Bandura, "is neither driven by inner forces or helplessly buffeted by environmental influence." Rather, he suggested that human self-regulation systems are a product of "a continuous reciprocal interaction" among one's behavior, the environmental consequences of that behavior, personal standards of conduct, and social as well as idiosyncratic rules relating human behavior to its goal-relevant consequences.[49] Thus, Bandura's theory embraces many of the concerns of rules as well as laws theorists. Its integrative nature makes it an important metatheoretical contribution to an understanding of persuasion.

Finally, the social learning perspective is important because it is an eminently useful theory of persuasion. It suggests several specific models of self-persuasion holding great promise as ways to alter human emotions, beliefs, and actions. Role-playing, modeling, desensitization, and behavior modification have all been employed successfully in a variety of settings. Thus, in addition to adding critically important theoretical and metatheoretical dimensions to our understanding of persuasion, social learning theory is a useful formulation for students whose principal interest is in the practice of persuasion.

NOTES

1. Whitman's behavior apparently was shaped not only by environmental reinforcements but also by physiological antecedents, since an autopsy revealed that he suffered from a brain tumor. However, most psychologists argue that environmental factors played a major role in influencing his aggressive tendencies. For an analysis of the external rewards and punishments contributing to Whitman's aggression, see Stephen Worchel and Joel Cooper, *Understanding Social Psychology*, 2nd ed. (Homewood, Ill.: The Dorsey Press, 1979), pp. 315–365.

2. See B. F. Skinner, *Science and Human Behavior* (New York: Free Press, 1953).

3. The learning of behaviors as a consequence of rewards and punishments typically is called instrumental learning, or operant conditioning, as distinguished from classical conditioning. The latter learning process occurs when an affectively neutral stimulus takes on the same emotional valence as an unconditioned one, that is, a stimulus that naturally elicits a positive or negative emotional response.

4. Leonard W. Doob, "The Behavior of Attitudes," *Psychological Review* 54 (1947): 135–156. Robert Weiss' and Arthur Staats' philosophical approaches parallel that of Doob. See Robert Frank Weiss, "Persuasion and the Acquisition of Attitudes: Models from Conditioning and Selective Learning," *Psychological Reports* 11 (1962): 709–732; and Arthur W. Staats, "Social Behaviorism and Human Motivation: Principles of the Attitude–Reinforcer-Discriminative System," in *Psychological Foundations of Attitudes,* ed. Anthony G. Greenwald, Timothy C. Brock, and Thomas M. Ostrom (New York: Academic Press, 1968), pp. 33–66.

5. Albert Bandura, *Social Learning Theory* (Morristown, N.J.: General Learning Press, 1971), p. 2. Used by permission. Also see Albert Bandura, *Social Learning Theory* (Englewood Cliffs, N.J.: Prentice-Hall, 1977).

6. Bandura, 1971, pp. 2–3. Used by permission.

7. Ibid., p. 3. Used by permission.

8. Ibid. Used by permission.

9. Ibid., p. 10. Used by permission. It should be noted that Bandura is not the only learning theorist to develop a rules-based approach. For another rules account of learning, see Staats, pp. 47–50.

10. Bandura, 1971, p. 5. Used by permission.

11. Ibid., p. 4. Used by permission.

12. Ibid., p. 3. Used by permission.

13. Ibid., pp. 3–4, p. 33. Used by permission.

14. Ibid., p. 3. Used by permission.

15. Ibid. Used by permission.

16. Ibid. Used by permission.

17. Ibid., p. 35. Used by permission.

18. Ibid., p. 7. Used by permission.

19. Ibid., p. 8. Used by permission.

20. Ibid., p. 27. Used by permission.

21. Ibid., pp. 27–28. Used by permission.

22. Ibid., p. 28. Used by permission.

23. Ibid., p. 31. Used by permission.

24. Ibid., p. 28. Used by permission.

25. Joseph W. Eaton and Robert J. Weil, *Culture and Mental Disorders* (New York: Free Press, 1955).

26. Charles C. Hughes et al., *People of Cove and Woodlot: Communities from the Viewpoint of Social Psychology* (New York: Basic Books, 1960).

27. Bandura, 1971, pp. 34–35. Used by permission.

28. Ibid., p. 33. Used by permission.

29. Jacob L. Moreno, *Who Shall Survive?*, 2nd ed. (New York: Beacon House, 1953).

30. George A. Kelly, *The Psychology of Personal Constructs* (New York: W. W. Norton, 1955).

31. Irving L. Janis and Leon Mann, "Effectiveness of Emotional Role-Playing in Modifying Smoking Habits and Attitudes," *Journal of Experimental Research in Personality* 1 (1965): 84–90.

32. Leon Mann, "The Effects of Emotional Role-Playing on Desire to Modify Smoking Habits," *Journal of Experimental Social Psychology* 3 (1967): 334–348.

33. Janis and Mann, p. 88.

34. Leon Mann and Irving L. Janis, "A Follow-up Study on the Long-Term Effects of Emotional Role-Playing," *Journal of Personality and Social Psychology* 8 (1968): 339–342.

35. Albert Bandura, Dorothea Ross, and Sheila A. Ross, "Vicarious Reinforcement and Imitative Learning," *Journal of Abnormal and Social Psychology* 67 (1963): 601–607.

36. See Robert A. Baron, "Attraction Toward the Model and Model's Competence as Determinants of Adult Imitative Behavior," *Journal of Personality and Social Psychology* 14 (1970): 345–351.

37. See David G. Perry and Kay Bussey, "The Social Learning Theory of Sex Differences: Imitation is Alive and Well," *Journal of Personality and Social Psychology* 37 (1979): 1699–1712.

38. See Baron; and Milton E. Rosenbaum and Irving F. Tucker, "Competence of the Model and the Learning of Imitation and Nonimitation," *Journal of Experimental Psychology* 63 (1962): 183–190.

39. See Charles W. Turner and Leonard Berkowitz, "Identification with Film Aggressor (Overt Role Taking) and Reactions to Film Violence," *Journal of Personality and Social Psychology* 21 (1972): 256–264.

40. See Peter A. Fehrenbach, David J. Miller, and Mark H. Thelen, "The Importance of Consistency of Modeling Behavior upon Imitation: A Comparison of Single and Multiple Models," *Journal of Personality and Social Psychology* 37 (1979): 1412–1417.

41. See Fehrenbach, Miller, and Thelen.

42. Joseph Wolpe is credited with developing the strategy of desensitization as a psychotherapeutic method. See Joseph Wolpe, *The Practice of Behavior Therapy* (Elmsford, N.Y.: Pergamon Press, 1973); and Joseph Wolpe, *Psychotherapy by Reciprocal Inhibition* (Stanford, Calif: Stanford University Press, 1958).

43. See Bernard Migler and Joseph Wolpe, "Automated Self-Desensitization: A Case Report," *Behavior Research and Theory* 5 (1967): 133–135.

44. It should be noted that desensitization frequently is interpreted as a case of classical conditioning, not social learning. Within the former interpretation, relaxation functions as the unconditioned stimulus that naturally elicits positive emotions. The feared behavior, when paired with relaxation, is presumed to take on the emotional valence of relaxation.

45. Gordon Paul, *Insight versus Desensitization in Psychotherapy* (Stanford, Calif.: Stanford University Press, 1966).

46. For an example of a popular approach to behavior modification, see Jhan Robbins and Dave Fisher, *How to Make and Break Habits* (New York: Dell, 1973).

47. Sydnor B. Penick et al., "Behavior Modification in the Treatment of Obesity," *Psychosomatic Medicine* 33 (1971): 49–55.

48. For a summary of typical research conducted by social learning theorists, see Worchel and Cooper, pp. 343–349.

49. Bandura, 1971, p. 2. Used by permission.

PART 3

INFORMATION-PROCESSING THEORIES OF PERSUASION

CHAPTER 9

The Yale Theories
of Information Processing

In the presidential campaign of 1960, the Democratic candidate, Massachusetts' Senator John F. Kennedy, was far less well known than his Republican opponent, Vice-President Richard Nixon. Thus, Kennedy's overriding task was to establish himself as a credible contender for the highest office in the land. His big opportunity to do so came in a series of four televised debates between himself and Mr. Nixon during the fall of 1960. The first and most important debate was seen by between 70 and 85 million Americans, over 60 percent of the total adult population at the time. From 48 to 70 million people saw each of the remaining debates.

Public opinion polls showed that Senator Kennedy decisively won the first debate and came out far ahead of Mr. Nixon when the four debates were considered as a whole. In accounting for the perception that Senator Kennedy was the superior persuader, viewers reported first that the Senator had seemed vigorous and decisive, whereas Mr. Nixon came across as dull, plodding, and humorless. In short, Mr. Kennedy had captured the attention and imagination of viewers at Mr. Nixon's expense. Second, Senator Kennedy was seen as equally well informed as the more experienced Vice-President on a broad range of foreign and domestic issues. Third and finally, Mr. Kennedy's style of presentation was sincere, personal, and appealing to viewers. Generally, he was seen as a more believable source of information than his opponent. All these factors combined to create a perception that Mr. Kennedy was a credible and informed candidate, fully capable of leading America into the 1960s.[1]

The way viewers interpreted Mr. Kennedy's messages in the debates and the effect those interpretations had on perceptions highlight the major issues we will consider in this chapter. We will be concerned with the ways people alter their cognitive schematic structures and overt behaviors as a result of processing the information contained in persuasive messages. As we saw in Chapter 2, an information-processing perspective assumes that persuasive effects are the product of a person's selective attention to, interpretation of, and reconstructive memory storage of incoming messages. On the basis of their unique cognitive schemata, people "fill-in" their own meanings to external messages and respond to their self-created messages. In Chapter 1 we called these messages *self-generated response messages*. Although an external agent, as in our example, Mr. Kennedy, is the overt producer of a message, the recipient as interpreter and respondent plays a decisive role in determining the message's persuasiveness.

In this chapter, we will examine several information-processing models inspired by the work of theorists in the Yale tradition. The Yale approach provided the first systematic, theoretical examination of the persuasive effects of information processing. In our treatment of the Yale theories of information processing, we will (1) examine the original Yale model developed in the 1950s; (2) review two theoretical extensions of the Yale approach, including a cognitive response theory of persuasion; (3) survey research that examines the major variables presumed to mediate the persuasive effects of information processing; and (4) critique the Yale model.

THE YALE CHAIN OF RESPONSES MODEL

At the end of World War II, Carl Hovland, a professor of psychology at Yale University, gathered a group of colleagues and students around him and developed what has since become known as the Yale approach to persuasion and attitude change.[2] The Yale perspective is not a theory per se, but, rather, is a general approach to persuasion grounded in cognitive learning theory. Hovland and his associates assumed that adopting a new attitude after exposure to a persuasive message is essentially "a learning experience," and that such learning is contingent upon the provision of appropriate rewards.[3] For a persuader to change a person's opinion, they argued, "it is necessary to create greater incentives for making the new implicit response than for making the old one."[4]

Moreover, Hovland and his colleagues maintained that a "major basis for the acceptance of a given opinion is provided by arguments or reasons [in a message] which, according to the individual's own thinking habits, constitute 'rational' or 'logical' support for the conclusion."[5] The Yale theorists, then, considered attitude change to be a consequence of learning new information that, from the recipient's perspective, is believable and personally rewarding. As this analysis indicates, Hovland and his associates stressed both the learning of new information and the motivation to accept newly learned material. However, as a practical matter, the Yale theorists originally and erroneously assumed that learning and accepting new information would be correlated positively.

Building on these assumptions, they argued that the extent to which a person will be persuaded by a message is dependent on the following chain of learning responses: (1) *attention* to the persuasive message; (2) *comprehension* of its content; (3) *acceptance* of, or yielding to, what is comprehended; (4) *retention* of the position agreed to; and (5) *action* in accordance with the retained agreement. Although each of these five stages was regarded as theoretically important, Hovland and his colleagues focused most of their attention on the motivational factors affecting *acceptance* rather than on comprehension and the other stages.

The Yale Research Paradigm

In their search for factors affecting acceptance, Hovland and his associates centered their investigation on the question: "Who [source] says what [message] in which channel to whom [receivers] with what effect?"[6] They believed that the effectiveness of information processing in producing new attitudes was dependent, first, on the perceived characteristics of the *source* of new information. If, for example, the source is perceived as trustworthy or expert, then a person should more readily accept the recommended position than if the persuader comes across as unreliable or incompetent.

Second, the perceived strength and believability of a *message*'s arguments should affect the success of information processing. Third, *channel* factors, like the communication setting and the choice of medium, should have a significant impact on the persuasion process. Finally, the *receivers*' characteristics, such as initial attitudes, levels of ego involvement in the communication topic, and personality traits, were regarded as major factors affecting the adoption of a new attitude. After examining the major theoretical modifications of the Yale model, we will review the principal research findings of Hovland and his associates.

MCGUIRE'S TWO-STAGE MEDIATION MODEL

Because Yale theorists neglected the relationship between comprehension and acceptance, and because of his own interest in receiver characteristics, William McGuire introduced several modifications in the Yale model. His modifications clarified the relationship between comprehension and acceptance and indicated the effects of each on the final impact of any persuasive message. Moreover, McGuire's research and theorizing clarified the effects that a number of personality traits of recipients have on comprehension, acceptance, and persuasibility in general.

He began his work by reducing the complex, five-stage chain of information processing to a two-stage model.[7] He combined the first two steps, attention and comprehension, into a single factor, *reception* of message content. The second stage he labeled *yielding* to what is comprehended. McGuire considers that the probability of attitude change in response to a persuasive message is a positive function of two mediators, reception and yielding. A person changes an attitude or opinion, McGuire argues, "insofar as he effectively receives the message and yields to the point received."[8]

Thus, from his perspective, attitude or opinion change is not synonymous with yielding, but is, rather, a more general effect reflecting the probability of effective reception as well as yielding to what is received. McGuire's two-stage mediation model is summarized in the following equation:

$$Pr(O) = Pr(R) \times Pr(Y)$$

where Pr (O) represents the probability of opinion change; Pr (R), the probability of effective reception; and Pr (Y), the probability of yielding to what is received.[9]

The Compensatory Assumption

McGuire developed two major theoretical postulates to clarify the relative importance of reception and yielding in producing opinion change. The first he calls the *compensatory assumption*. It asserts that those characteristics of people relating positively to reception of a message tend to be negatively related to yielding. In other words, those traits that increase people's ability to comprehend will usually decrease their susceptibility to yielding to what is comprehended. For example, McGuire argues that the more intelligent people are, the better able they are to comprehend message content, even exceptionally complex material. However, the more intelligent a person, the less likely he or she is to yield to what is comprehended.

This effect occurs because more intelligent people usually have more information to bolster their initial opinion, are better able to detect flaws in the arguments used in messages, and generally have more self-confidence and consequently, a greater willingness to maintain an attitude discrepant with peer or authority sources. In a similar fashion, McGuire argues that anxiety is usually negatively related to reception and positively related to yielding, but that high self-esteem frequently has the opposite relationship to the two mediators. Because reception and yielding generally have opposite effects on persuasibility, McGuire maintains that the greatest opinion change following exposure to a persuasive message can be expected among people who have moderate levels of intelligence, anxiety, and the like. At low levels of intelligence, for instance, difficulty with reception interferes with opinion change, and at high levels the yielding factor diminishes persuasibility.

This relationship between personality traits and susceptibility to opinion change is curvilinear, taking the shape of an inverted-U. Fig. 9.1 depicts the general relationship between intelligence and opinion change as well as the relationship between intelligence and reception and intelligence and yielding. Note that the greatest opinion change is at the point where the reception and yielding curves intersect.

McGuire argues that the compensatory principle can be explained by referring to human adaptation processes. A "person should be open, but not too open, to outside influence if he is to thrive in the natural environment," McGuire notes.[10] Moreover, he concludes "that nature is deliciously equitable so that any characteristic which makes an individual vulnerable to social influence through one of the mediators tends to protect him from influence via another."[11]

The Situational Weighting Assumption

McGuire's second postulate on the relative effects of reception and yielding is called the *situational weighting assumption*. It asserts that the comparative importance of each of the two mediators of opinion change will vary as a function of the specific characteristics of a persuasive communication situation. In this regard, the

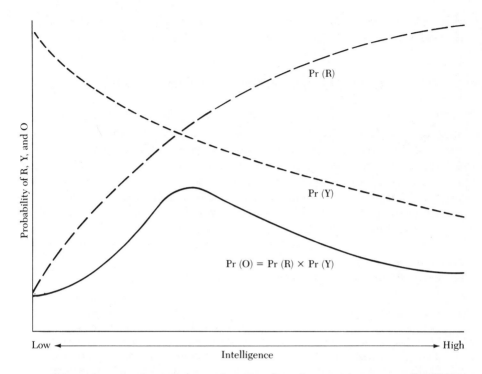

FIGURE 9.1   Opinion change as a function of intelligence of receiver. Adapted from William J. McGuire, "Personality and Susceptibility to Social Influence," in Handbook of Personality Theory and Research *by E. F. Borgatta and W. W. Lambert, eds., Rand McNally, 1968, p. 1145. Reprinted by permission.*

nature of the persuasive message itself, including how complex it is, is a particularly important situational variable. For example, some persuasive messages are simple and so easy to follow that most people should have no difficulty understanding them. In such a case, reception ought to be a relatively unimportant mediator of opinion change, and factors related to yielding or acceptance of the message content should carry the most weight in determining expected levels of attitude change.

Advertisements typify these relatively simple messages in that they usually consist of simple and repetitive slogans specifying one or two reasons why a product ought to be purchased. Sales pitches such as "Carleton cigarettes are lowest in tar and nicotine"; "Aspirin is the pain reliever recommended most by doctors"; and "Lite beer has one-third fewer calories than regular beer" exemplify this simplicity. The believability of these claims, rather than their comprehensibility, should determine effectiveness. In contrast, some persuasive messages are relatively complex, consisting of a series of logical arguments and subtle emotional appeals. In such cases, comprehension should be as important as the yielding factor in mediating the final persuasive effects.

In summary, McGuire's two-factor information-processing model considers attitude change to be a function of reception of the content of a persuasive message and yielding to the information. After examining one more information-processing model, we will review some of McGuire's major research findings.

GREENWALD'S COGNITIVE RESPONSE MODEL

The most recent information-processing theory inspired by the Yale tradition, Anthony Greenwald's cognitive response model,[12] is based on the same assumption that guided McGuire and the Yale theorists: attitude change is at least a partial function of the learning and retention of cognitive information. However, Greenwald disagrees with other theorists in the Yale tradition as to the source of the information learned by message recipients. Hovland and his colleagues, as well as McGuire, assumed that people learn new cognitive information from the *content* of the persuasive message itself.

Greenwald questions this assumption and argues that the most important source of cognitive content in any persuasion situation is not message content, but, rather, the interpretative reactions and covert messages produced by people in response to incoming messages. Thus, Greenwald reasons:

> When a person receives a communication, he may be expected to relate the new information to . . . existing attitudes, knowledge, [and] feelings. In the course of doing this, he likely rehearses substantial cognitive content beyond that of the persuasive message itself. [The] rehearsal and learning of cognitive responses to persuasion may be more fundamental to persuasion than is . . . learning of content [of the persuasive message itself].[13]

Based on these assumptions, Greenwald's cognitive response theory suggests that people adopt new attitudes and behaviors on the basis of the idiosyncratic messages *they* generate in response to externally produced messages. Given this view, the learning effects of a persuasive message may range from positive attitude change to a boomerang effect, or attitude change away from the advocated position. Positive attitude change can be expected when a person's predominant cognitive responses to a message support the advocated position. In contrast, a boomerang effect should result when a person produces messages contrary to the advocated position. Thus, Greenwald's cognitive response model easily explains the boomerang effect as a legitimate consequence of learning from self-produced countercognitions. In contrast, the more traditional Yale models must account for negative attitude change by referring to factors unrelated to learning message content.

Greenwald's model represents a landmark contribution to the understanding of persuasion as a function of processing new information. Clearly, his formulation suggests that information processing is a far more complex phenomenon than originally assumed. Other models in the Yale tradition regard the receiver as a relatively passive processer of incoming information. In contrast, Greenwald's theory suggests that people are, in fact, active agents generating their own messages in response to incoming information, that people respond to the messages they create for themselves. In the next section, we will review research findings bearing on the importance of cognitive responses as mediators of persuasive effects.

VARIABLES MEDIATING THE EFFECTS OF INFORMATION PROCESSING

Following the Yale theorists' original analysis, research from the late 1940s to date has focused on the persuasive impact of the source of a message, the message itself, the channel through which the message is sent, and the characteristics of recipients of messages. In this section, we will review the major research findings on the effects each of these four components has on information processing.

The Source

The extent to which people regard a persuader as an attractive and credible purveyor of information is an important mediator of persuasive effects. Applbaum, Berlo, Whitehead, McCroskey, and others have identified a number of perceived source characteristics that affect general persuasiveness. These include competence, or expertness; trustworthiness; objectivity; sociability; dynamism; physical attractiveness; and similarity, or perceived commonalities between the source and receiver.[14] Two classes of source characteristics have been studied extensively within an information-processing paradigm. The first class is usually labeled *credibility,* and it refers to all those perceived characteristics of a persuader that affect the believability of the content of his or her message. A person's perceived expertise on the issue at hand and his or her reputation as an honest and trustworthy source are the two variables most commonly associated with credibility.

The second class of variables relates to the *attractiveness* of the source of information; that is, the perceived characteristics of people that affect their likability, regardless of their competence with regard to the content of messages. Physical attractiveness and the degree to which a source and receiver have similar attitudes, interests, and experiences are the two variables most commmonly related to perceived attractiveness. We will now look at research on credibility and attractiveness.

Credibility

Hovland and Weiss were among the first researchers to examine the effects of source credibility on information processing. They treated credibility as a general factor encompassing elements of both expertise and trustworthiness. After premeasuring attitudes, the researchers presented several persuasive messages to people. Each message was attributed either to a high- or low-credibility source. For example, one message on the advisability of selling antihistamine drugs without a prescription was attributed either to *The New England Journal of Medicine* or to a mass circulation magazine. Another message on the practicality of building atomic submarines was attributed either to the eminent scientist, J. Robert Oppenheimer, or to *Pravda*. All messages were identical except for the alleged source. Hovland and Weiss measured attitude change and comprehension of the messages immediately after people were exposed to them; then they reassessed attitude change and measured retention one month later.

The results showed that source credibility had no effect on immediate comprehension or delayed retention of message information. People exposed to both the high- and low-credibility sources correctly answered between 80 percent and 85 percent of the items on an immediate comprehension test, and each group retained about 65 percent of the information one month later. In contrast, the effect of source credibility on acceptance, or attitude change, was radically different. As Figure 9.2 shows, immediately after exposure to the messages, the high-credibility sources elicited more attitude change than sources of questionable credibility. Twenty-three percent of the people exposed to high-credibility sources changed their opinions in the direction of the advocated positions, but only 6.6 percent of the receivers of low-credibility messages exhibited positive attitude change.

However, the effects of source credibility on attitude change were very short-lived. As Fig. 9.2 indicates, after one month there was a 10.7 percent decrease in agreement with the high-credibility sources and a 7.4 percent increase in agreement

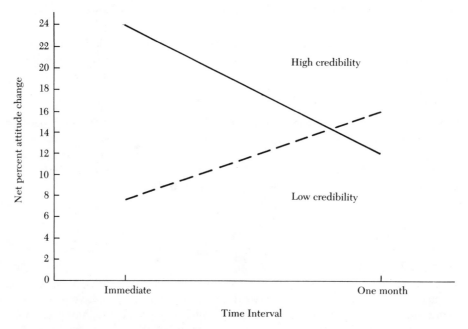

FIGURE 9.2 *Immediate and delayed agreement with positions advocated by high- and low-credibility sources. Adapted from Carl I. Hovland and Walter Weiss, "The Influence of Source Credibility on Communication Effectiveness."* Public Opinion Quarterly, *15, 1951–1952, p. 646. Reprinted by permission.*

with the messages attributed to the low-credibility sources. As a result of these shifts over time, four weeks after exposure to the messages, the two groups exhibited approximately the same level of attitude change.[15]

A delayed increase in agreement with a message, such as that observed in response to the low-credibility source, has been called a *sleeper effect*. To account for it, Hovland and Weiss postulated that, over time, the source of a message becomes dissociated from the message content. They concluded that source credibility has no effect whatsoever on comprehension and retention of message content, but that it has a decided impact on acceptance of what is learned. Specifically, low credibility interferes with message acceptance, and high credibility facilitates it. However, as the name and qualifications of the persuader are forgotten, interfering and facilitating effects disappear, leaving the recipient with the retained message content "which provides the basis for the [residual] opinion."[16] That the short-lived effects of source credibility are due to forgetting was supported by recall data collected by Hovland and Weiss. Immediately after message exposure, over 90 percent of the people who disagreed with the low-credibility source could recall the source's name. However, one month later only about 55 percent remembered the source's name.

Kelman and Hovland provided more substantial support for the hypothesis. They asked people to listen to a message about the treatment of juvenile delinquency. One group was told that the speaker was a juvenile court judge (high credibility), and another group was told the speaker was a drug pusher (low credibility). As in the Hovland and Weiss study, attitude measures were taken before, immediately after, and three weeks after exposure to the message. However, one-half of the receivers in each group were reminded of the source's identity after the three-week interval, but the other half got no reminder.

Consistent with Hovland's and Weiss' findings, the high-credibility source elicited significantly more immediate attitude change than the low-credibility source. Moreover, for those people who were allowed to forget the source's identity, agreement with the high-credibility source declined sharply after three weeks, and agreement with the negative communicator increased slightly, a duplication of Hovland's and Weiss' sleeper effect. However, for those people who were reminded of the source's qualifications, attitude change after three weeks was approximately the same as that exhibited immediately after exposure to the message.[17] Taken together, these findings suggest that the sustained retention of message-relevant arguments is more pertinent to long-run attitude change than is source credibility.

Cognitive Responding and the Short-Term Effects of Credibility   As we have just seen, source credibility has a decided impact on short-range acceptance of recommendations. This effect cannot be explained as a function of differences in learning message content since high- and low-credibility sources elicit equivalent comprehension. Paulette Gillig and Greenwald have proposed that the immediate effects of source credibility can be accounted for by referring, not to the learning of message content, but to the cognitive responses people make to messages. In three experiments, they found that when messages were presented by highly credible sources, the predominant cognitive responses were supportive argumentation. In contrast, low-credibility sources using the same messages elicited rejection and counterargumentation.[18] Apparently, high credibility stimulates supportive cognitive responses, and low credibility triggers negative cognitive responses.

In general, the short- and long-term effects of source credibility can be explained quite satisfactorily within an information-processing paradigm. In the short run, the credibility of the source is salient, and so long as it is, cognitive responses mediate the amount and direction of attitude change. The consequence is significantly greater short-term agreement with a high-credibility source than with a low-credibility one. Once positive and negative source credibility cues are forgotten, cue-relevant cognitive responses should diminish. As a result, any residual attitude change is a function of the extent to which people retain message content and their cognitive responses to that content. Since people exposed to high- and low-credibility sources retain approximately the same amount of message-relevant information, long-term attitude change for the two groups should be roughly equivalent.

The Multidimensional Quality of Credibility   Before examining the persuasive effects of attractiveness, it is important to underscore the point that source credibility is a multidimensional concept. Despite its use as a global factor in the research we examined, source credibility involves expertise, trustworthiness, and much more. Moreover, it is possible that a person may be perceived as honest and trustworthy, but not very competent. For example, one of the credibility problems that dogged former president Gerald Ford was the perception that he was an honest fellow, but lacked the competence to manage the highest office in the land. Conversely, a persuader may be seen as exceedingly competent, but untrustworthy. Although few people would argue with the notion that the leaders of organized crime are experts on illegal gambling and drug traffic, many would question their reputation for honesty and reliability.

Credibility, then, is a complex concept possessing many different dimensions. The greater the number and quality of a communicator's favorable characteristics, the more likely he or she will be to influence positively the final effects of information processing.

Attractiveness

Attractiveness refers to those characteristics of a person affecting his or her likability, regardless of competence or credibility. It is a common experience to be personally atttracted to certain individuals, and yet regard them as uninformed. For example, during the 1980 presidential election campaign, many Americans responded to Jimmy Carter as a warm and personable man; yet, a substantial number of voters questioned his competence to deal with domestic and foreign policy problems.

Conversely, we often respect others for their competence and judgment, yet find them thoroughly unlikable. In the presidential campaign of 1968, few Americans doubted Richard Nixon's competence. Nevertheless, many voters perceived him as cold, aloof, and unappealing. Finally, many people are perceived as both credible and likable, a mix of qualities that should promote maximal persuasiveness. Whether a person is perceived as simply likable or as likable *and* credible, attractiveness profoundly affects the way people process information.

Physical Attractiveness   Two dimensions of attractiveness have been investigated extensively within an information-processing paradigm: physical attractiveness; and similarity, or perceived commonalities, between communicating parties. Let's look first at the persuasive effects of physical attractiveness. Research indicates that physically attractive people generally are more influential persuaders than unattractive people especially with opposite-sex receivers.[19] There is some evidence that with same-sex receivers, under certain conditions, unattractive sources may be more influential than attractive ones.[20] This exception to the attractiveness-persuasiveness rule usually occurs when the communicating parties are members of the same peer group. In such a situation, Dion found that people often expect attractive peers of the same sex to behave more deceitfully than attractive opposite-sex peers or unattractive same-sex peers.[21] Nevertheless, the bulk of prior research indicates that, in most circumstances, physical attractiveness adds to persuasiveness regardless of the sex of the receiver.

The reasons for this have been explored in a number of studies. Generally, research shows that physically attractive persons are more influential, not because of attractiveness per se, but because they have a number of additional characteristics disposing them to be more effective communicators than unattractive individuals. Thus, Ellen Bercheid and Elaine Walster have hypothesized that physically attractive and unattractive persons experience quite different socialization processes, leading to the development of differing social and communication skills, self-concepts, personality traits, and status and achievement levels.[22] To partially test this hypothesis, Goldman and Lewis conducted an experiment in which subjects were asked to engage in three, five-minute telephone conversations with unseen, attractive and unattractive individuals. Results showed that the physically attractive persons were rated as more socially skilled and as more adept communicators than the unattractive persons.[23]

In a more elaborate field study, Chaiken found that physically attractive persuaders were significantly more fluent speakers than unattractive ones and had a faster speech rate than their unattractive counterparts, two variables McCroskey and others had previously linked to persuasiveness.[24] Moreover, Chaiken found that physically attractive people, relative to unattractive ones, had higher Scholastic Aptitude Test (SAT) scores and higher grade point averages in college. Finally, the physically attractive communicators exhibited a more favorable self-concept than the unattractive ones, seeing themselves as more persuasive, attractive, interesting, and more optimistic about getting an excellent job after graduation.[25] This evidence suggests that attractive individuals are more persuasive than unattractive persons, not merely because of their attractiveness, but because they have communication skills and other attributes disposing them to be particularly effective persuaders.

Similarity   A second factor affecting the attractiveness and likability of a source is perceived similarities between persuaders and receivers. Research indicates that people get more message acceptance if receivers see them as similar to themselves in attitudes, backgrounds, and experiences. In a study of perceived attitudinal similarity, Bercheid found that substantial, positive attitude change occurred when people perceived that persuaders held opinions similar to their own on the communication topic and vice versa.[26]

In a field experiment, Brock studied the effects of similarity of experience on purchasing behavior in a retail paint store in Ohio. All the salespersons were asked to try to persuade customers to purchase a particular brand of paint. Some salespersons established themselves as similar to the customers in terms of their past experience in selecting and using paints, but as not especially expert in the paint business. Others informed customers that they were very well informed about paints, but that their own experiences were quite dissimilar from those of the customers. Results showed that customers purchased significantly more paint from the first group than the second.[27]

The Relationship between Attractiveness and Credibility   To conclude discussion of source attractiveness, let's consider the similarities and differences between source attractiveness and source credibility as mediators of information processing and message acceptance. Norman compared the differential information-processing effects of attractiveness and credibility on agreement with a message. All subjects were female and were exposed to messages arguing that it is healthful to sleep fewer than eight hours per night. For one group of subjects, the source was a physically attractive, male undergraduate who was similar in age and background to the receivers. For another group, the source was portrayed as a 43-year-old, male professor of physiological psychology who had recently coauthored a book on the functions of sleep. One-half of the subjects in each group read a general message containing no specific arguments to support the conclusion that small amounts of sleep are beneficial, and the other half read a message that contained six arguments supporting the conclusion.

Results showed that the two sources were equally effective in getting people to agree with them. However, the effect of message content was quite different. The expert source was significantly more influential when his message contained arguments than when he presented no reasons for the acceptance of his recommendations. In contrast, the presentation of arguments had no effect on agreement with the attractive source.[28] These results indicate the persuasive impact of a credible source is dependent, at least in part, on the audience's processing and responding to message content. However, the persuasive impact of an attractive source appears to be independent of message content. The implications of these findings for the short- and long-term effects of source attractiveness are relatively straightforward. An attractive person should be equally or, as in Brock's study, more effective than a credible source in gaining short-run acceptance. However, given the absence of any message-relevant effects, long-term acceptance of the recommendations of an attractive source should not be expected.

The Message

The content of a persuasive message and people's cognitive responses to it are regarded as critical determinants of attitudinal and behavioral effects. In this section, we will consider message variables that are important mediators of information processing and persuasive effects. First, we will look at research bearing on the relative importance of message content versus cognitive responses to content as mediators of attitude change, a critical theoretical issue raised by Greenwald's cognitive response model. Then we will explore the persuasive effects of several specific message variables—among these, frequency of exposure to a message, one- versus two-sided argumentation, the inclusion of evidence in messages, and fear appeals.

Message Content versus Cognitive Responses to Content

Although all information-processing theorists regard attitude change as a function of the learning and retention of information, they disagree about the source of the learned information. You will recall that Hovland and his colleagues, as well as McGuire, assumed that people learn new information from the *content* of the messages to which they are exposed. In contrast, Greenwald argued that people's idiosyncratic *cognitive responses* to incoming messages are more important sources of information than message content. Although research supports the position that both information sources are important mediators of message acceptance, the weight of the evidence suggests that cognitive responses are the more powerful determinants of attitude change.

In one test of content versus cognitive responding, Cacioppo and Petty asked a group of college students to listen to a taped message advocating an increase in tuition at their university. After hearing the speech, the subjects were asked to collect their thoughts and list all the actual cognitions that had occurred to them during the presentation. Additionally, they were asked to classify their thoughts as either supportive of the persuasive message, opposed to the message, or neutral and irrelevant to the message. Finally, they were asked to list all the message arguments they could recall. As Table 9.1 shows, attitude change was positively correlated with supportive cognitive responses, negatively related to counterargumentation, and bore no relation to recall of message content or neutral cognitive responses.[29]

In a second study, rather than using the "thought-listing" procedure, Cacioppo and Petty took electrophysiological measures of covert linguistic activity while subjects listened to a persuasive message. They used an electromyogram (EMG) to monitor oral

TABLE 9.1: CORRELATIONS AMONG ATTITUDE CHANGE, COGNITIVE RESPONSES, AND RECALL OF MESSAGE CONTENT

Message variable	Attitude change°
Counterarguments	$-.56$[a]
Supportive arguments	$.45$[a]
Neutral arguments	$.03$
Recall of message content	$-.01$

°Correlation coefficients with the superscript *a* are statistically significant at $p<.05$. Coefficients without superscripts are statistically unreliable.

and facial indices of subvocal speech activity. In one experiment, the subjects' covert linguistic activity was monitored during the anticipation and presentation of either a counterattitudinal, a proattitudinal, or an attitudinally neutral persuasive message. After hearing the messages, the subjects were asked to express their attitudes toward the recommendations in the message, to list everything they had thought about during the messages, and to rate each thought as favorable, unfavorable, or neutral and irrelevant toward the messages.

Results showed that *oral* EMG activity, and therefore subvocal speech, was elevated when subjects expected a counterattitudinal message, indicating anticipatory counterarguing. In contrast, oral EMG activity remained stable when subjects anticipated either the proattitudinal or neutral message. However, during the actual presentation of all three messages, oral EMG activity increased significantly above basal levels. Furthermore, measures of *facial* EMG activity confirmed that the affective tone of the subjects' covert linguistic activity was positive during the presentation of the proattitudinal and neutral messages, but that the counterattitudinal message elicited negative subvocal speech. Importantly, electrophysiological activity correlated positively with self-reported covert cognitions. As in the first study, attitudes toward the messages correlated negatively with counterargumentation, positively with supportive cognitions, but were unrelated to recall of message content.[30]

Long-Term Effects   The results of these two studies are restricted to the *immediate* effects of message content and cognitive responses. What can we expect the long-term effects of the two variables to be? Love examined people's cognitive responses while they were exposed to a persuasive message, rather than after exposure as in the aforementioned studies. His aim was to assess the relationship between attitude change, message content, and the content of cognitive responses, both immediately and one week after people were exposed to a persuasive message.

After determining initial attitudes, Love divided his subjects into two groups. One group read a persuasive message on admitting Puerto Rico as the fifty-first state, and the other group was exposed to a message advocating popular election of the secretary of state. Each message contained three main arguments, each in separate paragraphs. Following each paragraph, a blank space was provided for the subjects to write a one-sentence reaction to the argument. This procedure elicited a sample of cognitive responses produced *during* receipt of the persuasive message. After reading and responding to the messages, the subjects' opinions were reassessed, and they were given a test for recall of message content as well as for their cognitive reactions to the messages.

One week later, the same subjects were recruited for an ostensibly different experiment, at which time their attitudes were remeasured and recall tests readministered. Among other things, the data were analyzed for correlations between delayed attitude change and retention of the cognitive responses to the messages; and delayed attitude change and retention of the arguments in the persuasive messages. The results showed that the best predictor of long-term persuasive effects was retention of cognitive responses, with correlations between delayed attitude change and retained cognitive reactions being +.45 and +.30 for the Puerto Rico and secretary of state issues, respectively. Correlations between delayed opinion change and retention of message content were an insignificant +.15 and −.09 for the statehood and election topics, respectively.[31] These findings confirm Greenwald's original notion that cognitive responses to messages are more important mediators of long-term, as well as immediate attitude change, than is message content.

Evidence on the Effects of Message Content Although cognitive responses to messages appear to be more critical to attitude change than message content, a number of studies have confirmed that comprehension of message content can, in some cases, have a strong independent effect on message acceptance. For example, Eagly, in a series of three well-designed experiments, varied the extent to which tape-recorded persuasive messages could be easily comprehended and measured attitude change as a function of comprehension. Results showed that attitude change increased significantly as comprehension of the messages increased.[32] Consistent with Eagly's findings, Watts and McGuire observed a high, positive correlation between attitude change and recall of the arguments in a message both immediately and one week after people were exposed to a persuasive communication.[33]

In general, research indicates that both message content and cognitive responses to it mediate attitude change. However, all research that has assessed the *relative* influence of *both* sources of information strongly suggests that a person's cognitive responses to messages are the most reliable predictors of immediate and long-range attitude change.

Frequency of Exposure to Messages

Message repetition is a common persuasive strategy employed by advertisers. Brand names, musical jingles, or catchy slogans are repeated endlessly on television, radio, and in print, since conventional wisdom holds that the more people are exposed to a particular message, the more likely they are to comprehend it, accept its arguments, and purchase the recommended product. However, considerable research and theorizing suggest that the "more is better" proposition may not be entirely justified.

Several theorists have proposed that a curvilinear (inverted-U) relationship exists between repeated exposure to a message and attitude change. For instance, Daniel Berlyne and David Stang have suggested that, initially, repeated message exposure gives people an opportunity to learn new information about an object or idea, and that this learning should lead to increased liking or positive attitude change toward the advocated position. However, with continued repetition, the theorists suggest that boredom, tedium, and satiation should develop, leading to a decrease in liking for the message.[34] Thus, agreement with a message *should* be greatest at *moderate* levels of exposure.

Cacioppo and Petty tested this hypothesis. Three groups of subjects heard a taped message either one, three, or five times. For each of the groups, the researchers assessed attitude change, message recall, and cognitive responses to the message, including supportive arguments and counterargumentation. Results confirmed that attitude change was significantly greater for people who heard the message three times than for the single-exposure or the five-exposure group. However, the research failed to con-

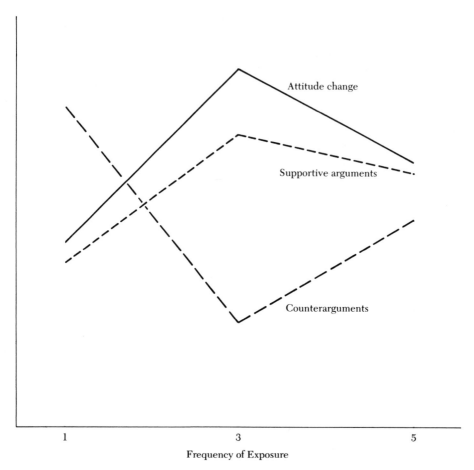

Frequency of Exposure

FIGURE 9.3   *Attitude change, supportive argumentation, and counterargumentation as a function of frequency of exposure to persuasive messages. Adapted from John T. Cacioppo and Richard Petty, "Effects of Message Repetition and Position on Cognitive Response, Recall, and Persuasion," Journal of Personality and Social Psychology, 37, 1979, p. 103. Copyright 1979 by the American Psychological Association. Reprinted by permission.*

firm the original prediction that positive attitude change is a direct function of people's learning new information from message content. Indeed, results showed that the greatest increase in attitude change (between one and three repetitions) was associated with no change in learning, whereas the greatest increase in learning (between three and five repetitions) was associated with a decrease in attitude change.

On the other hand, attitude change was a direct function of the receivers' cognitive responses. As Fig. 9.3 shows, for people who heard the message only one time, counterarguments predominated, and favorable responses were low. In contrast, counterargumentation declined dramatically and supportive argumentation increased sharply among individuals who heard the message three times. Finally, among people who heard the message five times, the ratio of counter to supportive arguments was equivalent to that for subjects who heard the message only once.[35]

This research suggests that attitude change resulting from message repetition is a two-stage process, involving an initial increase, then a decrease in attitude change with more frequent exposure. Apparently, initial cognitive responses to new information are often defensive in nature, but become more favorable as a person thinks about the arguments and realizes their favorable implications. However, at high exposure levels, boredom sets in, and people again attack the message that has now become offensive to them.

One-Sided versus Two-Sided Argumentation

A major question persuasive communicators face is whether to present only their side of an issue or to mention opposing arguments as well. Some advertisers, for instance, restrict their sales pitches to the positive features of their own products, but others refer to the qualities of rival products in an attempt to demonstrate the superiority of their own. Similarly, some politicians focus their messages on the merits of their own positions and programs, and others adopt a strategy of comparing an opponent's programs with their own ideas. To determine which strategy is the most effective, we must examine those variables affecting the two approaches.

The comparative effectiveness of one- versus two-sided messages was one of the first questions investigated by Hovland and his Yale colleagues. In a study conducted for the U.S. government, Hovland, Lumsdaine, and Sheffield presented radio messages to over 600 soldiers in the U.S. Army soon after Germany's defeat in World War II. The War Department was concerned that American soldiers were not properly motivated to continue the war against Japan after victory in Europe. Consequently, the purpose of the radio message was to convince the men that it would take at least two more years to conclude the war with Japan.

Hovland and his associates had one group of soldiers listen to a 15-minute message presenting only the government's side of the issue; another group heard a two-sided presentation. Results showed that the message presenting arguments for both sides of the issue produced significantly more attitude change than the one-sided message among individuals who were initially opposed to the advocated position. In contrast, the one-sided message produced significantly more agreement than the two-sided message among men who initially agreed with the government's point of view. In addition, the better educated men were more favorably affected by the presentation of both sides, whereas the less well-educated soldiers agreed more with the message containing only supporting arguments.[36]

Lumsdaine and Janis extended these findings in an experiment that investigated the long-range effects of one- versus two-sided messages. The two researchers were interested in finding out which type of message would be most effective in helping people withstand future counterattacks on their attitudes. Results showed that, regardless of the receivers' initial attitudes, a two-sided message was significantly more effective in producing attitude change that could withstand later countercommunications.[37] Apparently, the initial learning of arguments for the other side stimulates cognitive responses that prepare people to effectively combat those arguments in future messages.

In summary, if a short-range effect is sought, a two-sided presentation elicits greater agreement than a one-sided message among people opposed to the message. In contrast, a one-sided presentation should be more effective among partisan individuals. However, if a long-term effect is desired, a two-sided message is preferred, regardless of a person's initial attitude.

Evidence in Messages

James McCroskey defines *evidence* in a message as "factual statements [and opinions] originating from a source other than the speaker . . . that are offered in support of the speaker's claims."[38] Although conventional wisdom holds that using evidence increases a message's persuasive impact, this is not always the case. McCroskey and his associates isolated several key variables that determine whether evidence will promote increased agreement with a message. First, regarding *immediate* effects, they found that including documented evidence in messages has little impact if the source is high in credibility, but that it can substantially increase the short-term persuasiveness of low-credibility sources. Presumably, the latter gain stature by demonstrating that others support their positions, whereas the former do not need the opinions of others to buttress their recommendations.

Second, McCroskey and his colleagues demonstrated that evidence has little immediate impact on attitude change if the audience is familiar with the information, but that novel supporting material may increase immediate agreement. Third, reliable evidence has little immediate, persuasive impact if a message is delivered poorly, but if supporting materials are effectively delivered, they enhance agreement. Finally, McCroskey and his associates showed that the inclusion of evidence enhances *long-term* attitude change regardless of the source's initial credibility, the quality of delivery, and the like. This result parallels the finding of Hovland and his associates that source characteristics are forgotten readily, but that message content is retained for longer periods of time.[39]

Fear Appeals in Messages

The use of message strategies arousing fear for one's health and safety is a common practice in persuasion. The American Cancer Society and other organizations concerned with public health rely heavily on appeals designed to arouse the fear of disease and early death. Likewise, law enforcement and other government agencies encourage people to drive safely and take other measures to protect their lives and property. The widespread use of fear appeals and their apparent effectiveness have led a number of researchers in the information-processing tradition to study their efficacy in producing attitude and behavior change.

With a few exceptions,[40] research has confirmed that arousing *moderate* fear for health and safety facilitates cognitive alteration and behavior change. Thus, as fear appeals in a message progress from low to moderate levels, people are increasingly persuaded. However, when fear appeals become exceedingly intense, people often exhibit avoidance reactions and thereafter show declining attitudinal or behavioral alteration.

McGuire explains this curvilinear (inverted-U) relationship by arguing that fear arousal and yielding are positively related: as fear arousal intensifies, a person feels more insecure and is therefore more prone to yield to persuasion. In contrast, he maintains that fear arousal and receptivity are inversely correlated: as fear arousal intensifies, people become more withdrawn and preoccupied with their problems. Distracted by personal worries, a person should be less receptive to a persuasive message. Because of these contrasting mediational effects, McGuire argues that a moderate level of fear arousal should yield the most effective results.[41]

Qualifying Factors Related to Fear Arousal   Although considerable research supports McGuire's ideas, three qualifications should be stipulated. First, some research suggests that the facilitative effects of fear arousal are short-lived. For instance, Leventhal and Niles found that the fear engendered by exposure to motion pictures of automobile accidents dissipated within a 24-hour period,[42] and Mewborn observed considerable decay in emotional arousal within 10 minutes after people were exposed to a film on venereal disease.[43] This finding has two implications. First, if fear arousal is to have long-term effects, it may be necessary to periodically reexpose people to fear-arousing stimuli. Second, additional evidence suggests that initial exposure to very high fear appeals may produce more sustained effects than a moderately fearful message,[44] presumably because the decay rate of intense fear is slower than for moderate fear arousal. Thus, if long-term effects are desired, it may be wiser to expose people initially to intense rather than moderate fear appeals.

A second qualification of the proposition that fear arousal is an effective persuader comes from research indicating that arousal of fear *alone* is not sufficient to produce immediate or long-term attitude and behavior change. Rather, transitory fear arousal must be accompanied by variables related to a person's more enduring cognitive processes. At least two cognitive components must be included in a fear-arousing message if attitude and behavior change are to be facilitated. First, the fear-arousing message must convince people that the recommended preventive measures are *highly effective*. Without the inclusion of a workable remedy, the arousal of fear should be ineffectual. Rogers and Mewborn confirmed this in an experiment using three different fear-arousing communication topics: smoking and lung cancer; automobile accident injuries; and venereal disease. Their results showed that increases in fear appeals from mild to high levels were increasingly effective when people were convinced the recommended action could avert the predicted danger. However, when they did not believe in the effectiveness of the remedy, increases in fear arousal either had no effect or produced a boomerang effect on acceptance of the recommended measures.[45]

Second, people must be provided with *specific instructions* about how to take the recommended action. Leventhal, Singer, and Jones conducted an experiment aimed at inducing students to get a free tetanus shot at a local health center. The vaccination was described as an absolutely effective preventive measure against contraction of tetanus. One group of subjects was exposed to a high fear appeal on the dangers of tetanus, a second group received a mild fear appeal, and a control group received no message. One-half of the subjects in each group were given detailed instructions about getting the shot, how and when to go to the health center, and the like. The other half got a general recommendation that they ought to go get the shot. Results showed that 28 percent of the students who were given specific instructions and who received either of the two fear-arousing messages got tetanus injections. In contrast, only 3 percent of the subjects given vague instructions and a fear-arousing message chose to get a shot. Finally, in the control group receiving no fearful message, nobody complied with either the specific or vague recommendations to get a tetanus shot.[46]

This study indicates that, although some level of fear arousal is a necessary motivator, it is not sufficient to produce behavioral compliance. Rather, fear arousal of either a moderate or high level, coupled with specific recommendations about an effective remedy, are required if the message is to succeed. In general, this research strongly suggests that if fear appeals are to be effective, they must be accompanied by information verifying the effectiveness of the remedy as well as specific instructions regarding the taking of recommended preventive measures.

The third and final qualification to the general rule that moderate fear arousal is conducive to persuasion concerns *individual differences* among people. The most effective level of fear arousal (low, moderate, or high) varies as a function of the particular characteristics of message receivers. For instance, research suggests that low rather than moderate fear appeals are most effective among people who suffer from chronic anxiety, but that nonanxious people are equally persuaded by moderate and high fear appeals.[47] Another variable affecting fear arousal is the extent to which people believe they are actually vulnerable to the danger depicted in a message. Generally, low fear appeals work best with people who feel exceedingly vulnerable, and very intense fear arousal is most effective among persons who feel relatively invulnerable to danger or disease.[48]

From an information-processing perspective, fear appeals have an important motivational function. However, their effectiveness in eliciting attitude and behavior change depends, not on emotional arousal alone, but on a person's processing cognitive information about suggested remedies. Moreover, any long-term effects of fearful messages should be a function of the retention of relevant cognitive information, which is more enduring than emotional arousal.

The Channel

Communication *channels* refer to the human senses enabling us to transmit messages. Although messages may be transmitted by touch, taste, and smell, the channels most frequently employed in persuasion are sight and sound. Information-processing research has focused on how a channel affects the reception of, cognitive responses to, and acceptance of persuasive message content.

Two channel-related variables have been studied extensively by information-processing researchers: noise in the channel and the choice of medium to relay a message. Let's review major research findings relevant to these two variables.

Noise in the Channel: Distraction Effects

Channel noises, or distraction effects, are analogous to static on the radio or telephone and consist of visual or auditory stimuli that compete with the visual and auditory stimuli associated with a persuasive message. Typical examples of competing stimuli are the sound and visual effects accompanying the verbal messages in television advertisements.

Most distraction studies have used visual stimuli like lighting effects or audiovisual stimuli like films to distract people while they listen to persuasive messages. Generally, research has confirmed that competing noises have quite different effects on message comprehension and attitude change. Although distraction significantly diminishes message comprehension, it often increases immediate acceptance by inhibiting counterarguing.

Osterhouse and Brock demonstrated this effect by having college students listen to a counterattitudinal message advocating a doubling of tuition at their university. Some subjects listened to a taped message without distraction, and other listeners were distracted by a series of flashing lights. The researchers measured message comprehension, attitude change, and assessed the extent to which the receivers subvocally counterargued against the message. Results showed that the distracted receivers comprehended the message more poorly than did the nondistracted ones. However, the distracted subjects counterargued significantly less and exhibited substantially greater attitude change toward the message than did nondistracted subjects.[49]

This and similar studies have shown that the crucial mediator between distraction and immediate attitude change is not message comprehension, but rather cognitive responses to persuasive messages. Thus, when the dominant cognitive response to a message is expected to be counterargumentation, distraction should significantly increase immediate attitude change. However, as Petty, Wells, and Brock have demonstrated, when the dominant cognitive response is expected to be supportive argumentation, distraction may diminish immediate acceptance.[50]

These findings suggest that a persuader who expects to face a hostile audience can improve the chances for successful persuasion by using competing stimuli during message presentation. Televised political advertisements often do this by combining a candidate's message with numerous attention-diverting sound and visual effects. Likewise, banners and background music at a speaking event can distract people from the content of the speaker's message. On the other hand, if a persuader expects agreement, channel noise may diminish immediate attitude change by inhibiting supportive cognitive responses.

Although channel noise can significantly increase immediate attitude change in response to a counterattitudinal message, some research indicates that its long-term effects may be counterproductive. Watts and Holt investigated the delayed effects of distraction by measuring message comprehension and attitude change both immediately and one week after subjects were exposed to a persuasive message. Results showed that distracted subjects initially exhibited significantly more attitude change than nondistracted ones. However, one week later the pattern of results was reversed. Additionally, nondistracted subjects showed significantly greater immediate comprehension and delayed retention of the message than their distracted counterparts.

Watts and Holt concluded that attitude change among distracted receivers dissipates rapidly because they do not learn the reasons for the new or altered opinions. In contrast, nondistracted receivers exhibit longer-term attitude change because they retain message-relevant information.[51] In summary, cognitive responses mediate short-

**TABLE 9.2: MEAN ATTITUDE CHANGE
AS A FUNCTION OF MEDIUM
AND MESSAGE DIFFICULTY**

	Simple message	Complex message
Written	2.94	4.73
Audiotape	3.75	2.32
Videotape	4.78	3.02

Higher means indicate greater attitude change.

term distraction effects; however, long-term distraction effects appear to be correlated with the learning and retention of information relevant to a persuasive message.

Choice of Medium

Generally, research shows that televised messages using sight *and* sound produce greater attitude change than radio messages.[52] However, audio messages produce greater acceptance than printed ones.[53] These findings are qualified by the complexity of the message being communicated.

You will recall that McGuire argues that for very simple messages, factors associated with yielding should be more important than message comprehension. However, for complex messages, factors related to comprehension should be as important as yielding.[54] Since considerable evidence suggests that written materials are more readily comprehended than the same materials presented in other forms,[55] McGuire's analysis leads to the conclusion that very complex messages may produce more attitude change when presented in written form. On the other hand, simple messages should produce greater attitude change when presented on television or radio since comprehension is of minimal importance and yielding should be facilitated by the attention-getting qualities of the audio or audiovisual medium.

Chaiken and Eagly tested this hypothesis by varying the complexity of a persuasive message and the medium for its presentation. Subjects were exposed to a simple or a complex message that either was printed, audiotaped, or videotaped. The results, presented in Table 9.2, indicate that people were more persuaded by the simple message when it was videotaped, but were more influenced by the complex message when it was written.[56] In this regard, it is interesting to note that political candidates rarely discuss complex issues on television or radio. The difficult issues are usually covered in position papers, whereas simple slogans and image manipulations are reserved for television and radio. Chaiken's and Eagly's research supports the validity of this approach to information processing.

The Receiver

The individual characteristics of message recipients exert a profound influence on how they process information. The central importance of the receiver has been underscored throughout this chapter by the finding that cognitive responses to messages are more important determinants of attitude change than is message content. Since we have already presented much research on the role of people as information processers, we will restrict ourselves here to a brief review of three variables affecting human persuasibility: enduring personality traits; levels of ego involvement with the communication issue; and initial attitudes toward the advocated position.

Personality Traits

You will recall that McGuire argues that any enduring personality trait has an opposite effect on comprehension and one's general susceptibility to what is comprehended. For example, an individual who is high in self-esteem or self-confidence presumably can better comprehend messages but resists yielding to what is comprehended. Conversely, people with a low self-esteem are more easily influenced but are less willing or able to engage in a careful examination of the arguments in a message. Moreover, chronic anxiety and ego defensiveness tend to be positively related to yielding but negatively correlated with comprehension. In general, the greatest attitude change should occur when any one enduring personality trait is present in moderation.

Research has confirmed this curvilinear relationship (inverted-U) between personality traits and yielding. For example, Cox and Bauer investigated the relationship between persuasibility and level of self-esteem among 297 middle-aged housewives. Results showed that 45 percent of the women who were high in self-esteem conformed to the recommendations in a persuasive message, 62 percent of those who had moderate self-esteem complied, and 37 percent of subjects with low self-esteem accepted the persuader's recommendations.[57] Research on the relationship between other enduring personality traits and persuasibility has confirmed the same pattern.[58]

Involvement with the Communication Issue

When a person is ego involved with the communication issue, his or her attitudes have implications for the self-concept and other central values. Generally, a high level of ego involvement is associated with extensive information processing and an enhanced motivation to generate cognitive responses. Petty and Cacioppo found that when ego-involved subjects are exposed to a message contrary to their initial attitudes, they generate many more counterarguments and exhibit significantly less acceptance of the advocated position than their less involved counterparts.

On the other hand, when involved individuals are exposed to messages consistent with their basic attitudes, they generate many more supportive cognitions and show substantially greater attitude change than less involved people.[59] These findings suggest that issue involvement can either enhance or diminish persuasion depending on the type of cognitive responses a particular message elicits.

Initial Attitude Relative to Message Topic

As our discussion of ego involvement has suggested, the amount of discrepancy between a person's initial attitude toward an issue and the position advocated in a persuasive message profoundly affects his or her persuasibility. In general, research indicates that as discrepancy increases, agreement will increase up to moderate levels of discrepancy, but at extreme discrepancy levels it declines. Thus, the usual relationship between discrepancy and attitude change is curvilinear (inverted-U) in nature.[60]

A CRITICAL APPRAISAL OF THE YALE PERSPECTIVE

As the first information-processing theory of persuasion, the original Yale model was a landmark contribution to our understanding of human responses to symbols. Moreover, as we have seen, it has had enormous heuristic value, stimulating an ambitious research program into the persuasive effects of message sources, message characteristics, channel factors, and the characteristics of message recipients. Indeed, much of our current, empirical knowledge about persuasive effects may be traced to the systematic research of Yale theorists in the 1950s and 1960s. Despite these enormous contributions, the Yale approach has serious limitations.

First, the three models we examined—the Yale model, McGuire's two-stage mediational model, and Greenwald's cognitive response model—are, in many respects, atheoretical. Although they are all loosely grounded in cognitive learning theory, none explains systematically *why* people process information as they do. Rather, the information they have generated is more descriptive and correlational than explanatory. Since his approach focuses on active learning from self-produced messages, Greenwald's cognitive response model fares a bit better than Hovland's and McGuire's formulations on this score. However, the cognitive response approach, like its theoretical progenitors, really tells us more about *covariation* between self-generated messages and their effects than it does about *why* covert cognitions generate cognitive realignments and behavior changes.

The second problem with the Yale perspective concerns its reliance on cognitive learning theory to explain persuasive effects. Cognitive learning theory assumes that cognitive schemata develop *after* some overt response has consistently been rewarded. Thereafter, internal states are presumed to mediate overt behavior. Thus, although cognitive learning theory allows that cognitive processes direct human action, it still assumes that cognitive processes are formed and controlled largely by external rewards and punishments. This theoretical orientation led Hovland and his associates, as well as McGuire, to focus on what messages "do to" people, rather than what people "do with" messages.

Consequently, Hovland and McGuire applied causal, mechanistic assumptions to purposive human action. For example, they assumed that fear appeals in messages cause people to act to maintain health and safety. Similarly, a high-credibility source was presumed to cause immediate acceptance of persuasive recommendations. As we argued in Chapter 3, responses such as these are purposive actions, not causally determined phenomena. People typically act to achieve goals they deem personally satisfying. For instance, the desire to maintain health and safety undoubtedly motivates people to respond positively to fear appeals in messages; and value-expressive goals may underlie favorable reactions to competent and attractive persuaders. We believe the application of causal assumptions to purposive phenomena diminishes the meaningfulness of the explanations generated by Hovland's and McGuire's theories.

Greenwald, of course, broke with this mechanistic tradition, preferring to emphasize what people "do with" messages, rather than what messages "do to" people. Thus, his cognitive response approach focuses on people as choice-laden, self-directed agents who respond to their personalized interpretations and goal-oriented cognitive responses to externally produced messages. For that reason, we believe the cognitive response model is the most valuable theoretical contribution arising from the Yale model. Certainly, Greenwald's approach is quite compatible with our own action-oriented approach to persuasive communication.[61]

NOTES

1. For a detailed discussion of the persuasive impact of the Kennedy–Nixon debates, see Elihu Katz and Jacob J. Feldman, "The Debates in the Light of Research: A Survey of Surveys," in *The Process and Effects of Mass Communication*, ed. Wilbur Schramm and Donald F. Roberts (Urbana, Ill.: University of Illinois Press, 1971), pp. 701–753.

2. The Yale approach to persuasion in detailed in Carl I. Hovland, Irving L. Janis, and Harold H. Kelley, *Communication and Persuasion* (New Haven, Conn.: Yale University Press, 1953).

3. Ibid., pp. 10–11.

4. Ibid., p. 11.

5. Ibid.

6. This verbal model of persuasion is attributed to Harold D. Lasswell. See Lasswell, "The Structure and Function of Communication in Society," in *The Communication of Ideas*, ed. Lyman Bryson (New York: Institute for Religious and Social Studies, 1948), p. 37.

7. McGuire's information-processing model is detailed in William J. McGuire, "Personality and Attitude Change: An Information-Processing Theory," in *Psychological Foundations of Attitudes*, ed. Anthony G. Greenwald, Timothy C. Brock, and Thomas M. Ostrom (New York: Academic Press, 1968), pp. 171–196; and William J. McGuire, "Personality and Susceptibility to Social Influence," in *Handbook of Personality Theory and Research*, ed. Edgar F. Borgatta and William W. Lambert (Chicago: Rand McNally, 1968), pp. 1130–1187.

8. McGuire, "Personality and Susceptibility," p. 1143.

9. In the original statement of this equation, McGuire included a third predictor variable, $Pr\ (K)$, which he termed a residual factor representing the probability that any processes other than reception and yielding will affect opinion change. However, as a practical matter, McGuire ignored this third predictor.

10. McGuire, "Personality and Susceptibility," p. 1171.

11. McGuire, "Personality and Attitude Change," p. 182.

12. Greenwald's cognitive response model is detailed in Anthony G. Greenwald, "Cognitive Learning, Cognitive Response to Persuasion, and Attitude Change," in *Psychological Foundations of Attitude*, pp. 147–170. Also see Richard E. Petty, Thomas M. Ostrom, and Timothy C. Brock, *Cognitive Responses in Persuasion* (Hillsdale, N.J.: Lawrence Erlbaum, in press).

13. Greenwald, "Cognitive Learning," p. 149.

14. For discussions of factors of source credibility, see Ronald L. Applbaum and Karl W. E. Anatol, "Dimensions of Source Credibility: A Test for Reproducibility," *Speech Monographs* 40 (1973): 231–237; Ronald L. Applbaum and Karl W. E. Anatol, "The Factor Structure of Source Credibility as a Function of the Speaking Situation," *Speech Monographs* 39 (1972): 216–223; David K. Berlo, James B. Lemert, and Robert J. Mertz, "Dimensions for Evaluating the Acceptability of Message Sources,"

Public Opinion Quarterly 33 (1969–1970): 563–576; Jack L. Whitehead, Jr., "Factors of Source Credibility," *Quarterly Journal of Speech* 54 (1968): 59–63; and James C. McCroskey, "Scales for the Measurement of Ethos," *Speech Monographs* 33 (1966): 65–72.

15. Carl I. Hovland and Walter Weiss, "The Influence of Source Credibility on Communication Effectiveness," *Public Opinion Quarterly* 15 (1951): 635–650.

16. Ibid., p. 648.

17. Herbert C. Kelman and Carl I. Hovland, " 'Reinstatement' of the Communicator in Delayed Measurement of Opinion Change," *Journal of Abnormal and Social Psychology* 48 (1953): 327–335. It should be noted that some researchers have questioned whether the passage of time actually results in a true sleeper effect, that is, an actual *increase* in agreement with a low-credibility source. For analyses of this dispute, see Paulette M. Gillig and Anthony G. Greenwald, "Is It Time to Lay the Sleeper Effect to Rest?" *Journal of Personality and Social Psychology* 29 (1974): 132–139; and Charles L. Gruder, et al., "Empirical Tests of the Absolute Sleeper Effect Predicted from the Discounting Cue Hypothesis," *Journal of Personality and Social Psychology* 36 (1978): 1061–1074.

18. Gillig and Greenwald.

19. For examples of relevant research, see Joann Horai, Nicholas Naccari, and Elliot Fatoullah, "The Effects of Expertise and Physical Attractiveness upon Opinion Agreement and Liking," *Sociometry* 37 (1974): 601–606; Mark Snyder and Myron Rothbart, "Communicator Attractiveness and Opinion Change," *Canadian Journal of Behavioral Science* 3 (1971): 377–387; and Judson Mills and Eliot Aronson, "Opinion Change as a Function of the Communicator's Attractiveness and Desire to Influence," *Journal of Personality and Social Psychology* 1 (1965): 173–177.

20. Karen K. Dion and Steven Stein, "Physical Attractiveness and Interpersonal Influence," *Journal of Experimental Social Psychology* 14 (1978): 97–108.

21. Karen K. Dion, "Physical Attractiveness and Children's Evaluation of Peers' Behavior: What is Beautiful is Occasionally Suspect" (unpublished MS, University of Toronto, 1978).

22. Ellen Berscheid and Elaine Walster, "Physical Attractiveness," in *Advances in Experimental Social Psychology*, ed. Leonard Berkowitz (New York: Academic Press, 1974).

23. William Goldman and Philip Lewis, "Beautiful Is Good: Evidence that the Physically Attractive Are More Socially Skillful," *Journal of Experimental Social Psychology* 13 (1977): 125–130.

24. See Norman Miller et al., "Speed of Speech and Persuasion," *Journal of Personality and Social Psychology* 34 (1976): 615–624; and James C. McCroskey and R. Samuel Mehrley, "The Effects of Disorganization and Non-fluency on Attitude Change and Source Credibility," *Speech Monographs* 36 (1969): 13–21.

25. Shelly Chaiken, "Communicator Physical Attractiveness and Persuasion," *Journal of Personality and Social Psychology* 37 (1979): 1387–1397.

26. Ellen Berscheid, "Opinion Change and Communicator–Communicatee Similarity and Dissimilarity," *Journal of Personality and Social Psychology* 4 (1966): 670–680.

27. Timothy C. Brock, "Communicator–Recipient Similarity and Decision Change," *Journal of Personality and Social Psychology* 1 (1965): 650–654.

28. Ross Norman, "When What Is Said Is Important: A Comparison of Expert and Attractive Sources," *Journal of Experimental Social Psychology* 12 (1976): 294–300.

29. John T. Cacioppo and Richard E. Petty, "Effects of Message Repetition and Position on Cognitive Response, Recall, and Persuasion," *Journal of Personality and Social Psychology* 37 (1979): 97–109.

30. John T. Cacioppo and Richard E. Petty, "Attitudes and Cognitive Responses: An Electrophysiological Approach," *Journal of Personality and Social Psychology* 37 (1979): 2181–2199.

31. Robert Love's research is reported in Greenwald, "Cognitive Learning," pp. 163–165.

32. Alice H. Eagly, "Comprehensibility of Persuasive Arguments as a Determinant of Opinion Change," *Journal of Personality and Social Psychology* 29 (1974): 758–773.

33. William A. Watts and William J. McGuire, "Persistence of Induced Opinion Change and Retention of the Inducing Message Contents," *Journal of Abnormal and Social Psychology* 68 (1964): 233–241.

34. Daniel E. Berlyne, "Novelty, Complexity, and Hedonic Value," *Perception and Psychophysics* 8 (1970): 279–286; and David J. Stang, "The Effects of Mere Exposure on Learning and Affect," *Journal of Personality and Social Psychology* 31 (1975): 7–13.

35. Cacioppo and Petty, "Effects of Message Repetition."

36. Carl I. Hovland, Arthur A. Lumsdaine, and Fred D. Sheffield, "The Effects of Presenting 'One Side' versus 'Both Sides' in Changing Opinions on a Controversial Subject," in *Experiments on Mass Communication* (Princeton, N.J.: Princeton University Press, 1949), pp. 201–227.

37. Arthur A. Lumsdaine and Irving L. Janis, "Resistance to 'Counterpropaganda' Produced by One-sided and Two-sided 'Propaganda' Presentations," *Public Opinion Quarterly* 17 (1953): 311–318.

38. James C. McCroskey, "A Summary of Experimental Research on the Effects of Evidence in Persuasive Communication," in *The Process of Social Influence*, ed. Thomas D. Beisecker and Donn W. Parson (Englewood Cliffs, N.J.: Prentice-Hall, 1972), p. 320.

39. McCroskey, pp. 318–328.

40. See Irving L. Janis and Seymour Feshbach, "Effects of Fear-Arousing Communications," *Journal of Abnormal and Social Psychology* 48 (1953): 78–92. In this initial test of Hovland's hypothesis, Janis and Feshbach found that minimal fear appeals were more effective than moderate or strong fear arousal in promoting acceptance of recommendations on dental hygiene.

41. McGuire, "Personality and Susceptibility."

42. Howard Leventhal and Patricia Niles, "Persistence of Influence for Varying Durations of Exposure to Threat Stimuli," *Psychological Reports* 16 (1965): 223–233.

43. C. Ronald Mewborn, "Effects of Threat and Reassurance upon Attitude Change" (unpublished M.A. thesis, University of South Carolina, 1975).

44. Howard Leventhal, "Fear Communications in the Acceptance of Preventive Health Practices," in *Experiments in Persuasion*, ed. Ralph L. Rosnow and Edward J. Robinson (New York: Academic Press, 1967), p. 180.

45. Ronald W. Rogers and C. Ronald Mewborn, "Fear Appeals and Attitude Change: Effects of a Threat's Noxiousness, Probability of Occurrence, and the Efficacy of Coping Responses," *Journal of Personality and Social Psychology* 34 (1967): 54–61.

46. Howard Leventhal, Robert Singer, and Susan Jones, "Effects of Fear and Specificity of Recommendation upon Attitudes and Behavior," *Journal of Personality and Social Psychology* 2 (1965): 20–29.

47. Janis and Feshbach.

48. Patricia Niles, "The Relationship of Susceptibility and Anxiety to Acceptance of Fear-Arousing Communications" (Ph.D. diss., Yale University, 1964).

49. Robert A. Osterhouse and Timothy C. Brock, "Distraction Increases Yielding to Propaganda by Inhibiting Counterarguing," *Journal of Personality and Social Psychology* 15 (1970): 344–358.

50. Richard E. Petty, Gary L. Wells, and Timothy C. Brock, "Distraction Can Enhance or Reduce Yielding to Propaganda: Thought Disruption versus Effort Justification," *Journal of Personality and Social Psychology* 34 (1976): 874–884.

51. William A. Watts and Lewis E. Holt, "Persistence of Opinion Change Induced under Conditions of Forewarning and Distraction," *Journal of Personality and Social Psychology* 37 (1979): 778–789.

52. Kenneth D. Fransden, "Effects of Threat Appeals and Media of Transmission," *Speech Monographs* 30 (1963): 101–104.

53. Hadley Cantril and Gordon W. Allport, *The Psychology of Radio* (New York: Harper, 1935).

54. McGuire, "Personality and Susceptibility."

55. For example, see C. Edward Wilson, "The Effect of Medium on Loss of Information," *Journalism Quarterly* 51 (1974): 111–115.

56. Shelly Chaiken and Alice H. Eagly, "Communication Modality as a Determinant of Message Persuasiveness and Message Comprehensibility," *Journal of Personality and Social Psychology* 34 (1976): 605–614.

57. Donald F. Cox and Raymond A. Bauer, "Self-Confidence and Persuasibility in Women," *Public Opinion Quarterly* 28 (1964): 453–466.

58. For a summary of studies concerned with enduring personality traits other than self-esteem, see McGuire, "Personality and Susceptibility." It should be noted that the relationship McGuire postulates between personality traits and persuasibility applies only to chronic or dispositional traits, not to temporary or acute traits that may be induced experimentally. For a discussion of the relationship between acute and chronic personality traits and the relationship of both to persuasibility, see McGuire, "Personality and Susceptibility," pp. 1157–1161.

59. Richard E. Petty and John T. Cacioppo, "Issue Involvement Can Increase or Decrease Persuasion by Enhancing Message-Relevant Cognitive Responses," *Journal of Personality and Social Psychology* 37 (1979): 1915–1926.

60. For relevant studies, see Jonathan L. Freedman, "Involvement, Discrepancy, and Change," *Journal of Abnormal and Social Psychology* 69 (1964): 290–295; and Eliot Aronson, Judith A. Turner, and J. Merrill Carlsmith, "Communicator Credibility and Communication Discrepancy as Determinants of Opinion Change," *Journal of Abnormal and Social Psychology* 67 (1963): 31–36.

61. It should be noted that cognitive response theory has been the object of several methodological criticisms. Since these criticisms are detailed in Chapter 12 of this book, they are not considered here.

CHAPTER *10*

Information Integration Theory

On October 16, 1962, U.S. intelligence reports verified that the Soviet Union was placing intermediate-range ballistic missiles on the island of Cuba. In Washington, an official response had to be formulated. Some of President John F. Kennedy's advisers argued for a massive military attack on Cuba, but others urged diplomacy and restraint. Based on his belief that the Russian leader, Nikita Khrushchev, was a reasonable man who would not risk nuclear war, the President took an intermediate approach. He ordered a naval blockade to prevent Soviet ships from reaching Cuba with their military cargo. This strategy, Kennedy reasoned, would give both him and the Russian leader some extra time and a measure of flexibility in dealing with the missile crisis.

Khrushchev's initial reaction to the blockade was one of defiance. He insisted that Soviet ships en route to Cuba would continue and that any attempt to stop them would be resisted with military force. Thus, it seemed Kennedy's assessment of Khrushchev was misguided. However, on the evening of October 26, the crisis climate changed radically. A letter written by Khrushchev arrived from Moscow, indicating that an arrangement might be worked out to avoid confrontation. In an almost fraternal tone, the Soviet leader insisted that "what we want is not to destroy your country but to compete peacefully." He went on to say that only defensive missiles were being sent to Cuba to protect the country against a possible U.S. invasion. Finally, he concluded, "This is my proposal. No more weapons to Cuba and those within Cuba withdrawn or destroyed, and you reciprocate by withdrawing your blockade and agree not to invade Cuba." Within hours after this message was received, a second, curiously contradictory letter arrived. It had a decidedly belligerent tone and indicated that the blockade would be defied. Khrushchev declared that the missiles in Cuba would remain until there was a reciprocal removal of U.S. missiles from Turkey. This second letter implied that the naval blockade was putting the superpowers on the path to war.

On the morning of October 27, the people who gathered to consult with President Kennedy had before them two inconsistent pieces of information. The first conveyed good will and suggested that Khrushchev yearned for peace. The second was bellicose and hinted at war. The President and his advisers were faced with determining which of the two letters represented the Russian leader's true intentions. To do this, they had to carefully interpret both letters and then integrate that information with all other available material. There were three ways to integrate the available information. First, the President's advisers could assume that the difference between the two messages indicated a change of mind by the Soviet leader. In this case, the most recent message would carry the most weight. Second, they could assume that the two pieces of information were equally valid representations of Khrushchev's mood. Based on this assumption, they could either "add" or "average" the information in the two letters to form an opinion of his intentions, an approach that would probably lead to the conclusion that Khrushchev's position was somewhere between peaceful resolution and military confrontation.

Finally, the advisers could conclude that the first letter was more in line with their prior knowledge of Khrushchev as a reasonable man and, therefore, was the more accurate reflection of his intentions. On the assumption that the most recent message represented Khrushchev's true intentions, the majority of the President's advisers urged that the country prepare for war. However, the President's brother, Robert, and adviser, Theodore Sorensen, suggested that the President should simply disregard the second message. They argued that the first letter was more consistent with previous assessments of the Soviet leader and that a response to this initial message should be drafted, making no mention of the second letter.

Kennedy accepted this somewhat unusual suggestion, and he wrote an acceptance of Khrushchev's first proposal. As it turned out, Robert Kennedy's and Sorensen's assessment was correct. On October 28, Khrushchev cabled that he would begin dismantling the missiles in Cuba under international supervision. In return, the United States pledged it would neither invade Cuba nor allow itself to be used as a base for launching such an invasion. In this fashion, a potentially disastrous superpower confrontation was avoided.[1]

The judicious way Kennedy and his advisers integrated available information to determine Khrushchev's intentions illustrates the approach to persuasion we will explore in this chapter. Information integration theory looks at how we integrate new pieces of information into preexisting cognitive schemata to create, reinforce, and change attitudes or schematic assumptions. As our example indicated, the relative believability or weight assigned each item of new *and* prior information is a crucial determinant of the resulting attitude. If Kennedy's advisers had treated both of Khrushchev's messages as equally believable, they would have formed a quite different opinion from the one ultimately adopted. And had they attached a greater importance to the last message nuclear war could have resulted.

In our treatment of information integration theory, we will: (1) examine its basic assumptions and differentiate it from the Yale model of information processing; (2) explore research illustrating the persuasive effects of information integration; (3) review the expectancy-value model, one especially useful information integration theory; and (4) critically evaluate information integration approaches to persuasion.

THE INFORMATION INTEGRATION
APPROACH TO PERSUASION

Information integration theory, as developed by Norman Anderson, Martin Fishbein, and others[2] assumes that attitude formation, reinforcement, and change are functions of how individuals combine, or integrate, all available information relevant to an attitudinal object. The attitudinal object may be a person, such as a political candidate, an idea, like abortion, or a commercial product. The available information shaping one's attitude toward any object consists of all new information about that object, as well as one's preexisting memory stores of relevant materials. It is important to note that attitudes are shaped only by information that is *salient* to people at any one moment. Although innumerable bits of new and preexisting information are always relevant to any attitudinal object, only that information a person attends to will be used to shape attitudes. As this description suggests, information integration theory regards people as information processers whose attitudes are a function of how they integrate salient, new information into preexisting cognitive schemata.

The Weight and Value of Information

Information integration theory assumes that people assign two parameters—weight and value—to each item of information they process. *Weight* is defined as a person's subjective belief in the truth of the information. Thus, it represents an informational item's relative believability. *Value* is defined as a person's affective evaluation of a piece of information, and it may range from extremely positive to extremely negative. Weight combined with value determines the relative *importance* an individual attaches to any informational item.[3] Mathematically, the importance of any piece of information can be expressed as follows:

$$I_i = w_i \times v_i$$

where I_i is the relative importance of any one item (i) of information; w_i is its assigned weight; and v_i refers to its value. Thus, I (importance) is a function of the weight of information multiplied by assigned value.

To illustrate the concept, *weight*, suppose I find out that one of the U.S. senators from my state favors a massive increase in national defense spending. If my prior knowledge of the senator indicates that she or he consistently favors large defense expenditures, I will probably assign a good deal of weight to the new information and assume that it is probably true. However, if I know that the senator previously has opposed increases in military spending or that the senator's record is inconsistent on the issue, I will probably place less weight on the new information and conclude that it may or may not be true.

To understand the notion, *value*, suppose I am strongly opposed to an increase in military spending. In this case, I should negatively evaluate information that the senator favors it. Now, for the sake of simplicity, suppose that I must express an attitude toward my senator on the basis of this single item of information about his or her military spending policy. If I believe the new information is true, that is, I give it a lot of weight, and given my negative evaluation of it, my attitude toward the senator should be extremely unfavorable. On the other hand, if I don't believe the information, that is, I assign it a low truth probability or little weight, my attitude toward the senator is likely to be unchanged even though the value assigned the information is extremely negative.

This example is, of course, quite unrealistic in that any attitude is a function not of one bit, but of multiple bits of information regarding an attitudinal object. In the case of an elected official, he or she is associated with numerous, often unrelated, issues. According to information integration theory, our composite attitudinal schemata toward the official will be a function of the weighted combination of all pertinent new and prior information we have about him or her at any one time. Mathematically, a composite attitude is expressed as:

$$A = \sum_{i=1}^{n} w_i \times v_i$$

where A refers to the composite attitude; w_i and v_i represent the weight and value, respectively, assigned to each salient item (i) of information; $\sum$ denotes that all weighted and valued items of information (items i through n) are summed; and n refers to the total number of salient pieces of information relevant to attitude A.[4]

The Changing Nature of Attitude Composites

It is important to understand that our composite attitude toward any object, for example, a public official, will fluctuate over time as we are exposed to new information about the attitudinal object. Depending on the weights and values we assign to new items of incoming information, our attitude will vary in strength and degree of favorableness. One need only follow public opinion polls for several months to see that attitudes toward public issues and officeholders fluctuate sharply as a function of new information.

New information produces such fluctuations because all of our information is interdependent. The weight and value, hence, the importance, of any single item of information is affected profoundly by the weight and value attached to each other salient piece of information. The following example illustrates this concept.

During the summer of 1979, gasoline shortages and soaring inflation were highly salient, national issues. The apparent inability of the Carter administration to deal with these problems led to one of the lowest presidential approval ratings ever recorded by public opinion polls. However, in November of that year, Iranian militants captured the American embassy in Teheran and took the embassy staff hostage. And in late December 1979, the Soviet Union invaded Afghanistan, assassinated its leader, and installed a new regime. These two events drew angry reactions from the American public and led to a refocusing of attention from domestic to foreign policy issues in the first few months of 1980. This new information led to a temporary decline in the weights and values Americans attached to domestic issues. Consequently, Mr. Carter's approval rating rose nearly 30 percentage points in January 1980, the largest single increase in the history of American public opinion polling.

Clearly, the importance of any one item of information is highly dependent on the importance attached to all other information a person possesses. Furthermore, the example indicates that the weight and value attached to an informational item is at least a partial function of its salience at any one moment. Indeed, the introduction of new information almost always affects the salience of prior information. As the case of former President Carter's popularity ratings indicated, the introduction of new information often reduces the salience of old items of information, usually because new information competes with, contradicts, or otherwise nullifies its impact.

INFORMATION INTEGRATION: ADDING VERSUS AVERAGING

Since the inception of the information integration approach to persuasion, theorists have disagreed about the precise way people combine information to develop an attitude. The debate focuses on whether people psychologically "sum" all the information relevant to an attitudinal object or whether they "average" information to arrive at an opinion. Anderson is the foremost proponent of an averaging model,[5] and Fishbein and Robert Wyer are associated with the additive, or summation, approach.[6]

Mathematically, an additive model assumes an attitude is the sum of the weight and value product (that is, the importance) associated with all items of salient information. The formula for the summation model appeared on page 244. Anderson's averaging model and its conceptual relationship with the additive model can be represented mathematically as:

$$A = \frac{\sum_{i=1}^{n} w_i \times v_i}{\sum n}$$

where the numerator is the summation model formula and the denominator is the total number (n) of salient information units, each weighted for its importance to the individual.

Information integration theorists point out two situations where summation and averaging assumptions appear to make contradictory predictions about the persuasive effects of information integration. The first concerns what are called "set-size effects" and may be illustrated with the following example. Suppose that I have two pieces of information that are highly favorable toward some person, product, or idea, and then learn two additional, equally favorable, items of information about the same attitudinal object. Assuming all four items of information are judged equally important, a summation model predicts that the addition of two more favorable items to the initial set will increase the favorableness of my attitude toward the object. In contrast, an averaging model predicts no increase in favorableness.

To clarify, let's assign a numerical value to each of the four items of information, a value representing our perception of the importance (weight multiplied by value) of each piece of information. Suppose we assign a constant 4 to each informational item, using a scale ranging from 1–5, with 1 meaning "least favorable" and 5, "most favorable." The summation model predicts an increase in favorableness from 8 to 16 when two new items of information are added. But the averaging model predicts a constant rating of 4, regardless of whether two or four items of information are the basis of one's opinion.

A second situation where the summation and averaging models apparently contradict one another occurs when mildly favorable information is added to a set of highly favorable items of information. According to the summation model, this addition will strengthen attitudes, but according to the averaging formulation, it will lower them. Similarly, adding mildly unfavorable information to a highly unfavorable set should weaken attitudes according to the additive model, but strengthen them according to the averaging model. To illustrate, suppose I must form an attitude toward some hypothetical person based on the following two items of information: the person is intelligent and friendly. Suppose further that, on a 5-point scale ranging from 1, "least favorable" to 5, "most favorable", I give intelligence an importance rating of 3 and friendliness a rating of 4. To complicate the situation, I unexpectedly receive a third item of information about this hypothetical person, namely, that the individual has a reserved disposition. Suppose I give this information an importance rating of 2, indicating that I consider it a positive personality trait but less important than friendliness and intelligence.

If we assume that people form attitudes by summing all available information, my attitude toward this hypothetical person should become more favorable, increasing from 7 to 9, with the addition of the extra bit of positive information. However, if we adopt an averaging model, my attitude should decline from 3.5 to 3.0 as a result of the additional piece of information. Note, however, that the averaging model would also predict an intensified attitude if the new information were more favorable than the average favorability of the original information set. The same predictions and assumptions we have applied to a set of favorable information applies to sets of unfavorable information.

Resolving the Adding versus Averaging Controversy

Although most attempts to assess the relative merits of the additive and averaging formulations have been inconclusive, one experiment deserves mention. Anderson[7] provided subjects with information about hypothetical persons in the form of either two or four descriptive adjectives, all of which had previously been rated for favorableness by an independent sample of 100 subjects. The adjectives had been rated either as highly favorable (H), moderately favorable (M+), moderately unfavorable (M−), or low in favorability (L). Based on the adjectives they were given, subjects expressed an attitude toward several hypothetical persons.

Anderson constructed sets of information allowing tests between the adding and averaging models in each of the two types of situations described above. First, he examined set-size effects by comparing the persuasive impact of HH versus HHHH sets and LL versus LLLL sets. The second comparison he made explored the effects of adding mildly favorable or unfavorable adjectives to sets of highly favorable or unfavorable ones, respectively (HH versus HHM⁺M⁺ and LL versus LLM⁻M⁻). The following illustrates the types of information used in the experiment:

HH	Intelligent, good-natured
HHHH	Intelligent, good-natured, wise, friendly
HHM⁺M⁺	Intelligent, good-natured, reserved, obedient
LL	Hostile, conceited
LLLL	Hostile, conceited, belligerent, self-centered
LLM⁻M⁻	Hostile, conceited, meek, withdrawing

Results indicated that the first type of comparison, the set-size effects, conformed to the predictions of the summation model. Four highly favorable pieces of information produced a more positive attitude toward the hypothetical persons than did two highly favorable adjectives (HHHH>HH). Similarly, four highly unfavorable adjectives produced a more negative attitude than did two highly unfavorable items (LLLL<LL). (This result is consistent with that obtained by Anderson and Fishbein.[8]) In contrast, the second comparison appeared to favor the averaging model. Adding two mildly favorable pieces of information to two highly favorable adjectives reduced attitudinal intensity toward the hypothetical persons (HH>HHM⁺M⁺), but adding two mildly unfavorable adjectives to two highly unfavorable ones resulted in more positive attitudes (LL<LLM⁻M⁻).

In assessing the relative merits of the two integration models, two conclusions are possible. First, as Anderson's study implied, it is possible that the two models are not contradictory formulations, but rather apply to different information-integration tasks. Thus, in some circumstances, people may form or change attitudes by adding all salient information, but in other circumstances an averaging pattern is followed.

Second, an examination of each model's assumptions suggests that both may account satisfactorily for the effects described in Anderson's experiment. Consider the case of adding mildly favorable or unfavorable information to HH or LL sets. Although the averaging model appears to give the best account of the observed effects, an additive model can also accommodate them. Specifically, when mildly favorable information is added to highly favorable information, a summation model would predict a decrease in attitudes *if* we assume that people assign negative evaluations to mildly favorable information *in the context of highly favorable information*. Alternately, people may assign a positive evaluation to mildly unfavorable information *in the context of highly unfavorable information*. This "contrast effect" is a well-established concept in psychophysics and occupies a central place in the social judgment–involvement theory we will consider in Chapter 11.[9]

To illustrate this contrast effect, let's look, both in isolation and in context, at some adjectives similar to those Anderson used in his study. Suppose the only information I have about a hypothetical person is that he or she is "meek." In isolation, I will probably regard meekness as a mildly unfavorable personality trait. However, if I learn that the same individual is "hostile" and "conceited," meekness will probably begin to look like a positive attribute in that highly negative context. Moreover, mildly favorable adjectives should be similarly affected in an analogous context. As this analysis indicates, it is plausible that both an additive and an averaging model can account satisfactorily for the effects of adding mildly polarized to highly polarized information.

What about set-size effects where equally favorable information is added to an initial set? Both Anderson's and Fishbein's studies indicate that adding more positive information enhances an initially favorable attitude, and the addition of unfavorable information to an already unfavorable set results in a more negative attitude. Although the summation model appears to best explain this effect, Anderson argues that his averaging formulation can accommodate it equally well. He contends that when one takes into account an individual's opinion prior to receiving any information, the averaging model makes the same set-size prediction as the adding formulation. When forming an attitude about a hypothetical person, Anderson assumes one's initial opinion is numerically equal to zero.

To illustrate Anderson's explanation, let's assume that each item of favorable information a person receives is rated as a constant 2 in terms of favorability. According to Anderson's calculations, when a person has only two items of information, and where 0 is the initial attitude, his or her attitude toward a hypothetical person should be 1.33 $(0 + 2 + 2 \div 3)$. However, when two additional items of information are received, the averaging model correctly predicts that one's attitude should be more favorable, in this case increasing to 1.60 $(0 + 2 + 2 + 2 + 2 \div 5)$.[10] Thus, when initial opinion is incorporated into the averaging model, it appears to account for set-size effects as well as the summation model.

We may conclude that both the adding and the averaging models can account for the two information-processing effects we have discussed in this section. Moreover, given that both the weight and value of each item of information can fluctuate widely, depending on informational context and individual differences, Fishbein argues that "both models can account for any obtained result."[11] Even so, we believe it is more profitable to view the two models as equally reasonable perspectives on the nature of information integration that are applicable to different areas of persuasive effects.

INTEGRATION THEORY CONTRASTED WITH THE YALE APPROACH

Information integration theory and the Yale approach have many conceptual similarities because both construe persuasive effects as a function of information processing. However, the two theories differ in several important respects. First, information integration theory is a more particularized, or microcosmic, approach to attitude formation, reinforcement, and change than are the theories inspired by the Yale tradition. Information integration theory focuses on the ways individuals combine and assess multiple bits of information to arrive at a composite, schematic structure. Moreover, integration theory emphasizes how each piece of information affects every other informational unit in a person's perceptual field. In contrast, theories patterned after the Yale model represent a more global, or macrocosmic, approach to persuasion. As discussion in Chapter 9 indicated, the Yale theories focus on general processes and broad response patterns affecting cognitive and behavior change. They were designed neither to predict and explain the persuasive effects of multiple items of information nor to assess their relative contributions to a person's composite attitudes.

A second important difference between the Yale models and information integration theory is that the latter is a far more quantitative approach to persuasion. Yale theories are essentially qualitative, but information integration theory focuses on a precise mathematical description and explanation of how information is combined to influence attitudes. Integration theorists aim to precisely predict the amount of attitude change that can be expected in any well-defined, persuasive communication situation.

A final difference is that each theory claims a different generative force for persuasive effects. Theories inspired by the Yale tradition rely heavily on the somewhat mechanistic, cognitive learning theory to explain attitude formation, reinforcement, and change. In contrast, the generative forces claimed by information integration theorists are only loosely related to learning effects. These theorists construe persuasive effects as a function of a special kind of rule-following behavior, specifically, those rules we use to process, interpret, and integrate information.

These rules include: (1) those governing the selective perception and interpretation of incoming information; (2) rules governing the organization and reconstructive storage of information in memory, including rules defining relations among memory-based bits of information; and (3) rules governing the integration of incoming information, including rules guiding the processes by which new information is reconstructively combined with old information to create, reinforce, and change cognitive structures.[12]

In summary, information integration theory is a particularized, quantitative approach to persuasion focusing on the effects of multiple items of persuasive information. In contrast, the Yale approach emphasizes the effects of more global mediating processes and is especially useful in analysis of the effects of a single persuasive communication. Finally, unlike the Yale theories that rely on cognitive learning theory to explain persuasive effects, information integration theory explains persuasive effects by referring to the rules humans follow when they interpret and integrate multiple bits of information.

INFORMATION INTEGRATION AND PERSUASION: SOME RESEARCH FINDINGS

Having examined the concepts supporting information integration theory, we need to consider some of its persuasive effects. We will explore two topics: (1) the persuasive effects of the order of presentation of incoming information; and (2) variables affecting the weight and value people attach to items of information in a single persuasive message.

The Order of Presentation of Information: Primacy–Recency Effects

When individuals are exposed sequentially to two or more blocks of information, will they attach more importance to the first item of information or the last, or will they be affected equally by all the information in the sequence? When the initial items of information in a sequence have the greatest persuasive impact, the result is called a *primacy effect;* on the other hand, the term *recency effect* is applied when the last items are more persuasive. Because of its practical importance, the primacy–recency question has interested students of persuasion for more than 50 years.[13] In a political campaign, for instance, it is common for each candidate to try to get his or her views on important issues to the electorate before opponents do. This strategy is based on the assumption that the first information voters receive will have a greater persuasive impact than will later information. Likewise, smear tactics in business, government, and politics are based on the assumption that an initial charge of misconduct against a rival will have a greater impact than will a later refutation of the allegation.

In contrast, many politicians plan their campaign strategies on the assumption that the last word is more important than initial messages. Thus, media blitzes on election eve are common, based on the belief that the last information voters receive will have a disproportionate influence on their attitudes and behaviors. The essence of the primacy–recency controversy concerns the relative weight and value people assign to items of information as a function of their sequential position. This issue is especially amenable to investigation within an information integration paradigm.

Solomon Asch was one of the first information integration theorists to study the primacy–recency question. In one classic experiment, he gave subjects six items of information about a hypothetical person, arranging the information in terms of increasing or decreasing favorability. Half of the subjects received the following sequence of information: the person is intelligent; industrious; impulsive; critical; stubborn; and envious. The order was reversed for the other half. After exposure to the information, all subjects expressed their attitude toward the hypothetical person on an eight-point scale ranging from "highly favorable" to "highly unfavorable." The results showed a primacy effect. Attitudes were more favorable when the favorable information appeared first and more negative when the unfavorable information was presented first.[14]

Using informational inputs differing from Asch's, Luchins also found support for the primacy effect. He had subjects read two paragraphs, both describing the behaviors of a hypothetical boy named Jim. In the first paragraph, Jim's behaviors reflected an outgoing, affable person, and in the second paragraph he was portrayed as a quiet, more introverted young man. Subjects who read the extroverted description and then the introverted one saw Jim as more gregarious and sociable than did subjects who read the paragraphs in reverse order.[15]

Numerous later investigations, using similar experimental procedures, have also indicated that there may be a general tendency for individuals to place a greater weight and value on the initial items of information in a sequence.[16] Given this apparent tendency, most recent research has focused on the following: (1) identifying plausible theoretical explanations for the primacy effect; and (2) isolating variables that can break the power of primacy and result in a recency effect.

Explanations for the Primacy Effect

Four theoretical explanations have been proposed to account for the tendency of individuals to place more importance on the initial information appearing in a sequence: (1) the change in meaning hypothesis; (2) the attention decrement theory; (3) the discounting hypothesis; and (4) the inferential belief explanation.

The Change in Meaning Hypothesis   Asch explains the primacy effect in terms of what he calls a "change in meaning" or "directed impression." *The change in meaning hypothesis* stipulates that the first information in a sequence sets up the context in which later information is interpreted; thus, meaning is dependent on the context in which a bit of information appears. Regarding the primacy effect, this implies that early information provides the context that influences the meaning of later information.[17] Numerous studies have confirmed Asch's common-sense assumption.[18]

The Attention Decrement Hypothesis   A number of theorists, including Anderson and Ralph Stewart, have argued that the primacy effect is best explained as a function of attention decrement. According to the *attention decrement hypothesis*, people pay less attention to information coming late in a sequence than they do to initial material. Consequently, they assign a lower weight or truth probability to each successive piece of information.[19] Several studies support this hypothesis. All of them introduced conditions encouraging subjects to pay equal attention to all the information in a sequence. Theoretically, this tactic should eliminate the primacy effect, if, in fact, the primacy effect is due to attention decrement.

For example, Anderson and Hubert told all the subjects in a study that they were required to recall *all* the information in a sequence, and Stewart asked subjects to evaluate the attitudinal object after receiving each piece of information about it. Results of each study appeared to support the attention decrement hypothesis. Primacy effects disappeared when subjects were required to focus attention on all the information in a sequence. In fact, both studies reported a recency effect, that is, later information had a greater persuasive effect than earlier material.[20] This result is, of course, inconsistent with the attention decrement hypothesis since there should be no order effects at all if equal attention is paid to each item of information in a sequence.

Recent research has cast doubt on the validity of the attention decrement hypothesis. Studies on recall of sequential information, a measure directly related to attention, have established that recall follows a curvilinear, U-shaped pattern. People easily remember initial and later information in a sequence, but do not retain intermediate material very well. Moreover, later information tends to be recalled better than information presented first.[21]

Dreben, Fiske, and Hastie recently demonstrated that recall of sequential information and attitude formation and change are quite independent of one another. In one experimental condition, subjects were asked to form an opinion after hearing a sequence of information. Results showed a strong primacy effect: initial information had the greatest impact on opinions. However, recall followed a U-shaped curve, with a strong recency effect and some primacy.[22] Thus, although later information was attended to and retained more than initial information, the first information presented produced the stronger persuasive effect. These results are consistent with research discussed in Chapter 9 showing little correlation between the learning of the content of messages and subsequent attitude change.

The Discounting Hypothesis   Unlike the other two theories we have discussed, the *discounting hypothesis* is applicable only when an information sequence contains contradictory information. Anderson, the foremost proponent of the discounting hypothesis, argues that people discount inconsistent information, that is, assign it a low weight or truth probability. Based on this assumption, if negative information follows positive information, the negative material will be discounted and conversely. Thus, the primacy effect is regarded as a consequence of inconsistency resolution.[23] Logically, inconsistency resolution could be achieved equally well by discounting or assigning a low truth probability either to the early or late information. However, it has been argued that it is easier to discount later information than it is to change the impression created by the initial material.[24] If this assumption holds, then discounting should lead to a primacy effect.

Tests of the discounting hypothesis have yielded conflicting results. Although Anderson and Jacobson reported results supporting the hypothesis,[25] Hendrick and Costantini found contrary evidence. They presented subjects with six items of information about a hypothetical person and varied the magnitude of consistency between the first three items and the last three. After the information was presented, subjects evaluated the person on an eight-point scale. Using the discounting hypothesis, the greater the amount of inconsistency between the sets of information, the stronger the primacy effect should be. However, Hendrick and Costantini found that all sequences of information produced primacy effects, and that the effect was no greater for highly inconsistent and highly consistent informational sequences.[26] Even so, research into the discounting hypothesis's account of the primacy effect has neither confirmed nor convincingly disproved the theory.

The Inferential Belief Formation Hypothesis   The last explanation for the primacy effect focuses on the effect of covert message production in response to sequential information. Advocated by Fishbein, the *inferential belief formation hypothesis* suggests order of presentation has a powerful influence upon the formation of *inferential beliefs*—beliefs not directly tied to the content of message, but, rather, representing a person's responses to incoming messages based on past experience. As this description implies, inferential beliefs are analogous to the notion of cognitive responses discussed in Chapter 9. Fishbein argues that presenting information in a descending order of favorability should generate more positive inferential beliefs, but that presenting unfavorable information first should lead to more negative inferential beliefs. In both cases, of course, a primacy effect is expected.[27]

Jaccard and Fishbein found some support for this hypothesis. They presented subjects with 12 items of information about a hypothetical person; six were positive and six negative. Some subjects read the sequence of information with the positive information presented first, and others were exposed initially to the negative material. After subjects indicated their attitudes toward the person on a seven-point scale ranging from "like" to "dislike," the researchers took several additional measures. Subjects were asked to recall as much of the received information as they could. In addition, each subject was asked to write down anything *else* "you think might characterize the person described." Finally, the subjects' attitudes toward the hypothetical person were correlated with: (1) all the information they recalled correctly; (2) all information recalled plus all cognitive responses they listed; and (3) the 12 items of information that were given the subjects, whether recalled or not. Results showed a primacy effect. Moreover, the subjects' attitudes bore a high positive correlation (+.67) with recalled plus inferred beliefs, but attitudes correlated more poorly with correctly recalled information (+.47) and with the actual information provided (+.48).[28]

This research, and that of Asch and Anderson and Barrios,[29] support the notion that the information presented first in a sequence has a disproportionate influence on cognitive responding or the formation of inferential beliefs. If this is the case, the inferential belief hypothesis could logically account for either a primacy or a recency effect when a sequence contains inconsistent information. If initial information elicits cognitive responses congruent with it, a primacy effect is expected. However, if the first information elicits counterargumentation, then a recency effect seems likely since the later information should be consistent with a person's initial cognitive reactions. Unfortunately, there is as yet no evidence to confirm or disprove this speculation.

In summary, all four theoretical explanations examined have contributed to our understanding of why primacy effects predominate. Of the four approaches, the change in meaning hypothesis has received repeated empirical support. In contrast, the attention decrement, discounting, and inferential belief formation hypotheses all have some empirical support, but are, overall, weaker explanations for the primacy effect. Moreover, both the discounting and inferential belief accounts can explain either a primacy or a recency effect. This reduces their credibility as theoretical explanations for a *pervasive* tendency toward primacy. At the same time, that they can account for both effects makes the two hypotheses more general explanations of the varied effects of information integration than either of the other two theories considered.

Variables Promoting a Recency Effect

Despite an apparent pervasive tendency for the first information presented in a sequence to have the greatest persuasive impact, this is not always the case. The well-documented power of "eleventh hour" advertising in political campaigns to influence voting choices is testimony to the presence and persuasive power of recency effects. In this section, we will look at three categories of variables that promote recency: (1) attentional variables; (2) intervening factors; and (3) perceptual variables.

Directed Attention   Any tactic encouraging people to carefully consider all the information in a sequence increases the probability of a recency effect. Anderson and Hubert obtained a recency effect when subjects were led to believe they would have to recall all the information in a sequence.[30] In a more recent study, Dreben and others observed a recency effect under the same conditions.[31] A recency effect has also been obtained when people are asked to respond with an opinion after each item of information is presented rather than after all information is received.[32] This continuous mode of responding presumably prompts people to focus attention on all the later information in a sequence.

Luchins demonstrated a third strategy that encourages people to carefully consider all items of information and, therefore, promotes a recency effect. He found that warning people of the possible dangers of first impressions (for example, that snap judgments are sometimes incorrect) produces a recency effect. Moreover, he obtained recency effects whether or not the warning was given before any information was presented or given between two blocks of inconsistent information.[33] Hovland and his associates documented a fourth tactic that can encourage people to focus on all information and thereby produce a recency effect. They found that when people are aware that there are two or more sides to an issue, they tend not to *fully* commit themselves until all sides have been heard. In contrast, if people can be induced to commit themselves publicly after hearing one side of an issue, a primacy effect almost always results.[34]

In summary, a recency effect tends to occur when people are encouraged to carefully weigh all the information in a sequence. This effect can be accomplished by leading people to believe they must remember all the information, having them respond to each item of information as it is presented, warning of the hazards of first impressions, or making sure that they are aware an issue has at least two sides. Clearly, many of these conditions are present in the "real-life" practice of persuasion. For example, voters usually are aware there are two or more sides to issues in political campaigns. Moreover, they frequently react to issues on a continuous basis. Finally, juries in civil or criminal trials are warned by the court of the danger of first impressions and the need to attend to both sides of the issue at law. As this analysis indicates, recency effects occur quite often; primacy effects do not always prevail.

Intervening Variables   Distraction and elapsed time also tend to create recency effects. When a person is *distracted* between the presentation of initial and late information, the probability increases that later information will have the greatest persuasive impact. Dreben, and others, as well as Luchins, examined the effects of distraction by having some subjects perform a mathematics task between the reception of two sets of information; other subjects were not distracted. Results showed a primacy effect for the nondistracted subjects and recency for distracted subjects.[35] Presumably, intermediate distraction weakens people's memories of initial information, prompting the assignment of a greater weight or truth probability to the most recent information received. Luchins showed that *increasing the amount of time*, without distraction, between the presentation of a first and second block of information can produce a recency effect.[36] Presumably, delay, like distraction, leads to the forgetting of initial information and a recency effect occurs.

As with directed attention variables, distraction and delay are present in many persuasive situations. Distraction, including the reception of unrelated information, frequently occurs between units of related material. Moreover, time intervals between messages in politics, government, and the like, are often quite lengthy. In general, the greater the intervening delay and distraction between blocks of information, the greater the persuasive impact of the latest information.

Perceptions of Replacement Information A final variable promoting a recency effect concerns the replacement value of information. Edward Jones and George Goethals suggest that when later information is seen as a replacement for initial information, a recency effect will occur. In contrast, a primacy effect is likely when later information is not so perceived.[37] Let's illustrate this notion in the context of a hypothetical presidential election campaign. Suppose the challenger states that inflation is increasing at an annual rate of 14 percent and blames the incumbent administration for its inability to deal with the problem. The incumbent later responds with information showing that the rate of inflation is actually declining as a result of the current administration's economic policies. If I perceive the incumbent's information as new data replacing that of the challenger, a recency effect should occur. However, if I regard the incumbent's statement as a political ploy containing no updated information, a primacy effect ought to result.

Our earlier discussion of the Cuban missile crisis is relevant to this issue. Recall that most of President Kennedy's advisers regarded Khrushchev's second letter as replacement information. As a consequence, they found it more persuasive, and a recency effect occurred for them. In contrast, Robert Kennedy and Theodore Sorensen did not treat the second message as replacement information; they continued to place greater weight on the first letter. Because their perceptions violated the usual tendency to see later information as replacement material, their counsel to the President stands today as ingenious and historic advice.

Differential Weighting of Information in a Single Message

We have now considered the persuasive effects resulting from the order of presenting sequential messages. In this section, we will look at two classes of variables affecting the relative weights or truth probabilities people attach to items of information within a single message: context variables and context-free factors. Both sets influence the persuasive effect of information.

Context Effects

Context refers to the configuration of information within which a single piece of information appears. You will remember from an earlier discussion that the weight and value assigned to any one item of information are dependent on all other information salient to a person at any one moment. Thus, context should profoundly affect the importance a person will attach to information.

The effect of context on the differential weighting of information has been demonstrated many times. In a representative study, Hamilton and Zanna gave subjects information about a hypothetical person that had earlier been judged as: (1) moderately favorable information, for example, "The person is proud and daring;" (2) moderately unfavorable information, such as "The person is indecisive and conformist;" and (3) neutral information, for example, "The individual is outspoken and self-contented." This information was presented to subjects in the context of other information that either was highly favorable (H), moderately favorable (M⁺), moderately unfavorable (M⁻), or highly unfavorable (L). The results, presented in Figure 10.1, confirmed expectations: the connotative meaning of each piece of information was highly dependent on the meaning of the configuration of information in which it appeared. Moreover, favorable attitudes toward the hypothetical person declined as context favorableness diminished.[38]

Two theoretical explanations for context effects have been proposed. Asch's *change of meaning hypothesis*, as extended by Thomas Ostrom, is one. According to the Asch–Ostrom interpretation, any one piece of information can have a variety of meanings, each with different weight and value implications. When a bit of information is presented in the context of other information, certain of its possible meanings are judged inappropriate. Thus, its final meaning is what a person judges to be appropriate, given its context. Since the weight and value attached to the information are dictated by its meaning, it follows that importance is determined to a large extent by context.[39]

To illustrate, suppose I am told that a person is "daring." Suppose further that I learn this information in the context of other information alleging the person is also

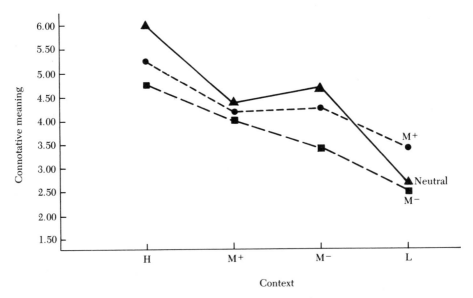

FIGURE 10.1   *Mean estimates of the connotative meaning of three types of information. Adapted from David C. Hamilton and Mark P. Zanna, "Context Effects in Impression Formation: Changes in Connotative Meaning,"* Journal of Personality and Social Psychology, 29, 1974, p. 653. Copyright 1974 by the American Psychological Association. Reprinted by permission.

"conceited" and "reckless." In this context, "daring" is likely to be judged as an unfavorable characteristic. In contrast, if I am told the individual is also "courageous" and "diligent," "daring" will probably be judged more favorably. It should be clear from these examples that the more *ambiguous* an item of information, the greater the role context has in defining or changing its meaning. Indeed, Wyer found that highly ambiguous words such as *cautious, meticulous,* and *choosy* were more often defined contextually than less ambiguous terms like *innocent, courteous,* and *self-centered.*[40]

Anderson has proposed a second explanation for context effects. Called the *generalized halo effect hypothesis,* his interpretation holds that each piece of information has a context-free, denotative meaning. However, Anderson argues that some portion of the meaning of the total collection of information generalizes to each component piece of information. More formally, he contends that the meaning and, thus, the importance of any item of information is the weighted average of its meaning in isolation plus the meaning of the total informational context in which it appears.[41]

Tests of the relative merits of the two theories have been notably inconclusive. Indeed, Ostrom has argued that this comparative research has been unprofitable since neither theory is specific enough to generate unequivocally different predictions of context effects.[42]

Context-Free Effects

A number of studies have investigated whether some types of information are assigned greater weights regardless of context. Four categories of informational variables have been identified as carrying a greater context-free weight than others. First, *negative information* appears to be believed more readily than positive or favorable information.[43] To illustrate, suppose I receive two pieces of information about my congressman. One item of information indicates that my representative has consistently supported all the issues and public projects I favor. The other information alleges that my married representative has been having an affair with a staff member. Much research in the area of information integration indicates that I will place a greater weight and value on the negative information than on the favorable material. As a consequence, I should like my representative less.

The *extremity of emotion* attached to information is a second variable affecting context-free weighting. Information that is highly charged with positive or negative emotion is believed more readily than information with less emotional intensity.[44] Thus, if a candidate for public office is praised as a good parent and spouse, this information ought to be weighted more heavily than less emotionally charged material, such as information that the candidate is a good businessperson or has lots of prior experience.

Third, *novel information* usually has more context-free weight than familiar information.[45] For example, describing a priest or minister as "moral" should have little novelty, since the clergy are generally presumed to be moral people. This information should have little impact on one's attitude toward the priest or minister. However, if we learn that some priest or minister is "immoral," such information is very novel and, therefore, should have a substantial impact on one's attitudes toward the individual.

Wyer has noted that the precise psychological reasons for the high believability of novel information are unclear. One explanation is that novel material is simply more informative, in that it clearly differentiates the object being described from others in the same class. If this is the case, novel information can be expected to carry more weight "independent of the characteristics of the information presented with it."[46] On the other hand, Wyer notes that the novelty of a piece of information may affect its salience, and thus the relative attention paid to it when presented in combination with other information.[47] If this last speculation is more reasonable, then novel information is not context free, and its weight depends upon the relative novelty of accompanying information. In this instance, novelty effects can be more accurately described as context, not context-free, effects.

Finally, *individual differences* among receivers of information often prompt people to assign vastly different weights to a single piece of information, regardless of context.[48] For example, one person may consistently weigh information about the "competence" and "intelligence" of public officials more heavily than material concerning their "likability" or "morality." In contrast, another person may regard information about the morality of officeholders as more important than any other information. If these two people were presented with information about a public figure's "competence" and "morality," we can expect the second person to weigh the "morality" information more heavily than the first. This effect should occur regardless of the context in which the information appears.

THE EXPECTANCY-VALUE THEORY
OF PERSUASION

We have now considered the nature of information integration theory and examined the persuasive effects resulting from the presentation of both sequential and simultaneous information. In this section, we will briefly outline the tenets of one specific information integration theory, Fishbein's expectancy-value model,[49] a formulation that has proved a particularly useful approach to persuasive communication.

According to Fishbein, beliefs are the basic informational units we integrate in order to create, reinforce, or change attitudes. A *belief* is a statement linking an object to an attribute of the object. For example, the belief that "cigarette smoking causes lung cancer" causally links the attribute *lung cancer* to the object *cigarette smoking*. Similarly, the belief that "solar energy is a renewable resource" descriptively links the attribute *renewable resource* to the object *solar energy*. As these examples indicate, the attribute of an object may be either a property or characteristic or it may be one of its consequences.

Like any other piece of information, a belief has both a weight, termed by Fishbein an *expectancy* that the belief is true, and a positive or negative evaluation, called a *value*. As to the belief that "cigarette smoking causes lung cancer," I may attach a weight, or expectancy, of .90, meaning that I am 90 percent sure that cigarette smoking does, in fact, cause lung cancer. With respect to value, I will most certainly evaluate such a belief negatively. In the case of the belief that "solar energy is a renewable resource," I surely will regard the proposition as 100 percent certain. Regarding value, I may evaluate the information positively or be quite indifferent to it. Like other information integration theorists, Fishbein considers that a person's attitude toward any object is a function of the believability (expectancy) of all salient beliefs plus the positive or negative evaluation (value) attached to each belief. As we indicated earlier in this chapter, Fishbein regards an attitude as the sum, not the average, of all the salient beliefs a person has, each weighted for its importance (expectancy multiplied by value) to him or her.[50]

According to Fishbein, a persuasive message is nothing more than a complex series of belief statements, called *source beliefs*, regarding some attitudinal object. Each source belief has weight and a positive or negative value. Corresponding to each source belief is what Fishbein calls a *proximal belief*, the receiver's subjective expectancy that the object mentioned by a source, in fact, has the attribute specified in the message plus the receiver's evaluation of that attribute. In short, a proximal belief is a person's estimate of how true a source's statements are, plus one's positive or negative emotional reaction to a source's claims. In addition to proximal beliefs, a person has a set of what Fishbein calls external beliefs. *External beliefs*, analogous to the notion of cognitive responses discussed in Chapter 9, consist of salient beliefs that are relevant to the communication topic, but do not correspond directly with the belief statements contained in a persuasive message.

To be successful, a persuasive message must change proximal and relevant external beliefs in the direction of source beliefs. There are three major strategies for changing these beliefs. First, a source may attempt to alter the believability, expectancy, or weight a person attaches to a proximal or external belief. For example, if someone wished to persuade me to give up cigarette smoking, he or she might try to convince me that there is a 100 percent rather than a 90 percent probability that cigarette smoking causes lung cancer. Second, a source may attempt to alter the value a person attaches to a belief. Thus, suppose I feel indifferent toward solar energy as a renewable resource, and at the same time I am 100 percent sure that it is, in fact, renewable. If someone wished to persuade me to support solar research, he or she should try to convince me to place a positive rather than a neutral value on the use of renewable resources.

Finally, proximal and external beliefs can be changed by introducing new attributes to a person's original set of beliefs. To persuade someone to stop smoking, for instance, a persuader might stress, not only that cigarette smoking causes lung cancer, but also that it is an air pollutant, is irritable to nonsmokers, dulls one's senses, and the like. By adding more negative attributes to an attitudinal object, the persuader increases the probability that a person will alter proximal or external beliefs, and, consequently, change relevant behavior patterns.

In general, Fishbein's expectancy-value theory is a specialized summation model of information integration focusing on beliefs as the basic building blocks of human cognitive schemata. Because it specifies the kind of relationship that exists between the source's beliefs and those held by receivers, it makes some rather precise predictions about how to alter cognitions and behaviors. For that reason, the expectancy-value theory has considerable promise as a model of persuasive communication.

A CRITICAL APPRAISAL OF INFORMATION
INTEGRATION THEORY

Unlike most theories of persuasion we have considered, information integration theory has generated relatively little substantive criticism. Indeed, it presently is enjoying immense popularity. What little critical commentary there is has usually been directed toward methodological issues.

For instance, information integration theory's highly quantitative nature has been greeted with considerable skepticism by some traditional theorists in persuasion. The basic argument advanced by such critics is that precise mathematical prediction is either impossible or meaningless in such an inexact social science as persuasion. This argument obviously is appealing when applied to the responses of individual people. Clearly, no statistical formulation can predict precisely how any *one* person will react to some message. Indeed, such equations do not claim that ability. By definition, the usefulness of any statistical formula is limited to estimating the probable responses of a typical person in a well-defined population and under certain clearly specified boundary conditions.

Thus, quantitative theories of persuasion are generalizations about how people will probably respond, given certain messages and the information integration rules operable under clearly stipulated conditions. In this regard, they differ little from the numerous qualitative theories we have considered in this book. Both kinds of theories are generalizations allowing us to deduce the probable responses of particular people who fall within the population covered by the generalizations. The primary difference between quantitative and qualitative theories is that the former attempts to place a precise mathematical value on the probability that a particular response will occur. In contrast, qualitative theories leave probability levels unspecified. As this discussion suggests, we regard this criticism of information integration theory as spurious, since it is an indictment of all types of theoretical generalizations.

Despite our defense of information integration theory, we believe it has some serious limitations. One concerns the nature of much of the research upon which the theory presently is based. As our discussions have shown, most of the studies supporting information integration theory utilize items of information about *hypothetical* persons as a basis for drawing conclusions about the nature of information integration and its persuasive consequences. For that reason, it may be argued that information integration theory is more pertinent to non–ego-involving, even trivial, impressions than to well-structured attitudinal schemata.

Presently, such an argument is moot. Past research has neglected the dynamics of information integration as it relates to well-structured cognitive schemata. Conceptually, there is no reason to suspect that information integration theory is limited to peripheral attitudes. Nevertheless, the generalizability of the theory requires empirical confirmation. Thus, future research must test the predictions of information integration theory in the arena of ego-involving, complex cognitive structures. Only then can we draw firm conclusions about the precise area to which information integration theory is applicable.

Beyond this major complaint, information integration theory appears to be a promising approach to the study of persuasion. Unlike the early Yale theorists, information integration theorists focus on what people "do with" external information, not what messages "do to" them. They are interested in how people go about actively "filling-in," or assigning meaning to, external symbols on the basis of their personalized schematic assumptions, including goals and desires. The ultimate aim of integration theorists is to isolate those rule structures governing: (1) the selective perception and interpretation of incoming information; (2) the organization and reconstructive storage of information in memory; and (3) the reconstructive integration of new messages with old, memory-based information. Finally, information integration theorists are interested in the types of new cognitive schemata that emerge from these rule-guided integration processes.

As this discussion indicates, the information integration approach is quite compatible with our own view of people as active, goal-directed agents. Moreover, the perspective is consistent with our cognitive schematic view of external phenomena, including the re-created nature of incoming persuasive messages.

NOTES

1. For complete accounts of the deliberations associated with the Cuban missile crisis, see Robert F. Kennedy, *Thirteen Days: A Memoir of the Cuban Missile Crisis* (New York: W. W. Norton, 1969); and Roger Hilsman, *To Move a Nation: The Politics of Foreign Policy in the Administration of John F. Kennedy* (Garden City, N.Y.: Doubleday, 1967), pp. 159–229.

2. See Norman H. Anderson, "Integration Theory and Attitude Change," *Psychological Review* 78 (1971): 171–206; Norman H. Anderson, "A Simple Model for Information Integration," in *Theories of Cognitive Consistency: A Sourcebook*, ed. Robert P. Abelson et al. (Skokie, Ill.: Rand McNally, 1968), pp. 731–741; Martin Fishbein and Icek Ajzen, *Belief, Attitude, Intention and Behavior* (Reading, Mass.: Addison-Wesley, 1975); and Robert S. Wyer, Jr., *Cognitive Organization and Change: An Information Processing Approach* (Hillsdale, N.J.: Lawrence Erlbaum Associates, 1974).

3. For discussion of these two parameters, see Anderson, "Integration Theory," pp. 172–174; and Fishbein and Ajzen, pp. 222–228.

4. This formula is equivalent to Fishbein's expectancy-value model of attitude. For a description of his model, see Fishbein and Ajzen, pp. 222–223.

5. Anderson, "Integration Theory," pp. 180–182.

6. Fishbein and Ajzen, pp. 229–235; Wyer, pp. 263–321.

7. Norman H. Anderson, "Averaging versus Adding as a Stimulus-Combination Rule in Impression Formation," *Journal of Experimental Psychology* 70 (1965): 394–400.

8. Lynn R. Anderson and Martin Fishbein, "Prediction of Attitude from the Number, Strength, and Evaluative Aspect of Beliefs about the Attitude Object: A Comparison of Summation and Congruity Theories," *Journal of Personality and Social Psychology* 2 (1965): 437–443.

9. For discussions of the "contrast effect," see Carolyn W. Sherif, Muzafer Sherif, and Roger E. Nebergall, *Attitude and Attitude Change: The Social Judgment-Involvement Approach* (Philadelphia, Pa.: W. B. Saunders, 1965); and Muzafer Sherif and Carl I. Hovland, *Social Judgment: Assimilation and Contrast Effects in Communication and Attitude Change* (New Haven, Conn.: Yale University Press, 1961).

10. Norman H. Anderson, "Averaging Model Analysis of Set Size Effect in Impression Formation," *Journal of Experimental Psychology* 75 (1967): 158–165.

11. Fishbein and Ajzen, p. 231.

12. For a discussion of some rules of information integration, see Wyer, pp. 2–5.

13. Frederick Hansen Lund conducted the first experimental investigation of the primacy–recency issue. See "The Psychology of Belief: A Study of its Emotional and Volitional Determinants," *Journal of Abnormal and Social Psychology* 20 (1925): 174–196.

14. Solomon E. Asch, "Forming Impressions of Personality," *Journal of Abnormal and Social Psychology* 41 (1946): 258–290.

15. Abraham S. Luchins, "Primacy–Recency in Impression Formation," in *The Order of Presentation in Persuasion*, ed. Carl I. Hovland et al. (New Haven, Conn.: Yale University Press, 1957), pp. 33–61.

16. For examples, see Ralph H. Stewart, "Effect of Continuous Responding on the Order Effect in Personality Impression Formation," *Journal of Personality and Social Psychology* 1 (1965): 161–165; and Norman H. Anderson and Stephen Hubert, "Effects of Concomitant Verbal Recall on Order Effects in Personality Impression Formation," *Journal of Verbal Learning and Verbal Behavior* 2 (1963): 379–391.

17. Asch.

18. For examples, see Martin F. Kaplan, "Context Effects in Impression Formation: The Weighted Averaging versus the Meaning-Change Formulation," *Journal of Personality and Social Psychology* 19 (1971): 92–99; and Robert S. Wyer, Jr., and Stanley F. Watson, "Context Effects in Impression Formation," *Journal of Personality and Social Psychology* 12 (1969): 22–33.

19. Norman H. Anderson, "Primacy Effects in Personality Impression Formation Using a Generalized Order Effect Paradigm," *Journal of Personality and Social Psychology* 2 (1965): 1–9; and Stewart.

20. Anderson and Hubert; and Stewart.

21. See Roberta L. Klatzky, *Human Memory: Structures and Processes* (San Francisco: W. H. Freeman, 1975).

22. Elizabeth K. Dreben, Susan T. Fiske, and Reid Hastie, "The Independence of Evaluative and Item Information: Impression and Recall Order Effects in Behavior-Based Impression Formation," *Journal of Personality and Social Psychology* 37 (1979): 1758–1768.

23. Norman H. Anderson and Ann Jacobson, "Effect of Stimulus Inconsistency and Discounting Instructions in Personality Impression Formation," *Journal of Personality and Social Psychology* 2 (1965): 531–539.

24. Clyde Hendrick and Arthur F. Costantini, "Effects of Varying Trait Inconsistency and Response Requirements on the Primacy Effect in Impression Formation," *Journal of Personality and Social Psychology* 15 (1970): 158–167.

25. Norman H. Anderson, "Application of a Linear-Serial Model to a Personality-Impression Task Using Serial Presentation," *Journal of Personality and Social Psychology* 10 (1968): 354–362; and Anderson and Jacobson.

26. Hendrick and Costantini.

27. Fishbein and Ajzen, pp. 250–253.

28. James J. Jaccard and Martin Fishbein, "Inferential Beliefs and Order Effects in Personality Impression Formation," *Journal of Personality and Social Psychology* 31 (1975): 1031–1040.

29. Asch; and Norman H. Anderson and Alfred A. Barrios, "Primacy Effects in Personality Impression Formation," *Journal of Abnormal and Social Psychology* 63 (1961): 346–350.

30. Anderson and Hubert.

31. Dreben, Fiske, and Hastie.

32. Stewart; and Dreben, Fiske, and Hastie.

33. Abraham S. Luchins, "Experimental Attempts to Minimize the Impact of First Impressions," in *The Order of Presentation in Persuasion*, pp. 62–75.

34. See Carl I. Hovland and Wallace Mandell, "Is There a 'Law of Primacy in Persuasion'?" in *The Order of Presentation in Persuasion*, pp. 13–22; and Carl I. Hovland, Enid H. Campbell, and Timothy Brock, "The Effects of 'Commitment' on Opinion Change Following Communication," in *The Order of Presentation in Persuasion*, pp. 23–32.

35. Dreben, Fiske, and Hastie; and Luchins, "Experimental Attempts to Minimize."

36. Luchins, "Experimental Attempts to Minimize."

37. Edward E. Jones and George R. Goethals, *Order Effects in Impression Formation: Attribution Context and the Nature of the Entity* (Morristown, N.J.: General Learning Press, 1971).

38. David L. Hamilton and Mark P. Zanna, "Context Effects in Impression Formation: Changes in Connotative Meaning," *Journal of Personality and Social Psychology* 29 (1974): 649–654.

39. See Thomas M. Ostrom, "Meaning Shift in the Judgment of Compound Stimuli" (unpublished MS, Ohio State University, 1967).

40. Robert S. Wyer, Jr., "Changes in Meaning and Halo Effects in Personality Impression Formation," *Journal of Personality and Social Psychology* 29 (1974): 829–835.

41. Norman H. Anderson, "Two More Tests against Change of Meaning in Adjective Combinations," *Journal of Verbal Learning and Verbal Behavior* 10 (1971): 75–85.

42. Thomas M. Ostrom, "Between-Theory and Within-Theory Conflict in Explaining Context Effects in Impression Formation," *Journal of Experimental Social Psychology* 13 (1977): 492–503.

43. See Michael H. Birnbaum, "The Nonadditivity of Personality Impressions," *Journal of Experimental Psychology* 102 (1974): 543–561; Bert H. Hodges, "Effect of Valence on Relative Weighting in Impression Formation," *Journal of Personality and Social Psychology* 30 (1974): 378–381; and Gregg C. Oden and Norman H. Anderson, "Differential Weighting in Integration Theory," *Journal of Experimental Psychology* 89 (1971): 152–161.

44. See Peter Warr and Paul Jackson, "The Importance of Extremity," *Journal of Personality and Social Psychology* 32 (1975): 278–282; and Peter Warr, "Inference Magnitude, Range, and Evaluative Directions as Factors Affecting Relative Importance of Cues in Impression Formation," *Journal of Personality and Social Psychology* 30 (1974): 191–197.

45. See Robert S. Wyer, Jr., "Information Redundancy, Inconsistency, and Novelty and Their Role in Impression Formation," *Journal of Experimental Social Psychology* 6 (1970): 111–127.

46. Wyer, *Cognitive Organization*, p. 223.

47. Ibid., pp. 223–228.

48. See Thomas M. Ostrom and Deborah Davis, "Idiosyncratic Weighting of Trait Information in Impression Formation," *Journal of Personality and Social Psychology* 37 (1979): 2025–2043.

49. What follows is a highly condensed description of the expectancy-value model. For a detailed description, see Fishbein and Ajzen, pp. 222–228, 387–509.

50. Fishbein's mathematical formula for predicting attitude can be found in Fishbein and Ajzen, p. 223.

CHAPTER *11*

Judgmental Theories of Persuasion

During the 1980 presidential election campaign, a primary aim of Jimmy Carter's media messages was to create the perception that his Republican opponent, Ronald Reagan, was a simple-minded, dangerous man likely to lead the nation into nuclear war. Mr. Carter's political advertisements included such messages as: "No matter how many advisers and assistants, a president can never escape the responsibility of truly understanding an issue himself. That is the only way a presidential decision can be made and the only way this president has ever made one"; and "President Carter—the people have come to respect his dedication, his foresight, his stability, and his good sense."[1] This approach was designed to get viewers to pass *judgments* on the competency of the two candidates. Mr. Carter's media consultants hoped their candidate would be judged as intelligent and stable, and that Mr. Reagan would be judged a reckless warmonger, without stability, intelligence, or good sense. Mr. Carter's advisers reasoned that once these judgments were made, they would shape subsequent attitudes and voting behavior.

Although this media strategy did not get Mr. Carter reelected, it illustrates the approach to persuasion we will examine in this chapter. We will consider how human judgments of external bits of information affect attitude and behavior change. Judgmental theories of persuasion are similar to other information-processing models in that persuasive effects are presumed to result from the integration of new information into preexisting cognitive structures. However, they differ from the other approaches we have considered because they focus exclusively on human judgment as the prime mediator of information-processing effects. We will explore two judgmental theories: Muzafer Sherif's social judgment–involvement approach; and Timothy Brock's commodity theory. Although the two differ considerably, both emphasize the interdependence of judgmental processes and persuasive communication.

THE SOCIAL JUDGMENT–INVOLVEMENT THEORY
OF PERSUASION

Before detailing the basic tenets of social judgment theory, we must examine briefly the nature of human judgmental processes. Three variables are associated with any judgment. The first consists of some *external stimulus* to be judged. It may be a person, as in the case of political candidates like Mr. Carter or Mr. Reagan, or it may be some object or event. As students of persuasion, the external stimuli that interest us are persuasive messages and associated bits of incoming information.

The second variable associated with judgment is the set of internal *cognitive schemata* people use to judge external phenomena. Sherif refers to this schematic set as a "frame of reference," by which he means the unique perspective and internal standards a person uses to interpret and judge incoming information.[2] The third and final aspect of human judgment is the *judgment* itself. It is the conclusion a person reaches about an external stimulus as it has been perceived, interpreted, and subjectively reconstructed in memory.[3] Let's now turn our attention to the characteristics of social judgment–involvement theory.

Latitudes of Acceptance, Rejection, and Noncommitment

As developed by Sherif and his associates, social judgment–involvement theory rests on the fundamental assumption that judgmental processes as we have described them are central to an understanding of attitude change.[4] From its perspective, persuasion is a two-stage process. First, following exposure to a persuasive message, a person judges the advocated position relative to his or her own position. Second, after this judgmental process, attitude change occurs, with its magnitude dependent on the judged discrepancy between a person's own position and that espoused in the message. In the first judgmental stage, social judgment–involvement theory assumes that a person's initial attitude toward a persuasive message is a powerful internal *anchor*, or standard, for judging the discrepancy between a message and a person's own position. Using this anchor, a person may decide that the position advocated in a persuasive message falls into one of three attitudinal zones, or categories: the latitude of acceptance; the latitude of rejection; or the latitude of noncommitment.[5]

The *latitude of acceptance* is defined as one's own anchor attitude plus all those attitudinal positions clustered around the anchor that are judged to be acceptable or tolerable. To illustrate, suppose my preferred position on the issue of women's rights is that sexual equality should be constitutionally guaranteed. If I hear a speech urging passage of the Equal Rights Amendment, I obviously will judge this position to fall within my latitude of acceptance. Additionally, messages advocating different but related measures, such as federal affirmative action programs in education or state statutes guaranteeing equal pay for equal work, will probably fall within my latitude of acceptance as well. These latter measures are less extreme than I would prefer; yet they are close enough to my initial position that I will probably find them acceptable. Indeed, on any one issue, most of us have a range of acceptable positions. When a position advocated in a persuasive message falls within one's latitude of acceptance, it is usually judged fair, unbiased, and credible.

The latitude of rejection is that band of positions advocated in persuasive messages that a person judges as intolerable or totally unacceptable. For example, if I oppose nuclear power as an alternative energy source, I most surely will judge messages advocating the construction of new nuclear plants negatively. Likewise, antiabortionists usually turn a deaf ear to proabortion advocates. When an advocated position falls within the latitude of rejection, its message is almost always judged unfair, biased, and incredible.

Finally, the *latitude of noncommitment* is a residual category to which we consign all those advocated positions not categorized as either acceptable or objectionable. Positions in this category include those about which we hold no strong attitudes and those upon which we have not fully decided. For instance, we often see both positive and negative features in certain policies. We may fear the potential hazards of nuclear energy, yet believe it is an essential supplemental energy source. Or we may support equal rights for women, but oppose women in military combat. On such issues, our attitudes are ambivalent and often fall into the latitude of noncommitment. Although the latitude of noncommitment is usually an intermediate zone separating the latitudes of acceptance and rejection, it need not be so. For example, the latitude of acceptance for many people may be in the middle of an attitudinal continuum, reflecting a moderate stance on an issue. In such a case, there should be two latitudes of rejection, one at each extreme of the attitudinal continuum. Each of these rejection zones would then be separated from the latitude of acceptance by a latitude of noncommitment.

In summary, judgmental processes concern the ways people categorize persuasive messages relative to their own anchor positions, or initial attitudes. Any one attitudinal position may be judged as falling within the latitudes of acceptance, rejection, or noncommitment.

The Effect of Ego Involvement on Judgmental Processes

The degree to which a person's attitude is *ego involving* exerts a profound influence on judgmental, or categorization, processes. Sherif and Hadley Cantril define an *ego-involved attitude* as a social value that an individual strongly identifies with and incorporates as a part of himself or herself.[6] Ego-involving attitudes, then, have strong implications for one's self-identity and central value system. For example, activists in antiabortion, gun control, or feminist movements usually have ego-involved attitudes with regard to these special interests. In contrast, less active supporters of these causes normally have less intense attitudes. As these examples indicate, public commitment to a cause is often associated with ego-involving attitudes. In a later discussion, we will see that Sherif and his associates consistently equated ego involvement with membership in a known group committed to a specific cause.

The principal effect of ego involvement on judgmental processes is to broaden considerably one's latitude of rejection. For the highly involved person, his or her attitude is an extremely strong anchor. Such people tend to judge almost any position different from their own as completely unacceptable, even those only slightly differ-

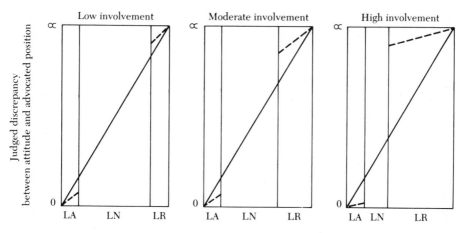

FIGURE 11.1   *Judgmental distortions as a function of ego involvement. The unbroken diagonal line represents the "correct" judgment of discrepancy. The broken lines are theoretically predicted distorted judgments of discrepancy. LA refers to latitude of acceptance; LN denotes latitude of noncommitment; and LR refers to latitude of rejection. Adapted from Charles A. Kiesler, Barry E. Collins, and Norman Miller,* Attitude Change *(New York: John Wiley & Sons, Inc., 1969), p. 247. Reprinted by permission.*

ent. Put another way, the ego-involved person usually does not make a "true" judgment of the discrepancy between his or her own position and those advocated in persuasive messages. Rather, as Figure 11.1 shows, "true" discrepancy is underestimated within one's latitude of acceptance, and overestimated within the latitude of rejection. Moreover, Figure 11.1 also indicates that such judgmental distortion occurs even at low levels of involvement and increases in a linear fashion with increasing ego involvement.[7]

To illustrate judgmental distortion, let's consider some hypothetical opponents of abortion who are highly involved with the issue. Such individuals often minimize minor differences between themselves and other "right-to-lifers" so long as everybody supports the basic cause, say a constitutional amendment to ban abortion. Indeed, many "right-to-life" political action groups support candidates for public office solely on the basis of the candidate's position on abortion. On the other hand, the fervent "right-to-lifer" tends to treat what are actually moderate pro-abortion positions as if they were extremely proabortion. For example, the public official who supports abortion only when a woman's physical or mental health is threatened is usually rejected as strenuously as the abortion-on-demand proponent. These same judgmental displacements can be observed among individuals in other ego-involved groups like proabortion lobbies, anti– and pro–gun control groups, and so forth.

Clearly, highly ego-involved people tend to see attitudinal positions as either black or white, as totally acceptable or unacceptable. They perceive few shades of gray or middle-ground positions. As a result, they have a very narrow latitude of noncommitment, and they inevitably consider far more positions objectionable than acceptable.

Thus, an ego-involved person's latitude of rejection is extremely wide relative to that of less involved individuals, and it expands at the expense of the latitude of noncommitment.

Ego Involvement: Assimilation and Contrast Effects

Social judgment–involvement theory explains these judgmental distortions by referring to two psychophysical principles, called the assimilation effect and the contrast effect. The *assimilation effect* refers to a person's tendency to subjectively minimize the discrepancy between an anchor attitude and other positions judged to be close to it. On the other hand, the *contrast effect* denotes a person's tendency to subjectively maximize the discrepancy between an anchor attitude and positions judged to be different. By referring to some examples of weight-judging tasks, we can explain the psychophysical bases for these two principles.

In an early weight-judging experiment, Sherif, Taub, and Hovland asked subjects to judge the weight of six cubes. In the initial phase of the study, the subjects were given no standard, or anchor, weight to use as a comparison for estimating the weight of the cubes. Results showed that weight estimates were relatively accurate. In a second stage of the experiment, other subjects were told that the heaviest cube, weighing 141 grams, should be used as a standard for judging the weight of the other five. As a result, subjects judged all the cubes to be heavier than they actually were. This piling up of cubes next to the anchor illustrates the assimilation effect. All the cubes were judged similar to the anchor weight; that is, they were perceived as heavier than they actually were. In the final phase of the study, additional subjects were given a very heavy cube, weighing 347 grams, and were instructed to use it as a standard or anchor weight for estimating the weight of the other cubes. In this situation there was a contrast effect. All the cubes were now judged to be different from the anchor weight, that is, as lighter than they actually were.[8]

From the social judgment perspective, an initial attitudinal position serves as an anchor or standard for judging other attitudinal positions in much the same way that physical weights function as anchors for estimating other weights. When other attitudinal positions are close to an anchor attitude, that is, they fall within the latitude of acceptance, people judge them to be closer to their own attitude than they actually are—the assimilation effect. In contrast, when attitudinal positions are different from an anchor attitude, that is, they fall into the latitude of rejection, they are judged more discrepant from the attitudinal anchor than they actually are—the contrast effect. According to social judgment–involvement theory, the more ego involved one's initial attitude, the greater its power as an anchor; consequently, the judgmental distortions associated with assimilation and contrast effects are far greater.

Attitude Change and Social Judgment–Involvement Principles

We noted at the beginning of our discussion that social judgment–involvement theory sees persuasion as a two-stage process. As we have seen, the first stage involves a judgment about the position advocated in a persuasive message relative to a person's anchor attitude. Once this judgmental phase is over, the second stage, attitude change, begins.

If an advocated position falls within a person's latitude of acceptance, we can expect attitude change as a consequence of the assimilation process. People accept the advocated position because they see it as close to their own preferred position. Accordingly, so long as an advocated position falls within the latitude of acceptance, the greater the actual discrepancy between that position and a person's anchor attitude, the greater the expected attitude change.

This prediction rests on two premises. First, when an advocated position is extremely close to an initial attitude, only a small amount of change is possible. As discrepancy increases, the potential for attitude change goes up. Second, the assimilation principle assumes that discrepancy is increasingly minimized as a function of the distance of an advocated position from one's own. Thus, the most discrepant position a source may advocate within the latitude of acceptance, the greater the expected attitude change. And, as we might expect, these attitudinal effects are intensified when the message recipient is ego involved.

When an advocated position falls within the latitude of rejection, no attitude change is expected. Indeed, Sherif and his associates argue that messages falling within this region are likely to reinforce a person's initial attitudes or perhaps produce a boomerang effect because of the contrast effect. The discrepancy between an anchor attitude and an advocated position is subjectively maximized. The advocated position is rejected more strenuously than otherwise might be the case. Moreover, so long as a message falls within the latitude of rejection, the less the actual discrepancy between an anchor attitude and the advocated position, the greater the contrast effect. Thus, moderately discrepant positions are judged just as extreme as highly discrepant messages and high ego involvement intensifies such contrast effects.

Finally, if an advocated position falls within the latitude of noncommitment, substantial attitude change can be expected. As with all social judgment phenomena, this prediction is tempered by levels of ego involvement. Persons whose egos are highly involved have a very narrow latitude of noncommitment. Those positions that ordinarily appear in a noninvolved person's latitude of noncommitment are rejected by involved people. Thus, low to moderately involved people will place more advocated positions within their latitudes of noncommitment and will be more readily persuaded than involved individuals.

As our discussion suggests, an inverted-U relationship is predicted between attitude change and the extent to which a message is discrepant from a person's initial attitude. When an advocated position is quite close to an initial attitude, only a small amount of change is possible. But with increasing discrepancy within the latitude of acceptance, attitude change should increase. However, once an advocated position becomes so discrepant that it falls into the latitude of rejection, attitude change declines sharply. Generally, the greatest amount of attitude change can be expected at moderate levels of discrepancy, and many of these moderately discrepant positions fall into a person's latitude of noncommitment.

This information suggests that attempts to change the attitudes of highly ego-involved individuals are usually counterproductive; they only harden deeply held attitudes. Thus, persuasive campaigns are most effective when messages are directed toward people who are minimally or moderately involved in an issue. For example, in election campaigns, successful politicians usually secure a majority by reinforcing the attitudes of "the faithful" in their own party and by soliciting uncommitted voters. Few serious attempts are made to convert die-hard opponents. From the social judg-ment–involvement perspective, this strategy involves directing messages toward: (1) ego-involved individuals who place the politician's message within their latitude of acceptance; and (2) low to moderately involved persons who place the politician's mes-sage within the latitude of noncommitment.

Social Judgment and Attitude Change: A Case Study

To close this discussion, let's consider a typical study conducted within the social judgment–involvement paradigm. In the 1950s, Hovland, Harvey, and Sherif conduct-ed an elaborate field study in Oklahoma shortly after a referendum passed prohibiting the sale of alcoholic beverages. The study used subjects who were deeply involved on one or the other side of the prohibition issue as well as people who held moderate positions. Involved "drys," those who strongly supported prohibition, were solicited from the Women's Christian Temperance Union, the Salvation Army, and several reli-gious colleges in the area. There were 183 "drys." Twenty-five extreme "wets," those who strongly opposed prohibition, were selected from among the acquaintances of the three experimenters. Finally, 250 subjects, mostly university students, with moderate stands on the issue were recruited.

The subjects participated in two sessions. In the first session, their latitudes of acceptance, rejection, and noncommitment were determined by having them sort nine attitudinal statements ranging from extremely "wet" to extremely "dry" into one of the three categories. In addition, they were asked to indicate their most- and least-preferred position on the prohibition issue. One to three weeks later, the subjects lis-tened to one of three tape-recorded messages: a moderately "wet" position on the prohibition issue; an extremely "wet" message; and an extremely "dry" communica-tion. Afterwards, these three measures were taken: (1) the listeners' judgments as to the position advocated in the message; (2) their evaluation of the message source's fairness and objectivity, and (3) the amount of attitude change that occurred.

Generally, results confirmed the predictions made by social judgment–involve-ment theory. First, the ego-involved "wets" and "drys" had much wider initial lati-tudes of rejection than did moderate subjects. Second, the "wets" judged the moderate-ly "wet" message as much "drier" than it actually was. In contrast, the "drys" judged the same message as advocating a much "wetter" position than it did. These judgmen-tal distortions reflected contrast effects. Third, the farther a message was from the subject's own positions, the more biased and unfair the source was rated. Fourth and finally, attitude change reflected the judgmental effects just discussed. Among those who heard the "wet" communication, the net percentage of change in the direction advocated was 4.3 percent for the "drys" versus 28.3 percent for the moderates. For those exposed to the "dry" message, the net percentages of change were 4.0 percent for the "wets" and 13.8 percent for the moderates. Overall, attitude change among moderates was about twice as much as among ego-involved subjects.[9]

This study, and a number of similar ones,[10] support the basic predictions of social judgment–involvement theory, whose central assumption is that attitude change is mediated by the judgments people make about the position advocated in a persuasive message. Moreover, the extent of a person's ego involvement is presumed to affect judgments and consequently the amount of attitude change. Finally, ego-involved individuals are presumed to have exceedingly broad latitudes of rejection, rendering them quite unresponsive to persuasion. All of these major assumptions appear to be reflected in the results of the Oklahoma prohibition study.

A Critical Appraisal of Social Judgment–Involvement Theory

Despite its contributions to an understanding of persuasion, the social judgment–involvement theory has several serious deficiencies. One of the more vexing of these concerns the conceptual and operational nature of ego involvement, the theory's central construct. As the prohibition study illustrated, Sherif and his associates consistently equated high ego involvement with membership in groups known to hold extreme positions on issues.[11] And by doing so, they introduced into their research at least four confounding variables, any one of which could account for the experimental results attributed to ego involvement. Thus, confounding effects, in general, are a criticism of social judgment–involvement theory.

Confounding Effects

First, it is probable that members of involved groups differ from other people on a variety of *characteristics other than ego involvement*. For example, in the Sherif study, members of the WCTU and the Salvation Army probably differed from the moderate college students on such dimensions as open-mindedness or dogmatism, education, age, and perhaps intelligence. Any one of these factors conceivably could explain why they changed their attitudes less than the students. It is well known, for instance, that dogmatism sharply diminishes receptivity and yielding to persuasion.[12] Moreover, older persons normally have more fixed attitudes than the young.

And, as earlier discussion of McGuire's information-processing model indicated, lower intelligence is associated with a diminished capacity to comprehend complex messages such as those presented on the prohibition issue, and thus may decrease acceptance. In sum, Sherif's research leaves unclear the precise reasons for the lower level of attitude change among members of the "dry" groups. Although ego involvement alone might have produced the effect, it is equally plausible that other variables or a combination of factors, with ego involvement being one among many contributors, led to lower levels of attitude change.

A second variable with which ego involvement has been confounded is *extremity of opinion*, and again Sherif's study is illustrative. The "wets" and the "drys" held opinions at the two extremes of the attitudinal continuum, but extremity of opinion and issue involvement are by no means logically equivalent. For instance, it is possible for a "middle-of-the roader" to be highly ego involved. Conversely, an individual holding an extreme position may be only minimally involved with the issue.[13] A third confounding variable is *public commitment* by virtue of known group membership. Although public commitment often is associated with ego involvement, it need not be. As we saw in an earlier treatment of group interaction, people frequently comply publicly with group norms; yet they do not internalize them. Thus, public commitment was confounded with ego involvement in the prohibition and related studies.

A fourth confounding variable has to do with *differing types of attitudes* held by ego-involved people and moderates. You will recall from Chapter 2 that attitudes often fulfill different goals for people. For some people, particular attitudes have an ego-defensive function, protecting them against harsh external and internal realities. For others, the same attitude may have a value-expressive function, allowing them to publicly display their central values. For yet a third group, it may have an instrumental function, enabling them to achieve desired external rewards.

Rules-oriented theorists argue that when goals constituting the motivational bases for attitudes differ, the persuasive techniques for changing them must conform.[14] In the prohibition study, it is plausible that antidrinking attitudes served an ego-defensive function for "drys." For them, liquor may have represented a lack of self-control, licentiousness, and sin, and support of prohibition may have served as an ego defense against these frailties of the flesh. If this speculation is reasonable, the lengthy (15-minute) informational message that Sherif used to persuade the "drys" may have been an inappropriate strategy. Rather, self-insight procedures and the offer of emotional support to allay deeply held fears would have been the more appropriate strategy for altering ego-defensive attitudes.[15]

On the other hand, subjects with moderate positions toward prohibition should have been more amenable to the traditional tactics used in the study. In contrast to the "drys," the position of the "wets" may have fulfilled a value-expressive or, perhaps, an instrumental goal. They may have valued freedom of choice or, alternately, the social benefits of liquor. The persuasive messages Sherif used that stressed the health, religious, and financial benefits of prohibition may have been irrelevant to these particular value-expressive and instrumental goals. Generally then, the low levels of attitude change among the extreme groups may have resulted from the use of messages containing contextually irrelevant rules.

In summary, the first problem associated with social judgment–involvement theory concerns the innumerable variables that may have been confounded with the central construct, *ego involvement.* Confounding effects preclude unequivocal conclusions about the judgmental and attitudinal effects of involvement.

Conceptual Ambiguity

A second major problem attending social judgment–involvement theory is the ambiguous relationship between judgmental processes and attitudinal effects. Social judgment–involvement theory assumes a sequential and causal relationship between judgment and later attitude change: judgmental processes are presumed to occur first, and afterwards, to mediate attitude change. But the fact that judgment and attitude change consistently covary does not mean that attitude change is *caused* by judgmental phenomena; nor does covariation even confirm that judgmental processes temporally precede attitude change. Indeed, the judgmental response may follow attitude alteration, or the two processes may co-occur.

Alternative Explanations

Because of these deficiencies, several alternative explanations for social judgment effects have been proposed. First, the covariation between judgmental processes and attitude change may be explained as a function of inconsistency resolution rather than assimilation and contrast effects. When judgments change, people may bring attitudes into line with their new perceptions, or, conversely, a change in attitude may prompt judgmental changes to restore desired cognitive consistency. If this is the case, social judgment effects may be explained entirely without reference to assimilation and contrast.

Another alternative explanation, developed by Harry Upshaw, is called the *variable perspective theory* of judgment. Upshaw has rejected assimilation and contrast effects as generative forces underlying judgment and attitude change. Rather, he argues that people perceive messages differently because they have differing cognitive schemata or perspectives on attitudinal issues. People do not perceptually distort the position in a message. Instead, we label attitudinal positions differently because of our varying frames of reference. Thus, from Upshaw's view, judgmental effects reflect differences in how people *describe* rather than how they *perceive* symbolic stimuli.[16]

Richard Petty and John Cacioppo have offered yet another explanation. They argue that ego involvement prompts people to generate a large number of favorable cognitions or covert responses to messages falling within their latitude of acceptance. From this perspective, the preponderance of positive cognitive responses elicited by proattitudinal messages and not an assimilation effect is responsible for positive attitude change. Similarly, Petty and Cacioppo argue that involved people generate many counterarguments in response to messages falling within their latitude of rejection; hence, learning through counterarguing, not judgmental contrast, is responsible for the boomerang effect within the latitude of rejection. Petty and Cacioppo found support for this alternative explanation of social judgment effects in an experiment in which college students heard either a proattitudinal or a counterattitudinal message about mixed-sex dormitory visitation privileges.[17]

Rules and Social Judgment Theory

It should be clear that social judgment–involvement theory is, in many ways, highly mechanistic. First, the judgmental process itself is regarded as almost autonomous, involving an unconscious operation of the psychophysical principles of assimilation and contrast. Second, the relation between judgment and attitude change is assumed to be a causal one, and therefore, beyond the control of the message receiver. Thus, people are treated as relatively passive responders to external causal phenomena.

This perspective is obviously incompatible with our own. Moreover, as we have already shown, social judgment effects can be accounted for easily within several, reason-based theoretical frameworks. They can be explained by referring to ego-defensive, instrumental, and value-expressive goals; by appealing to the need for consistency; and by applying the cognitive response model of information processing. All these explanations are actional in nature and are, therefore, from our perspective, more appealing accounts of persuasive effects than those posited by social judgment–involvement theory.

Despite its serious flaws and its incompatibility with our own views, social judgment–involvement theory has been an influential approach to persuasive communication. It formalized, for the first time, a systematic relationship between attitudes, actions, and human judgment; and called attention to the power of ego involvement as a mediator of judgment, attitude change, and overt behavior. Further, social judgment–involvement theory has placed in sharp focus the critical relationship between attitude change and the extent to which an advocated position departs from a person's initial attitudinal schemata. Finally, by developing and applying the concept, *frame of reference,* social judgment–involvement theorists made one of the first attempts to demonstrate the pervasive influence of cognitive schemata on people's judgments of the external world. This departure from a logical positivist view of external reality is a landmark contribution.

A COMMODITY THEORY OF PERSUASION

As the name implies, Brock's commodity theory is based on an economic model of human behavior and applies traditional economic principles like supply and demand to persuasive communication.[18] From an economic perspective, the information contained in a persuasive message is viewed as a *commodity;* that is, anything that is valuable or useful to a person and that can be conveyed from one person to another. Persuasive information, then, is a commodity only when it is both useful and conveyable. Thus, for an investment broker, information about the stock market is a commodity, but it should not be for a farmer who has no stock investments. On the other hand, information about the weather during planting season is a commodity from the farmer's perspective but probably not from the view of the businessperson.

According to commodity theory, persuasion is a two-stage process, just as was the case with social judgment–involvement theory. The first stage involves a judgment as to the value of a particular item of persuasive information. Once this value judgment is made, it is presumed to mediate attitude change toward the position advocated in the persuasive message. The greater the judged value of the information, the greater the positive attitude change toward the advocated position. Commodity theory assumes that an item of information will be judged as increasingly valuable the costlier it is to obtain.

This cost is a function of a piece of information's *perceived unavailability.* Perceived unavailability is related to two classes of variables: scarcity and effort. *Scarcity* occurs when information is restricted or withheld from an interested public. Classified government documents and censored material like pornographic films, books, and magazines are examples of scarce information. *Effort* refers to the energy that must be exerted in order to obtain and transmit information. Thus, if a small town resident drives a long distance to a major city to see an X-rated film, it should be perceived as more entertaining than if it were showing in several local theatres. The transmission of information also requires effort. Suppose that a theatre or bookstore owner has to go to court to secure the right to show a certain film or sell particular kinds of magazines. In such a circumstance, these items should be regarded as more valuable than they would be were the source not required to expend any energy to transmit them.

As this description indicates, a piece of information is judged valuable when it is difficult to obtain. Brock sees perceived unavailability of information as a function of what he calls *commodification*—situational variables augmenting perceived unavailability. The judged value of information is expected to increase with its increasing commodification, and this judged value, in turn, mediates attitude change. Brock discusses four commodification factors—scarcity, effort, restriction, and delay—that enhance perceived unavailability and hence, the judgmental and attitudinal effects of persuasive information. Let's examine these four commodification factors.

The Persuasive Effects of Scarcity

Brock developed two hypotheses about the judgmental and attitudinal effects of scarcity. First, he argues that "a message will increase in .effectiveness as the perceived number of co-recipients, relative to the total number of potential co-recipients, declines."[19] This means that the receiver of a certain piece of information is one of a small number out of a large pool of people interested in receiving the information. Limited offer advertising and sales strategies are often based on this principle. Typically, the potential consumer is informed by mail or telephone that he or she is one of a "lucky few" who has the chance to subscribe to a new insurance policy, buy stocks in gold, or purchase retirement or vacation property in Arizona. The perception that these opportunities are available to only a small group out of a large interested population should enhance their value and increase the probability that the customer will take advantage of them.

Fromkin and Brock conducted a field study to test this hypothesis. Subjects were 112 staff members of a private summer camp in Ontario, Canada. They heard a taped message by a fictitious person, Dr. Benjamin Rosenberg, arguing for a midnight curfew for all staff members. One group of listeners was told that only a few of the 112 staff members were permitted to hear the speech, but another group believed that everybody was welcome to listen. In addition, groups were told that either 90 percent or 9 percent of the staff members in nine other private camps were strongly interested in hearing Dr. Rosenberg's comments. The results, shown in Table 11.1, confirmed the hypothesis. Dr. Rosenberg's position on a curfew created the most favorable reactions among those who had been told that only a few staffers had been permitted to hear the message and who also believed that many others desired to hear it. In contrast, the least attitudinal effects were observed in the group that was told everybody was allowed to hear the message and that believed few others cared about it.[20]

TABLE 11.1: MEAN ATTITUDES TOWARD MESSAGE AS A FUNCTION OF SCARCITY

Condition	Attitude°	Number of subjects
Few recipients, many interested others	39.93	12
Many recipients, many interested others	21.60	12
Few recipients, few interested others	24.75	13
Many recipients, few interested others	20.96	11

° The higher the mean score, the more favorable the attitude.

Brock's second scarcity hypothesis states that "a message will increase in effectiveness to the extent the recipient perceives that few other communicators exist who might have delivered the same message."[21] Sales promotion pitches stating that a product can *only* be obtained at store X or is manufactured *only* by company Y conform to this principle. The advertisement for microwave ovens that states "If it's not an Amana, it's not a Radarange" captures the flavor of this technique. Generally, this principle suggests that a message will be especially valuable and effective if the source can convince the listeners that he or she is uniquely qualified to transmit a particular item of information.

The Persuasive Effects of Effort

There are three commodification hypotheses related to effort and its effects on perceived unavailability. First, "a message will increase in effectiveness the greater the degree of coercion upon the communicator needed to bring about disclosure."[22] This hypothesis speaks directly to the issue of *censorship*. For instance, previously censored information about the clandestine activities of the FBI and the CIA obtained under court order should be very valuable and effective relative to the same information freely dispensed by these agencies. Similarly, the censorship and restriction of pornographic materials in our society should increase their perceived value.[23]

Brock and Becker demonstrated this censorship hypothesis experimentally. College women heard an experimenter take a rigged phone call in which he advocated a position that was either acceptable or unacceptable to the listeners. For half of the women, the experimenter took the call in their presence, and for the other half, he ran to his nearby office, saying, "I can't talk about this here." Results showed that the overheard message was significantly more effective in producing attitude change than the unconcealed one, so long as the advocated position was proattitudinal. However, overhearing was not more effective for the counterattitudinal message.[24] This study suggests that efforts to censor or conceal messages increase the value of acceptable or useful messages. But, apparently, subjects did not expect the counterattitudinal message to be useful to them. Under other circumstances, however, counterattitudinal information might be perceived as valuable.

Thus far, we have discussed the attitudinal effects of concealment or censorship when people actually are exposed to the content of previously censored messages. Considerable research indicates that censorship can have a powerful effect on attitudes even though people never read or hear the censored messages. For example, Worchel and Arnold initially told 144 students at the University of North Carolina they intended to play a taped speech for them arguing that "police should never be allowed on university campuses." The experimenters then apologetically told some of the students that either the YMCA-YWCA (a positive censor) or the local chapter of the John Birch Society (a negative censor) had strongly objected to the speech and "asked that we not be allowed to use it in our study." The issue of censorship was not mentioned to a control group. At this point, attitudes toward the "police on campuses" issue were measured on a 21-point scale, where 1 represented "strongly agree" and 21 signified "strongly disagree." Although the control group's attitudes averaged 9.38 toward the message, the attitudes of students who thought the John Birch group or the YMCA-YWCA had censored the speech were 5.53 and 6.88, respectively.[25] Thus, censorship without exposure resulted in attitude change toward the censored position, with the most change directed toward the position censored by a disliked group.

Brock's second effort hypothesis suggests that "a message will increase in effectiveness the greater the perceived effort involved for the communicator . . . to transmit it."[26] The writings of Russian dissidents like Aleksandr Solzhenitsyn may owe much of their popularity and acceptance to the obvious and painful efforts of these authors to see their works published outside the Soviet Union. Similarly, business and government "whistle-blowers" who risk losing their jobs in order to report corruption or mismanagement should be especially persuasive. Government secrets and classified documents leaked to the press at considerable risk likewise should be valued highly.

Beyond these situations, considerable evidence shows that speakers who argue for positions obviously opposed to their own personal interests are particularly effective persuaders. To argue against one's vested interests is costly, entailing sacrifice and risk. As a result, such messages are perceived as valuable and effective. Walster, Aronson, and Abrahams demonstrated this by exposing high school students to messages advocating either an increase or a decrease in the power of the judicial system. Each message was attributed either to a criminal, who would stand to gain from decreasing and lose from increasing the courts' power; or to a prosecutor, who would gain from an increase but lose from a decrease in judicial power. The results showed that the "criminal" was significantly more effective than the "prosecutor" in arguing for an increase in judicial power. In contrast, the "prosecutor" produced more attitude change when arguing for a reduction of judicial power.[27] In general, this evidence suggests that the greater the effort communicators exert to transmit their messages, the more effective will be the results.

Brock's last effort hypothesis states that "a message will increase in effectiveness the greater the magnitude of the recipient's effort to obtain the information or to understand (decode) it."[28] Thus, if a person expends considerable effort to see an X-rated film or, alternately, must file suit under the Freedom of Information Act to secure a desired government document, the film and the document should be especially entertaining or persuasive. Zimbardo and Ebbesen tested this hypothesis by having two groups read aloud a persuasive message under varying effort levels. The effort level was manipulated by using delayed auditory feedback during the readings. For the low-effort group, the feedback volume was very low and the delay interval of one second was longer than optimal disruption time. For the high-effort group, the feedback was very loud and the delay of two-tenths of a second provided maximal disruption.

After the readings were over, the two groups were asked to work in a telephone bank for a committee allegedly working against the legalization of certain psychedelic drugs, the topic of the persuasive message they read. Eight of the 11 subjects in the high-effort condition agreed to help, but only 1 of 12 in the low-effort condition complied. Moreover, the average amount of time subjects volunteered for telephoning was 1.5 hours in the high-effort group, but only 5 minutes in the low-effort one.[29] These findings support Brock's final effort hypothesis.

In summary, the effort hypotheses suggest: (1) that persuasive messages will be particularly valuable and effective when they are censored; (2) that the greater the pressure needed to bring about disclosure of censored information, the more persuasive the information; and (3) the more effort required to transmit or to receive information, the greater its value and persuasive impact.

The Persuasive Effects of Restriction

As with the effort propositions, restriction hypotheses have considerable implications for censorship. *Restriction* occurs when information is available only to a select few and forbidden to others. Confidential memoranda and classified documents meant for a small, organizational elite are examples of restricted information. Films with explicit sex or violence often are restricted to adults or to adolescents only *if* accompanied by parents. Indeed, the uniform film-rating system is an example of graduated restriction. As you probably are aware, "G" rated films are for everybody regardless of age; "PG" rated movies are also open to everyone, but parental permission for children is suggested. The "R" rating denotes films for adults and persons under 17 who are accompanied by a parent or adult guardian. An "X" designation means that the film is restricted to adults. Commodity theory predicts that the greater the restriction placed on information, the more valuable and persuasive it will be. Applied to films, judged value should increase from "G" to "X" rated productions.

Brock outlines two restriction hypotheses. The first states that "a message will increase in effectiveness in proportion to the amount of accompanying reasons opposing disclosure."[30] Presumably the more reasons, or excuses, offered for restricting information the greater will be its judged value. Thus, if adolescents are kept from seeing an erotic film because it "appeals to prurient interests," "will stimulate antisocial behavior," "will corrupt community standards of acceptable morality," and so forth, it should be judged more desirable than when a single reason for restriction is given. Whether or not the reasons against disclosure are believable presumably is irrelevant.

That a source presents multiple reasons for censorship implies a strong commitment to restrict the information. The perception of such a commitment increases the judged value and persuasiveness of the restricted information.

Brock's second restriction hypothesis suggests that "a message will increase in effectiveness the greater the restrictions set by the communicator on further transmission."[31] Among other things, this hypothesis has implications for rumor transmission. Suppose you are given a piece of hot information about the unusual sexual habits of a professor at your university and you are urged not to "tell a soul." Brock's hypothesis suggests that this information should be more persuasive than if you felt free to tell everyone what you had heard. Yoder confirmed the effectiveness of transmission restriction by having students at Ohio State University observe some ongoing research projects. Half of the student observers had to sign an oath, pledging not to reveal the details to anybody. No such restriction was placed on the other student observers. After inspecting the research, subjects were asked to evaluate its merits. Restricted subjects judged the research significantly more valuable than did nonrestricted students.[32]

The Persuasive Effects of Delay

The final commodification factor discussed by Brock concerns the impact of delay in receiving information. Brock's single delay hypothesis states that "a message will increase in effectiveness the greater the delay by the communicator."[33] Thus, the longer one must wait to obtain desired information, the more persuasive it will be. Wicklund, Cooper, and Linder tested the delay hypothesis by telling subjects they were going to hear a tape-recorded counterattitudinal message. One group was told to expect a delay of 15 minutes, and others were told they would hear the speech in 1 minute. Results showed significantly greater attitude change toward the forthcoming message with a 15-minute delay than a 1-minute delay.[34]

The facilitative effects of delay on judged value may be restricted to moderate periods of delay. Exceptionally long delays could result in a loss of interest. If interest is lost, the information is, by definition, no longer a commodity, and should not be more highly valued because of unavailability. In this case, one might speculate an inverted-U relationship between delay and persuasiveness, with the greatest persuasion occurring at moderate levels of delay. However, if information continues to interest potential recipients, increasingly long delays should increase judged value and message effectiveness.

A Critical Appraisal of Commodity Theory

Commodity theory's application of a classical economic model to persuasive phenomena is both novel and insightful, broadening our understanding of persuasion in ways that other theories have not. Moreover, commodity theory is implicitly rules-based since scarce information is seen as more goal-satisfying than widely available material. And because it focuses on the active power of human perception and judgment to mediate persuasive communication, it is quite consistent with our own actional approach. Despite its contributions, commodity theory is not without conceptual flaws.

Two of these deficiencies are particularly serious. First, as was the case with social judgment–involvement theory, the precise relationship between judgmental processes assessing the *value* of a commodity and *effectiveness*, or attitude change, is extremely ambiguous. Brock has neither distinguished between the two constructs nor clarified their relation to one another. Thus, the rule-related, or goal-satisfying, relation we have assumed in this chapter reflects *our* interpretation of the relation that logically ought to obtain between the two.

The conceptual confusion surrounding the two variables is apparent in Brock's original statement of the theory. He began his monograph by noting that "effectiveness . . . is considered interchangeable with . . . value."[35] However, near the end of his discussion, he concludes that "in retrospect, it has seemed unnecessarily restrictive to equate value and effectiveness."[36] In a later statement of commodity theory, Fromkin and Brock returned to the original interpretation, suggesting that "the value of an informational stimulus, such as a message, is here defined as its effectiveness in producing acceptance."[37] Finally, in an even later treatment, Fromkin and Brock simply refuse to take a position and note that "the value of . . . a communication is defined [either] as its effectiveness in producing acceptance *or* its [judged] desirability" (emphasis added).[38] Our interpretation of the relation between value and effectiveness is that personal goals prompt people to judge scarce information as valuable; and that judged value, in turn, mediates a message's effectiveness. This interpretation was not based on Brock's theorizing. Rather, it is meant to be a clarifying contribution to commodity theory's approach to persuasive communication.

A second, related flaw in commodity theory is Brock's failure to specify the generative force producing responses to scarce information. As Brock admits, "At present the theory lacks a dynamic explanatory principle."[39] Thus, as Brock articulates the theory, we can *predict* that scarcity will result in increasing value and effectiveness, but we cannot *explain* why. Social judgment–involvement theory explains effects by referring to judgmental assimilation and contrast, but commodity theory posits no parallel explanatory mechanism. Thus, it is presently useful only for purposes of prediction. We will now expand the view that commodity-seeking actions are rules-based by offering an appropriate explanatory theory.

A THEORETICAL BASIS FOR COMMODITY EFFECTS: PSYCHOLOGICAL REACTANCE THEORY

Developed by Jack Brehm, psychological reactance theory is a rules-based approach that addresses human responses to threatened or lost freedoms.[40] Its central premise is that people have an intrinsic desire or goal to be free to believe and behave as they wish. When a person's freedom of thought or action is threatened or eliminated, he or she experiences a psychological discomfort called *reactance*. Reactance motivates a person to act to maintain or regain jeopardized freedom. Threatened or lost freedom may be restored in one of two ways. First, a person can sometimes restore freedom *directly*. For example, the child whose mother forbids the eating of candy can ignore the threat and eat the candy anyway. Similarly, a person who wants a restricted government document may bring suit under the Freedom of Information Act to obtain it.

Second, when direct restoration is impossible, a freedom may be regained *indirectly* by valuing the lost or threatened freedom more highly than otherwise would be the case. If, for example, the mother of our hypothetical child throws away all the forbidden candy, the child will probably come to value it more positively, seeing it as far more tasty than it ordinarily might be. Moreover, threatening to throw away the candy should enhance its perceived value. Likewise, the person who cannot obtain classified information may restore a *perception* of control by coming to value the document even more favorably. In short, reactance theory predicts that freedom can be restored indirectly by increasing the judged value of and adopting more positive attitudes toward freedoms that are threatened or lost.

This indirect means of restoring a perception of freedom applies nicely to the predictions of commodity theory. It suggests that when desired information is censored, restricted, delayed, or is otherwise difficult to obtain, a perception of freedom may be restored by coming to value the information more highly. From this perspective, the generative force for commodity effects is a desire to think and act freely without external constraint. A threat to, or loss of, freedom should produce discomfort or reactance, motivating one to act to maintain or regain freedom. Such restoration is accomplished indirectly by coming to value the desired information more highly and adopting a more positive attitude toward the position advocated in the forbidden message.

As we indicated earlier, Brock has not suggested this interpretation. Thus, it represents our effort to extend commodity theory by positing a rules-based explanatory principle for predicted effects. Of course, reactance as a motivational basis for commodity effects is probably not the only theory that could explain commodity phenomena, but it is one highly plausible explanation for the effects of scarce information. For that reason, we offer it as an extension of the commodity approach to persuasive communication.

NOTES

1. Robert G. Kaiser, "Candidates on TV: Reagan Goes Low-Key, Carter Goes Dramatic," *The Washington Post*, 9 September 1980, p. A2.

2. Muzafer Sherif, "A Study of Some Social Factors in Perception," *Archives of Psychology*, No. 187 (1935).

3. For a fuller discussion of judgmental processes, see Harry S. Upshaw, "The Personal Reference Scale: An Approach to Social Judgment," in *Human Judgment and Decision Processes*, ed. Martin F. Kaplan and Steven Schwartz (New York: Academic Press, 1975), pp. 315–371.

4. Social judgment–involvement theory is detailed in Carolyn W. Sherif, Muzafer Sherif, and Roger E. Nebergall, *Attitude and Attitude Change: The Social Judgment-Involvement Approach* (Philadelphia, Pa.: W. B. Saunders Company, 1963); and Muzafer Sherif and Carl I. Hovland, *Social Judgment: Assimilation and Contrast Effects in Communication and Attitude Change* (New Haven, Conn.: Yale University Press, 1961).

5. For a full discussion of these judgmental categories, see Sherif, Sherif, and Nebergall, pp. 18–59.

6. Muzafer Sherif and Hadley Cantril, *The Psychology of Ego-Involvements* (New York: John Wiley, 1947), pp. 126–127.

7. That some judgmental distortion occurs at all levels of ego involvement was demonstrated by Marisa Zavalloni and Stuart W. Cook, "Influence of Judges' Attitudes on Ratings of Favorableness of Statements about a Social Group," *Journal of Personality and Social Psychology* 1 (1965): 43–54. Sherif and associates originally argued that distortion occurs only at extreme levels of involvement.

8. Muzafer Sherif, Daniel Taub, and Carl I. Hovland, "Assimilation and Contrast Effects of Anchoring Stimuli on Judgments," *Journal of Experimental Psychology* 55 (1958): 150–155. An interesting demonstration of contrast effects using social rather than physical phenomena can be found in Douglas T. Kenrick and Sara E. Gutierres, "Contrast Effects and Judgments of Physical Attractiveness: When Beauty Becomes a Social Problem," *Journal of Personality and Social Psychology* 38 (1980): 131–140.

9. Carl I. Hovland, O. J. Harvey, and Muzafer Sherif, "Assimilation and Contrast Effects in Reactions to Communication and Attitude Change," *Journal of Abnormal and Social Psychology* 55 (1957): 244–252.

10. For similar studies, see Sherif, Sherif, and Nebergall.

11. In studies of the 1956 and 1960 presidential campaigns, ego involvement again was equated with membership in known groups. See Sherif, Sherif, and Nebergall.

12. See Norman Miller, "Involvement and Dogmatism as Inhibitors of Attitude Change," *Journal of Experimental Social Psychology* 1 (1965): 121–132.

13. In later publications, Sherif and his associates recognized this possibility. See Sherif, Sherif, and Nebergall.

14. See Daniel Katz, "The Functional Approach to the Study of Attitudes," *Public Opinion Quarterly* 24 (1960): 163–204.

15. See Charles G. McClintock, "Personality Syndromes and Attitude Change," *Journal of Personality* 26 (1958): 479–593; and Daniel Katz, Irving Sarnoff, and Charles McClintock, "Ego-Defense and Attitude Change," *Human Relations* 9 (1956): 27–45.

16. See Upshaw; and Thomas M. Ostrom and Harry S. Upshaw, "Psychological Perspective and Attitude Change," in *Psychological Foundations of Attitudes*, ed. Anthony G. Greenwald, Timothy C. Brock, and Thomas M. Ostrom (New York: Academic Press, 1968), pp. 217–242; and Harry S. Upshaw, "The Effects of Variable Perspectives on Judgments of Opinion Statements for Thurstone Scales: Equal-Appearing Intervals," *Journal of Personality and Social Psychology* 2 (1965): 60–69. For an experimental test of Upshaw's Model, see Steven I. Sherman, Karin Ahlm, and Leonard Berman, "Contrast Effects and Their Relation to Subsequent Behavior," *Journal of Experimental Social Psychology* 14 (1978): 340–350.

17. Richard E. Petty and John T. Cacioppo, "Issue Involvement Can Increase or Decrease Persuasion by Enhancing Message-Relevant Cognitive Responses," *Journal of Personality and Social Psychology* 37 (1979): 1915–1926.

18. Brock's commodity theory is detailed in Timothy C. Brock, "Implications of Commodity Theory for Value Change," in *Psychological Foundations of Attitudes*, pp. 243–275.

19. Ibid., p. 248.

20. Howard L. Fromkin and Timothy C. Brock, "A Commodity Theory Analysis of Persuasion," *Representative Research in Social Psychology* 2 (1971): 47–57.

21. Brock, p. 248.

22. Ibid., p. 249.

23. For an analysis of the implications of commodity theory for pornographic or erotic materials, see Howard L. Fromkin and Timothy C. Brock, "Erotic Materials: A Commodity Theory Analysis of the

Enhanced Desirability that May Accompany Their Unavailability," *Journal of Applied Social Psychology* 3 (1973): 219–231.

24. Timothy C. Brock and Lee Alan Becker, "Ineffectiveness of 'Overheard' Counterpropaganda," *Journal of Personality and Social Psychology* 2 (1965): 654–660.

25. Stephen Worchel and Susan E. Arnold, "The Effects of Censorship and Attractiveness of the Censor on Attitude Change," *Journal of Experimental Social Psychology* 9 (1973): 365–377.

26. Brock, p. 249.

27. Elaine Walster, Eliot Aronson, and Darcy Abrahams, "On Increasing the Persuasiveness of a Low Prestige Communicator," *Journal of Experimental Social Psychology* 2 (1966): 325–342.

28. Brock, p. 249.

29. Philip G. Zimbardo and E. B. Ebbesen, "Experimental Modification of the Relationship Between Effort, Attitude, and Behavior," *Journal of Personality and Social Psychology* 16 (1970): 207–213.

30. Brock, p. 250.

31. Brock.

32. M. R. Yoder, "The Effect of Unavailability and Communication Restriction upon the Evaluation of a Prospective Experience" (M.A. diss., Ohio State University, 1967).

33. Brock, p. 250.

34. Robert A. Wicklund, Joel Cooper, and Darwyn E. Linder, "Effects of Expected Effort of Attitude Change Prior to Exposure," *Journal of Experimental Social Psychology* 3 (1967): 416–428.

35. Brock, p. 248.

36. Ibid., p. 272.

37. Fromkin and Brock, "A Commodity Theory Analysis," p. 47.

38. Fromkin and Brock, "Erotic Materials," p. 222.

39. Brock, p. 272.

40. Psychological reactance theory is detailed in Jack W. Brehm, *A Theory of Psychological Reactance* (New York: Academic Press, 1966); and Robert A. Wicklund, *Freedom and Reactance* (Hillsdale, N.J.: Lawrence Erlbaum, 1973).

CHAPTER 12

Theories of Inducing Resistance to Counterpersuasion

After barely beating Ronald Reagan for the 1976 Republican presidential nomination, Gerald Ford entered the general election campaign as a decided underdog against Democrat Jimmy Carter. President Ford's aides immediately set about plotting a strategy to overcome Mr. Carter's popularity. They presented their ideas to Mr. Ford in a 120-page book dubbed "the battle plan." According to this plan, Ford's campaign should paint Mr. Carter as another Richard Nixon—"slick, media-oriented and power hungry, a candidate that takes positions based on polls, not principles." To cut into his popularity, the book advised that voters be forewarned that Mr. Carter would try to sell himself as "all things to all people," that he would "avoid specifics on issues," refusing to take any substantive position on the critical problems facing the nation.

By forewarning voters about Mr. Carter's presumed chameleon nature, Mr. Ford's advisers hoped to undermine the American people's view of him as a substantial and sincere man. Moreover, they planned to portray Mr. Ford as a solid, steady, "working President," a man concerned exclusively with issues. If successful, this forewarning should make voters more receptive to Mr. Ford's persuasive appeals, and at the same time, more resistant to the counterpersuasion of Jimmy Carter.[1]

Although Mr. Ford did not successfully execute this well-laid plan, the strategy does highlight the main issue we will consider in this chapter. Heretofore, our primary emphasis has been on how persuasion induces positive attitude and behavior change. In this chapter, we will take a different direction and explore several approaches to inducing resistance to *counterpersuasive messages*, messages that conflict with favored positions. As we will see, inducing resistance to counterpersuasion is a dynamically different process from inducing positive attitude change. Indeed, some techniques that produce very little positive attitude change on a particular issue can be exceedingly effective in inducing long-range resistance to counterpersuasion on the same issue.

We will look at three information-processing approaches to inducing resistance to counterpersuasion: (1) William McGuire's inoculation theory; (2) a three-factor model of resistance; and (3) a cognitive response model of resistance. Each theory will then be evaluated.

INDUCING RESISTANCE TO COUNTERPERSUASION: AN OVERVIEW

As we have said, *counterpersuasion* consists of messages that conflict with presently held attitudes. Usually, it takes the form of deliberate campaigns to dismantle deeply held value systems and alter enduring cognitive schemata. Because of its highly intentional nature, counterpersuasion is often labeled "counterpropaganda," or more simply, "propaganda." Powerful nations usually spend considerable money on counterpersuasive campaigns. For example, Radio Free Europe and the Voice of America continually beam messages to Communist countries in an effort to persuade them of the virtues of democracy. In recent years, Castro's Cuba similarly has made a concentrated effort to spread Marxist messages to other Caribbean, South American, and African countries. On a less grand scale, political parties in this country devote large sums of money, especially around election time, to try to convert the opposition and to win independent voting blocs. In this chapter, we will consider strategies designed to neutralize counterpersuasive campaigns.

Techniques for inducing resistance to counterpersuasion normally are quite different from positive persuasive appeals such as those used in counterpersuasive messages themselves. Indeed, some factors producing the most attitude change to begin with do not necessarily produce greater resistance to later counterattack. In fact, the opposite is often the case. Those strategies most effective in producing immediate attitude change are sometimes least effective in neutralizing counterpersuasion. For example, as we found in Chapter 9's discussion of message variables, one-sided messages produce far greater initial attitude change among partisan receivers than two-sided presentations. However, two-sided arguments are substantially more effective among those same partisans in inducing resistance to future counterpersuasion. Thus, we may conclude as McGuire does that "studying resistance to persuasion is not simply the inverse of studying persuasion itself."[2] Clearly, quite different dynamics underlie the two processes.

Two factors are critical to inducing resistance to counterpersuasion. First, an individual must be *motivated* to resist counterattacks. As we will find, one of the most effective motivators is threat, including a forewarning of impending counterpersuasion. Recall that Mr. Ford's 1976 "battle plan" aimed to forewarn voters of Mr. Carter's alleged changeability on issues and thereby motivate them to resist his upcoming persuasive campaign. In addition to motivation, a person must have the *information* necessary to counterargue against impending persuasive attacks. By citing instances of Mr. Carter's wishy-washy stance on issues and cases of Mr. Ford's adherence to principle, the Ford campaign hoped to give voters the information they would need to counterargue successfully against Mr. Carter's messages. Throughout this chapter, we will explore approaches to providing the necessary motivation and information for effective resistance to counterpersuasion.

MCGUIRE'S INOCULATION THEORY

McGuire's inoculation theory focuses on deeply accepted, enduring attitudes and values, those a "person has seldom, if ever heard attacked."[3] Examples of these types of cognitive schemata include: "Democracy is the best form of government"; "Communism is bad"; "I am an honest person"; and "There is a God." Many of our stereotyped beliefs about ourselves and others are representative of attitudes and values we take to be inviolate. But precisely because we regard them as unassailable, they are extremely vulnerable to counterpersuasive attack. Their vulnerability stems in part from the dynamics of *selective exposure:* the tendency of individuals to avoid information that conflicts with personal attitudes and values. According to McGuire,

> People tend to defend their beliefs by avoiding exposure to counterarguments rather than developing positive support for the beliefs. As a consequence of the ideological 'aseptic' environment that results, the person tends to remain highly confident about his beliefs but also highly vulnerable to strong counterattacks when forced exposure occurs.[4]

McGuire's theory, then, addresses only those attitudes people accept so completely they regard them as unassailable.

He theorizes that persuasive attacks against such beliefs are particularly effective because people are unprepared to make appropriate defensive responses. They cannot muster adequate defenses for two reasons: (1) they are *unpracticed* in defending these beliefs because they have never been called upon to defend them and because they lack the necessary information and arguments to build an effective defense; and (2) they are *unmotivated* to find supportive information and to practice a defense because they regard their beliefs as unassailable. To overcome this vulnerability and make people more resistant to counterpersuasion, McGuire suggests that, *prior* to counterpersuasion, they must be motivated and informed. *Motivation* to build and practice defensive responses can be supplied by making people aware of the vulnerability of their beliefs. Put another way, a person's faith in his or her beliefs must be threatened to some degree. An obvious way to threaten is to attack the beliefs people regard as invulnerable. In addition to motivation/threat, people must acquire the *information* necessary to build and practice an effective defense; it may be given directly or people may secure it on their own. After receiving this motivational and informational defensive pretreatment, people should be able to resist later counterattack on their beliefs.

As this name of his theory implies, McGuire likens this threat plus information defensive pretreatment to biological immunization processes. He notes:

> In the biological situation, the person is typically made resistant to some attacking virus by pre-exposure to a weakened dose of the virus. This mild dose stimulates his defenses so that he will be better able to overcome any massive viral attack to which he is later exposed. [But the dose must not be] so strong that [it] will itself cause the disease.[5]

As applied to counterpersuasion, the threatening pretreatment must be strong enough to stimulate defensive measures, but not so threatening that it destroys the person's faith in his or her beliefs. In summary, inoculation against counterpersuasion consists of a mild attack on a person's beliefs and the provision of information necessary to defend them. This "inoculation" should motivate a person to construct an effective defense for later use.

McGuire's theory deals exclusively with beliefs "that have been maintained in a 'germ free' ideological environment."[6] It does not deal with controversial attitudes that previously have been subjected to attack and counterattack. For that reason, McGuire chose to work with *cultural truisms*, defined as "beliefs that are so widely shared within the person's social milieu that he would not have heard them attacked, and indeed would doubt that an attack were possible."[7] After extensive pretesting, he settled on health truisms such as "It's a good idea to brush your teeth after every meal if at all possible"; "Mental illness is not contagious"; and "The effects of penicillin have been, almost without exception, of great benefit to mankind" for use in experimental tests of inoculation theory. McGuire explored three general issues in his inoculation research: (1) the optimal amount of threat needed in defensive pretreatments; (2) the effect of a person's active versus passive participation in defensive pretreatments; and (3) the persistence, or long-term efficacy, of defensive pretreatments. It is to these three general issues that we now turn our attention.

Magnitude of Threat in Defensive Pretreatments

McGuire studied two pretreatment defenses with varying threat levels. The first, called the *supportive defense*, is nonthreatening and consists of giving people several arguments to support their beliefs. The second, the *refutational defense*, threatens believers by advancing arguments that attack beliefs, but then refutes the threatening arguments. The refutational defense is presumed to be threatening enough to stimulate defenses, but not so strong as to overwhelm deeply held, but substantively fragile, beliefs.

McGuire studied two variants of the refutational defense. The first, called the *refutational-same* pretreatment, mentions and then refutes the same arguments to be used in subsequent counterattacks. The *refutational-different* pretreatment advances and refutes arguments different from the ones planned for later counterpersuasion. McGuire introduced this variation to determine whether resistance to persuasion derives only from the general motivational effect of threat or whether it requires the useful supportive material provided by the refutations. Finally, he explored the immunization effects of adding either forewarnings of impending attack or supportive reassurances about the rightness of beliefs to supportive and refutational defenses.

McGuire and Papageorgis examined the relative effectiveness of supportive versus refutational-same defenses in creating resistance to counterpersuasion. In a defensive pretreatment session, one group of 128 subjects received arguments supporting their beliefs (supportive defense), and another 132 subjects heard arguments against their beliefs along with refutations of the arguments (refutational-same defense). A third group of 260 subjects was given no pretreatment (control group). Two days later, the two experimental groups and one-half of the control subjects read a 1000-word counterattack on their beliefs that used the same arguments as those in the refutational-same treatment.

TABLE 12.1: MEAN BELIEF
LEVELS AS FUNCTIONS OF
PRETREATMENT AND ATTACK °

Condition	Means†
Refutational-same	10.33
Supportive	7.39
Attack, no pretreatment	6.64
No attack, no pretreatment control	12.62

° All belief levels were measured on a 15-point scale, where 15 represents complete acceptance of the belief and 1 denotes complete rejection.

† The higher the mean, the stronger the belief.

As Table 12.1 shows, the more threatening refutational-same defense was superior to the supportive defense. In fact, the mean belief level of 10.33 among the refutational-defense subjects was only slightly lower than the 12.62 mean belief score of the control subjects whose beliefs were never attacked. The supportive defense was less successful in inducing resistance. Indeed, the supportive subjects' mean belief level after the attack was not reliably different from the mean belief score of the attacked control subjects who received no pretreatment at all.[8] This study clearly underscores the overriding importance of motivation induced by threat in conferring resistance to persuasion.

Another experiment by Papageorgis and McGuire compared the effectiveness of refutational-same and refutational-different defensive pretreatments. All 73 subjects participating in the study read 600-word essays that presented and then refuted two arguments against their beliefs. As in the previous study, a control group received no pretreatment. One week later, half of the subjects read an attack using the same arguments that previously had been refuted, and the other half read messages containing novel attacking arguments. Finally, part of the control group read an attack on their beliefs.

As in the first study, results showed that counterpersuasion was very damaging when not preceded by a defensive pretreatment. The no–pretreatment control group exposed to counterpersuasion had a mean belief level of 5.73 (on a 15-point scale where 15 meant complete acceptance of the beliefs and 1 denoted complete rejection) compared to a mean of 13.23 for the control subjects whose beliefs were not attacked. Both of the refutational defenses conferred appreciable resistance to counterpersuasion. When the attack was preceded by a refutational-same defense, the mean belief level was 9.25, and it was 8.70 among the refutational-different subjects. The mean belief levels in these last two groups were significantly higher than the 5.73 mean of the no–pretreatment control group, and they were not significantly different from one another.[9] This study strongly supports inoculation theory's focus on the role of mildly threatening attacks as a defensive motivator. Indeed, the resistance to novel attacks was equivalent to that produced by attacks on previously refuted arguments. Apparently, when properly motivated, people can easily summon their own supportive information to combat counterpersuasion. Clearly, this study suggests that externally supplied support is quite unnecessary.

External Threats and Reassurances

To explore further the immunizing effects of threat, McGuire examined the impact of adding external threats or reassurances to the various defensive pretreatments. It was expected that threat would enhance resistance, especially for the supportive defense since it confers little or no motivation to resist counterpersuasion. Reassurances, on the other hand, ought to undermine resistance in all pretreatment conditions. To test the effects of threat, McGuire and Papageorgis administered either supportive, refutational-same, or refutational-different defensive pretreatments to 96 subjects. Later, all subjects read an attacking counterpersuasion. Half of the subjects in a "no forewarning" condition were not told that their beliefs would shortly be attacked. The other subjects in the "forewarning" condition were told that the aim of the experiment was to determine how persuasible they were and that their beliefs would shortly be attacked.

As Table 12.2 shows, forewarning of attack significantly enhanced resistance to counterpersuasion. Across all three defense conditions, the mean belief level among the forewarned subjects was 11.67 compared to 10.93 for subjects not forewarned, a statistically reliable difference. As expected, forewarning was particularly effective among subjects who got the supportive defense. Forewarning added some moderate resistance among the refutational defense subjects who were already motivated by the threatening defensive pretreatments.[10]

To explore the effects of reassurance, Anderson administered the three defensive pretreatments to 96 subjects. Instead of forewarning, half of the subjects were given reassuring feedback—they were told that other subjects had agreed unanimously that the beliefs used in the study were true beyond any doubt. The balance of the subjects

TABLE 12.2: MEAN BELIEF LEVELS AS A FUNCTION OF FOREWARNING °

	Supportive defense	Refutational-same defense	Refutational-different defense	Combined effects
Forewarning	12.09	11.79	11.12	11.67
No fore-warning	10.11	11.68	10.98	10.93

° The higher the mean, the greater the resistance to persuasion. Complete adherence to beliefs is indicated by 15.

received no reassuring feedback. As expected, reassurance undermined all varieties of defensive pretreatment. After each group's beliefs were attacked, the mean belief level among reassured subjects was 10.63, compared with 11.53 for unreassured ones.[11]

These studies confirm inoculation theory's central claim that threat is the generative force behind successful resistance to counterpersuasion. Clearly, supportive material is useful only if combined with motivation-inducing threat. Moreover, McGuire's research has shown that, when properly motivated, people readily generate their own supportive counterarguments.

Active versus Passive Participation in Defensive Pretreatments

Given the well-documented superiority of active over passive participation in promoting positive attitude change, McGuire was interested in the effect of this variable on creating resistance to persuasion. In the inoculation paradigm, active participation involves instructing individuals to generate their own belief-supporting arguments in the supportive pretreatment. In the refutational-defense treatments, active participation requires people to think up arguments against their own beliefs, then to refute the self-generated arguments. McGuire developed several hypotheses concerning the effects of having people generate their own defensive pretreatments. He began by recalling that vulnerability to counterpersuasion on cultural truisms stems from a practice/information deficit and a motivational deficiency.

Given these two deficits, he argues that active participation in defensive pretreatments ought to operate in opposite ways on practice/information and motivation. As to practice/information, McGuire suggests active participation in constructing pretreatment should be less effective than passive receipt of supportive information because believers have a woefully inadequate repertoire of information with which to construct arguments. In the passive mode, the believer is provided with the information he or she lacks. In contrast, active participation in the construction of pretreatment defenses should be more motivational than passive participation. As McGuire puts it, "the very poorness of the believer's performance . . . should bring home to him how inadequately based is his confidence in the truism. This should motivate him to correct this state of affairs."[12]

Based on this analysis, McGuire made some rather subtle and complicated deductions. First, he argues that, across all types of defensive pretreatments, passive rather than active participation theoretically should be more effective in creating resistance. He based this conclusion on the belief that the detrimental effects of active participation on information acquisition should outweigh its motivational advantage, which he felt would be far less potent than motivation generated by external threat. Second, McGuire contends that active participation might be helpful with supportive defenses since they lack a motivational dimension. Third, he argues that active participation should increase the effectiveness of refutational-different defenses since these rely solely on motivation to stimulate defenses against counterattacks. Enhanced motivation should increase the generation of supportive material as well as counterarguments. Fourth and finally, McGuire claims that active participation should be less effective than passive participation in refutational-same pretreatments. The refutational-same, unlike the refutational-different pretreatment, owes its effectiveness to two factors: the motivation induced by threat and the provision of useful information for resisting counterattacks. Unlike active involvement, passive participation supplies helpful information. Since the refutational-same pretreatment is itself motivational, the additional information supplied by passive participation should confer the most resistance.[13]

McGuire conducted several experiments to test these deductions. In the first study, he and Papageorgis set up four participation levels in defensive pretreatments, ranging from purely passive reading of the pretreatment to writing one's own pretreatment without any guidance whatsoever. Refutational-same and supportive pretreatments were included in the experimental design. Results confirmed McGuire's predictions concerning refutational-same pretreatments. Passive reading conveyed considerably more resistance to counterattack than did active writing (11.33 versus 9.33 on a 15-point scale). However, among subjects receiving the supportive pretreatment, the resistance conferred by the two modes was roughly equivalent (7.56 and 7.23 for passive and active participation, respectively). Finally, when resistance levels created by both supportive and refutational-same defenses were combined, passive participation was the superior mode.[14] This result supports McGuire's view that the informational disadvantages of active participation outweigh its motivational value.

In a second experiment, McGuire confirmed his notion that active involvement is preferable to passive participation in refutational-different defensive treatments, but that the opposite holds for refutational-same defenses. Within the refutational-same conditions, mean belief levels after attack were 10.66 with active participation and 11.47 when participation was passive. In contrast, when defenses were refutational-different, active participation resulted in a mean belief level after attack of 11.42, and passive participation, in a mean belief level of 10.62.[15]

All of these results support McGuire's rather complicated reasoning on the issue of active versus passive participation in constructing defenses. In general, when a pretreatment depends exclusively on *either* motivation (refutational-different) *or* information (supportive), active rather than passive participation confers more resistance to counterpersuasion. In contrast, when a pretreatment's effectiveness is based on both motivation and information (refutational-same), the passive receipt of threats and supportive arguments is apparently superior to attempts to actively generate both.

The Persistence of Defensive Pretreatments

As a final consideration, McGuire's inoculation theory looks at the long-term effectiveness of induced resistance to counterpersuasion. To understand his persistence predictions, recall that immunization efficacy is dependent on threats that motivate people to seek and assimilate supportive information, and on the actual accumulation of such bolstering material. McGuire argues that persistence effects depend on whether resistance is conferred by stimulating motivation or supplying supportive information or both. He made the general prediction that resistance induced by pretreatments relying solely on motivation should follow a curvilinear (inverted-U) pattern: resistance should be relatively low immediately after a threatening pretreatment, rise over time, and ultimately drop off. In explaining this prediction, he notes that

> once a threat has motivated the previously overconfident believer to accumulate belief-bolstering material, he will still need time before he can act effectively on his motivation, since material relevant to these uncontroverted truisms is relatively scarce in the ordinary ideological environment. Hence, the believer will continue to accumulate additional material for a considerable time after being exposed to the threatening [defensive pretreatment].[16]

The accumulation of supportive information should continue and resistance should grow as long as threat-induced motivation is present. However, as time passes without counterattack, the threat should become less salient. Consequently, "the induced motivation to accumulate material will itself tend to decay."[17] The result should be first a rising, then a falling resistance level, the classic inverted-U pattern.

In contrast to threat-induced persistence trends, persistence created by supplying supportive information should decline linearly. In this case, persistence should be a direct function of retention of the bolstering material. Since retention follows an ordinary forgetting pattern, informational resistance should be greatest right after the pretreatment, then show a sharp and rapid drop over time, a typical inverse linear relationship between time and persistence of effect.

Given these two predictions about persistence as a function of motivational versus informational resistance, McGuire argues that the precise pattern of persistence depends on whether resistance is actively or passively conferred. Since the effectiveness of active-participation defenses is based solely on the threatening, motivational dimension of resistance, all types of active defenses—whether supportive, refutational-same, or refutational-different—should follow an inverted-U pattern. Hence, in this mode, the greatest resistance to counterattacks is not immediate, but occurs some time after pretreatment. Delay gives the motivated believer time to accumulate supportive data.

In contrast, predictions regarding passively conferred resistance depend on the particular defensive pretreatment used. Any resistance conferred by reading or hearing a supportive defense derives exclusively from retention of bolstering information. Thus, in the absence of motivation, a sharp and rapid linear decline in resistance is predicted. Since the refutational-different defense is based exclusively on the motivating-threat mechanism, a passive refutational-different defense should show the same inverted-U pattern as the three types of active defenses. Finally, the passive refutational-same pretreatment depends on both motivation and information. Thus, its persistence trend should be a composite of the supportive and the refutational-different time patterns. There should be a slight linear decline initially since the forgetting of supportive material is largely offset by the bolstering motivational mechanism. After this, persistence should fall rapidly as threat and information are both forgotten.

McGuire conducted several experiments to test these persistence predictions. To examine the passive-participation hypotheses, he had 480 subjects read either a supportive, a refutational-same, or a refutational-different pretreatment. The subjects' beliefs were then attacked either immediately, two days, or seven days later. As Figure 12.1 shows, the results were as predicted. What small resistance the supportive defense conferred decayed almost completely within two days—at both the two- and seven-day

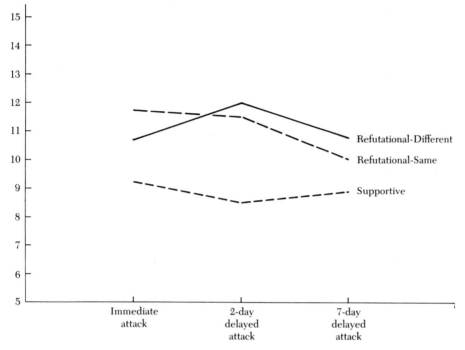

FIGURE 12.1   Persistence of resistance to persuasion conferred by three types of passive defenses. One control group (n=80) receiving neither pretreatment nor attack scored 11.74; a second control group (n=80) receiving no pretreatment but a counterattack scored 8.49. (On the 15-point scale, 15 represents complete acceptance and 1 represents complete rejection.)

intervals, the supportive subjects' mean belief level (8.51 and 8.82, respectively) was approximately the same as that of control subjects who were attacked but received no pretreatment. For the refutational-same group, the conferred resistance declined steadily but at a slower rate than supportive resistance. Finally, the predicted inverted-U trend in the refutational-different condition was confirmed. Resistance to attack two days later was greater than resistance to immediate attacks or attacks one week later.[18]

In a second study, McGuire tested the persistence of actively versus passively conferred resistance. A total of 288 subjects received either an active or a passive defensive pretreatment. Within each of these two conditions, some subjects got a supportive defense, others a refutational-same, and the balance a refutational-different defense. The subjects' beliefs were then attacked either immediately or one week later. The results, shown in Table 12.3, confirmed that all three active defenses yielded greater resistance one week later, rather than immediately after pretreatment. In contrast, only the refutational-different, passive defense resulted in greater long-term than immediate resistance. Finally, combined effects show that the passive pretreatments induced more immediate resistance to persuasion, but that the active mode produced greater long-term resistance.[19] This finding suggests that the choice of pretreatment will depend on

TABLE 12.3: MEAN BELIEF LEVELS AS FUNCTIONS OF TIME OF ATTACK AND ACTIVE VERSUS PASSIVE DEFENSES

Type of pretreatment	Active defense		Passive defense	
	Immediate attack	One week later	Immediate attack	One week later
Supportive	8.30	9.89	9.72	9.47
Refutational-same	9.61	10.13	12.12	10.42
Refutational-different	9.77	9.98	9.61	9.99
All three combined	9.22	10.00	10.48	9.96

15.00 indicates complete adherence to beliefs.

From William J. McGuire, "Inducing Resistance to Persuasion: Some Contemporary Approaches," in *Experiments in Persuasion* by Ralph L. Rosnow and Edward J. Robinson, eds., Academic Press, 1967, p. 226. Reprinted by permission.

whether one wishes to induce temporary or long-range resistance to counterpersuasion.

A Critical Appraisal of Inoculation Theory

McGuire's inoculation theory is a significant contribution to our understanding of persuasion. It was the first systematic attempt to explore the dynamics of resisting counterpersuasion; and it remains the most extensive and thoroughly researched theory of resistance in the literature of persuasion. Indeed, as we will see, most other resistance theories take McGuire's notions of threat and information as starting points. Thus, other resistance theories represent extensions and elaborations of the fundamental tenets of inoculation theory.

Despite the breadth and creativity of McGuire's thinking, inoculation theory has several serious limitations. First, its generalizability is not yet clear. McGuire himself limits the application of inoculation theory to cultural truisms, beliefs so strongly held they are perceived as unassailable. However, he never proved empirically that this limitation is warranted. Attempts by other researchers to demonstrate the generalizability of inoculation strategies to more controversial beliefs have been inconclusive.[20] At present, inoculation theory is limited to conferring resistance to attack on cultural truisms, stereotypes, and other ideas that previously have not been questioned. Although a considerable number of religious, social, and political beliefs fall into this classification, many other attitudes are excluded. Whether this exclusion is justified awaits empirical demonstration.

A second problem with inoculation theory concerns McGuire's assumption that resistance to persuasion derives from the ability and willingness of people to *counterargue* against future attacks. Despite the centrality of this counterargument assumption,

McGuire provided no direct evidence that his motivational and informational pretreatments, in fact, increased the ability and willingness of people to counterargue against persuasive attacks. Moreover, even if we assume that counterarguing increases after pretreatment, McGuire never explicitly showed that it is the crucial mediator of conferred resistance. Indeed, there are plausible alternatives to McGuire's counterargument explanation. It is possible that the net effect of defensive pretreatments, especially the refutational variety, is to inform believers that the arguments against their beliefs are typically weak and ineffectual. For example, a typical argument used by McGuire against the truism that "toothbrushing is healthful" was: "Too frequent brushing tends to damage the gums and expose vulnerable parts of the teeth to decay"—hardly a belief-shattering argument!

Given these kinds of attacks, refutational pretreatments may create in people a mental set to judge all antitruism arguments as poor and to discredit them as weak and unworthy of consideration. This explanation is quite different from McGuire's assumption that resistance occurs because believers generate counterarguments against attacking messages. The alternative explanation suggests that, instead of counterarguing, believers simply dismiss attacks judged to be poor. Because McGuire did not verify the existence of active counterarguing, inoculation theory is vulnerable to alternative explanations like this.

Third, McGuire's reliance on the biological analogy is flawed in several respects. Some researchers argue that there really is no such thing as a "germ-free" belief, one never before attacked by counterarguments. According to this view, belief systems are interrelated in much the same way as organs of the human body. A viral attack on one organ inevitably affects other organs. Applying this analogy to belief systems, an attack on peripheral beliefs related to a truism should affect the truism as well. Although "democracy is the best form of government" may be an unattacked truistic belief for many Americans, related beliefs have probably been called into question. Certainly Watergate and Vietnam have pointed to the American government's capacity for error and corruption. Attacks on beliefs related to a truism no doubt affect the truism as well.[21]

One additional issue related to McGuire's use of a biological analogy is especially important. Although he patterned most of his inoculation strategies after the biological analogy, he strayed from that focus in certain instances. For example, his predictions regarding the efficacy of active versus passive defensive pretreatments neither follow from nor illuminate the utility of the analogy. And though such flaws may have few serious, practical implications, they do diminish inoculation theory's conceptual coherence.

A fourth criticism of inoculation theory appears to relate to McGuire's departures from the biological analogy in formulating predictions. In developing hypotheses about the relative effectiveness of active versus passive participation in pretreatments, McGuire's reasons for a number of predictions were never entirely clear. For example, his general prediction that passive pretreatments should be more effective than active ones had no firm theoretical or empirical justification. In fact, his explanation amounted to an expression of personal belief that the detrimental effects of active participation on information acquisition ought to be dominant over its motivational value.[22] Equally unclear was his rationale for predicting that active participation should be effective with the refutational-different, but not the refutational-same defense.[23] His departure from the biological analogy when formulating these active–passive predictions can easily account for their conceptual fuzziness. Other predictions such as the expected superiority of refutational over supportive defenses flowed clearly and directly from the analogy with biological immunization processes. In contrast, the active-passive predictions have no biological counterpart. Once having strayed from the biological analogy, a coherent rationale for some predictions apparently was difficult to summon.

Inoculation Theory and Rules

Finally, we must critically examine inoculation theory in relation to our action-oriented, rules-based conception of persuasion. McGuire's focus on externally supplied immunizing pretreatments represents a highly mechanistic, laws approach to explaining purposive behavior. The parallel between biological inoculation and the "hypodermic needle" theory of persuasion is so obvious it requires little elaboration. McGuire clearly assumed people were relatively passive creatures whose belief-supportive as well as goal-oriented motivation had to be "injected into them" by an external agent. Such a causal approach is obviously at odds with our own.

However, it is interesting that, although McGuire approached persuasion from a mechanistic, causal view, much of his research yielded data that is quite consistent with an actional approach. For example, the finding that people, when properly motivated, require no external assistance to muster their own defenses against persuasion conforms to an active, goal-directed view of human nature. Moreover, his confirmation that active participation in one's own defensive pretreatment has far more lasting effects than passive immunization is consistent with our perspective. Finally, the theoretical assumption that active counterarguing is the crucial mediator of resistance to persuasion is congruent with an actional view of persuasive communication. Thus, McGuire perhaps unwittingly provided support for the view that people are active, goal-directed processers of persuasive information.

OTHER MODELS OF RESISTANCE TO PERSUASION

As we noted earlier, most other theories of resistance to persuasion are extensions or elaborations of McGuire's inoculation theory. The two models we will now consider are no exception. The first theory, a three-factor model, incorporates McGuire's central postulates as one of three classes of variables related to the creation of resistance. The second, a cognitive response approach, focuses on counterarguing and elaborates on the role of covert cognitive responses in creating resistance to counterattack. Both theories depart from McGuire's formulation by considering resistance to attacks on controversial, as well as generally accepted, beliefs and values.

A Three-Factor Model of Resistance to Persuasion

Developed by Michael Burgoon and his associates, the three-factor model is a relatively recent formulation.[24] According to it, resistance to counterpersuasion is mediated by three factors. The first factor, incorporating the basic principles of inoculation theory, considers the amount of *threat* and motivation required to generate counterarguing. Second, resistance is affected by the degree to which a message fulfills or violates a person's *expectations* of appropriate communication behaviors. Finally, the *context* in which the persuasive communication occurs is presumed to mediate resistance to counterattack.

Since the first factor duplicates McGuire's work, we will focus on the second and third factors. As we will see, both expectancy and context variables are expected to promote resistance to the extent that they threaten people and, thereby, motivate them to counterargue. Although these resistance factors go beyond the basic constructs of inoculation theory, both ultimately depend on McGuire's central notions of threat and motivation to counterargue for their effectiveness in conferring resistance. For that reason, Burgoon's three-factor model may be regarded only as an extension and elaboration of inoculation theory.

Violation of Expectations and Resistance

Burgoon's resistance model assumes that people generally have a set of expectations concerning any source's communication behaviors. Moreover, these expectancy sets should affect both initial responses to messages and future resistance to counterattacks on message-relevant attitudes. Suppose, for example, that people initially expect a source to be untrustworthy, arrogant, and the like. If the source unexpectedly exhibits positive behaviors, people typically overestimate the favorableness of the behaviors and perceive them as more positive than they actually are. This *positive violation of expectations* should reduce immediate resistance to persuasion, that is, promote immediate, positive attitude change toward the advocated position, but should *enhance* long-range resistance to attack on one's attitudes. For, as Burgoon argues, the realization that one's attitudes can be successfully attacked and undermined by a positive source should threaten a person. That threat ought to increase one's motivation to muster counterarguments against future attacks on beliefs.

In contrast, a *negative violation of expectations* should increase immediate resistance to persuasion, that is, inhibit immediate attitude change, but reduce long-term resistance on the same attitudinal issue. To illustrate, suppose a person initially expects a source to exhibit positive communication behaviors, for example to be honest, competent, and likable. If the source unexpectedly appears negative, people should exaggerate the unanticipated negative qualities, perceiving him or her as more negative than is actually the case. This contrast effect should inhibit immediate attitude change. However, the source's poor performance should be quite nonthreatening to people and, thus, inhibit counterargumentation. As a result, people should be especially vulnerable to future persuasion by a competent or likable source.

Miller and Burgoon tested these assumptions by leading some subjects to expect a high-intensity counterattitudinal message that used inflammatory language (negative expectancy). Other subjects were told to expect a low-intensity message, one advancing moderate and reasonable arguments (positive expectancy). Subjects with the negative expectancy sets were unexpectedly exposed to a positive, low-intensity message, whereas positive expectancy subjects unexpectedly got a negative, high-intensity communication. At a later experimental session, all subjects were exposed to a moderately intense persuasive message advocating the same counterattitudinal position as the first message, but using different arguments.

Results confirmed the researchers' predictions. People receiving a positive violation of expectancy were initially persuaded to accept the position advocated in the message, but resisted later persuasion, reverting to preexperimental attitudes. Apparently, the first positive counterattitudinal message showed people their attitudes were vulnerable to attack, and presumably that motivated them to muster counterarguments for use against later attacks. In contrast, people receiving a negative violation of expectations showed little initial attitude change and no resistance to a later, more reasonable, attack on their attitudes. Apparently, the nonthreatening nature of the first message provided no motivation to muster counterarguments, leaving them vulnerable to later counterpersuasion.[25]

Persuasion Context and Resistance

Burgoon and his colleagues argue that any threatening context variable motivates counterarguing and should create resistance to future persuasion. More particularly, Burgoon focused on those context factors he expected would distract or not distract people from counterarguing. In searching for distraction-related variables, Burgoon and associates concluded that the *critical response set*, created by giving people instructions about those aspects of a forthcoming communication they should focus on, is a crucially important context variable. People can be told to focus either on the *source* or the *message content*. In addition, they may be instructed to look either for *negative* or for *positive* source or message characteristics.

Burgoon predicts that these preexposure instructions should affect levels of resistance to an initial message and to later counterattacks. He speculates that if a person is instructed to criticize source attributes and look for negative characteristics, he or she should be unpersuaded by an initial message, but vulnerable to later counterattack. Two factors account for this prediction. First, people should not feel threatened by a negatively evaluated speaker, and little initial attitude change should result. However, because they don't feel threatened, people should not be motivated to guard against future counterpersuasion. Second, looking for negative source characteristics should distract individuals from counterarguing against message content, leaving them vulnerable to later attack.

On the other hand, Burgoon predicts that attention to positive source characteristics should initially lower resistance and result in positive attitude change, but should enhance long-term resistance to counterattack. The threat engendered by the realization that one's beliefs are vulnerable to attack by a credible, likable speaker should motivate people to muster counterarguments during the time delay between exposure to a first and second message. These counterarguments should shift attitudes back to their position prior to exposure to the first communication.

Regarding message content, if people are asked to positively evaluate the arguments in a message, they should show little initial resistance and change positively toward the message they rate high in quality. However, they should exhibit considerable resistance to later persuasion on the same attitudinal issue for two reasons. First, the nature of the critical response set focuses attention on the attacking arguments. Second, the recognition that there are cogent arguments against their attitudes should threaten and motivate people to prepare counterarguments for use against future attacks. In contrast, if people are induced to negatively evaluate message content, they should show considerable initial and long-term resistance to persuasion. The long-term resistance should stem not from threat but from the nature of the critical response task itself: to critically counterargue against the message. The accumulation of counterarguments during exposure to a first message should provide an informational arsenal for combating future attacks. However, without a threatening dimension, resistance presumably should not persist for long periods of time.

Burgoon and his associates tested these hypotheses using two counterattitudinal messages arguing for the legalization of heroin. Subjects were students, and faculty members unfamiliar to them were used as speakers. Prior to hearing the first message, subjects were asked either to positively or negatively evaluate source characteristics or,

TABLE 12.4: MEAN ATTITUDES IN RESPONSE
TO TWO COUNTERATTACKS

Groups	First message	Second message
Negative set toward message	10.83	10.78
Positive set toward message	11.83	10.78
Negative set toward source	10.26	13.11
Positive set toward source	12.36	11.53

Attitudes were the summed responses of subjects on four 7-point scales, with 4 indicating the least agreement with the message and 28 signifying the greatest agreement. Thus, the lower the mean, the greater the resistance to persuasion.

Adapted from M. Burgoon, M. Cohen, M. D. Miller, and C. L. Montgomery, "An Empirical Test of Resistance to Persuasion," *Human Communication Research*, 5, 1978, p. 34. Reprinted by permission.

alternately, the message content. Two to three days later, subjects heard a second message advocating the legalization of heroin. The results, shown in Table 12.4, generally confirmed predictions. Both a positive and a negative critical response set toward message content led to considerable resistance to the second message. Likewise, a positive evaluation of source characteristics led to strong resistance. In contrast, a negative response set toward source qualities did not create resistance.[26] These results suggest that preinstruction to focus on the threatening aspects of initial messages induces resistance to future attack. In contrast, preinstruction designed to distract people from mustering counterarguments should diminish long-term resistance.

A Critical Appraisal of the Three-Factor Model

Burgoon's three-factor model is an interesting and informative extension of McGuire's inoculation theory because it expands our view of what constitutes an effective defensive pretreatment. McGuire limited his view of pretreatments to either supportive or refutational messages. Burgoon's theorizing suggests this approach may be unnecessarily narrow in that any message or context variable that stimulates counterarguing can properly be viewed as a defensive pretreatment. Additionally, Burgoon's three-factor model is not limited, as is inoculation theory, to truisms; it encompasses controversial attitudes as well. This extension makes the three-factor model applicable to a wider variety of persuasive phenomena than is inoculation theory.

Despite its value, the three-factor theory has several limitations. The most damaging problem relates to the model's central construct, counterarguing. Despite an exclusive dependence on counterarguing as a mediator of resistance, Burgoon and his associates have not attempted to directly measure the actual production of counterarguments. (Recall that this criticism applies to inoculation theory as well.) Montgomery and Burgoon recently tried to explain away this flaw by arguing that "attempts at measuring counterarguing have been relatively unproductive in past research,"[27] a claim we believe is unfounded. Future research must measure counterarguing as a function of expectancy violations and critical response sets. Until this is accomplished, the three-factor model is vulnerable to the same kinds of alternative explanations earlier attributed to inoculation theory.

A second criticism of the model probably reflects its newness. Presently, the two critical resistance factors, expectancy violation and context, are relatively undeveloped theoretically and untested empirically. In fact, theoretical postulates related to context variables are currently limited to predictions about critical response sets, an exceedingly narrow interpretation of context. Other context variables that lead to resistance must be articulated, integrated into the theory, and tested. In addition, many different types of expectancy violations should be explored and incorporated into the model. Presently, violations related to language intensity are the only ones to have been explored systematically. Furthermore, following McGuire's lead, the effect of active participation in the construction of one's own defenses should be investigated. Finally, Burgoon and his associates have yet to address the long-term persistence of effects created by expectancy violations and context variables. Given some time for development and testing, these problems may be solved.

Finally, we must examine the three-factor model in relation to our action-oriented view of persuasive communication. Like McGuire's theory, Burgoon's formulation is causal and mechanistic in tone. As we have seen, its focus is on "threatening" and "pretreating" relatively passive people so they can better defend themselves against external persuasive assaults. Thus far, little effort has been made to integrate more actional dimensions into the model. But despite its "hypodermic needle" quality, the theory's focus on active counterarguing is consistent with an action-oriented approach to persuasive communication.

A Cognitive Response Model of Resistance to Persuasion

Developed by Richard Petty and John Cacioppo, the cognitive response model, like Burgoon's theory, relies on McGuire's notion of motivation to counterargue as a crucial mediator of resistance to persuasion.[28] Like Burgoon's model, the cognitive response approach applies to all types of attitudes, including those subjected to prior counterattack and not just truisms. However, unlike both inoculation theory and the three-factor model, Petty's and Cacioppo's theory does not emphasize causal, externally imposed pretreatments to motivate people to resist persuasion. Rather, the cognitive response model focuses on: (1) motivating people to *think* about their own attitudinal positions; and (2) allowing them sufficient *time* prior to a persuasive attack to develop their own idiosyncratic defenses against counterpersuasion. These defenses consist of positive arguments supporting a person's own attitudes, a defensive factor deemphasized by McGuire and Burgoon, as well as counterarguments to refute antagonistic positions.

According to cognitive response theory, a primary motivational cue is to *forewarn* people of an impending attack, a strategy originally suggested by McGuire and Papageorgis.[29] Presumably, people will use the time period between the warning and the attacking message to consider supportive and refutational arguments. These anticipatory responses should lead to resistance to later counterpersuasion. It is critically important to note that, unlike McGuire and Burgoon, Petty and Cacioppo do not regard forewarning as a threatening strategy designed to stimulate latent defensive antibodies. Rather, they see forewarning as just one means of focusing attention on a certain attitudinal issue and motivating a person to think carefully about the issue; it is a useful, but not a necessary condition for promoting resistance to persuasion. As Petty and Cacioppo put it, "It is not the forewarning per se that produces resistance to persuasion, but the fact that persons are motivated by the warning to consider more fully their own positions."[30] And anything, including self-motivation, that gets a person to think about some attitudinal issue and to covertly argue and counterargue should create resistance to future counterpersuasion.

A final, important feature of cognitive response theory is methodological in nature. Unlike inoculation theory and Burgoon's three-factor model, cognitive response theorists have formulated specific procedures for directly measuring supportive and counterarguments against a persuasive attack. Two of these measurement procedures were discussed in Chapter 9 when we considered Anthony Greenwald's cognitive response theory. The first is a "thought listing" procedure in which people are asked to list all the covert cognitions that occur to them prior to and during exposure to a persuasive message. These covert thoughts are later classified as supportive arguments, counterarguments, or neutral points irrelevant to the persuasive message. The second measurement technique is physiological in nature. An electromyogram (EMG) is used to monitor oral and facial indices of subvocal speech activity prior to and during exposure to a persuasive message. The EMG is capable of identifying the presence of covert argumentation and of detecting the affective tone, either positive or negative, of a person's covert speech activity. As we saw in Chapter 9, both methods have been used successfully to measure the covert production of arguments.

Some Experimental Tests of the Cognitive Response Model

Petty and Cacioppo conducted a study in which undergraduates were exposed to a counterattitudinal message arguing that "seniors, graduating in 1978 and beyond, be required to pass a comprehensive examination in their declared major." Some students were given a 5¼-minute forewarning of the impending message. Others were forewarned immediately prior to the speech, and a third group received no forewarning. The thought-listing procedure was used to measure covert argumentation. After exposure to the counterpersuasion, attitudes were measured on an 11-point scale, with 1 indicating "do not agree at all" and 11 denoting "agree completely."

The results showed that unwarned subjects were more persuaded by the attack (a mean attitude of 8.80) than subjects who received the 5¼-minute forewarning (mean attitude of 6.55). Importantly, subjects warned just prior to the attack recorded a mean attitude of 9.15, higher than that of either of the other groups. A check on covert argument production showed that subjects receiving the 5¼-minute forewarning generated substantially more counterarguments and supportive arguments than did either of the other two groups. In contrast, these two groups produced twice as many neutral or irrelevant thoughts as the subjects receiving advanced warning.[31] Beyond demonstrating the effectiveness of forewarning in creating resistance, this study underscored the importance of time to think before an attack. Without adequate time to generate supportive and refutational material, just-warned subjects showed somewhat less resistance to counterpersuasion than did individuals who received no warning at all.

In a second study, Petty and Cacioppo questioned whether forewarning is necessary to motivate people to think up defenses for their attitudes. Some undergraduates were warned 3 minutes ahead of an impending attack on their attitudes concerning student housing, and others were not warned. In addition, a third group of subjects was not forewarned, but was asked to think for 3 minutes about student housing. The thought-listing procedure was again used to measure covert argumentation. After hearing a counterattitudinal message, attitudes were measured on an 11-point scale, where 1 indicated "totally disagree" and 11 meant "totally agree."

The results, displayed in Table 12.5, reconfirmed that forewarning plus time to think leads to resistance and generates substantial supportive and counterargumentation when compared to the responses of unwarned subjects. Of primary interest was the finding that merely thinking about the topic with no threat or forewarning generated resistance equivalent to that shown by the warned subjects. Additionally, thinking

TABLE 12.5: MEAN ATTITUDES AND COGNITIVE RESPONSES AS FUNCTIONS OF FOREWARNING AND THINKING

Measures	No forewarning	Forewarning	Thinking without forewarning
Attitude°	6.27	4.20	4.60
Counterarguments	.00	3.46	2.67
Supportive arguments	.00	2.20	1.73
Neutral thoughts	4.93	.27	.60

°The higher the mean, the less the resistance to counterpersuasion.

Adapted from Richard E. Petty and John T. Cacioppo, "Forewarning, Cognitive Responding, and Resistance to Persuasion," *Journal of Personality and Social Psychology*, 35, 1977, p. 652. Copyright 1977 by the American Psychological Association. Reprinted by permission.

without forewarning resulted in substantial topic-relevant arguing and a small number of irrelevant thoughts.[32] Thus, this study successfully demonstrated the importance of time and thought, independent of threat, in creating resistance to counterpersuasion.[33]

In a final set of experiments, Cacioppo and Petty demonstrated the use of physiological techniques to measure covert argumentation after forewarning and during counterpersuasion. Subjects were forewarned 1 minute before hearing a taped message arguing either for stricter control of alcoholic beverages or stricter hours for coed dormitory visitation. Oral and facial electromyograms (EMGs) were used to measure subvocal speech prior to the forewarning (to establish a baseline for comparison), during the period between forewarning and exposure to the message, and finally, during actual exposure to the 2-minute counterattitudinal message.

The results showed that oral EMG activity, and therefore subvocal speech, was elevated significantly above the basal levels when subjects were waiting for the message, indicating anticipatory argumentation. During the actual presentation of the message, oral EMG activity was again significantly higher than basal levels. Moreover, measures of facial EMG activity confirmed that the affective tone of the subjects' covert linguistic activity was predominantly negative, indicating the presence of substantial counterarguing prior to and during exposure to counterpersuasion. Importantly, Cacioppo and Petty found that EMG activity correlated positively with self-reported, covert arguing as indicated by the thought-listing procedure.[34] This study is significant because it confirmed directly that thought and covert argumentation are present prior to an expected attack and during the attack itself. Moreover, the study provided support for the validity of the thought-listing procedure as a mode of detecting thought and subvocal arguing against persuasion.

A Critical Appraisal of the Cognitive Response Model

From our perspective, the cognitive response model of resistance is appealing because of its actional orientation. Unlike McGuire's and Burgoon's formulations, it does not rely on elaborately planned, externally provided pretreatments to create resistance to persuasion. Rather, it emphasizes that people can muster their own defenses against counterpersuasion if given sufficient time to think carefully about their attitudinal stances. Although forewarning is perceived as a useful motivator of thought, its presence is not regarded as essential. Moreover, when forewarning is employed, its motivational utility does not derive from threat. Rather, forewarning is seen as just one of many strategies that can motivate people to consider carefully their attitudinal positions. Other strategies include self-motivation to think about an issue and any nonthreatening external factor that makes an attitudinal issue salient to a person. From the cognitive response perspective, providing time for people to construct unique, goal-oriented defenses against persuasion is the crucial mediator of resistance. As such, the cognitive response model is an important contribution to an action-oriented approach to creating resistance to persuasion.

Additionally, cognitive response theorists have made the singularly important contribution of providing and validating two specific strategies for directly measuring covert arguing and counterarguing.[35] Thus, cognitive response theory, in comparison to inoculation theory and the three-factor model, is not so vulnerable to alternative explanations for observed effects.

Nevertheless, cognitive response theory is not without problems, a primary one relating to the probable long-term effects of time and thought in creating resistance to persuasion. McGuire's research established that threatening pretreatments are substantially more effective in conferring long-term resistance than nonthreatening ones. Since cognitive response theory does not rely on threat as a motivator, the question of persistence of induced effects must be raised. In a study not directly concerned with resistance to persuasion, Watts and Holt presented some evidence bearing on this problem. They found that forewarning does, in fact, depress immediate attitude change in response to a first message, a result duplicating Petty's and Cacioppo's work. However, on measuring attitude change one week later, they discovered that attitudes had returned to their initial positive level.[36] Although these results suggest that the effects of forewarning and thought are short-lived, they must be interpreted with care. The subjects in the Watts and Holt study were not exposed to a second attack one week after the first. Thus, we cannot be certain that, had they been reattacked, they would not have mustered appropriate defenses against delayed counterpersuasion. Given these uncertainties, future research must determine how long the effect of time and thought, independent of threat, may be expected to persist.

A second problem with the cognitive response model concerns procedures for measuring covert arguing. Although both the thought-listing and the EMG procedures have been validated in several studies, each has generated some criticism. For example, it has been argued that the thought-listing procedure may produce covert responses that would not occur naturally without an experimental request. And, it is possible that the EMG technique, requiring subjects to be attached to monitoring equipment, may produce positive or negative linguistic activity unrelated to the persuasive event. Although cognitive response theorists have presented impressive evidence to support the validity and reliability of each of these two procedures, additional methodological refinement would remove all doubt.

NOTES

1. Jules Witcover, *Marathon: The Pursuit of the Presidency 1972–1976* (New York: Viking Press, 1977), pp. 534–535.

2. William J. McGuire, "Inducing Resistance to Persuasion: Some Contemporary Approaches," in *Advances in Experimental Social Psychology*, ed. Leonard Berkowitz (New York: Academic Press, 1964), p. 192.

3. McGuire, "Inducing Resistance," p. 200.

4. William J. McGuire, "The Effectiveness of Supportive and Refutational Defenses in Immunizing and Restoring Beliefs against Persuasion," *Sociometry* 24 (1961): 184.

5. McGuire, "Inducing Resistance," p. 200.

6. Ibid.

7. Ibid., p. 201.

8. William J. McGuire and Demetrios Papageorgis, "The Relative Efficacy of Various Types of Prior Belief-Defense in Producing Immunity against Persuasion," *Journal of Abnormal and Social Psychology* 62 (1961): 327–337. The reason for the superiority of the refutational over the supportive defense in conferring resistance to persuasion may explain the relative superiority of two-sided versus one-sided messages in creating resistance. The two-sided message, in mentioning counterarguments, may be seen as threatening and thus may motivate people to build defenses against future attack. One-sided messages, like supportive defenses, contain no such threatening dimensions.

9. Demetrios Papageorgis and William J. McGuire, "The Generality of Immunity to Persuasion Produced by Pre-Exposure to Weakened Counterarguments," *Journal of Abnormal and Social Psychology* 62 (1961): 475–481.

10. William J. McGuire and Demetrios Papageorgis, "Effectiveness of Forewarning in Developing Resistance to Persuasion," *Public Opinion Quarterly* 26 (1962): 24–34.

11. Lynn R. Anderson, unpublished research described in McGuire, "Inducing Resistance," pp. 212–213.

12. McGuire, "Inducing Resistance," p. 216.

13. The rationales for McGuire's predictions regarding active versus passive participation lack the clarity and cogency of the other hypotheses we have covered. We will address this issue when we evaluate inoculation theory. For McGuire's discussion of the active–passive participation, see McGuire, "Inducing Resistance," pp. 215–221.

14. McGuire and Papageorgis, "The Relative Efficacy."

15. William J. McGuire, "Resistance to Persuasion Conferred by Active and Passive Prior Refutation of the Same and Alternative Counterarguments," *Journal of Abnormal and Social Psychology* 63 (1961): 326–332.

16. McGuire, "Inducing Resistance," p. 222.

17. Ibid.

18. William J. McGuire, "Persistence of the Resistance to Persuasion Induced by Various Types of Prior Defenses," *Journal of Abnormal and Social Psychology* 64 (1962): 241–248.

19. This experiment is reported in McGuire, "Inducing Resistance," pp. 225–227.

20. For example, see Bert Pryor and Thomas M. Steinfatt, "The Effects of Initial Belief Level on Inoculation Theory and Its Proposed Mechanisms," *Human Communication Research* 4 (1978): 217–230.

21. This argument was advanced by Thomas M. Steinfatt, "Resistance to Persuasion" (unpublished MS, Michigan State University, 1970).

22. See McGuire, "Inducing Resistance," pp. 217–218.

23. Ibid., pp. 219–220.

24. The three-factor model is articulated in Michael Burgoon et al., "An Empirical Test of a Model of Resistance to Persuasion," *Human Communication Research* 4 (1978): 27–39; Michael D. Miller and Michael Burgoon, "The Relationship between Violations of Expectations and the Induction of Resistance to Persuasion," *Human Communication Research* 5 (1979): 301–313; and Charles L. Montgomery and Michael Burgoon, "The Effects of Androgyny and Message Expectations on Resistance to Persuasive Communication," *Communication Monographs* 47 (1980): 56–57.

25. Miller and Burgoon.

26. Burgoon et al.

27. Montgomery and Burgoon, p. 67.

28. For an explanation of the model see Richard E. Petty and John T. Cacioppo, "Forewarning, Cognitive Responding, and Resistance to Persuasion," *Journal of Personality and Social Psychology* 35 (1977): 645–655.

29. McGuire and Papageorgis, "Effectiveness of Forewarning."

30. Petty and Cacioppo, p. 645.

31. Ibid.

32. Ibid.

33. For further evidence bearing on the attitudinal effects of time and thought, see Abraham Tesser and Mary Charles Conlee, "Some Effects of Time and Thought on Attitude Polarization," *Journal of Personality and Social Psychology* 31 (1975): 262–270.

34. John T. Cacioppo and Richard E. Petty, "Attitudes and Cognitive Responses: An Electrophysiological Approach," *Journal of Personality and Social Psychology* 37 (1979): 2181–2199.

35. See Cacioppo and Petty; Petty and Cacioppo; and Bobby J. Calder, Chester A. Insko, and Ben Yandell, "The Relation of Cognitive and Memorial Processes to Persuasion in a Simulated Jury Trial," *Journal of Applied Social Psychology* 4 (1974): 62–93.

36. William A. Watts and Lewis E. Holt, "Persistence of Opinion Change Induced under Conditions of Forewarning and Distraction," *Journal of Personality and Social Psychology* 37 (1979): 775–789.

PART *4*

NEW DIRECTIONS
IN PERSUASION

CHAPTER 13

New Theoretical Directions in Persuasion: A Critical Appraisal

James B. Conant has observed that "the history of science demonstrates beyond a doubt that the really revolutionary and significant advances come not from empiricism, but from new theories."[1] Conant's assessment underscores the crucial role played by theory in the development of knowledge in any field. We have seen throughout this book that theory serves at least two important functions for scholars and practitioners of persuasion. First, it organizes and systematizes available knowledge about persuasive behaviors and effects. As Abraham Kaplan puts it, theory allows us to make sense of "what would otherwise be inscrutable or unmeaning empirical findings."[2] Second, theory has a heuristic function, suggesting new frontiers for investigation and new ways of thinking about familiar patterns of communication behavior.

In this chapter, we will critically assess the current status of theory in persuasion and examine the new directions in which it is presently moving. Finally, we will discuss some unfinished tasks, including our own view of the direction persuasion theory ought to take in the 1980s. Thus, the chapter represents a personal critique of what is and our views of what ought to be in persuasion theory. In undertaking this task, we hope to develop a critical focus for assessing the values and limitations of the diverse theories we have examined throughout this book.

NEW THEORETICAL DIRECTIONS

During the 1960s and early 1970s, theoretical advances in persuasion centered around what might be called general theories of social influence. Such theories claimed to explain an exceedingly wide range of persuasive phenomena. A number of them appealed to some internal arousal state as the essential motivator of persuasive effects, and all of them embraced, in varying degrees, a number of mechanistic assumptions about people and their relation to the external environment. Thus, a common assumption was that some external stimulus "causes" cognitive and behavioral responses, either directly or indirectly by arousing an internal motivational state. Although Leon Festinger's cognitive dissonance theory keynoted this general theoretical era, other approaches such as social judgment–involvement theory and cognitive learning theories attracted a considerable following.

During the 1970s, interest in these general theories declined markedly because of three developments in persuasion. First, empirical research convincingly demonstrated that most general theories, in fact, lack the generality they originally were thought to possess. For instance, we saw in Chapter 5 that cognitive dissonance theory, rather than being the general formulation its author supposed, actually applies to a rather limited area of counterattitudinal behavior. The counterattitudinal advocate must have a perception of choice, perform for an unattractive sponsor, exert substantial effort, enact behaviors causing harm to others, receive little or no compensation for a counterattitudinal act, and the like. Obviously, few naturally occurring persuasive situations meet these stringent boundary requirements. Other general theories have suffered similar empirical shrinkage. For instance, Alice Eagly and Samuel Himmelfarb argue that social judgment–involvement theory has little or no relevance to any communication phenomena "that cannot be readily conceptualized and operationalized in terms of their influence on latitudes of acceptance and rejection."[3] Thus, one reason for the diminished interest in general theories of persuasion is that they are not really general at all. Indeed, many are quite limited in scope.

A second reason for the declining interest in general theories is their loss of *unique* explanatory power. A number of appealing alternative theories have been proposed to account for the effects many general theories purported to explain. At least six alternative explanations for dissonance phenomena have arisen, including the incentive, self-perception, and impression management theories discussed in Chapter 5. Likewise, social judgment–involvement theory has been challenged by several alternative explanations, including cognitive response theory covered in Chapter 9 and Chapter 12. Finally, Skinnerian learning theories have been reinterpreted by social learning theorists like Albert Bandura whose approach we considered in Chapter 8. The loss of a unique explanatory capacity reduced considerably the utility of many general theories of persuasion.

Third and finally, early general theories of persuasion have fallen into disrepute because of their overwhelmingly mechanistic approach to human behavior, an approach regarded by many students of human behavior as too simplistic to account for the complexities of people's responses to messages. Many of the more recent alternative explanations just mentioned are actional in nature. For instance, the impression management explanation of dissonance phenomena focuses on the motivational properties of self-presentational goals. Similarly, the cognitive response account of social judgment effects, as well as Bandura's reinterpretation of learning theories, stress the reason-based nature of human responses to messages.

Replacing general theories are a growing number of *limited-range* theories, claiming to explain a relatively narrow domain of communicative behavior. Some of these theories, covered in this book, are Jack Brehm's reactance theory that considers only the consequences of lost freedoms; Anthony Greenwald's cognitive response model, focusing exclusively on the effects of self-generated messages; William McGuire's inoculation theory that addresses resistance to counterpersuasion; and social comparison theory, focusing on group conformity and polarization effects. The reader will note that, with a few exceptions like McGuire's formulation, most of these limited-range theories depend much less on mechanistic assumptions than the older theories of persuasion.[4]

This description of current limited-range theories reflects several new directions persuasion theorists presently are pursuing. The contemporary literature suggests at least three areas of theoretical interest that legitimately may be called "new directions." As such, each represents a dominant theme in the current literature and, at the same time, involves a clear break with past practices. These new lines of thought are: (1) a focus on information processing and the cognitive schematic processes underlying responses to messages; (2) an interest in self-generated cognitive and behavior changes; and (3) a concern with rules, or reason-based, approaches to persuasive communication. All three directions signal an abandonment of causal and logical positivist assumptions in favor of an actional view of people and a cognitive schematic approach to the external environment. Let's examine each of these approaches.

Information Processing and Cognitive Schemata

The past decade has witnessed a growing interest in information-processing approaches to persuasion. These approaches emphasize the cognitive schematic processes underlying message responses. Theorists and researchers are attempting to understand how cognitive schemata direct attention to certain aspects of messages, how they guide interpretation or the filling-in of personal meaning to messages, and how they direct the reconstructive storage of interpreted information in memory.[5] Our discussion of the cognitive bases of persuasion in Chapter 2 summarized many of these research findings.

This focus on how people interpret and reconstructively create messages for themselves and then respond to their own symbolic creations is a clear break with the logical positivist perspective on persuasive phenomena. You will recall from Chapter 3 that logical positivists consider the external environment, including persuasive messages, as an uninterpreted "reality" capable of "causing" effects in people exposed to it. In sharp contrast, the cognitive schematic view suggests that "reality" is, in fact, a construction of humans, who bring their uniquely personal assumptions and beliefs to bear on symbolic stimuli. Human action and persuasive effects are responses to self-created messages.

As a theoretical direction, the cognitive schematic approach assumes that persuasive effects are a product of the interpretive transformations people perform on the symbols conveyed in messages. This approach to theory-building contrasts sharply with early general theories that relegated messages to the role of uninterpreted stimuli capable of directly producing responses or indirectly influencing human action by arousing some internal state, like dissonance. In short, the cognitive schematic view suggests that persuasion theories ought to be based on the assumption that people change as a function of their unique cognitive responses to persuasive information.

A number of theories reviewed in this book reflect the cognitive schematic view of persuasive communication. Eugene Burnstein's information-processing theory of group polarization effects considered in Chapter 7, Norman Anderson's and Martin Fishbein's information integration theories covered in Chapter 10, Greenwald's cognitive response model discussed in Chapter 9 and Chapter 12, and Timothy Brock's commodity theory covered in Chapter 11 are pertinent examples.

Self-Generated Cognitive and Behavior Change

During the past five years, there has been a resurgence of interest in self-generated persuasive effects, in the effects of what we called in Chapter 1 original self-generated messages, those constructed by a person without external inducement.[6] In one sense, this theoretical direction is not really new at all since investigations of active participatory persuasion, including role-playing, date to World War II. But even so, the revitalized interest in self-produced persuasion classifies as a new direction for two reasons.

First, current research and theorizing do not rely, as did earlier work, on elaborate external inducements to engage people in self-persuasion. Earlier studies used structured psychodramatic exercises, contrived group discussions, and the like; but presently the focus is on more naturally occurring processes of self-persuasion. For example, Abraham Tesser typically investigates self-persuasion simply by asking people to take a few minutes to think about some issue. He has demonstrated repeatedly that nondirected thought produces a significant strengthening of initial attitudes, and that the longer people think, the greater the number of covert arguments they generate, and the more marked are the self-persuasive effects.[7]

There are also theoretical reasons for classifying the present interest in self-persuasion as a new direction. Early role-playing studies were essentially atheoretical in that researchers demonstrated the efficacy of self-generated messages without determining *why* they worked. In contrast, current research is guided by clear theoretical notions specifying why self-generated messages produce attitude and behavior change. The dominant theoretical paradigm is a cognitive schematic, information-processing one. Tesser has best elaborated it. He argues that "thought, under the direction of a schema, produces changes in beliefs, and these changes are often in the direction of greater schematic . . . consistency." Moreover, he contends, as we did in Chapter 2, that "attitudes are a function of one's beliefs." Tesser concludes his theoretical analysis of thought-induced self-persuasion by noting, "Since thought tends to make beliefs more evaluatively consistent [with one's cognitive schemata] and attitudes are a function of beliefs, thought will tend to polarize attitudes."[8]

Many of the theories reviewed in this book focus on self-generated information processing to explain cognitive and behavior changes. Incentive theory covered in Chapter 5, self-attribution theory considered in Chapter 6, social comparison and information-processing theories of group persuasion discussed in Chapter 7, and the persuasive models derived from social learning theory outlined in Chapter 8, all rely on original self-produced messages to explain attitude and behavior changes.

This new interest in active participatory, self-generated persuasion is a turning from a mechanistic view of people as passive reactors to external messages. Rather, it sees people as self-directed agents in control of their own cognitive and behavioral destiny. As such, it is an important new contribution to theorizing about persuasion and human action.

Rules-Based Approaches to Persuasion

We noted in discussion in Chapter 3 that the laws approach is the oldest theoretical tradition in persuasion, and that it has generated many more persuasion theories than has the relatively new rules approach. Although there currently are more laws than rules-based formulations, the present trend is toward the development of explicit rules-based theories to account for purposive human action.

Although recent rules-based theories rarely employ the term *rule*[9] and they often use lawlike language, the generative forces they specify are, in fact, goal oriented and reason based. For example, the impression management approach discussed in Chapter 5, and its conceptual cousin, social identity theory covered in Chapter 6, both explicitly claim that the generative force responsible for attitude and behavior change is the desire to present a positive public self-image. Similarly, the social comparison explanation for group conformity and polarization effects, discussed in Chapter 7, states that the generative force motivating attitude reinforcement and change is the desire to present socially acceptable attitudes to similar others. These three theories appeal to socially shared rules as the motivational bases for cognitive realignment and behavior change.

Other rules-based theories refer to idiosyncratic, as well as social, prescriptions for behavior. For example, psychological reactance theory, covered in Chapter 11, specifies that the personal desire to feel free to act as one wishes is the essential motivator of attitude change. Daniel Katz' functional theory, discussed in Chapter 2, argues that people adopt attitudes and behaviors for one or more of four reasons: to satisfy value-expressive, instrumental, knowledge, or ego-defensive needs. And incentive theory, considered in Chapter 5, states that we act to gain rewards and minimize punishments. Also, we saw that Brock's commodity theory, covered in Chapter 11, argues that people adopt positive attitudes toward those messages they expect will be personally useful to them. Finally, Bandura's social learning theory, addressed in Chapter 8, is an explicit rules-based approach. Recall that he argues that the essence of human behavior is the search for "if–then" rules specifying those actions one ought to take to maximize rewards and minimize unfortunate consequences.

Most of the rules-based perspectives examined in this book have been articulated since 1970. That theorists are beginning to explain purposive human actions from a teleological, rather than a causal, perspective is an important new contribution to persuasive communication theory.

FUTURE THEORETICAL DIRECTIONS IN PERSUASION: SOME UNFINISHED TASKS

We have seen that new directions in persuasion theory include a preference for limited-range theories, a focus on information processing, an interest in self-generated persuasive effects, and a concern with rules-based accounts of purposive responses to messages. These developments all signal a break with mechanistic and logical positivist assumptions in favor of an actional view of people and a cognitive schematic approach to persuasive messages. Despite the promise of these new approaches, several vexing problems must be solved, including: (1) the need to reconceptualize our thinking and revamp the language we use to describe persuasive communication; (2) the need for a general rules-based account of purposive persuasive actions; and (3) the need for a systematic methodology for studying rule-governed behaviors in persuasion.

Overhauling How We Think and Talk about Persuasion

There is substantial agreement among linguists that the language we use to describe a phenomenon structures the way we think about it; and conversely, that the cognitive assumptions we apply to an area of experience influence the language we select to describe that experience.[10] We believe that the discipline of persuasion presently suffers from a self-perpetuating syndrome wherein the use of inappropriate language to describe persuasive phenomena fosters erroneous assumptions about the nature of the persuasion process. Moreover, the application of erroneous assumptions leads us, in a circular fashion, to misdescribe the nature of persuasive communication.

This unfortunate state of affairs has, in our judgment, led to misunderstandings about the nature of persuasion, both by serious students of social influence and by the public as well. This many faceted problem originates in the traditional association of persuasion with the laws approach to theory and research. We will be considering two of the more serious aspects of the problem. We believe that both can be corrected only by radically overhauling how we think and talk about the process of persuasive communication.

Let's look first at the tendency of many contemporary persuasion theorists, even those whose approaches are implicitly rules-based, to describe *purposive* human action in the language of laws and to apply causal assumptions to behaviors that, in fact, are prompted by reasons. To illustrate the dimensions of this problem, recall that a typical law in persuasion states that some persuasive strategy, say high source-credibility, *causes* certain effects in people, for instance, compliance with recommendations. As we argued in Chapter 3, the phenomenon to be explained in this generalization, agreement with a credible communicator, behaves purposively, not causally, and should be described as such. People accept credible recommendations because they expect that doing so will fulfill goals or help them avoid undesirable consequences. Through past experiences, people undoubtedly learn that, *as a rule*, accepting the recommendations of credible communicators is more beneficial than going along with persuaders whose competence or trustworthiness is questionable. Or, alternatively, some people may feel that identifying with a competent persuader projects their ideal self-concepts as reasonable individuals. In either case, when people encounter a credible communicator, they typically act on the basis of these contextually relevant rules, or goal-oriented prescriptions, for behaving. Thus, in this case, compliance is not caused by high source-credibility, but rather is prompted by rules relevant to communicator credibility.

From the rules perspective, message strategies and responses are not causally linked, but, rather, covary because of a particular strategy's capacity to activate relevant rules that, in turn, generate responses. Relevant rules, not the persuasive strategy itself, generate purposive action. In our judgment, this conceptualization is a more meaningful description of the bases of purposive action than the laws assumption that message strategies cause responses.

Hence, we believe it is necessary to revise our ways of thinking and talking about persuasion. As a first step, we must abandon the view that persuasion theories describe *causal* connections between message strategies and *purposive* responses. Instead, we suggest that persuasion theories should be reconceptualized as generalizations describing probable covariations between persuasive strategies and purposive responses, given the nature of the contextually relevant rules in operation. If one accepts the view that people are choice-laden agents, who act to achieve their goals rather than react to the vagaries of external message strategies, then a purposive theory in persuasion cannot logically be construed otherwise. In our judgment, such a reconceptualization, accompanied by appropriate descriptive language, should greatly clarify the nature of the process of persuasive communication.

A second facet of the language–thought problem in persuasion also represents a legacy of the laws approach. Because laws theorists typically have applied mechanistic assumptions and used causal language to describe social influence processes, persuasion often is regarded by professionals and laypersons alike as a one-way process of influence, in which a persuader deliberately produces changes in one or more other persons.

This mechanistic view has led many people to regard persuasion as suspect, as a form of social manipulation. Indeed, professional writers in persuasion often perpetuate this view by including elaborate sections in their works on the "ethics of persuasion." These dissertations typically caution the student of persuasion to develop a "set of ethical and moral standards" to guide them when using the powerful tool of persuasion.[11] Our point here is not to eschew moral considerations in communicative relationships. To the contrary, we believe meaningful communication requires mutually agreeable standards for behaving. Rather, we are suggesting that a preoccupation with ethics may indicate an underlying assumption that persuasion is a unidirectional, causal form of influence designed to victimize choiceless people. Certainly, one rarely finds a similar preoccupation in books on dyadic communication, interpersonal communication, or small group communication, all subdisciplines that traditionally have not been associated with the causal laws approach.

Persuasion's historical association with causal laws is also reflected in the tendency of many professionals to view persuasion as manipulative communication that is somehow set apart from other forms of communicative interaction. The approach adopted in this book, of course, represents a rejection of this dichotomy. We regard persuasion as a developmental process of social influence among people who share a sense of control over the interaction and a perception of choice to accept or reject their interpretation of others' messages. From this perspective, persuasion as a process of mutual influence is the stuff of which interpersonal communication, small group communication, and the like are made.[12]

The Need for a General Rules-Based Approach
to Persuasion

As we have seen, there are several rules-based theories of persuasion. Some are explicitly rules-related, and others are only implicit, couched in the language of laws. Although the increasing appeal to human goals to explain action in response to messages is promising, the field of communication has yet to produce a *general* rules-based theoretical perspective on purposive persuasive phenomena.[13]

Such a general theory should serve three important functions. First, it would provide a broad structure or theoretical umbrella under which current, often disparate, rules-based theories of persuasion could be organized, systematized, and hierarchically integrated with one another. Second, it would represent a new world view of persuasion, including a new set of actional assumptions and a new language appropriate to the purposive nature of persuasion—in short, a new framework for thinking and talking about persuasive communication, a sorely needed advance. Finally, a general rules-based perspective on persuasion should have enormous heuristic value, suggesting new ways of conceptualizing old patterns of persuasive interaction.

In Chapter 3, we advanced some guidelines for constructing a general rules-based perspective. An axiomatic form was suggested as especially appropriate. You will recall that axiomatic theory is an interrelated, hierarchically ordered set of propositions, including axioms assumed to be true, and theorems deduced from the axioms that are empirically testable. Of course, to develop a rules-based perspective based on the axiomatic form, we must first specify axioms. From a rules perspective, these most certainly would include: (1) the belief that humans are self-directed agents with a capacity for choice; (2) the belief that much human action is rule governed, that is, people are goal oriented and strive to maximize rewards and minimize punishments; and (3) the belief that persuasive messages are a creation of human cognitive schematic structures.

A general rules-based approach to persuasion would also entail reconceptualizing the nature of persuasive messages. They would have to be seen as sets of symbols whose twin purposes are: (1) to make contextually relevant human goals salient; and (2) to stipulate those actions a person must take, should take, or must not take in order to achieve salient goals. Thus, from a rules perspective, *persuasive communication is reconceptualized as a symbolic activity involving the coordination of human action according to contextually relevant rules.*

Following the stipulation of axioms and a reconceptualization of the nature of persuasive communication, rule-related theorems could then be deduced and empirically tested. One such theorem suggested in Chapter 3 was: Given their choice-laden and goal-oriented nature, people will comply with persuasive messages specifying contextually relevant rules, or prescriptions, for achieving goals more often than they will comply with messages stipulating contextually irrelevant rules. Innumerable other theorems could be deduced from the general axioms underpinning a rules-based view of persuasive communication.

After developing a general set of axioms and theorems, the next task of persuasive theorists would be to develop interrelated axioms and theorems relevant to particular areas of persuasion. These areas might include *dyadic persuasion,* or two-person influence; *small-group persuasion,* involving more than two communicators engaged in face-to-face interaction; *public persuasion,* entailing one or more persuaders and a relatively large audience; *organizational persuasion,* involving an interrelated system of small communicating groups; and *mass persuasion,* entailing the physical separation of communicating parties.

Some of the axioms and theorems relevant to these disparate areas of persuasion would be the same, others would be different. One obvious difference concerns the types of rules peculiar to different contexts. For instance, small-group and organizational persuasion should be dominated by socially shared rules, but dyadic, public, and mass persuasion should mix social and idiosyncratic rule-structures. However, across all persuasive forms, a rules-based perspective requires that persuasion be seen as symbolic activity involving the coordination of human action according to contextually relevant rules.

This reconceptualization should prompt professionals and laypersons alike to assume a more realistic view of the role of persuasion in all human interaction. As a general term, *human communication* has been described as "the coordinated management of meaning," focusing "on the coordination procedures by which individuals intermesh their own action with those of someone else" to produce shared meanings.[14] Assuming this view is reasonable, it should be apparent that that coordination is accomplished largely by mutual, social influence processes. Persuasive coordination strategies may range from subtle influence among friends or lovers to blatant attempts by advertisers to manipulate consumer buying behaviors. Whether subtle or manipulative, the coordinated management of meaning is, from our perspective, a product of mutual persuasive interaction.

These proposals are merely a first step. The task of constructing a full-blown general rules account of persuasive phenomena remains unfinished. Thus, a clear theoretical imperative is the generation of this new "world view" of persuasion and human purposive action.

The Need for a Systematic Methodology for Studying Rules in Persuasion

In our discussion of research methods in Chapter 4, two methodological deficiencies associated with the rules perspective were mentioned. First, we noted that rules researchers currently lack a well-developed methodology for identifying rules. This difficulty is particularly acute in the case of idiosyncratic rules, involving personalized ways of fulfilling goals. The problem is further complicated because many rules researchers disagree as to whether rules should be defined from the perspective of the rule-user or the observer of others' rule-following behavior. Although most rules researchers opt for determining rules from the view of the rule-user, the methodology is problematic since people are often not consciously aware of the specific rules prompting their behavior.

As this analysis suggests, an important task facing rules-oriented persuasion theorists is to develop a unified set of research tools for locating and verifying both socially shared and idiosyncratic rules. Fortunately, using both naturalistic and correlational research methods, rules theorists are making progress in this area.[15]

A second methodological deficiency in the rules perspective concerns the tendency of many rules researchers to shy away from the experimental methodology because of its association with laws research. As we argued in Chapter 4, this practice is misguided and self-defeating since it deprives rules researchers of a powerful tool for establishing generative links between goals and actions. We believe that rules researchers, by applying actional assumptions to the experimental methodology, can revitalize it and use it in the discovery and verification of rules. By experimentally manipulating contextually relevant rules in messages, researchers can both identify rules and confirm the generative relationship between rules and the purposive actions they prompt. Such a revitalization would, in our judgment, represent a major contribution to the methodological arsenal rules researchers presently possess.

NOTES

1. James B. Conant, *Modern Science and Modern Man* (New York: Columbia University Press, 1952), p. 53.

2. Abraham Kaplan, *The Conduct of Inquiry* (San Francisco: Chandler Publishing, 1964), p. 302.

3. Alice H. Eagly and Samuel Himmelfarb, "Current Trends in Attitude Theory and Research," in *Readings in Attitude Change*, ed. Samuel Himmelfarb and Alice Hendrickson Eagly (New York: John Wiley, 1974), p. 596.

4. For a fuller discussion of the preference for limited-range theories, see Eagly and Himmelfarb, pp. 595–601.

5. For a summary of recent trends in information processing, see E. Tory Higgins, C. Peter Herman, and Mark P. Zanna, eds., *Social Cognition: The Ontario Symposium* (Hillsdale, N.J.: Lawrence Erlbaum, 1981).

6. For a summary of recent research on self-generated persuasion, see Abraham Tesser, "Self-Generated Attitude Change," in *Advances in Experimental Social Psychology*, ed. Leonard Berkowitz (New York: Academic Press, 1978), pp. 289–338.

7. See Tesser; Abraham Tesser and Christopher Leone, "Cognitive Schemas and Thought as Determinants of Attitude Change," *Journal of Experimental Social Psychology* 13 (1977): 340–356; and Abraham Tesser and Mary Charles Conlee, "Some Effects of Time and Thought on Attitude Polarization," *Journal of Personality and Social Psychology* 31 (1975): 262–270.

8. Tesser, p. 290.

9. A noticeable exception is a very recent formulation by Kathleen Kelley Reardon. She argues that human action is generated by rules of *appropriateness, consistency,* and *effectiveness.* See *Persuasion: Theory and Context* (Beverly Hills, Calif.: Sage Publications, 1981).

10. For example, see Lev Semenovich Vygotsky, *Thought and Language*, trans. Eugenia Hanfmann and Gertrude Vakar (Cambridge, Mass.: MIT Press, 1962); Benjamin L. Whorf, "The Relations of Habitual Thought and Behavior to Language," in *Language, Thought and Reality*, ed. John B. Carroll (Cambridge, Mass.: MIT Press, 1956), pp. 134–159; and Jean Piaget, *The Language and Thought of the Child*, trans. Marjorie Worden (New York: Harcourt, Brace & World, 1926).

11. For some examples, see Erwin P. Bettinghaus, *Persuasive Communication* (New York: Holt, Rine-

hart & Winston, 1980), pp. 14–19; Charles U. Larson, *Persuasion: Reception and Responsibility* (Belmont, Calif.: Wadsworth, 1979), pp. 248–275; Wayne C. Minnick, *The Art of Persuasion* (Boston: Houghton Mifflin, 1968), pp. 278–288; and Richard L. Johannesen, ed., *Ethics and Persuasion: Selected Readings* (New York: Random House, 1967).

12. A similar perspective is taken in Gerald R. Miller and Michael Burgoon, "Persuasion Research: Review and Commentary," in *Communication Yearbook 2*, ed. Brent D. Ruben (New Brunswick, N.J.: Transaction Books, 1978), pp. 29–47.

13. Kathleen Reardon's approach, mentioned in note 9, is quite comprehensive in scope and, therefore, may be regarded by many persuasion theorists as a *general* rules theory of persuasion. See *Persuasion*, especially Chapters 1 and 5.

14. W. Barnett Pearce, "The Coordinated Management of Meaning: A Rules-Based Theory of Interpersonal Communication," in *Explorations of Interpersonal Communication*, ed. Gerald R. Miller (Beverly Hills, Calif.: Sage Publications, 1976), p. 24.

15. For a discussion of methodologies presently available to rules researchers, see Susan B. Shimanoff, *Communication Rules: Theory and Research* (Beverly Hills, Calif.: Sage Publications, 1980), pp. 137–198.

CHAPTER 14

New Directions in the Practice of Persuasion

It is common to hear the terms *theory* and *practice* contrasted as if *theory* means something impractical or unrealistic, and *practice* refers to the "real" world. Throughout this book, we have rejected such a dichotomy. We agree with a statement attributed to psychologist Kurt Lewin that, in persuasion, as in all facets of life, "there is nothing so practical as a good theory." In this chapter, we expect to demonstrate the wisdom of Lewin's dictum. Although our discussion will focus on the practice of persuasion, our primary purpose is to demonstrate that theories are essential for understanding why some persuasive attempts succeed, and others fail.

In considering the practice of persuasion, we will: (1) examine some of the major differences between face-to-face and mass persuasion; (2) consider several new directions in the practice of mass persuasion, including political persuasion and commercial advertising; (3) explore some new directions in the practice of interpersonal, face-to-face persuasion, in part by presenting case studies of religious conversion and ideological indoctrination; (4) look at how the practice of mass and interpersonal persuasion conforms to or diverges from the theoretical models covered in this book; and (5) evaluate the contributions theories make to understanding persuasion practices.

FACE-TO-FACE PERSUASION AND MASS PERSUASION

The practice of persuasion takes the form either of face-to-face interaction or mass media persuasion. Face-to-face persuasion is characterized by direct contact between the communicating parties. Feedback, or the responses of each communicator to the messages of the other, is rapid and continuous. In contrast, the mass media are characterized by the interposition of either an electronic device or the printed page between communicating parties; thus, feedback occurs on a delayed basis.

Before considering some of the major differences between face-to-face and mass persuasion, it will be useful to see how the two modes pervade our lives. Certainly, face-to-face persuasion is an integral part of our daily lives. So long as two or more people are together in groups, mutual interaction and persuasive influence are inevitable. Such groups include the interpersonal dyad, the primary family unit, peer and neighborhood groups, business, political, and social organizations, and large institutions, such as educational centers and religious orders. All of our interpersonal relationships, our basic values, and ultimately, our self-concepts, emerge and evolve over a lifetime of communicating with other people.

Aside from interpersonal persuasion, we are all bombarded daily with mass media messages attempting to sell us products, people, and ideas. Of the major media forms, television is by far the most pervasive. Currently, there are over 112 million television sets in the United States, reaching well over 95 percent of the homes in America.[1] Bower reported that the average television set is on between six and seven hours per day and that, during the prime evening hours, all major national demographic groups are represented proportionately.[2] During prime time, viewers typically are exposed to from 60 to 90 commercial advertisements, public service announcements, political messages, and other persuasive appeals.

In contrast to television's growing audience, newspaper and magazine readership has declined, particularly during the 1970s, which saw a marked increase in non-readers.[3] Likewise, radio ranks third among Americans as a source of information and believability, behind television and newspapers.[4] The influence of television vis-à-vis the other media probably reflects a general change in America's entertainment habits. For instance, in 1938, a Gallup poll showed that reading was the most popular evening entertainment. However, by 1974, Gallup reported that only 14 percent of those persons interviewed preferred reading, whereas 46 percent said they liked to spend their evening hours watching television.[5]

In general, if one considers all mass media forms to which we are exposed, it is estimated that each of us pays some attention to about 76 advertisements during an average day, and probably comes into physical contact with many more.[6]

Differences Between the Influence Modes

Having examined the pervasiveness of face-to-face and mass persuasion, it is now time to look at some of the major differences between the two. Differences can be grouped into two categories: the *means* of social influence each employs; and the kinds of *effects* the two modes typically produce.

As to means of social influence, mass media persuaders rely almost exclusively on persuasive appeals or *information control* to effect change, but interpersonal persuaders often mix persuasive appeals and coercive strategies, entailing *information control and reinforcement control,* respectively. These differences occur primarily because mass media communicants are physically separated from one another, whereas face-to-face communicators interact directly. Consider the case of the media advertiser. The designers of commercials and political advertisements can't reward or punish their physically remote, anonymous viewers and readers. And since they don't control reinforcements, advertisers must rely on warnings or mendations to get people to accept recommended actions.

In contrast, face-to-face communicators not only control information about naturally occurring reinforcements, but they also often have the explicit power to reward and punish one another for accepting or rejecting recommendations. For example, we saw in Patty Hearst's conversion that the members of the Symbionese Liberation Army used reinforcement controls and persuasive appeals to accomplish their objectives. Such an opportunity to reward and punish is rarely available to mass media persuaders since their messages are directed toward anonymous, remote audiences.

As with means, the kinds of *effects* typically produced by face-to-face and mass persuasion also diverge. Although interpersonal persuasion is an effective means of generating basic cognitive *changes* in people,[7] the primary effect of mass persuasion is to *reaffirm* preexisting attitudes, norms, and cultural values.[8] Indeed, mass persuaders rarely attempt to alter fundamental cognitive schemata or basic values. Rather, mass media persuasion typically is directed toward channeling, or "canalizing," preexisting cognitive and behavior patterns into paths promoting the sale of particular products or political candidates.[9]

For example, most of us have been socially conditioned to use deodorants, colognes, and so on. Advertisers make no attempt to reshape these behavior patterns. Rather they offer us what they hope are new and more exciting ways to enact established ways of behaving. Slogans like "Secret—the deodorant that's made for a woman," and "Aqua Velva—A man needs to smell like a man," illustrate this strategy. Similarly, political advertising is often aimed at identifying the candidate with the values, attitudes, and fantasies of the electorate. In *The Selling of the President 1968,* Joe McGinnis discussed one of Richard Nixon's television commercials that illustrates this identification strategy. The advertisement used a series of flashing pictures and a voice-over from Mr. Nixon. Said McGinnis:

> Nixon would say his same old tiresome things but no one would have to listen. The flashing pictures would be carefully selected to create the impression that somehow Nixon represented competence, respect for tradition, serenity, faith that the American people were better than people anywhere else, and that all these problems others shouted about meant nothing in a land blessed with the tallest building, strongest armies, biggest factories, cutest children, and rosiest sunsets in the world. Even better: through association with these pictures, Richard Nixon could *become* these very things.[10]

In summary, face-to-face persuasion mediates change, as in religious conversion or ideological indoctrination, a conclusion further documented in later discussion. In contrast, mass persuasion is especially useful for linking new ideas and products with old values and well-established patterns of behavior.

THE PRACTICE OF MASS PERSUASION

In contrasting face-to-face with mass persuasion, we have seen that the mass media, relying on information control, are particularly useful for reaffirming basic values and for linking new ideas and courses of action with well-established schemata. Let's look at some examples of mass persuasion as it is used in political and commercial advertising.

Political Persuasion and Image Making

A primary function of mass persuasion in political campaigns is the making and maintaining of a candidate's image—the creation of an appearance of competence, strength, sincerity, and the like. As a media adviser to former President Nixon once put it: "It's not what's *there* [within the candidate] that counts, it's what's projected—and carrying it one step further, it's not what [the candidate] projects, but rather what the voter receives." The response of the media viewer, he continues, "is to the image, not the man."[11] The mass media, especially television, are well suited for building and maintaining political images for at least three reasons, each of which we will illustrate with case studies taken from the 1976 and 1980 presidential election campaigns.

First, as we suggested earlier, the mass media are an especially effective means of linking a candidate with the basic values, ideals, and longings of the electorate. Moreover, this linking strategy is usually accomplished through the use of nonverbal symbols rather than verbal ones. Recall Richard Nixon's identification strategy just discussed. Similarly, many of the strategies Jimmy Carter used during the 1976 campaign exemplify this linking tactic. Mr. Carter often appeared in television commercials in casual clothes, including blue jeans and work shirts. He was filmed with his wife and family, working on his farm or attending religious services, all of which buttressed Mr. Carter's image as a Washington outsider, a good husband and father, a born again Christian and a farmer. The aura of casualness, simplicity, and sincerity he projected seemed to signal a return to the agrarian values upon which Americans have always fantasized the country was founded. By linking himself with the central values of many ordinary Americans, a person the press had referred to barely two years before as "Jimmy Who?" was elected to the highest office in the land.[12]

These examples suggest a second reason for the media's effectiveness in building, and sometimes breaking, positive political images. The mass media, especially television, are more effective in projecting notions about a candidate's character than in illuminating his or her qualifications for office. For example, in the 1980 presidential primary campaigns, former Texas governor John Connally outspent all his Republican rivals in buying television time to detail his background in government and qualifications to be president. Despite this expenditure of money and effort, Mr. Connally's connections with the Nixon White House and his image as a shady, "Texas wheeler-dealer" prevailed and derailed his candidacy. Similarly, Democratic contender, Massachusetts Senator Edward Kennedy, had great difficulty in getting the American public to listen to his programs for dealing with the nation's economic problems because of the Chappaquiddick incident and the resulting image of him as a reckless man.

In contrast, Mr. Carter exploited the character issue to his advantage during the primaries. His television advertisements consisted almost entirely of messages such as "You may not always agree with President Carter, but you'll never find yourself wondering whether he's telling you the truth"; and "President Carter. He keeps his word." One television advertisement used in the 1980 New York Democratic primary was particularly pointed. The only visual display in the advertisement was a New York ballot showing the names of Jimmy Carter and Edward M. Kennedy. An announcer then delivered this message:

> A man brings two things to a presidential ballot. He brings his record, and he brings himself. Who he is is frequently more important than what he's done. In the voting booth the voter must weigh both record and character before deciding. Often it's not easy. And the voter winds up asking—"Is this the *person* I really want in the White House for the next four years?"

Such advertisements concluded with the message: "President Carter. He's a solid man in a sensitive job."[13]

Third and finally, the media are especially effective in image building because they can create the *appearance* of competence in a political candidate even though carefully and deliberately avoiding any explicit demonstration of competence. This strategy is usually accomplished with ambiguous verbal messages, along with nonverbal symbols like music or visual images that distract viewers from the content of a candidate's message. One of Jimmy Carter's strategies in the 1976 presidential primary campaign illustrates this tactic. After winning a string of impressive primary victories, Carter's campaign began to falter in April of 1976. He finished a poor fourth in the important New York primary, capturing only 12.8 percent of the popular vote. And during the same month, he won the Wisconsin primary by a mere 1 percent over his closest competitor.

At this point, Carter's advisers were forced to consider what was going wrong. Pat Caddell, Carter's pollster, came up with some answers. His public opinion surveys showed that anywhere from 33 to 43 percent of the voters believed Jimmy Carter was "wishy-washy" and "fuzzy" on the issues. He was perceived either as avoiding discussion of specific issues or as constantly changing his position on them, depending on the particular audience he was addressing. Caddell argued that if these public attitudes went unchecked they would inevitably "lead to perceptions" of Carter as incompetent, untrustworthy, and dishonest.

Carter's advisers moved immediately to combat this problem. Gerald Rafshoon, Carter's chief media adviser, came up with a cut-rate plan to combat the image problem. He took Carter's existing television spots, all of which were deliberately vague on issues and contained a number of nonverbal distracters, and had an announcer read new introductions to them: "Jimmy Carter on the issue of health care"; "Jimmy Carter on the issue of unemployment"; and the like. Rafshoon also had the announcer read a new closing to the commercials: "If you see this *critical issue* the way Jimmy Carter does, then vote for him." Obviously, this clever manipulation of words did not clarify

Carter's position on the issues, but it substantially sharpened his *image* as a competent candidate for president.[14]

To recapitulate, mass persuasion is especially effective in building political images because it can visually link a candidate to cherished values, highlight character issues, and create the appearance of competence, even as it deliberately avoids specific issues.

Commercial Advertising

Advertising uses persuasive communication to promote the sale of commercial goods and services. Nonverbal symbols play a major role in commercial advertising, especially in television advertisements. Indeed, as we have pointed out elsewhere, the verbal dimension of much advertising often is limited to the repetition of a simple, but catchy slogan or musical jingle containing the brand name of the product. "Campbell soup is *Mmmm Mmmm* good"; and "Tums for the tummy" are typical examples. Sound effects, the physical setting, the attractiveness of the people in the commercials, and other visual displays generally carry the burden of selling many products and services.

Although the verbal dimensions of commercial messages typically are short and appear rather innocuous, they often are carefully constructed to convey impressions and create expectations about products or services that are either meaningless or misleading.[15] This usually is accomplished through the use of ambiguous language or nonsensical sentence constructions. Consider the following slogan once used by the Scott paper company to promote its bathroom tissue: "Scott makes it better for you." The implication is, of course, that Scott tissue is superior in quality to all comparable products. However, "better" can mean almost anything—better than other brands of bathroom tissue, better than Scott tissue used to be, or better than sandpaper for accomplishing its purposes! The slogan is deliberately vague, allowing the receiver to fill-in preferred implications.

The use of nonsense sentences in advertising slogans also can create confusing, but often very pleasant, feelings about a product. For example, the Clairol company once advertised its hair care product, Condition, in this way: "Condition actually makes your hair feel stronger.... Revitalizes your hair's inner strength, outer beauty." Or consider an advertisement once used to promote Calvert whiskey: "Calvert's Soft Whiskey—it does anything any other whiskey can do. It just does it softer." On the face of it, the two messages are logically inscrutable. What does a whiskey do when it "does it softer?" And how do you explain "hair feeling stronger"?

In an insightful analysis of television advertising, Herbert Krugman argues that such media advertising is effective because its content *is* "meaningless, nonsensical," and "uninvolving."[16] Given advertising's trivial, innocuous content, he maintains that our critical faculties, and therefore, our usual defenses against persuasive appeals are lowered. Consequently, we gradually absorb the pleasant implications of advertising messages without critical involvement. Further, he suggests that the endless repetition of meaningless slogans may in the long run alter our perception of a product, triggering purchasing behavior and then the realization of our changed frame of mind. For example, the Coca-Cola slogans, "Coke adds life" and "Have a Coke and a smile," may gradually become associated in our minds with vigor, youth, and the remembrance of good times with good friends. From Krugman's perspective, then, the trivial and nonsensical nature of commercial advertisements is a crucial persuasive ploy, fostering uncritical acceptance of many meaningless or misleading claims.

Commercial Advertising and Subliminal Persuasion

For over two decades, an influence strategy called subliminal persuasion has attracted considerable popular interest. Trade publications such as Vance Packard's best seller, *The Hidden Persuaders*, and, more recently, Wilson Key's books *Subliminal Seduction* and *Media Sexploitation* have been largely responsible for the subject's catching the public's fancy.[17] *Subliminal persuasion*, a highly controversial topic, typically is defined as influence that takes place without conscious awareness. According to students of subliminal persuasion, all of us are continually affected by symbolic stimulation that is undetectable by our five senses.

The public's interest in subliminal persuasion was first piqued by a quasi experiment conducted at a movie house in Fort Lee, New Jersey, in the fall of 1957. During the showing of the film, *Picnic*, James Vicary, a marketing researcher, flashed on the screen for 1/3000 of a second the messages, "Drink Coca-Cola" or "Hungry? Eat popcorn." He repeated the messages every five seconds throughout the film. The time exposure was so brief the messages were not detectable by the human eye; they were subliminal, below the level of conscious perception. After continuing his research for six weeks, Vicary reported that Coca-Cola sales in the theatre lobby increased by 57.7 percent and popcorn sales rose 18.1 percent.[18]

A more recent demonstration of the potential effectiveness of subliminal persuasion took place in 1979 when about 50 department stores in the United States and Canada installed what its inventor, Hal Becker, calls his "little black box." Basically a sound mixer like those used by disc jockeys, the box mingles bland music with subliminal antitheft messages such as "I am honest" and "I will not steal." Repeated 9,000 times an hour at a very low volume, the words are barely audible. After using the device on a trial basis for nine months, one East Coast department store chain reported a 37 percent drop in shoplifting for a savings of $600,000.[19]

Although these examples are isolated uses of subliminal persuasion, Key argues that all commercial advertisers, in fact, make extensive use of the technique. He suggests they do this by embedding written messages and images in advertisements, especially those appearing in magazines and other print media. The vast majority of the messages and images Key claims to have identified are sexual in nature. According to him, words like *sex*, as well as sexual images, such as erogenous zones, are airbrushed into advertisements for all sorts of products, including items as mundane as Ritz crackers. Although these messages are not readily visible, Key believes they are sexually arousing, and stimulate people to buy the advertised products.[20]

Key tested his hypothesis by showing over 1,000 adults a full-page advertisement for Gilbey's London Dry Gin that had appeared in the July 5, 1971, edition of *Time* magazine. The advertisement featured a frosty bottle of gin and a glass of gin and tonic on ice. The word *SEX* and images, such as male and female genitals, seemed to have been airbrushed into the photograph. All viewers were asked to express their feelings on seeing the advertisement. Whereas 38 percent of them reported seeing nothing but the bottle and glass and having no particular feelings about the photograph, 62 percent described themselves as feeling "satisfied," "sensuous," "sexual," "romantic," "stimulated," "aroused," "excited," or "horny." Key took this finding as support for his thesis.[21]

Methodological Problems with Subliminal Research

As interesting as these popular demonstrations of subliminal persuasion are, the reader will recognize that they are not terribly convincing from a scientific point of view. Two major problems are apparent. First, none of the three "experiments" used a control group to generate comparative baseline data. In all three cases, a control group would have consisted of people not exposed to any subliminal stimulation. For example, if Key had asked an additional 1000 persons to express their current feelings *without* showing them the Gilbey advertisement, it is entirely possible that about 62 percent might have reported feelings of satisfaction or excitement, and the balance might have said they were feeling little emotion at the time.

Similarly, Vicary did not compare his data on Coca-Cola and popcorn sales with sales in other comparable theatres where *Picnic* was shown without the subliminal stimulation. It is possible that sales in other theatres increased during the six-week test period because of the theme or setting of the movie or even by chance. If that were the case, one could not conclude that the increased sales in the target theatre were due to the subliminal messages. Finally, as to Mr. Becker's black box, it is possible that thefts were generally low in all department stores in 1979 or low in the 50 target stores for other reasons. Of course, it is also possible that the effects observed in each of the three studies were, in fact, due to subliminal persuasion. But even so, the studies' unscientific procedures make it impossible to establish what generative force was responsible for the observed effects.

A second problem with Key's research, not shared with the other two, is that he failed to measure the later buying behaviors of his subjects. Assuming he had done so and found that the 62 percent reporting arousal actually bought more Gilbey's gin, say over the next month, than the 38 percent who said they felt nothing, a better case might be made for his hypothesis. Since such follow-up research was not conducted, Key's test proved little, if anything, about the influence of subliminal stimulation.

The Current Status of Knowledge about Subliminal Persuasion

Despite its serious methodological shortcomings, Key's work has established that advertisers frequently embed erotic messages in their advertisements. However, whether these messages are actually perceived, consciously or unconsciously, by most viewers has not been established. Moreover, if perceived, whether the perceptions actually influence feelings and later actions has never been confirmed.

Only recently has there been a scientific effort to investigate the effects of subliminal persuasion. Wilson had female subjects listen to a taped passage from Daphne DuMaurier's *The Birds*.[22] Subjects used stereo headphones, and the passage was played into the subjects' right ears. Additionally, subjects were given a written copy of the passage and asked to edit it by slashing through all words in the written text not corresponding to the oral version. They were further instructed to "focus their complete attention on the literary passage" since it was expected to contain many errors, and "to ignore any extraneous sounds, regardless of the source.[23]

About 30 seconds after the taped passage had begun and without forewarning, Wilson played into the subjects' left ears a simple, low-volume melody containing six tones. After the editing phase of the experiment was over, Wilson again played a six-tone melody for the subjects, including three tones previously used and three new ones. He then asked subjects to indicate after each tone whether they had heard it during the editing task. Results showed that subjects could not differentiate between the familiar and novel tones above a chance level of recognition. Thus, they apparently were not consciously aware of the previously heard tones. However, they rated them as significantly more pleasant than the novel ones, confirming the hypothesis that familiarity breeds liking. In summarizing his findings, Wilson concluded that the "results suggest that an individual's positive feelings toward a previously encountered object are not dependent on consciously knowing or perceiving the object as familiar."[24] Any recognition of the previously heard tones was, he argued, "not at a level of conscious awareness."[25]

Wilson's findings are nonetheless preliminary, and considerably more scientific work must be done to confirm or disprove the efficacy of subliminal persuasion. Thus, we must conclude that subliminal persuasion, although an interesting direction in the practice of persuasion, is presently an unproved phenomenon.

Commercial Advertising and Consumer Information Processing

Developed within the last five years, the consumer information-processing (CIP) approach to advertising is a radical departure from the traditional techniques we have discussed so far. Instead of focusing on what advertising strategies "do to" consumers, CIP is a cognitive schematic approach emphasizing what consumers "do with" the information contained in advertisements. As Robert Chestnut puts it, the CIP paradigm addresses the question: "How is information (be it an advertisement, a sales presentation, or the product itself) processed within the framework of consumer problem-solving behavior?"[26]

As a cognitive schematic approach to advertising, the CIP approach focuses on the impact of human "perception, conscious evaluation, and long-term memory" on responses to commercial messages.[27] Because of its newness and the fact that the business community has reacted to the approach with considerable skepticism, few practical applications of CIP presently are available.[28] Thus, although it is an exciting new direction in advertising and is entirely compatible with what we know about humans as active agents, it is not yet a dominant trend in mass persuasion.

A Critical Assessment of Mass Persuasion Practices

It should be clear from our discussion that current practices in mass persuasion are, in many ways, highly mechanistic and at odds with much recent persuasive theory. Indeed, it is difficult to think of a more mechanistic approach than subliminal advertising since it assumes the total absence of conscious awareness in the persuasion process.[29] And even the more traditional strategies using innocuous and nonsensical messages to lull consumers into passive acceptance smack of the "hypodermic needle" approach to persuasion, an approach mass communication theorists disavowed at least 20 years ago.[30] Indeed, as late as 1977, Lutz and Swasy noted that the practice of persuasion in the marketplace has rarely "moved beyond the [Skinnerian] black box model."[31] So too, many political persuaders, albeit to a lesser extent than commercial advertisers, take a mechanistic approach to selling candidates to the electorate. As we saw, their focus frequently is on manipulating verbal and nonverbal symbols on the assumption they will cause positive perceptions and favorable voting patterns.

In general, we must conclude that, excepting the limited use of the CIP advertising model and some political persuasive tactics we will highlight shortly, "new" directions in the practice of mass persuasion are not really new at all. Rather, practitioners of mass persuasion still operate, for the most part, on a causal laws model of persuasion.

Let's briefly relate a few of the mass persuasion practices we have reviewed to some of the theories covered in this book. For instance, advertising practices aimed at lowering consumers' resistance to persuasion are suggested by William McGuire's inoculation theory, covered in Chapter 12. Recall that McGuire argues people will be vulnerable to persuasion so long as they are unmotivated to defend their positions. Moreover, he maintains that the best way to motivate people is to threaten their existing beliefs. By employing nonthreatening, innocuous, and nonsensical messages, commercial advertisements apparently are quite effective in lowering consumers' usual defenses against persuasive communication.

Political persuaders depart substantially from a mechanistic model when they employ strategies that identify a candidate with the values and goals of the electorate. This practice can be understood in the context of Daniel Katz' functional theory, discussed in Chapter 2. Katz argues that people adopt attitudes and enact behaviors that project their values and help them reach desired goals. By linking candidates with a voter's personal goals, political persuaders are utilizing the rules-based assumption underpinning Katz' theory, as well as Albert Bandura's social learning theory covered in Chapter 8.

The consumer information-processing approach may be understood within the context of several information-processing approaches we have considered, including Norman Anderson's and Martin Fishbein's information integration theories, discussed in Chapter 10, and Anthony Greenwald's cognitive response model, covered in Chapter 9. Each of these perspectives assumes that persuasive effects are a product of people's unique interpretations and cognitive responses to incoming information.

Finally, many mass persuasion practices we considered, notably subliminal persuasion, can be understood only within "hypodermic needle" approaches to persuasion. B.

F. Skinner's stimulus–response (S–R) theory best explains the projected effects of subliminal persuasion. Recall that Skinner assumes that persuasive effects are unmediated by cognitive processes and, additionally, are quite independent of conscious human awareness.

As we have seen, the practice of mass persuasion is, for the most part, at considerable odds with recent theory in persuasion. However, the consumer information-processing approach to advertising and many practices in political persuasion are promising since they regard people as something more than passive reactors to media messages.

THE PRACTICE OF INTERPERSONAL PERSUASION

Interpersonal persuasion differs from mass persuasion in several critical respects. First, interpersonal persuasion is a face-to-face phenomenon, involving mutual interaction and influence among the communicating parties. Because of this quality, communication channels other than sight and sound may be used for transmitting messages. The most frequently used additional channel is touch, although taste and smell occasionally may be employed. Furthermore, the face-to-face nature of interpersonal persuasion involves rapid verbal and nonverbal feedback. As this description implies, interpersonal persuasion is a dynamic, developmental communication process.

Second, interpersonal persuasion is distinguished from mass persuasion by its capacity to effect substantial alteration in enduring cognitive schemata and behavior patterns, as well as to reaffirm old ways of believing and behaving. We have seen that mass persuasion is more effective in doing the latter. Third and finally, interpersonal persuasion, unlike mass persuasion, is often accompanied by coercive influence strategies, as well as psychological and physiological arousal states that render people more susceptible to legitimate persuasive influence. For instance, intense interpersonal interaction frequently stimulates affective arousal that, in turn, makes people more amenable to persuasion.[32]

Let's look at some case studies illustrating the persuasive form. We will consider first the role of interpersonal persuasion in religious conversion and then examine a case of ideological indoctrination.

Religious Conversion: A Case Study

Conversion is defined as a persuasive process whereby people give up one ordered view of the world for another. It is almost exclusively a product of face-to-face interpersonal persuasion, and it requires active involvement on the part of the convert, who in the final analysis, persuades himself or herself of the value of new visions and the worth of new ways. This active involvement often produces arousal states that render people more susceptible to symbolic appeals. We will now examine the dynamics of conversion within a major American religious sect, the Unification Church of Reverend Sun Myung Moon.

The Moon Movement

Over 10,000 young Americans are among the half million followers of one of the fastest growing religious sects in the United States—the Moon Unification Church. Religion and politics are interwoven in Reverend Sun Myung Moon's writings, and Communism is considered the earthly embodiment of Satan. The Unification Church has vast real estate holdings in the United States and runs well over 100 "awareness training centers" throughout the country.

The process of soliciting converts to the Unification Church typically begins with what seems to be a chance encounter with a devoted "Moonie." Potential recruits are usually invited to spend a weekend at an awareness training center, often a farm located in an out-of-the-way area. The unsuspecting guests are usually promised a weekend of musical entertainment, refreshments, and a chance to share their ideas with others. The invitations are always low key. The happy, smiling Moonies convey a sense that the weekend retreat will be entertaining and consciousness raising and that the potential recruit may choose or not choose to participate as judgment dictates.

It is well known that many weekend guests never return. They give up family, friends, and former social and religious beliefs to devote themselves to the Unification Church's goal of conquering evil and spreading love in the world. How is this conversion so quickly accomplished? Philip Zimbardo and his associates studied the persuasive strategies used at Moonie awareness training centers and have provided some of the following details.[33]

The Persuasive Dynamics of Conversion

First, the young people who visit awareness training centers typically are lonely, alienated, and directionless. They desire companionship, structure, and meaning in their lives. Second, guests are immediately involved in structured group interaction with true believers. These Moonies are role models of happiness, vitality, and sincerity. Moreover, group games, singing, and intimate conversation create a highly cohesive atmosphere. Zimbardo argues that, given their initial sense of isolation, many potential converts rapidly become deindividuated, or submerged in the group; that is, they shed their negative self-identities and take on the "happy and loving" group persona.

Third, social rewards are dispensed freely, including smiles, approval, praise, physical contact, and love. Zimbardo maintains that the

> intensity of the emotional and physical experience is exhilarating and alters one's time perspective so as to expand the present and diminish past concerns and future apprehensions. With that change in one's temporal orientation, out goes reflection, past commitments to the world you left behind, and anxiety about what is to come. Instead, there is the mindless joy in the impulsive pleasures of the here-and-now, of living for the moment.[34]

Undoubtedly, the physical isolation of the awareness training centers from more familiar environments heightens this "here-and-now" arousal state. (The temporal disorientation and emotional arousal Zimbardo describes is, of course, very similar to many drug-induced states found to sharply increase susceptibility to persuasion.[35])

Fourth and finally, guests hear many lectures detailing the teaching of the Reverend Moon. The lecturers' only request is that guests keep an "open mind." This uncritical mind set, coupled with physiological arousal and time disorientation, make people especially vulnerable to influence. Moreover, Zimbardo argues that simple, easy-to-follow demands, like the request to keep an open mind, "recreates the passivity, dependence, and obedience of childhood." After complying with minimal requests in such a childlike atmosphere, he notes that "attitudes fall into line to justify compliant actions."[36]

As a result of these intense, emotionally arousing persuasion processes, many "ordinary" young Americans annually persuade themselves to desert their old environs for a life on some street corner selling carnations and salvation for the Reverend Moon. Moreover, it should be clear that the persuasive tactics we have discussed are not the work of some sinister persuader or charismatic messiah. Rather, they are really quite ordinary, differing little from persuasive strategies used in more "respectable" American institutions like the home, the school, or established religious organizations. Indeed, the Moonie conversion strategies are effective largely *because* they are mundane, ordinary, and nonthreatening. Moreover, dramatic and rapid conversion occurs because guests actively and freely participate in their own conversion. Apparently, new converts usually internalize their new beliefs and become true believers since amazingly few voluntarily desert the church after their conversion experience.

Ideological Indoctrination: A Case Study

Ideological indoctrination, sometimes called brainwashing, is usually described as a deliberately planned and systematic use of symbols and related psychological and physiological coercive techniques to alter deeply held values and well-established behavior patterns. Thus, indoctrination and conversion have the same goal: the substitution of one ordered view of the world for another. Moreover, both programs usually try to create certain psychological and physiological states that render people particularly susceptible to symbolic appeals. The temporal disorientation induced in potential recruits at Moonie training centers is a pertinent example. However, the tactics used in the conversion process are, as we saw in our discussion of the Moon movement, subtle and few in number. In contrast, indoctrination programs use a fairly large number of blatantly, often brutally, coercive techniques for rendering people mentally and physically susceptible to symbolic appeals. The typical ideological indoctrination program includes a generous mix of legitimate persuasive communication and physical and psychological coercion.

The ideological indoctrination program we are going to examine took place between 1950 and 1953 during the Korean conflict. Hundreds of U.N. soldiers, mostly Americans, were taken as prisoners of war by the Chinese Communists. For three years, the Chinese engaged in a systematic attempt to convert the Americans to the Chinese Communist ideology. Our account of this indoctrination program is based on

Edgar Schein's study. Schein based his findings on psychiatric interviews conducted in Korea during August 1953 when the prisoners were being repatriated.[37]

Initial Indoctrination Strategies

From the time of capture until they were housed in a permanent camp, two indoctrination strategies were used to render the prisoners more susceptible to later persuasion. The first may be called a *positive violation of expectations*. Having heard rumors of the brutal treatment of prisoners by the North Koreans, the soldiers expected severe punishment, even death, upon capture by the Chinese. However, according to Schein,

> These fears were... quickly dispelled by the friendly attitude of the Chinese soldiers. ... Some men reported that their Chinese captors approached them with outstretched hands, saying "Congratulations. You've been liberated." It was made clear to [each] man that he could now join forces with other "fighters for peace."... This friendly attitude and the emphasis on "peace" was the first and perhaps the most significant step in making the prisoners receptive to the more formal indoctrination which was to come later.[38]

The second initial strategy consisted of great *physical hardship and psychological pressure*, coupled with *promises* that the stress could be brought to an end by a "cooperative" attitude. The men were forced to march an average of 20 miles a night toward the prison camp where they were to be housed. The food was bad and medical care was nonexistent. Schein reports that during the marches "the men became increasingly disorganized and apathetic. Their only realistic hope was to get to prison camp where, it was hoped, conditions would be better."[39] This physical and psychological debilitation, coupled with promises of improvement, left the men particularly susceptible to later indoctrination.

The Prison Camp: Manipulation of the Social Setting

Once the captives reached the permanent prison camp, the Chinese manipulated the social setting to undermine social support structures and to emotionally isolate each prisoner. First, the men were segregated by rank, "in what appeared to be a systematic attempt to undermine the internal structure of the group by removing its leaders." The Chinese also put a special emphasis "on undermining all friendships, emotional bonds, and group activities." Any informal groups that sprang up among the prisoners were "systematically broken up."[40]

In addition to prohibiting the formation of social bonds, information was severely restricted. Only Communist newspapers, radio broadcasts, and magazines were available to the prisoners. The delivery of mail and contact with visitors from outside the camp were sharply curtailed. Schein concludes that the consequence of this social and emotional isolation was that each man was prevented "from validating any of his beliefs, attitudes, and values through meaningful interaction with other men at a time when these were under heavy attack from many sources, and when no accurate information was available."[41]

The Indoctrination Program: Passive Persuasive Strategies

Once encamped, the Chinese used two broad categories of persuasion or information control strategies on the prisoners: the first a passive source-oriented mode and the other an active participatory approach. The passive approach consisted of requiring the men to attend daily lectures lasting from two to three hours. The lectures, as well as films and leaflets, attacked the United Nations and the United States on various political, social, and economic issues, and glorified the achievements of Communist countries. The men were also exposed to testimonials and confessions from other prisoners, including a number of Air Force officers, who ostensibly supported the Communist cause. These confessions appeared to be a far more effective attack on existing values, beliefs, and attitudes than the lectures, that often were simplistic and contained obviously incorrect information about the United States.

The Indoctrination Program: Active Persuasive Strategies

According to Schein, the most effective persuasive technique used by the Chinese was active in nature, one "in which each prisoner of war was encouraged to participate in a way that would make it more possible for him to accept some of the new points of view."[42] The Chinese used several different strategies of active self-persuasion.

The first consisted of *group discussions* following lectures. After a lecture,

> the men were then required to break up into squads, go to their quarters, and discuss the material for periods of two hours or more. At the end of the discussion, each squad had to provide written answers to questions handed out during the lecture—the answers, obviously, which had already been provided in the lecture. To "discuss" the lecture thus meant, in effect, to rationalize the predetermined conclusions.[43]

Schein reports that "the fact that many men were unclear about why they were fighting in Korea was a good lever for such discussions."[44]

A second active participatory strategy was *interrogation*. One effective interrogation technique was to have the men write out their own questions and then answer them. Additionally, the Chinese got complete personal histories of each prisoner, including economic background, social class, and the like. During interrogation, the Chinese tried to relate each man's personal life, particularly any social or economic setbacks he had experienced, to the capitalistic system of government.

Another useful interrogation technique was the creation of a friendly atmosphere. In some cases, the interrogator lived in the same quarters with his subject and offered warmth and companionship. Interrogations often lasted for days, even weeks. Schein reports that a main objective of the Chinese seemed to be to get the prisoner talking, no matter what he was talking about. The discussions sometimes became effective didactic sessions because of the friendly relationship which the interrogator built up. If there were any weakness or inconsistency in a man's belief systems, once he lowered his guard and began to examine them critically, he was in danger of being overwhelmed by the arguments of the instructor.[45]

A third active participation technique to get the prisoners to question their beliefs was confession and *self-criticism*. Initially, the Chinese would encourage the men to confess to trivial offenses and then criticize themselves for their transgressions. Schein reports that "men who had confessed at first to trivial offenses soon found themselves having to answer for relatively major ones."[46]

Fourth and finally, *rewards and punishments* were meted out for participation, or lack of it, in the indoctrination program. For example, highly valued items like cigarettes or fresh fruit were offered as prizes in essay-writing contests that dealt with certain aspects of world politics. Winning essays, selected on the basis of agreement with the Communist point of view, were published in the camp newspaper or magazine. Threats of punishments were used when prisoners failed to cooperate, including threats of death, nonrepatriation, torture, reprisals against families, reductions in food and medications, and imprisonment. The only one of these that was carried out with any consistency was imprisonment in the form of solitary confinement.

General Characteristics of the Chinese Indoctrination Program

Schein summarizes some of the more important features of the Chinese indoctrination program, one of which is *repetition*. Schein writes:

> One of the chief characteristics of the Chinese was their immense patience in what they were doing; they were always willing to make their demand or assertion over and over again. . . . Many men pointed out that most of the techniques gained their effectiveness by being used in this repetitious way until the prisoner could no longer sustain his resistance.[47]

A second feature of the program was the *pacing of demands*. Schein notes that

> in the various kinds of responses that were demanded of the prisoners, the Chinese always started with trivial, innocuous ones and, as the habit of responding became established, gradually worked up to more important ones. Thus, after a prisoner had once been "trained" to speak or write out trivia, statements on more important issues were demanded of him. This was particularly effective in eliciting confessions, self-criticisms, and information during interrogation.[48]

Third, as we saw, the prisoners' *active participation* was a crucial characteristic of the indoctrination program. "It was never enough for the prisoners to listen and absorb," writes Schein. "Some kind of verbal or written response was always demanded."[49]

Fourth and finally, Schein notes that in their indoctrination program, "the Chinese made a considerable effort *to insert their new ideas into old and meaningful contexts*" (emphasis Schein's).[50] Knowing a man's personal history enabled an interrogator to determine what might be a significant context for the particular prisoner with whom he was dealing. In this regard, any prior misfortune a person might have suffered "served as an ideal starting place for undermining democratic attitudes and instilling communistic ones."[51]

Schein summarizes his analysis of the Chinese indoctrination program by arguing that "taken singly, there is nothing new or terrifying about the specific techniques used by the Chinese; they invented no mysterious devices for dealing with people."[52] Although the program included more blatantly coercive elements than those used in most persuasive situations, Schein argues that all the Chinese techniques were actually strikingly similar to strategies used in many institutions in our own society, including "religious orders, prisons, [and] educational centers."[53] On the basis of his research, he concludes that "the only novelty in the Chinese methods was the attempt *to use a combination of all these techniques and apply them simultaneously* in order to gain complete control over significant portions of the physical and social environment of a group of people" (emphasis Schein's).[54]

Measuring the Success of the Chinese Program

Schein notes that the success of the Chinese indoctrination program is difficult to assess. From a behavioral perspective, it is well documented that the majority of the prisoners collaborated at one time or another with their captors. That 21 prisoners refused repatriation perhaps is suggestive of the "Stockholm Syndrome," a phenomenon in which hostages come to love and admire their captors. However, Schein speculates that most of the prisoners, although irrevocably changed by their experience, were probably never completely converted to the Chinese Communist ideology.

A Critical Assessment of Interpersonal Persuasion Practices

It should be apparent that the practice of interpersonal persuasion reflects recent theoretical advances far more than the practice of mass communication. For the most part, interpersonal persuasion is founded on an actional view of humans. Two of its features support this conclusion. First, we have seen that interpersonal persuasion emphasizes people's active participation in social influence processes, with self-influence strategies predominating. Second, interpersonal persuasion operates on the assumption that people are goal-directed agents, always striving to maximize rewards and avoid punishments. The emphasis that conversion and indoctrination processes place on rewards and punishments reflects this notion.

Many of the persuasive strategies used by the Moonies and the Chinese Communists may be understood in the context of some of the action-oriented theories explored in this book. First, the rules-based group theory of social comparison, covered in Chapter 7, readily explains many of the persuasive strategies we have described. Much of the success of the Moonies' conversion process is due to the normative, or rules-based, power of groups to dispense social rewards and punishments and to the process of deindividuation, or submergence in the group. And consistent with social comparison theory, the indoctrination program of the Chinese Communists began with the systematic tearing down of the prisoners' social reality, as defined by group consensus. Losing the support of similar others with whom they could compare and validate opinions made the prisoners especially susceptible to later symbolic appeals. By breaking up group structures, the Chinese eradicated the social rules that had previously coordinated the attitudes and actions of the prisoners of war.

Second, information-processing theories, including Greenwald's cognitive response model discussed in Chapter 9, figure prominently in both religious conversion and ideological indoctrination. Recall that the Moonies and the Chinese controlled the information available to their targets, limiting it to material consistent with the preferred point of view. The extensive use of lectures by both groups illustrates this strategy. Furthermore, the Chinese forced their captives to make overt cognitive responses to the lecture materials, either orally or in writing.

Third, attribution theory, covered in Chapter 6, explains the success of many of the strategies used by the Moonies and the Chinese Communists. In both cases, potential converts were removed from their old physical and social environment—potential Moonie converts came willingly, but obviously the prisoners of war were forced into a new environment. However, in each case, the persuaders had total power to arrange environmental cues so as to increase the probability that potential converts would infer their behavior reflected a belief in its rightness. Moreover, we saw that the Chinese made extensive use of what we called the "foot-in-the-door" attribution strategy. By initially asking for small commitments, the Chinese increased the chances that the prisoners would later accede to larger and more important demands.

Fourth, techniques of counterattitudinal advocacy, discussed in Chapter 5, were used extensively, particularly by the Chinese in the form of self-criticisms. By any number of theoretical accounts, including the reason-based incentive and impression management explanations, this tactic ought to have increased the probability that attitudes would fall into line with actions. Finally, the principles of social learning, covered in Chapter 8, explain many of the tactics used by the Moonies and the Chinese. Social learning theory suggests that people follow practical rules, enabling them to maximize benefits and avoid misfortune. Although the Chinese blatantly used rewards and punishments, implicit in the Moonie conversion process is the promise that acceptance of the new dogma will maximize happiness and lead to self-fulfillment and peace of mind. Clearly, the smiling, happy, true believers serve as powerful role models for potential converts.

Beyond a congruence with recent theoretical directions in persuasion, interpersonal persuasion has a number of other critical features. First, it is almost always accompanied by coercion designed to render people more susceptible to later symbolic appeals. Coercive tactics range from the blatant to the subtle, from death threats from the Chinese to the Moon technique of inducing temporal disorientation. But as useful as these nonpersuasive influence strategies are, persuasion alone can effect internalization or the private acceptance of new ways of thinking and acting.

Second, both of the case studies we presented reveal that interpersonal persuasion is a dynamic, developmental process. Both persuader and receiver are actively involved in the process of change. Third, we have seen that interpersonal persuasion techniques, even those used in settings as restrictive as a prisoner of war camp, are rarely novel, sinister, or mysterious. Rather, they are, for the most part, quite ordinary, much like the persuasive strategies used by all of us in our everyday comings and goings. Fourth, our two case studies illustrate that interpersonal persuasion is largely a matter of self-persuasion and involves a person's perception of choice to accept or reject new ideologies. That most of the prisoners of war, despite three years of intense indoctrination that included physical brutality, remained unconverted testifies to the self-directional, choice-laden nature of human beings.

Clearly, the practice of interpersonal persuasion is far more consistent with an actional view of humans than is mass persuasion. The use of mechanistic strategies, like the lectures given by the Chinese, is usually ineffective. In contrast, action-based strategies, including active participatory forms of self-influence, seem quite effective in changing cognitive schemata and overt human action.

NOTES

1. Don R. Pember, *Mass Media in America*, 2nd ed. (Chicago: Science Research Associates, 1977), p. 189.

2. Robert T. Bower, *Television and the Public* (New York: Holt, Rinehart & Winston, 1973).

3. Pember, pp. 125–126.

4. Ibid., p. 155.

5. Ibid., p. 348.

6. Charles Winick, "Sex and Advertising," in *Mass Media: The Invisible Environment Revisited*, ed. Robert J. Glessing and William P. White (Chicago: Science Research Associates, 1976), p. 122.

7. For example, see A. W. van den Ban, "A Revision of the Two-Step Flow of Communication Hypothesis," *Gazette* 10 (1964): 237–249; Franklin R. Knower, "Experimental Studies of Changes in Attitudes I: A Study of the Effect of Oral Argument on Changes of Attitude," *Journal of Abnormal and Social Psychology* 6 (1935): 315–347; and Hadley Cantril and Gordon Allport, *The Psychology of Radio* (New York: Harper & Row, 1935).

8. For example, see Joseph T. Klapper, *The Effects of Mass Communication* (Glencoe, Ill.: The Free Press, 1960); and Raymond A. Bauer, "Limits of Persuasion," *Harvard Business Review* 36 (1958): 105–110.

9. The term *canalization* was used to describe this media function in a classic article by Paul F. Lazarsfeld and Robert K. Merton, "Mass Communication, Popular Taste, and Organized Social Action," in *The Communication of Ideas*, ed. Lyman Bryson (New York: Institute for Religious and Social Studies, 1948).

10. Joe McGinniss, *The Selling of the President 1968* (New York: Trident Press, 1969), p. 83.

11. Ibid., p. 31.

12. See Jules Witcover, *Marathon: The Pursuit of the Presidency 1972–1976* (New York: The Viking Press, 1977); and Martin Schram, *Running for President: A Journal of the Carter Campaign* (New York: Pocket Books, 1976).

13. Robert G. Kaiser, "Reselling of Carter: A Living Room Pitch for the President," *The Washington Post*, 18 March 1980, p. A-3.

14. Schram, pp. 141–142.

15. The following analysis draws heavily on Samm Sinclair Baker, "Advertising: The Permissible Lie," in *Mass Culture Revisited,* ed. Bernard Rosenberg and David Manning White (New York: Van Nostrand Reinhold, 1971), pp. 359–376.

16. Herbert E. Krugman, "The Impact of Television Advertising: Learning without Involvement," in *The Process and Effects of Mass Communication,* ed. Wilbur Schramm and Donald F. Roberts (Urbana, Ill.: University of Illinois Press, 1971), pp. 484–494.

17. Vance Packard, *The Hidden Persuaders* (New York: David McKay, 1957); Wilson Bryan Key, *Subliminal Seduction: Ad Media's Manipulation of a Not So Innocent America* (New York: New American Library, 1973); and Wilson Bryan Key, *Media Sexploitation* (New York: New American Library, 1976).

18. Herbert Brean, "'Hidden Sell' Techniques Are Almost Here," *Life,* 31 March 1958, pp. 102–114.

19. "Secret Voices: Messages that Manipulate," *Time,* 10 September 1979, p. 71.

20. See Key, *Subliminal;* and Key, *Media.*

21. Key, *Subliminal,* pp. 4–7.

22. William Raft Wilson, "Feeling More than We Can Know: Exposure Effects without Learning," *Journal of Personality and Social Psychology* 37 (1979): 811–821.

23. Ibid., pp. 813–814.

24. Ibid., p. 818.

25. Ibid., p. 819.

26. Robert W. Chestnut, "Persuasive Effects in Marketing: Consumer Information Processing Research," in *Persuasion: New Directions in Theory and Research,* ed. Michael E. Roloff and Gerald R. Miller (Beverly Hills, Calif.: Sage Publications, 1980), p. 268.

27. Chestnut, p. 271.

28. For examples, see Jacob Jacoby and Joel C. Olsen, "Consumer Response to Price: An Attitudinal Information Processing Perspective," in *Moving Ahead with Attitude Research,* ed. Yoram Wind and Marshall G. Greenberg (Chicago: American Marketing Association, 1977); and James R. Bettman, "Issues in Designing Consumer Information Environments," *Journal of Consumer Research* 2 (1975): 169–177.

29. It should be noted that some theorists argue that much persuasion takes place without awareness. See Michael E. Roloff, "Self-Awareness and the Persuasion Process: Do We Really Know What We're Doing?" in *Persuasion: New Directions,* pp. 29–66.

30. For some early theoretical statements, see Raymond A. Bauer, "The Obstinate Audience: The Influence Process from the Point of View of Social Communication," *American Psychologist* 19 (1964): 319–328; and W. Phillips Davison, "On the Effects of Communication," *Public Opinion Quarterly* 23 (1959): 360.

31. R. J. Lutz and J. L. Swasy, "Integrating Cognitive Structure and Cognitive Response Approaches to Monitoring Communication Effects," *Advances in Consumer Research* 5 (1977): 363.

32. For evidence that interaction with others can trigger physiological arousal, see Robert B. Zajonc, "Social Facilitation," *Science* 149 (1965): 269–274.

33. Philip G. Zimbardo, E. B. Ebbesen, and Christina Maslach, *Influencing Attitudes and Changing Behavior,* Second Edition. © 1977, Addison-Wesley Publishing Company, pp. 184–189. Reprinted by permission.

34. Ibid., p. 185. Reprinted by permission.

35. For a discussion of the effects of altered physiological states on persuasive effects, see Robert N. Bostrom, "Altered Physiological States: The Central Nervous System and Persuasive Communication," in *Persuasion: New Directions*, pp. 171–196.

36. Zimbardo, Ebbesen, and Maslach, p. 185. Reprinted by permission.

37. Edgar H. Schein, "The Chinese Indoctrination Program for Prisoners of War: A Study of Attempted 'Brainwashing,'" *Psychiatry* 19 (1956): 149–172. Reprinted by permission of the William Alanson White Psychiatric Foundation, Inc., 1610 New Hampshire Avenue, N.W., Washington, D.C., 20009. Also see Edgar H. Schein, Inge Schneier, and Curtis H. Barker, *Coercive Persuasion* (New York: W. W. Norton, 1961).

38. Schein, pp. 150–151. Reprinted by permission.

39. Ibid., p. 151. Reprinted by permission.

40. Ibid., pp. 153–154. Reprinted by permission.

41. Ibid., p. 155. Reprinted by permission.

42. Ibid., p. 157. Reprinted by permission.

43. Ibid. Reprinted by permission.

44. Ibid., p. 155. Reprinted by permission.

45. Ibid., pp. 158–159. Reprinted by permission.

46. Ibid., p. 159. Reprinted by permission.

47. Ibid., pp. 162–163. Reprinted by permission.

48. Ibid., p. 163. Reprinted by permission.

49. Ibid. Reprinted by permission.

50. Ibid. Reprinted by permission.

51. Ibid. Reprinted by permission.

52. Ibid., p. 172. Reprinted by permission.

53. Schein, Schneier, and Barker, p. 285.

54. Schein, p. 172. Reprinted by permission.

Bibliography

ABELSON, ROBERT P. "Script Processing in Attitude Formation and Decision Making." *Cognition and Social Behavior.* Ed. John S. Carroll and John W. Payne. Potomac, Md.: Lawrence Erlbaum, 1976.

————. "Modes of Resolution of Belief Dilemmas." *Journal of Conflict Resolution* 3 (1959): 343–352.

ADAIR, JOHN G., AND SCHACTER, BRENDA S. "To Cooperate or To Look Good?: The Subjects' and Experimenters' Perceptions of Each Others' Intentions." *Journal of Experimental Social Psychology* 8 (1972): 74–85.

ADLER, KEITH. "An Evaluation of the Practical Syllogism as a Model of Man for Human Communication Research." *Communication Quarterly* 21 (1978): 8–18.

AJZEN, ICEK. "Attitudinal vs. Normative Messages: An Investigation of the Differential Effects of Persuasive Communications on Behavior." *Sociometry* 34 (1971): 263–280.

AJZEN, ICEK, and FISHBEIN, MARTIN. "The Prediction of Behavior from Attitudinal and Normative Variables." *Journal of Experimental Social Psychology* 6 (1970): 466–487.

ALLEN, VERNON L., and LEVINE, JOHN M. "Social Support and Conformity: The Role of Independent Assessment of Reality." *Journal of Experimental Social Psychology* 7 (1971): 48–58.

ALLEN, VERNON L., and WILDER, DAVID A. "Social Comparison, Self-Evaluation, and Conformity to the Group." *Social Comparison Processes: Theoretical and Empirical Perspectives.* Ed. Jerry M. Suls and Richard L. Miller. Washington, D.C.: Hemisphere Publishing, 1977, pp. 196–201.

ANDERSEN, KENNETH E. *Persuasion: Theory and Practice.* Boston: Allyn & Bacon, 1971.

ANDERSON, LYNN R., and FISHBEIN, MARTIN. "Prediction of Attitude from the Number, Strength, and Evaluative Aspect of Beliefs about the Attitude Object: A Comparison of Summation and Congruity Theories." *Journal of Personality and Social Psychology* 2 (1965): 437–443.

ANDERSON, NORMAN H. "Integration Theory and Attitude Change." *Psychological Review* 78 (1971a): 171–205.

————. "Two More Tests against Change of Meaning in Adjective Combinations." *Journal of Verbal Learning and Verbal Behavior* 10 (1971b): 75–85.

————. "A Simple Model for Information Integration." *Theories of Cognitive Consistency: A Sourcebook.* Ed. Robert P. Abelson, et al. Skokie, Ill.: Rand McNally, 1968a, pp. 731–741.

————. "Application of a Linear–Serial Model to a Personality–Impression Task Using Serial Impression." *Journal of Personality and Social Psychology* 10 (1968b): 354–362.

————. "Averaging Analysis of Set Size Effect in Impression Formation." *Journal of Experimental Psychology* 75 (1967): 158–165.

————. "Primacy Effects in Personality Impression Formation Using a Generalized Order Effect Paradigm." *Journal of Personality and Social Psychology* 2 (1965a): 1–9.

————. "Averaging versus Adding as a Stimulus-Combination Rule in Impression Formation." *Journal of Experimental Psychology* 70 (1965b): 394–400.

ANDERSON, NORMAN H., and BARRIOS, ALFRED A. "Primacy Effects in Personality Impression Formation." *Journal of Abnormal and Social Psychology* 63 (1961): 346–350.

ANDERSON, NORMAN H., and HUBERT, STEPHEN. "Effects of Concomitant Verbal Recall on Order Effects in Personality Impression Formation." *Journal of Verbal Learning and Verbal Behavior* 2 (1963): 379–391.

ANDERSON, NORMAN H., and JACOBSON, ANN. "Effect of Stimulus Inconsistency and Discounting Instructions in Personality Impression Formation." *Journal of Personality and Social Psychology* 2 (1965): 531–539.

ANDERSON, ROSEMARIE; MANOOGIAN, SAM THOMAS; and REZNICK, J. STEVEN. "The Undermining and Enhancing of Intrinsic Motivation in Preschool Children." *Journal of Personality and Social Psychology* 34 (1976): 915–922.

APPLBAUM, RONALD L., and ANATOL, KARL W. E. "Dimensions of Source Credibility: A Test for Reproducibility." *Speech Monographs* 40 (1973): 231–237.

————. "The Factor Structure of Source Credibility as a Function of the Speaking Situation." *Speech Monographs* 39 (1972): 216–223.

ARONSON, ELIOT. "Dissonance Theory: Progress and Problems." *Theories of Cognitive Consistency: A Sourcebook.* Ed. Robert P. Abelson, et al. Skokie, Ill.: Rand McNally, 1968, pp. 5–27.

ARONSON, ELIOT, and MILLS, JUDSON. "The Effects of Severity of Initiation on Liking for a Group." *Journal of Abnormal and Social Psychology* 59 (1959): 177–181.

ARONSON, ELIOT; TURNER, JUDITH A.; and CARLSMITH, JAMES M. "Communicator Credibility and Communication Discrepancy as Determinants of Opinion Change." *Journal of Abnormal and Social Psychology* 67 (1963): 31–36.

ASCH, SOLOMON E. "Effects of Group Pressures upon Modification and Distortion of Judgments." *Readings in Social Psychology.* 3rd ed. Ed. Eleanor E. Maccoby, Theodore M. Newcomb, and Eugene L. Hartley. New York: Holt, Rinehart & Winston, 1958.

————. *Social Psychology.* New York: Prentice-Hall, 1952.

————. "Forming Impressions of Personality." *Journal of Abnormal and Social Psychology* 41 (1946): 258–290.

AYER, A. J., ed. *Logical Positivism.* New York: The Free Press, 1958.

BAILEY, KENNETH D. "Evaluating Axiomatic Theories." *Sociological Methodology.* Ed. Edgar F. Borgatta. San Francisco: Jossey-Bass, 1970, pp. 48–71.

BAKER, SAMM SINCLAIR. "Advertising: The Permissible Lie." *Mass Culture Revisited.* Ed. Bernard Rosenberg and David Manning White. New York: Van Nostrand Reinhold, 1971, pp. 359–376.

BANDURA, ALBERT. *Social Learning Theory.* Englewood Cliffs, N.J.: Prentice-Hall, 1977.

————. *Social Learning Theory.* Morristown, N.J.: General Learning Press, 1971.

BANDURA, ALBERT; ROSS, DOROTHEA; and ROSS, SHEILA A. "Vicarious Reinforcement and Imitative Learning." *Journal of Abnormal and Social Psychology* 67 (1963): 601–607.

BANUAZIZI, ALI, and MOVAHEDI, SIAMAK. "Interpersonal Dynamics in a Simulated Prison: A Methodological Analysis." *American Psychologist* 30 (1975): 152–160.

BARNLUND, DEAN C.   "A Transactional Model of Communication." *Language Behavior: A Book of Readings*. Ed. Johnnye Akin, et al. The Hague, The Netherlands: Mouton and Company, 1970, pp. 53–71.

BARON, REUBEN M.   "Attitude Change through Discrepant Action: A Functional Analysis." *Psychological Foundations of Attitudes*. Ed. Anthony G. Greenwald, Timothy C. Brock, and Thomas M. Ostrom. New York: Academic Press, 1968, pp. 297–326.

BARON, ROBERT A.   "Attraction Toward the Model and Model's Competence as Determinants of Adult Imitative Behavior." *Journal of Personality and Social Psychology* 14 (1970): 345–351.

BARON, ROBERT STEVEN, and ROPER, GARD.   "A Reaffirmation of a Social Comparison View of Choice Shifts, Averaging, and Extremity Effects in Autokinetic Situations." *Journal of Personality and Social Psychology* 33 (1976): 521–530.

BARTLETT, FREDERICK C.   *Remembering: A Study in Experimental and Social Psychology*. London: Cambridge University Press, 1932.

BATESON, NICHOLAS.   "Familiarization, Group Discussion, and Risk Taking." *Journal of Experimental Social Psychology* 2 (1966): 119–129.

BAUER, RAYMOND A.   "The Obstinate Audience: The Influence Process from the Point of View of Social Communication." *American Psychologist* 19 (1964): 319–328.

————— .   "Limits of Persuasion." *Harvard Business Review* 36 (1958): 105–110.

BAUMHART, RAYMOND.   *An Honest Profile*. New York: Holt, Rinehart & Winston, 1968.

BECKMAN, LINDA.   "Effects of Students' Performance on Teachers' and Observers' Attributions of Causality." *Journal of Educational Psychology* 61 (1970): 76–82.

BEM, DARYL J.   "Self-Perception Theory." *Advances in Experimental Social Psychology*. Ed. Leonard Berkowitz. New York: Academic Press, 1972, pp. 1–62.

————— .   "An Experimental Analysis of Self-Persuasion." *Journal of Experimental Social Psychology* 1 (1965): 199–218.

BEM, DARYL J., and FUNDER, DAVID C.   "Predicting More of the People More of the Time: Assessing the Personality of Situations." *Psychological Review* 85 (1978): 485–501.

BEM, DARYL J., and LORD, CHARLES G.   "Template Matching: A Proposal for Probing the Ecological Validity of Experimental Settings in Social Psychology." *Journal of Personality and Social Psychology* 37 (1979): 833–843.

BEM, DARYL J., and McCONNELL, H. KEITH.   "Testing the Self-Perception Explanation of Dissonance Phenomena: On the Salience of Premanipulation Attitudes." *Journal of Personality and Social Psychology* 14 (1970): 23–31.

BENWARE, CARL, and DECI, EDWARD L.   "Attitude Change as a Function of the Inducement for Espousing a Proattitudinal Communication." *Journal of Experimental Social Psychology* 11 (1975): 271–278.

BERG, KENNETH R.   "Ethnic Attitudes and Agreement with a Negro Person." *Journal of Personality and Social Psychology* 4 (1966): 216–220.

BERGER, CHARLES R.   "The Covering Law Perspective as a Theoretical Basis for the Study of Human Communication." *Communication Quarterly* 25 (1977): 7–18.

————— .   "Toward a Role Enactment Theory of Persuasion." *Speech Monographs* 39 (1972): 260–267.

BERGER, CHARLES R., and CALABRESE, RICHARD J.   "Some Explorations in Initial Interaction and Beyond: Toward a Developmental Theory of Interpersonal Communication." *Human Communication Research* 1 (1975): 99–112.

BERLO, DAVID K.; LEMERT, JAMES B.; and MERTZ, ROBERT J.   "Dimensions for Evaluating the Acceptability of Message Sources." *Public Opinion Quarterly* 33 (1969–1970): 563–576.

BERLYNE, DANIEL E.   "Novelty, Complexity, and Hedonic Value." *Perception and Psychophysics* 8 (1970): 279–286.

BERNE, ERIC.   *Transactional Analysis in Psychotherapy*. New York: Grove Press, 1961.

BERSCHEID, ELLEN.   "Opinion Change and Communicator–Communicatee Similarity and Dissimilarity." *Journal of Personality and Social Psychology* 4 (1966): 670–680.

BERSCHEID, ELLEN, and WALSTER, ELAINE.   "Physical Attractiveness." *Advances in Experimental Social Psychology*. Ed. Leonard Berkowitz. New York: Academic Press, 1974.

BETTINGHAUS, ERWIN P.   *Persuasive Communication*. 3rd ed. New York: Holt, Rinehart & Winston, 1980.

BETTMAN, JAMES R.   "Issues in Designing Consumer Information Environments." *Journal of Consumer Research* 2 (1975): 169–177.

BIRNBAUM, MICHAEL H.   "The Nonadditivity of Personality Impressions." *Journal of Experimental Psychology* 102 (1974): 543–561.

BODAKEN, EDWARD M.; PLAX, TIMOTHY G.; PILAND, RICHARD W.; and WEINER, ALLEN N.   "Role Enactment as a Socially Relevant Explanation of Self-Persuasion." *Human Communication Research* 5 (1979): 203–214.

BOSTROM, ROBERT N.   "Altered Physiological States: The Central Nervous System and Persuasive Communications." *Persuasion: New Directions in Theory and Research*. Ed. Michael E. Roloff and Gerald R. Miller. Beverly Hills, Calif.: Sage Publications, 1980, pp. 171–196.

BOVEE, HARLEY H.   *Report of the 1954 Windshield Pitting Phenomenon in the State of Washington*. Seattle: Environmental Research Laboratory, University of Washington, 10 June 1954.

BOWER, ROBERT T.   *Television and the Public*. New York: Holt, Rinehart & Winston, 1973.

BRADLEY, GIFFORD WEARY.   "Self-Serving Biases in the Attribution Process: A Re-examination of the Fact or Fiction Question." *Journal of Personality and Social Psychology* 35 (1978): 56–71.

BREAN, HERBERT.   " 'Hidden Sell' Techniques Are Almost Here." *Life*, 31 March 1958, pp. 102–114.

BREHM, JACK W.   *A Theory of Psychological Reactance*. New York: Academic Press, 1966.

BREHM, JACK W., and COHEN, ARTHUR R., eds.   *Explorations in Cognitive Dissonance*. New York: John Wiley, 1962.

BREMBECK, WINSTON L., and HOWELL, WILLIAM S.   *Persuasion: A Means of Social Change*. 2nd ed. Englewood Cliffs, N.J.: Prentice-Hall, 1976.

BROCK, TIMOTHY C.   "Implications of Commodity Theory for Value Change." *Psychological Foundations of Attitudes*. Ed. Anthony G. Greenwald, Timothy C. Brock, and Thomas M. Ostrom. New York: Academic Press, 1968, pp. 243–275.

————— .   "Communicator–Recipient Similarity and Decision Change." *Journal of Personality and Social Psychology* 1 (1965): 650–654.

BROCK, TIMOTHY C., and BECKER, LEE ALAN.   " 'Debriefing' and Susceptibility to Subsequent Experimental Manipulations." *Journal of Experimental Social Psychology* 2 (1966): 314–323.

————— .   "Ineffectiveness of 'Overheard' Counterpropaganda." *Journal of Personality and Social Psychology* 2 (1965): 654–660.

BROWN, ROGER.   *Social Psychology*. New York: Free Press of Glencoe, 1965.

BURGOON, MICHAEL; COHEN, MARSHALL; MILLER, MICHAEL D.; and MONTGOMERY, CHARLES L.   "An Empirical Test of a Model of Resistance to Persuasion." *Human Communication Research* 4 (1978): 27–39.

BURNSTEIN, EUGENE, and VINOKUR, AMIRAM.   "Persuasive Argumentation and Social Comparison as Determinants of Attitude Polarization." *Journal of Experimental Social Psychology* 13 (1977): 315–332.

BURNSTEIN, EUGENE; VINOKUR, AMIRAM; and TROPE, YAACOV.   "Interpersonal Comparison versus Persuasive Argumentation: A More Direct Test of Alternative Explanations for Group Induced Shifts in Individual Choice." *Journal of Experimental Social Psychology* 9 (1973): 236–245.

BUSS, ALLAN R. "On the Relationship between Causes and Reasons." *Journal of Personality and Social Psychology* 37 (1979): 1458–1461.

————. "Causes and Reasons in Attribution Theory: A Conceptual Critique." *Journal of Personality and Social Psychology* 36 (1978): 1311–1321.

CACIOPPO, JOHN T., and PETTY, RICHARD R. "Effects of Message Repetition and Position on Cognitive Response, Recall, and Persuasion." *Journal of Personality and Social Psychology* 37 (1979a): 97–109.

————. "Attitudes and Cognitive Responses: An Electrophysiological Approach." *Journal of Personality and Social Psychology* 37 (1979b): 2181–2199.

CALDER, BOBBY J.; INSKO, CHESTER A.; and YANDELL, BEN. "The Relation of Cognitive and Memorial Processes to Persuasion in a Simulated Jury Trial." *Journal of Applied Social Psychology* 4 (1974): 62–93.

CAMPBELL, DONALD T. "Stereotypes and the Perception of Group Differences." *American Psychologist* 22 (1967): 817–829.

————. "Social Attitudes and Other Acquired Behavioral Dispositions." *Psychology: A Study of a Science.* Ed. Sigmund Koch. New York: McGraw-Hill, 1963, pp. 97–172.

CAMPBELL, DONALD T., and STANLEY, JULIAN C. *Experimental and Quasi-Experimental Designs for Research.* Chicago: Rand McNally, 1963.

CANN, ARNIE; SHERMAN, STEVEN J.; and ELKES, ROY. "Effects of Initial Request Size and Timing of Second Request on Compliance: The Foot in the Door and the Door in the Face." *Journal of Personality and Social Psychology* 32 (1975): 774–882.

CANTOR, NANCY, and MISCHEL, WALTER. "Traits as Prototypes: Effects on Recognition Memory." *Journal of Personality and Social Psychology* 35 (1977): 39–48.

CANTRIL, HADLEY. "The Invasion from Mars." *The Process and Effects of Mass Communication.* Ed. Wilbur Schramm and Donald F. Roberts. Urbana, Ill.: University of Illinois Press, 1971, 579–595.

CANTRIL, HADLEY, and ALLPORT, GORDON W. *The Psychology of Radio.* New York: Harper, 1935.

CARLSMITH, J. MERRILL; COLLINS, BARRY E.; and HELMREICH, ROBERT C. "Studies in Forced Compliance: The Effects of Pressure for Compliance on Attitude Change Produced by Face-to-Face Role Playing and Anonymous Essay Writing." *Journal of Personality and Social Psychology* 4 (1966): 1–13.

CARR, LESTER, and ROBERTS, S. O. "Correlates of Civil-Rights Participation." *Journal of Social Psychology* 67 (1965): 259–267.

CATTELL, RAYMOND B., ed. *Handbook of Multivariate Experimental Psychology.* Chicago: Rand McNally, 1966.

CHAIKEN, SHELLY. "Communicator Physical Attractiveness and Persuasion." *Journal of Personality and Social Psychology* 37 (1979): 1387–1397.

CHAIKEN, SHELLY, and EAGLY, ALICE H. "Communication Modality as a Determinant of Message Persuasiveness and Message Comprehensibility." *Journal of Personality and Social Psychology* 34 (1976): 605–614.

CHAPANIS, NATALIA P., and CHAPANIS, ALPHONSE. "Cognitive Dissonance: Five Years Later." *Psychological Bulletin* 61 (1964): 1–22.

CHESTNUT, ROBERT W. "Persuasive Effects in Marketing: Consumer Information Processing Research." *Persuasion: New Directions in Theory and Research.* Ed. Michael E. Roloff and Gerald R. Miller. Beverly Hills, Calif.: Sage Publications, 1980, pp. 267–283.

CIALDINI, ROBERT B.; VINCENT, JOYCE E.; LEWIS, STEPHEN K.; CATALAN, JOSÉ; WHEELER, DIANE; and DARBY, BETTY LEE. "Reciprocal Concessions Procedure for Inducing Compliance: The Door-in-the-Face Technique." *Journal of Personality and Social Psychology* 31 (1975): 206–215.

COHEN, ARTHUR R.   "An Experiment on Small Rewards for Discrepant Compliance and Attitude Change." *Explorations in Cognitive Dissonance*. Ed. Jack W. Brehm and Arthur R. Cohen. New York: John Wiley, 1962, pp. 73–78.

COHEN, CLAUDIA E., and EBBESEN, E. B.   "Observational Goals and Schema Activation: A Theoretical Framework for Behavior Perception." *Journal of Experimental Social Psychology* 15 (1979): 305–329.

COLLINS, BARRY E., and GUETZKOW, HAROLD.   *A Social Psychology of Group Processes for Decision Making*. New York: John Wiley, 1964.

CONANT, JAMES B.   *Modern Science and Modern Man*. New York: Columbia University Press, 1952.

COOK, THOMAS D., and PERRINI, BARTON F.   "The Effects of Suspiciousness of Deception and the Perceived Legitimacy of Deception on Task Performance in an Attitude Change Experiment." *Journal of Personality* 39 (1971): 204–224.

COOK, THOMAS D.; BEAN, BOBBY J.; FREY, ROBERT; KROVETZ, MARTIN L.; and REISMAN, STEPHEN R.   "Demand Characteristics and Three Conceptions of the Frequently Deceived Subject." *Journal of Personality and Social Psychology* 14 (1970): 185–195.

COOPER, HARRIS M.   "Statistically Combining Independent Studies: A Meta-Analysis of Sex Differences in Conformity Research." *Journal of Personality and Social Psychology* 37 (1979): 131–146.

COOPER, JOEL.   "Personal Responsibility and Dissonance: The Role of Foreseen Consequences." *Journal of Personality and Social Psychology* 18 (1971): 354–363.

COOPER, JOEL, and WORCHEL, STEPHEN.   "Role of Undesired Consequences in the Arousal of Cognitive Dissonance." *Journal of Personality and Social Psychology* 37 (1979): 1179–1185.

COOPER, JOEL; DARLEY, JOHN M.; and HENDERSON, JAMES E.   "On the Effectiveness of Deviant- and Conventionally-Appearing Communicators: A Field Experiment." *Journal of Personality and Social Psychology* 29 (1974): 752–757.

COX, DONALD F., and BAUER, RAYMOND A.   "Self-Confidence and Persuasibility in Women." *Public Opinion Quarterly* 28 (1964): 453–466.

CRANO, WILLIAM D., and MESSÉ, LAWRENCE A.   "When Does Dissonance Fail? The Time Dimension in Attitude Measurement." *Journal of Personality* 38 (1970): 493–508.

CROCKETT, WALTER H.   "Cognitive Complexity and Impression Formation." *Progress in Experimental Personality Research*. Ed. Brandon A. Maher. New York: Academic Press, 1965.

CRONKHITE, GARY.   *Persuasion: Speech and Behavioral Change*. Indianapolis: Bobbs-Merrill, 1965.

CRONKHITE, GARY L.   "Autonomic Correlates of Dissonance and Attitude Change." *Speech Monographs* 33 (1966): 392–399.

CRONKHITE, GARY, and LISKA, JO.   "Symposium: What Criteria Should Be Used to Judge the Admissibility of Evidence to Support Propositions in Communication Research? Introduction." *Western Journal of Speech Communication* 41 (1977): 3–8.

CULLEN, DALLAS M.   "Attitude Measurement by Cognitive Sampling." Ph.D. dissertation, Ohio State University, 1968.

CUSHMAN, DONALD P.   "The Rules Perspective as a Theoretical Basis for the Study of Human Communication." *Communication Quarterly* 25 (1977): 30–45.

CUSHMAN, DONALD, and WHITING, GORDON C.   "An Approach to Communication Theory: Toward Consensus on Rules." *The Journal of Communication* 22 (1972): 217–238.

D'ANDRADE, ROY G.   "Trait Psychology and Componential Analysis." *American Anthropologist* 67 (1965): 215–228.

DAVISON, W. PHILLIPS.   "On the Effects of Communication." *Public Opinion Quarterly* 23 (1959): 343–360.

DAYTON, C. MITCHELL.   *The Design of Educational Experiments*. New York: McGraw-Hill, 1970.

DECI, EDWARD L.   *Intrinsic Motivation*. New York: Plenum Press, 1975.

_____ . "Intrinsic Motivation, Extrinsic Reinforcement and Inequity." *Journal of Personality and Social Psychology* 22 (1972): 113–120.

_____ . "Effects of Externally Mediated Rewards on Intrinsic Motivation." *Journal of Personality and Social Psychology* 18 (1971): 105–115.

DEJONG, WILLIAM. "An Examination of Self-Perception Mediation of the Foot-in-the-Door Effect." *Journal of Personality and Social Psychology* 37 (1979): 2221–2239.

DE LAMATER, JOHN A. "A Definition of 'Group.'" *Small Group Behavior* 5 (1974): 30–44.

DELIA, JESSE G. "Constructivism and the Study of Human Communication." *Quarterly Journal of Speech* 63 (1977a): 66–83.

_____ . "Alternative Perspectives for the Study of Human Communication." *Communication Quarterly* 25 (1977b): 46–62.

DELIA, JESSE G.; CLARK, RUTH ANNE; and SWITZER, DAVID E. "Cognitive Complexity and Impression Formation in Informal Social Interaction." *Speech Monographs* 41 (1974): 299–308.

DEUTSCH, MORTON, and GERARD, HAROLD B. "A Study of Normative and Informational Social Influence on Individual Judgment." *Journal of Abnormal and Social Psychology* 51 (1955): 629–636.

DIENER, ED. "Deindividuation, Self-Awareness, and Disinhibition." *Journal of Personality and Social Psychology* 37 (1979): 1160–1171.

DIENER, EDWARD; FRASER, SCOTT C.; BEAMAN, ARTHUR L.; and KELEM, ROGER T. "Effects of Deindividuation Variables on Stealing among Halloween Trick-or-Treaters." *Journal of Personality and Social Psychology* 33 (1976): 178–183.

DION, KAREN K. "Physical Attractiveness and Children's Evaluation of Peers' Behavior: What Is Beautiful Is Occasionally Suspect." Unpublished MS, University of Toronto, 1978.

DION, KAREN K., and STEIN, STEVEN. "Physical Attractiveness and Interpersonal Influence." *Journal of Experimental Social Psychology* 14 (1978): 97–108.

DITTES, JAMES E., and KELLEY, HAROLD H. "Effects of Different Conditions of Acceptance upon Conformity to Group Norms." *Journal of Abnormal and Social Psychology* 53 (1956): 100–107.

DOOB, LEONARD W. "The Behavior of Attitudes." *Psychological Review* 54 (1947): 135–156.

DRAY, WILLIAM. *Laws and Explanation in History.* London: Oxford University Press, 1957.

DREBEN, ELIZABETH K.; FISKE, SUSAN T.; and HASTIE, REID. "The Independence of Evaluative and Item Information Effects in Behavior-Based Impression Formation." *Journal of Personality and Social Psychology* 37 (1979): 1758–1768.

DUVAL, SHELLEY, and WICKLUND, ROBERT A. *A Theory of Objective Self Awareness.* New York: Academic Press, 1972.

EAGLY, ALICE H. "Comprehensibility of Persuasive Arguments as a Determinant of Opinion Change." *Journal of Personality and Social Psychology* 29 (1974): 758–773.

EAGLY, ALICE H., and HIMMELFARB, SAMUEL. "Current Trends in Attitude Theory and Research." *Readings in Attitude Change.* Ed. Samuel Himmelfarb and Alice Hendrickson Eagly. New York: John Wiley, 1974, pp. 594–610.

EATON, JOSEPH W., and WEIL, ROBERT J. *Culture and Mental Disorders.* New York: Free Press, 1955.

EBON, MARTIN, ed. *The World's Weirdest Cults.* New York: New American Library, 1979.

EHRLICH, HOWARD J. "Attitudes, Behavior, and the Intervening Variables." *American Sociologist* 4 (1969): 29–34.

ELASHOFF, JANET D., and SNOW, RICHARD E. *Pygmalion Reconsidered.* Worthington, Ohio: Charles A. Jones, 1971.

ELMS, ALAN C., and JANIS, IRVING L. "Counter-Norm Attitudes Induced by Consonant versus Dissonant Conditions of Role-Playing." *Journal of Experimental Research in Personality* 1 (1965): 50–60.

ENZLE, MICHAEL E., and ROSS, JUNE M. "Increasing and Decreasing Intrinsic Interest with Contingent Rewards: A Test of Cognitive Evaluation Theory." *Journal of Experimental Social Psychology* 14 (1978): 588–597.

FAZIO, RUSSELL H., and ZANNA, MARK P. "Attitudinal Qualities Relating to the Strength of the Attitude–Behavior Relationship." *Journal of Experimental Social Psychology* 14 (1978): 398–408.

FAZIO, RUSSELL H.; ZANNA, MARK P.; and COOPER, JOEL. "Dissonance and Self-Perception: An Integrative View of Each Theory's Proper Domain of Application." *Journal of Experimental Social Psychology* 13 (1977): 464–479.

FEHRENBACH, PETER A.; MILLER, DAVID J.; and THELEN, MARK H. "The Importance of Consistency of Modeling Behavior upon Imitation: A Comparison of Single and Multiple Models." *Journal of Personality and Social Psychology* 37 (1979): 1412–1417.

FESTINGER, LEON. *A Theory of Cognitive Dissonance*. Evanston, Ill.: Row, Peterson, 1957.

———. "A Theory of Social Comparison Processes." *Human Relations* 7 (1954): 117–140.

———. "Informal Social Communication." *Psychological Review* 57 (1950): 271–282.

FESTINGER, LEON, and CARLSMITH, JAMES M. "Cognitive Consequences of Forced Compliance." *Journal of Abnormal and Social Psychology* 58 (1959): 203–210.

FESTINGER, LEON; PEPITONE, ALBERT; and NEWCOMB, THEODORE. "Some Consequences of Deindividuation in a Group." *Journal of Abnormal and Social Psychology* 47 (1952): 382–389.

FILLENBAUM, SAMUEL. "Prior Deception and Subsequent Experimental Performance: The 'Faithful' Subject." *Journal of Personality and Social Psychology* 4 (1966): 532–537.

FILLENBAUM, SAMUEL, and FREY, ROBERT. "More on the 'Faithful' Behavior of Suspicious Subjects." *Journal of Personality* 38 (1970): 43–51.

FISHBEIN, MARTIN. "The Prediction of Behaviors from Attitudinal Variables." *Advances in Communication Research*. Ed. C. David Mortensen and Kenneth K. Sereno. New York: Harper & Row, 1973, pp. 3–31.

FISHBEIN, MARTIN, and AJZEN, ICEK. *Belief, Attitude, Intention and Behavior*. Reading, Mass.: Addison-Wesley, 1975.

———. "Attitudes Towards Objects as Predictors of Single and Multiple Behavioral Criteria." *Psychological Review* 81 (1974): 59–74.

FISHBEIN, MARTIN, and HUNTER, RONDA. "Summation versus Balance in Attitude Organization and Change." *Journal of Abnormal and Social Psychology* 69 (1964): 505–510.

FISHBEIN, MARTIN, and RAVEN, BERTRAM H. "The AB Scales: An Operational Definition of Belief and Attitude." *Human Relations* 15 (1962): 35–44.

FOSS, ROBERT O., and DEMPSEY, CAROLYN B. "Blood Donation and the Foot-in-the-Door Technique: A Limiting Case." *Journal of Personality and Social Psychology* 37 (1979): 580–590.

FOTHERINGHAM, WALLACE C. *Perspectives on Persuasion*. Boston: Allyn & Bacon, 1966.

FRANSDEN, KENNETH D. "Effects of Threat Appeals and Media of Transmission." *Speech Monographs* 30 (1963): 101–104.

FREEDMAN, JONATHAN L., and FRASER, SCOTT C. "Compliance without Pressure: The Foot-in-the-Door Technique." *Journal of Personality and Social Psychology* 4 (1966): 195–202.

FROMKIN, HOWARD L., and BROCK, TIMOTHY C. "Erotic Materials: A Commodity Theory Analysis of the Enhanced Desirability that May Accompany Their Unavailability." *Journal of Applied Social Psychology* 3 (1973): 219–231.

———. "A Commodity Theory Analysis of Persuasion." *Representative Research in Social Psychology* 2 (1971): 47–57.

GAES, GERALD G.; KALLE, ROBERT J.; and TEDESCHI, JAMES T. "Impression Management in the Forced Compliance Situation: Two Studies Using the Bogus Pipeline." *Journal of Experimental Social Psychology* 14 (1978): 493–510.

GANZ, JOAN SAFRON. *Rules: A Systematic Study*. Paris: Mouton, 1971.

GAUTHIER, DAVID P. *Practical Reasoning*. Oxford: The Clarendon Press, 1963.

GERARD, HAROLD B., and MATHEWSON, GROVER C. "The Effects of Severity of Initiation on Liking for a Group: A Replication." *Journal of Experimental Social Psychology* 2 (1966): 278–287.

GERGEN, KENNETH J.; GERGEN, MARY M.; and BARTON, WILLIAM H. "Deviance in the Dark." *Psychology Today* 7 (1973): 129–130.

GILBERT, G. M. "Stereotype Persistence and Change among College Students." *Journal of Abnormal and Social Psychology* 46 (1951): 245–254.

GILLIG, PAULETTE M., and GREENWALD, ANTHONY G. "Is It Time to Lay the Sleeper Effect to Rest?" *Journal of Personality and Social Psychology* 29 (1974): 132–139.

GLASER, BARNEY G., and STRAUSS, ANSELM L. *The Discovery of Grounded Theory: Strategies for Qualitative Research*. Chicago: Aldine, 1967.

GLASS, GENE V. "Primary, Secondary, and Meta-Analysis Research." *Educational Researcher* 5 (1976): 3–8.

GOETHALS, GEORGE R., and DARLEY, JOHN M. "Social Comparison Theory: An Attributional Approach." *Social Comparison Processes: Theoretical and Empirical Perspectives*. Ed. Jerry M. Suls and Richard L. Miller. Washington: Hemisphere Publishing, 1977, pp. 259–278.

GOETHALS, GEORGE R.; COOPER, JOEL; and NAFICY, ANAHITA. "Role of Foreseen, Foreseeable, and Unforeseeable Behavior Consequences in the Arousal of Cognitive Dissonance." *Journal of Personality and Social Psychology* 37 (1979): 1178–1185.

GOLDMAN, WILLIAM, and LEWIS, PHILIP. "Beautiful Is Good: Evidence that the Physically Attractive are More Socially Skillful." *Journal of Experimental Social Psychology* 13 (1977): 125–130.

GOTTLIEB, GIDON. *Logic of Choice: An Investigation of the Concepts of Rules and Rationality*. New York: Macmillan, 1968.

GRAHAM, BRADLEY, and McCOMBS, PHIL. "The Energy Mess: How We Got There." *The Washington Post*, 8 July 1979, p. A1.

GREENWALD, ANTHONY G. "Cognitive Learning, Cognitive Response to Persuasion, and Attitude Change." *Psychological Foundations of Attitudes*. Ed. Anthony G. Greenwald, Timothy C. Brock, and Thomas M. Ostrom. New York: Academic Press, 1968, pp. 147–170.

GREENWALD, ANTHONY G., and ALBERT, ROSITA D. "Acceptance and Recall of Improvised Arguments." *Journal of Personality and Social Psychology* 8 (1968): 31–34.

GROSS, ALAN E.; RIEMER, BARBARA S.; and COLLINS, BARRY E. "Audience Reaction as a Determinant of the Speaker's Self-Persuasion." *Journal of Experimental Social Psychology* 9 (1973): 246–256.

GRUDER, CHARLES L.; COOK, THOMAS D.; HENNIGAN, KAREN M.; FLAY, BRIAN R.; ALESSIS, CYNTHIA; and HALAMAJ, JEROME. "Empirical Tests of the Absolute Sleeper Effect Predicted from the Discounting Cue Hypothesis." *Journal of Personality and Social Psychology* 36 (1978): 1061–1074.

GUILFORD, J. P., and FRUCHTER, BENJAMIN. *Fundamental Statistics in Psychology and Education*. New York: McGraw-Hill, 1973.

HALE, CLAUDIA, and DELIA, JESSE G. "Cognitive Complexity and Social Perspective-Taking." *Communication Monographs* 43 (1976): 195–203.

HAMILTON, DAVID C., and ZANNA, MARK P. "Context Effects in Impression Formation: Changes in Connotative Meaning." *Journal of Personality and Social Psychology* 29 (1974): 649–654.

HANEY, CRAIG; BANKS, CURTIS; and ZIMBARDO, PHILIP. "Interpersonal Dynamics in a Simulated Prison." *International Journal of Criminology and Penology* 1 (1973): 69–97.

HANSON, NORWOOD RUSSEL. *Patterns of Discovery*. Cambridge: Cambridge University Press, 1958.

HARE, A. PAUL. *Handbook of Small Group Behavior*. New York: Free Press, 1976.

HARRÉ, ROMANO, and SECORD, PAUL F. *The Explanation of Social Behavior*. Oxford: Basil Blackwell, 1972.

HARRISON, RANDALL. "Nonverbal Communication: Explorations into Time, Space, Action, and Object." *Dimensions in Communication*. Ed. J. H. Campbell and H. W. Hepler. Belmont, Calif.: Wadsworth, 1970, pp. 256–271.

HARVEY, JOHN H., and TUCKER, JALIE A. "On Problems with the Cause–Reason Distinction in Attribution Theory." *Journal of Personality and Social Psychology* 37 (1979): 1441–1446.

HAWES, LEONARD C. *Pragmatics of Analoguing: Theory and Model Construction in Communication*. Reading, Mass.: Addison-Wesley, 1975.

HEBERLEIN, THOMAS A., and BLACK, J. STANLEY. "Attitudinal Specificity and the Prediction of Behavior in a Field Setting." *Journal of Personality and Social Psychology* 33 (1976): 474–479.

HEMPEL, CARL G. *Aspects of Scientific Explanation: And Other Essays in the Philosophy of Science*. New York: Free Press, 1965.

HENDRICK, CLYDE, and COSTANTINI, ARTHUR F. "Effects of Varying Trait Inconsistency and Response Requirements on the Primacy Effect in Impression Formation." *Journal of Personality and Social Psychology* 15 (1970): 158–167.

HIEDER, FRITZ. *The Psychology of Interpersonal Relations*. New York: John Wiley, 1958.

HIGGINS, E. TORY; HERMAN, C. PETER; and ZANNA, MARK P., eds. *Social Cognition: The Ontario Symposium*. Hillsdale, N.J.: Lawrence Erlbaum, 1981.

HIGGINS, E. TORY; RHOLES, WILLIAM S.; and JONES, CARL R. "Category Accessibility and Impression Formation." *Journal of Experimental Social Psychology* 13 (1977): 141–154.

HIGGINS, E. TORY; RODEWALT, FREDERICK; and ZANNA, MARK P. "Dissonance Motivation: Its Nature, Persistence, and Reinstatement." *Journal of Experimental Social Psychology* 15 (1979): 16–34.

HILSMAN, ROGER. *To Move a Nation: The Politics of Foreign Policy in the Administration of John F. Kennedy*. Garden City, N.Y.: Doubleday, 1967.

HIMMELFARB, SAMUEL, and EAGLY, ALICE HENDRICKSON, eds. *Readings in Attitude Change*. New York: John Wiley, 1974.

HODGES, BERT H. "Effect of Valence on Relative Weighting in Impression Formation." *Journal of Personality and Social Psychology* 30 (1974): 378–381.

HOLLANDER, EDWIN P. "Conformity, Status and Idiosyncrasy Credit." *Psychological Review* 65 (1958): 117–127.

HOLMES, DAVID S. "Amount of Experience in Experiments as a Determinant of Performance in Later Experiments." *Journal of Personality and Social Psychology* 7 (1967): 403–407.

HOLMES, DAVID S., and APPELBAUM, ALAN S. "Nature of Prior Experimental Experience as a Determinant of Performance in a Subsequent Experiment." *Journal of Personality and Social Psychology* 14 (1970): 195–202.

HORAI, JOANN; NACCARI, NICHOLAS; and FATOULLAH, ELLIOT. "The Effects of Expertise and Physical Attractiveness upon Opinion Agreement and Liking." *Sociometry* 37 (1974): 601–606.

HOVLAND, CARL I., and MANDELL, WALLACE. "Is There a 'Law of Primacy in Persuasion'?" *The Order of Presentation in Persuasion*. Ed. Carl I. Hovland, et al. New Haven, Conn.: Yale University Press, 1957, pp. 13–22.

HOVLAND, CARL I., and WEISS, WALTER. "The Influence of Source Credibility on Communication Effectiveness." *Public Opinion Quarterly* 15 (1951): 635–650.

HOVLAND, CARL I.; CAMPBELL, ENID H.; and BROCK, TIMOTHY. "The Effects of 'Commitment' on Opinion Change Following Communication." *The Order of Presentation in Persuasion*. Ed. Carl I. Hovland, et al. New Haven, Conn.: Yale University Press, 1957, pp. 23–32.

HOVLAND, CARL I.; HARVEY, O. J.; and SHERIF, MUZAFER.   "Assimilation and Contrast Effects in Reactions to Communication and Attitude Change." *Journal of Abnormal and Social Psychology* 55 (1957): 244–252.

HOVLAND, CARL I.; JANIS, IRVING L.; and KELLEY, HAROLD H.   *Communication and Persuasion*. New Haven, Conn.: Yale University Press, 1953.

HOVLAND, CARL I.; LUMSDAINE, ARTHUR A.; and SHEFFIELD, FRED D.   "The Effects of Presenting 'One Side' versus 'Both Sides' in Changing Opinions on a Controversial Subject." *Experiments on Mass Communication*. Princeton, N.J.: Princeton University Press, 1949, pp. 201–227.

HUGHES, CHARLES C.; TREMBLAY, MARC-ABELARD; and RAPOPORT, ROBERT N.   *People of Cove and Woodlot: Communities from the Viewpoint of Social Psychology*. New York: Basic Books, 1960.

HULL, CLARK L.   *Principles of Behavior*. New York: Appleton-Century, 1943.

HUME, DAVID.   *Enquiries Concerning Human Understanding*. Oxford: The Clarendon Press, 1902.

HUNTER, EDWARD.   *Brainwashing in Red China*. New York: Vanguard, 1941.

HYMAN, HERBERT H.   "The Psychology of Status." *Archives of Psychology*, No. 269 (1942).

ITTELSON, WILLIAM H., and CANTRIL, HADLEY.   *Perception: A Transactional Approach*. New York: W. W. Norton, 1954.

JACCARD, JAMES J., and FISHBEIN, MARTIN.   "Inferential Beliefs and Order Effects in Personality Impression Formation." *Journal of Personality and Social Psychology* 31 (1975): 1031–1040.

JACOBS, ROBERT C., and CAMPBELL, DONALD T.   "The Perpetuation of an Arbitrary Tradition through Several Generations of a Laboratory Microculture." *Journal of Abnormal and Social Psychology* 62 (1961): 649–658.

JACOBY, JACOB, and OLSON, JERRY C.   "Consumer Response to Price: An Attitudinal Information Processing Perspective." *Moving Ahead with Attitude Research*. Ed. Yoram Wind and Marshall G. Greenberg. Chicago: American Marketing Association, 1977, pp. 73–86.

JAMES, WILLIAM.   *Psychology*. New York: Holt, 1892.

JANIS, IRVING L.   *Victims of Groupthink: A Psychological Study of Foreign-Policy Decisions and Fiascoes*. Boston: Houghton Mifflin, 1972.

JANIS, IRVING L., and FESHBACH, SEYMOUR.   "Effects of Fear-Arousing Communications." *Journal of Abnormal and Social Psychology* 48 (1953): 78–92.

JANIS, IRVING L., and GILMORE, J. BARNARD.   "The Influence of Incentive Conditions on the Success of Role Playing in Modifying Attitudes." *Journal of Personality and Social Psychology* 1 (1965): 17–27.

JANIS, IRVING L., and MANN, LEON.   "A Conflict-Theory Approach to Attitude Change and Decision Making." *Psychological Foundations of Attitudes*. Ed. Anthony G. Greenwald, Timothy C. Brock, and Thomas M. Ostrom. New York: Academic Press, 1968, pp. 327–360.

————.   "Effectiveness of Emotional Role-Playing in Modifying Smoking Habits and Attitudes." *Journal of Experimental Research in Personality* 1 (1965): 84–90.

JOHANNESEN, RICHARD L., ed.   *Ethics and Persuasion: Selected Readings*. New York: Random House, 1967.

JOHNSON, ROBERT O., and DOWNING, LESLIE L.   "Deindividuation and Valence of Cues: Effects on Prosocial and Antisocial Behavior." *Journal of Personality and Social Psychology* 37 (1979): 1532–1538.

JONES, EDWARD E., and DAVIS, KEITH E.   "From Acts to Dispositions: The Attribution Process in Person Perception." *Advances in Experimental Social Psychology*. Ed. Leonard Berkowitz. New York: Academic Press, 1965.

JONES, EDWARD E., and GERARD, HAROLD B. *Foundations of Social Psychology*. New York: John Wiley, 1967.

JONES, EDWARD E., and GOETHALS, GEORGE R. *Order Effects in Impression Formation: Attribution Context and the Nature of the Entity*. Morristown, N.J.: General Learning Press, 1971.

JONES, EDWARD E., and NISBETT, RICHARD E. *The Actor and the Observer: Divergent Perceptions of the Causes of Behavior*. Morristown, N.J.: General Learning Press, 1971.

JUDD, CHARLES M., and KULIK, JAMES A. "Schematic Effects of Social Attitudes on Information Processing and Recall." *Journal of Personality and Social Psychology* 38 (1980): 569–578.

KAHLE, LYNN R., and BERMAN, JOHN J. "Attitudes Cause Behaviors: A Cross-Lagged Panel Analysis," *Journal of Personality and Social Psychology* 37 (1979): 315–321.

KAISER, ROBERT G. "Candidates on TV: Reagan Goes Low-Key, Carter Goes Dramatic," *The Washington Post*, 9 September 1980, p. A2.

KANT, IMMANUEL. *Critique of Pure Reason*. Trans. N. Kemp Smith. London: Macmillan, 1929.

————. *Critique of Practical Reason and Other Works*. Trans. T. K. Abbott. New York: Longman's, 1909.

————. *Anthropology from a Pragmatic Point of View*. Berlin: Reimer, 1902.

KAPLAN, ABRAHAM. *The Conduct of Inquiry*. San Francisco: Chandler, 1964.

KAPLAN, MARTIN F. "Context Effects in Impression Formation: The Weighted Averaging versus the Meaning–Change Formulation." *Journal of Personality and Social Psychology* 19 (1971): 92–99.

KASSARJIAN, HAROLD H., and COHEN, JOEL B. "Cognitive Dissonance and Consumer Behavior." *California Management Review* 8 (1965): 55–64.

KATZ, DANIEL. "The Functional Approach to the Study of Attitudes." *Public Opinion Quarterly* 24 (1960): 163–204.

KATZ, DANIEL, and BRALY, KENNETH. "Racial Stereotypes of 100 College Students." *Journal of Abnormal and Social Psychology* 28 (1933): 280–290.

KATZ, DANIEL; SARNOFF, IRVING; and McCLINTOCK, CHARLES. "Ego-Defense and Attitude Change." *Human Relations* 9 (1956): 27–45.

KATZ, ELIHU, and FELDMAN, JACOB J. "The Debates in the Light of Research: A Survey of Surveys." *The Process and Effects of Mass Communication*. Ed. Wilbur Schramm and Donald F. Roberts. Urbana, Ill.: University of Illinois Press, 1971, pp. 701–753.

KELLEY, HAROLD H. "The Process of Causal Attribution." *American Psychologist* 28 (1973): 107–128.

————. "Attribution in Social Interaction." *Attribution: Perceiving the Causes of Behavior*. Ed. Edward E. Jones, et al. Morristown, N.J.: General Learning Press, 1972.

————. "Attribution Theory in Social Psychology." *Nebraska Symposium on Motivation*. Ed. David Levine. Lincoln, Neb.: University of Nebraska Press, 1967.

————. "Two Functions of Reference Groups." *Readings in Social Psychology*. 2nd ed. Ed. Guy E. Swanson, Theodore M. Newcomb, and Eugene L. Hartley. New York: Holt, Rinehart & Winston, 1952.

KELLY, GEORGE A. *The Psychology of Personal Constructs*. New York: W. W. Norton, 1955.

KELMAN, HERBERT C. "Attitudes Are Alive and Well and Gainfully Employed in the Sphere of Action." *American Psychologist* 29 (1974): 310–324.

————. "Compliance, Identification, and Internalization: Three Processes of Attitude Change." *Journal of Conflict Resolution* 2 (1958): 51–60.

KELMAN, HERBERT C., and HOVLAND, CARL I. "'Reinstatement' of the Communicator in Delayed Measurement of Opinion Change." *Journal of Abnormal and Social Psychology* 48 (1953): 327–335.

KENNEDY, ROBERT F. *Thirteen Days: A Memoir of the Cuban Missile Crisis.* New York: W. W. Norton, 1969.

KENNY, DAVID A. "Cross-Lagged Panel Correlation: A Test for Spuriousness." *Psychological Bulletin* 82 (1975): 887–903.

KENRICK, DOUGLAS T., and GUTIERRES, SARA E. "Contrast Effects and Judgments of Physical Attractiveness: When Beauty Becomes a Social Problem." *Journal of Personality and Social Psychology* 38 (1980): 131–140.

KERCKHOFF, ALAN C.; BACK, KURT W.; and MILLER, NORMAN. "Sociometric Patterns in Hysterical Contagion." *Sociometry* 28 (1965): 2–15.

KERLINGER, FRED N. *Foundations of Behavioral Research.* New York: Holt, Rinehart & Winston, 1964.

KERLINGER, FRED N., and PEDHAZUR, ELAZAR J. *Multiple Regression in Behavioral Research.* New York: Holt, Rinehart & Winston, 1973.

KEY, WILSON BRYAN. *Media Sexploitation.* New York: New American Library, 1976.

————. *Subliminal Seduction: Ad Media's Manipulation of a Not So Innocent America.* New York: New American Library, 1973.

KIESLER, CHARLES A., and KIESLER, SARA B. *Conformity.* Reading, Mass.: Addison-Wesley, 1969.

KIESLER, CHARLES A.; COLLINS, BARRY E.; and MILLER, NORMAN. *Attitude Change: A Critical Analysis of Theoretical Approaches.* New York: John Wiley, 1969.

KIESLER, CHARLES A.; NISBETT, RICHARD E.; and ZANNA, MARK P. "On Inferring One's Beliefs from One's Behavior." *Journal of Personality and Social Psychology* 11 (1969): 321–327.

KIM, JAI-ON, and KOHOUT, FRANK J. "Special Topics in General Linear Models." *Statistical Package for the Social Sciences.* Ed. Norman Nie, et al. New York: McGraw-Hill, 1975, pp. 368–397.

KING, STEPHEN W. *Communication and Social Influence.* Reading, Mass.: Addison-Wesley, 1975.

KLAPPER, JOSEPH T. *The Effects of Mass Communication.* Glencoe, Ill.: The Free Press, 1960.

KLATZKY, ROBERTA L. *Human Memory: Structures and Processes.* San Francisco: W. H. Freeman, 1975.

KNAPP, MARK L. *Social Intercourse: From Greeting to Goodbye.* Boston: Allyn & Bacon, 1978.

KNOWER, FRANKLIN R. "Experimental Studies of Changes in Attitudes I. A Study of The Effect of Oral Argument on Changes of Attitude." *Journal of Abnormal and Social Psychology* 6 (1935): 315–347.

KOZIOL, RONALD. "Patty's Story: Why I Joined the SLA." *Chicago Tribune,* 6 February 1976, p. 1, p. 10.

KRAUT, ROBERT E. "Effects of Social Labeling on Giving to Charity." *Journal of Experimental Social Psychology* 9 (1973): 551–562.

KRECH, DAVID; CRUTCHFIELD, RICHARD S.; and BALLACHEY, EGERTON, L. *Individuals in Society: A Textbook of Social Psychology.* New York: McGraw-Hill, 1962.

KRUGLANSKI, ARIE W. "Causal Explanation, Teleological Explanation: On Radical Particularism in Attribution Theory." *Journal of Personality and Social Psychology* 37 (1979): 1447–1457.

————. "Much Ado about the 'Volunteer Artifacts.'" *Journal of Personality and Social Psychology* 28 (1973): 348–354.

KRUGMAN, HERBERT E. "The Impact of Television Advertising: Learning Without Involvement." *The Process and Effects of Mass Communication.* Ed. Wilbur Schramm and Donald F. Roberts. Urbana, Ill.: University of Illinois Press, 1971, pp. 485–494.

KUIPER, N. A., and ROGERS, T. B. "Encoding of Personal Information: Self–Other Differences." *Journal of Personality and Social Psychology* 37 (1979): 499–514.

LAMM, HELMUT, and MYERS, DAVID G.   "Group Induced Polarization of Attitudes and Behavior." *Advances in Experimental Social Psychology*. Ed. Leonard Berkowitz. New York: Academic Press, 1978, pp. 145–195.

LANGER, ELLEN J.   "Rethinking the Role of Thought in Social Interaction." *New Directions in Attribution Research*. Ed. John H. Harvey, William Ickes, and Robert F. Kidd. Hillsdale, N.J.: Lawrence Erlbaum, 1978, pp. 35–58.

————. "The Illusion of Control." *Journal of Personality and Social Psychology* 32 (1975): 311–328.

LANGER, ELLEN; BLANK, ARTHUR; and CHANOWITZ, BENZION.   "The Mindlessness of Ostensibly Thoughtful Action: The Role of 'Placebic' Information in Interpersonal Attraction." *Journal of Personality and Social Psychology* 36 (1978): 635–642.

LA PIÉRE, RICHARD T.   "Attitudes vs. Action." *Social Forces* 13 (1934): 230–237.

LARSON, CHARLES U.   *Persuasion: Reception and Responsibility*. 2nd ed. Belmont, Calif.: Wadsworth, 1979.

LASSWELL, HAROLD D.   "The Structure and Function of Communication in Society." *The Communication of Ideas*. Ed. Lyman Bryson. New York: Institute for Religious and Social Studies, 1948, pp. 37–51.

LAY, CLARRY H., and JACKSON, DOUGLAS N.   "Analysis of the Generality of Trait Inferential Relationships." *Journal of Personality and Social Psychology* 12 (1969): 12–21.

LAZARSFELD, PAUL F., and MERTON, ROBERT K.   "Mass Communication, Popular Taste, and Organized Social Action." *The Communication of Ideas*. Ed. Lyman Bryson. New York: Institute for Religious and Social Studies, 1948.

LE BON, GUSTAV.   *The Crowd*. London: Allen and Unwin, 1903.

LENIHAN, K. J.   "Perceived Climates as a Barrier to Housing Desegregation." Unpublished MS, Columbia University, 1965.

LEPPER, MARK R.; GREENE, DAVID; and NISBETT, RICHARD E.   "Undermining Children's Intrinsic Interest with Extrinsic Rewards: A Test of the 'Overjustification' Hypothesis." *Journal of Personality and Social Psychology* 28 (1973): 129–137.

LERBINGER, OTTO.   *Designs for Persuasive Communication*. Englewood Cliffs, N.J.: Prentice-Hall, 1972.

LEVENTHAL, HOWARD.   "Fear Communications in the Acceptance of Preventive Health Practices." *Experiments in Persuasion*. Ed. Ralph L. Rosnow and Edward J. Robinson. New York: Academic Press, 1967, pp. 168–192.

LEVENTHAL, HOWARD, and NILES, PATRICIA.   "Persistence of Influence for Varying Durations of Exposure to Threat Stimuli." *Psychological Reports* 16 (1965): 223–233.

LEVENTHAL, HOWARD; SINGER, ROBERT; and JONES, SUSAN.   "Effects of Fear and Specificity of Recommendation upon Attitudes and Behavior." *Journal of Personality and Social Psychology* 2 (1965): 20–29.

LEVINGER, GEORGE, and SCHNEIDER, DAVID J.   "Test of the 'Risk is a Value' Hypothesis." *Journal of Personality and Social Psychology* 11 (1969): 165–169.

LEWIN, KURT.   "Group Decision and Social Change." *Basic Readings in Social Psychology*. Ed. Harold M. Proshansky and Bernard Seidenberg. New York: Holt, Rinehart & Winston, 1965.

LEWIS, STEVEN A.; LANGAN, CHARLES J.; and HOLLANDER, EDWIN P.   "Expectation of Future Interaction and the Choice of Less Desirable Alternatives in Conformity." *Sociometry* 35 (1972): 440–447.

LINDER, DARWYN E.; COOPER, JOEL; and JONES, EDWARD E.   "Decision Freedom as a Determinant of the Role of Incentive Magnitude in Attitude Change." *Journal of Personality and Social Psychology* 6 (1967): 39–45.

LINGLE, JOHN H., and OSTROM, THOMAS M.   "Thematic Effects of Attitude on the Cognitive Processing of Attitude Relevant Information." *Cognitive Responses in Persuasion*. Ed. Richard E. Petty, Thomas M. Ostrom, and Timothy C. Brock. Hillsdale, N.J.: Lawrence Erlbaum, in press.

LINGLE, JOHN H.; GEVA, NEHEMIA; OSTROM, THOMAS M.; LEIPPE, MICHAEL R.; and BAUM-GARDNER, MICHAEL H.   "Thematic Effects of Person Judgments on Impression Organization." *Journal of Personality and Social Psychology* 37 (1979): 674–687.

LORD, CHARLES G.   "Schemas and Images as Memory Aids: Two Modes of Processing Social Information." *Journal of Personality and Social Psychology* 38 (1980): 257–269.

LUCHINS, ABRAHAM S.   "Primacy–Recency in Impression Formation." *The Order of Presentation in Persuasion*. Ed. Carl I. Hovland, et al. New Haven, Conn.: Yale University Press, 1957a, pp. 33–61.

_____.   "Experimental Attempts to Minimize the Impact of First Impressions." *The Order of Presentation in Persuasion*. Ed. Carl I. Hovland, et al. New Haven, Conn.: Yale University Press, 1957b, pp. 62–75.

LUMSDAINE, ARTHUR A., and JANIS, IRVING L.   "Resistance to 'Counterpropaganda' Produced by One-sided and Two-sided 'Propaganda' Presentations." *Public Opinion Quarterly* 17 (1953): 311–318.

LUND, FREDERICK HANSEN.   "The Psychology of Belief: A Study of its Emotional and Volitional Determinants." *Journal of Abnormal and Social Psychology* 20 (1925): 174–196.

LUTZ, R. J., and SWASY, J. L.   "Integrating Cognitive Structure and Cognitive Response Approaches to Monitoring Communication Effects." *Advances in Consumer Research* 5 (1977): 363–371.

McARTHUR, LESLIE ANN; KIESLER, CHARLES A.; and COOK, BARRY P.   "Acting on an Attitude as a Function of a Self-Precept and Inequity." *Journal of Personality and Social Psychology* 12 (1969): 295–302.

McCAULEY, CLARK, and JACQUES, SUSAN.   "The Popularity of Conspiracy Theories of Presidential Assassination: A Bayesian Analysis." *Journal of Personality and Social Psychology* 37 (1979): 637–644.

McCLEARY, RICHARD; HAY, JR., RICHARD A.; MEIDINGER, ERROL E.; and McDOWALL, DAVID.   *Applied Times Series Analysis for the Social Sciences*. Beverly Hills, Calif.: Sage Publications, 1980.

McCLINTOCK, CHARLES G.   "Personality Syndromes and Attitude Change." *Journal of Personality* 26 (1958): 479–593.

McCROSKEY, JAMES C.   "A Summary of Experimental Research on the Effects of Evidence in Persuasive Communication." *The Process of Social Influence*. Ed. Thomas D. Beisecker and Donn W. Parson. Englewood Cliffs, N.J.: Prentice-Hall, 1972, pp. 318–328.

_____.   "Scales for the Measurement of Ethos." *Speech Monographs* 33 (1966): 65–72.

McCROSKEY, JAMES C., and MEHRLEY, R. SAMUEL.   "The Effects of Disorganization and Nonfluency on Attitude Change and Source Credibility." *Speech Monographs* 36 (1969): 13–21.

McCROSKEY, JAMES C., and YOUNG, THOMAS J.   "The Use and Abuse of Factor Analysis in Communication Research." *Human Communication Research* 5 (1979): 375–382.

McDERMOTT, VIRGINIA.   "The Literature on Classical Theory Construction." *Human Communication Research* 2 (1975): 83–103.

McGINNISS, JOE.   *The Selling of the President 1968*. New York: Trident Press, 1969.

McGUIRE, WILLIAM J.   "The Concept of Attitudes and Their Relations to Behaviors." *Perspectives on Attitude Assessment: Surveys and Their Alternatives*. Ed. H. Wallace Sinaiko and L. A. Broedling. Champaign, Ill.: Pendleton, 1976.

_____.   "The Yin and Yang of Progress in Social Psychology: Seven Koan." *Journal of Personality and Social Psychology* 26 (1973): 446–456.

_____.   "Personality and Susceptibility to Social Influence." *Handbook of Personality Theory and Research*. Ed. Edgar F. Borgatta and William W. Lambert. Chicago: Rand McNally, 1968a, pp. 1130–1187.

————. "Personality and Attitude Change: An Information-Processing Theory." *Psychological Foundations of Attitudes.* Ed. Anthony G. Greenwald, Timothy C. Brock, and Thomas M. Ostrom. New York: Academic Press, 1968b, pp. 171–196.

————. "Inducing Resistance to Persuasion: Some Contemporary Approaches." *Advances in Experimental Social Psychology.* Ed. Leonard Berkowitz. New York: Academic Press, 1964, pp. 191–229.

————. "Persistence of the Resistance to Persuasion Induced by Various Types of Prior Defenses." *Journal of Abnormal and Social Psychology* 64 (1963): 241–248.

————. "Resistance to Persuasion Conferred by Active and Passive Prior Refutation of the Same and Alternative Counterarguments." *Journal of Abnormal and Social Psychology* 63 (1961a): 326–332.

————. "The Effectiveness of Supportive and Refutational Defenses in Immunizing and Restoring Beliefs against Persuasion." *Sociometry* 24 (1961b): 184–197.

McGUIRE, WILLIAM J., and PAPAGEORGIS, DEMETRIOS. "Effectiveness of Forewarning in Developing Resistance to Persuasion." *Public Opinion Quarterly* 26 (1962): 24–34.

————. "The Relative Efficacy of Various Types of Prior Belief-Defense in Producing Immunity against Persuasion." *Journal of Abnormal and Social Psychology* 63 (1961): 327–337.

MacNEIL, MARK K., and SHERIF, MUZAFER. "Norm Change over Subject Generations as a Function of Arbitrariness of Prescribed Norms." *Journal of Personality and Social Psychology* 34 (1976): 762–773.

McNEMAR, QUINN. "Opinion–Attitude Methodology." *Psychological Bulletin* 43 (1946): 289–374.

MANN, LEON. "The Effects of Emotional Role Playing on Desire to Modify Smoking Habits." *Journal of Experimental Social Psychology* 3 (1967): 334–348.

MANN, LEON, and JANIS, IRVING L. "A Follow-up Study on the Long-Term Effects of Emotional Role Playing." *Journal of Personality and Social Psychology* 8 (1968): 339–342.

MARKUS, HAZEL. "Self-Schemata and Processing Information about the Self." *Journal of Personality and Social Psychology* 35 (1977): 63–78.

MARSHALL, GARY D., and ZIMBARDO, PHILIP G. "Affective Consequences of Inadequately Explained Physiological Arousal." *Journal of Personality and Social Psychology* 37 (1979): 970–988.

MASLACH, CHRISTINA. "Negative Emotional Biasing of Unexplained Arousal." *Journal of Personality and Social Psychology* 37 (1979): 953–969.

MASLING, JOSEPH. "Role-Related Behavior of the Subject and Psychologist and its Effects upon Psychological Data." *Nebraska Symposium on Motivation.* Ed. David Levine. Lincoln, Neb.: University of Nebraska Press, 1966, pp. 67–103.

MASSAD, CHRISTOPHER M.; HUBBARD, MICHAEL; and NEWTSON, DARREN. "Selective Perception of Events." *Journal of Experimental Social Psychology* 15 (1979): 513–532.

MEDALIA, NAHUM Z., and LARSEN, OTTO N. "Diffusion and Belief in a Collective Delusion: The Seattle Windshield Pitting Epidemic." *American Sociological Review* 23 (1958): 180–186.

MELDEN, ABRAHAM IRVING. *Free Action.* London: Routledge and Kegan Paul, 1961.

MEWBORN, C. RONALD. "Effects of Threat and Reassurance upon Attitude Change." Unpublished Master's thesis, University of South Carolina, 1975.

MIGLER, BERNARD, and WOLPE, JOSEPH. "Automated Self-Desensitization: A Case Report." *Behavior Research and Theory* 5 (1967): 133–135.

MILGRAM, STANLEY. *Obedience to Authority: An Experimental View.* New York: Harper & Row, 1974.

MILLER, DANIEL R., and SWANSON, GUY E. *Inner Conflict and Defense.* New York: Holt, Rinehart & Winston, 1960.

MILLER, GERALD R.   "On Being Persuaded: Some Basic Definitions." *Persuasion: New Directions in Theory and Research.* Ed. Michael E. Roloff and Gerald R. Miller. Beverly Hills, Calif.: Sage Publications, 1980, pp. 11–28.

————.   "The Current Status of Theory and Research in Interpersonal Communication." *Human Communication Research* 4 (1978): 164–178.

————.   "Interpersonal Communication: A Conceptual Perspective." *Communication* 2 (1975): 93–105.

————.   *An Introduction to Speech Communication.* Indianapolis: Bobbs-Merrill, 1972.

————.   "Research Setting: Laboratory Studies." *Methods of Research in Communication.* Ed. Philip Emmert and William D. Brooks. Boston: Houghton Mifflin, 1970, pp. 77–104.

————.   "A Crucial Problem in Attitude Research." *Quarterly Journal of Speech* 53 (1967): 235–240.

MILLER, GERALD R., and BERGER, CHARLES R.   "On Keeping the Faith in Matters Scientific." *Western Journal of Speech Communication* 42 (1978): 44–57.

MILLER, GERALD R., and BURGOON, MICHAEL.   "Persuasion Research: Review and Commentary." *Communication Yearbook* 2. Ed. Brent D. Ruben. New Brunswick, N.J.: Transaction Books, 1978, pp. 29–47.

————.   *New Techniques of Persuasion.* New York: Harper & Row, 1973.

MILLER, GERALD R., and STEINBERG, MARK.   *Between People: A New Analysis of Interpersonal Communication.* Chicago: Science Research Associates, 1975.

MILLER, MICHAEL D., and BURGOON, MICHAEL.   "The Relationship between Violations of Expectations and the Induction of Resistance to Persuasion." *Human Communication Research* 5 (1979): 301–313.

MILLER, NORMAN.   "Involvement and Dogmatism as Inhibitors of Attitude Change." *Journal of Experimental Social Psychology* 1 (1965): 121–132.

MILLER, NORMAN; MARUYAMA, GEOFFREY; BEABER, REX JULIAN; and VALONEE, KEITH.   "Speed of Speech and Persuasion." *Journal of Personality and Social Psychology* 34 (1976): 615–624.

MILLS, JUDSON, and ARONSON, ELIOT.   "Opinion Change as a Function of the Communicator's Attractiveness and Desire to Influence." *Journal of Personality and Social Psychology* 1 (1965): 173–177.

MINNICK, WAYNE C.   *The Art of Persuasion.* Boston: Houghton Mifflin, 1968.

MINSKY, MARVIN.   "A Framework for Representing Knowledge." *The Psychology of Computer Vision.* Ed. Patrick Henry Winston. New York: McGraw-Hill, 1975.

MISCHEL, THEODORE, ed.   *Human Action.* New York: Academic Press, 1969.

MONGE, PETER R.   "The Systems Perspective as a Theoretical Basis for the Study of Human Communication." *Communication Quarterly* 25 (1977): 19–29.

MONGE, PETER R., and DAY, PATRICK D.   "Multivariate Analysis in Communication Research." *Human Communication Research* 1 (1976): 201–220.

MONTGOMERY, CHARLES L., and BURGOON, MICHAEL.   "The Effects of Androgyny and Message Expectations on Resistance to Persuasive Communication." *Communication Monographs* 47 (1980): 56–67.

MOORE, BERT S.; SHERROD, DRURY R.; LIU, THOMAS J.; and UNDERWOOD, BILL.   "The Dispositional Shift in Attribution over Time." *Journal of Experimental Social Psychology* 15 (1979): 553–569.

MORENO, JACOB L.   *Who Shall Survive?* 2nd ed. New York: Beacon House, 1953.

MORTENSEN, C. DAVID.   "A Transactional Paradigm of Verbalized Social Conflict." *Perspectives on Communication in Social Conflict.* Ed. Gerald R. Miller and Herbert W. Simons. Englewood Cliffs, N.J.: Prentice-Hall, 1974, pp. 90–124.

MOSCOVICI, SERGE, and ZAVALLONI, MARISA.   "The Group as a Polarizer of Attitudes." *Journal of Personality and Social Psychology* 12 (1969): 125–135.

MYERS, DAVID G.   "Polarizing Effects of Social Comparison." *Journal of Experimental Social Psychology* 14 (1978): 554–563.

————.   "Summary and Bibliography of Experiments on Group-Induced Response Shift." *Catalog of Selected Documents in Psychology* 3 (1973): 123.

MYERS, DAVID G., and KAPLAN, MARTIN F.   "Group-Induced Polarization in Simulated Juries." *Personality and Social Psychology Bulletin* 1 (1976): 63–66.

MYERS, DAVID G., and LAMM, HELMUT.   "The Group Polarization Phenomenon." *Psychological Bulletin* 83 (1976): 602–627.

MYERS, DAVID G.; WOJCICKI, SANDRA BROWN; and AARDEMA, BOBETTE S.   "Attitude Comparison: Is There Ever a Bandwagon Effect?" *Journal of Applied Social Psychology* 7 (1977): 341–347.

NEL, ELIZABETH; HELMREICH, ROBERT; and ARONSON, ELIOT.   "Opinion Change in the Advocate as a Function of the Persuasibility of His Audience: A Clarification of the Meaning of Dissonance." *Journal of Personality and Social Psychology* 12 (1969): 117–124.

NEWTSON, DARREN A.   "Foundations of Attribution: The Perception of Ongoing Behavior." *New Directions in Attribution Research*. Ed. John H. Harvey, William J. Ickes, and Robert F. Kidd. Hillsdale, N.J.: Lawrence Erlbaum, 1976.

————.   "Attribution and the Unit of Perception of Ongoing Behavior." *Journal of Personality and Social Psychology* 28 (1973): 28–38.

NEWTSON, DARREN, and ENQUIST, GRETCHEN.   "The Perceptual Organization of Ongoing Behavior." *Journal of Experimental Social Psychology* 12 (1976): 847–862.

NIDORF, LEWIS J., and CROCKETT, WALTER H.   "Cognitive Complexity and the Integration of Conflicting Information in Written Impressions." *Journal of Social Psychology* 66 (1965): 165–169.

NILES, PATRICIA.   "The Relationship of Susceptibility and Anxiety to Acceptance of Fear-Arousing Communications." Ph.D dissertation, Yale University, 1964.

NOFSINGER, JR., ROBERT E.   "A Peek at Conversational Analysis." *Communication Quarterly* 25 (1977): 12–20.

NORMAN, DONALD A.   *Memory and Attention*. 2nd ed. New York: John Wiley, 1976.

NORMAN, ROSS.   "When What Is Said Is Important: A Comparison of Expert and Attractive Sources." *Journal of Experimental Social Psychology* 12 (1976): 294–300.

————.   "Affective–Cognitive Consistency, Attitudes, Conformity, and Behavior." *Journal of Personality and Social Psychology* 32 (1975): 83–91.

NUTTIN, JR., JOZEF M.   *The Illusion of Attitude Change: Toward a Response Contagion Theory of Persuasion*. London: Academic Press, 1975.

ODEN, GREGG C., and ANDERSON, NORMAN H.   "Differential Weighting in Integration Theory." *Journal of Experimental Psychology* 89 (1971): 152–161.

ORNE, MARTIN T.   "On the Social Psychology of the Psychological Experiment: With Particular Reference to Demand Characteristics and Their Implications." *American Psychologist* 17 (1962): 776–783.

OSTERHOUSE, ROBERT A., and BROCK, TIMOTHY C.   "Distraction Increases Yielding to Propaganda by Inhibiting Counterarguing." *Journal of Personality and Social Psychology* 15 (1970): 344–358.

OSTROM, THOMAS M.   "Between-Theory and Within-Theory Conflict in Explaining Context Effects in Impression Formation." *Journal of Experimental Social Psychology* 13 (1977): 492–503.

————.   "Meaning Shift in the Judgment of Compound Stimuli." Unpublished MS, Ohio State University, 1967.

OSTROM, THOMAS M., and DAVIS, DEBORAH.   "Idiosyncratic Weighting of Trait Information in Impression Formation." *Journal of Personality and Social Psychology* 37 (1979): 2025–2043.

OSTROM, THOMAS M., and UPSHAW, HARRY S.   "Psychological Perspective and Attitude Change." *Psychological Foundations of Attitudes*. Ed. Anthony G. Greenwald, Timothy C. Brock, and Thomas M. Ostrom. New York: Academic Press, 1968, pp. 217–242.

PACKARD, VANCE.   *The Hidden Persuaders*. New York: David McKay, 1957.

PAGE, RICHARD A., and MOSS, MARTIN K.   "Attitude Similarity and Attraction: The Effects of the Bogus Pipeline." *Bulletin of the Psychonomic Society* 5 (1975): 63–65.

PAICHELER, GENEVIÈVE.   "Norms and Attitude Change I. Polarization and Styles of Behavior." *European Journal of Social Psychology* 6 (1976): 405–427.

PAPAGEORGIS, DEMETRIOS, and MCGUIRE, WILLIAM J.   "The Generality of Immunity to Persuasion Produced by Pre-Exposure to Weakened Counterarguments." *Journal of Abnormal and Social Psychology* 62 (1961): 475–481.

PAUL, GORDON.   *Insight versus Desensitization in Psychotherapy*. Stanford, Calif.: Stanford University Press, 1966.

PEARCE, W. BARNETT.   "The Structure of the Social Order: A Review of Research about Communication Rules." Unpublished MS, University of Massachusetts, 1978.

————.   "Metatheoretical Concerns in Communication." *Communication Quarterly* 25 (1977a): 3–6.

————.   "Naturalistic Study of Communication: Its Function and Form." *Communication Quarterly* 25 (1977b): 51–56.

————.   "The Coordinated Management of Meaning: A Rules-Based Theory of Interpersonal Communication. *Explorations in Interpersonal Communication*. Ed. Gerald R. Miller. Beverly Hills, Calif.: Sage Publications, 1976, pp. 17–35.

PEARCE, W. BARNETT, and CRONEN, VERNON E.   *Communication, Action, and Meaning: The Creation of Social Realities*. New York: Praeger, 1980.

PEARCE, W. BARNETT; HARRIS, LINDA M.; and CRONEN, VERNON E.   "The Coordinated Management of Meaning: Human Communication Theory in a New Key." *Rigor and Imagination: Essays on Communication from the Interactional View*. Ed. John Weakland and Carol Wilder-Mott. New York: Praeger, in press.

PEMBER, DON R.   *Mass Media in America*. 2nd ed. Chicago: Science Research Associates, 1977.

PENICK, SYDNOR B.; FILION, ROSS; FOX, SONJA; and STUNKARD, ALBERT J.   "Behavior Modification in the Treatment of Obesity." *Psychosomatic Medicine* 33 (1971): 49–55.

PERLOFF, RICHARD M., and BROCK, TIMOTHY C.   " 'And Thinking Makes it So:' Cognitive Responses in Persuasion." *Persuasion: New Directions in Theory and Research*. Ed. Michael E. Roloff and Gerald R. Miller. Beverly Hills, Calif.: Sage Publications, 1980, pp. 67–99.

PERRY, DAVID G., and BUSSEY, KAY.   "The Social Learning Theory of Sex Differences: Imitation is Alive and Well." *Journal of Personality and Social Psychology* 37 (1979): 1699–1712.

PETTY, RICHARD E., and CACIOPPO, JOHN T.   "Issue Involvement Can Increase or Decrease Persuasion by Enhancing Message-Relevant Cognitive Responses." *Journal of Personality and Social Psychology* 37 (1979): 1915–1926.

————.   "Forewarning, Cognitive Responding, and Resistance to Persuasion." *Journal of Personality and Social Psychology* 35 (1977): 645–655.

PETTY, RICHARD E.; HARKINS, STEPHEN G.; and WILLIAMS, KIPLING D.   "The Effects of Group Diffusion of Cognitive Effort on Attitudes: An Information-Processing View." *Journal of Personality and Social Psychology* 38 (1980): 81–92.

PETTY, RICHARD E.; WELLS, GARY L.; and BROCK, TIMOTHY C.   "Distraction Can Enhance or Reduce Yielding to Propaganda: Thought Disruption versus Effort Justification." *Journal of Personality and Social Psychology* 34 (1976): 874–884.

PETTY, RICHARD E.; OSTROM, THOMAS M.; and BROCK, TIMOTHY, eds.   *Cognitive Responses in Persuasion*. Hillsdale, N.J.: Lawrence Erlbaum, in press.

PIAGET, JEAN. *The Language and Thought of the Child.* Trans. Marjorie Warden. New York: Harcourt, Brace, and World, 1926.

PLINER, PATRICIA; HART, HEATHER; KOHL, JOANNE; and SAARI, DORY. "Compliance Without Pressure: Some Further Data on the Foot-in-the-Door Technique." *Journal of Experimental Social Psychology* 10 (1974): 17–22.

PRESS, ALLEN N.; CROCKETT, WALTER H.; and DELIA, JESSE G. "The Effect of Cognitive Complexity and of the Perceiver's Set upon the Organization of Impressions." Unpublished MS, Kansas State University, 1974.

PRUITT, DEAN G. "Choice Shifts in Group Discussion: An Introductory Review." *Journal of Personality and Social Psychology* 20 (1971a): 339–360.

———. "Conclusions: Toward an Understanding of Choice Shifts in Group Discussion." *Journal of Personality and Social Psychology* 20 (1971b): 495–510.

PRYOR, BERT, and STEINFATT, THOMAS M. "The Effects of Initial Belief Level on Inoculation Theory and Its Proposed Mechanisms." *Human Communication Research* 4 (1978): 217–230.

QUIGLEY-FERNANDEZ, BARBARA, and TEDESCHI, JAMES T. "The Bogus Pipeline as a Lie Detector: Two Validity Studies." *Journal of Personality and Social Psychology* 36 (1978): 247–256.

RABBIE, JACOB M.; BREHM, JACK W.; and COHEN, ARTHUR R. "Verbalization and Reactions to Cognitive Dissonance." *Journal of Personality* 27 (1959): 407–417.

REDL, FRITZ. "The Phenomenon of Contagion and 'Shock Effect' in Group Therapy." *Searchlight on Delinquency.* Ed. K. R. Eissler. New York: International Universities Press, 1949.

REARDON, KATHLEEN KELLEY. *Persuasion: Theory and Context.* Beverly Hills, Calif.: Sage Publications, 1981.

REGAN, DENNIS T., and FAZIO, RUSSELL. "On The Consistency between Attitudes and Behavior: Look to the Method of Attitude Formation." *Journal of Experimental Social Psychology* 13 (1977): 28–45.

ROBBINS, JHAN, and FISHER, DAVE. *How to Make and Break Habits.* New York: Dell, 1973.

ROGERS, RONALD W., and MEWBORN, C. RONALD. "Fear Appeals and Attitude Change: Effects of a Threat's Noxiousness, Probability of Occurrence, and the Efficacy of Coping Responses." *Journal of Personality and Social Psychology* 34 (1976): 54–61.

ROGERS, T. B.; KUIPER, N. A.; and KIRKER, W. S. "Self-Reference and the Encoding of Personal Information." *Journal of Personality and Social Psychology* 35 (1977): 677–688.

ROKEACH, MILTON. *Beliefs, Attitudes, and Values.* San Francisco: Jossey-Bass, 1968.

ROKEACH, MILTON, and KLIEJUNAS, PETER. "Behavior as a Function of Attitude-Toward-Object and Attitude-Toward-Situation." *Journal of Personality and Social Psychology* 22 (1972): 194–201.

ROLOFF, MICHAEL E. "Self-Awareness and the Persuasion Process: De We Really Know What We're Doing?" *Persuasion: New Directions in Theory and Research.* Ed. Michael E. Roloff and Gerald R. Miller. Beverly Hills, Calif.: Sage Publications, 1980, pp. 29–66.

ROSENBAUM, MILTON E., and TUCKER, IRVING F. "Competence of the Model and the Learning of Imitation and Nonimitation." *Journal of Experimental Psychology* 63 (1962): 183–190.

ROSENBERG, MILTON J. "The Conditions and Consequences of Evaluation Apprehension." *Artifact in Behavioral Research.* Ed. Robert Rosenthal and Ralph L. Rosnow. New York: Academic Press, 1969.

———. "When Dissonance Fails: On Eliminating Evaluation Apprehension from Attitude Measurement." *Journal of Personality and Social Psychology* 1 (1965): 28–42.

ROSENKRANTZ, PAUL S., and CROCKETT, WALTER H. "Some Factors Influencing the Assimilation of Disparate Information in Impression Formation." *Journal of Personality and Social Psychology* 2 (1965): 397–402.

ROSENTHAL, ROBERT. "Interpersonal Expectations: Effects of the Experimenter's Hypothesis." *Arti-

fact in Behavioral Research. Ed. Robert Rosenthal and Ralph L. Rosnow. New York: Academic Press, 1965, pp. 181–277.

ROSENTHAL, ROBERT, and JACOBSON, LENORE. *Pygmalion in the Classroom: Teacher Expectation and Pupils' Intellectual Development.* New York: Holt, Rinehart & Winston, 1968.

ROSENTHAL, ROBERT, and ROSNOW, RALPH L. "The Volunter Subject." *Artifact in Behavioral Research.* Ed. Robert Rosenthal and Ralph L. Rosnow. New York: Academic Press, 1969, pp. 59–118.

ROSNOW, RALPH L., and ROSENTHAL, ROBERT. "Volunteer Subjects and the Results of Opinion Change Studies." *Psychological Reports* 19 (1966): 1183–1187.

ROSS, LEE. "The Intuitive Psychologist and his Shortcomings: Distortions in the Attribution Process." *Advances in Experimental Social Psychology.* Ed. Leonard Berkowitz. New York: Academic Press, 1977.

ROSS, LEE; BIERBRAUER, GÜNTER; and HOFFMAN, SUSAN. "The Role of Attribution Processes in Conformity and Dissent: Revisiting the Asch Situation." *American Psychologist* 31 (1976): 148–157.

ROSSITER, CHARLES M. "The Validity of Communication Experiments Using Human Subjects: A Review." *Human Communication Research* 1 (1976): 197–206.

ROTHBART, MYRON; FULERO, SOLOMON; JENSEN, CHRISTINE; HOWARD, JOHN; and BIRRELL, PAMELA. "From Individual to Group Impressions: Availability Heuristics in Stereotype Formation." *Journal of Experimental Social Psychology* 14 (1978): 237–255.

ROYCE, JOSEPH R. *The Encapsulated Man.* New York: Van Nostrand Reinhold, 1964.

SANDERS, GLENN S., and BARON, ROBERT S. "Is Social Comparison Irrelevant for Producing Choice Shifts?" *Journal of Experimental Social Psychology* 13 (1977): 303–314.

SARNOFF, IRVING. "Reaction Formation and Cynicism." *Journal of Personality* 28 (1960): 129–143.

SCHACHTER, STANLEY. "Deviation, Rejection and Communication." *Journal of Abnormal and Social Psychology* 46 (1951): 190–207.

SCHACHTER, STANLEY, and SINGER, JEROME E. "Cognitive, Social, and Physiological Determinants of Emotional State." *Psychological Review* 69 (1962): 379–399.

SCHANK, ROGER, and ABELSON, ROBERT. *Scripts, Plans, Goals, and Understanding.* Hillsdale, N.J.: Lawrence Erlbaum, 1977.

SCHATZMAN, LEONARD, and STRAUSS, ANSELM L. *Field Research: Strategies for a Natural Sociology.* Englewood Cliffs, N.J.: Prentice-Hall, 1973.

SCHEIDEL, THOMAS M. *Persuasive Speaking.* Glenview, Ill.: Scott, Foresman, 1967.

SCHEIN, EDGAR H. "The Chinese Indoctrination Program for Prisoners of War: A Study of Attempted 'Brainwashing'," *Psychiatry* 19 (1956): 149–172.

SCHEIN, EDGAR H.; SCHNEIER, INGE; and BARKER, CURTIS H. *Coercive Persuasion.* New York: W. W. Norton, 1961.

SCHLENKER, BARRY R. "Group Members' Attributions of Responsibility for Prior Group Performance." *Representative Research in Social Psychology* 6 (1975): 98–108.

SCHLENKER, BARRY R., and RIESS, MARC. "Self-Presentations of Attitudes Following Commitment to Proattitudinal Behavior." *Human Communication Research* 5 (1979): 325–334.

SCHNEIDER, DAVID J. "Implicit Personality Theory: A Review." *Psychological Bulletin* 79 (1973): 294–309.

SCHNEIDER, DAVID J.; HASTROF, ALBERT H.; and ELLSWORTH, PHOEBE C. *Person Perception.* 2nd ed. Reading, Mass.: Addison-Wesley, 1979.

SCHOPLER, JOHN, and BATESON, NICHOLAS. "A Dependence Interpretation of the Effects of Severe Initiation." *Journal of Personality* 30 (1962): 633–649.

SCHRAM, MARTIN. *Running for President: A Journal of the Carter Campaign.* New York: Pocket Books, 1976.

SCHRAMM, WILBUR. "The Nature of Communication between Humans." *The Process and Effects of Mass Communication*. Ed. Wilbur Schramm and Donald F. Roberts. Urbana, Ill.: University of Illinois Press, pp. 3–53.

SCHRAMM, WILBUR, and ROBERTS, DONALD F. "Social Consequences of Mass Communication." *The Process and Effects of Mass Communication*. Ed. Wilbur Schramm and Donald F. Roberts, Urbana, Ill.: University of Illinois Press, 1971, pp. 519–523.

SCOTT, ROBERT L. "Communication as an Intentional, Social System." *Human Communication Research* 3 (1977): 258–268.

SCOTT, WILLIAM A. "Attitude Change by Response Reinforcement: Replication and Extension." *Sociometry* 22 (1959): 328–335.

————. "Attitude Change through Reward of Verbal Behavior." *Journal of Abnormal and Social Psychology* 55 (1957): 72–75.

"Secret Voices: Messages That Manipulate." *Time*, 10 September 1979, p. 71.

SELIGMAN, CLIVE; BUSH, MALCOLM; and KIRSCH, KENNETH. "Relationship between Compliance in the Foot-in-the-Door Paradigm and Size of First Request." *Journal of Personality and Social Psychology* 33 (1976): 517–520.

SHAW, MARVIN E. *Group Dynamics: The Psychology of Small Group Behavior*. 2nd ed. New York: McGraw-Hill, 1976.

SHAW, MARVIN E.; ROTHSCHILD, GERALD H.; and STRICKLAND, JOHN F. "Decision Processes in Communication Nets." *Journal of Abnormal and Social Psychology* 54 (1957): 323–330.

SHEPARD, CLOVIS R. *Small Groups: Some Sociological Perspectives*. San Francisco: Chandler, 1964.

SHERIF, CAROLYN W.; SHERIF, MUZAFER; and NEBERGALL, ROGER E. *Attitude and Attitude Change: The Social Judgment–Involvement Approach*. Philadelphia: W. B. Saunders, 1965.

SHERIF, MUZAFER. "A Study of Some Social Factors in Perception." *Archives of Psychology*, No. 187 (1935).

SHERIF, MUZAFER, and CANTRIL, HADLEY. *The Psychology of Ego-Involvements*. New York: John Wiley, 1947.

SHERIF, MUZAFER, and HOVLAND, CARL I. *Social Judgment: Assimilation and Contrast Effects in Communication and Attitude Change*. New Haven: Yale University Press, 1961.

SHERIF, MUZAFER; TAUB, DANIEL; and HOVLAND, CARL I. "Assimilation and Contrast Effects of Anchoring Stimuli on Judgments." *Journal of Experimental Psychology* 55 (1958): 150–155.

SHERMAN, STEVEN J.; AHLM, KARIN; and BERMAN, LEONARD. "Contrast Effects and Their Relation to Subsequent Behavior." *Journal of Experimental Social Psychology* 14 (1978): 340–350.

SHIMANOFF, SUSAN B. *Communication Rules: Theory and Research*. Beverly Hills, Calif.: Sage Publications, 1980.

SHWEDER, RICHARD A. "Illusory Correlation and the MMPI Controversy." *Journal of Consulting and Clinical Psychology* 45 (1977): 917–924.

SIEGEL, ALBERTA E., and SIEGEL, SIDNEY. "Reference Groups, Membership Groups, and Attitude Change." *Group Dynamics*. Ed. Dorwin Cartwright and Alvin Zander. Evanston, Ill.: Row, Peterson, 1960, pp. 232–240.

SIGALL, HAROLD; ARONSON, ELIOT; and VAN HOOSE, THOMAS. "The Cooperative Subject: Myth or Reality?" *Journal of Experimental Social Psychology* 6 (1970): 1–10.

SILVERMAN, IRWIN, and SCHULMAN, ARTHUR D. "A Conceptual Model of Artifact in Attitude Change Studies." *Sociometry* 33 (1970): 97–107.

SILVERMAN, IRWIN; SHULMAN, ARTHUR D.; and WIESENTHAL, DAVID L. "Effects of Deceiving and Debriefing Psychological Subjects on Performance in Later Experiments." *Journal of Personality and Social Psychology* 14 (1970): 203–212.

SIMONS, HERBERT W. "The Carrot and Stick as Handmaidens of Persuasion in Conflict Situations."
Perspectives on Communication in Social Conflict. Ed. Gerald R. Miller and Herbert W. Simons. Englewood Cliffs, N.J.: Prentice-Hall, 1974.

————. "Persuasion and Attitude Change." *Speech Communication Behavior: Perspectives and
Principles.* Ed. Larry L. Barker and Robert J. Kibler. Englewood Cliffs, N.J.: Prentice-Hall, 1971, pp.
227–248.

SINGER, JEROME E. "Social Comparison-Progress and Issues." *Journal of Experimental Social Psychology* 1 (1966): 103–110.

SKINNER, B. F. *Science and Human Behavior.* New York: Macmillan, 1953.

SMITH, EWART E. "The Power of Dissonance Techniques to Change Attitudes." *Public Opinion
Quarterly* 25 (1961a): 626–639.

————. "Methods of Changing Consumer Attitudes: A Report of Three Experiments." Project
Report, Quartermaster Food and Container Institute for the Armed Forces. PRA Rpt. 61–2, 1961.

SMITH, MARY JOHN. "A Practical Reasoning Model of Human Communication." Unpublished MS,
University of Virginia, 1979.

SMITH, MARY JOHN, and GABBARD-ALLEY, ANNE. "Attitudinal Freedom, Crowding, and Chronological Age." Unpublished MS, University of Virginia, 1979.

SNOW, RICHARD E. "Unfinished Pygmalion." *Contemporary Psychology* 14 (1969): 197–199.

SNYDER, MARK, and CUNNINGHAM, MICHAEL R. "To Comply or Not to Comply: Testing the
Self-Perception Explanation of the 'Foot-in-the-Door' Phenomenon." *Journal of Personality and Social
Psychology* 31 (1975): 64–67.

SNYDER, MARK, and ROTHBART, MYRON. "Communicator Attractiveness and Opinion Change."
Canadian Journal of Behavioral Science 3 (1971): 377–387.

SNYDER, MARK, and SWANN, JR., WILLIAM B. "Behavioral Confirmation in Social Interaction:
From Social Perception to Social Reality." *Journal of Experimental Social Psychology* 14 (1978): 148–
162.

SNYGG, DONALD, and COMBS, ARTHUR W. *Individual Behavior: A Perceptual Approach to Behavior.* New York: Harper & Row, 1959.

SPINNER, BARRY; ADAIR, JOHN G.; and BARNES, GORDON E. "A Reexamination of the Faithful
Subject Role." *Journal of Experimental Social Psychology* 13 (1977): 543–551.

SRULL, THOMAS K., and WYER, JR., ROBERT S. "The Role of Category Accessibility in the Interpretation of Information about Persons: Some Determinants and Implications." *Journal of Personality
and Social Psychology* 37 (1979): 1660–1672.

STAATS, ARTHUR W. "Social Behaviorism and Human Motivation: Principles of the Attitude-
Reinforcer-Discriminative System." *Psychological Foundations of Attitudes.* Ed. Anthony G. Greenwald,
Timothy C. Brock, and Thomas M. Ostrom. New York: Academic Press, 1968, pp. 33–66.

STANG, DAVID J. "The Effects of Mere Exposure on Learning and Affect." *Journal of Personality
and Social Psychology* 31 (1975): 7–13.

————. "Conformity, Ability, and Self-Esteem." *Representative Research in Social Psychology* 3
(1972): 97–103.

STEINER, IVAN D. *Group Process and Productivity.* New York: Academic Press, 1972.

STEINFATT, THOMAS M. "Resistance to Persuasion." Unpublished MS. Michigan State University,
1970.

STEWART, RALPH H. "Effects of Continuous Responding on the Order Effect in Personality Impression Formation." *Journal of Personality and Social Psychology* 1 (1965): 161–165.

STONER, JAMES A. F. "A Comparison of Individual and Group Decisions Involving Risk." Unpublished Master's thesis, Massachusetts Institute of Technology, 1961.

STRICKER, LAWRENCE J.; JACOBS, PAUL I.; and KOGAN, NATHAN. "Trait Interrelations in Implicit Personality Theories and Questionnaire Data." *Journal of Personality and Social Psychology* 30 (1974): 198–207.

SUMMERS, GENE F., ed. *Attitude Measurement.* Chicago: Rand McNally, 1970.

TANNENBAUM, PERCY H. "Experimental Method in Communication Research." *Introduction to Mass Communication Research.* Ed. Ralph O. Nafziger and David M. White. Baton Rouge, La.: Louisiana State University Press, 1963, pp. 51–77.

TARDE, GABRIEL. *The Laws of Imitation.* New York: Holt, 1903.

TAYLOR, CHARLES. *The Explanation of Behaviour.* London: Routledge and Kegan Paul, 1961.

TAYLOR, MARYLEE C. "Race, Sex, and the Expression of Self-Fulfilling Prophecies in a Laboratory Teaching Situation." *Journal of Personality and Social Psychology* 37 (1979): 897–912.

TAYLOR, SHELLEY E. "On Inferring One's Attitudes from One's Behavior: Some Delimiting Conditions." *Journal of Personality and Social Psychology* 31 (1975): 126–131.

TAYLOR, SHELLEY E., and CROCKER, JENNIFER. "Schematic Bases of Social Information Processing." *Social Cognition: The Ontario Symposium.* Ed. E. Tory Higgins, C. Peter Herman, and Mark P. Zanna. Hillsdale, N.J.: Lawrence Erlbaum, 1981, pp. 89–134.

TEDESCHI, JAMES T. "Threats and Promises." *The Structure of Conflict.* Ed. Paul Swingle. New York: Academic Press, 1970, pp. 155–191.

TEDESCHI, JAMES T., and LINDSKOLD, SVENN. *Social Psychology: Interdependence, Interaction and Influence.* New York: John Wiley, 1976.

TEDESCHI, JAMES T., and ROSENFELD, PAUL. "Communication in Bargaining and Negotiation." *Persuasion: New Direction in Theory and Research.* Ed. Michael E. Roloff and Gerald R. Miller. Beverly Hills, Calif.: Sage Publications, 1980, pp. 225–248.

TEDESCHI, JAMES T.; GAES, GERALD G.; and SILVERMAN, L. "Impression Management Theory and the Forced Compliance Paradigm." Unpublished MS, State University of New York at Albany, 1976.

TEDESCHI, JAMES T.; SCHLENKER, BARRY R.; and BONOMA, THOMAS V. "Cognitive Dissonance: Private Raciocination or Public Spectacle?" *American Psychologist* 26 (1971): 685–695.

TESSER, ABRAHAM. "Self-Generated Attitude Change." *Advances in Experimental Social Psychology.* Ed. Leonard Berkowitz. New York: Academic Press, 1978, pp. 289–338.

TESSER, ABRAHAM, and CONLEE, MARY CHARLES. "Some Effects of Time and Thought on Attitude Polarization." *Journal of Personality and Social Psychology* 31 (1975): 262–270.

TESSER, ABRAHAM, and LEONE, CHRISTOPHER. "Cognitive Schemas and Thought as Determinants of Attitude Change." *Journal of Experimental Social Psychology* 13 (1977): 340–356.

THORNTON, D. A., and ARROWOOD, A. JOHN. "Self-Evaluation, Self-Enhancement, and the Locus of Social Comparison." *Journal of Exprimental Social Psychology*, supplement 1 (1966): 40–48.

TRIANDIS, HARRY C. *Attitude and Attitude Change.* New York: John Wiley, 1971.

TRIPLETT, NORMAN. "The Dynamogenic Factors in Pacemaking and Competition." *American Journal of Psychology* 9 (1897): 507–533.

TUCKER, RAYMOND K., and CHASE, LAWRENCE J. "Canonical Correlation in Human Communication Research." *Human Communication Research* 3 (1976): 86–96.

TURNER, CHARLES W., and BERKOWITZ, LEONARD. "Identification with Film Aggressor (Overt Role Taking) and Reactions to Film Violence." *Journal of Personality and Social Psychology* 21 (1972): 256–264.

UPSHAW, HARRY S. "The Personal Reference Scale: An Approach to Social Judgment." *Human Judgment and Decision Processes.* Ed. Martin F. Kaplan and Steven Schwartz. New York: Academic Press, 1975, pp. 315–371.

————. "The Effects of Variable Perspective on Judgments of Opinion Statements for Thurstone Scales: Equal-Appearing Intervals." *Journal of Personality and Social Psychology* 2 (1965): 60–69.

URANOWITZ, SEYMOUR W. "Helping and Self-Attributions: A Field Experiment." *Journal of Personality and Social Psychology* 31 (1975): 852–854.

VAN DEN BAN, A. W. "A Revision of the Two-Step Flow of Communication Hypothesis." *Gazette* 10 (1964): 237–249.

VINOKUR, AMIRAM, and BURNSTEIN, EUGENE. "The Effects of Partially Shared Persuasive Arguments on Group Induced Shifts: A Group Problem Solving Approach." *Journal of Personality and Social Psychology* 29 (1974): 305–315.

VON WRIGHT, GEORG H. *Explanation and Understanding.* Ithaca, N.Y.: Cornell University Press, 1971.

————. "The Logic of Practical Discourse." *Contemporary Philosophy.* Ed. Raymond Klikansky. Italy: La Nuava Italia Editrice, 1968, pp. 141–165.

VYGOTSKY, LEV SEMENOVICH. *Thought and Language.* Trans. Eugenia Hanfmann and Gertrude Vakar. Cambridge, Mass.: MIT Press, 1962.

WALLACE, JOHN. "Role Reward and Dissonance Reduction." *Journal of Personality and Social Psychology* 3 (1966): 305–312.

WALLACH, MICHAEL A.; KOGAN, NATHAN; and BEM, DARYL J. "Diffusion of Responsibility and Level of Risk Taking in Groups." *Journal of Abnormal and Social Psychology* 68 (1964): 263–274.

WALSTER, ELAINE, and BERSCHEID, ELLEN. "The Effects of Time on Cognitive Consistency." *Theories of Cognitive Consistency: A Sourcebook.* Ed. Robert P. Abelson, et al. Skokie, Ill.: Rand McNally, 1968, pp. 599–608.

WALSTER, ELAINE; ARONSON, ELIOT; and ABRAHAMS, DARCY. "On Increasing the Persuasiveness of a Low Prestige Communicator." *Journal of Experimental Social Psychology* 2 (1966): 325–342.

WARNER, LYLE G., and DEFLEUR, MELVIN L. "Attitude as an Interactional Concept: Social Constraint and Social Distance as Intervening Variables between Attitudes and Action." *American Sociological Review* 34 (1969): 153–167.

WARNER, REBECCA M.; KENNY, DAVID A.; and STOTO, MICHAEL. "A New Round Robin Analysis of Variance for Social Interaction Data." *Journal of Pesonality and Social Psychology* 37 (1979): 1742–1757.

WARR, PETER. "Inference Magnitude, Range, and Evaluative Directions as Factors Affecting Relative Importance of Cues in Impression Formatioñ." *Journal of Personality and Social Psychology* 30 (1974): 191–197.

WARR, PETER, and JACKSON, PAUL. "The Importance of Extremity." *Journal of Personality and Social Psychology* 32 (1975): 278–282.

WATSON, JOHN B. *Psychology from the Standpoint of a Behaviorist.* Philadelphia: J. B. Lippincott, 1924.

WATSON, ROBERT I. "Investigation into Deindividuation Using a Cross-Cultural Survey Technique." *Journal of Personality and Social Psychology* 25 (1973): 342–345.

WATTS, WILLIAM A. "Relative Persistence of Opinion Change Induced by Active Compared to Passive Participation." *Journal of Personality and Social Psychology* 5 (1967): 4–15.

WATTS, WILLIAM A., and HOLT, LEWIS W. "Persistence of Opinion Change Induced under Conditions of Forewarning and Distraction." *Journal of Personality and Social Psychology* 37 (1979): 778–789.

WATTS, WILLIAM A., and McGUIRE, WILLIAM J. "Persistence of Induced Opinion Change and Retention of the Inducing Message Contents." *Journal of Abnormal and Social Psychology* 68 (1964): 233–241.

WEARY, GIFFORD. "Self-Serving Attributional Biases: Perceptual or Response Distortions?" *Journal of Personality and Social Psychology* 37 (1979): 1418–1420.

WEBER, STEPHEN J., and COOK, THOMAS D. "Subject Effects in Laboratory Research: An Examination of Subject Roles, Demand Characteristics, and Valid Inference." *Psychological Bulletin* 77 (1972): 273–295.

WEIGEL, RUSSELL H., and NEWMAN, LEE S. "Increasing Attitude-Behavior Correspondence by Broadening the Scope of the Behavioral Measure." *Journal of Personality and Social Psychology* 33 (1976): 793–802.

WEISS, ROBERT FRANK. "Persuasion and the Acquisition of Attitudes: Models from Conditioning and Selective Learning." *Psychological Reports* 11 (1962): 709–732.

WHEELER, LADD. "Toward a Theory of Behavioral Contagion." *Psychological Review* 73 (1966): 179–192.

WHEELER, LADD, and CAGGIULA, ANTHONY R. "The Contagion of Aggression." *Journal of Experimental Social Psychology* 2 (1966): 1–10.

WHEELER, LADD, and SMITH, SEWARD. "Censure of the Model in the Contagion of Aggression." *Journal of Personality and Social Psychology* 6 (1967): 93–98.

WHEELER, LADD; SHAVER, KELLY G.; JONES, RUSSELL A.; GOETHALS, GEORGE R.; COOPER, JOEL; ROBINSON, JAMES E.; GRUDER, CHARLES L.; and BUTZINE, KENT W. "Factors Determining the Choice of Comparison Other." *Journal of Personality and Social Psychology* 5 (1969): 219–232.

WHITE, THEODORE H. *Breach of Faith: The Fall of Richard Nixon.* New York: Atheneum Publishers, 1975.

WHITEHEAD, JR., JACK L. "Factors of Source Credibility." *Quarterly Journal of Speech* 54 (1968): 59–63.

WHORF, BENJAMIN L. "The Relations of Habitual Thought and Behavior to Language." *Language, Thought, and Reality.* Ed. John B. Carroll. Cambridge, Mass.: MIT Press, pp. 134–159.

WICKER, ALAN W. "An Examination of the 'Other Variables' Explanation of Attitude–Behavior Inconsistency." *Journal of Personality and Social Psychology* 19 (1971): 18–30.

———. "Attitudes versus Actions: The Relationship of Verbal and Overt Behavioral Responses to Attitude Objects." *Journal of Social Issues* 25 (1969): 1–78.

WICKLUND, ROBERT A. "Objective Self-Awareness." *Advances in Experimental Social Psychology.* Ed. Leonard Berkowitz. New York: Academic Press, 1975, pp. 233–275.

———. *Freedom and Reactance.* Hillsdale, N.J.: Lawrence Erlbaum, 1973.

WICKLUND, ROBERT A., and BREHM, JACK W. *Perspectives on Cognitive Dissonance.* Hillsdale, N.J.: Lawrence Erlbaum, 1976.

WICKLUND, ROBERT A.; COOPER, JOEL; and LINDER, DARWYN E. "Effects of Expected Effort on Attitude Change Prior to Exposure." *Journal of Experimental Social Psychology* 3 (1967): 416–428.

WILLIAMS, EDWIN P., and RAUSH, HAROLD L., eds. *Naturalistic Viewpoints in Psychological Research.* New York: Holt, Rinehart & Winston, 1969.

WILMOT, WILLIAM W. *Dyadic Communication: A Transactional Perspective.* Reading, Mass.: Addison-Wesley, 1975.

WILSON, C. EDWARD. "The Effects of Medium on Loss of Information." *Journalism Quarterly* 51 (1974): 111–115.

WILSON, WILLIAM RAFT. "Feeling More than We Can Know: Exposure Effects Without Learning." *Journal of Personality and Social Psychology* 37 (1979): 811–821.

WINICK, CHARLES. "Sex and Advertising." *Mass Media: The Invisible Environment Revisited.* Ed. Robert J. Glessing and William P. White. Chicago: Science Research Associates, 1976, pp. 122–126.

WITCOVER, JULES. *Marathon: The Pursuit of the Presidency 1972–1976.* New York: Viking Press, 1977.

WOLPE, JOSEPH. *The Practice of Behavior Therapy.* Elmsford, N.Y.: Pergamon Press, 1973.

————. *Psychotherapy by Reciprocal Inhibition.* Stanford, Calif.: Stanford University Press, 1958.

WORCHEL, STEPHEN, and ANDREOLI, VIRGINIA. "Facilitation of Social Interaction through Deindividuation of the Target." *Journal of Personality and Social Psychology* 36 (1978): 549–557.

WORCHEL, STEPHEN, and ARNOLD, SUSAN E. "The Effects of Censorship and Attractiveness of the Censor on Attitude Change." *Journal of Experimental Social Psychology* 9 (1973): 365–377.

WORCHEL, STEPHEN, and COOPER, JOEL. *Understanding Social Psychology.* Homewood, Ill.: The Dorsey Press, 1979.

WORD, CARL H.; ZANNA, MARK P.; and COOPER, JOEL. "The Nonverbal Mediation of Self-Fulfilling Prophecies in Social Interaction." *Journal of Experimental Social Psychology* 10 (1974): 109–120.

WRIGHTSMAN, LAWRENCE. "Wallace Supporters and Adherence to 'Law and Order'." *Journal of Personality and Social Psychology* 13 (1969): 17–22.

WYER, JR., ROBERT S. *Cognitive Organization and Change: An Information Processing Approach.* Hillsdale, N.J.: Lawrence Erlbaum, 1974a.

————. "Changes in Meaning and Halo Effects in Personality Impression Formation." *Journal of Personality and Social Psychology* 29 (1974b): 829–835.

————. "Information Redundancy, Inconsistency, and Novelty and Their Role in Impression Formation." *Journal of Experimental Social Psychology* 6 (1970a): 111–127.

————. "The Prediction of Evaluations of Role Occupants as a Function of Favorableness, Relevance, and Probability Associated with Attributes of these Occupants." *Sociometry* 33 (1970b): 79–96.

WYER, JR., ROBERT S., and WATSON, STANLEY F. "Context Effects in Impression Formation." *Journal of Personality and Social Psychology* 12 (1969): 22–23.

WYER, JR., ROBERT S.; HENNINGER, MARILYN; and HINKLE, RONALD. "An Informational Analysis of Actors' and Observers' Belief Attributions in a Role-Playing Situation." *Journal of Experimental Social Psychology* 13 (1977): 199–217.

YODER, M. R. "The Effects of Unavailability and Communication Restriction upon the Evaluation of a Prospective Experience." Unpublished master's thesis, Ohio State University, 1967.

ZAJONC, ROBERT B. "Social Facilitation." *Science* 149 (1965a): 269–274.

————. "The Requirements and Design of a Standard Group Task." *Journal of Experimental Social Psychology* 1 (1965b): 71–88.

ZAJONC, ROBERT B., and SALES, STEPHEN M. "Social Facilitation of Dominant and Subordinate Responses." *Journal of Experimental Social Psychology* 2 (1966): 160–168.

ZAJONC, ROBERT B.; WOLOSIN, ROBERT J.; WOLOSIN, MYRNA A.; and SHERMAN, STEVEN J. "Individual and Group Risk Taking in a Two-Choice Situation." *Journal of Experimental Social Psychology* 4 (1968): 89–107.

ZANNA, MARK P., and COOPER, JOEL. "Dissonance and the Pill: An Attribution Approach to Studying the Arousal Properties of Dissonance." *Journal of Personality and Social Psychology* 29 (1974): 703–709.

ZANNA, MARK P., and KIESLER, CHARLES A. "Inferring One's Beliefs from One's Behavior as a Function of Belief Relevance and Consistency of Behavior." *Psychonomic Science* 24 (1971): 283–285.

ZAVALLONI, MARISA, and COOK, STUART W. "Influence of Judges' Attitudes on Ratings of Favorableness of Statements about a Social Group." *Journal of Personality and Social Psychology* 1 (1965): 43–54.

ZIMBARDO, PHILIP G. *The Psychological Power and Pathology of Imprisonment.* Statement prepared for the U.S. House of Representatives Committee on the Judiciary, Subcommittee No. 3, Robert Kastemeyer, Chairman. Unpublished MS, Stanford University, 1971.

————. "The Human Choice: Individuation, Reason, and Order versus Deindividuation, Impulses, and Chaos." *Nebraska Symposium on Motivation.* Ed. William J. Arnold and David Levine. Lincoln, Neb.: University of Nebraska Press, 1969, pp. 237–307.

ZIMBARDO, PHILIP G., and EBBESEN, E. B. "Experimental Modification of the Relationship between Effort, Attitude, and Behavior." *Journal of Personality and Social Psychology* 16 (1970): 207–213.

ZIMBARDO, PHILIP G.; EBBESEN, E. B.; and MASLACH, CHRISTINA. *Influencing Attitudes and Changing Behavior.* 2nd ed. Reading, Mass.: Addison-Wesley, 1977.

ZIMBARDO, PHILIP G.; WEISENBERG, MATISYOHU; FIRESTONE, IRA; and LEVY, BURTON. "Communicator Effectiveness in Producing Public Conformity and Private Attitude Change." *Journal of Personality* 33 (1965): 233–255.

Author Index

Subject Index

Actionalism. *See* Actional model of man
Actional model of man, 58–59, 81
Action versus motion, 58–59, 81, 145
Active participatory models, 18–19, 23, 117–209, 331–332, 334–335
Adding versus averaging models, 245–248
Advertising
  commercial, 325–328
  and consumer information processing, 328
  political, 323–325
  and subliminal persuasion, 326–328
Affect, 38–39. *See also* Emotion
Anthropomorphic model of man, 81. *See also* Actional model of man
Assimilation effect, 268
Attention decrement hypothesis, 251–252
Attitude
  and behavior, 44–49
  centrality of, 39–41
  and cognitive schemata, 38–39, 51
  defined, 38
  and ego involvement, 266–268
  formation of, 41–43
  functions of, 43–44
  measurement of, 97
  strength of, 39–41
Attitude and behavior change
  and attribution processes, 145–147
  and centrality, 40–41
  and cognitive responses, 17–18, 218–219, 221–222, 225–229, 232–233, 235, 252–253
  and commodification, 274–275
  and counterattitudinal advocacy, 123–128, 130–131, 134–135, 136–137
  and functions of attitude, 44

  and group processes, 165–167, 171, 174–176, 182–185
  and information integration, 243–245
  and proattitudinal advocacy, 151–154
  self-generated, 312–313
  and social judgment-involvement processes, 268–271
  and social learning processes, 194–205
  and stereotypes, 42–43
  and thought, 181, 301–303, 312
  and the Yale information-processing paradigm, 214–219
Attribution theory. *See also* Self-perception theory
  a critical appraisal of, 159–160
  described, 143–144
  dispositional versus situational attributions, 143–145, 147–148
  and the foot-in-the-door phenomenon, 149–151
  and a model of persuasion, 143–147
  in practice, 337
  and proattitudinal advocacy, 151–155
  and self-attributions, 143–148
  and a two-factor emotional model, 155–159
Autokinetic effect, 167
Axiom, 75
Axiomatic theory, 74–77

Behavioral contagion, 182–183
Behavioral intentions, 48
Behavior change. *See* Attitude and behavior change
Behaviorism, 58–60, 192–193
Behavior modification, 203–205